Kristin

May the Master bless you

always and ever

Chetanananda

April 2, 2011

Mahendra Nath Gupta

The Recorder of
The Gospel of Sri Ramakrishna

M. at Bel-tala in Dakshineswar on 23 February 1927

Mahendra Nath Gupta

The Recorder of
The Gospel of Sri Ramakrishna

Tava kathāmritam tapta jivanam kavibhir-iditam kalmashāpaham;
Shravana-mangalam shrimad-ātatam bhuvi grnanti ye bhuridā janāh.
Bhagavata 10:31:9

"O Lord, your nectar-like words relieve the burning misery of afflicted souls. Your words, which poets have sung in verses, destroy the sins of worldly people forever. Blessed are they who hear of your vast glory. Blessed indeed are those who speak of you. How unparalleled is their bounty!"

Swami Chetanananda

Vedanta Society of St. Louis

Copyright © 2011 Vedanta Society of St. Louis

Library of Congress Cataloging-in-Publication Data

Chetanananda, Swami.
  Mahendra Nath Gupta (M.) : the recorder of the Gospel of Sri Ramakrishna / Swami Chetanananda. -- 1st ed.
    p. cm.
  Includes bibliographical references (p.   ) and index.
  ISBN 978-0-916356-94-1 (hardcover : alk. paper) -- ISBN 978-0-916356-95-8 (pbk. : alk. paper)
  1. Gupta, Mahendra Nath, 1855-1932. 2. Ramakrishna, 1836-1886. Kathamrta.
  3. Ramakrishna, 1836-1886--Disciples--Biography. 4.
Hindus--India--Biography. I. Title.
  BL1175.G785C54 2011
  294.5'55092--dc22
  [B]
                              2010053407

FIRST EDITION 2011

Printed in Canada

Those who wish to learn in greater detail about the teachings contained in this book may write to:

Vedanta Society of St. Louis
205 S. Skinker Blvd.
St. Louis, MO 63105, U.S.A.

www.vedantastl.org

Contents

Reminiscences

List of Illustrations

Preface

Every year on New Year's Day, thousands of people assemble at the Cossipore garden house to observe the anniversary of that historical event when Ramakrishna blessed many householder devotees in 1886, saying, "Be illumined." On one such anniversary, 1 January 1960, a well-known orator spoke eloquently about the purpose of Ramakrishna's coming to this world. He said that the Master came to help householders because they need more help than monks, who have renounced everything for God. Moreover, he pointed out that, on that Kalpataru Day, the Master blessed householders only and not monks. Swami Gambhirananda, a learned monk of the Ramakrishna Order, was presiding over the meeting. He got up at the end and remarked: "Ramakrishna came neither for householders nor for monks. He came to help those who sincerely want to realize God." This is a wonderful statement. God-realization does not depend on the colour of one's cloth; it depends on one's longing and love.

This book is the story of a householder who lived with his wife and children and at the same time became a rishi, a great spiritual teacher. He demonstrated that however difficult married life might be, it need not be an obstacle to God-realization. One can practise the Martha way (the active life) and the Mary way (the contemplative life) simultaneously. This ideal householder learned this technique from the Godman of Dakshineswar.

The name of this householder was Mahendra Nath Gupta, but he is better known as M., the recorder of *The Gospel of Sri Ramakrishna*. In the course of his first few meetings with the Master, this is how he introduced himself to Ramakrishna: "I am married and have children. I live in a joint family with my father, stepmother, and brothers, and we have many problems. I am a peace-loving person and cannot bear the family squabbles and pettiness anymore. I sometimes feel like committing suicide, and so does my wife. I am the headmaster of a school and carry a lot of responsibility. As a result of my Western education, I am not comfortable with image worship, and this is why I attend the lectures of Keshab Chandra Sen [a leader of the Brahmo Samaj]. I am depressed, and I feel no peace or joy. In fact, I do not know in which direction to move. I am a householder, submerged in worldly problems. From time to time I think I shall become a mendicant, but it is not possible for me to renounce my wife and children, and my duties. I am stuck in maya. Please show me the way out."

And this is how Ramakrishna answered him: "Do all your duties, but keep your mind on God. Live with all — with wife and children, father and mother — and serve them. Treat them as if they were very dear to you, but know in your heart of hearts that they do not belong to you. If you enter the world without first cultivating love for God, you will be entangled more and more....Let the boat be in water, but let there be no water in the boat; let an aspirant live in the world, but let there be no worldliness in him."

M. was impressed with this gospel of hope, and like a peacock addicted to opium, he became addicted to the Master's words. Previously, M. had developed the habit of keeping a diary, so for the next five years (1882-1886) he filled the pages of his diaries with conversations between the Master and his devotees. It was these conversations that later took the form of *The Gospel of Sri Ramakrishna*. The Master's nectar-like words captivated M., and as he drank them in he felt they made him immortal. In fact, he strongly believed that anyone who imbibed these immortal words of the Master would become immortal.

M. was a great observer, and he described what he saw with great care. The following are a few of the things that M. observed about the Master: First, Ramakrishna was simple, pure, and the embodiment of renunciation; second, his life was based on truth and thus his speech and mind were united; third, his words had the power to solve human problems; fourth, his joyful face, humour, and spiritual power could immediately uplift even those who were depressed and could fill them with bliss; and fifth, his singing, dancing, and samadhi were captivating.

Transformation comes through love and devotion, meditation and self-dedication. After his first encounter with Ramakrishna, M. forgot his family problems and found direction in life. His I-consciousness gradually became saturated with Ramakrishna-consciousness. If this had not been so, he could never have produced *The Gospel of Sri Ramakrishna*, which is unique in the world's religious literature. Faithfully and vividly, M. recorded the Master's samadhi and meditation, prayer and worship, visions and revelations, actions and devotion, purity and renunciation, singing and dancing, humour and mimicry, sadhana and pilgrimage, behaviour and psychology, teachings and philosophy, and social and scientific outlook. But most important, M. recorded Ramakrishna's conversations with God, as well as his talks with the people who came to him, and incidents that showed his love and empathy for others and his fervent concern for those who acted in his divine drama. In later days M. told someone: "After meeting Sri Ramakrishna, I completely forgot my past. His towering personality and spiritual energy erased my sad memories."

Krishna says in the Gita that God incarnates "when religion declines and irreligion prevails." But he does not come alone. He brings along some special people who act in different roles of his divine play. He also brings someone to record his life and message.

As other Incarnations of God had someone to record their teachings, perhaps M. was this same great soul born again for that very purpose. Ramakrishna recognized M. at first sight, and the comments he made about M. at different times indicate that he knew M. was not an ordinary person: "I recognized you on hearing you read the *Chaitanya Bhagavata.* You are my own. The same substance, like father and son....Before you came here, you didn't know who you were. Now you will know."

"Once [in a vision] I saw Gauranga and his devotees singing kirtan in the Panchavati. I think I saw Balaram there and you too."

"Yes, I know everything: what your Ideal is, who you are, your inside and outside, the events of your past lives, and your future."

"I can see from the signs of your eyes, brows, and face that you are a yogi. You look like a yogi who has just left his seat of meditation."

Ramakrishna made M. an ideal householder. The Master knew that it was not possible for householders to renounce fully, so he advised them to adopt *gārhasthya-sannyās*, which means outwardly performing the duties of a householder but inwardly practising renunciation and keeping the mind on God. The Master referred to the gopis as an example. They performed their household duties and at the same time kept their minds on Krishna. M. used to say: "The Master saturated my mind with the colour ochre."

Although M. did not wear an ochre robe, he led his life like a rishi of ancient India. He created a second Naimisharanya [a famous hermitage in ancient India, where the Bhagavata was taught] on the roof of Thakur Bari (his parental home) and also on the roof of his school, the Morton Institution. He lived at Thakur Bari until 1905, and then he moved to a room in the attic of his school. He planted tulsi, plumeria, and other flowering plants in big tubs on both roofs to create an Ashrama atmosphere like that of the Vedic age. His shrine on the roof of Thakur Bari still exists.

As Ramakrishna empowered Vivekananda to teach humanity, so he empowered M. Regarding M., Ramakrishna once said in an ecstatic mood, addressing the Divine Mother: "Mother, why have You given him only one *kala* [a small part] of power? Oh, I see. That will be sufficient for Your work." Another time the Master remarked about M.: "This man has no ego." Where there is ego there is no God, and where there is God there is no ego. Ramakrishna had effaced M.'s ego forever, and thus he became a perfect instrument. After the Master's passing away, M. became a collector, preserver, and distributor of Ramakrishna's life and message. But he did not take any credit, as he was an embodiment of humility. He described himself merely as "His Master's Voice," like the famous logo of the gramophone company, in which a dog listens to his master's voice coming from the phonograph through a black horn.

M. was truly blessed. He quite often quoted this utterance of Ramakrishna: "As children inherit the wealth of their parents, so those who meditate on me will inherit my treasures." Ramakrishna's treasures are discrimination, renunciation, knowledge, devotion, unselfish love, and samadhi — and M. was one of those who truly inherited them. The reader will find in this book how to love not only God, but also the guru, the devotees, and the Bhagavata (the Holy Scriptures). In fact, M. was the living voice of the Bhagavata.

I wish to express my gratitude to my proofreaders, my typesetter, my designer, and those who corrected the manuscript on the computer. I also gratefully acknowledge the help that I received from my editors: Kim Saccio-Kent, a freelance editor in San Francisco; Linda Prugh, an English teacher in Kansas City; Pravrajika Shuddhatmaprana, a nun of the Vedanta Society of Southern California; Chris Lovato, Associate Professor, University of British Columbia, Vancouver; and Ralph Hile, a devotee in Kansas City, who also made the index.

Materials have been collected from so many sources that it is difficult to mention each publisher's name. However, I thankfully acknowledge these important ones: Kathamrita Bhavan (Calcutta), Srima Trust (Chandigarh), General Printers and Publishers (Calcutta), Grantha Bharati (Calcutta), Udbodhan Office (Calcutta), Advaita Ashrama (Calcutta), Ramakrishna-Vivekananda Centre (New York), and Gangotri Parishad (Calcutta). I am grateful to Dipak Gupta, a great grandson of M., who answered many of my questions about M., and allowed me to take precious historical photographs from the family archives.

All biographers of M. are indebted to Swami Nityatmananda who, in his *Srima Darshan* (vols. 1-16), recorded innumerable conversations with and observations of M. I express my special indebtedness to him.

The reader will find that some quotes are used more than once. Such repetition was necessary in order to preserve continuity of ideas.

Finally, I must mention that devotion is contagious. Devotion manifests in many ways, such as through worship of God, holy company, chanting and praying, spiritual talks, longing for God, self-surrender, and taking delight in the Atman. The reader will find in this book that M.'s overflowing devotion was palpable, and it manifested through his untiring talks about his Master given over the course of nearly half a century. During his lifetime, M. touched and transformed thousands of people, and his immortal recordings and conversations still inspire and uplift innumerable people in the East and the West. As long as the sun and moon exist, so long will Ramakrishna's name and gospel exist — and so will the name of M., a humble householder who dissolved his existence into that of the Master.

Chetanananda

Vedanta Society of St. Louis
Kalpataru Day, 1 January 2011

Mahendra Nath Gupta (M.) in his younger days

Prologue

Every avatar or divine incarnation comes with a chronicler who records the avatar's life and teachings. Valmiki wrote Ramachandra's life and teachings in the Ramayana, Vyasa wrote Krishna's life and message in the Bhagavata and the Mahabharata. Buddha's and Christ's lives and messages were recorded by their disciples. According to the divine plan, Mahendra Nath Gupta (known as M.) was earmarked to record the gospel of Ramakrishna, the avatar of this present age.

Observing Ramakrishna, sometimes 24 hours a day for a number of years, M. recorded in the pages of his diary the Master's daily routine, conversations, and way of life. He presented the divine drama of Ramakrishna, showing how an avatar eats and sleeps, talks and behaves, laughs and cries, sings and dances, worships and prays, meditates and goes into samadhi. Such minute details and vivid descriptions of an avatar are unique in religious history. For his contributions, M. deserves not only respect and appreciation, but also humanity's adoration.

In *Ramakrishna and His Disciples* Christopher Isherwood wrote about M. and his immortal record, *The Gospel of Sri Ramakrishna*:

> One of M.'s great virtues as a biographer is his candour. We have seen how he describes his humiliation during his second visit to Ramakrishna. Elsewhere in the *Gospel*, he tells how Ramakrishna praised him and treated him with affection. A self-consciously humble man might have omitted the praise. But there is a more genuine lack of egotism in M.'s simple relation of fact.
>
> M. is equally candid about Ramakrishna himself. His firm belief in the divinity of Ramakrishna's nature was just what stopped him from presenting his Master as the glorified figure of a holy man. Anything that Ramakrishna says or does is sacred to him; therefore he omits nothing, alters nothing. In his pages, we encounter Ramakrishna as an authentic spiritual phenomenon; by turns godlike and childlike, sublime and absurd, now expounding the highest philosophy, now telling funny animal-stories as parables, now singing and dancing, now staggering in ecstasy like a drunkard, now admonishing his devotees with the mature

wisdom of a father, now dropping his wearing-cloth and walking naked like a baby....

If I had to use one single word to describe the atmosphere of the *Gospel* narrative, it would be the word *Now*. The majority of us spend the greater part of our lives in the future or the past — fearing or desiring what is to come, regretting what is over. M. shows us a being who lives in continuous contact with that which is eternally present. God's existence has no relation to past or future; it is always of *now*. To be with Ramakrishna was to be in the presence of that *Now*. Not everybody who visited Dakshineswar was aware of this. M. was aware, from the first; and he never ceased to be thankful for the privilege he was enjoying. He describes every scene of his narrative with a thankful wonder that he — the ordinary unworthy schoolmaster — should have been permitted to take part in it....

M. would have been overwhelmed, no doubt, if he could have known that Aldous Huxley would one day compare him to Boswell and call his *Gospel* "unique in the literature of hagiography."[1]

In the divine drama of Ramakrishna, Mahendra Nath Gupta performed one of the main roles, but he himself wanted to act in disguise. He tried to efface his identity in the pages of the *Gospel* by assuming various names, such as a Master (a school teacher), Mani, Manimohan, Mohini, Mohinimohan, Mahim, a Bhakta (a devotee), a Sevak (a servant), an Englishman (an English-educated man). During his second visit to Dakshineswar, Ramakrishna crushed M.'s ego completely, thereby making him the perfect messenger. As a flute player can play a flute only if it is hollow, so God works through those souls who have no ego within. Thus M. became an instrument in the hands of Ramakrishna and recorded his gospel.

Swami Prabhananda has attempted to reveal the true M. behind the various pseudonyms that he assumed in the Gospel:

1. *Master* — M.'s regular form. Master is a loving schoolteacher; he is learned, humble, and sweet.
2. *A Devotee* — a harmless gentleman who is struggling to survive in the ocean of worldly life. He is striving for his own liberation.
3. *Mohini* — a middle-class Bengali householder with family problems. He is grief-stricken over his son's death and concerned about his wife's unusual behaviour.
4. *Mani* — a curious inquirer into life. He is an independent person, prone to reading poetry and philosophy.[2]

The above four characters in the *Gospel* reflect each aspect of M.'s personality. If one could bring together these characters, one would understand M. completely.

M. said, "I recorded whatever I heard with my own ears from the Master's lips and whatever I saw of his life with my own eyes." Though M. remains hidden in the pages of the *Gospel*, at the same time he is a part of every scene. The title of the Bengali *Gospel* is *Sri Sri Ramakrishna Kathamrita* (literally, the nectar-like words of Sri Ramakrishna). Instead of acknowledging himself as the author, he specified *Srima Kathita*, or "told by Srima." This appears to mean that the account was recorded by Srima (M.'s penname), but the words have a deeper meaning. In Sanskrit, *Sri* means endowed with all divine qualities, *ma* means God; and in Bengali, *kathita* means *was told*. In other words, this record of Ramakrishna was told by God. To M., Ramakrishna was God. M. dedicated his entire being to his beloved Master, and he even offered the authorship of his magnum opus to him. M.'s life is so interwoven with Ramakrishna's in the *Gospel* that M. will be remembered as long as Ramakrishna is.

In 1924 a brahmachari, under the guidance of Swami Shuddhananda, began to collect biographical information on Sri Ramakrishna's close devotees. On 2 June he visited M. The interview was recorded by Swami Nityatmananda in his *Srima Darshan*.

Brahmachari: "Please tell me your father's name."

M. (*irritably*): "It is not necessary to talk about that."

Brahmachari: "Where did you go for study?"

M.: "I studied at the Hare School and then Presidency College. I was born on Friday, 14 July 1854. I met the Master in 1882 when I was 28 years old."

Brahmachari: "Please tell me something about your early life."

M.: "It is useless to record those things. Please write about my connection with the Master's life and leave aside everything else."

Brahmachari: "No, it is valuable to know about your early life. People want to see the evolution of a person. Only a few can grasp the abstract truth."

M.: "If you want to know the greatest event in my life that is my meeting with Sri Ramakrishna Paramahamsa. I stayed at my sister's house in Baranagore for three or four days. One of those days I went to visit the Dakshineswar temple garden, where I met the Master. My brother-in-law, Kaviraj Ishan Chandra Majumdar, knew the Master and was his physician."

Brahmachari: "How many brothers have you?"

M. (*indignantly*): "Why are you asking all these unnecessary questions? Did the Master ask anyone, 'Who was your father?' or 'What did your brother do?'

"You see, a biography is not a collection of facts or events; it is the history of one's mind and soul. These you will find in the four volumes of *Sri Ramakrishna Kathamrita.**

"Thomas Macaulay** remarked: 'It is not necessary to write the life of James Boswell;*** it is interfused with the life of Samuel Johnson.' N.N. Ghosh, the editor of the *Indian Mirror*, remarked while reviewing the Bengali gospel [*Kathamrita*]: 'It happened only once in the history of the world when Boswell wrote the biography of Dr. Johnson. It was the life of a literary man. But this gospel is the record of a person who would talk with God day and night, sometimes in a room packed with devotees. Revealing himself, he said that Satchidananda had descended in this very body.'

"My life story — the unfolding of my life and soul — is embedded in the contents of *Sri Sri Ramakrishna Kathamrita*. I was present in all these scenes. My mind was influenced by all the scenes described and the words narrated therein."[3]

---

*The fifth volume of *Sri Sri Ramakrishna Kathamrita* came out after M.'s passing away.
**An English writer and statesman who was active in the mid-1800s.
***A Scottish lawyer and biographer of the English lexicographer, Samuel Johnson, both of whom lived in the 1700s.

—1—
(M.)

Early Life (1854-1874)

It is extremely difficult to write about a man who was reticent, self-effacing, humble, reluctant to speak about himself, and preferred to be hidden from the public gaze. There is a saying: "The more secret it is, the stronger and more fruitful it becomes; the more it is expressed, the weaker and more superficial it becomes." For this reason mystics and true spiritual aspirants like to remain anonymous. Mahendra Nath Gupta (known as M.) wanted to be hidden but failed: His immortal work, *The Gospel of Sri Ramakrishna*, made him famous.

People from all over the world flocked to see M., and he would talk to them only about God. When they would ask, "Please tell us something about Sri Ramakrishna," he would quote the conversation between the disciple and the teacher in the Kena Upanishad: The disciple said, "Teach me the Upanishad," and the preceptor remained silent for a while and then replied, "I have already told you the Upanishad."[1] By this, Mahendra meant that as he knew only Ramakrishna and nothing else, whatever came through his lips was about him. If anyone asked M. about his personal life, he would invariably turn the conversation to Ramakrishna. He infused his identity with his beloved guru and acted as his Master's voice throughout the rest of his life.

M. was born on Friday, 14 July 1854, at 5:55 a.m. The place of his birth was at Shivanarayan Das Lane, Shimulia, in North Calcutta, and it is very close to Swami Vivekananda's birthplace. Coincidentally, at that time Ramakrishna was living in that same area, helping his brother by performing rituals in private homes.

M.'s father, Madhusudan Gupta, was a pious man and worked in the Calcutta High Court. His mother, Swarnamayi Devi, was extremely devoted to God. It is said that she had this special child after worshipping Lord Shiva and praying to Him for a long time. Madhusudan and Swarnamayi had five sons and six daughters: Kailashchandra, Khirodvasini, Saudamini, Kshetramohan, Ramanmohini, Manmohini, Akshaykumar, Binodini, Mahendra Nath, Durgamani, and Kishori. (Kishori also became a devotee of Ramakrishna.)

Shortly after M.'s birth, Madhusudan bought a house nearby at 13/2 Guruprasad Chaudhury Lane, which M. later named Thakur Bari, the Lord's House. Now it is also known as Kathamrita Bhavan, the House of the Kathamrita. M. was handsome and had a fair complexion. He was very dear to his parents and neighbours. His primary school teacher was also fond of him because of his sweet nature and intelligence. From an early age, M.'s calm face, large and distinctive eyes, gentle voice, and charming personality attracted others.

M. had a sharp intellect, keen powers of observation, a poetic imagination, and above all a prodigious, photographic memory. Even in his old age he could recall his childhood incidents in great detail. One day he reminisced: "Once I went with my mother to Rishra, to my maternal uncle's house, and we attended the Chariot Festival of Jagannath at Mahesh. On our way back we stopped at the Dakshineswar temple garden of Rani Rasmani. I was then 4 years old. The temple was all white then, new and glistening. While going around the temple, I lost sight of my mother in the crowd and was crying for her on the temple porch. Immediately a handsome brahmin came out of the temple and, touching my head, consoled me. Then he called out: 'Whose child is this? Where has his mother gone?' Most probably he was Sri Ramakrishna, because at that time [in 1858] he was the priest in the Kali temple."[2]

M. had religious and mystical inclinations from his childhood. When he was 5 years old, he would climb to the roof of the house to gaze at the vastness of the sky or to experience the torrential rains of the monsoon. He loved to attend Durga Puja, the Chariot Festival, Ganga Puja, and other religious festivals. He had deep love and respect for his parents and teachers. At the age of 10 he read in the Mahabharata that one should love and worship one's family guru, so when the family priest visited their home, M. bowed down to him and served him personally. On 5 October 1864, there was a terrible cyclone in Calcutta. Years later, on 14 July 1885, Ramakrishna asked M.: "Do you remember the great storm of the month of Ashwin?" Surprised, M. replied: "Yes, sir. I was very young at that time — 9 or 10 years old. I was alone in a room while the storm was raging, and I prayed to God."

M. recorded in the *Gospel*: "Why did the Master suddenly ask me about the great storm of Ashwin? Does he know that I was alone at that time, earnestly praying to God with tears in my eyes? Does he know all this? Has he been protecting me as my guru since my very birth?"[3]

M. was a very gentle and tender-hearted boy. He recalled: "When I was 8 or 10 years old, I went to Kalighat [in South Calcutta] with my mother. As I watched the goat sacrifice I thought that when I was grown up, I would stop this practice. I was ambitious at that time. Now, in old age, I understand that everything happens by the will of God. No one can contradict the law of God."[4]

After finishing his primary education, M. studied at Vidyasagar's school on Shankar Ghosh Lane for a brief period. At the age of 10 he met Ishwar Chandra Vidyasagar, the great Bengali educator, philanthropist, and social reformer. M. was then admitted to the Hare School, which was highly regarded in Calcutta. At this time he met Keshab Chandra Sen, the famous Brahmo leader. When M. was 12 years old, Michael Madhusudan Datta returned from England and visited one of M.'s relatives who lived nearby. M. and his friends were seated on the veranda. Michael shook hands with them and said with a smile, "Well, gentlemen, how do you do?"[5] Michael was a great poet and playwright, and he introduced blank verse in Bengali literature. M. always had deep regard for intellectuals and national heroes. Until he met Sri Ramakrishna, he was a hero worshipper.

In 1867, when he was in the seventh grade, he started to keep a diary. The following entries show his religious nature: "I got up in the morning and prostrated before my parents." "As usual, on my way to school I saluted Mother Kali and Mother Shitala."[6]* *The Gospel of Sri Ramakrishna* originated from this habit of keeping a diary, and M. himself commented about his great work, "I was an apprentice for fifteen years."[7]

M. was a brilliant student. He always stood first or second in his class at the Hare School. In 1870 he passed the Matriculation examination at Calcutta University and stood second. He then entered Presidency College, receiving a merit scholarship. In 1872 he stood fifth in his F.A examination, and in 1874 he received a B.A. degree and secured the third position in the University of Calcutta. In college, M. was a favourite of C.H. Tawney, a well-known professor of English who later became the

*On his way to school M. would bow down at the temple of the Divine Mother near the College Street market.

Director of Public Instruction. Tawney returned to England upon his retirement, but he and M. corresponded regularly. Tawney later wrote a brochure on Ramakrishna.

During his college years, M. had a passion for meeting eminent people. For example, he met Bankim Chandra Chattopadhyay, the famous Bengali novelist. At the Presidency College, Surendra Nath Banerjee (who later became a national leader) was the vice president of the Students' Association, and M. was the secretary. When Surendra returned from England after receiving his I.A.S. (Indian Administrative Service) degree, M. went to see him at his Taltala residence in Calcutta to ask him about that course and about living abroad. He wanted to receive that degree himself because it would lead to a prestigious position in the British government. He also visited Devendra Nath Tagore, father of the poet Rabindra Nath Tagore and the leader of the Adi Brahmo Samaj. Among all the leaders for whom he felt a special attraction were Bankim Chandra, Ishwar Chandra Vidyasagar, and Keshab Chandra Sen. He regularly attended Keshab's Brahmo Samaj services and was inspired by his sermons.

In addition to his admiration for distinguished people, M. had a great love of learning. He studied literature, philosophy, history, economics, science, religion, astronomy, and ayurvedic medicine. He was well versed in Eastern and Western philosophy, as well as the English, Bengali, and Sanskrit languages; he also took some courses in French. He studied the philosophical schools of India, including the Jaina and Buddhist traditions. Moreover, he studied the New Testament so thoroughly that he could quote many passages from memory. Long after Ramakrishna had passed away, a Christian minister once expressed his amazement at the depth of M.'s knowledge of the Bible. M. told him politely, "Sir, we lived with Christ [to M., Ramakrishna and Christ were the same], so we understand his teachings a little."[8]

Only an excellent student can be an excellent teacher. A true teacher needs a wide range of knowledge so that he can speak with authority to his students. M.'s hunger for knowledge was so intense that he was not satisfied with the books assigned for his college courses. He also studied the Ramayana, Mahabharata, and the Puranas, and he memorized hymns to gods and goddesses. Though he received a Western education at college, he did not neglect the deep cultural and spiritual heritage of ancient India. His imaginative mind also delved into the poetic beauty and wisdom of Sanskrit literature, such as the *Kumara-sambhava, Abhijnana Shakuntalam, Bhatti-kavya, Kadambari, Uttara-Ramacharita,* and so on. He memorized many verses from these works, especially those describing the hermitages of ancient rishis. Among the Sanskrit poets, he gave a high position to Kalidasa.

M. recalled: "During my college years, I was beside myself when I read the description of Shiva's meditation in the *Kumara-sambhava*. The poet Kalidasa wrote: 'Standing at the door of Shiva's cottage, His attendant Nandi protects His meditation. Holding a gold cane in his left hand and placing his right index finger on the lips, Nandi looks as if he is warning all beings, trees, beasts, and birds not to make any noise or they will be punished. Out of fear, the trees remain like motionless pictures; the birds, dumb; the beasts, calm; and the bees, silent.'"[9]

In college, when M. read Kalidasa's play *Shakuntala*, he became absorbed in the description of Sage Kanwa's Ashrama. M.'s heart became flooded with knowledge, renunciation, devotion, and compassion. He said: "When I read the scene in which Shakuntala leaves Kanwa's Ashrama, I burst into tears. I knew it was a poet's imagination, yet that vivid description overwhelmed me. I wondered at how beautifully the Divine Mother's power operates in this world."[10] M. was not a dry intellectual. He had a loving, sensitive heart.

During his college days, he also read *Sri Chaitanya Charitamrita* (The Life of Chaitanya) and was inspired by Chaitanya's transcendental divine love. Years later, he said to a devotee: "Read *Chaitanya Charitamrita*. Before I went to Sri Ramakrishna, I read that book like a madman."[11] After receiving his B.A. degree, M. attended law school. Apart from the regular law courses, he studied the laws of ancient sages, such as the Manu Samhita, Yajnavalkya Samhita, Parashara Samhita, and Brihaspati Samhita. Unfortunately, financial issues and family problems kept him from completing his study of law.

In 1873, while M. was still attending Presidency College, he married Nikunja Sen, the daughter of Thakur Charan Sen, a cousin of Keshab Chandra Sen. It is said that Professor Tawney told Keshab about M.'s genius and predicted a bright future for him. On the strength of this recommendation, Keshab arranged his relative's marriage with M.

As a Householder and School Teacher

Everything that happens is part of a great plan of Providence. M. married and entered the life of a householder at the age of nineteen. After graduating from college in 1874, he began to study law. However, he had to abandon his studies for two reasons: First, his father could no longer afford to pay his educational expenses; and, as M. and his wife were living in the joint family, they were supposed to contribute to the family's finances. Second, the couple began to get drawn into squabbles, which are common in families where selfishness prevails. The independent-minded M. soon realized that, as he was now married, he should no longer live on the incomes of his father and brother. His dream to finish law school and go to England to earn an I.A.S. degree was shattered, and he started to face the reality of his life.

Since money is necessary in a householder's life, M. had to find a job. He soon found a position in a British merchant firm in Calcutta where his father was also employed. But it was difficult for him to continue that kind of office work, as it was contrary to his nature. After a couple of years he left Calcutta because he was hired as headmaster of Narail High School in Jessore, which is now in Bangladesh. He was a natural teacher and he soon received widespread recognition as an ideal educator. M. developed a wonderful method of teaching. He would first explain the subject to his students in a simple way so that they could grasp it easily. He knew beforehand which parts would be difficult for them to understand, so he used examples to clarify those sections. Although he was then in his early 20s, he was serious, mature, and could grasp the students' psychology very well. M.'s reputation spread, and several high schools and colleges offered him more money if he would teach for them.

M. later told the following story of an incident that happened while he was working in Narail as a young headmaster. Once Bhudev Chandra Mukhopadhyay, a school inspector, came to investigate the Narail High School. After the school closed for the day, M. took him to see Ratan Roy, the local landlord and secretary of the school. Ratan was then relaxing in his parlour in casual clothing and did not know that Mukhopadhyay was the school inspector. The wealthy landlord casually and indiscreetly asked Mukhopadhyay, "What is your monthly salary?"

"Twelve hundred rupees [a huge sum in those days]," answered Mukhopadhyay.

Embarrassed, Ratan immediately stood up and asked his servant to give him a chair and refreshments.[1]

In January 1880 M. became the headmaster and superintendent of Metropolitan High School in Shyampukur, which was owned by Ishwar Chandra Vidyasagar. But as soon as M. moved back in with his father and brothers in their Calcutta home, the family squabbles began again. M. was a peace-loving man. He could not bear the pettiness and abrasiveness among the women and children of their joint family. During this period M.'s mother died. This was a terrible blow. His mother had generally smoothed over the differences between family members and resolved arguments between her daughters-in-law and her grandchildren. Later, M. commented on his family life: "It is difficult to live in a joint family with several women. They cannot live together harmoniously. They quarrel and fight; they become angry and jealous. Sometimes they release their anger by slapping their children. When they are piqued and emotionally upset, they cry and blow their noses. Everyone is selfish and busy with his or her own affairs. One can recognize a true relative only when one is in danger."[2]

M. was endowed with a soft, loving, and poetic nature, yet he also had a critical mind. When Providence revealed to him the nastiness and pettiness of his family life, he craved peace the way a drowning man struggles for air. M. desperately sought peace, which is an essential aspect in human life. During this time, M. made Keshab Chandra Sen his ideal. He began to attend Keshab's lectures at the Brahmo Samaj. Keshab's passionate sermons and prayers greatly inspired him, as he acknowledged later: "I was deeply drawn to him. He was then visiting Sri Ramakrishna with his followers and preaching the immortal teachings of the Master without mentioning his name. I considered Keshab to be a god."[3] Keshab first wrote about Ramakrishna in the *Indian Mirror* in March 1875. In the same year, he wrote about the Master in detail in *Dharmatattwa*.

M. tried to forget the loss of his mother and escape his family difficulties by studying the literature of different religions. He studied the Upanishads and Gita, the Bhagavata and other Puranas, the Tantra scriptures, and basic books of Indian philosophy. He also acquired a fair knowledge of ayurveda and astronomy in addition to Western philosophy.

Before M. met Ramakrishna in early 1882, he had four children — three sons and a daughter. Later, he and his wife had three more daughters. Though outwardly M. was a householder, inwardly he was like a monk, full of intense devotion to God and renunciation of the world. Sometimes he would get up at night and, taking his bed roll, would leave his home to sleep on the open veranda of the Calcutta University Senate Hall among the homeless people of the city. When asked why, he explained, "The idea of home and family clings to one and does not leave easily."[4]

It is difficult for a bird to be caged, or a lion to be confined in a zoo. M. was desperately trying to free himself from the troublesome bondage of family life. One night, on Saturday, 18 February 1882, at 10:00 p.m., M. decided to leave home. M's wife knew her husband's mental condition, and she did not want him to be alone at this critical time. She went out secretly into the street to accompany him. Both left home without extra clothes or any belongings, and M. did not bring his diary. As his mind was in great turmoil, he did not even think of writing in his diary. However, some days after arriving at his sister's house at Baranagore, he began to write some notes on a scrap of paper:

> 18th Feb., Saturday, 1882 — I am forced to leave home with family for Baranagore.
> 19th Feb. '82, Sunday — Birthday Festival of the Lord celebrated by Ram, Suresh. (I absent)
> 23rd Feb. '82, Thursday — On steamer with Cook and Keshab.
> 26th Feb. '82, Sunday (?) Was it on this day that I first saw the Lord.
> 4th March '82 — Saturday — Doljatra.
> 11th & 12th March — Saturday & Sunday — Convocation.
> 19th March, Sunday — Amabasya — Return home with father.[5]

These entries record the dates when M. left home and when he first met Sri Ramakrishna. It is likely that after he returned home on 19 March

1882, he began to write in his diary details about his meetings with the Master. Previously M. had noted that his first meeting with the Master was in March 1882, but later he changed this and wrote "26th Feb, Sunday 1882." Although M. stayed with his sister in Baranagore for a month, it seems he continued to work at his school. The Master's birthday fell on 19 February and he was not present for it, so he must have met the Master the following Sunday, on 26 February 1882.

M. later recalled his desperate condition:

> At that time I could not get along with my father and brothers at home. Though I tried my best to serve them, they mistreated me very much. Unable to bear the mental agony any longer, I decided to leave home and commit suicide. One night at ten o'clock I left with my wife in a hired carriage. I asked the driver to take us to Baranagore, where my sister lived, but on the way, near Shyambazar, a wheel of the carriage came off. We then went to a friend's house and got a cold reception. He thought we wanted to stay at his house overnight. Finally I was able to get another carriage, and we reached Baranagore at midnight.
>
> The next afternoon [actually Sunday, 26 February 1882] I went for a walk with my nephew Sidhu, and we visited several gardens on the bank of the Ganges. Feeling tired and depressed, I sat down in a garden. Sidhu then said: "Uncle, let us go to Rasmani's garden. A holy man lives there." We entered through the main gate of the temple garden at Dakshineswar. It was half an hour before sunset.
>
> Having a poetic mind, I was deeply impressed with the beautiful flower garden. I picked some flowers and was overwhelmed by their fragrance. After some time we entered Sri Ramakrishna's room.
>
> The Master was seated on his small cot and the devotees were on the floor. I didn't know any of them. The first thing I heard from the Master's lips was: "When, hearing the name of God once, you shed tears and your hair stands on end, then you may know for certain that you do not have to perform any more karma."[6]

(M.)

First Meetings with Ramakrishna

Everything in this world has a beginning and an end. Seasons change. The Earth rotates through day and night. Empires rise and fall. Human beings go through prosperity and poverty, separation and union, birth and death. Misery and happiness follow one after the other. It is impossible to find anyone who is always happy or always miserable. When M.'s misery had reached its peak, Providence provided him with divine bliss, which he enjoyed for the next four and a half years, and then he shared it with others for another fifty years.

The Omniscient Mother knew that M. had been born with a mission to record the gospel of Ramakrishna, the avatar of this age. The reader will find M.'s detailed entries in *The Gospel of Sri Ramakrishna*, but we shall present here some highlights of his first four memorable meetings. In the *Gospel*, we see M.'s power of observation, his keen memory, and his love and devotion for his guru. M.'s poetic imagination cast the temple garden of Dakshineswar as a divine abode and Ramakrishna as a living god, enacting his divine drama. One hundred and twenty-five years have passed, yet still we can visualize Ramakrishna's living presence in Dakshineswar.

On Sunday, 26 February 1882,* the Divine Mother bestowed her grace on M. by sending him to Ramakrishna, in the temple garden of

---

*Regarding the dates of M.'s first meetings with the Master, there is a discrepancy in the earlier editions of *Sri Sri Ramakrishna Kathamrita*, as well as in *The Gospel of Sri Ramakrishna* translated by Swami Nikhilananda. On Saturday night, 18 February 1882, M. left home with his wife to go to his sister's home at Baranagore, and (*cont.*)

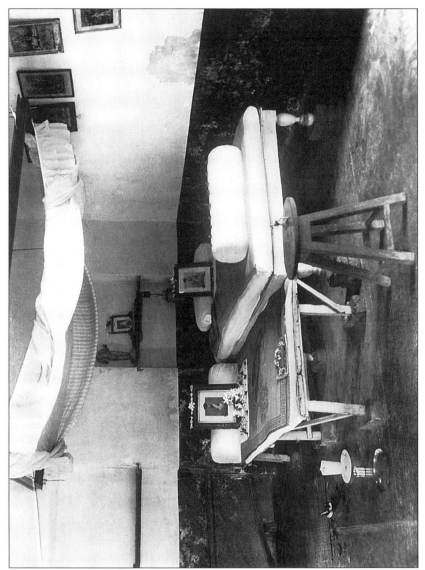

Ramakrishna's bedroom at Dakshineswar, where M. met the Master on 26 February 1882.

Dakshineswar. When M. entered Ramakrishna's room for the first time, he saw the Master seated facing the east and devotees seated on the floor facing him. He was talking of God, with a smile on his face. M. saw a room full of people silently drinking in the words that flowed from him like nectar.

Ramakrishna was saying: "When, hearing the name of Hari or Rama once, you shed tears and your hair stands on end, then you may know for certain that you do not have to perform such devotions as the *sandhya* anymore. Then only will you have a right to renounce rituals; or rather rituals will drop away of themselves. Then it will be enough if you repeat only the name of Rama or Hari, or even simply Om."[1]

M. was overwhelmed by Ramakrishna's charming personality and his spiritual talk, and he was also impressed seeing the gorgeous temples and beauty of the garden. His agitated mind became calm on hearing the sweet music of the vesper services in the Shiva, Radha-Krishna, and Kali temples. The maid Brinde used to light the oil lamp and burn incense in the Master's room in the evening. At that time she would close the doors and windows of the room so that mosquitoes could not get in. As soon as she came out, M. returned from the temples and inquired about the Master.

M.: "Is the holy man in?"

Brinde: "Yes, he's in the room."

M.: "How long has he lived here?"

Brinde: "Oh, he has been here a long time."

M.: "Does he read many books?"

Brinde: "Books? Oh, dear no! They're all on his tongue."

M.: "Perhaps it is time for his evening worship. May we go into the room? Will you tell him we are anxious to see him?"

Brinde: "Go right in, children. Go in and sit down."[2]

It is amazing that on the first day an illiterate maid introduced M., who was so proud of his learning, to Ramakrishna who had no formal

(cont.) on Sunday, 19 March 1882, he returned home with his father. When he left his home in tremendous mental anguish, he did not carry his diary. He recorded his first visits with the Master later on some scrap paper and forgot to write the exact dates. In the first edition of the *Kathamrita*, M. wrote that his first visit was in "March 1882"; in the seventh edition, he changed it to "February-March." He was a man of truth so he was trying to pinpoint the exact dates. (See the copies of M.'s diary and his own handwriting starting on page 252.) Later, based on M.'s writing and thorough research, Kathamrita Bhavan (the publisher) fixed the dates of M.'s first four visits as 26 February 1882; 28 February 1882 (M. wrote in his English translation, "A couple days after, at about eight in the morning, M. called again."); 5 March 1882; and 6 March 1882. Anyone who is interested in the entire account, should read *Srimar Jivan Darshan* by Dr. Abhay Chandra Bhattacharya, p. 364-69. — Author

education. Upon entering the room, M. and his companion Sidhu saw Ramakrishna seated on his cot in an ecstatic mood. The Master asked them to sit down and inquired where they were from. Then finally he said, "Come again."

M.'s second visit to Ramakrishna took place two days later on the southeast veranda of the Master's room at eight o'clock in the morning on Tuesday, 28 February 1882. The barber had just arrived to trim the Master's hair and beard. Seeing M., the Master said: "So you have come. That's good. Sit down here." The Master's skin was so delicate that he could not have a clean shave with a razor. The barber would simply trim his hair and beard with a scissors. While having his hair cut, the Master inquired about M.'s present residence and learned that he was staying with his sister and brother-in-law, Ishan Kaviraj, who was the Master's physician.

The Brahmo leader Keshab Chandra Sen was then a hero of Bengal. Knowing he was not well, the Master inquired of M. about his health and expressed his concern: "I made a vow to worship the Mother with green coconut and sugar on Keshab's recovery.* Sometimes, in the early hours of the morning, I would wake up and cry before Her: 'Mother, please make Keshab well again. If Keshab doesn't live, whom shall I talk with when I go to Calcutta?' And so it was that I resolved to offer Her the green coconut and sugar." M. was touched by the Master's guileless nature, genuine emotions, and unselfish love for others.

Then the Master spontaneously made a statement regarding the duties of a householder that had particular meaning for M. — but without any knowledge of M.'s family trouble and mental condition. The Master said: "Pratap's brother came here. He stayed a few days. He had nothing to do and said he wanted to live here. I came to know that he had left his wife and children with his father-in-law. He has a whole brood of them! So I took him to task. Just fancy! He is the father of so many children! Will people from the neighbourhood feed them and bring them up? He isn't even ashamed that someone else is feeding his wife and children, and that they have been left at his father-in-law's house. I scolded him very hard and asked him to look for a job. Then he was willing to leave here."[3]

In the following scene, M. described in detail how Ramakrishna crushed his ego. This proves how honest M. was, since most people would try to hide such unflattering remarks. First, Ramakrishna asked, "Are you married?" Hearing his reply in the affirmative, the Master cried out: "Oh! Ramlal! Alas, he is married! May the Lord help him."[4]

M. thought: "Is it such a wicked thing to get married?"

*This is a typical Bengali custom.

The Master then asked, "Have you any children?"

"Yes, sir, I have children."

Upset, the Master said: "Ah me! He even has children!" M. felt that a terrible blow had been dealt to his ego.

The Master was sorry to hear that M. was bound by family ties, with a wife and children. He had recognized M.'s true nature. Looking affectionately at M.'s face, he said: "You see, you have certain good signs. I know them by looking at a person's forehead, his eyes, and so on. The eyes of yogis — those that in previous incarnations passed their days in communion with God — have an unusual look. In the case of some it seems as if they have just left their seat of divine contemplation."[5]

Then the Master inquired: "Tell me, now, what kind of person is your wife? Has she spiritual attributes, or is she under the power of avidya?"

M: "She is all right. But I am afraid she is ignorant."

Master (*with evident displeasure*): "And you are a man of knowledge!"

When Ramakrishna made this exclamation, M.'s ego, for the second time, received a rude shock. He learned from the Master that to know God is knowledge, and not to know Him, ignorance. Previously he had believed that one could only gain knowledge from books and schools.

The Master then asked: "Well, do you believe in God with form or without form?"

M., rather surprised, said to himself: "How can one believe in God without form when one believes in God with form? And if one believes in God without form, how can one believe that God has a form? Can these two contradictory ideas be true at the same time? Can a white liquid like milk be black?"

M: "Sir, I like to think of God as formless."

Master: "Very good. It is enough to have faith in either aspect. You believe in God without form; that is quite all right. But never for a moment think that this alone is true and all else is false. Remember that God with form is just as true as God without form. But hold fast to your own conviction."

The assertion that both are equally true amazed M., because Aristotelian logic had taught him that yea is always yea and nay is always nay. He had never learned such a profound lesson from his books. Thus his ego received a third blow. But since it was not yet completely crushed, he came forward to argue with the Master. M. was influenced to some extent by the Brahmos who saw the worship of images as mere idolatry.

M: "Sir, suppose one believes in God with form. Certainly He is not the clay image!"

Master (*interrupting*): "But why clay? It is an image of Spirit."

M. could not quite understand the significance of this "image of Spirit."

"But, sir," he said to the Master, "one should explain to those who worship the clay image that it is *not* God, and that, while worshipping it, they should have God in view and not the clay image. One should not worship clay."

Master (*sharply*): "That's the one hobby of you Calcutta people — giving lectures and bringing others to the light! Nobody ever stops to consider how to get the light himself. Who are you to teach others?

"He who is the Lord of the Universe will teach everyone.... Suppose there is an error in worshipping the clay image; doesn't God know that through it He alone is being invoked? He will be pleased with that very worship. Why should you get a headache over it? You had better try for knowledge and devotion yourself."

This time M. felt that his ego was completely crushed. His analytical mind was convinced that the Master had spoken the truth. In his diary he later recorded: "This was M.'s first argument with the Master, and happily his last."

If a bamboo flute is not completely hollow, a flute player cannot produce any music with it. Similarly if there is ego in a person, God cannot spread His message through him or her. For that reason the Master eradicated M.'s raw ego.

During this second visit M. asked Ramakrishna four vital questions of human life. The Master's answers need no commentary. One can see how the Master incorporated in his teachings parables, symbols, songs, stories, folklore, myths, scientific reasoning, day-to-day household examples, and examples from nature and the behaviour of animals and humans. He seldom quoted from the scriptures. He taught from his personal experience and explained the deep truths of spiritual life in an utterly simple way. This captivated M. Never before had he met such a man.

M: "How, sir, may we fix our minds on God?"

Master: "Repeat God's name and sing His glories, and keep holy company; and now and then visit God's devotees and holy men. The mind cannot dwell on God if it is immersed day and night in worldliness, in worldly duties and responsibilities; it is most necessary to go into solitude now and then and think of God. To fix the mind on God is very difficult in the beginning unless one practises meditation in solitude. When a tree is young it should be fenced all around; otherwise it may be destroyed by cattle.

"To meditate, you should withdraw within yourself or retire to a secluded corner or to the forest. And you should always discriminate between the Real and the unreal. God alone is real, the Eternal Substance; all else is unreal, that is, impermanent. By discriminating thus, one should shake off impermanent objects from the mind."

M: "How ought we to live in the world?"

Master: "Do all your duties, but keep your mind on God. Live with all — with wife and children, father and mother — and serve them. Treat them as if they were very dear to you, but know in your heart of hearts that they do not belong to you.

"A maidservant in the house of a rich man performs all the household duties, but her thoughts are fixed on her own home in her native village. She brings up her Master's children as if they were her own. She even speaks of them as 'my Rama' or 'my Hari.' But in her own mind she knows very well that they do not belong to her at all.

"The tortoise moves about in the water. But can you guess where her thoughts are? There on the bank, where her eggs are lying. Do all your duties in the world, but keep your mind on God.

"If you enter the world without first cultivating love for God, you will be entangled more and more. You will be overwhelmed with its danger, its grief, its sorrows. And the more you think of worldly things, the more you will be attached to them.

"First rub your hands with oil and then break open the jack-fruit; otherwise they will be smeared with its sticky milk. First secure the oil of divine love, and then set your hands to the duties of the world.

"But one must go into solitude to attain this divine love. To get butter from milk you must let it set into curd in a secluded spot; if it is too much disturbed, milk won't turn into curd. Next, you must put aside all other duties, sit in a quiet spot, and churn the curd. Only then do you get butter.

"Further, by meditating on God in solitude the mind acquires knowledge, dispassion, and devotion. But the very same mind goes downward if it dwells in the world. In the world there is only one thought: 'woman and gold.'

"The world is water and the mind milk. If you pour milk into water they become one; you cannot find the pure milk anymore. But turn the milk into curd and churn it into butter. Then, when that butter is placed in water, it will float. So, practise spiritual discipline in solitude and obtain the butter of knowledge and love. Even if you keep that butter in the water of the world the two will not mix. The butter will float.

"Together with this, you must practise discrimination. 'Woman and gold' is impermanent. God is the only Eternal Substance. What does a man get with money? Food, clothes, and a dwelling-place — nothing more. You cannot realize God with its help. Therefore money can never be the goal of life. That is the process of discrimination."

M: "Is it possible to see God?"

Master: "Yes, certainly. Living in solitude now and then, repeating God's name and singing His glories, and discriminating between the Real and the unreal — these are the means to employ to see Him."

M: "Under what conditions does one see God?"

Master: "Cry to the Lord with an intensely yearning heart and you will certainly see Him. People shed a whole jug of tears for wife and children. They swim in tears for money. But who weeps for God? Cry to Him with a real cry.

"Longing is like the rosy dawn. After the dawn out comes the sun. Longing is followed by the vision of God.

"God reveals Himself to a devotee who feels drawn to Him by the combined force of these three attractions: the attraction of worldly possessions for the worldly man, the child's attraction for its mother, and the husband's attraction for the chaste wife. If one feels drawn to Him by the combined force of these three attractions, then through it one can attain Him.

"The point is, to love God even as the mother loves her child, the chaste wife her husband, and the worldly man his wealth. Add together these three forces of love, these three powers of attraction, and give it all to God. Then you will certainly see Him."

After four days M. again returned to Dakshineswar (Sunday, 5 March 1882). M. was still staying at his sister's house in Baranagore. Ever since he first saw Ramakrishna, M.'s thoughts had been all about him: He saw his joyful form everywhere, and the Master's nectar-like words rang in his ears. M. kept wondering how this poor brahmin could have penetrated so deeply into these profound subjects. He had met no one else who explained such subtle truths so simply.

At about 3:00 or 4:00 in the afternoon he came to the garden at Dakshineswar and saw that Ramakrishna was sitting on the small cot in his room, which was full of devotees who had come to visit him on their day off. M. had not been introduced to anyone as yet, so he found a seat on one side of the group. He noticed that the Master was smiling and talking with the devotees. M. was amazed as he observed how the Master offered commonsense solutions to vital problems in day-to-day life, and how he used stories in giving his answers.

The Master said: "God dwells in all beings. But you must be intimate only with good people; you must keep away from the evil-minded. God is even in the tiger; but you cannot embrace the tiger on that account."[6] Saying this, the Master told the parable of "the Mahut Narayana" who asked the people to run away from the mad elephant. A brahmachari did not run away because he had learned from his guru that all are God, and so, he felt, was the elephant. But the mad elephant injured him, and he was taken to the monastery. When he told his guru his reason for not running away from the elephant, the guru replied, "My child, it is true that the elephant God was coming, but the mahut God forbade you to stay there."[7]

A devotee asked: "Sir, if a wicked man is about to do harm, or actually does so, should we keep quiet then?"

The Master replied: "A man living in society should make a show of tamas to protect himself from evil-minded people. But he should not harm anybody in anticipation of harm likely to be done him."[8] In this connection the Master told a marvelous story: A snake that used to attack some cowherd boys became transformed by the influence of a holy man. It renounced violence completely. When the cowherd boys realized this, they almost killed it. The holy man later heard what had happened and scolded the snake: "What a shame! You are such a fool! I asked you not to bite, but I did not forbid you to hiss. Why didn't you scare them by hissing?"[9]

Only a good student can be a good teacher. In the *Gospel*, we find a learned headmaster as the student of an uneducated temple priest. Later, M. would say, "I learned from the Master how to teach." M. was deeply affected by the Master's description of four kinds of human beings: "Those bound by the fetters of the world, the seekers after liberation, the liberated, and the ever-free."

The Master vividly described these four kinds of people:

Suppose a net has been cast into a lake to catch fish. Some fish are so clever that they are never caught in the net. They are like the ever-free. But most of the fish are entangled in the net. Some of them try to free themselves from it, and they are like those who seek liberation. But not all the fish that struggle succeed. A very few do jump out of the net, making a big splash in the water. Then the fishermen shout, "Look! There goes a big one!" But most of the fish caught in the net cannot escape, nor do they make any effort to get out. On the contrary, they burrow into the mud with the net in their mouths and lie there quietly, thinking, "We need not fear anymore; we are quite safe here." But the poor things do not know that the fishermen will drag them out with the net. These are like the men bound to the world.

The bound souls are tied to the world by the fetters of "woman and gold." They are bound hand and foot. Thinking that "woman and gold" will make them happy and give them security, they do not realize that it will lead them to annihilation. When a man thus bound to the world is about to die, his wife asks, "You are about to go; but what have you done for me?" Again, such is his attachment to the things of the world that, when he sees the lamp burning brightly, he says: "Dim the light. Too much oil is being used." And he is on his deathbed!

The bound souls never think of God. If they get any leisure they indulge in idle gossip and foolish talk, or they engage in fruitless work. If you ask one of them the reason, he answers, "Oh, I cannot keep still; so I am making a hedge." When time hangs heavy on their hands they perhaps start playing cards.[10]

There was deep silence in the room. M. then observed that the Master not only had identified the problem in spiritual life but also provided the solution.

A Devotee: "Sir, is there no help, then, for such a worldly person?"

Master: "Certainly there is. From time to time he should live in the company of holy men, and from time to time go into solitude to meditate on God. Furthermore, he should practise discrimination and pray to God, 'Give me faith and devotion.' Once a person has faith he has achieved everything. There is nothing greater than faith."[11]

During this third visit, M. saw the Master in samadhi. He wrote:

Sri Ramakrishna was standing still, surrounded by a few devotees, and Narendra was singing. M. had never heard anyone except the Master sing so sweetly. When he looked at Sri Ramakrishna he was struck with wonder; for the Master stood motionless, with eyes transfixed. He seemed not even to breathe. A devotee told M. that the Master was in samadhi. M. had never before seen or heard of such a thing. Silent with wonder, he thought: "Is it possible for a man to be so oblivious of the outer world in the consciousness of God? How deep his faith and devotion must be to bring about such a state!"[12]

The next day (Monday, 6 March 1882) was a holiday for M. When he arrived at 3:00 p.m., Ramakrishna was in his room talking to Narendra, Bhavanath, and other young disciples. No sooner had M. entered the room than the Master laughed aloud and said: "There! He has come again." M. bowed low before him and sat near the boys on the floor. Previously he used to salute with folded hands as English-educated persons did. But that day he learned how to bow down on the floor.

The Master then explained the cause of his laughter to the boys: "A man once fed a peacock with a pill of opium at four o'clock in the afternoon. The next day, exactly at that time, the peacock came back. It had felt the intoxication of the drug and returned just in time to have another dose. (*All laugh*.)"[13]

Instead of being embarrassed, M. appreciated the Master's apt illustration. Even at home he had been unable to banish the thought of Ramakrishna for a moment. He had counted the minutes until he could return to Dakshineswar. M. noticed that the Master was in a jovial mood with his young disciples. After singing a song, he went into samadhi. This was the second time M. saw the Master in samadhi.

At five o'clock M. was walking around the temple garden. He met the Master and Narendra at the southern ghat of the goose pond. The Master said to Narendra: "Look here, come a little more often. You are a newcomer. On first acquaintance people visit each other quite often, as is the case with a lover and his sweetheart. (*Narendra and M. laugh*.) So please come, won't you?"[14]

"Yes, sir, I shall try," replied Narendra with a smile.

After the vesper service, M. saw the Master pacing alone in the natmandir in front of the Kali temple. The single lamp in the spacious natmandir blended light and darkness into a kind of mystic twilight, in which the figure of the Master could be dimly seen.

While walking, the Master asked M.: "What do you think of me? How many 'annas' of knowledge of God have I?" M. replied: "I don't understand what you mean by 'annas.' But of this I am sure: I have never before seen such knowledge, ecstatic love, faith in God, renunciation, and catholicity anywhere."

The Master was pleased with M.'s understanding of him, as M. was to be the future recorder of his gospel.

When M. was about to take his leave, the Master invited him to visit him at Balaram Bose's house in Calcutta. M. agreed and left. But when he reached the main gate of the garden, M. turned back. Seeing him, the Master inquired: "What makes you come back?"

M. replied: "Perhaps the house you asked me to go to belongs to a rich man. They may not let me in. I think I had better not go. I would rather meet you here."

Master: "Oh, no! Why should you think that? Just mention my name. Say that you want to see me; then someone will take you to me."

M. nodded his assent, saluted the Master, and took his leave.

"Just mention my name ... then someone will take you to me" — this is very significant. Ramakrishna is telling not only M. but all lost and confused people how to reach him. Doors will open in all directions for anyone who repeats the Master's name — whether the door is to a wealthy man's mansion or to a poor man's cottage. As a prince has free access to any room in the palace and gatekeepers open the door for him with a salute, so Mahamaya opens the door of liberation for the disciples and devotees of an avatar. The avatar is the ruler of maya.

The Guru and the Disciple

When the earth is tormented by scorching heat, Mother Nature sends rain. So when human beings can no longer bear their agony, and all their efforts fail, they desperately seek divine help. That is the beginning of true religious life. The gracious Lord then comes forward as a guru to help those souls. M. described how God's grace came to him:

> Seven or eight days after my first meeting with the Master, he was walking through the courtyard of the Kali temple and I said to him, "It is better to take one's life than to suffer such terrible pain." At once he replied: "Why do you say so? You have a guru. Why do you worry? Your guru is always behind you. He can remove your suffering by a mere wish. He makes everything favourable. A juggler threw a rope with many knots in it in front of a thousand people, and none could untie a single knot. But the juggler immediately removed all the knots just by a jerk of his hand. Don't worry. The guru will remove all your obstacles." What agony I was suffering, but I had found the Master. How he guided my life! Later my father came. We were reconciled with love and affection, and he took me back home. In retrospect we see that God is all-auspicious, but we judge things superficially. It was my family problems and my desire to commit suicide that led me to God.[1]

M. was truly fortunate that he found his guru, Ramakrishna. The Katha Upanishad says: "Wonderful is the expounder and rare the hearer; rare indeed is the experiencer of the Atman taught by an able preceptor."[2]

Ramakrishna (1836-1886) at Dakshineswar in 1884

M. was an ideal disciple and passionate lover of truth. On 11 March 1882, M.'s father took him back home; on the same day M. went to Balaram's house to meet the Master as he had been instructed. M. was new and shy by nature, so he quietly observed the Master in the company of his devotees. He was also impressed by Balaram's humility.

Circumstances kept M. from visiting the Master for a few weeks, but on 2 April 1882 he met the Master at a devotee's house in Calcutta. There he learned that a guru is essential for God-realization. Ramakrishna described a true guru: "Anyone and everyone cannot be a guru. A huge timber floats on the water and can carry animals as well. But a piece of worthless wood sinks if a man sits on it, and drowns him. Therefore in every age God incarnates Himself as the guru, to teach humanity. Satchidananda alone is the guru."[3]

That afternoon the Master went to Keshab Sen's house, accompanied by M. and others. When a pandit was introduced to him, the Master remarked: "Yes, I can see inside him through his eyes, as one can see the objects in a room through a glass door."[4] M. understood that the Master was all-knowing. At the outset the Master recognized M.'s greatness and knew his mission. So now that he was seeing M. again after a few weeks, he told Keshab (*pointing to M.*): "Will you please ask him why he doesn't come to Dakshineswar anymore? He repeatedly tells me he is not attached to his wife and children."[5] Ramakrishna even asked M. to write to him if he could not come. Frequent visits from then on helped the guru-disciple relationship to develop.

It is interesting to observe how a dropout opened a school and a headmaster became his student. It is true that Ramakrishna, who had renounced formal education, opened a school for God-realization in the temple garden of Dakshineswar, and M., the headmaster of Vidyasagar's school, became his student.

Swami Vivekananda remarked: "The man at whose feet I sat all my life — and it is only a few ideas of his that I try to teach — could [hardly] write his name at all. All my life I have not seen another man like that, and I have travelled all over the world. When I think of that man, I feel like a fool, because I want to read books and he never did. He never wanted to lick the plates after other people had eaten. That is why he was his own book."[6]

M. was a wonderful disciple and he absorbed the Master's teachings like a dry sponge. On the Master's side, he saw the signs of a yogi in M. and gave him some preliminary lessons on 24 August 1882.

Master: "A little spiritual discipline is necessary in order to know what lies within."

M.: "Is it necessary to practise discipline all through life?"

Master: "No. But one must be up and doing in the beginning. After that one need not work hard. The helmsman stands up and clutches the rudder firmly as long as the boat is passing through waves, storms, high wind, or around the curves of a river; but he relaxes after steering through them. As soon as the boat passes the curves and the helmsman feels a favourable wind, he sits comfortably and just touches the rudder. Next he prepares to unfurl the sail and gets ready for a smoke. Likewise, the aspirant enjoys peace and calm after passing the waves and storms of 'woman and gold.'

"Some are born with the characteristics of the yogi; but they too should be careful. It is 'woman and gold' alone that is the obstacle; it makes them deviate from the path of yoga and drags them into worldliness. Perhaps they have some desire for enjoyment. After fulfilling their desire, they again direct their minds to God and thus recover their former state of mind, fit for the practice of yoga.

"'Woman and gold' alone is the obstacle to yoga. Always analyse what you see. What is there in the body of a woman? Only such things as blood, flesh, fat, entrails, and the like. Why should one love such a body?"

Master (to M.): "The mind of the yogi is always fixed on God, always absorbed in the Self. You can recognize such a man by merely looking at him. His eyes are wide open, with an aimless look, like the eyes of the mother bird hatching her eggs. Her entire mind is fixed on the eggs, and there is a vacant look in her eyes. Can you show me such a picture?"

M.: "I shall try to get one."*

Master: "Perform your duties in an unselfish spirit. Always try to perform your duties without desiring any result."

M.: "Sir, may I make an effort to earn more money?"

Master: "It is permissible to do so to maintain a religious family. You may try to increase your income, but in an honest way. The goal of life is not the earning of money, but the service of God. Money is not harmful if it is devoted to the service of God."

M.: "How long should a man feel obliged to do his duty towards his wife and children?"

Master: "As long as they feel pinched for food and clothing. But one need not take the responsibility of a son when he is able to support himself. When the young fledgling learns to pick its own food, its mother pecks it if it comes to her for food."

* Unfortunately, M. could not get that picture during the Master's lifetime, but later he had one made and kept it in his house. (A copy is on page 438.)

M.: "How long must one do one's duty?"

Master: "The blossom drops off when the fruit appears. One doesn't have to do one's duty after the attainment of God, nor does one feel like doing it then."[7]

On 16 October 1882, M. described how the Master gave him instruction in a dream.

Master (*to M.*): "Do you ever have dreams?"

M.: "Yes, sir. The other day I dreamt a strange dream. I saw the whole world enveloped in water. There was water on all sides. A few boats were visible, but suddenly huge waves appeared and sank them. I was about to board a ship with a few others, when we saw a brahmin walking over that expanse of water. I asked him, 'How can you walk over the deep?' The brahmin said with a smile: 'Oh, there is no difficulty about that. There is a bridge under the water.' I said to him, 'Where are you going?' 'To Bhawanipur, the city of the Divine Mother,' he replied. 'Wait a little,' I cried. 'I shall accompany you.'"

Master: "Oh, I am thrilled to hear the story!"

M.: "The brahmin said: 'I am in a hurry. It will take you some time to get out of the boat. Good-bye. Remember this path and come after me.'"

Master: "Oh, my hair is standing on end! Please be initiated by a guru as soon as possible."[8]

M. later said: "Unlike other gurus, the Master did not make disciples by initiating with a mantra. He could make people realize God by a mere wish, or a word, or a touch, so there was no necessity for a mantra." M. also said: "The Master asked some, those who had doubts and did not have sufficient faith, to receive a mantra. He again said to some: 'You don't need a mantra. Just visit this place.' People take a mantra for God-realization. When you are seeing God in front of you, what is the need of a mantra?" However, M. admitted that the Master wrote a seed mantra on his tongue with his finger.[9] M. also mentioned that the Master gave a mantra to some disciples. For example, he gave Narendra a Ram mantra at the Cossipore garden house.[10]

In the beginning, M.'s wife was displeased that her husband was deeply involved with the Master. On 17 October 1882 M. asked: "What should one do if one's wife says: 'You are neglecting me; I shall commit suicide'?"

Master (*in a serious tone*): "Give up such a wife if she proves an obstacle in the way of spiritual life. Let her commit suicide or anything else she likes. The wife that hampers her husband's spiritual life is an ungodly wife."

Immersed in deep thought, M. stood leaning against the wall. Narendra and the other devotees remained silent a few minutes. The Master exchanged several words with them; then, suddenly going to M., he whispered in his ear: "But if a man has sincere love for God, then all come under his control — the king, wicked persons, and his wife. Sincere love of God on the husband's part may eventually help the wife to lead a spiritual life. If the husband is good, then through the grace of God the wife may also follow his example."

This had a most soothing effect on M.'s worried mind.[11]

Ramakrishna strove to make M. understand the guru-disciple relationship, and he also wanted to pour all his ideas and wisdom into him. On 22 October 1882 M. described Keshab's interpretation of Durga Puja to the Master. Keshab had said that anyone who could install the Mother in his or her heart, would automatically attain Lakshmi (wealth), Saraswati (knowledge), Kartika (strength), and Ganesha (success). Listening to this description, the Master understood that those who want to fulfill their desires worship the Mother in that manner. He said to M.: "Don't go hither and thither. Come here alone. Those who belong to the inner circle of my devotees will come only here."[12] As a small plant needs a fence around it to protect its growth, so the Master put a fence around M. so that he might not be confused.

Ramakrishna classified his devotees into two groups. The first group seeks liberation. About the second group, he said to M.: "They are satisfied if they can know two things: first, who I am; second, who they are and what their relationship to me is. You belong to this second group."[13] Sometimes the Master told him, "You will achieve everything just by thinking of me." And again: "He who thinks of me will attain my wealth, as children inherit their parents' wealth. My wealth is: knowledge, devotion, discrimination, renunciation, pure love, and samadhi."[14] Thus Ramakrishna gradually revealed to the inner circle of his devotees that he was the avatar and they were his playmates, born to carry out various aspects of his mission. As the limbs are part of the body, so the disciples of his inner circle were part of himself. If the disciples understood this and meditated on him, their minds would be permeated by Ramakrishna-consciousness. According to the Vedas, "One becomes exactly like Him upon whom one meditates."[15]

Christ said, "Except a man be born again, he cannot see the kingdom of God."[16] By this he meant spiritual rebirth. In Hinduism, one attains a second birth upon initiation into spiritual life. This rebirth is necessary to get rid of unhealthy or worldly samskaras and develop new spiritual samskaras. For this reason, Ramakrishna began to transform M.'s life, so that he would be the ideal man to record his message. In this connection, M. cited the example of a coral island. This island is formed by the hard, stony skeletons of certain marine polyps, which are deposited in extensive masses that form reefs and atolls in tropical seas. People on a coral island do not realize that previously there was an ocean where their homes now exist. In the same way, the constant recollectedness of Ramakrishna buried M.'s old samskaras, and as a result, for five years, he was absorbed in the divine realm of the Master. And he recorded everything in his diary, which eventually took the form of *The Gospel of Sri Ramakrishna*.

After living with the Master for some time and observing his samadhi, M. was anxious to have some sort of spiritual experience. On 5 June 1883 the Master said to M.: "Yes, God can be seen. X has had a vision of God. But don't tell anyone about it. Tell me, which do you like better, God with form, or the formless Reality?"

> M.: "Sir, nowadays I like to think of God without form. But I am also beginning to understand that it is God alone who manifests Himself through different forms."
>
> Master: "Will you take me in a carriage someday to Mati Sil's garden house at Belgharia? When you throw puffed rice into the lake there, the fish come to the surface and eat it. Ah! I feel so happy to see them sport in the water. That will awaken your spiritual consciousness too. You will feel as if the fish of the human soul were playing in the Ocean of Satchidananda. In the same manner, I go into an ecstatic mood when I stand in a big meadow. I feel like a fish released from a bowl into a lake.
>
> "Spiritual discipline is necessary in order to see God. I had to pass through very severe discipline. How many austerities I practised under the bel-tree! I would lie down under it, crying to the Divine Mother, 'O Mother, reveal Thyself to me.' The tears would flow in torrents and soak my body."[17]

Ramakrishna did not just preach religion; he taught his disciples how to practise it through examples or by describing his own experiences. On 18 June 1883 Ramakrishna went to Panihati to attend a Vaishnava festival. M., Rakhal, and other devotees went with him.

> Sri Ramakrishna, accompanied by the devotees, took a carriage to return to Dakshineswar. They were going to pass the temple garden of Mati Sil on the way. For a long time the Master had been asking M. to take him to the reservoir in the garden in order that he might teach him how to meditate on the formless God. There were tame fish in the reservoir. Nobody harmed them. Visitors threw puffed rice and other bits of food into the

water, and the big fish came in swarms to eat the food. Fearlessly the fish swam in the water and sported there joyously.

Coming to the reservoir, the Master said to M.: "Look at the fish. Meditating on the formless God is like swimming joyfully like these fish, in the Ocean of Bliss and Consciousness."[18]

Ramakrishna taught M. how to realize God as well as how to live in the world. On 15 June 1883 M. told the Master: "At mealtime, sometimes a cat stretches out its paw to take the fish from my plate. But I cannot show any resentment." Immediately the Master replied: "Why? You may even beat it once in a while. What's the harm? A worldly man should hiss, but he shouldn't pour out his venom. He mustn't actually injure others. But he should make a show of anger to protect himself from enemies. Otherwise they will injure him. But a sannyasi need not even hiss."[19]

On 26 September 1883 M. had a long talk with the Master. The Master asked: "Do you ever dream of me?"

M.: "Yes, sir. Many times."
Master: "How? Did you dream of me as giving you instruction?"
M. remained silent.
Master: "If you ever see me instructing you, then know that it is Satchidananda Himself that does so."
M. related his dream experiences to Sri Ramakrishna, who listened to them attentively.
Master (*to M.*): "That is very good. Don't reason anymore. You are a follower of Shakti."[20]

M. constantly immersed himself in the spiritual atmosphere of the Dakshineswar temple garden and absorbed the Master's teachings. On 9 December 1883 M. was in deep meditation on the veranda of the nahabat in Dakshineswar. He later recorded:

Sri Ramakrishna was standing in the road by the side of the nahabat. He was on his way to his room, having come from the pine-grove. He saw M. seated on the veranda of the nahabat, behind the screen, absorbed in meditation.
Master: "Hello! You are here? You will get results very soon. If you practise a little, then someone will come forward to help you."
M. looked up at the Master, startled; he remained sitting on the floor.
Master: "The time is ripe for you. The mother bird does not break the shell of the egg until the right time arrives. What I told you is indeed your Ideal."
Sri Ramakrishna again mentioned to M. his spiritual Ideal.

Master (*to M.*): "If you practise only a little, someone will come forward to tell you the right path. Observe the Ekadashi.

"You are my very own, my relative; otherwise, why should you come here so frequently?

"Once I saw the companions of Chaitanya, not in a trance but with these very eyes. Formerly I was in such an exalted state of mind that I could see all these things with my naked eyes; but now I see them in samadhi. I saw the companions of Chaitanya with these naked eyes. I think I saw you there, and Balaram too. You must have noticed that when I see certain people I jump up with a start. Do you know why? A man feels that way when he sees his own people after a long time."

M. remained silent. The Master himself gave the reply.

Master: "Could you come here unless you belonged to my inner circle? That means you all are my own relatives, my own people — like father and son, brother and sister.

"I do not tell you everything. If I did, would you come here anymore?"[21]

Observing the Master's blazing renunciation, and tormented by family problems, M. sometimes felt driven to renounce the world. On 3 August 1884 the Master said to M.:

"The important thing is somehow to cultivate devotion to God and love for Him. What is the use of knowing many things? It is enough to cultivate love of God by following any of the paths. When you have this love, you are sure to attain God. Afterwards, if it is necessary, God will explain everything to you and tell you about the other paths as well. It is enough for you to develop love of God. You have no need of many opinions and discussions. You have come to the orchard to eat mangoes. Enjoy them to your heart's content. You don't need to count the branches and leaves on the trees."

M: "I now desire that my activities may be much reduced and that I may devote myself greatly to God."

Master: "Ah! Certainly your desire will be fulfilled. But a jnani can live unattached in the world."

M: "True, sir. But one needs special power to lead an unattached life."

Master: "That is also true. But perhaps you wanted the worldly life. Now you should pray to God that your worldly duties may be reduced. And you will achieve the goal if you renounce mentally.

"Tell me, what is the meaning of renunciation?"

M: "Renunciation does not mean simply dispassion for the world. It means dispassion for the world and also longing for God."

Master: "You are right. You no doubt need money for your worldly life; but don't worry too much about it. The wise course is to accept what comes of its own accord. Don't take too much trouble to save money. Those who surrender their hearts and souls to God, those who are devoted to Him and have taken refuge in Him, do not worry much about money. As they earn, so they spend. The money comes in one way and goes out the other. This is what the Gita describes as 'accepting what comes of its own accord.'"[22]

Buddha described himself as a farmer who sowed the seed of religion in the hearts of his followers. Christ declared himself to be the shepherd who knew his sheep (his followers) and guided them. Ramakrishna tried to make human beings perfect. Swami Vivekananda described his method: "His principle was: first form character, first earn spirituality, and results will come of themselves. His favourite illustration was: 'When the lotus opens, the bees come of their own accord to seek the honey; so let the lotus of your character be full-blown, and the results will follow.' This is a great lesson to learn."[23]

Ramakrishna tested M. in many ways and finally took him into his inner circle. Swami Saradananda wrote about Ramakrishna's method of testing a prospective disciple:

When a man first came to the Master, he observed him very closely. If he felt attracted to the visitor, he talked about spiritual matters with him and asked him to visit occasionally. As the days passed and the visits continued, unknown to the visitor, the Master would examine the formation of his body and his limbs, the nature of his thoughts, the degree of his attachment to lust and gold, the magnitude of his worldly desires, and the extent to which the visitor's mind was being drawn towards him. After the Master had collected these data by keenly observing the man's movements, actions, and conversations, he arrived at a firm conclusion about the visitor's latent spirituality. Thus, the Master became convinced of a man's character after having seen him a few times. If the Master felt that he needed to know hidden facts about the man's inner nature, he would then use his subtle yogic vision to learn about them. He once told us about this: "When I am alone in the early hours of the morning, I think of your spiritual welfare. The Divine Mother then shows me how far one devotee has advanced on the spiritual path, why another cannot make progress, and so on." From this, however, do not conclude that his yogic power was active only at that time. Other conversations indicated that he could ascend to high states of spiritual consciousness and obtain similar visions at will. He told us, "Just as by merely looking at a glass case one can see all of its contents, so I can know the inmost thoughts and tendencies — indeed everything about someone — merely by looking at that person."[24]

Swami Vivekananda once said that Ramakrishna could make hundreds of Vivekanandas from a handful of dust. M. made a similar statement: "A potter kneads the clay and gives shape to pots and plates; and again at his will he breaks them and gives shape to other things. Similarly, Ramakrishna would play with human minds. He could make and unmake human minds at his will." From the very beginning Ramakrishna began to shape M.'s mind for a specific purpose: recording his gospel. For that reason, the Master first smashed M.'s ego, and then advised M. not to reason too much.

On 2 January 1884, the Master told M. directly:

"Through too much reasoning your spiritual life will be injured; you will at last become like Hazra. I used to roam at night in the streets all alone, and cry to the Divine Mother, 'O Mother, blight with Thy thunderbolt my desire to reason!' Tell me that you won't reason anymore."

M.: "Yes, sir. I won't reason anymore."

Master: "Everything can be achieved simply through love of God…. Weeping, I prayed to the Mother: 'O Mother, reveal to me what is contained in the Vedas and the Vedanta. Reveal to me what is in the Purana and the Tantra.' One by one She has revealed all these to me.

"Another day She showed me an ocean. Taking the form of a salt doll, I was going to measure its depth. While doing this, through the grace of the guru I was turned to stone. Then I saw a ship and at once got into it. The helmsman was the guru. I hope you pray every day to Satchidananda, who is the Guru. Do you?"

M: "Yes, sir."

Master: "The guru was the helmsman in that boat. I saw that 'I' and 'you' were two different things. Again I jumped into the ocean, and was changed into a fish. I found myself swimming joyfully in the Ocean of Satchidananda.

"These are all deep mysteries. What can you understand through reasoning? You will realize everything when God Himself teaches you. Then you will not lack any knowledge."[25]

M.'s steadfast devotion for his guru made him an ideal disciple.

With Ramakrishna in Various Places

We are accustomed to seeing pictures or images of Ramakrishna in monastery temples, on the altars of shrines in private homes, hanging on the walls of our rooms, and on our desks. But is he limited to these places only? The Master once said, "I will be worshipped from house to house." But now his presence has spread everywhere. Now one can see his photograph in the thatched huts of village farmers, in the mansions of wealthy people in the cities, in caves and cottages in the Himalayas, in shops, and in taxis. His image is even carried in travellers' purses and wallets.

Just as Ramakrishna loved to travel through the streets of Calcutta and along village roads, he also enjoyed travelling along various religious paths. He showed people how to move through this impermanent world. However, his body was very delicate, so once he lamented: "Gaur and Nitai carried the message of God from door to door, and I cannot go anyplace without a carriage." Driven by his desire to rescue people from the whirlpool of maya, he often visited his devotees, walking or travelling by palanquin, bullock cart, horse carriage, or train. Whenever he heard of anyone who had sincere longing for God, he would rush to see that person. He did not care about formal invitations, and he disregarded social etiquette. His attitude was: "Well, you are a devotee and think of God, so I have come to see you." He said, "If a man takes one step towards God,

God comes a hundred steps towards him." A devotee once said, "I did not take even one step, but the Master took hundreds of steps and came to me."

Although Ramakrishna was absorbed most of the time in a divine mood, on occasion he would travel around Calcutta in search of souls hungry for God. Once he said to M.: "You don't want anything from me, but you love to see me and hear my words. My mind also dwells on you. I wonder how you are and why you don't come. Could you give me your address?"[1] Thus collecting the devotees' addresses, the Master moved through the streets of Calcutta to look after their welfare. Sometimes the devotees' intense longing pulled Ramakrishna from Dakshineswar to Calcutta, even at night. If someone found it difficult to visit him in Dakshineswar, the Master would send for that person when visiting another devotee's home in Calcutta.

Human beings live on their memories. Clinging to their memories, they smile and cry; they ruminate over the past and dream about the future. Some memories remain dormant, while others are vividly active. We may not see the physical presence of Ramakrishna in Kamarpukur and Jayrambati, in Varanasi and Vrindaban, or in the lanes and streets of Calcutta, but those places, houses, and streets still exist. If we live in those cities, we walk through those streets every day and see the places connected with Ramakrishna. But we are so burdened with family responsibilities, or perhaps with poverty and mental anguish, that we have no time to evoke the Master's presence in our memories. While moving here and there, if someone reminds us that the Master came to this house or walked through this street, then momentarily at least he becomes manifest in our mind and we feel his presence.

After the passing away of the Master, M., the recorder of *The Gospel of Sri Ramakrishna*, lived on his memories of him. He would bow down to the house on Bechu Chatterjee Street where the Master's elder brother had once run a school. He also paid his respects to the house of the Mitra family at Jhamapukur where the Master had once worked as a priest. Observing his companions' surprise, M. would say, "Do you know that anyone who walks through this street will become a yogi?"[2] People who did not understand M.'s divine madness thought he was unbalanced.

Not only did M. live on the memories of Ramakrishna, but he also recorded in vivid language his guru's life in his immortal book, *The Gospel of Sri Ramakrishna*. In this chapter we shall visualize Ramakrishna's movements through the streets of Calcutta. Based on M.'s accounts and on the records that other eyewitnesses have left, we shall follow the holy footprints of the Master. While mentally moving with him, we shall listen to his fascinating conversations and learn many interesting things that his keen mind reveals. It will not always be pleasant to travel with him. Most of the time he will be in a state of God-intoxication. While travelling with him, we will be anxious that he might have an accident at any moment.

Human life is guided by social norms and conventions and controlled by injunctions and prohibitions. These rules and regulations make the journey of life mechanical and monotonous. Truly, life is dull and joyless without freedom. This is why our modern urban civilization seems superficial and artificial. Although Ramakrishna lived on the outskirts of Calcutta, the capital of British India at that time, he was not at all affected by its materialistic civilization. His mind dwelt in God, so he walked his own path, without concern for public opinion.

During the 19th century, a tremendous commotion was going on in Calcutta, sparked by the materialism of the West. The trend of Western civilization was towards lust and gold, greed and sense enjoyment. Calcutta, the citadel of Indian culture, was turned upside down. In fact, the whole of Indian society was shaken because its national ideals, system of education, and religion were being attacked by Western civilization.

Ramakrishna observed that, in general, the worldly people of Calcutta had been hypnotized by the West. To break the spell they were under, Ramakrishna began visiting places here and there in Calcutta. He visited the Maidan (Central Park) and Fort William; he went to the theatres; he visited the houses of the rich as well as of the poor. If the mountain will not go to Muhammad, Muhammad must go to the mountain. So Ramakrishna went uninvited to the homes of people in Calcutta and talked to them about God. He reminded them again and again of the goal of human life. Once he said: "Wherever there is any trouble in the Divine Mother's empire, I shall have to rush there to stop it, like a government officer."[3]

Now we shall travel with Ramakrishna using our imagination. We shall listen to him talk while going by horse carriage or while walking in the streets of Calcutta. We shall not enter anyone's house, because it is not proper to enter someone's home uninvited. We shall observe his movements and learn from him how to walk with God. We are indebted to M., who has left us these wonderful street scenes and immortal words of the Master. We shall present to the reader excerpts from M.'s invaluable record, and occasionally, we shall add our own comments.

A Visit to Ishwar Chandra Vidyasagar

M. described the Master's visit to Ishwar Chandra Vidyasagar, which took place on 5 August 1882:

Ramakrishna had long wanted to visit Ishwar Chandra Vidyasagar, a great scholar, educator, writer, and philanthropist. Learning from M. that he was a teacher at Vidyasagar's school, the Master asked: "Can you take me to Vidyasagar? I should like very much to see him." M. told Ishwar Chandra of Ramakrishna's wish, and the pandit gladly agreed that M. should bring the Master some Saturday afternoon at four o'clock.

On the afternoon of August 5 the Master left Dakshineswar in a hackney carriage, accompanied by Bhavanath, M., and Hazra. Vidyasagar lived in Badurbagan, in Central Calcutta, about six miles from Dakshineswar. The carriage crossed the Baghbazar bridge and then reached Amherst Street via Shyambazar. On the way the Master joyfully talked with his companions; but as the carriage neared Vidyasagar's house his mood suddenly changed. He was overpowered with divine ecstasy. Not noticing this, M. pointed out the garden house where Raja Rammohan Roy had lived. The Master was annoyed and said, "I don't care about such things now." He was going into an ecstatic state.

The carriage stopped in front of Vidyasagar's house. The Master alighted, supported by M., who then led the way. In the courtyard were many flowering plants. As the Master walked to the house he said to M., like a child, pointing to his shirt-button: "My shirt is unbuttoned. Will that offend Vidyasagar?" "Oh, no!" said M. "Don't be anxious about it. Nothing about you will be offensive. You don't have to button your shirt." He accepted the assurance simply, like a child.[4]

Ramakrishna had a prolonged conversation with Vidyasagar. While talking to Vidyasagar about Brahman, Ramakrishna said: "What Brahman is cannot be described. All things in the world — the Vedas, the Puranas, the Tantras, the six systems of philosophy — have been defiled, like food that has been touched by the tongue, for they have been read or uttered by the tongue. Only one thing has not been defiled in this way, and that is Brahman." In this connection he cited the example of a salt doll that wanted to tell others how deep the ocean was. But no sooner did it get into the water than it melted.

When one is illumined, one becomes silent. The Master gave examples from what he had seen around himself, such as: "The bee buzzes as long as it is not sitting on a flower. It becomes silent when it begins to sip honey. An empty pitcher makes a gurgling sound when it is dipped in water. When it fills up it becomes silent."

After leaving Vidyasagar, the Master met with one of his devotees, as M. narrated:

Ramakrishna then took leave of Vidyasagar, who with his friends escorted the Master to the main gate, leading the way with a lighted candle in his hand. Before leaving the room, the Master prayed for the family's welfare, going into an ecstatic mood as he did so.

As soon as the Master and the devotees reached the gate, they saw an unexpected sight and stood still. In front of them was a bearded gentleman of fair complexion. No sooner did he see the Master than he fell prostrate before him.

When he stood up the Master said: "Who is this? Balaram? Why so late in the evening?"

Balaram: "I have been waiting here a long time, sir."

Master: "Why didn't you come in?"

Balaram: "All were listening to you. I didn't like to disturb you."

The Master got into the carriage with his companions.

Vidyasagar (*to M.*): "Shall I pay the carriage hire?"

M.: "Oh, don't bother, please. It is taken care of."

Vidyasagar and his friends bowed to Ramakrishna, and the carriage started for Dakshineswar. But the little group, with the venerable Vidyasagar at their head holding the lighted candle, stood at the gate and gazed after the Master until he was out of sight.[5]

Boat Trips with Keshab Chandra Sen

Ramakrishna travelled by steamboat thrice with Keshab Chandra Sen. The first trip was in 1881 and Hriday was with him. The Master enjoyed the jhak-jhak sound of the steamer. Someone requested the Master to look through the telescope of the steamer, but he said: "My mind is now attached to God. How can I withdraw it from Him and put it on this telescope?" The second trip took place on 23 February 1882. On that day Keshab came to the Master at Dakshineswar with Reverend Joseph Cook, Miss Pigot (an American missionary), Nagendra Nath Gupta (the editor of the *Tribune*), Prince Gajendranarayan of Coochbehar, Pratap Majumdar, and other Brahmo devotees. Observing the Master's unceasing samadhi and ecstatic mood, Pratap remarked: "Good heavens! It is as if he were possessed by a ghost!"[6]

M. provided a detailed description of the third boat trip, which took place on 27 October 1882:

It was Friday, the day of the Lakshmi Puja. Keshab Chandra Sen had arranged a boat trip on the Ganges for Sri Ramakrishna.

About four o'clock in the afternoon the steamboat with Keshab and his Brahmo followers cast anchor in the Ganges alongside the Kali temple at Dakshineswar.... Some disciples of Keshab entered [the Master's room]. Bowing before the Master, they said to him: "Sir, the steamer has arrived. Keshab Babu has asked us to take you there." A small boat was to carry the Master to the steamer. No sooner did he get into the boat than he lost outer consciousness in samadhi. Vijay was with him.

M. was among the passengers. As the boat came alongside the steamer, all rushed to the railing to have a view of Sri Ramakrishna. Keshab became anxious to get him safely onboard. With great difficulty the Master was brought back to consciousness of the world and taken to a cabin in the steamer.... He said to himself in a whisper: "Mother, why have You brought me here? They are hedged around and not free. Can I free them?"[7]

On that day the Master described the mystery of Kali, sang many songs, and held the Brahmos spellbound with his illuminating talk and humour.

M.'s narrative continued:

The boat cast anchor at Kayalaghat [in Calcutta] and the passengers prepared to disembark. On coming outside they noticed that the full moon was up. The trees, the buildings, and the boats on the Ganges were bathed in its mellow light. A carriage was hailed for the Master, and M. and a few devotees got in with him. The Master asked for Keshab. Presently the latter arrived and inquired about the arrangements made for the Master's return to Dakshineswar. Then he bowed low and took leave of Sri Ramakrishna.

The carriage drove through the European quarter of the city. The Master enjoyed the sight of the beautiful mansions on both sides of the well-lighted streets. Suddenly he said: "I am thirsty. What's to be done?" Nandalal, Keshab's nephew, stopped the carriage before the India Club and went upstairs to get some water. The Master inquired whether the glass had been well washed. On being assured that it had been, he drank the water.

As the carriage went along, the Master put his head out of the window and looked with childlike enjoyment at the people, the vehicles, the horses, and the streets, all flooded with moonlight. Now and then he heard European ladies singing at the piano. He was in a very happy mood.

The carriage arrived at the house of Suresh Mitra, who was a great devotee of the Master and whom he addressed affectionately as Surendra. He was not at home.

The members of the household opened a room on the ground floor for the Master and his party. The cab fare was to be paid; Surendra would have taken care of it had he been there. The Master said to a devotee: "Why don't you ask the ladies to pay the fare? They certainly know that their master visits us at Dakshineswar. I am not a stranger to them."[8]

If someone now were to follow the same route that Ramakrishna took in 1882, he would see many changes. The names of some streets are different; cars and buses have replaced horse carriages, and electric lights have replaced gas lights; the British government in India is no more.

After Mathur's death, the Master's carriage fare was paid by one of the devotees who could afford the expense. The Master's humorous remark, asking for the fare at Surendra's house, makes us laugh. But then we remember with awe how an avatar visited the houses of his devotees for their benefit.

Ramakrishna at the Circus

Ramakrishna prayed to the Divine Mother, "Mother, don't make me a dry monk." We are amazed when we find that the Master, who was mostly in a state of divine intoxication, went to Calcutta to see the circus on 15 November 1882. Sometimes we plan to meet our friends at a particular place and time and then go to a theatre or a movie house. The Master did the same thing, as M. recorded in the *Gospel*:

> Sri Ramakrishna, accompanied by Rakhal and several other devotees, came to Calcutta in a carriage and called for M. at Vidyasagar's school where he was teaching. Then they all set out for the Maidan. Sri Ramakrishna wanted to see the Wilson Circus. As the carriage rolled along the crowded Chitpore Road, his joy was very great. Like a little child he leaned first out of one side of the carriage and then out of the other, talking to himself as if addressing the passers-by. To M. he said: "I find the attention of the people fixed on earthly things. They are all rushing about for the sake of their stomachs. No one is thinking of God."
>
> They arrived at the circus. Tickets for the cheapest seats were purchased. The devotees took the Master to a high gallery, and they all sat on a bench. He said joyfully: "Ha! This is a good place. I can see the show well from here." There were exhibitions of various feats. A horse raced around a circular track over which large iron rings were hung at intervals. The circus rider, an Englishwoman, stood on one foot on the horse's back, and as the horse passed under the rings, she jumped through them, always alighting on one foot on the horse's back. The horse raced around the entire circle, and the woman never missed the horse or lost her balance.
>
> When the circus was over, the Master and the devotees stood outside in the field, near the carriage. Since it was a cold night he covered his body with his green shawl.
>
> Sri Ramakrishna said to M.: "Did you see how that Englishwoman stood on one foot on her horse, while it ran like lightning? How difficult a

feat that must be! She must have practised a long time. The slightest care-lessness and she would break her arms or legs; she might even be killed. One faces the same difficulty leading the life of a householder. A few succeed in it through the grace of God and as a result of their spiritual practice. But most people fail. Entering the world, they become more and more involved in it; they drown in worldliness and suffer the agonies of death. Therefore spiritual practice is extremely necessary; otherwise one cannot rightly live in the world."[9]

Every one of the Master's actions was meaningful. He went to see the circus and then used an example from it to tell his devotees how one could attain perfection through practice.

The Festival in Panihati

On 18 June 1883, the Master attended a Vaishnava festival with some of his disciples. M. described the event:

Sri Ramakrishna had been invited to the great religious festival at Panihati near Calcutta. This "Festival of the Flattened Rice" was inaugurated by Raghunath Das, a disciple of Chaitanya. It is said that Raghunath used to run away from home, secretly practise his devotions, and enjoy the bliss of spiritual ecstasy. One day Nityananda said to him: "Thief! You run away from home and enjoy the love of God all alone. You hide it from us. I shall punish you today. You must arrange a religious festival and entertain the devotees with flattened rice." Since then the festival has been annually celebrated at Panihati by the Vaishnavas.

The Master had been invited by Mani Sen who was the custodian of the [Radha-Krishna] temple. Ram, M., Rakhal, Bhavanath, and a few other disciples went with the Master in a carriage. On his way to Panihati Sri Ramakrishna was in a light mood and joked with the youngsters. But as soon as the carriage reached the place of the festival, the Master, to the utter amazement of the devotees, shot into the crowd. He joined the kirtan party and danced, totally forgetting the world. Every now and then he stood still in samadhi, carefully supported by Navadwip Goswami for fear he might fall to the ground. Thousands of devotees were gathered together for the festival.... The crowd seemed to become infected by the Master's divine fervour and swayed to and fro, chanting the name of God, until the very air seemed to reverberate with it. Drums, cymbals, and other instruments produced melodious sounds.... Flowers were showered from all sides on his feet and head. The shouting of the name of Hari was heard even at a distance, like the rumbling of the ocean.[10]

Top: Panihati festival ground, Bottom: Kankurgachi Yogodyana

Travelling by Carriage with the Master

On 21 July 1883, M. joined the Master on a trip to Calcutta. He wrote:

It was about four o'clock in the afternoon when Sri Ramakrishna, with Ramlal and one or two other devotees, started from Dakshineswar for Calcutta in a carriage. As the carriage passed the gate of the Kali temple, they met M. coming on foot with four mangoes in his hand. The carriage stopped and M. saluted the Master. Sri Ramakrishna was going to visit some of his devotees in Calcutta.

Master (*to M., with a smile*): "Come with us. We are going to Adhar's house."

M. got joyfully into the carriage. Having received an English education he did not believe in the tendencies inherited from previous births. But he had admitted a few days before that it was on account of Adhar's good tendencies from past births that he showed such great devotion to the Master. Later on he had thought about this subject and had discovered that he was not yet completely convinced about inherited tendencies. He had come to Dakshineswar that day to discuss the matter with Sri Ramakrishna.

Master: "Well, what do you think of Adhar?"

M.: "He has great yearning for God."

Master: "Adhar, too, speaks very highly of you."

M.: "I haven't much faith in rebirth and inherited tendencies. Will that in any way injure my devotion to God?"

Master: "It is enough to believe that all is possible in God's creation. Never allow the thought to cross your mind that your ideas are the only true ones, and that those of others are false. Then God will explain everything.

"What can man understand of God's activities?...Once, when I was explaining God's actions to someone, God suddenly showed me the lake at Kamarpukur. I saw a man removing the green scum and drinking the water. The water was clear as crystal. God revealed to me that Satchidananda is covered by the scum of maya. He who puts the green scum aside can drink the water."

The carriage came to the crossing at Shobhabazar in Calcutta. The Master continued, saying: "Sometimes I find that the universe is saturated with the Consciousness of God, as the earth is soaked with water in the rainy season. Well, I see so many visions, but I never feel vain about them."

M. (*with a smile*): "That you should speak of vanity, sir!"

Master: "Upon my word, I don't feel vanity even in the slightest degree.... Have you found anyone else resembling me — any pandit or holy man?"

M.: "God has created you with His own hands, whereas He has made others by machine. All others He has created according to law."

Master (*laughing, to Ramlal and the other devotees*): "Listen to what he is saying!"

Sri Ramakrishna laughed for some time, and said at last, "Really and truly I have no pride — no, not even the slightest bit."[11]

Like a child, the Master laughed, and his joy was contagious.

The Master had an open mind, and he always loved to learn new things. He once said: "As long as I live so long do I learn." M.'s narrative shows this aspect of Ramakrishna, as the conversation continues on the way to Calcutta:

Master: "Do you believe in English astronomy?"

M.: "It is possible to make new discoveries by applying the laws of Western astronomy. Observing the irregular movement of Uranus, the astronomers looked through their telescopes and discovered Neptune shining in the sky. They can also foretell eclipses."

Master: "Yes, that is so."

The carriage drove on. They were approaching Adhar's house. Sri Ramakrishna said to M.: "Dwell in the truth and you will certainly realize God."

M.: "You said the other day to Navadwip Goswami: 'O God, I want Thee. Please do not delude me with Thy world-bewitching maya. I want to realize Thee.'"

Master: "Yes, one should be able to say that from one's innermost soul." [12]

After giving M. this valuable advice, the Master entered Adhar's parlour. Afterwards, the Master visited the houses of Jadu Mallick and Khelat Ghosh. In both homes he talked about God and sang devotional songs. He finally returned to Dakshineswar late at night.

The Master's Keen Power of Observation

When Ramakrishna moved through the streets of Calcutta by horse carriage, he sometimes kept the doors open so he could observe the fashions and lifestyles of the people he saw. Nothing escaped his keen vision. On 7 September 1883 he said to M.:

"The other day I went to Calcutta. As I drove along the streets in the carriage, I observed that everyone's attention was fixed on low things. Everyone was brooding over his stomach and running after nothing but food. Everyone's mind was turned to 'lust and gold.' I saw only one or two with their attention fixed on higher things, with their minds turned to God."

M.: "The present age has aggravated this stomach-worry. Trying to imitate the English, people have turned their attention to more luxuries; therefore their wants have also increased."[13]

Ramakrishna felt great discomfort while hearing worldly conversation. On 9 September 1883 he said to M.:

"I see people coming to the Ganges to bathe. They talk their heads off about everything under the sun. The widowed aunt says: 'Without me they cannot perform the Durga Puja. I have to look after even the smallest detail. Again, I have to supervise everything when there is a marriage festival in the family, even the bed of the bride and groom.'"

M.: "Why should we blame them? How else will they pass the time?"

Master (*with a smile*): "Some people have their shrine rooms in their attics. The women arrange the offerings and flowers and make the sandal paste. But, while doing so, they never say a word about God. The burden of the conversation is: 'What shall we cook today? I couldn't get good vegetables in the market. That curry was delicious yesterday. That boy is my cousin. Hello there! Have you that job still? Don't ask me how I am. My Hari is no more.' Just fancy! They talk of such things in the shrine room at the time of worship!"[14]

A Visit to Kankurgachi

In India, people generally invite a holy person or a famous leader to inaugurate a new house or retreat centre. Ram Datta bought a garden house for a retreat and wanted the Master to inaugurate it. M. described Ramakrishna's first visit to the garden, on 26 December 1883:

Sri Ramakrishna, accompanied by Manilal Mallick, M., and several other devotees, was in a carriage on his way to Ram's new garden [Kankurgachi, in Calcutta]. The garden, which Ram had recently purchased, was next to Surendra's. Ram adored the Master as an incarnation of God. Manilal was a member of the Brahmo Samaj. The Brahmos do not believe in Divine Incarnations.

Master (*to Manilal*): "In order to meditate on God, one should try at first to think of Him as free from *upadhis*, limitations. God is beyond upadhis. He is beyond speech and mind. But it is very difficult to achieve perfection in this form of meditation.

"But it is easy to meditate on an Incarnation — God born as man. Yes, God in man. The body is a mere covering. It is like a lantern with a light burning inside, or like a glass case in which one sees precious things."

Arriving at the garden, the Master got out of the carriage and accompanied Ram and the other devotees to the sacred tulsi grove. Standing

near it, he said: "How nice! It is a fine place. You can easily meditate on
God here."

Sri Ramakrishna sat down in the house, which stood to the south of
the lake. Ram offered him a plate of fruit and sweets, which he enjoyed
with the devotees. After a short time he went around the garden.

Next Sri Ramakrishna proceeded towards Surendra's garden. He
walked on foot a little distance and saw a sadhu sitting on a couch under
a tree. At once he went up to the holy man and joyfully began a conversation with him.

Master: "To which order of monks do you belong? Have you any title
-- Giri, Puri, or the like?"

Sadhu: "People call me a paramahamsa."

Master: "That is good. 'I am Shiva' — that is a good attitude. But I
must tell you something else. The process of creation, preservation, and
destruction that is going on day and night is due to Shakti, the Power
of God. This Primal Power and Brahman are one and the same. Shakti
cannot exist without Brahman, just as waves cannot exist without water.
There cannot be any instrumental music without an instrument."

After a pleasant conversation with the sadhu, the Master returned to
the carriage, the holy man walking with him. Sri Ramakrishna looked
upon him as a friend of long acquaintance, and they walked arm in arm.[15]

This amazing scene shows how simple and natural was the Master's
human aspect. After the party reached Surendra's garden, the Master said
to Ram: "Bring this sadhu to Dakshineswar when you come."

Visits to Ishan

M.'s poetic faculty was given free rein in his vivid descriptions of the
Master's actions and his surroundings. Although these events took place
in the 1880s, we still see them very clearly, as if they were happening in
front of us.

On the morning of the Master's visit to Ishan's house in Calcutta on
27 December 1883, M. described a scene that has some similarities to
Krishna's journey to Hastinapur as ambassador of the Pandavas with a
proposal to try to avert the Kurukshetra war:

The temple garden was filled with the sweet music of the dawn service,
which mingled with the morning melody from the nahabat. Leaving his
bed, Sri Ramakrishna chanted the names of God in sweet tones. Then he
bowed before the pictures of the different deities in his room and went to
the west porch to salute the Ganges.

Some of the devotees who had spent the night at the temple garden came to the Master's room and bowed before him. M. had been staying there two weeks.

Sri Ramakrishna said to M.: "I have been invited to Ishan's this morning. Baburam will accompany me, and you too." M. made ready to go with the Master.

At eight o'clock the carriage hired for the Master stood waiting in front of the nahabat. On all sides plants and trees were in flower, and the river sparkled in the sunlight of the bright winter's day. The Master bowed once more before the pictures. Then, still chanting the name of the Divine Mother, he got into the carriage, followed by M. and Baburam. The devotees took with them Sri Ramakrishna's woolen shawl, woolen cap, and small bag of spices.

Sri Ramakrishna was very happy during the trip and enjoyed it like a child. About nine o'clock the carriage stopped at the door of Ishan's house. Ishan and his relatives greeted the Master and led him to the parlour on the first floor.[16]

M. described the events of 25 June 1884:

It was the day of the Rathayatra, the Chariot Festival of the Hindus. At Ishan's invitation Sri Ramakrishna went to his house in Calcutta. For some time the Master had had a desire to meet Pandit Shashadhar Tarkachudamani, who had been staying with one of Ishan's neighbours. So it was decided that he would visit the pandit in the afternoon.[17]

M. continued:

About four o'clock in the afternoon the Master left in a carriage for the house where Pandit Shashadhar was staying. As soon as Sri Ramakrishna got into the carriage he went into samadhi. His physical frame was very tender as a result of the austerities he had undergone during the long years of his spiritual discipline and his constant absorption in God-consciousness. The Master would suffer from the slightest physical discomfort and even from the vibration of worldly thoughts around him. Once Keshab Chandra Sen had said that Sri Ramakrishna, Christ, and Sri Chaitanya belonged to a delicate species of humanity that should be kept in a glass case and protected from the vulgar contact of the world.

It was the rainy season, and a fine drizzle of rain had made the road muddy. The sky was overcast. The devotees followed the carriage on foot. As the carriage stopped in front of the house, the host and his relatives welcomed the Master and took him upstairs to the drawing-room. There the Master met the pandit.[18]

Although the Master had not had any formal education, his words of wisdom would burst forth with similes, scintillating like fireworks. The Master told the pandit: "When the fruit appears the blossom drops off. Love of God is the fruit, and rituals are the blossom." He also said: "When the lamp is lighted the moths come in swarms. They don't have to be invited. In the same way, the preacher who has a commission from God need not invite people to hear him.... At Kamarpukur I have seen people measuring grain. It lies in a heap. One man keeps pushing grain from the heap towards another man, who weighs it on a scale. So the man who weighs doesn't run short of grain. It is the same with the preacher who has received a commission from God. As he teaches people, the Divine Mother Herself supplies him with fresh knowledge from behind. That knowledge never comes to an end."[19]

After a long conversation with the pandit, the Master returned to Ishan's house before dusk. After a while, the Master was prepared to leave. M. described the scene:

> Ishan and the other devotees stood by the Master. They were waiting to bid him good-bye. Sri Ramakrishna said to Ishan: "Live in the world like an ant. The world contains a mixture of truth and untruth, sugar and sand. Be an ant and take the sugar."
> "Again, the world is a mixture of milk and water, the bliss of God-consciousness and the pleasure of sense-enjoyment. Be a swan and drink the milk, leaving the water aside.
> "Live in the world like a waterfowl. The water clings to the bird, but the bird shakes it off. Live in the world like a mudfish. The fish lives in the mud, but its skin is always bright and shiny.
> "The world is indeed a mixture of truth and make-believe. Discard the make-believe and take the truth."
> Sri Ramakrishna got into the carriage and left for Dakshineswar.[20]

Ramakrishna at the Theatre

Sri Ramakrishna was planning to go to a performance of *Chaitanyalila* (The Life of Chaitanya) at the Star Theatre on 21 September 1884. Mahendra Mukherji was to take him to Calcutta in his carriage. They were talking about choosing good seats. Some suggested that one could see the performance well from the one-rupee gallery. Ram said: "Oh, no! I shall engage a box for him." The Master laughed. Some of the devotees said that public women took part in the play. They took the parts of Nimai, Nitai, and others.

Master (*to the devotees*): "I shall look upon them as the Blissful Mother Herself. What if one of them acts the part of Chaitanya? An imitation custard-apple reminds one of the real fruit.... I was once taken to the Maidan in Calcutta to see a balloon go up. There I noticed a young English boy leaning against a tree, with his body bent in three places. It at once brought before me the vision of Krishna and I went into samadhi."[21]

The Master later told M. privately: "What Ram says applies to rajasic people. What is the use of reserving an expensive seat?"

M. continued his description of that day:

> About five o'clock that afternoon Sri Ramakrishna was on his way to Calcutta. M., Mahendra Mukherji, and a few other devotees accompanied him in Mahendra's carriage. Thinking of God, the Master soon went into an ecstatic mood. After a long time he regained consciousness of the world. He observed: "That fellow Hazra dares teach me! The rascal!" After a short pause he said, "I shall drink some water." He often made such remarks in order to bring his mind down to the sense plane.
>
> Mahendra (to M.): "May I get some refreshments for him?"
>
> M.: "No, he won't eat anything now."
>
> Master (still in ecstatic mood): "I shall eat."
>
> Mahendra took the Master to his flour-mill located at Hatibagan. After a little rest Sri Ramakrishna was to go to the theatre.... Sri Ramakrishna washed his face. A smoke was prepared for him. He said to M.: "Is it dusk now? If it is, I won't smoke. During the twilight hour of the dusk you should give up all other activities and remember God." Saying this he looked at the hairs of his arm. He wanted to see whether he could count them. If he could not, it would be dusk.[22]

Every one of the Master's words and actions has deep meaning. Muslims pray punctually five times a day. Orthodox Hindus repeat the Gayatri mantra three times a day. Some practise spiritual disciplines at sunrise and sunset, and some do purascharana* from sunrise to sunset. Maintaining punctuality in spiritual disciplines is extremely important. It is called kshana rahasya — that is, observing the mystery of time. For example, we have set times for breakfast, lunch, and dinner. As a result, our stomachs demand food at those times. Similarly, if we set aside time for meditation at 6:00 a.m. and 6:00 p.m., our minds will automatically demand spiritual food at those times. The Master did not have a watch. He saw how villagers determined morning by hearing the singing of the birds and evening by seeing whether one can still see the hairs on the arm.

Let us resume M.'s narrative:

*Repeating the mantra a certain number of times a day, then methodically increasing the amount daily, followed by a similar decrease, according to the phase of the moon.

About half past eight in the evening the carriage with the Master and the devotees drew up in front of the Star Theatre on Beadon Street. The Master was accompanied by M., Baburam, Mahendra, and two or three others. They were talking about engaging seats, when Girish Chandra Ghosh, the manager of the theatre, accompanied by several officials, came out to the carriage, greeted the Master, and took him and the party upstairs. Girish had heard of the Master and was very glad to see him at the theatre. The Master was conducted to one of the boxes. M. sat next to him; Baburam and one or two devotees sat behind.

The hall was brilliantly lighted.... Sri Ramakrishna was filled with joy and said to M., with his childlike smile: "Ah, it is very nice here! I am glad to have come. I feel inspired when I see so many people together. Then I clearly perceive that God Himself has become everything."

M.: "It is true, sir."

Master: "How much will they charge us here?"

M.: "They won't take anything. They are very happy that you have come to the theatre."

Master: "It is all due to the grace of the Divine Mother."

After the performance, a devotee stopped the Master as he was about to enter a carriage. He asked him how he had enjoyed the play. Smiling, the Master replied: "I found the representation the same as the real."

M.'s narrative continued:

The carriage proceeded towards Mahendra's mill. Suddenly Sri Ramakrishna went into an ecstatic mood and murmured to himself in loving tones: "O Krishna! O Krishna! Krishna is knowledge! Krishna is soul! Krishna is mind! Krishna is life! Krishna is body! O Govinda, Thou art my life! Thou art my soul!"

The carriage reached the mill. Mahendra fed the Master tenderly, with various dishes. With Mahendra and a few other devotees, Sri Ramakrishna left in the carriage for the Dakshineswar temple garden. The Master was in a happy mood. He sang a song about Gauranga and Nitai.

Mahendra: "Please bless me that I may have love for God."

Master: "You are generous and artless. One cannot realize God without sincerity and simplicity. God is far, far away from the crooked heart."

Near Shyambazar, Mahendra bade the Master good-bye, and the carriage continued on its way.[23]

The Annakuta Festival in Barabazar

Two days after the annual Kali puja, the Marwaris of the Barabazar section in Calcutta celebrated the Annakuta festival. (Annakuta means "hill of food.") During this festival a vast quantity of cooked food is offered to the deity and later distributed among devotees and the poor.

M. described how the Master took part in the festival, on 20 October 1884:

> Sri Ramakrishna had been invited by the Marwari devotees to the ceremony at 12 Mallick Street. It was the second day of the bright fortnight of the moon. The festival connected with the worship of Kali, known as the "Festival of Light," was still going on at Barabazar.
>
> About three o'clock in the afternoon M. and the younger Gopal came to Barabazar. M. had in his hand a bundle of cloths he had purchased for Sri Ramakrishna. Mallick Street was jammed with people, bullock-carts, and carriages. As M. and Gopal approached 12 Mallick Street they noticed Sri Ramakrishna in a carriage, which could hardly move because of the jam. Baburam and Ram Chattopadhyay were with the Master. He smiled at M. and Gopal.
>
> Sri Ramakrishna alighted from the carriage. With Baburam he proceeded on foot to the house of his host, M. leading the way. They saw the courtyard of the house filled with big bales of clothes, which were being loaded into bullock-carts for shipment. The Marwari host greeted the Master and led him to the third floor of the house. A painting of Kali hung on the wall. Sri Ramakrishna bowed before it. He sat down and became engaged in conversation with the devotees. One of the Marwaris began to stroke his feet. The Master asked him to stop. After reflecting a minute he said, "All right, you can stroke them a little." His words were full of compassion.[24]

The picture of Barabazar that M. painted with words is over 120 years old, but anyone who visits that area of Barabazar now will see the same scene. The streets are still jammed with traffic, only now horse carriages and bullock-carts have been replaced by handcarts, jeeps, and trucks. And visitors will see the angry and disgusted faces of the drivers of carts, cars, and trucks instead of the smiling face of Ramakrishna.

We shall wait on the sidewalk of Mallick Street till the Master returns from the house. M. continued:

> Sri Ramakrishna took leave of the host. It was evening and the street was jammed as before with people and vehicles. He said: "Let us get out of the carriage. It can go by a back street." Proceeding on foot, he found that a betel-leaf seller had opened his stall in front of a small room that looked like a hole. One could not possibly enter it without bending one's head. The Master said: "How painful it is to be shut in such a small space! That is the way of worldly people. And they are happy in such a life."

The carriage came up after making the detour. The Master entered it with Baburam, M., and Ram Chattopadhyay. The younger Gopal sat on the roof of the carriage.

A beggar woman with a baby on her arm stood in front of the carriage waiting for alms. The Master said to M., "Have you any money?" Gopal gave her something.

The carriage rolled along Barabazar. Everywhere there were signs of great festivity. The night was dark but illuminated with myriads of lights. The carriage came to the Chitpur Road, which was also brightly lighted. The people moved in lines like ants. The crowd looked at the gaily decorated stores and stalls on both sides of the road. There were sweetmeat stores and perfume stalls. Pictures, beautiful and gaudy, hung from the walls. Well-dressed shopkeepers sprayed the visitors with rose water. The carriage stopped in front of a perfume stall. The Master looked at the pictures and lights and felt happy as a child. People were talking loudly. He cried out: "Go forward! Move on!" He laughed. He said to Baburam with a loud laugh: "Move on! What are you doing?" The devotees laughed too. They understood that the Master wanted them to move forward to God and not to be satisfied with their present state.

The carriage drove on. The Master noticed that M. had brought some cloths for him. M. had with him two pieces of unbleached and two pieces of washed cloth. But the Master had asked him only for the unbleached ones. He said to M.: "Give me the unbleached ones. You may keep the others. All right. You may give me one of them."

M.: "Then shall I take back one piece?"

Master: "Then take both."

M.: "As you please, sir."

Master: "You may give me those when I need them. You see, yesterday Beni Pal wanted me to carry away some food for Ramlal. I told him I couldn't. It is impossible for me to lay up for the future."

M.: "That's all right, sir. I shall take back the two pieces of washed cloth."

Referring to a devotee, Sri Ramakrishna said: "I said to him yesterday, 'Tomorrow I shall go to Barabazar; please meet me there.' Do you know what he said? He said: 'The tram fare will be one anna. Where shall I get it?' He had been to Beni Pal's garden yesterday and had officiated there as a priest. No one had asked him to do it. He had put on the show himself. He wanted people to know that he was a member of the Brahmo Samaj. (*To M.*) Can you tell me what he meant when he said that the tram would cost him one anna?"

The conversation turned to the Annakuta festival of the Marwaris.

Master (*to the devotees*): "What you have seen here one sees at Vrindaban too.... Did you notice the Marwaris' devotion? That is the real

Hindu ideal. That is the Sanatana Dharma. Did you notice their joy when they carried the image in procession? They were happy to think that they bore the throne of God on their shoulders.

"The Hindu religion alone is the Sanatana Dharma. The various creeds you hear of nowadays have come into existence through the will of God and will disappear again through His will. They will not last forever."

M. was going home. He saluted the Master and got out of the carriage near Shobhabazar. Sri Ramakrishna proceeded to Dakshineswar in a happy mood.[25]

During this trip we saw the Master reveal his strict renunciation. We also felt pity for that miserly man who rejected an avatar's invitation because he did not want to spend one anna for the tram fare. Some people consider a small donation to a charity for religious purposes to be a waste of money, but they do not hesitate to spend a lot of money for a vacation, shopping, eating in a restaurant, going to the movies, and so on. This is the nature of worldly people.

At Balaram Bose's House

During Sri Ramakrishna's time, Dakshineswar was a village and there was no regular transport system between it and Calcutta. People had to travel there by foot, carriage, or boat. For this reason the Master needed a place in Calcutta where he could meet on a regular basis with his devotees who lived in the city. Balaram Bose's house served that purpose.

M. described the following meeting at Balaram's house, which took place on 11 March 1885:

Balaram was indeed blessed among the householder disciples of the Master. Sri Ramakrishna often described him as a *rasaddar*, or supplier of stores, appointed by the Divine Mother to take care of his physical needs. Balaram's house in Calcutta had been sanctified many times by the Master's presence. There he frequently lost himself in samadhi, dancing, singing, or talking about God. Those of the Master's disciples and devotees who could not go to Dakshineswar visited him there and received his instruction. And so it happened that whenever the Master was at Balaram's house, the devotees would gather there. It was the Master's chief vineyard in Calcutta. It was here that the devotees came to know each other intimately.

The shadow of evening fell on Calcutta. For the moment the noise of the busy metropolis was stilled. Gongs and conch-shells proclaimed the evening worship in many Hindu homes. Devotees of God set aside their worldly duties and turned their minds to prayer and meditation. This joining of day and night, this mystic twilight, always created an ecstatic mood in the Master.

The devotees seated in the room looked at Sri Ramakrishna as he began to chant the sweet name of the Divine Mother. After the chanting he began to pray. Every word of this prayer, uttered from the depths of his soul, stirred the minds of the devotees. The melody of his voice and the childlike simplicity of his face touched their hearts very deeply.

Girish invited the Master to his house, saying that he must go there that very night.

It was nine o'clock in the evening when the Master was ready to start for Girish's house. Since Balaram had prepared supper for him, Sri Ramakrishna said to Balaram: "Please send the food you have prepared for me to Girish's. I shall enjoy it there." He did not want to hurt Balaram's feelings.

As the Master was coming down from the second floor of Balaram's house, he became filled with divine ecstasy. He looked as if he were drunk. Narayan and M. were by his side; a little behind came Ram, Chuni, and the other devotees. No sooner did he reach the ground floor than he became totally overwhelmed. Narayan came forward to hold him by the hand lest he should miss his footing and fall. The Master expressed annoyance at this. A few minutes later he said to Narayan affectionately: "If you hold me by the hand people may think I am drunk. I shall walk by myself."

Girish's house was not far away. The Master passed the crossing at Bosepara Lane. Suddenly he began to walk faster. The devotees were left behind. Presently Narendra was seen coming from a distance. At other times the Master's joy would have been unbounded at the thought of Narendra or at the mere mention of his name; but now he did not even exchange a word with his beloved disciple.

Girish stood at the door to welcome the Master. As Sri Ramakrishna entered the house, Girish fell at his feet and lay there on the floor like a rod. At the Master's bidding he stood up, touching the Master's feet with his forehead. Sri Ramakrishna was taken to the drawing-room on the second floor. The devotees followed him and sat down, eager to get a view of the Master and listen to every word that fell from his lips.

As Sri Ramakrishna was about to take the seat reserved for him, he saw a newspaper lying near it. He signed to someone to remove the paper. Since a newspaper contains worldly matters — gossip and scandal — he regarded it as unholy. After the paper was removed he took his seat.[26]

On 24 April 1885, the Master was on his way to Girish's house with some devotees when some people made a remark that he overheard. Laughing, he said to M.: "What are these people saying? 'There comes

Paramahamsa's battalion!' What these fools say!"[27] Public opinion or criticism did not bother the Master: his mind was above the pairs of opposites, beyond praise or blame.

Ramakrishna's Compassion

Sri Ramakrishna had infinite love and compassion for everyone and everything, even animals. He would go to Calcutta by horse carriage, but he had deep feeling for those horses. The Master did not allow too many passengers in his carriage. The Master would tell devotees who asked for a ride, "No, there is no room in this carriage." He would ask them to hire a carriage for themselves or to come by boat. He felt that it would be hard for the horses to pull too many people.

Swami Akhandananda wrote in his reminiscences: "The Master would always visit Calcutta by the hired carriage of Beni Pal of Baranagore because his horses were strong and healthy. The Master felt pain if the coachman whipped the horses. He cried out, 'Uh! Someone is hitting me.' Beni Pal always supplied his best horses for the carriage that the Master would be riding in. The coachman did not whip the horses; he only made some noise and shook the reins."[28]

M. often recorded the love and concern the Master had for his devotees, as this incident of 6 April 1885 shows:

> Sri Ramakrishna was on his way in a carriage to Devendra's house in Nimu Goswami's Lane. The younger Naren, M., and one or two other devotees were with him. The Master felt great yearning for Purna. He began to talk of the young disciple.
>
> Master (*to M.*): "A great soul! Or how could he make me do japa for his welfare? But Purna doesn't know anything about it."
>
> M. and the other devotees were amazed at these words.
>
> The carriage proceeded to Devendra's house. Once Sri Ramakrishna had said to Devendra at Dakshineswar, "I have been thinking of visiting your house one day." Devendra had replied: "The same idea came to my mind today, and I have come here to ask that favour of you. You must grace my house this Sunday." "But," the Master had said, "you have a small income. Don't invite many people. The carriage hire will also run to a big amount." Devendra had answered, laughing: "What if my income is small? 'One can run into debt to eat butter.'" At these words Sri Ramakrishna had laughed a long time.
>
> Soon the carriage reached Devendra's house. Sri Ramakrishna said to him: "Devendra, don't make elaborate arrangements for my meal. Something very simple will do. I am not very well today."[29]

In the Bible we have read the parable of the ten virgins who were waiting for the bridegroom to appear. All of the women fell asleep while their lamps burnt on. At midnight when the bridegroom appeared, only the five virgins who had brought an extra supply of oil for their lamps were ready to attend the wedding feast. The five foolish virgins were excluded from the feast. We find a similar incident in *The Gospel of Sri Ramakrishna*. After a beautiful conversation about God at Devendra's house the Master was about to leave. M.'s record continues: "Devendra and the other devotees took the Master to his carriage. Seeing that one of his neighbours was sound asleep on a bench in the courtyard, Devendra woke him up. The neighbour rubbed his eyes and said, 'Has the Paramahamsa come?' All burst into laughter. The man had come a long time before Sri Ramakrishna's arrival, and because of the heat had spread a mat on the bench and lain down, and soon fell sound asleep.

"Sri Ramakrishna's carriage proceeded to Dakshineswar. He said to M. happily, 'I have eaten a good deal of ice-cream; bring four or five cones for me when you come to Dakshineswar.'"[30]

Visiting Devotees in Calcutta

On another occasion M. recorded:

It was about three o'clock in the afternoon. Sri Ramakrishna was sitting in Balaram's drawing-room with the devotees.... Narayan and certain other devotees had remarked to the Master that Nanda Bose, an aristocrat of Baghbazar, had many pictures of gods and goddesses in his house. Hence Sri Ramakrishna intended to pay a visit to Nanda's house in the afternoon [28 July 1885]. A brahmin woman [Golap-ma] devoted to the Master lived nearby. She often came to see him at Dakshineswar. She was extremely sorrowful over the death of her only daughter, and the Master had agreed to go to her house. She had invited him with great earnestness. From her house the Master was to go to the house of Ganu's mother [Yogin-ma], another devotee....

He was ready to go to Nanda Bose's house. A palanquin was brought for him, and he got into it repeating the name of God. He had put on a pair of black-varnished slippers and a red-bordered cloth. As Sri Ramakrishna sat down in the palanquin, M. put the slippers by his side. He accompanied the palanquin on foot....

They entered the gate of Nanda's house, crossed the spacious square, and stopped in front of the building. The members of the family greeted the Master. He asked M. to hand him the slippers and then got out of the palanquin and entered the large hall. It was a very spacious room. Pictures of gods and goddesses were hanging on all sides....

A picture of Keshab's Navavidhan hung on the wall. Suresh Mitra, a beloved householder disciple of the Master, had had it painted. In this picture Sri Ramakrishna was pointing out to Keshab that people of different religions proceed to the same goal by different paths.

Master: "That was painted for Surendra."

Prasanna's father (*smiling*): "You too are in that picture."

Master (*smiling*): "Yes, it contains everything. This is the ideal of modern times."

The master of the house had not yet shown any sign of serving Sri Ramakrishna with refreshments. Sri Ramakrishna himself said to Nanda: "You see, you should offer me something to eat. That is why the other day I said to Jadu's mother: 'Look here. Give me something to eat.' Otherwise it brings harm to the householder."[31] [It is a custom that if a holy man visits a home, the owner must offer him something to eat or at least a glass of water.]

Nanda ordered some sweets. After having refreshments the Master left for Golap-ma's house. M.'s narrative continued:

The Master arrived at the house of the brahmin lady who was grief-stricken on account of her daughter's death. It was an old brick house. Entering the house, the Master passed the cowshed on his left. He and the devotees went to the roof, where they took seats. People were standing there in rows. Others were seated. They were all eager to get a glimpse of Sri Ramakrishna.

The brahmani had a sister; both of them were widows.... The brahmani had been busy all day making arrangements to receive Sri Ramakrishna.... The brahmani's sister came to the Master and saluted him. She said: "Sister has just gone to Nanda Bose's house to inquire the reason for your delay in coming here. She will return presently."

The brahmani came and saluted the Master. She was beside herself with joy. She did not know what to say. In a half-choked voice she said: "This joy is too much for me. Perhaps I shall die of it."

She was talking like this when her sister came up and said: "Come down, sister! How can I manage things if you stay here? Can I do it all by myself?"

But the brahmani was overwhelmed with joy. She could not take her eyes from the Master and the devotees.

After a while she very respectfully took Sri Ramakrishna to another room and offered him sweets and other refreshments. The devotees were entertained on the roof.

It was about eight o'clock in the evening. Sri Ramakrishna was ready to leave.... A man showed the way with a light. At places it was dark.[32]

After visiting the house of Ganu's mother, the Master returned to Balaram's house. M. described the scene:

He [Ramakrishna] was resting in the small room to the west of the drawing-room. It was quite late, almost a quarter to eleven.... M. was stroking the Master's feet. They talked together.

Master (*referring to the brahmani and her relatives*): "Ah! How happy they were!"

M.: "How amazing! A similar thing happened with two women at the time of Jesus. They too were sisters, and devoted to Christ. Martha and Mary."

Master (*eagerly*): "Tell me the story."

M.: "Jesus Christ, like you, went to their house with his devotees. At the sight of him one of the sisters was filled with ecstatic happiness.... The other sister, all by herself, was arranging the food to entertain Jesus. She complained to the Master, saying: 'Lord, please judge for yourself — how wrong my sister is! She is sitting in your room and I am doing all these things by myself.' Jesus said: 'Your sister indeed is blessed. She has developed the only thing needful in human life: love of God.'"

Master: "Well, after seeing all this, what do you feel?"

M.: "I feel that Christ, Chaitanyadeva, and yourself — all three are one and the same. It is the same Person that has become all these three."

Master: "Yes, yes! One! One! It is indeed one. Don't you see that it is He alone who dwells here (*pointing to himself*) in this way."

M.: "You explained clearly, the other day, how God incarnates Himself on earth."

Master: "Tell me what I said."

M.: "You told us to imagine a field extending to the horizon and beyond. It extends without any obstruction; but we cannot see it on account of a wall in front of us. In that wall there is a round hole. Through the hole we see a part of that infinite field."

Master: "Tell me what that hole is."

M.: "You are that hole. Through you can be seen everything — that Infinite Meadow without any end."

Sri Ramakrishna was very much pleased. Patting M.'s back, he said: "I see you have understood that. That's fine!"

M.: "It is indeed difficult to understand that. One cannot quite grasp how God, Perfect Brahman that He is, can dwell in that small body."

The Master quoted from a song:

> Oh, no one at all has found out who He is;
> Like a madman from door to door He roams,
> Like a poor beggar He roams from door to door.[33]

Sri Ramakrishna loved to visit holy places, including the houses of his devotees in Calcutta. But it was not so easy to accompany him. Swami Turiyananda recalled:

> One day Mathur Babu was returning to Janbazar in his deluxe phaeton,* bringing Sri Ramakrishna with him. When the carriage reached Chitpur Road the Master had a wonderful vision. He felt that he had become Sita, and that Ravana was kidnapping him. Seized by this idea, he merged into samadhi. Just then the horses tore loose from their reins and stumbled and fell. Mathur Babu could not understand the reason for such a mishap. When Sri Ramakrishna returned to normal consciousness, Mathur told him about the accident with the horses. Sri Ramakrishna then said that while in ecstasy he perceived that Ravana was kidnapping him, and that Jatayu** was attacking Ravana's chariot and trying to destroy it. After hearing this story, Mathur Babu said, "Father, how difficult it is even to go with you through the street!"[34]

Sri Ramakrishna was not only a great teacher, but also a great learner. Once he went to visit the Calcutta Zoo. He said: "I went into samadhi at the sight of the lion, for the carrier of the Mother awakened in my mind the consciousness of the Mother Herself."[35]

After visiting the Calcutta Museum, he said: "I was shown fossils. A whole animal has become stone! Just see what an effect has been produced by company! Likewise, by constantly living in the company of a holy man one verily becomes holy."[36]

Ramakrishna described his visit to the studio of Bengal Photographers in Calcutta: "Today [10 December 1881] I enjoyed very much the machine by which a man's picture is taken. One thing I noticed was that the impression doesn't stay on a bare piece of glass, but it remains when the glass is stained with a black solution. In the same way, mere hearing of spiritual talk doesn't leave any impression. People forget it soon afterwards. But they can retain spiritual instruction if they are stained inside with earnestness and devotion."[37]

---

*A light, four-wheeled carriage.
**The great bird who had attempted to rescue Sita.

—6—
(M.)

Christmas Vacation with Ramakrishna

Roughly 125 years have passed since Ramakrishna lived in the temple garden of Dakshineswar, yet when we visit Dakshineswar we can see the same image of the Divine Mother Kali that Ramakrishna worshipped; the same image of Krishna that he worshipped, and which he repaired; the same image of Shiva that he embraced. We can enter Ramakrishna's room and see the cots on which he sat and slept; his collection of pictures still hangs on the walls. We can bathe at the Chandni Ghat where he used to bathe; we can sit in the Panchavati and under the bel tree where he practised severe disciplines. When we walk over the courtyard tiles, we know that God in human form once walked over them. How blessed are those tiles! Now we try to remember Ramakrishna through japa and meditation; how wonderful it would be if we could live there with him for a few days!

When Ramakrishna lived in Dakshineswar, Calcutta was the capital of India. (Delhi became the capital in 1912.) Although Dakshineswar was only four or five miles away, very few people from Calcutta went to see him. It is said that there is always a shadow under a lamp. The nearest relatives may not understand the greatness of an illumined soul, but people far away recognize him and search him out. People in India go to the mountains and visit holy places while on vacation. They spend much money, time, and energy on these trips, but they are not interested in meeting a great soul who lives nearby.

Travel is very important in human life. Vacations relieve monotony and stress, reinvigorate us, and give us a break from ordinary life. When we are away from home, we feel relaxed and at least temporarily experience freedom from our daily routine and worldly duties. The joy of this freedom refreshes our body and mind.

From 14 December 1883 to 5 January 1884, M., spent his Christmas vacation with Ramakrishna at Dakshineswar. However, he recorded the events for only fourteen of the twenty-three days.

On 9 December 1883 M. was meditating on the western veranda of the nahabat. While returning from the pine grove, the Master saw M. and said: "Hello! You are here? You will get results very soon. If you practise a little, then someone will come forward to help you." M. looked up at the Master with joy and hope. The Master continued: "The time is ripe for you. The mother bird does not break the shell of the egg until the right time arrives."[1] M. had read many books on religion and philosophy, but had not found peace of mind. From this point on the Master's company brought a new turn to M.'s life.

The Master started walking towards the Panchavati, accompanied by M. No one else was with them. While listening to the Master's spiritual experiences, M. took a couple of leaves from a tree in the Panchavati and put them in his pocket.

> Master: "See there — that branch has been broken. I used to sit under it."
> M.: "I took a young twig from that tree — I have it at home."
> Master (*with a smile*): "Why?"
> M.: "I feel happy when I look at it. After all this is over, this place will be considered very holy."[2]

M. was inspired after talking to the Master and decided to spend his Christmas vacation practising spiritual disciplines under the Master's guidance. On Friday, 14 December 1883, at 9:00 a.m., M. arrived at Dakshineswar and bowed down to the Master. On 9 December the Master had said to M.: "If an aspirant practises a little spiritual discipline, then someone comes forward to help him." The Master's words penetrated M.'s mind; later he repeated them to the devotees who came after the Master's passing.

Late that afternoon, M. and Ramakrishna stood on the south side of the nahabat, talking:

Northern Nahabat at Dakshineswar, where M. spent his Christmas vacation in 1883-84 in the upper room.

Master: "Where will you sleep? In the hut in the Panchavati?"

M.: "Won't they let me have the room on the upper floor of the nahabat?"

M. selected the nahabat because he had a poetic temperament. From there he could see the sky, the Ganges, the moonlight, and the flowers in the garden.

Master: "Oh, they'll let you have it. But I suggested the Panchavati because so much contemplation and meditation have been practised there and the name of God has been chanted there so often."[3]

Before M.'s vacation, the Master had told him: "You should not eat every day at the guesthouse of the Kali temple. The guesthouse is intended to supply free food to monks and the destitute. Bring your own cook with you." M. had accordingly done so. The Master arranged a place for the man to cook and he asked Ramlal to speak to the milkman about milk. The Master suggested that M. eat plain rice, vegetables, and milk. During sadhana one's mind should not dwell on rich and fancy food. The Bhagavata says: *Jitam sarvam, jite rase* — One who has controlled the tongue has controlled everything.

When a flower blooms, bees come of their own accord. People came to hear the Master talk about God, even though he did not advertise himself. A schoolteacher came one afternoon with a group of students. The Master glanced at M. and said: "One attains God when one feels yearning for Him. An intense restlessness is needed. Through it the whole mind goes to God.

"One must have childlike faith — and the intense yearning that a child feels to see his mother. That yearning is like the red sky in the east at dawn. After such a sky the sun must rise. Immediately after that yearning one sees God."[4]

He then told the story of Jatila, a little boy who was afraid to walk through the forest to school. His mother asked him to call on his elder brother, Madhusudana [Krishna], if he became afraid. The boy had complete faith in his mother's words. The next day, on his way to school, he cried out, "Brother Madhusudana." Krishna then appeared and walked with him to school. After telling that story to the devotees, the Master said, "One must have this childlike faith, this yearning."

M. described the first evening he spent at Dakshineswar:

Late at night M. sat alone in the nahabat. The sky, the river, the garden, the steeples of the temples, the trees, and the Panchavati were flooded with moonlight. Deep silence reigned everywhere, broken only by the melodious murmuring of the Ganges. M. was meditating on Sri Ramakrishna.

At three o'clock in the morning M. left his seat. He proceeded towards the Panchavati as Sri Ramakrishna had suggested. He did not care for the nahabat anymore and resolved to stay in the hut in the Panchavati.

Suddenly he heard a distant sound, as if someone were wailing piteously, "Oh, where art Thou, Brother Madhusudana?" The light of the full moon streamed through the thick foliage of the Panchavati, and as he proceeded he saw at a distance one of the Master's disciples [Latu] sitting alone in the grove, crying helplessly, "Oh, where art Thou, Brother Madhusudana?"

Silently M. watched him.[5]

When most people go on a pilgrimage during their vacation, they move around the whole day, eat at restaurants to enjoy good food, buy various souvenirs for friends and family, watch movies or plays, and sleep in comfortable beds at night. M.'s vacation was quite different: The Master had created a hunger for God in his mind, so he slept very little and he tried to be absorbed in God all the time.

Saturday, 15 December 1883

Ordinary people try to hide their shortcomings, but M. was absolutely honest and did not hide anything. In the *Gospel* he even recorded the scoldings that he received from the Master. Ramakrishna was all-knowing, so he knew what was good for his disciples. On the second morning of M.'s vacation, he told M. bluntly:

Master: "Aren't you ashamed of yourself? You have children, and still you enjoy intercourse with your wife. Don't you hate yourself for thus leading an animal life? Don't you hate yourself for dallying with a body which contains only blood, phlegm, filth, and excreta? He who contemplates the Lotus Feet of God looks on even the most beautiful woman as mere ash from the cremation ground."

M. sat there silently, hanging his head in shame.

Master: "A man who has tasted even a drop of God's ecstatic love looks on 'woman and gold' as most insignificant....One gradually obtains that love for God if one but prays to Him with a yearning heart and always chants His name and glories."[6]

Later, the Master remarked: "Those who are my own will not be angry even if scolded. They will come back again."

M.'s account continued:

It was ten o'clock in the morning....The Master went to the temple accompanied by M. Entering the shrine, the Master sat before the image.

He offered a flower or two at the feet of the Divine Mother. Then he put a flower on his own head and began to meditate. He sang a song to the Divine Mother:

> Thy name, I have heard, O Consort of Shiva, is the destroyer of our fear,
> And so on Thee I cast my burden: Save me! Save me, O kindly Mother![7]

M. later wrote that Ramakrishna, while singing that song, had dedicated him to the Divine Mother.

Sunday, 16 December 1883

The description of Ramakrishna and his surroundings that M. presented in the *Gospel* are so vivid that they can help us in our meditation. For example, here he writes of the events that took place on Sunday, 16 December 1883:

> Sri Ramakrishna was seated with M. on the semicircular porch of his room at about ten o'clock in the morning. The fragrance of gardenias, jasmines, oleanders, roses, and other flowers filled the air....
>
> [The Master went into an ecstatic mood.] His body became motionless and his mind stopped functioning; tears streamed down his cheeks. After a while he said, "O Mother, make me like Sita, completely forgetful of everything — body and limbs —, totally unconscious of hands, feet, and sense organs — only the one thought in her mind, 'Where is Rama?'"
>
> M. wondered: "Was the Master inspired by the ideal of Sita to teach M. the yearning that a devotee should feel for God?"[8]

In the afternoon the Master told some devotees:

> "Maya is nothing but 'woman and gold.' A man attains yoga when he has freed his mind from these two. The Self — the Supreme Self — is the magnet; the individual self is the needle. But the magnet cannot attract the needle if the needle is covered with clay."
>
> Mukherjee: "How can one remove it?"
>
> Master: "Weep for God with a longing heart. Tears shed for Him will wash away the clay. When you have thus freed yourself from impurity, you will be attracted by the magnet. Only then will you attain yoga."[9]

At the time of his sadhana, whenever the Master saw the sunset he would weep, saying, "Mother, another day is gone in vain; still Thou art not revealed unto me." The Master told M. many stories about how sunsets reminded him of his longing, so in the *Gospel* we find many descriptions of the sunset and evening hours.

It was evening. Sri Ramakrishna was meditating on the Divine Mother and chanting Her holy name. The devotees also went off to solitary places and meditated on their Chosen Ideals. Evening worship began at the temple garden in the shrines of Kali, Radha-Krishna, and Shiva.

It was the second day of the dark fortnight of the moon. Soon the moon rose in the sky, bathing temples, trees, flowers, and the rippling surface of the Ganges in its light. The Master was sitting on the couch and M. on the floor. The conversation turned to the Vedanta.

M.: "Is the world unreal?"

Master: "Why should the universe be unreal? That is a speculation of the philosophers. After realizing God, one sees that it is God Himself who has become the universe and all living beings.

"The Divine Mother revealed to me in the Kali temple that it was She who had become everything. She showed me that everything was full of Consciousness. The Image was Consciousness, the altar was Consciousness, the water-vessels were Consciousness, the doorsill was Consciousness, the marble floor was Consciousness — all was Consciousness.

"I found everything inside the room soaked, as it were, in Bliss — the Bliss of Satchidananda. I saw a wicked man in front of the Kali temple; but in him also I saw the Power of the Divine Mother vibrating.

"That was why I fed a cat with the food that was to be offered to the Divine Mother. I clearly perceived that the Divine Mother had become everything — even the cat."[10]

M. was dumbfounded. He had never heard anything like this before. Earlier, M. had asked, "Is the world unreal?" The Master had not replied by quoting scriptures or by explaining his answer with logic and philosophy. M.'s Western education could not solve this riddle: Where does matter end and Consciousness begin? Ramakrishna's experience of Oneness revealed the truth of the Chandogya Upanishad: *Sarvam khalu idam Brahma* — Verily, everything is Brahman.

Monday, 17 December 1883

It was about eight o'clock in the morning. Ramakrishna was in his room with M.

Master: "The whole thing in a nutshell is that one must develop ecstatic love for Satchidananda....One must become mad with love in order to realize God. But that love is not possible if the mind dwells on 'woman and gold.'...Gauri used to say that when a man attains ecstatic love of God all the pores of the skin, even the roots of the hair, become like so many sexual organs, and in every pore the aspirant enjoys the happiness of communion with the Atman."[11]

M. felt intense renunciation and expressed his desire to become a monk. He described Ramakrishna's reaction: "The Master fixed his gaze on M. and said, 'By renouncing everything?'"

M.: "What can a man achieve unless he gets rid of Maya?..."

Both remained silent a few minutes.[12]

Tuesday, 18 December 1883

M. had a tremendous power of observation. Like a shadow, he followed Ramakrishna day and night. His own overwhelming desire to experience samadhi impelled him to meticulously record the instances in which he saw the Master go into samadhi: "It was a winter morning, and the Master was sitting near the east door of his room, wrapped in his moleskin shawl. He looked at the sun and suddenly went into samadhi. His eyes stopped blinking and he lost all consciousness of the outer world. After a long time he came down to the plane of the sense world."[13]

The Master's samadhi reminded M. of this passage from the Gayatri mantra: *Om tat savitur varenyam bhargo devasya dhimahi* — I meditate on the luminous One who dwells in the solar region.

Later that day, the Master and some devotees went to Calcutta:

Sri Ramakrishna had vowed to offer green coconut and sugar to Siddheswari, the Divine Mother, for Rakhal's welfare. He asked M. to pay for the offerings.

That afternoon the Master, accompanied by M., Rakhal, and some other devotees, set out in a carriage for the temple of Siddheswari in Calcutta. On the way offerings were purchased. On reaching the temple, the Master asked the devotees to offer the fruit and sugar to the Divine Mother. They saw the priests and their friends playing cards in the temple. Sri Ramakrishna said: "To play cards in the temple! One should think of God here."[14]

We find in the Bible that Jesus went into the temple of God, cast out everyone who bought and sold in the temple, overthrew the tables of the moneychangers, and said: "It is written, 'My house shall be called the house of prayer; but ye have made it a den of thieves.'"[15] Like Christ, Ramakrishna could not bear hypocrisy, and he was outspoken about it.

Ramakrishna left the temple and went to see his wealthy devotee, Jadu Mallick. When they arrived, they found Jadu surrounded by his admirers, well-dressed dandies. Jadu welcomed the Master. M. described their conversation:

Master (*with a smile*): "Why do you keep so many clowns and flatterers with you?"

Jadu (*smiling*): "That you may liberate them." (*Laughter.*)[16]

Wednesday, 19 December 1883

The places where Christ and Buddha lived have become holy. Even now people from all over the world visit those places and try to absorb their presence. Ramakrishna lived in the temple garden of Dakshineswar for thirty years. M. tried to preserve the Master's presence and the panoramic beauty of the temple garden through his powerful, photographic memory and his poetic imagination. After 125 years, M.'s vivid descriptions still bring Ramakrishna and his surroundings to life for us:

> It was nine o'clock in the morning. Sri Ramakrishna was talking to M. near the bel tree at Dakshineswar. This tree, under which the Master had practised the most austere sadhana, stood in the northern end of the temple garden. Farther north ran a high wall, and just outside was the government magazine. West of the bel tree was a row of tall pines that rustled in the wind. Below the trees flowed the Ganges, and to the south could be seen the sacred grove of the Panchavati. The dense trees and underbrush hid the temples. No noise of the outside world reached the bel tree.[17]

Now that bel tree, the pine grove, and the big banyan that was in the Panchavati are gone. This wonderful place that was made sacred by Ramakrishna's sadhana is full of vendors. There is now a brick building near the bel tree, and another wall has been built between the bel tree and the Panchavati. Almost the entire area has been filled with restaurants and shops. To see this is very painful for the devotees. Time — the devourer of all — has swallowed that beautiful temple garden. If God wills, someone may come forward to restore the temple according to M.'s description. We now return to M.'s narrative:

> Sri Ramakrishna went to the Panchavati on his way back to his room. M. accompanied him. It was about ten o'clock.
>
> M.: "Sir, is there no spiritual discipline leading to realization of the Impersonal God?"
>
> Master: "Yes, there is. But the path is extremely difficult. After intense austerities the rishis of olden times realized God as their innermost consciousness and experienced the real nature of Brahman. But how hard they had to work! They went out of their dwellings in the early morning and all day practised austerities and meditation. Returning home at nightfall, they took a light supper of fruit and roots."[18]

M. had a busy life. He was the headmaster of a school; he had a wife and children and other family responsibilities. During this vacation he was trying his utmost to focus on his spiritual practices.

After saluting the Master, M. went to a secluded place under the bel tree. He carried his prayer carpet and a jug of water with him.

> At midday, finding that M. had not yet returned, Sri Ramakrishna started towards the bel tree; but on reaching the Panchavati he met M. carrying his prayer carpet and water jug.
>
> Sri Ramakrishna said to M.: "I was coming to look for you. Because of your delay I thought you might have scaled the wall and run away. I watched your eyes this morning and felt apprehensive lest you should go away like Narayan Shastri. Then I said to myself: 'No, he won't run away. He thinks a great deal before doing anything.'"[19]

Sometimes we wonder if God thinks of us. Ramakrishna's life reveals the great love and concern he had for his devotees. He always thought of their welfare. As God attracts devotees, so also devotees attract God. Love is reciprocal. If you love, you will be loved — this is the law. M. wrote:

> Following Sri Ramakrishna's direction, M. spent the night in the hut at the Panchavati. In the early hours of the morning he was singing alone:
> I am without the least benefit of prayer and austerity, O Lord!
> I am the lowliest of the lowly; make me pure with Thy hallowed touch.
> One by one I pass my days in hope of reaching Thy Lotus Feet,
> But Thee, alas, I have not found.
> Suddenly M. glanced towards the window and saw the Master standing there. Sri Ramakrishna's eyes became heavy with tears as M. sang the line: "I am the lowliest of the lowly; make me pure with Thy hallowed touch."[20]

M. felt the Master's grace.

Friday, 21 December 1883

M. described his morning with Ramakrishna: "In the morning the Master and M. were conversing alone under the bel tree. The Master told him many secrets of spiritual discipline, exhorting him to renounce 'woman and gold.' He further said that the mind at times becomes one's guru."[21]

In the afternoon the Master advised a monk who was a worshipper of the formless God: "Dive deep; one does not get the precious gems by merely floating on the surface. God is without form, no doubt; but He also has form. By meditating on God with form one speedily acquires devotion; then one can meditate on the formless God."[22]

Saturday, 22 December 1883

M.'s family life caused him much pain; he had even contemplated suicide. But he forgot all of his problems when he was with Ramakrishna. The Master's immortal words brought him peace.

M. recorded a conversation that took place in the morning:

> A devotee: "Sir, how does one obtain love for God?"
> Master: "Go forward. The king dwells beyond the seven gates. You can see him only after passing through all the gates.
> "At the time of the installation of Annapurna at Chanak, I said to Dwarika Babu: 'Large fish live in the deep water of a big lake. Throw some spiced bait into the water; then the fish will come, attracted by its smell; now and then they will make the water splash.' Devotion and ecstatic love are like the spiced bait."[23]

Sometimes we ask ourselves: How can we love God if we have not seen Him?

The Master said: "God sports in the world as man. He incarnates Himself as man as in the case of Krishna, Rama, and Chaitanya....If you seek God, you must seek Him in the Incarnations....One needs spiritual practice in order to know God and recognize Divine Incarnations."

That afternoon, the Master said: "To love an Incarnation of God — that is enough."[24]

Sunday, 23 December 1883

After the midday meal Sri Ramakrishna rested a few minutes in his room. M. was sitting on the floor. The Master was delighted to hear the music that was being played in the nahabat. He then explained to M. that Brahman alone has become the universe and all living beings.

Master: "I perceive that living beings are like different flowers with various petals. They are also revealed to me as bubbles, some big, some small."

While describing in this way the vision of different divine forms, the Master went into an ecstatic state and said: "I have become! I am here!" Uttering these words he went into samadhi. His body was motionless. He remained in that state a long time and then gradually regained partial consciousness of the world. He began to laugh like a boy and pace the room. His eyes radiated bliss as if he had seen a wondrous vision. His gaze was not fixed on any particular object, and his face beamed with joy. Still pacing the room, the Master said: "I saw the paramahamsa who stayed under the banyan tree walking thus with just such a smile. Am I too in that state of mind?"

Master (*to M*): "One attains this state immediately after freeing oneself of all grief and desire."

(*To the Divine Mother*): "Mother, Thou hast done away with my worship. Please see, Mother, that I don't give up all desire."[25]

According to Vedanta, a person attains samadhi when the mind becomes free from desire. Cessation of desire, dissolution of the mind, and illumination — these three things happen simultaneously. We are always tormented by innumerable desires that we cannot get rid of. Ramakrishna, however, prayed to have some desires so that his mind would stay in the world and he could teach and awaken the spiritual consciousness of earnest souls.

Monday, 24 December 1883

At eight o'clock in the morning Sri Ramakrishna and M. were talking together in the pine grove at the northern end of the temple garden. This was the eleventh day of M.'s stay with the Master.

It was winter. The sun had just risen. The river was flowing north with the tide. Not far off could be seen the bel tree where the Master had practised great spiritual austerities.

Master: "Not everyone can recognize an Incarnation. It is God alone who incarnates Himself as man to teach people the ways of love and knowledge. Well, what do you think of me?

"Once my father went to Gaya. There Raghuvir said to him in a dream, 'I shall be born as your son.' Thereupon my father said to Him: 'O Lord, I am a poor brahmin. How shall I be able to serve You?' 'Don't worry about it,' Raghuvir replied. 'It will be taken care of.'

"My sister, Hriday's mother, used to worship my feet with flowers and sandal paste. One day I placed my foot on her head and said to her, 'You will die in Benares [Varanasi].'

"Once Mathur Babu said to me: 'Father, there is nothing inside you but God....'

"I am shown everything beforehand. Once I saw Gauranga and his devotees singing kirtan in the Panchavati. I think I saw Balaram there and you too....I shall have to be born once more. Therefore I am not giving all knowledge to my companions. (*With a smile*) Suppose I give you all knowledge; will you then come to me again so willingly?"

"I recognized you on hearing you read the *Chaitanya Bhagavata*. You are my own. The same substance, like father and son.

"Before you came here, you didn't know who you were. Now you will know. It is God who, as the guru, makes one know."

Sri Ramakrishna stood up. There was silence all around, disturbed only by the gentle rustling of pine-needles and the murmuring of the Ganges. The Master went to the Panchavati and then to his room, talking all the while with M. The disciple followed him, fascinated. At the Panchavati Sri Ramakrishna touched with his forehead the raised platform around the banyan tree. This was the place of his intense spiritual discipline, where he had wept bitterly for the vision of the Divine Mother, where he had held intimate communion with Her, and where he had seen many divine forms.[26]

The Bhakti scriptures say, *Ādau shraddhā* — one first needs sincere faith in God. M. continually learned about spirituality from the Master's actions, words, and behaviour. And all this he related to the devotees who came after Ramakrishna's passing. The Master knew that M. was to be the recorder of his gospel, so he wanted M. to be present when he talked to others.

We continue with M.'s narrative:

Sri Ramakrishna was resting after his midday meal when Surendra, Ram, and other devotees arrived from Calcutta. It was about one o'clock. While M. was strolling alone under the pine trees, Harish came there and told him that the Master wanted him in his room. Someone was going to read from the *Shiva Samhita*, a book containing instructions about yoga and the six centres.[27]

We cannot learn everything by studying a book or a manual on our own. We cannot even learn the alphabet by ourselves. Similarly, in spiritual life we need an experienced teacher who has realized the truth. Here we see Ramakrishna in his role as teacher:

It was evening. The Master was sitting on the floor of his room with the devotees. He was talking to them about yoga and the six centres, which are described in the *Shiva Samhita*.

Master: "Ida, Pingala, and Sushumna are the three principal nerves. All the lotuses are located in the Sushumna. They are formed of Consciousness, like a tree made of wax — the branches, twigs, fruits, and so forth all of wax. The Kundalini lies in the lotus of the Muladhara. That lotus has four petals. The Primordial Energy resides in all bodies as the Kundalini. She is like a sleeping snake coiled up.... (*To M.*) The Kundalini is speedily awakened if one follows the path of bhakti. God cannot be seen unless She is awakened. Sing earnestly and secretly in solitude:

Waken, O Mother! O Kundalini, whose nature is Bliss Eternal!
Thou art the serpent coiled in sleep, in the lotus of the Muladhara."

M.: "Grief and distress of mind disappear if one has these experiences but once."

Master: "That is true. Distress of mind disappears forever. I shall tell you a few things about yoga. But you see, the mother bird doesn't break the shell until the chick inside the egg is matured. The egg is hatched in the fullness of time. It is necessary to practise some spiritual discipline. The guru no doubt does everything for the disciple; but at the end he makes the disciple work a little himself."[28]

Tuesday, 25 December 1883

Ramakrishna came to fulfill the ancient traditions, not to destroy them. It was the day of Ekadashi, when one is supposed to fast. The Master did not put too much emphasis on physical austerity, however; it is hard to think of God if one experiences hunger pangs.

Master (*to M.*): "One should fast on the eleventh day of the lunar fortnight. That purifies the mind and helps one to develop love of God. Isn't that so?"

M.: "Yes, sir."

Master: "But you may take milk and puffed rice."[29]

Wednesday, 26 December 1883

Ramakrishna visited Ram Datta's Kankurgachi Yogodyana with M. and other devotees. Ram received the Master when he got out of the carriage. Standing near the tulsi grove, the Master said: "How nice! It is a fine place. You can easily meditate on God here."[30]

Thursday, 27 December 1883

We know very little about the day-to-day activities of Buddha, Christ, or Chaitanya. For Ramakrishna, however, we have the *Gospel*, in which M. meticulously recorded the Master's daily routine, engagements, visitors, and conversation. Details, like those given here in the *Gospel*, help the reader to clearly visualize the Master:

> The temple garden was filled with the sweet music of the dawn service, which mingled with the morning melody from the nahabat. Leaving his bed, Sri Ramakrishna chanted the names of God in sweet tones. Then he bowed before the pictures of the different deities in his room and went to the west porch to salute the Ganges.
>
> Some of the devotees who had spent the night at the temple garden came to the Master's room and bowed before him. M. had been staying there two weeks.

Sri Ramakrishna said to M.: "I have been invited to Ishan's this morning. Baburam will accompany me, and you too." M. made ready to go with the Master.[31]

It is not possible to describe Ramakrishna's philosophy: He accepted all philosophical paths and said that they were complementary, not contradictory. All paths lead to the same goal. Ramakrishna was the embodiment of all religions, and he harmonized all yogas and philosophical paths.

At Ishan's house the Master spoke on various topics. He explained the three main schools of Vedanta philosophy (dualism, qualified nondualism, and nondualism) by citing Hanuman's attitude: "O Rama, sometimes I feel that You are the Master and I am Your servant. Sometimes I meditate on You as the whole and on myself as the part. But when I have the Knowledge of Reality, I see that I am You and You are I."[32]

That evening, the Master visited Ram's house. He taught the devotees assembled there how to pray: "Listen. I prayed to the Divine Mother for pure love. I said to Her: 'Here is Thy righteousness, here is Thy unrighteousness. Take them both and give me pure love for Thee. Here is Thy purity, here is Thy impurity. Take them both and give me pure love for Thee. O Mother, here is Thy virtue, here is Thy vice. Take them both and give me pure love for Thee.'"[33]

Saturday, 29 December 1883

M.'s record continues:

It was the day of the new moon, auspicious for the worship of the Divine Mother. At one o'clock in the afternoon Sri Ramakrishna got into a carriage to visit the temple of Kali at Kalighat....While the carriage was waiting near the north porch of the Master's room, M. went to the Master and said, "Sir, may I also go with you?"

Master: "Why?"

M.: "I should like to visit my home in Calcutta."

Sri Ramakrishna reflected a moment and said: "Must you go home? Why? You are quite all right here."

M. wanted to see his people a few hours, but evidently the Master did not approve.[34]

During M.'s second visit in March 1882, the Master had told him:

"If you enter the world without first cultivating love for God, you will be entangled more and more. You will be overwhelmed with its danger, its grief, its sorrows. And the more you think of worldly things, the more you will be attached to them.

"One must go into solitude to attain this divine love. To get butter from milk you must let it set into curd in a secluded spot: if it is too much disturbed, milk won't turn into curd. Next, you must put aside all other duties, sit in a quiet spot, and churn the curd. Only then do you get butter."[35]

Sunday, 30 December 1883

At three o'clock in the afternoon, while M. was walking back and forth under a tree, a devotee came to him and said that the Master had sent for him. M. went to Ramakrishna's room and found a number of devotees there. Ram, Kedar, and others had arrived from Calcutta. Ram had brought with him the Vedantist monk whom the Master had visited near Ram's garden a few days earlier.[36]

While talking about Brahman with the monk, the Master went into samadhi. Kedar told the monk: "Look at him, sir. This is samadhi." The monk had read of samadhi but had never seen it before.[37]

Monday, 31 December 1883

M. was witness to Ramakrishna's divine play. Like a playwright, he set the stage and the scene, and made the characters come to life through their wonderful dialogues with the Master. Later, he would tell the devotees, "I have seen one person in my life who would talk with God in front of me." M. wrote:

> In the evening…the Master remained in his room, absorbed in contemplation of the Divine Mother. After a while the sweet music of the evening worship in the temples was heard.
> A little later the Master began to talk to the Mother in a tender voice that touched the heart of M., who was seated on the floor. After repeating, "Hari Om! Hari Om! Om!", the Master said: "Mother, I don't want Brahmajnana. I want to be merry. I want to play."[38]

Wednesday, 2 January 1884

Jaygopal Sen, a Brahmo devotee, asked the Master: "How does one receive the grace of God?"

Master: "Constantly you have to chant the name and glories of God and give up worldly thoughts as much as you can.…I used to cry for God all alone, with a longing heart.…The thing is that one must love God. The attraction of the husband for the chaste wife, the attraction of the child for its mother, the attraction of worldly possessions for the worldly man — when a man can blend these three into one, and direct it all to God, then he gets the vision of God."[39]

That evening, the Master sat in his room with Rakhal and M. Ramakrishna had forbidden M. to indulge in reasoning, and now he explained why:

Master: "It is not good to reason too much. First comes God, and then the world. Realize God first; then you will know all about His world....

"Through too much reasoning your spiritual life will be injured; you will at last become like Hazra. I used to roam at night in the streets, all alone, and cry to the Divine Mother, 'O Mother, blight with Thy thunderbolt my desire to reason!' Tell me that you won't reason anymore."

M.: "Yes, sir. I won't reason anymore."

Master: "Everything can be achieved through bhakti alone. "You will realize everything when God Himself teaches you. Then you will not lack any knowledge."[40]

Friday, 4 January 1884

Sri Ramakrishna was sitting in his room. M. was still staying with the Master, devoting his time to the practice of spiritual discipline. He had been spending a great part of each day in prayer and meditation under the bel tree, where the Master had performed great austerities and had seen many wonderful visions of God.

Master (*to M.*): "One should assume a particular attitude towards God while praying to Him — the attitude of a friend or servant or son. I assume the attitude of a child. To me every woman is my mother. The divine Maya, seeing this attitude in an aspirant, moves away from his path out of sheer shame."[41]

Saturday, 5 January 1884

It was the twenty-third day of M.'s stay with Sri Ramakrishna. M. had finished his midday meal about one o'clock and was resting in the nahabat when suddenly he heard someone call his name three or four times. Coming out, he saw Sri Ramakrishna calling him from the veranda north of his room.

M. saluted the Master and they conversed on the south veranda.

Master: "I want to know how you meditate. When I meditated under the bel tree I used to see various visions clearly. One day I saw in front of me money, a shawl, a tray of sandesh, and two women. I asked my mind, 'Mind, do you want any of these?' I saw the sandesh to be mere filth. One of the women had a big ring in her nose. I could see both their inside and outside -- entrails, filth, bone, flesh, and blood. The mind did not want any of these — money, shawl, sweets, or women. It remained fixed at the Lotus Feet of God.

"No spiritual progress is possible without the renunciation of 'woman and gold.' I renounced these three: land, wife, and wealth....How can one expect to attain God without renunciation? Suppose one thing is placed upon another; how can you get the second without removing the first?"[42]

At dusk Ramakrishna went to the Kali temple; he was pleased to see M. meditating there. M. described the scene:

The evening worship was over in the temples. The Master returned to his room and sat on the couch, absorbed in meditation on the Divine Mother. M. sat on the floor. There was no one else in the room.

The Master was weeping and praying to the Mother with a voice choked with emotion: "Mother, may those who come to You have all their desires fulfilled! If you keep them in the world, Mother, then please reveal Yourself to them now and then. Otherwise, how will they live?"

Master (*to M.*): "Yes, I know everything: what your Ideal is, who you are, your inside and outside, the events of your past lives, and your future.

"I scolded you on learning that you had a son. Now go home and live there. Let them know that you belong to them. But you must remember in your heart of hearts that you do not belong to them nor they to you."

M. sat in silence.

Master (*to M.*): "The Nitya and Lila are the two aspects of the Reality. God plays in the world as man for the sake of His devotees. They can love God only if they see Him in a human form; only then can they show their affection for Him as their Brother, Sister, Father, Mother, or Child."[43]

During his vacation, M. had lived constantly with the Master and observed his divine and human aspects. He was a spectator of Ramakrishna's divine drama, and he sometimes acted in it as well. He loved the Master passionately, and his ego was completely absorbed in his beloved guru. That is why when he wrote the *Gospel* he tried to hide himself, referring to himself by various pseudonyms, such as Mani, Mohinimohan, an English-educated man, a devotee, and so on. He knew how to drink the nectar of the Master's divine words, so the *Gospel* is beautiful and sweet. It touches our inmost feelings. M. tried to preserve in the *Gospel* a record of the Master's meditation, samadhi, worship, prayers, dreams, visions, actions, devotion, purity, renunciation, singing, dancing, laughter, humour, sadhana, pilgrimage, dealings with human beings, psychology, philosophy, social and scientific outlook, and finally his message.

A painter puts several coats of paint on doors and on window frames to protect the underlying wood from rain and sun. Similarly, during the twenty-three days of M.'s visit, Ramakrishna put a spiritual coating on M.'s mind so that it would not be polluted by the world.

On the last day of his vacation, M. received the Master's blessings and left for home.

—7—
(M.)

Two New Entries from M.'s Diary

I

[This entry from M.'s diary was published in *Punya Darshan Srima* (Part 1:60-66) by Amiya Kumar Majumdar. Anil Kumar Gupta, a grandson of M., made it available to the author from M.'s diary. It seems Mr. Majumdar developed this entry following M.'s style. There were many entries in M.'s diary that he could not develop during his lifetime. Perhaps he was planning to publish more volumes of *Sri Ramakrishna Kathamrita*. — Translated from Bengali by the author.]

Friday, 28 December 1883

It was a memorable day. Sri Ramakrishna was talking with M. at the Panchavati in Dakshineswar.

Master: "You shouldn't reason anymore. Remember that in whatever way a man calls on God, He appears to him in that way. Worship God according to your own temperament. The goal of all paths is God, Who is attainable by all; but one will have to be sincere. This is mentioned in the Gita. One develops love and passion for God by constantly calling on Him and practising sadhana. Thus when a man attains love and devotion by God's grace, his mind becomes free from ego, which originates from ignorance.

"Man does not have the power to do anything by his own will. Everything follows God's will. Puppets dance well on the stage when pulled by strings, but they cannot move when a string snaps. Thus one should reflect and discriminate. Only then does ego go away from the mind.

"Wealthy aristocrats are puffed up with pride in their riches, which makes them forget God. He who thinks that God is the only reality and remains unattached to worldly possessions, that person alone attains Him. God becomes everything to the person who has renounced everything."

M. understood that one could not realize God as long as one is egotistical. He said: "It is extremely difficult to get rid of the ego. Without good fortune, one can neither be free from ego nor renounce everything. I don't like being a slave anymore. I wish my worldly duties were reduced so my mind could be focussed more on God."

Master: "You wanted to experience family life, so you are in the world. But it will be enough if you renounce mentally. Let me tell you your condition: Narada began to liberate each and all by bestowing the knowledge of Brahman. Then Brahma cursed Sanaka, Sanatana, and others and trapped them in maya in order to perpetuate his creation. You had some karma left, so you are in the world. I shall make you do some work. Please give up desires, which bring misery. However, you are making good progress. When you attain knowledge, you will realize that God exists eternally — past, present, and future. He is Satchidananda, without beginning or end. This world is the manifestation of His magical power of maya. I learned something about you last night that you will learn later.

"Know for certain that I and She (Kali of Dakshineswar) are one, and there is no difference. If you think of Her day and night, that will be thinking of me."

M. was speechless as he listened attentively to the Master.

Master: "Believe in the form of God. You belong to a Shakta family, so you should believe in Shakti. He who is Brahman, He is Shakti and also the Divine Mother. Without acknowledging Shakti, no one can understand what Brahman is. Brahman can become manifest only through Shakti. What is fire? It is something that has the power to burn. Fire would become useless if it could not burn. As fire and its power to burn are no different, so Brahman and Shakti are the same. When we describe them, they seem to be two different things, but in reality they are one. The One has become many; that is the manifestation of His power. When Shakti is inactive It is called Brahman — one without a second. When creation begins, that is Shakti. Brahman or Purusha can be compared to still water. The same water, moving in waves, may be compared to Shakti or Prakriti. Whatever you do, hear, see, or experience in this world, all are actions of Shakti. No one can realize the truth of Brahman without going through Shakti.

"This whole world is the lila of God — the manifestation of His Shakti. They are like the gem and its lustre. A gem is perceived by its lustre. Similarly, Brahman is recognized by observing the play of Shakti. If there were no Shakti, who could know Brahman? Who would adore Him? The dominant power of Brahman is called the Lord of the Universe. He is one and again many. When there is no activity, He becomes the sum total of everything. Again, when action (creation) begins, His power manifests — His infinite power creates everything. God is the sum total of everything in this universe. The contraction of power is Brahman; the expansion of power is Shakti. Meditation, concentration, sadhana, worship, ecstasy, devotion, and love — all are made possible by Shakti. Without Shakti, the power of God, one cannot see or think of anything. God manifests through His power. It is due to His power that He is Great and people adore Him. Without taking recourse in Shakti, how can you call on Him?

"Brahman is formless, devoid of qualities, beyond sight and thought. How can one see Him who is formless? How can one call on or pray to Brahman? Brahman and Shakti are indivisible — one entity with two names. When there was no creation, He was unknowable. When He set creation in motion, His power began to function. At that point, it became possible to perceive Him with the eyes and the mind. In other words, He became endowed with qualities. Brahman contains Shakti, or power. Without a container, how can power exist? As the container and the contained they are different, but truly they are indivisible. This is the inscrutable doctrine of the divisible and the indivisible.

"For example, a cup does not create itself. It was fabricated by a potter who used his or her own power. No object can be self-created, and no creator can do anything without power. And that power cannot exist without its source. All forms originated from Shakti: Kali, Durga, Radha are different names for the same Shakti. A deity has been named according to the activity of that deity. Shakti also manifests as an avatar through lila. He who is Brahman is also Rama, Krishna, and Shiva. How is it possible to realize Brahman without taking refuge in Shakti? The words that are used to call on Him, the sound that is used to worship Him — those are all functions of Shakti. You have originated from Shakti, and you move and walk by means of Her power. You have heard and understood the word *Brahman*; and by Shakti's grace you are eager to realize Brahman. If you give up Shakti now — the Divine Mother — who will sustain and protect you? Without the mother, a son cannot know a father's affection, or what a father is. The mother's affection nourishes the child. How could you renounce such a loving mother and hope to reach the father? The Divine

Mother is Brahmamayi: Call on Her intently. She will listen to your sincere prayer and reveal Herself to you without delay."

While talking about Brahman and Shakti, Sri Ramakrishna went into samadhi and his face glowed. Afterwards he prayed to the Divine Mother for M. in a choked voice: "Mother, illumine his heart, otherwise how will he awaken others? Why did you entangle him in the world? Mother, please show him that wonderful form of yours; otherwise how will he stay in this world?"

M. was overwhelmed as he gazed upon the Master's luminous form and heard him pray to the Divine Mother like a child. M. experienced the Master's unconditional love and grace for the devotees.

When he returned to normal consciousness, Sri Ramakrishna again said: "One can achieve everything through faith and devotion, but one must be sincere. Hold on to your faith and don't reason anymore. At present, please follow this instruction. Well, tell me: what is your attitude?"

M. remained silent.

Master: "You have two attitudes: Prahlada's attitude –– I am That — and the attitude of a servant. You see, Hazra used to say that I can see what is in another's mind. I wanted the Divine Mother to teach me the scriptures. I said to Her: 'Mother, tell me what is in the scriptures. I shall accept only what you teach me.' She has brought me much knowledge and showed me many visions. Please don't tell others what I have said.

"One should call on God. If you cannot think of Him all the time, at least call on Him twice a day. There is a glorious power in His name! The name of God helps one to reach God. God appears to the person who sincerely chants His name with a pure and simple heart. If a friend cordially invites a neighbour to his home, that neighbour will pay a visit. However, no one will accept an invitation offered rudely and with selfish motives. Similarly, God comes to a devotee who calls on Him sincerely."

Sri Ramakrishna left the Panchavati and returned to his room, accompanied by M. Devotees came one after another. Rakhal, Latu, Harish, Balaram, and a few others bowed down to the Master and sat on the floor.

The Master began talking about faith and the glory of the divine name.

Master: "The omnipresent God dwells in all beings. One whose mind dwells in Him is known as a devotee. God is indivisible. The heart of a devotee is God's dwelling place. God relieves devotees of all responsibility. The sage Durvasa was pleased with Duryodhana's hospitality and offered him a boon. The shrewd Duryodhana wanted Durvasa to become angry and curse the Pandavas, so he asked Durvasa and his 10,000 disciples to visit the Pandavas after Draupadi had finished her meal. When the hungry Durvasa went to the Pandavas' cottage and asked to be fed, Draupadi was terribly embarrassed and felt helpless. Endangered, Draupadi passionately prayed to Krishna, saviour of the helpless. When Krishna heard his devotee's intense prayer he could not remain aloof. He realized that his devotee Draupadi was in danger, so he rushed to rescue her.*

"God always responds if one calls on Him intently with a simple, pure, sincere heart. He always protects His devotees from danger and difficulties. He is graciously affectionate to his devotees."

M.: "Hanuman had such steadfast devotion to Ramachandra that when Rama took the form of Vishnu at Garuda's request, the form of Ramachandra that was imprinted on Hanuman's heart immediately changed [to that of Vishnu]."

Master: "Aha! Aha! That is the reason people say Hanuman is the only true devotee. Is it possible to find another devotee like Hanuman? He used to say: 'I don't know anything about the day of the week, the position of the stars, and so forth. I only meditate on Rama.'

"Is it possible to attain Rama without having as much devotion as Hanuman? When I was practising different religious paths, I took on the mood of Hanuman to attain Ramachandra. I completely became identified with Hanuman. At that time I hopped about like Hanuman and ate fruit with the peels. I tied my *dhoti* around my waist to make it look like a tail. Thus I attained perfection in that mood.

"Hanuman maintained Ramachandra's form in his heart with so much steadfast love and devotion that he could not accept any other form. For that reason, Hanuman cared for no other form of Vishnu except Ramachandra."

M.: "In the Bhagavata it is written that a low-class woman fruit vendor received Krishna's grace when she sold fruit to him. She was overwhelmed when Krishna revealed his luminous form to her and addressed her as mother; she was blessed as she held the child Krishna against her bosom. Then she gave all of her fruit to Krishna and returned

* The Sun God had given Draupadi a bowl that supplied an infinite quantity of food. But as soon as she finished her daily meal, no more food would appear. Draupadi asked the sage Durvasa to go to the Ganges and finish his spiritual practices, and then come back for food. Meanwhile, Krishna responded to Draupadi's call and asked for some food from her. She told him that she had no food. Krishna asked her to search inside the bowl. She found a few grains of rice and a little spinach. Krishna ate them and drank a little water. That filled up the stomachs of Durvasa and his disciples, and they never returned.

home with an empty basket, joyfully contemplating Krishna's luminous form. That woman was extremely poor and supported herself by selling fruit. On her way back home, her empty basket became full of gems by Krishna's grace. She felt her basket become heavy, so she set it down. She was amazed when she saw that her basket was full of jewels, but she remained even-minded. She thought to herself: 'The Blue Jewel [Krishna] who has attracted me today, he is my only gem — the Lord of the universe. Compared to that Blue Jewel, these gems are rubbish.'"

Master: "That fruit seller had earned good karma in her previous life, so she received Krishna's grace — and by his grace she realized that Krishna is the only reality. Everything else is his maya, transitory. She clearly understood that all those gems were impermanent, so she renounced them.

"God offers wealth to human beings to tempt them. All these riches are maya. A true devotee is not deluded by God's bewitching maya. He seeks only the owner of maya — God, the embodiment of all power and glory.

"When a man becomes rich with God's wealth, he becomes proud and egotistic. This egotism gives rise to lust, anger, and so on. The ego leads to a person's downfall and prevents God-realization. Once the eyes, the ears, the mouth, and other sense organs began to quarrel. Each one claimed that it was the greatest and the others were useless. Then each sense organ left the body by turns. You have seen the blind, the deaf, or the mute on the street; they function all right without having a particular sense organ. So it is to be understood that even though those sense organs are not the main parts of the body, they were still proud. The sense organs finally realized that the body survives without the senses, and they became humble. They returned to the body, abashed. Later, when the Atman departed from the body, the senses understood that they were inconsequential: The Atman is the source of their power.

"Although this Atman is not visible, It dwells in all. Its dwelling place is the human heart. When an egotistic man says, 'I have done this. Am I an ordinary man?' — he always points to his heart, the dwelling place of the Atman. He speaks in that manner because he is ignorant. But when he finally experiences the Atman and knows that he is the Atman, he will be free from ego. If he is still proud, he will be proud of his Atman — and this sort of pride has no faults.

"*Prarabdha karma* [action that is presently bearing fruit] causes human beings to come into this world, which is filled with sorrow. Human beings are heavily burdened by the results of karma. If a man wishes, he can easily escape the consequences of karma by bowing down to God with

sincere devotion twice a day. Take for example a man who is carrying a
load of ten maunds.* He cannot bring it down by himself or even with the
help of four or five people. There is nonetheless an easy way to unload
it: If he bows down his head to God at least twice a day, then that burden
will fall away.

"So I tell you, attain God by any means — either by fully surrendering
yourself to God, by removing the mind's impurities, by crying to Him,
by cultivating pure devotion, or by any other means. God will make you
understand everything. You will never again be deluded by His bewitching maya. By His grace you will realize that this world and its riches are
God's maya and therefore impermanent. You will then realize that God is
infinite, all-pervading. You will experience bliss — limitless, infinite bliss.
This bliss is not worldly sense pleasure. Worldly pleasure eventually
brings misery or emptiness. The joy that originates from God-realization
is uninterrupted, and it leads to infinite bliss that has no beginning or
end. God is infinite, so the bliss of God-realization is also infinite, limitless, eternal, and supreme."

After saying this, Sri Ramakrishna went into bhava samadhi. He then
prayed almost inaudibly: "Mother, I have taken refuge at Thy feet."

The devotees were overwhelmed as they witnessed the Master's
ecstasy. When he returned to normal consciousness, M. bowed down to
him and mentally prayed: "I bow down to that guru who has opened my
eyes, blinded by the darkness of ignorance, with the lancet of the light of
knowledge."

M. then went to the natmandir in front of the Kali temple and rolled
on the floor from one side to the other. Keeping the Master in mind, he
also bowed down to the deities of all the temples.[1]

II

[M. read from his diary during the weekly meeting of the Ramakrishna
Mission at Balaram's house in Calcutta on 22 August 1897. This talk was
summarized in the minutes of the Ramakrishna Mission. The author
translated this entry from the original Bengali, rearranged the text according to M.'s style, and made some additions from M.'s printed version in
some places to complete the theme or story.]

Monday, 9 March 1885

Sri Ramakrishna was going to Balaram's house in Calcutta from
Dakshineswar by carriage, accompanied by Narayan. They picked up M.

*One maund is equal to 82 pounds.

on the way. A boy bowed down to the Master, and Narayan told him that the boy's father earned one thousand rupees per month. The Master was happy that the son of a wealthy man had so much humility. Seeing Girish's son on the way, the Master saluted him.

When they reached Balaram's house, the Master went upstairs and found Balaram in bed. He had been ill.

Master (*to Balaram*): "You look pale. Is it from illness or lack of sleep?"

Balaram: "Sir, even you had a broken arm, and compared to you we are nothing."

Master: "As long as you have a human body, you will have to undergo disease and suffering."

Balaram was then taking medicine from a brahmachari at Dakshineswar. The Master asked Balaram to send him four annas' worth of some *harital-bhasma* (calx of orpiment, a kind of ayurvedic medicine). Holy Mother was then ill also. Balaram suggested that the brahmachari should diagnose the Holy Mother's disease.

Master: "No, that brahmachari is mad at the people in the Kali temple because the cashier took his medicine but did not pay him. Previously, that brahmachari was a very good person, but now he has been changed by practising medicine."

Mahendra Mukherjee, Paltu, and the younger Naren arrived.

Master (*to Mahendra Mukherjee*): "Well, you told me that you would take me to see the play *Prahlada Charitra*, but you did not show up. You didn't send the carriage either. Is it because you are embarrassed that you haven't visited me?"

Mahendra: "It is not like that. You asked me to send the carriage in the evening, but there was no performance that evening, so I didn't send it."

A relative of Balaram came to take his pregnant daughter home. The Master told him: "Your daughter is good-natured. It is said that one should not cross the river during pregnancy."

Balaram: "Sir, that is in an even-numbered month."

Master: "Well, I know one should not cross the river."

Master (*to Tulsiram*): "Please continue your studies. Narendra has read the Vedas and Vedanta philosophy at home.

"Girish has changed. He is now much better. Narendra visits him and they have many spiritual discussions. Chuni wants to repeat the Pranava (Om) mantra. I told him, 'If you wish you can repeat it, but it is not necessary.'"

The Master went to the toilet. After coming back he said to Dr. Pratap: "Your medicine is very effective. I am fully cured now."

Pratap: "It is my good fortune, sir."

Master (*to Mahendra Mukherjee*): "Please visit me in Dakshineswar. It is good to have holy company. Jadu's mother said, 'Father, you are a wonderful sadhu; you don't ask for money.' A young woman came to Dakshineswar. I was then pulling some weeds in the Panchavati and didn't look at her. She said: 'Hello, sadhu, I have been standing behind you for a long time. You have neither looked at me nor talked to me. I have visited many Ashramas. Wherever I went, everyone eagerly talked to me or asked me to stay at the Ashrama. You are a wonderful and detached monk. You didn't look at me even once!'

"Well, I must try to please everyone. Let me visit the inner apartment." The Master visited the women devotees there and allowed them to bow down to him, and then returned to the parlour.

Master (*to the devotees*): "Look, I can't touch a metal pot anymore. Can you tell me what is happening? The other day I went to answer the call of nature, but I could not carry my brass water pot, so I improvised a way to clean myself. A few days later I carried an earthen water cup for cleaning. Afterwards, I was a little apprehensive that the temple manager might think that I was feigning. One day I said to the Divine Mother, 'Why am I in such a state?' Another day I grabbed the brass water pot with a folded towel, but I had a terrible aching pain. I tried to eat my meals on a brass plate, but failed; so I eat on a leaf plate and look at the brass plate.

"In this Kaliyuga, jnana yoga is extremely difficult for householders. The path of devotion prescribed by Narada is the best for this age. Why should I play only one note on the flute? I will play different melodies through the flute's seven holes. I shall play: 'Āmār sādher kālāchānd — My dear luminous Blue One — Krishna...' There are many ways to reach God. I shall enjoy fish in various ways, such as fish soup, fish curry, pickled fish, fried fish, and so on.

"Jnana yoga cannot be practised when one is involved with women and the management of oil mills and brick-dust mills. A jnani is supposed to practise sadhana in seclusion; whereas the nature of a devotee is like a hemp smoker. A hemp smoker does not enjoy smoking alone; he loves the company of other hemp smokers."

Girish: "Sir, you talked about admission to a hospital."

Master: "A patient goes to the hospital on his own, but cannot leave until the doctor examines him carefully and releases him."

(*To a young devotee*): "Your father is like Hiranyakashipu, who did not allow his son Prahlada to chant God's name. You must love and respect your parents. However, one does not commit any sin if one disobeys parents who stand in the way of God. Several people have disobeyed their elders: For Rama's sake Bharat did not obey his mother Kaikeyi. Vibhishana went against the wishes of Ravana, his elder brother, to please Rama. The gopis did not obey their husbands when they were forbidden to visit Krishna. Prahlada disobeyed his father for God. Vali disregarded Shukracharya, his teacher, in order to please God. Shukadeva disobeyed Vyasa, his father, when the latter asked him to enter family life. Parashuram didn't listen to his parents when he left to practise austerities in Kailash. But one should be sincere.

"Narendra didn't believe in the Divine Mother. He considered Her to be an illusion of my brain. He listens to English-educated people, so he did not accept Mother. I told him to beg forgiveness from Her. Now he has a vision of light in meditation. Previously he banished all divine forms; now he accepts Mother. I told him, 'Look, Mother talks to me.'

"Nangta [Tota Puri] stayed at Dakshineswar for eleven months. I told him, 'Until I experience the truth of Vedanta, you cannot go.' He said: 'I feel the same way. I am unable to leave this place.' Nangta didn't believe in Mother. I said to him, 'See what happens to me.' Watching my bhava samadhi, he remarked: '*Daivi maya* — Ah, what a display of divine maya!' In a dream Mother told Nangta: 'You still have I-consciousness, and you don't accept Me.' Previously he would go to the Kali temple, but didn't bow down to Her. But on that day he bowed down to the Mother and exclaimed: 'Jai Kali Kalyāni — Victory to Kali, the auspicious Mother.' Previously he would say, 'Jai Ganesha, Jnana Ganesha — Victory to Ganesha — the wise One.'"

Afterwards the Master left for Girish's house. On the way he went into ecstasy and was staggering like a drunkard. When he reached the crossroad, he said: "Don't hold me. I shall be able to go myself.' Girish and Haripada were waiting at the corner of the lane. Seeing the Master, Girish rushed inside to say something and then escorted the Master to his living room upstairs. Many people were present.

Entering the room, the Master said: "Chaitanyadeva used to experience three spiritual states: the inmost, the semiconscious, and the conscious. In the inmost state he would see God and go into samadhi. He would be in the state of jada samadhi. In the semiconscious state he would become partially conscious of the outer world. In the conscious state he would sing the name and glories of God." Then in a low voice, the Master said: "Chaitanya also used to restrain his spiritual feeling in the presence of unsympathetic people."

Master: "'I' and 'mine' — these constitute ignorance. 'My house, my wealth, my learning, my possessions' — he attitude that prompts one to say such things comes from ignorance. If a visitor goes to a rich man's garden, the manager says to him, 'This is our house; this is our picture gallery; this is our furniture,' and so forth. But if the owner fires the manager for some misdeed and angrily orders him, 'Get out, right now,' he has no time to carry away even his mango-wood chest.

"God laughs on two occasions. He laughs when the physician says to the patient's mother: 'Don't be afraid, mother. I shall certainly cure your boy.' God laughs, saying to Himself, 'I am going to take his life, and this man says he will save it!' God laughs again when two brothers divide their land with a string, saying to each other, 'This side is mine and that side is yours.' He laughs and says to Himself, 'This whole universe belongs to Me, but they say they own this portion or that portion.'

"God does everything. The Sikh devotees told me that even the leaves cannot move without the will of God.

"I said to Keshab: 'Tell me, how many annas of knowledge of God have I?' Keshab replied, 'You have sixteen annas' [one hundred percent] worth of knowledge.' To this, I said: 'I don't value or believe your words because you are a family man with worldly desires. If Narada and Shukadeva had said that, I would believe it.'"

Master (*To Atul*): "'The devotee of Kali is a jivanmukta, full of Eternal Bliss' — this is the final word. She is full of the bliss of divine inebriation. The whole creation evolves from Her and dissolves into Her. Purusha or Brahman is unattached to good and evil. Good and evil apply to the jiva, the individual soul, as do righteousness and unrighteousness, but Brahman is not affected by them.

"One man may read the Bhagavata by the light of a lamp, another may commit forgery by that very light; but the lamp is unaffected. The sun remains the same but the other planets move around the sun.

"Harish meditates so deeply it is as if his body is lifeless. [Harish had renounced his wife and was living with Sri Ramakrishna in Dakshineswar.] I asked him to be a little kind to his wife. Harish said: 'You must excuse me on this point. This is not the place to show kindness. If I try to be sympathetic to her, there is a possibility of my forgetting the ideal and becoming entangled in the world. It is better to be kind to all beings.'

"People of small intellect seek occult powers — powers to cure disease, win a lawsuit, walk on water, and such things. As long as one has a body, one will get some kind of disease. But genuine devotees of God don't want anything except His lotus feet. God bestows immortality upon those who call on Him."

Pointing to an idle devotee, the Master jokingly said: "You are like 'Elder, the pumpkin-cutter.' You are neither a man of the world nor a devotee of God. That is not good. You must have seen the sort of elderly man who lives in a family and is always ready, day or night, to entertain the children. He sits in the parlour and smokes a hubble-bubble. With nothing in particular to do, he leads a lazy life. Now and then he goes to the inner court and cuts a pumpkin; for, since women do not cut pumpkins, they send the children to ask him to come and do it. That is the extent of his usefulness — hence his nickname, 'Elder, the pumpkin-cutter.'

"It is not good to have any ego. To eradicate the brahminical ego forever, I cleaned a toilet with a brush.

"A man is not considered to be a man just because he grows a beard and a moustache, or begets a child. Rather he is a genuine man who is endowed with manliness. Satchidananda alone is the male principle and everything else is the female principle."

Observing the silence among the devotees, the Master asked, "Where is the food?" After dinner, the Master said: "Please bring a good carriage, not like the one M. got for me. While I was returning to Dakshineswar, the door of that carriage flew open and the carriage tilted to one side; one of the horses had a stomach spasm, and the coachman tied it to the rear bumper. I got down on the street. At that time Trailokya's [Mathur's son] carriage was passing by, and I covered my face with my hand when I saw him. Finally, the other horse began to pull the carriage.

"An interesting thing happened at the Nandanbagan Brahmo festival. The organizers invited me with great devotion and said with folded hands, 'Sir, please bless our place with your holy feet.' I saw that some young girls of sixteen with socks and shoes on had arrived with books in their hands. I thought there would be a performance and those girls were the dancers. Dinner was served but nobody paid any attention to us. Upset, Rakhal blurted out, 'Sir, let us leave here and go to Dakshineswar.' I said to him: 'Keep quiet! The carriage hire is three rupees and two annas. Who will pay that? You haven't a penny, and you are making these empty threats! Besides, where shall we find food at this late hour of the night?' After a long time, they arranged our seats near a dirty corner where people keep their shoes. An immoral woman served the curry on our leaf plates. I could not eat it. I ate a luchi with salt and took some sweets. The boys went to our hosts to ask for the carriage hire. First they were put out, but at last they managed to get together three rupees. Our hosts refused to pay the extra two annas and said, 'No, that will do.'"[2]

The Stage for
Ramakrishna's Divine Play

I t is extremely important for the reader to know the history of the place in which Ramakrishna enacted his divine drama for thirty years. The Dakshineswar Kali temple was built by Rani Rasmani, a wealthy woman of Calcutta. In 1847 she had planned a pilgrimage to Varanasi. The night before her departure, the Divine Mother appeared to her in a dream and said: "You need not go to Varanasi. Install my image in a beautiful spot along the bank of the Ganges* and arrange for daily worship and food offerings to Me. I will manifest Myself within that image and accept your worship every day."[1]

Rani Rasmani bought a piece of land in Dakshineswar, a few miles north of Calcutta, and over the next eight years built a huge temple complex there. She spent an enormous amount of money to complete the temple and install its deities. Rasmani's design was unusual in that she included temples to Kali, Radha-Krishna, and Shiva, all in the same compound. Kali and Shiva temples are often built side by side, but traditionally a temple to Krishna is not included in the same compound. Perhaps Rasmani was intuitively following a divine plan: In the future Ramakrishna would come to the temple complex and practise different

*In another version of this incident it is said that Rasmani started her journey, and on the first night her party halted near Dakshineswar, where she had the dream.

religious paths, demonstrating the harmony of religions. On 31 May 1855, Ramkumar, Ramakrishna's elder brother, officiated over the dedication ceremony of the temple; Ramakrishna was also present on that occasion.

Sister Nivedita wrote: "Humanly speaking, without the temple of Dakshineswar there would have been no Ramakrishna; without Ramakrishna, no Vivekananda; and without Vivekananda, no Western mission [of Vedanta]."[2]

In the eyes of his devotees, Ramakrishna is still in Dakshineswar and Dakshineswar is still as it was in the 1880s. Of course, due to the passing of time some changes have taken place in the temple garden. The temples have deteriorated; most of the trees that grew during the Master's time are now dead; and crowds of pilgrims have overrun the formerly peaceful temple garden. Such changes are inevitable. We are thankful to M. (Mahendra Nath Gupta) for the vivid description of the temple garden that he included in the first part of *Sri Sri Ramakrishna Kathamrita* (*The Gospel of Sri Ramakrishna*). The description is in the Bengali version of the *Gospel*. I translated it in full in *Ramakrishna as We Saw Him* (Vedanta Society of St. Louis, 1990). In this chapter I shall present some excerpts from this description. M. began:

> It is Sunday. The devotees have the day off, so they come in large numbers to the temple garden to visit Sri Ramakrishna. His door is open to everybody, and he talks freely with all, irrespective of caste or creed, sect or age. His visitors are monks, paramahamsas [illumined souls], Hindus, Christians, Brahmos, the followers of Shakti and Vishnu, men and women. Blessed was Rani Rasmani! She, out of her religious disposition, built this beautiful temple garden and brought Sri Ramakrishna, the embodiment of divinity, to this place. She made it possible for people to see and worship this God-man.[3]

With these words M. invited suffering humanity to relax in the blissful abode of the Dakshineswar temple garden and listen to the immortal message of Ramakrishna. His intention was to imprint the setting of the temple garden on the minds of the audience before he presented the drama.

When one visits a holy place and worships the deities there, one's mind is purified and one then develops a longing to hear more about God. M. said:

> According to the scriptures, one should circumambulate a holy place at least three times because that makes an indelible impression on the mind

Early picture of the Temple Garden of Dakshineswar from the Ganges

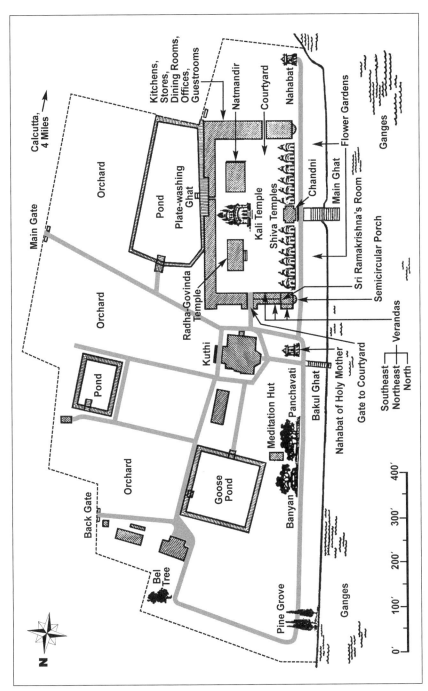

Map of Dakshineswar Temple Garden

of the pilgrim. But once is enough for those who have a good memory and a strong power of observation.

What should one do in a holy place? First, drink a little of the deity's sanctified water. Second, sit in front of the deity for a while. Third, sing or chant the glories of God. Fourth, feed the holy people. Fifth, bring some fruits and sweets to offer. Sixth, don't be stingy or cheat anybody.[4]

In the sixteen volumes of *Srima Darshan*, Swami Nityatmananda recorded conversations with M. and collected many of his memories of the Master that are not in the *Gospel*. In this chapter, some materials from those volumes have been used to complete the descriptions.

We often spend our money, time, and energy to visit a holy or historical place. We also hire a guide who explains the importance of that place, for otherwise our trip would be less meaningful. After Ramakrishna's passing away, M. took many people to Dakshineswar and acted as their guide.

In the eyes of a lover, everything related to the beloved is sweet and precious. M. tried to imprint his experiences with the Master on the minds of his visitors, thus giving them a taste of the divine bliss that he had enjoyed.

The Chandni (Porch)

The Dakshineswar Kali temple is on the Ganges, five miles north of Calcutta. One can travel by boat to Dakshineswar and disembark at the Chandni ghat to enter the temple complex. One is supposed to purify oneself with Ganges water before visiting the deities. It was here at the Chandni ghat that Ramakrishna would bathe. After Ramakrishna's passing, when M. visited Dakshineswar, he would come to this ghat and soak a towel in the water of the Ganges. When he returned home he would squeeze the towel and sprinkle that water on his visitors, reminding them that this water came from the spot where the Master used to bathe. Swami Nityatmananda wrote: "M. reached the Chandni ghat. He sat on the second step from the top, four yards from its northern end. He said: 'The Master sat here when Keshab Sen and his followers came.'"[5] The Master sat on this ghat as if he were a ferryman waiting for passengers who sincerely wanted to cross the turbulent ocean of maya.

Bhavatarini Kali

M. described the image in the Kali temple at Dakshineswar:

South of the Krishna temple is the Kali temple. The beautiful image of the Divine Mother is made out of black stone and Her name is "Bhavatarini," or the Saviour of the World. The floor of this temple is paved with white and black marble. A high altar, with steps to the south, is also made out of stone. Above this is a thousand-petalled lotus made of silver, on which Lord Shiva is lying, with his head to the south and feet to the north. The image of Shiva is made of white marble. On his chest stands the beautiful three-eyed image of Mother Kali, wearing a Varanasi silk sari and various ornaments.[6]

The height of the image is 33 ½ inches. M. later said about this image: "The Master told us that the sculptor of this image was Navin [Pal]. He would work on the image the whole day and eat one vegetarian meal at 3:00 p.m. He undertook severe austerities to make that image of Kali in Dakshineswar. That is the reason the image looks so alive. As the sculptor's heart was full of devotion, his hands transmitted that feeling to the stone image."[7] There are many Kali images in Bengal, but the image in Dakshineswar is special because the Master invoked the deity within it. He once checked to see if the Mother was alive by holding wisps of cotton near Her nostrils; as he did this, he saw the Mother breathing.

The image of Kali is much misunderstood by many Western people, who think She is terrible and frightening. Kali is the Shakti, or power of Brahman, by which He creates, preserves, and dissolves. She is the Cosmic Energy and manifests in both benign and destructive ways. She is the Divine Mother who loves all beings because all are Her children.

Kali's deep blue complexion represents the infinite; each strand of Her hair is a jiva, or individual soul. Her three eyes symbolize her knowledge of past, present, and future. Her white teeth symbolize sattva (peace); Her red tongue, rajas (activity). Her protruding tongue between the teeth reminds the viewer that one controls restlessness with calmness. Her necklace consists of fifty skulls, symbolic of the fifty letters of the Sanskrit alphabet, the origin of sound. Her upper-right hand grants fearlessness, as Her lower-right hand offers boons. She cuts human bondage with the sword in Her upper-left hand and imparts wisdom with the lower-left one, which holds a severed head. She is infinite, so she is naked, clad in space. Shiva is cosmic consciousness and Kali is cosmic energy. Shiva lies on His back beneath Kali's feet. No creation is possible without their union.

During his second visit to Dakshineswar, M. raised a question about the "clay" image of Kali, and Ramakrishna told him, "It is an image of Spirit." He further explained that God is both formless and with form, like water and ice.

The Terrace

There is a terrace between the steps of the Kali temple and the natmandir. "Sometimes the Master used to sit here alone or with the devotees facing the Mother, not far from the edge of the natmandir," wrote
M. One day Ramakrishna dedicated M. to the Mother by singing this
song:

> Thy name, I have heard, O Consort of Shiva, is the destroyer of our fear,
> And so on Thee I cast my burden: Save me! Save me! O kindly Mother![8]

Another day the Master was seated on the terrace, close to the eastern
columns of the natmandir, when he prayed:

> Mother, I don't want any physical enjoyment;
> Mother, I don't want name and fame;
> Mother, I don't want the eight occult powers;
> Mother, I don't want the other hundred powers;
> Mother, give me pure, unchanging, selfless devotion to You.
> Mother, may I never be deluded by Your bewitching maya.[9]

Natmandir (The Concert Hall)

M. described this building:

> In front of the Kali temple and just to the south is the spacious natmandir.
> It is rectangular and the terrace is supported by both inner and outer rows
> of columns. Theatrical performances take place here on special occasions,
> especially during the night of Kali Puja. On the front side of the roof of
> the natmandir there are images of Shiva and His followers, Nandi and
> Bhringi. Sri Ramakrishna used to salute Lord Shiva with folded hands
> before entering the Mother's temple, as if he were seeking His permis-
> sion to enter the temple.[10]

One day M. went to the natmandir, where he embraced the left column of the inner row on the north side of the building. He remained for
a while with closed eyes, then said to his companions: "This column has
been touched by the Master. While listening to the *yatra* performance of
Nilkantha, the Master embraced the column out of ecstasy."[11]

M. described a wonderful scene that he witnessed in the natmandir
during his fourth visit to Dakshineswar: "It was now late in the evening
and time for M.'s departure; but he felt reluctant to go and instead went in
search of Sri Ramakrishna. At last he found the Master pacing alone in the
natmandir in front of the Kali temple. A lamp was burning in the temple
on either side of the image of the Divine Mother. The single lamp in the

spacious natmandir blended light and darkness into a kind of mystic twi-light, in which the figure of the Master could be dimly seen. In the dim light the Master, all alone, was pacing the hall rejoicing in the Self — as the lion lives and roams alone in the forest."[12]

Krishna Temple and the Courtyard

M. wrote:

East of the Chandni and twelve temples is a large tiled courtyard. There are two temples in the middle of the courtyard — the Radhakanta [Krishna] temple on the north side and the Kali [Divine Mother] temple on the south side. In the Radhakanta temple there are two images on the altar — Radha and Krishna — standing and facing west. Steps lead from the courtyard into the sanctuary. The floor of this temple is paved with marble. Chandeliers hang from the ceiling of the veranda. They are usu-ally covered with red linen and used only during festive occasions. In front of the veranda is a row of columns.[13]

Ramakrishna became the priest of the Krishna temple after the previ-ous priest had slipped and dropped Krishna's image, breaking one of the feet. The Master subsequently repaired this image.

Once, while listening to the Bhagavata on the veranda of the Krishna temple, the Master had a vision: He saw a light emanate from the image, then touch him, and then touch the Bhagavata. He experienced the truth that the scripture, the devotee, and the deity are one. On another occa-sion, a photograph of Ramakrishna was taken as he sat in front of this temple. This photograph subsequently became the one most commonly worshipped by devotees in their shrines.

The Brahmos did not believe in God with form. When Keshab Sen and the Brahmos came to Dakshineswar, the Master would escort them to the temples. When they reached the Krishna temple, Ramakrishna would wrap part of his wearing cloth around his neck and bow down to Krishna from the courtyard, touching his forehead to the lower step of the temple. This is how he taught them to respect the deity.[14]

Blessed are the tiles in that courtyard! They were touched by the Master's feet thousands of times.

Twelve Shiva Temples

M. described them thus: The Chandni is located at the centre of twelve Shiva temples — six of them on the north and six on the south. Seeing the twelve temples from a distance, passengers in boats on the Ganges point out to one another: "Look! There is the temple garden of Rani Rasmani."[15]

It is said that the Master embraced the northern-most image of Shiva, which is situated near his room. Swami Saradananda wrote: "One day the Master entered one of the Shiva temples of Dakshineswar and began to recite the *Shiva-mahimnah*, a hymn in praise of the deity. He was beside himself in ecstasy as he recited the following verse: 'O Lord, if the blue mountain be the ink, the ocean the ink pot, the biggest branch of the celestial tree the pen, and the earth the writing-leaf, and if by taking this, the goddess of learning writes forever, even then the limit of Your glory can never be reached.'"[16]

Ramakrishna's Room

Ramakrishna spent fourteen years, from 1871 to 1885, in a room located at the northwest corner of the temple courtyard and immediately to the north of the Shiva temples.

After Ramakrishna's passing, M. would tell the devotees:

One should see everything connected with the Master in detail. For example, in the Master's room there are cots, a jar containing Ganges water, pictures of gods and goddesses — Kali, Krishna, Rama, Chaitanya and his kirtan party, Dhruva, Prahlad, Christ extending his hand to the drowning Peter, and a white marble image of Buddha, which was given to him by Rani Katyayani, the wife of Lalababu. There was a picture of the goddess of learning on the western wall. Whenever a new person would come, the Master would look at that picture and pray, "Mother, I am an unlettered person. Please sit on my tongue," and then he would speak to him. If a person can imprint these divine sights on his mind, he will have deep meditation, and even sitting at home he can live at Dakshineswar with the Master.[17]

One can feel the tangible spiritual atmosphere in this room. Here the Master had many visions, and he went into samadhi on countless occasions. This is where he received his visitors and disciples and talked to them about God. Unfortunately, during the centenary of the Dakshineswar temple garden in 1955, the Master's red cement floor was replaced with mosaic tile, so we can no longer walk on the same floor that he trod.

The Semicircular Porch

M. wrote:

To the west of this room is a semicircular veranda. Standing here facing west, Sri Ramakrishna would watch the holy river Ganges flow by. In front of the veranda is a narrow garden path running from north to south. On the other side of this path is the flower garden and then the embankment. From here, one can hear the sweet, melodious murmuring of the Ganges.[18]

M. later told Swami Nityatmananda: "Sometimes at 2:00 or 3:00 a.m., the Master would pace back and forth on the embankment. He said: 'At that time one can hear the *anahata* sound [music of the spheres]. Only the yogis can hear it.'"[19]

The Southeastern Veranda

Ramakrishna would walk through the southeastern veranda when he visited the temples. Ramlal recalled: "One day the Master was seated on the southeastern veranda of his room. All of a sudden, he saw the Divine Mother standing on the roof of the temple, wearing Her anklets, extending one of Her legs towards the courtyard. Immediately he cried out and forbade Her, waving his hands: 'Don't — don't go farther! You will fall.' Saying so, the Master went into samadhi."

One day Ramakrishna was resting on his bed while Baburam (later Swami Premananda) fanned him. Narendra (later Swami Vivekananda) sat smoking with Hazra on the southeastern veranda of the Master's room. Hazra said to Narendra: "You are all mere boys! You are visiting Sri Ramakrishna off and on, and he just keeps you satisfied with fruits and sweets. Hold him — press him — and get something [power, wealth, and so on] from him." As soon as the Master heard this from his room he jumped up from his bed, rushed to the veranda, and shouted: "Naren, come to my room right now. Don't listen to his calculating advice. The beggar pesters the rich man, saying: 'Sir, give me a pice! Give me a pice!' Being disgusted with the beggar, the rich man throws a small coin to him, saying, 'Take this and get out of here.' You are my very own. You will not have to ask for anything from me. Whatever I have is all yours."[20]

The Northern Veranda

M. described the importance of the northern veranda:

Here the devotees used to celebrate the Master's birthday. They would sing devotional songs in chorus and eat prasad with him. Keshab Chandra Sen and his followers often met with the Master here to talk about God. Afterwards the Master would feed them puffed rice, coconut, luchi [fried bread], and sweets. On this same spot Sri Ramakrishna, seeing Narendra [Swami Vivekananda], went into samadhi.[21]

During his third visit, M. heard Swami Vivekananda sing this song as he stood on the northern veranda:

Meditate, O my mind, on the Lord Hari,
The Stainless One, Pure Spirit through and through.
How peerless is the Light that in Him shines!
How soul-bewitching is His wondrous form!
How dear is He to all His devotees!
Ever more beauteous in fresh-blossoming love
That shames the splendour of a million moons,
Like lightning gleams the glory of His form,
Raising erect the hair for very joy.

M. described Ramakrishna's reaction:

The Master shuddered when this last line was sung. His hair stood on end, and tears of joy streamed down his cheeks. Now and then his lips parted in a smile. Was he seeing the peerless beauty of God, "that shames the splendour of a million moons?" Was this the vision of God, the Essence of Spirit? How much austerity and discipline, how much faith and devotion, must be necessary for such a vision![22]

Standing at the northeastern corner of this veranda, the Master would say good-bye to the Calcutta devotees. "One day," M. said, "I saw the Master sweeping the path next to the northern veranda with a broom. He told me, 'Mother walks here; that is why I am cleaning this path.'"[23]

The Northeastern Veranda

One day Ramakrishna was pacing back and forth on the northeastern veranda of his room in Dakshineswar. He was in a spiritual mood, completely oblivious of his surroundings. Mathur was then seated alone in a room of the kuthi (mansion) near the nahabat, and was watching him through a window. All of a sudden Mathur ran out of the kuthi, threw himself down at Ramakrishna's feet, and began to cry profusely.

"What are you doing?" said Ramakrishna in alarm. "You are an aristocrat and Rani Rasmani's son-in-law. What will people say if they see you acting like this? Calm yourself. Please, get up!"

Mathur gradually got control of himself and said: "Father [as he called Ramakrishna], I was watching you just now as you walked back and forth — I saw it distinctly: As you walked towards me you were no longer yourself. You were the Divine Mother Kali from the temple! Then, as you turned around and walked in the opposite direction, you became Lord Shiva! At first I thought it was some kind of optical illusion. I rubbed my eyes and looked again, but I saw the same thing. As often as I looked, I saw it!"[24]

The Nahabat (The Music Tower)

There are two nahabats in the temple garden, one on the south side and the other on the north side. M. described the music that came from one of these towers: "Early in the morning, before the eastern horizon becomes red, the *mangala-arati* [morning service] to the Divine Mother begins with the sweet sound of temple bells. In the nahabat, morning melodies are then played on the flageolet to the accompaniment of drums and cymbals. These are welcome sounds of love and joy for all, for the Mother of the Universe has awakened to bless Her beloved children."[25]

Ramakrishna's mother used to live in the upper room of the northern nahabat and the Holy Mother lived in the lower room. To protect her privacy, the veranda was screened with plaited bamboo mats, which cut off the sun and fresh air. The Holy Mother lived there like a caged bird. She would cook for the Master on the northern veranda and below the staircase of the nahabat. (*Pointing to the steps reaching the upper floor of the nahabat*) M. said: "The Holy Mother would sit here and repeat her mantra. As a result of her limited movement, she developed rheumatism that caused suffering all through her life. Her little room was filled with foodstuffs and other things; and sometimes women devotees also stayed there. Oh, what superhuman patience, perseverance, and self-control! Her self-sacrifice and service are incomparable."[26]

The Flower Gardens

M. described the beautiful temple gardens:

On the bank of the Ganges and just to the west of the Panchavati are a bel tree and a sweet-scented, milk-white *gulchi* [plumeria] flower tree. Sri Ramakrishna was very fond of *mallika* [a type of jasmine], *madhavi*, and gulchi. He brought a madhavi plant [a flowering creeper that Radha liked] from Vrindaban and planted it in the Panchavati. East of the goose pond and the kuthi is another pond around which are many flowering plants such as the *champak*, the five-faced hibiscus, the pendant hibiscus [resembling earrings], roses, and the *kanchan* [gold]. On a fence there is an *aparajita* [a blue flower used in the worship of the Divine Mother], and nearby are jasmine and *shefalika*.

West of the twelve Shiva temples, there are many flowering trees such as the white oleander, red oleander, rose, jasmine, and double-petalled jasmine. Also growing there are *dhutura* flowers, which are used for the worship of Shiva. Tulsi [basil] plants grow in brick vases between these flowering trees.

South of the nahabat are more double-petalled jasmine as well as other varieties of jasmine, gardenias, and roses. Two more flowering trees grow near the Chandni ghat: the lotus oleander and the *kokilak-sha*, or cuckoo-eyed flower. The colour of the latter resembles that of the eyes of a cuckoo. West of the Master's room there are quite a few plants: *Krishna-chura*, double-petalled jasmine, jasmine, gardenia, mallika, roses, hibiscus, white oleander, red oleander, five-faced hibiscus, china rose, and so on.

Formerly Sri Ramakrishna picked flowers for worship. One day when he was plucking bel leaves from a bel tree near the Panchavati, a layer of bark came off the tree. At that moment he experienced that God, who dwells in every being and every thing, must have felt pain at this. He never again picked bel leaves for worship. Another day while picking flowers he had a vision: He saw that the flowers of each tree formed a bouquet and all those bouquets hung around the neck of the cosmic form of Shiva. Thus he experienced that the worship of God is going on day and night. After that experience he could no longer pick flowers.[27]

M.'s description of the flower gardens makes us feel that we are roaming in the gardens of heaven.

The Bakul-tala

M. wrote:

West of the nahabat are a bakul tree and a bathing ghat. The women of the neighbourhood bathe at this ghat. In 1877 Sri Ramakrishna's aged mother passed away here. Following the Hindu custom, the Master's dying mother was taken to this ghat and the lower half of her body was immersed in the holy water of the Ganges. She breathed her last in the presence of her weeping son.[28]

M. told Swami Nityatmananda: "Holding the feet of his mother, the Master said: 'Mother, who are you that carried me in your womb?' The Master knew that he was an avatar, so he exclaimed in joy: 'You are not an ordinary woman.'"[29]

The Panchavati

M. described the Panchavati as it appeared in Ramakrishna's time:

A little north of the bakul tree is the Panchavati. This is a grove of five trees — banyan, pipal, ashoka, amalaki, and bel — which were planted under Sri Ramakrishna's supervision. After returning from his pilgrimage [in 1868] he spread the holy dust of Vrindaban around this place. The Master practised various kinds of sadhana [disciplines] in the Panchavati grove, sometimes going there alone at night. Later he often accompanied the devotees as they walked around the holy spot. East of the Panchavati

is a thatched hut [now a brick building], in which Sri Ramakrishna practised meditation and austerities [Advaita sadhana under Tota Puri].

Next to the Panchavati is an old banyan tree that has grown around a
pipal tree, both looking as if they were one tree. The banyan is an ancient
tree, and as a result there are many holes in it, which are the homes of
birds and other animals. Around this tree is a circular brick platform with
steps on two sides — north and south. The platform is used by people
who visit the temple garden and especially by those who wish to sit in
solitude and meditate on God with the holy Ganges flowing before them.
Sri Ramakrishna used to sit on the northwest corner of the platform and
practise various kinds of spiritual disciplines. He would cry to the Divine
Mother with a longing heart, as the cow longs for her calf.[30]

M. told Swami Nityatmananda: "European indigo planters used to
live here. This banyan tree and the platform existed during their time. This
platform was the first place where the Master practised intense sadhana.
Between the Panchavati and the old banyan tree was the madhavi creeper
that the Master brought from Vrindaban. He planted it himself."[31]

Swami Subodhananda told M. the following incident: "The Master
told me: 'I was then possessed by divine madness. One day I was weed-
ing in the Panchavati. I was unaware that a beautiful young woman was
standing behind me. Piqued, she said to me: "Hello, sadhu! I have been
standing behind you for such a long time and you have not looked at me
or talked to me! I have visited many Ashramas and everywhere people
are eager to talk to me and want me to live there. But you didn't even care
to look at me. You are a real sadhu."'"[32]

M. recalled this particular scene many times:

Sri Ramakrishna was going to the pine grove. After a few minutes, M. and
Latu, standing in the Panchavati, saw the Master coming back towards
them. Behind him the sky was black with the rain-cloud. Its reflection in
the Ganges made the water darker. The disciples felt that the Master was
God Incarnate, a Divine Child five years old, radiant with the smile of
innocence and purity. Around him were the sacred trees of the Panchavati
under which he had practised spiritual disciplines and had beheld visions
of God. At his feet flowed the sacred river Ganges, the destroyer of Man's
sins. The presence of this God-man charged the trees, shrubs, flowers,
plants, and temples with spiritual fervour and divine joy.[33]

Sadhan Kutir (Meditation Hut)

The sadhan kutir is situated east of the Panchavati. Here Tota Puri
initiated the Master into sannyasa, and here he attained nirvikalpa

samadhi. M. said: "It was a thatched hut with an earthen floor when the Master practised Vedanta sadhana there. Later it was rebuilt as a brick building and there was nothing inside. Now someone has installed a Shiva image there. So many things will crop up in the future. People will say that image was there during the Master's time. Thus it happens everywhere."[34]

Pine Grove and Bel-tala

M. described:

Going a little north of the Panchavati one reaches a fence of iron wire. North of this fence is the pine grove — a collection of four pine trees. Sri Ramakrishna and the devotees would use this place to answer the call of nature.

East of the pine grove is the bel-tala. Sitting under this bel tree, Sri Ramakrishna practised many difficult disciplines [especially tantric sadhanas under the guidance of the Bhairavi Brahmani]. To the north of the pine grove and bel tree is the high boundary wall of the temple garden, and on the other side of the wall is a government magazine [for munitions].[35]

Gazi-tala and the Main Gate

M. wrote:

There is a path running east to west between the northern portico of the courtyard and the kuthi. While walking east, one can see a beautiful pond with a concrete ghat on the right side. There is another ghat for this pond on the eastern side of the Kali temple, which is used to clean the sacred utensils and dishes. A pipal tree is next to the northern ghat. This place is called Gazi-tala. Long ago an old Muslim saint lived here, passing his days in the contemplation of God. His departed spirit is worshipped even today by Hindus and Muslims who live near the temple. [At the Gazi-tala Ramakrishna practised Islamic sadhana under the guidance of a Sufi named Govinda Roy.]

The main gate of the temple garden is a little east of the Gazi-tala. People who come from Alambazar or Calcutta enter the temple compound through this gate, and the people of Dakshineswar come through the northeastern gate, which is a little north of the main gate. A guard protects the main gate. When the Master would return late from Calcutta by carriage, sometimes even at midnight, the guard at the main gate would unlock the gate for him. Then the Master would invite the guard to his room and feed him fried bread and sweets which had been sent as prasad.[36]

Kuthi (Mansion)

M. described the mansion in which Ramakrishna lived for sixteen years:

> Coming out of the temple courtyard through the northern portico, one comes across a two-storeyed mansion called the kuthi. Whenever Rani Rasmani or her son-in-law Mathur and other relatives came to visit Dakshineswar, they stayed in this kuthi. During their lifetime Sri Ramakrishna lived [for sixteen years] in a room on the west side of the ground floor of this mansion. From this room one can go to the bakul-tala ghat and have a very good view of the Ganges.[37]

Swami Saradananda described a touching incident that took place on the roof of the kuthi. It is amazing how Sri Ramakrishna prayed for the disciples who acted in his divine drama:

> After the Master had attained all the spiritual experiences, divine inspiration prompted a new desire to arise intensely in the Master's mind. He became extremely anxious to meet the devotees he had seen previously in spiritual visions and to transmit his spiritual power into their hearts.
>
> The Master said: "In those days there was no limit to my yearning. During the daytime I could just manage to keep it under control. Severely tormented by the worthless, mundane talk of worldly people, I would wistfully anticipate the day when my beloved companions would arrive. I hoped to find solace in conversing with them about God and to lighten my heart by relating to them my own spiritual experiences. Every little incident would remind me of them, and thoughts of them completely engrossed me. I kept planning what I should say to this one and what I should give to that one, and so forth. When evening came, I couldn't control my feelings any longer. I was tortured by the thought that another day had passed and they still hadn't arrived! When the vesper service started, and the temples resounded with the ringing of bells and the blowing of conch shells, I would climb up to the roof of the kuthi [mansion] and cry out at the top of my voice, with the anguish of my heart: 'Come to me, my children! Where are you? I can't bear to live without you!' A mother never longed so for the sight of her child, or a friend for a friend, or a lover for his sweetheart, as I did for them. Oh, it was beyond all describing! And soon after this, they did at last begin to come."[38]

M. made a wonderful comment about Dakshineswar: "A spiritual fire is blazing intensely there, and whoever goes there will be purified. The body does not burn, but mental impurities are consumed in no time. Then a person can attain immortality. God himself, in a physical form, lived

there for thirty years! One can tangibly feel the spirituality at Dakshineswar."[39]

There is a beautiful verse in the *Sri Sri Chaitanya Charitamrita*: *Adyapiha
sei lila kare gora rai, kono kono bhagyavane dekhibare pai.* "Chaitanya is still
performing his divine play; only the fortunate ones can see it." Let us
pray to Ramakrishna to grant us the good fortune to be able to visualize
his divine play.

Service to the Master

Humility, the spirit of inquiry, and personal service rendered to the teacher are requirements of discipleship. Krishna says in the Gita: "Learn it [the Truth] by prostration, by inquiry, and by service. The wise, who have seen the Truth, will teach you that Knowledge."[1] There is also a saying: "One can attain God by service, worship, and humility." M. was endowed with all these qualities.

Very few people had the opportunity to serve Ramakrishna. He did not allow people to serve him who were not pure and guileless, who earned money through unfair means, who offered him food with ulterior motives, who lied, or who were of questionable character. On the other hand, the Master needed someone nearby to hold him when he would go into samadhi, or to carry his water pot, because he could not touch any metal.

On 20 June 1884 Ramakrishna said to M.: "You see, I am having some difficulty about my physical needs. It will be nice if Baburam lives with me. The nature of these attendants of mine is undergoing a change. Latu is always tense with spiritual emotion. He is about to merge himself in God. Rakhal is getting into such a spiritual mood that he can't do anything even for himself. I have to get water for him. He isn't of much service to me."[2] Moreover, Rakhal had to visit his home occasionally. Although several devotees lived with the Master, when he was in samadhi he could bear the touch of only certain people. On 30 June 1884 he told Baburam:

"Do stay with me. It will be very nice. In this mood I cannot allow others to touch me."

Baburam was a student at M.'s school. He was deemed a proper attendant for Ramakrishna because of his absolute purity. He was one of those fortunate souls whose touch the Master could accept during samadhi. Many were the occasions when he was found supporting the Master in that state lest he should fall and be injured. Later, Baburam reminisced: "Sri Ramakrishna was the embodiment of purity. A man earned a lot of money by taking bribes. One day this person touched the Master's feet while he was in samadhi and he cried out in pain. During the Master's samadhi we had to hold him so he would not fall, but we were afraid. We thought that if we were not pure enough, then, when we touched him during samadhi, he would publicly cry out in pain. So we prayed for purity. It was the Master's grace that I was allowed to live with him."[3]

Personal Service to the Master

M. had a family and could not stay with Ramakrishna constantly, but some of the disciples lived with the Master and served him. Whenever M. had an opportunity, he gave personal service to the Master. One day at Dakshineswar, when the Master had finished his meal, M. took his plate and glass and washed them. Being pleased, the Master remarked: "This attitude of serving is very good. It is nice to be practical in all circumstances. One should know how to cook, to wash utensils, to clean clothes, how to sweep and mop the floor, and so on."[4] Even after the Master's passing away M. used to visit the Ramakrishna Math at Baranagore to serve Ramakrishna's monastic disciples. He recalled: "The Master had just left the body. As usual I visited the Baranagore Math, sometimes on foot, because a share carriage was not always available. I would clean the monks' pots, pans, and dishes. I used to carry water from the pond and sometimes go to the market with Shashi Maharaj."[5]

In the *Gospel* M. recorded in various places that the Master had asked him to massage his feet or fan him or carry his water pot. We cannot resist presenting to the reader some of those wonderful scenes, which demonstrate how much affection the Master had for M.

8 June 1883 at Dakshineswar: "Lying on the mat and resting his head on a pillow, Sri Ramakrishna continued the conversation. He said to M.: 'My legs are aching. Please stroke them gently.' Thus, out of his infinite compassion, the Master allowed his disciple to render him personal service."[6]

On 7 March 1885 M. went with his wife to see the Master at Dakshineswar. Whenever he visited the Master, M. always carried some fruits or sweets for him. On that day he carried a basket of sandesh and the Master touched it, uttering the word "Om," and ate a little. Then he distributed the remainder among the devotees.

> Sri Ramakrishna sat with the devotees on the mat on the floor. He was smiling. He said to the devotees, "Please stroke my feet gently." They carried out his request. He said to M., "There is great significance in this." Placing his hand on his heart, the Master said, "If there is anything here, then through this service the ignorance and illusion of the devotees will be completely destroyed."
>
> Suddenly Sri Ramakrishna became serious, as if about to reveal a secret.
>
> Master (*to M.*): "There is no outsider here. The other day, when Harish was with me, I saw Satchidananda come out of this sheath. It said, 'I incarnate Myself in every age.' I thought that I myself was saying these words out of mere fancy. I kept quiet and watched. Again Satchidananda Itself spoke, saying, 'Chaitanya, too, worshipped Shakti.'... I saw that it is the fullest manifestation of Satchidananda; but this time the Divine Power is manifested through the glory of sattva."
>
> The devotees sat spellbound.
>
> It was dusk. Preparations were going on in the temples for the evening worship. The lamp was lighted in the Master's room and incense was burnt. Seated on the small couch, Sri Ramakrishna saluted the Divine Mother and chanted Her name in a tender voice. There was nobody in the room except M., who was sitting on the floor.
>
> Sri Ramakrishna rose from the couch. M. also stood up. The Master asked him to shut the west and north doors of the room. M. obeyed and stood by Sri Ramakrishna on the porch. The Master said that he wanted to go to the Kali temple. Leaning on M.'s arm, he came down to the terrace of the temple. He asked M. to call Baburam and sat down. After visiting the Divine Mother, the Master returned to his room across the courtyard, chanting, "O Mother! Mother! Rajarajesvari!"[7]

11 March 1885 at Balaram's house in Calcutta:

M. taught in a school in the neighbourhood. He often brought his young students to visit the Master at Balaram's house. On this day, having learnt of Sri Ramakrishna's arrival, M. went there at noon during the recess hours of the school. He found the Master resting in the drawing-room after his midday meal. Several young boys were in the room. M. prostrated himself before the Master and sat by his side....

The Master, looking a little thoughtful, asked M. to come nearer. He said, "Please wring out my wet towel and put my coat in the sun." Then he continued: "My legs and feet ache. Please rub them gently."

M. felt very happy to be given the privilege of rendering these services to the Master.[8]

Ramakrishna went to Balaram's house in Calcutta to attend the Chariot Festival and stayed there from 13 to 15 July 1885.

13 July 1885 at Balaram's house:

It was dusk. Lamps were lighted in the room. Sri Ramakrishna was meditating on the Divine Mother and chanting Her name in his melodious voice. The devotees sat around him. Since Balaram was going to celebrate the Chariot Festival at his house the following day, Sri Ramakrishna intended to spend the night there.

After taking some refreshments in the inner apartments, Sri Ramakrishna returned to the parlour. It was about ten o'clock. The Master said to M., "Please bring my towel from the other room." A bed was made for Sri Ramakrishna in the adjoining small room. About half past ten Sri Ramakrishna lay down to sleep. It was summertime. He said to M., "You had better bring a fan." He asked the disciple to fan him. At midnight Sri Ramakrishna woke up. He said to M., "Don't fan me anymore; I feel chilly."

It was the day [14 July 1885] of the Chariot Festival. Sri Ramakrishna left his bed very early in the morning. He was alone in the room, dancing and chanting the name of God. M. entered and saluted the Master. Other devotees arrived one by one. They saluted the Master and took seats near him.

It was about half past six in the morning. M. was going to bathe in the Ganges, when suddenly tremors of an earthquake were felt. At once he returned to Sri Ramakrishna's room. The Master stood in the drawing room. The devotees stood around him. They were talking about the earthquake. The shaking had been rather violent, and many of the devotees were frightened.

M: "You should all have gone downstairs."

Master: "Such is the fate of the house under whose roof one lives; and still people are so egotistic. (To M.) Do you remember the great storm of the month of Aswin?"

M: "Yes, sir. I was very young at that time — nine or ten years old. I was alone in a room while the storm was raging, and I prayed to God."

M. was surprised and said to himself: "Why did the Master suddenly ask me about the great storm of Aswin? Does he know that I was alone at that time earnestly praying to God with tears in my eyes? Does he know all this? Has he been protecting me as my guru since my very birth?"[9]

M. had a full-time job, a wife and children, and other duties. But his mind dwelt on the Master and followed him like a shadow. Whenever he found any opportunity, he tried to give him personal service.

Filled with intense spiritual fervour, the Master began to narrate his profound mystical and spiritual experiences, including visions of Shiva and Annapurna in Varanasi. While describing a vision of God, he went into samadhi. The devotees fixed their eyes on him. After a long time he regained consciousness of the world and resumed talking to the devotees.

Master (*to M.*): "What do you think I saw? I saw the whole universe as a shalagram,* and in it I saw your two eyes."

M. and the devotees listened in silent wonder.

On 14 July M. spent the night at Balaram's house to serve the Master. He later wrote: "It was four o'clock in the morning. Sri Ramakrishna was in bed in the small room next to the drawing room. M. was sitting on a bench in the outer veranda to the south of the room. A few minutes later Sri Ramakrishna came out to the veranda. M. saluted him."[10] It seems he spent a sleepless night, thinking that the Master might need some personal service.

14 March 1886 at the Cossipore garden house:

Sri Ramakrishna sat facing the north in the large room upstairs. It was evening. He was very ill. Narendra and Rakhal were gently massaging his feet. M. sat nearby. The Master, by a sign, asked him, too, to stroke his feet. M. obeyed.

That day Sri Ramakrishna was feeling very ill. At midnight the moonlight flooded the garden, but it could wake no response in the devotees' hearts. They were drowned in a sea of grief. They felt that they were living in a beautiful city besieged by a hostile army. Perfect silence reigned everywhere. Nature was still, except for the gentle rustling of the leaves at the touch of the south wind. Sri Ramakrishna lay awake. One or two devotees sat near him in silence. At times he seemed to doze.

M. was seated by his side. Sri Ramakrishna asked him by a sign to come nearer. The sight of his suffering was unbearable. In a very soft voice and with great difficulty he said to M: "I have gone on suffering so

---

*A stone emblem of Lord Vishnu.

much for fear of making you all weep. But if you all say: 'Oh, there is so much suffering! Let the body die,' then I may give up the body."

These words pierced the devotees' hearts. And he who was their father, mother, and protector had uttered these words! What could they say? All sat in silence.[11]

Shopping for the Master

Krishna said in the Gita: "Those persons who worship Me, meditating on their identity with Me and ever devoted to Me — to them I carry what they lack and for them I preserve what they already have."[12] Ramakrishna was completely dependent upon the Divine Mother. She provided everything for him. However, human beings show their love and gratitude by presenting gifts or money to their loved ones. The Master's suppliers were Mathur Nath Biswas, Shambhu Charan Mallick, Surendra Nath Mitra, and Balaram Basu. M. was headmaster of a school and was not wealthy enough to serve the Master with money like more affluent devotees. Nonetheless, the Master occasionally asked M. to buy some personal things for him, whereas he refused to accept money or any other gifts from some rich people.

"Whosoever offers Me," says Krishna, "with devotion, a leaf, a flower, a fruit, or water — that I accept, the pious offering of the pure in heart."[13] M. offered his heart and soul to Ramakrishna and also supplied some of the things that the Master used every day. When the Master had cancer, he was moved from Dakshineswar to Calcutta and then to Cossipore for treatment. Surendra paid the rent, and Balaram supplied his food. While living in Dakshineswar, the Master had always received six dhotis (wearing cloths) from the temple authorities every year. He had two dhotis for everyday use. The devotees supplied him with shirts. One set of clothes — a dhoti and a shirt — he kept reserved for his visits to Calcutta. The Master needed a towel and a short loin cloth (oil-dhoti), which he wore while smearing his body with oil before bathing.

On 18 October 1884 the Master said to M.: "Please bring two ordinary dhotis for my bath." On 20 October M. recorded:

> The Master noticed that M. had brought some cloths for him. M. had with him two pieces of unbleached and two pieces of washed cloth. But the Master had asked him only for the unbleached ones. He said to M.: "Give me the unbleached ones. You may keep the others. All right. You may give me one of them."
>
> M.: "Then shall I take back one piece?"
>
> Master: "Then take both."

M.: "As you please, sir."

Master: "You can give me those when I need them. You see, yesterday Beni Pal wanted me to carry away some food for Ramlal. I told him I couldn't. It is impossible for me to lay up for the future."

M.: "That's all right, sir. I shall take back the two pieces of washed cloth."

Master (*tenderly*): "Don't you see, if any desire arises in my mind, it is for the good of you all? You are my own. I shall tell you if I need anything."

M. (*humbly*): "Yes, sir."[14]

On 26 October 1884 Ramakrishna said to M: "Please bring me a couple of linen shirts. As you know, I cannot use everybody's things. I thought of asking Captain for the shirts, but you had better give them to me." M. felt highly gratified and said, "As you please, sir."[15]

On 9 November M. recorded:

It was the beginning of winter. Sri Ramakrishna had felt the need of some shirts and had asked M. to bring them. Besides two linen-cloth shirts, M. had brought another of a heavy material [twill], for which Sri Ramakrishna had not asked.

Master (*to M.*): "You had better take that one back with you. You can use it yourself. There is nothing wrong in that. Tell me, what kind of shirt did I ask you to bring?"

M: "Sir, you told me to get you plain ones. You didn't ask me to buy the heavier one."

Master: "Then please take that one back. (*To Vijay and the others*) You see, Dwarika Babu gave me a shawl. The Marwari devotees also brought one for me. I couldn't accept — "

Vijay interrupted the Master, saying: "That is right, sir. If a man needs a thing, he must accept it. And there must be a man to give it. Who but a man will give?"

Master: "The giver is the Lord Himself."[16]

M. carefully described the Dakshineswar temple garden, the stage for Ramakrishna's divine play. Ramakrishna's room has four doors and three windows, and is located in one of the nicest spots of the temple complex. The room is 21 feet from east to west, and 19 feet from north to south. The Master had two cots, one for sleeping and the other for sitting. Both are still there, as they were during his time. There are two bricks underneath each leg of the sleeping cot and one brick underneath each leg of the sitting cot. In his day there was no other furniture in his room except a stool and a cabinet for keeping sweets and fruits. Surendra supplied some carpets and bedrolls for the devotees who stayed overnight at Dakshineswar to serve the Master. The Master asked M. to buy a small water pot,* so that the devotees could drink water. On 20 August 1883 M. brought it to Dakshineswar.

When Ramakrishna had cancer, he was first moved to Calcutta and then to Cossipore for treatment. He needed a stool near his bed on which to keep some of his things, or for sitting. On 23 December 1885, M. recorded:

> Master (*to M.*): "Buy a stool for me. What will it cost?"
> M.: "Between two and three rupees."
> Master: "If a small wooden seat costs only twelve annas, why should you have to pay so much for a stool?"
> M.: "Perhaps it won't cost so much."
> Master: "Tomorrow is Thursday. The latter part of the afternoon is inauspicious. Can't you come before three o'clock?"
> M.: "Yes, sir, I shall."[17]

On 9 April 1886 M. recorded:

> Sri Ramakrishna sat on his bed in the big hall upstairs. It was evening. M. was alone in the room, fanning the Master. Latu came in a little later.
> Master (*to M.*): "Please bring a chadar for me and a pair of slippers."
> M.: "Yes, sir."
> Master (*to Latu*): "The chadar will cost ten annas, and then the slippers — what will be the total cost?"
> Latu: "One rupee and ten annas."
> Sri Ramakrishna asked M., by a sign, to note the price.

On 12 April 1886 M.'s diary runs:

> About five o'clock in the afternoon Sri Ramakrishna was sitting on the bed in his room in the Cossipore garden house. Shashi and M. were with him. He asked M., by a sign, to fan him. There was a fair in the neighbourhood in celebration of the last day of the Bengali year. A devotee, whom Sri Ramakrishna had sent to the fair to buy a few articles, returned. "What have you bought?" the Master asked him.
> Devotee: "Candy for five pice, a spoon for two pice, and a vegetable-knife for two pice."
> Master: "What about the penknife?"
> Devotee: "I couldn't get one for two pice."
> Master (*eagerly*): "Go quickly and get one!"

Chumki ghati is a pitcher-shaped metal water pot that is used for drinking water without touching it to the lips.

In the evening lamps were lighted in the house. Sri Ramakrishna sat on his bed, facing the north. He was absorbed in contemplation of the Mother of the Universe. M. was fanning Sri Ramakrishna. The Master said to him by signs, "Get a stone bowl for me that will hold a quarter of a seer of milk — white stone." He drew the shape of the bowl with his finger.

M.: "Yes, sir."

Master: "When eating from other bowls I get the smell of fish."

13 April 1886:

It was about eight o'clock in the morning. M. had spent the night at the garden house. After taking his bath in the Ganges he prostrated himself before Sri Ramakrishna.

Sri Ramakrishna's slippers were not comfortable. Dr. Rajendra Datta intended to buy a new pair and had asked for the measurement of his feet. The measurement was taken.

Sri Ramakrishna asked M., by a sign, about the stone bowl. M. at once stood up. He wanted to go to Calcutta for the bowl.

Master: "Don't bother about it now."

M.: "Sir, these devotees are going to Calcutta. I will go with them."

M. bought the bowl in Calcutta and returned to Cossipore at noon. He saluted the Master and placed the bowl near him. Sri Ramakrishna took the bowl in his hand and looked at it.[18]

Ramakrishna's life demonstrates how a paramahamsa, or an illumined soul, lives in the world. He had no money, no possessions, and no fancy things. He collected some holy pictures in his room in Dakshineswar; some of them are still there. He was happy to see the pictures of gods and goddesses. He said: "A perfect soul, even after attaining Knowledge, practises devotions or observes religious ceremonies to set an example to others. I go to the Kali temple and I bow before the holy pictures in my room; therefore others do the same."[19] On 24 September 1885 Ramakrishna fell ill, and soon afterwards he moved to Calcutta for treatment. Before he left, M. described the Master's loving gift to him: "A picture of Gauranga and Nitai hung on the wall of the Master's room. It was a picture of the two brothers singing devotional songs with their companions at Navadwip."

Ramlal (*to the Master*): "Then may I give him [*meaning M.*] the picture?"

Master: "Yes."[20] This picture is still kept in M.'s house.

Towards the End

When the Master moved to Shyampukur in Calcutta to be treated for cancer, Holy Mother took responsibility for the Master's diet, the young disciples nursed him and tended to his personal needs. M.'s duty was to go to the doctors every day, inform them of the Master's condition, and bring them to the Shyampukur house. Some other devotees handled the finances.

M. recalled: "The Master suffered from throat cancer for more than ten months. He had a terrible hemorrhage from his wound, but the devotees served him wholeheartedly. Holding the doctor's hand, he plaintively said, 'Please cure my disease.' But as soon as he felt a little better, he would talk about God. Finally he said, 'The Divine Mother will not keep this body anymore.'... The entire report of the Master's illness is in my diary. I recorded the amount of blood from each hemorrhage, the intensity of his pain, what he ate, and other things. Every day I carried that report to Dr. Mahendralal Sarkar."[21]

Although M. recorded all the details of the Master's illness in his diary, he did not publish all of them. The last entry in *The Gospel of Sri Ramakrishna* was dated 24 April 1886. The previous day (23 April 1886) was Good Friday, which is a day of mourning for Christians. M. elaborately described what happened on that day, including the following incident:

> It was evening. A lamp was lighted in the Master's room. Amrita Basu, a Brahmo devotee, came in. A garland of jasmine lay in front of the Master on a plantain-leaf. There was perfect silence in the room. A great yogi seemed to be silently communing with God. Every now and then the Master lifted the garland a little, as if he wanted to put it around his neck.
>
> Amrita (*tenderly*): "Shall I put it around your neck?"
> Sri Ramakrishna accepted the garland.[22]

At the Master's request, M. arrived the next day (24 April 1886) with his wife. She was grief-stricken over the death of their son. M. recorded:

> That day the Master several times allowed M.'s wife the privilege of waiting on him. Her welfare seemed to occupy his attention a great deal. In the evening the Holy Mother came to the Master's room to feed him. M.'s wife accompanied her with a lamp. The Master tenderly asked her many questions about her household. He requested her to come again to the garden house and spend a few days with the Holy Mother, not forgetting to ask her to bring her baby daughter. When the Master had finished his meal M.'s wife removed the plates. He chatted with her a few minutes. [This is a wonderful scene for meditation.]
> About nine o'clock in the evening Sri Ramakrishna was seated in his room with the devotees. He had a garland of flowers around his neck. He

told M. that he had requested his wife to spend a few days at the garden house with the Holy Mother. His kindness touched M.'s heart.

M. was fanning him. The Master took the garland from his neck and said something to himself. Then in a very benign mood he gave the garland to M."[23]

Here M.'s entries for the *Gospel* end. The human aspect of Ramakrishna revealed in such scenes is very moving. Despite his painful disease, he was thinking only of others' welfare. The Master assuaged the grief in M.'s wife's heart and also blessed the recorder of his gospel with a garland.

It is not known why M. did not publish the entries from his diary that described Ramakrishna's last days. Swami Saradananda also did not write about the Master's final days at Cossipore. When he was requested to complete *Sri Ramakrishna and His Divine Play*, he humbly said: "Perhaps it will never be completed. I am not getting inspiration from within. The Master made me write whatever he wanted."[24]

Human desires are insatiable. We are hungry to know more about our beloved Master, but at the same time we are unable to fathom God's will. We will remain ever grateful to M. and Swami Saradananda for the information that they have given us about the Master.

M. devoted himself completely to his guru, Sri Ramakrishna, and in this way he found fulfillment. The Master assigned different tasks to different disciples, and M.'s task was to record his gospel and spread it throughout the world. But there was another way in which M. served his guru. Serving the guru personally is praiseworthy, no doubt, but real service is in translating the guru's teachings into one's own life. M.'s other service was in personifying his guru's ideal of a true householder — one who lives in the world in a detached spirit while his mind remains on God. M. demonstrated this ideal householder life to the world.

Ramakrishna's Love for M.

Sometimes we wonder: Does God think of us? Does He listen to our prayers? Does He love us? This reminds me of the poem "Footprints in the Sand" by Ella H. Scharring-Hausen:

One night I dreamed I was walking
Along the beach with the Lord.
Many scenes from my life flashed across the sky.
In each scene I noticed footprints in the sand.
Sometimes there were two sets of footprints.
Other times there was only one.
This bothered me because I noticed that
During the low periods of my life when I was
Suffering from anguish, sorrow, or defeat,
I could see only one set of footprints,
So I said to the Lord, "You promised me,
Lord, that if I followed You,
You would walk with me always.
But I noticed that during the most trying periods
Of my life there has only been
One set of footprints in the sand.
Why, when I needed You most,
Have you not been there for me?"
The Lord replied,
"The times when you have seen only one set of footprints
is when I carried you."

This poem is very reassuring and encouraging. We may not see our Beloved in our day-to-day life, but our faith reminds us that the Lord is always with us as *antaryami*, the indwelling Self.

Once someone asked M., "What have you achieved from being with Ramakrishna?"

He replied, "Burning faith." This faith bound his mind to his guru throughout his life. Observing M.'s attraction for him and his unselfish love, the Master said to him: "You are my very own, my relative; otherwise, why should you come here so frequently?"[1] On another occasion he said to M.: "You don't want anything from me, but you love to see me and hear my words. My mind also dwells on you. I wonder how you are and why you don't come."[2] This statement from an avatar makes us hopeful. God really does love and care for us. All of our misgivings disappear because we realize that our love is reciprocated.

Ramakrishna said: "Sometimes God becomes the magnet and the devotee the needle, and sometimes the devotee becomes the magnet and God the needle. The devotee attracts God to him. God is the Beloved of His devotee and is under his control."[3]

On 25 June 1884, the Master told M.: "The other day I thought of going to your house. What is your address?" God thinks of His devotees. Uninvited, sometimes He visits sincere spiritual aspirants.

In the Gita, Krishna clearly states what human beings are supposed to do and what He will do for them: "With their mind fixed on Me, with their life absorbed in Me, enlightening one another about Me, and always conversing about Me, they derive satisfaction and delight. On those who are ever devoted to Me and worship Me with love, I bestow the yoga of understanding, by which they come to Me. Solely out of compassion for them, I, dwelling in their hearts, dispel with the shining lamp of wisdom the darkness born of ignorance."[4]

Human beings' love for God has been described in devotional scriptures and demonstrated in the lives of devotees and mystics, but God's love for human beings is not clearly recorded anywhere. Who would record it? God does not write books or articles. In 1916 Swami Premananda visited Swami Adbhutananda, a great mystic and a brother disciple, in Varanasi. Premananda said to Adbhutananda, "Please describe the Master's love for us."

Swami Adbhutananda responded: "Oh, that is inexpressible! How can a man understand God's love? When we listen to the reading of the Bhagavata we have some understanding of the love of the gopis of Vrindaban for Krishna. But just how much Sri Krishna loved them — of that we have no idea. Reading and hearing the scriptures can give us only an inkling of the depth of his love. The gopis were not aware of what attracted them to Krishna; they did not know the cause. Does iron know how the magnet attracts it?"[5]

In the Bhagavata, however, we get some glimpses of Krishna's love for the gopis. During the Raslila, when the gopis became proud, Krishna disappeared. They searched for Krishna, lamenting and crying loudly. When Krishna finally reappeared, they questioned his love for them, asking: "In this world, the first type of person returns love to the lover, the second type does not return love to the lover, and the third type remains indifferent to the lover. Among these three groups which do you belong to?"

Krishna replied: "I don't belong to any of them, because I am God. My love flows to all, as the sun shines on all. It is true I disappeared from your sight, but I was watching you all the time. I hid myself to intensify your love. This is my play. Your love surpasses my love because you have renounced everything for me and I have renounced nothing."[6]

Ramakrishna's love for M. manifested in many ways: When M. came to practise sadhana at Dakshineswar under the Master's guidance, the latter arranged a room for M. and a place for his servant to cook. Ramakrishna also asked Ramlal to speak to the milkman about supplying milk to M. On other occasions, the Master suggested that he eat sattvic food, such as rice, boiled vegetables with ghee, and milk. He asked M. to observe partial fasting on Ekadashi (the 11th day of the lunar fortnight) by eating only puffed rice with milk, because that purifies the mind and helps one to develop love of God. To strengthen M.'s devotion for God, the Master gave rice prasad of Jagannath to him and said: "Take this prasad regularly. Those who are devotees of God do not eat anything before taking the prasad."[7] Like a loving mother, the Master even asked M. to scrape his tongue after brushing his teeth.

M.'s wife and his stepmother did not get along, so M. left the joint household and rented an apartment near his school. The Master did not approve of this, and he reminded M. that the duty of a son is to look after his father. On 24 April 1885 the Master asked M.: "How is your wife? I noticed the other day that she was looking rather sickly. Give her soothing drinks to keep her nerves cool."

M.: "Green coconut milk, sir?"

Master: "Yes. A drink made of sugar candy is also good."

M.: "Since last Sunday I have been living at our house with my parents."

Master: "You have done well. It will be convenient for you to live at home. Since your parents live there, you won't have to worry so much about the family."[8]

The scripture says: "Speak the truth; speak pleasant words; and don't speak the unpleasant or harsh truth. But if you love someone, then speak the unpleasant truth." The Master loved M. and always thought about his welfare. But sometimes he scolded M. with harsh words. When M. came to practise sadhana at Dakshineswar, the Master expressed his abhorrence for those who enjoy sexual relationships while practising spiritual disciplines.

> He said to M.: "Aren't you ashamed of yourself? You have children, and still you enjoy intercourse with your wife. Don't you hate yourself for thus leading an animal life? Don't you hate yourself for dallying with a body which contains only blood, phlegm, filth, and excreta? He who contemplates the Lotus Feet of God looks on even the most beautiful woman as mere ash from the cremation ground. To enjoy a body which will not last and which consists of such impure ingredients as intestines, bile, flesh, and bone! Aren't you ashamed of yourself?"
>
> M. sat there silently, hanging his head in shame.
>
> The Master continued: "A man who has tasted even a drop of God's ecstatic love looks on 'woman and gold' as most insignificant. He who has tasted syrup made from sugar candy regards a drink made from treacle as a mere trifle. One gradually obtains that love for God if one but prays to Him with a yearning heart and always chants His name and glories."[9]

The beauty of Ramakrishna's method of teaching is that he always showed great love for his disciples, even when harsh methods were required to shatter the spell of maya. He knew human weaknesses very well, so he always pointed out solutions to overcome them. The Master was keen to share his spiritual heritage with M. so that he could be a good teacher. When M. did not visit him in Dakshineswar at his usual times, the Master would become deeply concerned. There is a saying: "It befits a man to discipline another whom he loves." On 25 June 1884 when M. met the Master in Calcutta, the latter said: "You used to come to Dakshineswar very frequently. But why have you become such a rare visitor? Perhaps you have become particularly friendly with your wife. Is it true? Why should I blame you? The influence of 'woman and gold' is everywhere. Therefore I pray, 'O Divine Mother, please don't make me a worldly man if I am to be born again in a human body."[10]

A man unburdens his heart to the one he loves. In *The Gospel of Sri Ramakrishna*, we find that the Master revealed his true nature and personal spiritual experiences to M. to a greater extent than he did to other disciples. Here are a few examples:

On 7 March 1885 the Master said to M.:

"There is no outsider here. The other day, when Harish was with me, I saw Satchidananda come out of this sheath [his body]. It said, 'I incarnate Myself in every age.' I thought that I myself was saying these words out of mere fancy. I kept quiet and watched. Again Satchidananda Itself spoke, saying, 'Chaitanya, too, worshipped Shakti.'"

The devotees listened to these words in amazement. Some wondered whether God Himself was seated before them in the form of Sri Ramakrishna. The Master paused a moment. Then he said, addressing M., "I saw that it is the fullest manifestation of Satchidananda; but this time the Divine Power is manifested through the glory of sattva."

The devotees sat spellbound.

Master (to M.): "Just now I was saying to the Mother, 'I cannot talk much.' I also said to Her, 'May people's inner consciousness be awakened by only one touch!' You see, such is the power of Yogamaya that She can cast a spell. She did so at Vrindaban. That is why Subol [Krishna's companion] was able to unite Sri Krishna and Radhika. Yogamaya, the Primal Power, has a power of attraction. I applied that power myself.

(To M.) "Well, do you think that those who come here are realizing anything?"

M: "Yes, sir, it must be so."[11]

On 21 July 1883 the Master said to M.:

"Can one ever understand the work of God? He is so near; still it is not possible for us to know Him. Balarama did not realize that Krishna was God."

M: "That is true, sir."

Master: "God has covered all with His maya. He doesn't let us know anything. Maya is 'woman and gold.' He who puts maya aside to see God, can see Him. Once, when I was explaining God's actions to someone, God suddenly showed me the lake at Kamarpukur. I saw a man removing the green scum and drinking the water. The water was clear as crystal. God revealed to me that Satchidananda is covered by the scum of maya. He who puts the green scum aside can drink the water.

"Let me tell you a very secret experience. Once I had entered the wood near the pine-grove, and was sitting there, when I had a vision of something like the hidden door of a chamber. I couldn't see the inside of the chamber. I tried to bore a hole in the door with a nail-knife, but did not succeed. As I bored, the earth fell back into the hole and filled it. Then suddenly I made a very big opening."

Uttering these words, the Master remained silent. After a time he said: "These are very profound words. I feel as if someone were pressing my mouth....I have seen with my own eyes that God dwells even in the sexual organ. I saw Him once in the sexual intercourse of a dog and a bitch.

"The universe is conscious on account of the Consciousness of God. Sometimes I find that this Consciousness wriggles about, as it were, even in small fish."[12]

On 7 September 1883 the Master described his experiences of Brahman to M.:

"One day I had the vision of Consciousness, nondual and indivisible. At first it had been revealed to me that there were innumerable men, animals, and other creatures. Among them there were aristocrats, the English, the Mussalmans, myself, scavengers, dogs, and also a bearded Mussalman with an earthenware tray of rice in his hand. He put a few grains of rice into everybody's mouth. I too tasted a little.

"Another day I saw rice, vegetables, and other food-stuff, and filth and dirt as well, lying around. Suddenly the soul came out of my body and, like a flame, touched everything. It was like a protruding tongue of fire and tasted everything once, even the excreta. It was revealed to me that all these are one Substance, the nondual and indivisible Consciousness."[13]

On 16 December 1883 the Master said to M.:

"Why should the universe be unreal? That is a speculation of the philosophers. After realizing God, one sees that it is God Himself who has become the universe and all living beings.

"The Divine Mother revealed to me in the Kali temple that it was She who had become everything. She showed me that everything was full of Consciousness. The Image was Consciousness, the altar was Consciousness, the water-vessels were Consciousness, the door-sill was Consciousness, the marble floor was Consciousness — all was Consciousness.

"I found everything inside the room soaked, as it were, in Bliss — the Bliss of Satchidananda. I saw a wicked man in front of the Kali temple; but in him also I saw the Power of the Divine Mother vibrating.

"That was why I fed a cat with the food that was to be offered to the Divine Mother. I clearly perceived that the Divine Mother Herself had become everything — even the cat. The manager of the temple garden wrote to Mathur Babu saying that I was feeding the cat with the offering intended for the Divine Mother. But Mathur Babu had insight into the state of my mind. He wrote back to the manager: 'Let him do whatever he likes. You must not say anything to him.'

"After realizing God, one sees all this aright — that it is He who has become the universe, living beings, and the twenty-four cosmic princi-ples. But what remains when God completely effaces the ego cannot be described in words. As Ramprasad said in one of his songs, 'Then alone will you know whether you are good or I am good!' I get into even that state now and then.

"A man sees a thing in one way through reasoning and in an alto-gether different way when God Himself shows it to him."[14]

When Ramakrishna was suffering from cancer at the Cossipore gar-den house, he knew that his days were coming to an end. He began to distribute his spiritual treasures among his disciples. M. described a won-derful scene:

"On the morning of December 23 [1885] Sri Ramakrishna gave unre-strained expression to his love for the devotees. He said to Niranjan, 'You are my father: I shall sit on your lap.' Touching Kalipada's chest, he said, 'May your inner spirit be awakened!' He stroked Kalipada's chin affec-tionately and said, 'Whoever has sincerely called on God or performed his daily religious devotions will certainly come here.' In the morning two ladies received his special blessing. In a state of samadhi he touched their hearts with his feet. They shed tears of joy. One of them said to him, weeping, 'You are so kind!' His love this day really broke all bounds. He wanted to bless Gopal of Sinthi and said to a devotee, 'Bring Gopal here.'"[15]

Children inherit their parents' wealth. M. inherited the spiritual trea-sures that Ramakrishna distributed freely to each and all. The Master also empowered him to teach people. On 22 July 1883 the Master was talking with the Divine Mother in an ecstatic mood: "O Mother, why hast Thou given him only a particle?" Remaining silent a few moments, he added: 'I understand it, Mother. That little bit will be enough for him and will serve Thy purpose. That little bit will enable him to teach people."[16]

On 5 January 1884 the Master prayed for M. as well as for others: "Mother, may those who come to You have all their desires fulfilled. But please don't make them give up everything at once, Mother. Well, You may do whatever You like in the end. If You keep them in the world, Mother, then please reveal Yourself to them now and then. Otherwise, how will they live? How will they be encouraged if they don't see You once in a while? But You may do whatever You like in the end."[17]

There is a saying, "The letter killeth." Truly, words of affection belittle love. Nowadays many people glibly say, "We love you, we miss you," but they do not mean it. True love can only be felt in the heart. M. felt

Ramakrishna's divine love, which connected him with the Master, till the last moment of his life. Ramakrishna said: "A man belches what he eats. If he eats radish, he belches radish." A lover wants to talk only about his or her beloved. M. showed his love for Ramakrishna by meditating, writing, and talking about the Master for nearly 50 years after his passing away

Last Days with Ramakrishna

Ramakrishna was born on 18 February 1836 and passed away on 16 August 1886. He enacted his divine play in three parts. The first act (1836 to 1852), his early life, he spent in his native village of Kamarpukur. The second (1852 to 1885), his adult life, he spent in Calcutta and nearby Dakshineswar, where he lived for thirty years. It was in Dakshineswar that he practised various sadhanas, attained illumination, and commenced his divine mission. In the third act (1885 to 1886), he spent the last months of his life in Calcutta and in nearby Cossipore, where he brought his divine drama to its close by laying the foundation for the future Ramakrishna Order.

In *Sri Ramakrishna and His Divine Play* Swami Saradananda wrote a detailed account of the Master's early life in Kamarpukur, his days in Calcutta and Dakshineswar, his sadhanas and spiritual experiences, his method of training his disciples, and his universal message to the world. Saradananda also wrote seven brief chapters describing the Master's life after he left Dakshineswar, but he was silent about his last days. M. chronicled the Master's life from 26 February 1882 to 24 April 1886 in *The Gospel of Sri Ramakrishna*. Although there were many entries in the diary upon which he based the *Gospel*, M. did not develop them all for publication. In the *Gospel* we find twenty-seven entries (two undated) between 26 September 1885 and 24 April 1886. M. too was reticent about the Master's passing away. Although both Saradananda and M. were asked to write about the Master's last days, both expressed their inability and unwillingness.

Swami Prabhananda wrote *Sri Ramakrishner Antyalila* (The Last Divine Play of Sri Ramakrishna) in Bengali in two volumes, which the Udbodhan Office published in 1985 and 1987. Prabhananda painstakingly extracted a colossal amount of information about the Master's last days from M.'s unpublished diary and other sources, but he could not supply a description of the Master's life between 26 May and 13 August, 1886. Nonetheless, we shall present the highlights of the Master's last days from *Sri Ramakrishner Antyalila*, and other sources, which show how M. played a very important role in this chapter of the Master's life.

Ramakrishna had promised Mathur that he would remain in Dakshineswar as long as his wife Jagadamba and son Dwarika were alive. But both of them had passed away by 1885,* so the Master was free to bid farewell to Dakshineswar. Sometime in April 1885 Ramakrishna began to feel some pain in his throat. Despite his discomfort, on 26 May he attended the Vaishnava festival in Panihati. When his pain became severe, several doctors were consulted for treatment. They diagnosed his condition as "clergyman's sore throat." Though the doctors forbade Ramakrishna to talk too much, he continued to teach. He never turned anybody away. He said: "Let me be condemned to be born over and over again, even in the form of a dog, if I can be of help to a single soul."[1] Towards the end of September his throat began to hemorrhage, so the devotees arranged for his treatment in Calcutta, as his doctors lived nearby.

The anonymous biographer of *The Life of Sri Ramakrishna* wrote: "There is a liquid beauty in the rising sun, there is a royal splendour in its midday blaze, and there is also an exquisite grace in its setting glow. So it is with the life of a great man. There is sweetness in its childhood and adolescence, there is resplendence in its maturity, and again there is a deep pathos in its last days."[2]

Ramakrishna left Dakshineswar on 26 September 1885 and stayed at Balaram's house in Baghbazar for seven days. Swami Saradananda wrote: "The devotees had rented a small house on Durgacharan Mukherjee Street in Baghbazar because one could see the Ganges from its roof. Soon they brought the Master to Calcutta. The Master had been accustomed to living in the spacious temple garden of Dakshineswar on the Ganges, and when he entered this tiny house he declined to stay there and immediately walked to Balaram's house on Ramkanta Basu Street. Balaram cordially

* Dwarika died in 1878 and Jagadamba died in 1880.

received him and invited him to stay there until a suitable house could be found. The Master agreed."[3]

At Balaram's House

Saturday, 26 September 1885: The Master came to Calcutta from Dakshineswar in the morning. He had lunch and dinner at Balaram's house, where he gargled with a medication that the doctor had prescribed. He said to M.: "I am coughing too much today." M. stayed in the Master's room that night.

Sunday, 27 September 1885: In the morning Harish rubbed oil on the Master's body; then the Master took his bath. Afterwards he went to see Lord Jagannath in the shrine and returned to his room. M. visited Ramakrishna after working at his job as the headmaster of a school run by Ishwar Chandra Vidyasagar. On this day the Master blessed a Vaishnava Babaji from Murshidabad by touching his chest.

Monday, 28 September 1885: At 9:30 a.m. M. visited the Master on his way to Vidyasagar's school. After bathing, the Master went to see Lord Jagannath in the shrine and then had some farina pudding, the only food he could eat. After M. left for work, four famous ayurvedic doctors — Gangaprasad, Gopimohan, Dwarikanath, and Navagopal — examined Ramakrishna's throat and diagnosed his condition as cancer. At 4:30 p.m. M. returned and informed the Master that Purna was coming. When Purna arrived, the Master was happy to see him and gave him some refreshments. He then asked Purna to massage his feet (thus he would transmit power to his disciples).

Ramakrishna was selective about whom he would allow to touch his feet. On 7 March 1885 he said to M. "There is great significance in this [the stroking of his feet]." Placing his hand on his heart, the Master said, "If there is anything here, then through this service the ignorance and illusion of the devotees will be completely destroyed."[4]

Dr. Pratap Majumdar visited the Master and gave him a homeopathic medicine.

Tuesday, 29 September 1885: M. visited Balaram's home in the morning and again in the afternoon.

Wednesday, 30 September 1885: M. came to see the Master on his way to Vidyasagar's school and learned about the house that had been rented in Shyampukur. Ramakrishna asked M. to check on whether it was a damp place.

Thursday, 1 October 1885: M. visited Ramakrishna on his way to Vidyasagar's school and stayed for an hour. He came back at 4:30 p.m. In the evening Pandit Shashadhar Tarkachudamani came to see the Master. M. stayed with Ramakrishna that night. The Master was in terrible pain and could not sleep. M. fanned him.

Friday, 2 October 1885: At 6:30 a.m. M. bathed in the Ganges, and upon his return he found the Master sleeping. At 7:00 a.m. the Master said to M., Balaram, and Gopal, "This body has no desire, so why should I keep it?" When M. was about to leave for work, Dr. Gangaprasad Sen arrived and prescribed medicine. Then Dr. Pratap Majumdar came to examine the Master's throat. Ramakrishna said to him, "Please visit me every morning." M. then left for Vidyasagar's school.

At the Shyampukur House

The devotees of Ramakrishna rented a house at 55 Shyampukur Street in North Calcutta so that he could be cared for more easily. The house was not far from Balaram's and M.'s homes. Kalipada Ghosh took responsibility for cleaning and decorating it, and all other tasks necessary to establish a household. He also hung pictures of gods and goddesses in the Master's bedroom, which was actually the parlour. Ramakrishna came to the house on Friday evening, 2 October 1885. Ram Chandra Datta lit a lantern to show the Master the holy pictures in his room. The Master went to see the dining room, where his attendants were eating their supper. Golap-ma took responsibility for cooking. Ramakrishna asked M. to make sure the windows were closed so that the cool air would not come into his room. He was happy and relieved.

Saturday, 3 October 1885: M. came in the morning and took care of some small things for the Master. He returned after work and noticed that Haripada was reading the Bhagavata to the Master. M. stayed that night to serve him.

Sunday, 4 October 1885: In the morning the Master asked M. to buy two pitchers, two earthen pots, and two wooden seats for the household. Around 3:00 p.m., the Master hemorrhaged three times. This was the first such incident since he had arrived in Calcutta. Niranjan, Devendra, and others were alarmed, but Narendra consoled them. Rakhal, Latu, Shashi, Sharat, Niranjan, Baburam, Kali, Jogin, Senior Gopal and others began to care for the Master around the clock, under Narendra's leadership. Some of them would eat at their homes, but otherwise they lived with the Master, ignoring their parents' orders.

Monday, 5 October 1885: M. arrived at the Shyampukur house in the morning and found the Master in bed, with Niranjan massaging his feet. The Master then took his bath. He asked M. to buy a comb for him. Dr.

TOP: Shyampukur House, where Ramakrishna initially stayed during his cancer treatment from 2 October to 11 December 1885.
BOTTOM: Ramakrishna's room at Shyampukur

Pratap Majumdar arrived, examined the Master, and prescribed some homeopathic medicines. Someone suggested calling Dr. Mahendralal Sarkar, a reputable homeopathic physician, but the Master was not interested because Dr. Sarkar had examined him earlier, and had pressed his tongue too hard.

Dhirendra told the Master, "Sir, M. is such a great devotee, but his eight-year-old son died and his wife has lost her mind." The Master remained silent and looked at M. with compassion.

Tuesday, 6 October 1885: M. arrived at 8:00 a.m. and heard the Master saying, "My throat feels as if it were cracking." He was anxiously waiting for Dr. Majumdar. Rakhal suggested rubbing old ghee [an ayurvedic remedy] externally on the Master's throat, and the Master consented. M. left for Vidyasagar's school at 10:00 a.m. and returned at 2:00 p.m.

That afternoon Surendra came to Shyampukur for the first time. He told Ramakrishna that he had not come earlier because it was hard for him to see his guru suffering.

At 7:00 p.m. the Master said: "It feels as if someone were piercing my throat with a knife." After talking for some time he asked, "Can you tell me why I have pain near the ear?" It seemed the Master's cancer had spread into that area. Niranjan arrived and asked the devotees to leave so that the Master could rest.

Wednesday, 7 October 1885: It was 10:00 a.m. Girish, M., and Senior Gopal were present in the Master's room. The Master again complained, "It feels as if someone is stabbing the wound with a knife." It was hard for him to swallow solid food. So far he had been eating rice gruel, farina, and milk. Girish suggested that he start drinking one and a half seers of milk, which would give him more strength.

Observing the Master's suffering, Girish cried profusely. The Master consoled him, wiping tears from his own eyes.

After Girish left, Ramakrishna lay down and began to perspire. He was drowsy. Meanwhile Dr. Majumdar arrived. Dhirendra served the Master rice and milk for lunch. The Master asked, "Why so much?"

M.: "Sir, it is good for you to eat a little more. Your body is weak." The Master looked at M. affectionately.

At 7:00 p.m. M. returned with Prankrishna Mukhopadhyay. As there was no palm-leaf fan nearby, M. began to fan the Master with a folded chadar. The Master motioned to Shashi to give a fan to M., who then fanned him with that palm-leaf fan.

Thursday, 8 October 1885: M. arrived in the afternoon. The Master told him: "Tomorrow is Friday. I need a barber." He then said: "I feel excruciating pain. Will drinking milk make it worse?" M. consoled him and told him not to worry. The Master walked around his room and said, "It hurts when I move." He fell asleep at 7:30 p.m. as Devendra massaged his feet. M. went home at 8:00 p.m.

Friday, 9 October 1885: M. arrived in the afternoon and found the Master asleep. Nandalal, Keshab Sen's nephew, was fanning him. After a while the Master got up. In the evening a monk visited the Master and the latter greeted him cordially. The Master was expecting Dr. Biharilal Bhaduri and Dr. Majumdar, but they did not come that day. Ramakrishna asked M. to lower the mosquito curtain around his bed. That night M. stayed with the Master.

Saturday, 10 October 1885: At 3:00 p.m. M. arrived and found that the Master's bleeding had stopped. He was feeling better. Senior Gopal and Jogin arrived from Dakshineswar and the Master asked them, "How is she [Holy Mother]?"

Senior Gopal answered: "She is fine. How are you?"

Purna visited the Master twice that day, which made the Master happy. M. gave Senior Gopal one rupee to whitewash the Master's room in Dakshineswar and stayed the night to care for the Master.

*   *   *

The following incident, recorded by Saradananda, apparently took place during this period:

> One day in Shyampukur the Master had an incredible vision. He saw his subtle body come out of his gross body and move around the room. He noticed some wounds on the back of its throat and was wondering how those wounds came to be, when the Divine Mother explained it to him: People who had committed various sins had become pure by touching him, thereby transferring their sins to his body and causing those wounds. At Dakshineswar the Master had sometimes told us that he would not hesitate to be born millions of times and suffer for the good of humanity. So it is not surprising that instead of being perturbed by this vision, he narrated it to us joyfully. We were moved by thus remembering and discussing his infinite grace, and the devotees, especially the younger ones, made special efforts to ensure that no newcomers bowed down to the Master or touched his feet until he had recovered his health. Some devotees, remembering their previous wayward lives, resolved not to touch the Master's pure body again. Narendra and a few others heard of the Master's vision and found in it the truth of vicarious atonement [in which one voluntarily takes upon oneself the suffering caused by the sins of others], a fundamental doctrine of Christianity, Vaishnavism, and other faiths. They began to think about this and to explore its possibilities.[5]

Another interesting incident took place during this time involving a famous actress. Binodini heard that the Master was ill, and she wanted to see him. The Master's visitors were very restricted, however, so she sought help from Kalipada, whom she knew through Girish. One evening she dressed herself as a European gentleman and went with Kalipada to see Ramakrishna. The Master laughed when he learned who the "European gentleman" really was. After praising Binodini's faith, devotion, and courage, the Master gave her some spiritual instructions and allowed her to touch his feet with her forehead. When they left the Master told the disciples about the trick that had been cleverly played on them.

*   *   *

Sunday, 11 October 1885: After his morning bath the Master began to laugh uninterruptedly. Everyone was puzzled. The Master said: "This joyful laugh is coming from inside."

That evening Ramakrishna went into ecstasy for the first time at the Shyampukur house. Later the Master said to M. and others: "Chant the name of Hari; perhaps that will reduce the disease." Afterwards the devotees conferred and decided to engage Dr. Mahendralal Sarkar to treat the Master. His fee was 16 rupees. M. was deputed to call on the doctor.

Monday, 12 October 1885: Dr. Sarkar had been a famous allopathic doctor, but changed his specialty to homeopathy. As the Master's system was so delicate, he could not tolerate allopathic medicine.

Dr. Sarkar had known Ramakrishna long before as "Mathur Babu's Paramahamsa." When M. brought Dr. Sarkar to Shyampukur, the Master greeted him respectfully. He checked the Master's pulse, examined his throat, and prescribed a homeopathic medicine. He took his fee of 16 rupees at this first visit. However, when he later learned that the devotees were paying for the Master's treatment, he said: "I shall treat him to the best of my ability, and to help you in your noble cause I won't accept any payment."[6] Dr. Sarkar soon became very close to the Master.

M. later said: "The Master suffered from throat cancer for more than ten months. He had terrible hemorrhaging from his wound, but the devotees served him wholeheartedly. Once, holding the doctor's hand, he plaintively said, 'Please cure my disease.' But as soon as he felt a little better, he would talk about God. Finally he said, 'The Divine Mother will not keep this body anymore.'... The entire report of the Master's illness is in my diary. I recorded the amount of blood from each hemorrhage, the intensity of his pain, what he ate, and other things. Every day I carried that report to Dr. Mahendralal Sarkar."[7]

Thursday, 15 October 1885: It was the first day of Durga Puja. M. arrived at the Shyampukur house at 4:00 p.m. and found Mani Mallick and other devotees in Ramakrishna's room. The Master asked Mani to send his sister Nandini to visit him. She was a wonderful devotee and had attained bhava samadhi by following the Master's instructions.

Friday, 16 October 1885: M. arrived at 7:30 a.m. The Master was experiencing ecstasy because of Durga Puja. He said to Devendra, "The whole world is absorbed in the bliss of Brahman, and I am lying in bed." Ramakrishna then began to notice the pictures in his room. He especially liked the three that depicted Gaur-Nitai, Shiva-Gauri, and Draupadi.

Saturday, 17 October 1885: Dr. Sarkar and a friend arrived, and Narendra entertained them with some devotional songs. At 7:00 p.m. the Master inquired about the time and then went into deep samadhi. Dr. Sarkar checked the Master's heart and his friend touched one of his eyes. There was no response. The men were dumbfounded. They admitted that science could not explain this phenomenon.

When they had left, the Master told the devotees that his subtle body had gone to Surendra's shrine to Durga along a luminous path, and he saw Surendra crying in front of the Divine Mother. He asked them to visit Surendra. When the devotees arrived there they learned that the Master's vision had been correct.

Sunday, 18 October 1885: Despite his illness the Master had a long conversation with Dr. Sarkar.[8]

Thursday, 22 October 1885: Dr. Sarkar became intrigued with the Master and he began to spend time with him, as M. describes in the *Gospel*:

Girish (*to the doctor, with a smile*): "You have already spent three or four hours here. What about your patients?"

Doctor: "Well, my practice and patients! I shall lose everything on account of your paramahamsa!" (*All laugh.*)

Master: "There is a river called the 'Karmanasha.'* It is very dangerous to dive into that river. If a man plunges into its waters he cannot perform any more action. It puts an end to his duties." (*All laugh.*)

Doctor (*to Girish, M., and the other devotees*): "My friends, consider me as one of you. I am not saying this as a physician. But if you think of me as your own, then I am yours."

(*To the Master*): "The illness you are suffering from does not permit the patient to talk with people. But my case is an exception. You may talk with me when I am here." (*All laugh.*)

*Literally, "destroyer of karma."

Master: "Please cure my illness. I cannot chant the name and glories of God."

Doctor: "Meditation is enough."

Master: "What do you mean? Why should I lead a monotonous life? I enjoy my fish in a variety of dishes: curried fish, fried fish, pickled fish, and so forth! Sometimes I worship God with rituals, sometimes I repeat His name, sometimes I meditate on Him, sometimes I sing His name and glories, and sometimes I dance in His name."[9]

Friday, 23 October, 1885: It was the day of the full moon, following Durga Puja, the worship of the Divine Mother. At 10:00 a.m. Ramakrishna was talking to M., who was helping him with his socks.

Master (*smiling*): "Why can't I cut my woolen scarf into two pieces and wrap them around my legs like socks? They will be nice and warm." M. smiled.

At 11:00 a.m. M. went to Dr. Sarkar's house to report on the Master's condition. The doctor was very eager to hear about Ramakrishna. When Dr. Sarkar later came to Shyampukur, he said to the Master: "I was much worried about you last night at three o'clock. It was raining. I said to myself: 'Who knows whether or not the doors and windows of his room are shut?'"

"Really?" said Ramakrishna. He was very pleased by the doctor's thoughtfulness and affection.[10]

Saturday, 24 October 1885: When Dr. Sarkar arrived at 1:00 p.m., the Master praised the homeopathic system of medicine. The doctor remarked: "In homeopathy, the physician has to check the symptoms of the disease against descriptions in the medical book. It is like Western music. The singer follows the score."

Ramakrishna wanted to have his samadhi evaluated from a scientific point of view. He said: "Well, when I am in samadhi I feel intoxicated, as if I were drunk with *siddhi* [sherbet made of marijuana]. What have you to say about that?"

Doctor (*to M.*): "In that state the nerve centres cease to function. Hence the limbs become numb. The legs become weak because all the energy rushes towards the brain. Life consists of the nervous system. There is a nerve centre in the nape of the neck called the medulla oblongata. If that is injured, one may die."

Narendra sang six songs at the Master's request, charming the doctor. The doctor then left.

That evening the Master went into samadhi and then slowly returned to normal. M. decided to spend the night there.[11]

Sunday, 25 October 1885: It was about 6:30 a.m. M. asked Ramakrishna about his health. He was on his way to Dr. Sarkar to report on the Master's condition. The Master said to M.: "Tell the doctor that during the early hours of the morning my mouth becomes filled with water and I cough. Also ask him if I may take a bath." M. then went to see the doctor, who came in the afternoon.

Doctor: "I have heard the story that you were once lying on the ground unconscious in samadhi when a wicked man kicked you with his boots."

Master: "You must have heard it from M. The man was Chandra Haldar, a priest of the Kali temple at Kalighat; he often came to Mathur Babu's house. One day I was lying on the ground in an ecstatic mood. The room was dark. Chandra Haldar thought I was feigning that state in order to win Mathur's favour. He entered the room and kicked me several times with his boots. It left black marks on my body. Everybody wanted to tell Mathur Babu about it, but I forbade them."

Doctor: "This is also due to the will of God. Thus you have taught people how to control anger and practise forgiveness."[12]

Monday, 26 October 1885: M. chronicled the events of this day in the *Gospel*:

It was about ten o'clock in the morning when M. arrived at the Shyampukur house on his way to Dr. Sarkar to report the Master's condition.

Dr. Sarkar had declared the illness incurable. His words cast gloom over the minds of the Master's devotees and disciples. With unflagging devotion and zeal they nursed the patient — their teacher, guide, philosopher, and friend. A band of young disciples, led by Narendra, was preparing to renounce the world and dedicate their lives to the realization of God and the service of humanity. People flocked to the Master day and night. In spite of the excruciating pain in his throat, he welcomed them all with a cheerful face. There seemed to be no limit to his solicitude for their welfare. His face beamed as he talked to them about God. Dr. Sarkar, seeing that conversation aggravated the illness, forbade him to talk to people. "You must not talk to others," the physician had said to the Master, "but you may make an exception in my case." The doctor used to spend six or seven hours in Sri Ramakrishna's company, drinking in every word that fell from his lips.

Master: "I am feeling much relieved. I am very well today. Is it because of the medicine? Then why shouldn't I continue it?"

M: "I am going to the doctor. I shall tell him everything. He will advise what is best."

Dr. Sarkar arrived at 1:00 p.m. and was pleased to hear that the Master was doing well. He had a long conversation with Ramakrishna and the devotees.[13]

Tuesday, 27 October 1885: The Master was feeling better. He said to M.: "The devotee looking on himself as Prakriti likes to embrace and kiss God, whom he regards as the Purusha. I am telling this just to you. Ordinary people should not hear these things."

M.: "God sports in various ways. Even this illness of yours is one of His sports. Because you are ill new devotees are coming to you."

Despite his illness, the Master continued to speak fiery words about renunciation. He ridiculed those who first make arrangements for their family and property, and then practise sadhana. Narendra's father had died, so he was trying to provide for his family.

The Master said: "When a man feels utter dispassion, he looks on the world as a deep well and his relatives as venomous cobras. Then he cannot think of saving money or making arrangements about his property. God alone is real and all else illusory. To think of the world instead of God!

"A woman was stricken with intense grief. She first tied her nose-ring in the corner of her cloth and then dropped to the ground, saying, 'Oh, friends, what a calamity has befallen me!' But she was very careful not to break the nose-ring."

All laughed. At these words Narendra felt as if he were struck by an arrow, and lay down on the floor. M. understood what was going through Narendra's mind and said with a smile: "What's the matter? Why are you lying down?"

The Master said to M., with a smile: "You remind me of a woman who felt ashamed of herself for sleeping with her brother-in-law and couldn't understand the conduct of those women who lived as mistresses of strangers. By way of excusing herself she said: 'After all, a brother-in-law is one's own. But even that kills me with shame. And how do these women dare to live with strangers?'"

M. himself had been leading a worldly life. Instead of being ashamed of his own conduct, he smiled at Narendra. That was why Sri Ramakrishna referred to the woman who criticized the conduct of immoral women, though she herself had illicit love for her brother-in-law.

It was 5:30 p.m. when Dr. Sarkar came to the Master's room, felt his pulse, and prescribed the necessary medicine. Many devotees were present and the conversation continued for a long time. Finally the Master said to Dr. Sarkar: "If you won't take offence, I shall tell you something. It is this: You have had enough of such things as money, honour, lecturing, and so on. Now for a few days direct your mind to God. And come here now and then. Your spiritual feeling will be kindled by hearing words about God."[14]

Thursday, 29 October 1885: M. reached Shyampukur at 10:00 a.m. As usual, he collected the Master's health report and then left for Dr. Sarkar's house. He and Dr. Sarkar returned to Shyampukur by carriage, visiting several patients along the way. When they arrived, Dr. Sarkar took the Master's pulse and inquired about his condition.

Master (*to Dr. Sarkar*): "I understand that you spoke of me as insane. That is why they (*pointing to M. and the others*) don't want to go to you."

Dr. Sarkar (*looking at M.*): "Why should I call you [meaning the Master] insane? But I mentioned your egotism. Why do you allow people to take the dust of your feet?"

M: "Otherwise they weep."

Dr. Sarkar: "That is their mistake. They should be told about it."

M: "Why should you object to their taking the dust of his feet? Doesn't God dwell in all beings?"

Dr. Sarkar: "I don't object to that. Then you must take the dust of everyone's feet."

M: "But there is a greater manifestation of God in some men than in others. There is water everywhere; but you see more of it in a lake, a river, or an ocean. Will you show the same respect to a new Bachelor of Science as you do to Faraday?"

Dr. Sarkar: "I agree with that. But why do you call him God?"

M: "Why do we salute each other? It is because God dwells in everybody's heart. You haven't given much thought to this subject."

Master (*to Dr. Sarkar*): "I have already told you that some people reveal more of God than others. Earth reflects the sun's rays in one way, a tree in another way, and a mirror in still another way. You see a better reflection in a mirror than in other objects. Don't you see that these devotees here are not on the same level with Prahlada and others of his kind? Prahlada's whole heart and soul were dedicated to God."

Dr. Sarkar did not reply. All were silent....

It was dusk. Sri Ramakrishna became absorbed in contemplation of God. For the time being he forgot all about his painful disease. After a long time he became aware of the outer world and said to M. in a whisper: "You see my mind was completely merged in the Indivisible Brahman. After that I saw many things. I found that the doctor will have spiritual awakening. But it will take some time. I won't have to tell him much."[15]

Friday, 30 October 1885: M. arrived at the Shyampukur house and collected the report of Ramakrishna's health. He then left to pick up the doctor; they arrived at noon. As usual Dr. Sarkar had a long conversation with the Master and the devotees. The Master was grateful for his free treatment, but he was giving the doctor spirituality in return. Ignoring Dr. Sarkar's high status, Ramakrishna told him a harsh truth because he loved him: "Mahindra Babu, what is this madness of yours about money? Why such attachment to wife? Why such longing for name and fame? Give up all these now, and direct your mind to God with whole-souled devotion. Enjoy the bliss of God."

Dr. Sarkar sat still, without uttering a word.[16]

Saturday, 31 October 1885: M. arrived at 9:00 a.m., and then left to report to Dr. Sarkar on the Master's health. At 11:00 a.m., Prabhudayal Mishra, a Quaker Christian, came to visit the Master. He said: "Jesus is not the son of Mary. He is God Himself. (*To the devotees*) Now he (*pointing to Sri Ramakrishna*) is as you see him — again, he is God Himself. You are not able to recognize him. I have seen him before in a vision, and now I see him directly with my eyes."

In an ecstatic mood, the Master shook hands with Mishra and blessed him, saying, "You will get what you are seeking."

Dr. Sarkar arrived soon afterwards and examined the Master. They had a discussion about God.[17]

Sunday, 1 November 1885: M. arrived in the morning to visit the Master. Captain Vishwanath Upadhyay, a devotee and an officer of the Nepalese government, visited the Master. They spoke about jnana and bhakti. Prabhudayal Mishra came to bid farewell to Ramakrishna, as he was leaving to perform austerities. Girish, Surendra, Devendra, Mahima, and Ramchandra arrived and the Master talked to them about longing for God.

In the afternoon M. returned from work and Dr. Sarkar came to see the Master. A misunderstanding had developed between Dr. Sarkar and the devotees regarding taking the dust of Ramakrishna's feet. Dr. Sarkar told the Master: "I shall not say anything to anyone. These people are angry with me." Meanwhile Girish took the dust of the Master's feet. The doctor said: "I have nothing to say. You people do whatever you like." Then Narendra sang a song, and the doctor said to the Master: "Please don't go into ecstasy. If you do, I shall leave."

Master: "What can I do? It comes spontaneously."

Dr. Sarkar examined the Master's throat and then left.

Monday, 2 November 1885: When M. arrived at 7:00 a.m. he heard that the Master's cough had become worse. Later on, at 5:00 p.m., he returned after work, and the Master told him that there was blood in his phlegm. Moreover, there was a piercing pain in his throat. He said: "This body is different from others' bodies. Sometimes I feel it will not last long. Let me awaken the consciousness of these people quickly."

Tuesday, 3 November 1885: The weather was cool in Calcutta. M. arrived at 6:00 p.m. Dr. Sarkar had not come for two days. The Master's throat had been bleeding, and the devotees were concerned. Girish and Narendra left to inform the doctor of Ramakrishna's condition. The Master said to M.: "Eating sattvic food is necessary for real meditation."

Wednesday, 4 November 1885: The Master was seriously ill. Dr. Sarkar was annoyed at the devotees and had not come for the past few days. However, he came to Shyampukur at 10:00 a.m. that morning to examine the Master and prescribe medicine. He and the Master had a long spiritual conversation, in which Ramakrishna described the signs of an illumined soul: "First, one experiences exuberant bliss and one's nature becomes like a child; second, one becomes calm and serene; and third, one becomes free from ego." M. left at 2:00 p.m. and returned three hours later. In the evening, when the lamps were lighted, the Master said to M.: "Now stop all your activities and think of God."

Friday, 6 November 1885: Dr. Sarkar did not understand why his treatment was not working. He thought perhaps the change of seasons was the cause and that his remedies might be more effective when winter came.

It was Kali Puja. Following the Master's instructions, M. went to the Siddheswari Kali temple in Thanthania and made a special offering. He came back to Shyampukur with prasad for the Master. Dr. Sarkar arrived at 2:00 p.m. Girish, M., and others entertained him by singing songs praising the Mother. At 7:00 that evening the devotees offered flowers to the Master and he went into samadhi. The devotees felt the presence of the Divine Mother in Ramakrishna.[18]

Saturday, 7 November 1885: M. arrived at 2:00 p.m. and found that everyone was resting. He then went to see the Master and learned that he had not been feeling well. Dr. Sarkar arrived. The Master said to him: "There is so much bleeding from the throat! The devotees are spending so much money. I think I should return to Dakshineswar."

Dr. Sarkar reassured him: "Please don't worry."

The two men then talked about knowledge and devotion. Narendra sang a couple of songs for the doctor.

Sunday, 8 November 1885: At 8:00 a.m., M. put some blood discharged from the Master's throat into a paper packet and took it to Dr. Sarkar. The doctor examined it and read M.'s report of the Master's condition. His throat had been bleeding the previous night and again in the morning.

Hazra came to visit the Master and the latter cheerfully told him, "Why don't you repeat a mantra and cure my disease?" Dr. Sarkar arrived that afternoon, examined the Master, and told his attendants not to worry. He did not stay long. M. stayed till midnight and then left for home.

Monday, 9 November 1885: The Master was gravely ill and the devotees' hearts were heavy. During the night he had had a lot of hemorrhaging. In the morning M. found blood on the Master's bed sheet. He wrote his report of the Master's condition and left for the doctor. In the meantime, Dr. Pratap Majumdar came to see Ramakrishna.

After making his report to Dr. Sarkar, M. went home and took his wife to the Pareshnath Jaina temple. Dr. Sarkar went to the Shyampukur house during M.'s absence. The Master told him: "Your medicine is not working. I shall take Pratap's medicine." At 3:00 p.m. M. went to Dr. Majumdar, and he recommended that Dr. Sarkar continue treating the Master. Observing the Master's condition, M. stayed with him that night.

Tuesday, 10 November 1885: In the morning M. went to Dr. Sarkar and collected the homeopathic medicine. At noon Dr. Sarkar visited the Master, and M. was present.

Master: "Let me keep one hundred twenty-five percent faith in you."

The doctor was pleased. He told Ramakrishna: "Please pray to God so that we may be free from anxiety about you." After a brief conversation the doctor left. In the evening the Master's throat hemorrhaged again, and his attendants were at a loss as to what to do.

Holy Mother heard of the Master's serious condition and came from Dakshineswar to help care for him. She suggested through Sharat that someone should pour cold water on the Master's head and put a wet towel on his abdomen. Although there was no privacy, from that day on Holy Mother began to stay in a small room on the upper floor at the Shyampukur house and took responsibility for cooking the Master's meals.

Friday, 13 November 1885: At 10:00 a.m. M. observed that the Master was in a serious mood.

Girish: "Please tell us which doctor we should call."

"I don't know," the Master replied. "I have no attachment to my body."

M. gathered information for Dr. Sarkar and then prepared to leave. On that day the Master had no bleeding, and he was not coughing, but had a throbbing pain in his wound. He easily ate some farina pudding. Before he left to see Dr. Sarkar, M. stood near the door and watched the Master eat. He wept a little as he thought of his pain.

Saturday, 21 November 1885: It was *Raspurnima*, the full moon night of autumn, celebrating the night that Krishna played with the gopis. There was a festive mood in Calcutta, but the Master's condition continued to deteriorate. Girish left to see the doctor.

At 4:30 p.m. the Master's throat began bleeding and he became extremely weak. His attendants did not know what to do. Rakhal held his own head and began to cry. The Master tried to console him.

Dr. Sarkar arrived. He carefully examined Ramakrishna and said: "This medicine will work. I spent the whole day researching his symptoms in my medical books." Dr. Sarkar had earlier suggested moving the Master to a spacious and clean place outside of Calcutta, rather than keeping him in the polluted city. The devotees had found a house for 100 rupees per month. M. now mentioned that proposal to Narendra in front of the doctor. However, the Master overheard the plan and vehemently opposed a move to such an expensive house. M. returned home with a heavy heart and could not sleep that night. He returned to the Shyampukur house when it was still dark.

Sunday, 22 November 1885: In the morning M. delivered the Master's health report to Dr. Sarkar, and then he returned to Shyampukur. During lunch, the Master said, "I feel extremely uneasy." He asked M. to massage his feet and then put socks on them. When Dr. Sarkar arrived, he told the Master, "You are definitely better today." The Master became somewhat cheerful. He walked feebly around in his room and then began to enter into ecstasy as he gazed at the picture of Mother Yashoda. He said to M.: "I feel terribly weak. My body is shaking. I feel nauseated. Shall I eat something?" Ramakrishna then inquired about Niranjan and learned that he, Gopal, and Bhupati had gone to Tarakeswar to offer worship to Shiva for his recovery. He smiled.

Sunday, 29 November 1885: At 6:00 a.m. M. arrived and found the Master asleep. He and Shashi went to visit Dr. Sarkar. Shashi gave the doctor details about Ramakrishna's condition. Dr. Sarkar then said: "If this is true, then he will die." The statement shocked both M. and Shashi. Shashi begged Dr. Sarkar: "The Master is suffering from excruciating pain. Please give him some effective medicine." After saying this, Shashi left the room. He had brought a sample of the Master's blood to show the doctor. The doctor then spoke frankly to M., "It seems that it is cancer." This was the first time that the doctor had openly declared Ramakrishna's disease to be cancer. M. was extremely upset. He said plaintively: "Sir, you must assure us that his suffering can be mitigated. Is there anything lacking in his care?"

"The nursing is going well," Dr. Sarkar replied, "but his suffering will increase day by day. You can go now."

M. left the doctor's residence. After walking for a while, he sat down on a bench in Wellington Square (now Subodh Mallick Square) and began to weep. He lamented, "O beloved Master, how shall I live without you?" Returning home, he told his wife everything, and then went back to the Shyampukur house. The Master was feeling a little better. M. went to Vidyasagar's school (100 Shyampukur Street) and read the notes that he had written on the Master's life in Kamarpukur.

At 5:00 p.m. M. returned to the Master and found him in great pain. He was restless. He told Surendra: "I have never felt such pain before." M. was very sad and felt helpless when he heard this. Soon Dr. Sarkar arrived.

Master: "It is very painful. Please give me some medicine."

The doctor examined Ramakrishna's throat and gave him some medicine. The Master then went into samadhi. After a while he told Dr. Sarkar: "I tried to suppress my ecstasy but failed. My mind merged into the Infinite. Nowadays I don't see any forms anymore." His face was shining with bliss.

Monday, 30 November 1885: The day had been uneventful. In the evening the Master was sitting up, surrounded by Narendra and other devotees. He said: "I see that everything is maya. This body is like a sheath. God is in everything and He has become everything." He was silent for a while, and then he said to Narendra: "I hesitate to give up this body lest you boys be submerged in grief." As they witnessed the Master's suffering, the devotees decided to begin ayurvedic treatment. Someone went to Dr. Navin Pal, who arrived at 10:00 p.m. He gave ayurvedic medicine to the Master and asked him to gargle with hot water. But the Master said: "No gargling — it hurts too much."

Tuesday, 1 December 1885: M. arrived at 2:00 p.m. from Vidyasagar's school. The Master told M. that he had been coughing the night before and needed medication. Sharat went to Dr. Sarkar and Dr. Pal.

The Master was impatient. He said: "Navin [Pal] has not yet come. What kind of person is he? I am depending on him." M. was ready to fetch the doctor, but the Master stopped him.

Wednesday, 2 December 1885: M. arrived at 12:30 p.m. and collected information on the Master's health for the doctors. Ramakrishna had been having difficulty swallowing food, and he was coughing and felt dizzy. M. left to deliver his reports, and returned at 5:30 p.m.

The Master may have been thinking about returning to Dakshineswar, because he sent Rakhal to see Trailokya Nath Biswas, Mathur's son and the caretaker of the Dakshineswar temple. However, the gatekeeper would not allow him to see Trailokya. Rakhal sent his message to him through someone else.

When Dr. Sarkar arrived, he asked about the Master's health in detail. As a man of science, he had a low opinion of ayurvedic medicine. Nonetheless, Dr. Sarkar and Dr. Pal both continued to treat the Master.

For the next two days the Master was tolerably well. Narendra said to the Master: "Let us go back to Dakshineswar. Mother Kali dwells there."

"Is not Kali here?" replied the Master.

Saturday, 5 December 1885: On his way to work, M. came to see the Master and found him sleeping. He heard that the previous night Ramakrishna's condition had been critical. He was shivering so much that even the quilt was not effective. His attendants were anxious and called Dr. Biharilal Bhaduri. Seeing Shashi and Rakhal weeping, the Master said: "Don't cry. Does the body last forever?"

M. had urgent business at Vidyasagar's school, so he wrote his report on the Master's health and sent it to Dr. Sarkar through another devotee. M. returned at 12:30 p.m. and found Girish and some others in the Master's room. Dr. Sarkar arrived shortly thereafter and learned that the Master was eating rice gruel and bathing daily. He did not approve of this. He then said that the air pollution in the Shyampukur area was terrible. The smog was most heavy in the mornings and evenings when people used their coal stoves. He suggested that the Master be moved to a garden house on the outskirts of Calcutta.

Narendra fed the Master. Dr. Sarkar observed that he was having difficulty swallowing even a liquid diet. When the doctor left, Ram Chandra told Ramakrishna: "Sir, Dr. Sarkar has suggested that we find a garden house outside Calcutta. Shall we look for it now?"

The Master consented: "Yes, find a place. Here I have no good digestion or appetite." Ram Chandra and the devotees began to search for a suitable place for the Master.

Sunday, 6 December 1885: Dr. Sarkar prescribed broth, which gave Ramakrishna some strength. The attendants and devotees were, for the time being, relieved. M. arrived at 8:00 a.m. and found the Master slowly walking around his room. He said that the meat soup was giving him some strength. The soup had been made from a goat that had been sacrificed in front of the Kali image.

Ram Chandra Datta went to Trailokya to ask for a room in the kuthi at Dakshineswar for Ramakrishna, but Trailokya would not provide one.

When Ram Chandra returned, he told the Master: "Trailokya refused. Shall we look for another place?"

Master: "Yes, find another place. I have no appetite here."

M. said to Ram, "Please go today."

Dr. Sarkar arrived at noon. He asked Narendra and others to sing some songs in an adjacent room. When Narendra began singing, the Master came into the room and joined the group. M. sang a song by Mirabai. The Master returned to his room when the singing was over.

Monday, 7 December 1885: M. was on his way to see the Master early in the morning when he encountered Narendra on the street. They walked to the Shyampukur house together. When the Master saw them, he said: "I had a thick hemorrhage last night and now I have a throbbing pain." Captain Upadhyay arrived. The Master talked to him briefly, and then washed his mouth. He cautioned his attendants that the rinse water should be disposed of hygienically. Narendra assured him that it would be.

The Master asked for a mirror. He then turned it around like a child and saw his emaciated body in it.

Master: "What next?"

M.: "Sir, your disease has taken a good turn and you will be cured."

Master: "What do you say?"

Narendra: "You are getting well."

Master: "Is that so?"

M.: "Yes, sir. Dr. Sarkar says that you are improving because you no longer bathe or eat rice gruel."

These remarks reassured the Master.

Tuesday, 8 December 1885: M. arrived at 5:00 p.m. and learned that Ramakrishna had coughed throughout the night and had a throbbing pain. Despite Dr. Sarkar's diagnosis, M. still believed that the Master's disease was clergyman's sore throat. He told the Master: "I believe that you have gotten the right medicine and your disease will be cured. No one has ever talked as much as you, and your singing is unparalleled."

Ramakrishna smiled. He then got up and began to walk slowly in his room. Suddenly he began throwing up blood. His attendants and devotees were alarmed. Narendra and Ram Chandra rushed to the room. M. couldn't bear the Master's suffering, so he left the room. But soon after, he came back and noticed that the Master had rallied. "Why does this happen?" the Master asked Narendra. "Perhaps the sore is drying up because I have not had a bath."

Ram Chandra said to the attendants: "Please do what the Master says now."

M. went home that night and sent his maidservant to clean the Shyampukur house.

Wednesday, 9 December 1885: The Master was feeling better. M. came by in the morning and then left to see Dr. Sarkar and Dr. Kali Kaviraj, another ayurvedic practitioner. Later M. returned to the Master and informed him of the doctors' suggestions.

Mahima Charan Chakrabarty found a garden house at 90 Cossipore Road in Cossipore for the Master. When Dr. Sarkar heard about the location of the garden house, he approved. The Master said to M.: "Now make arrangements to move."

Thursday, 10 December 1885: The Master appeared to be improving. M. arrived in the evening. The devotees told Ramakrishna that the Cossipore house would cost 80 rupees per month. Immediately the Master said: "I don't need such an expensive place. Let whatever is in my fate happen. It is better that I go back to Dakshineswar." After a long discussion the devotees persuaded Ramakrishna to agree to the move. Surendra promised to pay the rent and signed a six-month lease. The last night at Shyampukur passed smoothly. M. stayed at night.

Friday, 11 December 1885: At 5:00 a.m. M. took over the nursing duty from Shashi. While returning from the bathroom, the Master asked M.: "What does the doctor say? Is it cancer?" Avoiding the question, M. said, "Sir, it is cold here. Let us go inside the room." M. left at 6:30 a.m. After running several errands, he returned at 2:15 p.m.

Shashi told M. that Dr. Sarkar had arrived to see the Master.

Dr. Sarkar: "Now you are better. Please go to Cossipore and get well."

Master: "Will you visit me there? I know it is a little far."

Dr. Sarkar: "I want a report on your health every day, and I shall visit you occasionally."

In the afternoon Ramakrishna left for Cossipore by horse carriage with Holy Mother, Latu, Kali, and Senior Gopal. Other attendants took another carriage with the household belongings and necessities.

Ramakrishna had lived at the Shyampukur house for 70 days.

At the Cossipore Garden House

On 11 December at 10:00 p.m. M. and Girish arrived at the garden house in Cossipore by horse carriage. They entered the Master's room on the upper floor. A lantern was lit. There were many mosquitoes, so the Master was lying on his bed under the mosquito curtain. His bed consisted of a mat on the cement floor with a cotton carpet over it, and over

TOP: Cossipore garden house. Ramakrishna became the Kalpataru near the curve of the mango tree. BOTTOM: Ramakrishna's room at Cossipore, where he passed away on 16 August 1886.

that a mattress and sheet. His bed was situated in the southwest corner of the room, two yards from the western window.

Ramakrishna was awake. Girish and M. bowed down to him. He sat up and said: "I have no cough or wheezing sound in my chest, but my stomach is not normal. The ayurvedic doctor lives in Baghbazar. Will he be able to come here?"

M. replied: "Of course, he will come soon. He will take a carriage." Shortly after this, Girish and M. left for Calcutta.

At this time, Dr. Rajendralal Datta, a famous homeopathic doctor, began to treat the Master with Dr. Sarkar's approval. He prescribed Lycopodium 200, and this kept the Master well for about two weeks.

Sunday, 13 December 1885: The news spread that Ramakrishna had been moved to Cossipore. It was a holiday, so many devotees came there. At 2:00 p.m. M. arrived and bowed down to the Master, who was seated facing north. His body was thin, but he was cheerful. M. was suffering from blood dysentery. When Ramakrishna heard that M. was ill, he asked him to get some medicine from Ramlal. The Master assured him that within three days he would be cured. M. took his leave at 4:30 p.m.

Wednesday, 23 December 1885: M. arrived in the evening. The Master asked M. to buy a stool for him.

Master: "Well, can you tell how long it will take me to recover from this illness?"

M.: "It has been aggravated a little and will take some days."

Master: "How long?"

M.: "Perhaps five or six months."

Master: "So long? What do you mean?"

M.: "I mean, sir, for complete recovery."

Master: "Oh, that! I am relieved. Can you explain one thing? How is it that in spite of all these visions, all this ecstasy and samadhi, I am so ill?"

M.: "Your suffering is no doubt great, but it has a deep meaning."

Master: "What is it?"

M.: "A change is coming over your mind. It is being directed towards the formless aspect of God. Even your 'ego of Knowledge' is vanishing."

Master: "That is true. My teaching of others is coming to an end. I see that everything is Rama Himself.... This disease is showing me who belongs to the inner circle and who to the outer. Those who pay occasional visits and ask, 'How are you, sir?' belong to the outer circle."

(*To M.*) "When God assumes a human body for the sake of His devotees, many of His devotees accompany Him to this earth.... The Divine Mother also showed me in a vision the five suppliers of my needs.

"It was revealed to me in a vision that during my last days I should have to live on pudding. During my present illness my wife was one day feeding me with pudding. I burst into tears and said, 'Is this my living on pudding near the end, and so painfully?'"[19]

Saturday, 26 December 1885: M. arrived in the morning and met with the Master. Kishori, M.'s brother, was also a devotee. M. told the Master what Kishori had said to him: "My guru may leave me, but I shall not leave him."

"Wonderful!" Ramakrishna joyfully remarked.

Sunday, 27 December 1885: The Master was feeling much better. He sat up, surrounded by the devotees. Ram Chandra strongly believed that the Master's disease was mere pretense and that he could cure himself at any time. One moment he would be suffering from pain, and the next he would merge into samadhi. Ram, Nityagopal, and other devotees began to sing kirtan on the ghat of the western pond. As he listened to the kirtan, Ramakrishna went into deep samadhi. Afterwards he said: "I see my spiritual state is intact; only my disease has suppressed it.…It is Satchidananda who descends into the human body."

Monday, 28 December 1885: After work M. arrived at Cossipore and found Girish, Ram, and others talking with the ayurvedic doctor of Baghbazar. M. went upstairs to the Master and bowed down to him. The Master asked him to buy two glass bowls. He reminisced about how when he was young he would make clay images of Krishna with his flute, as well as other gods and goddesses. The devotees and disciples were singing and dancing downstairs, and with Ramakrishna's permission M. joined them.

Friday, 1 January 1886: Swami Saradananda described the events of this momentous day, when Ramakrishna became the Kalpataru, the "wish-fulfilling tree."

The Master felt better and expressed a desire to walk in the garden for a short while. Because it was a holiday, the householder devotees began arriving at the Cossipore garden after midday, individually and in groups. The Master came down from upstairs at 3:00 p.m.; there were more than thirty people talking amongst themselves inside the house and sitting under the trees in the garden. They all stood up reverently and bowed down when they saw him. The Master went out through the western door of the hall, descended onto the garden path, and proceeded slowly southward to the gate. The devotees followed him at a little distance. When he reached the midpoint of the path between the house and the gate, the Master saw Girish, Ram, Atul, and a few others under a tree on the west side of the path. They bowed down to him and came to him joyfully.

Before anyone had spoken a word, the Master addressed Girish, asking him: "Girish, what have you seen and understood [about me] that makes you say all these things [that I am an avatar, and so on] to everyone, wherever you go?" Unperturbed, Girish knelt down at the Master's feet, folded his hands before his raised face, and responded in a voice choked with emotion: "What more can I say of Him? Even the sages Vyasa and Valmiki could find no words to measure His glory!" Girish's sincere faith expressed in those words so moved the Master that he said to the devotees, while looking at Girish: "What more need I tell you? I bless you all. May you all be illumined!" He became overwhelmed by love and compassion for his devotees, and went into ecstasy after uttering those few words.[20]

M. was not present that afternoon, but he was at Cossipore in the evening. Ramakrishna said to the devotees: "Seven years ago, I thought that many people would come here [to himself], and a gatekeeper would have to control the crowd." At 7:00 p.m. M. took his leave and went with Mahima, whose house was nearby. Mahima told M.: "I have never seen another person in India like Ramakrishna Paramahamsa."

Saturday, 2 January 1886: The Kalpataru event had taken a toll on the Master's fragile body. M. arrived at 1:30 p.m. Ramakrishna asked Navagopal to give some blankets to his attendants, and he asked M. to massage his feet. The Master's sore had been aggravated and he was in pain. He put a small amount of ghee in his mouth, as one of his doctors had said it would lubricate the open sore.

Master: "I see I have become everything."

M.: "Yes sir. The Lord also said in the Gita (7:7): 'Everything is strung on Me as a row of gems on a thread.'"

M. left at 5:00 p.m.

Sunday, 3 January 1886: M. arrived in the afternoon and found Ram, Devendra, and other devotees in the Master's room. His throat hemorrhaged twice that day.

In the evening Harish brought the Master's meal, but the Master noticed that Harish had smelt the food so he could not eat it. Ramakrishna then chewed a myrobalan, which is a laxative, but stopped when M. reminded him of its effect.

Narendra brought Dr. Pratap to see the Master. He examined the wound and gave Ramakrishna some medicine.

Monday, 4 January 1886: M. arrived at 4:00 p.m. Narendra was in the Master's room. M. learned that Narendra had cried for God and begged

Ramakrishna to give him samadhi. Shashi told M. that the Master had had a lot of bleeding that day.

At 9:00 p.m. the Master got up from his bed and talked about Narendra's longing for God. M. spent the night there.[21]

Tuesday, 5 January 1886: M. arrived at 4:00 p.m. and found the Master seated on his bed. He talked about the renunciation of his young disciples and how they were unwilling to enter family life. Then the Master asked M.: "Well, all my joy, all my ecstasy — where are they now?"

M. replied: "Perhaps you are now in the state of mind that the Gita describes as beyond the three gunas."

Master: "Yes, the Divine Mother has put me into the state of a child. Tell me, won't the body live through this illness?"

M. remained silent.[22]

Wednesday, 6 January 1886: At 3:30 p.m. M. came to Cossipore with his wife and son. He heard the following story about his student Subodh:

> Hearing about the recent aggravation of the Master's throat pain, Subodh simply said: "Sir, you used to live in a damp room in Dakshineswar. As a result, it seems you have a sore throat because of the cold. Please take tea. Whenever we have sore throats, we drink tea and the soreness goes away. If you want, I can bring some good tea from my home." Immediately the childlike Master called Rakhal and said: "Look, I want to drink tea. This boy says that I will be cured if I drink tea." Rakhal said: "Sir, tea is very hot; it may aggravate your throat. You may not be able to bear it." "No, then it is not necessary," said the Master. He consoled Subodh, saying "Hot tea will not suit me." Subodh was moved by the Master's childlike nature.[23]

Thursday, 7 January 1886: Although M. had a full-time job as headmaster of Vidyasagar's school in Calcutta, almost every day he visited the Master in Cossipore — which is quite a distance from Calcutta. M. arrived at 4:30 p.m. The Master was teaching Narendra how to practise sadhana. Narendra asked M., "Well, you practised sadhana under the bel tree in Dakshineswar for a month. Can you tell me what you achieved?"

M. replied with a smile, "I achieved him [*pointing to the Master*]." The Master laughed.

Friday, 8 January 1886: M. arrived in the afternoon. Observing Narendra's longing for God, the Master asked him to sing a few songs praising Krishna. Narendra sang three songs. It was the Master's suppertime but his meal had not arrived. The Master sent M. downstairs to inquire about it. When the food was brought, Ramakrishna ate a small amount of farina pudding. After supper the Master asked M. to massage his feet. When he finished, M. covered Ramakrishna with a quilt and left.

Monday, 11 January 1886: Since 2 January the Master's illness had worsened. He was being treated by Navin Pal, an ayurvedic doctor, who was in the Master's room along with others. The Master softly said: "Enough! Let this body go. People call me an avatar, but now see his condition." After a while, he was in a joyful mood. Again he began to cough, but it soon stopped. Dr. Navin Pal left. The Master said to Rakhal: "You cry over my suffering. Let the body go soon." Then he said to M., "Mahindar, it is better to leave this world."

In the meantime Dr. Pratap Majumdar arrived and the Master asked him for a homeopathic medicine.

Tuesday, 12 January 1886: It was the day of makar-sankranti, an auspicious day.

Every year monks and pilgrims from all over India go to Gangasagar, the confluence of the Ganges and the Bay of Bengal, for a holy bath. Many pilgrims go by boat from the Jagannath ghat of Calcutta. Senior Gopal had a little money and wanted to acquire merit by offering cloths to holy people on that auspicious day; so he bought twelve pieces of cloth and twelve rosaries of rudraksha beads to distribute among the monks. He dyed the cloths the ochre colour himself. When the Master heard about it, he said to Gopal: "You will attain a thousand times more merit if you present those ochre cloths and rosaries to my children rather than giving them to the monks at Jagannath ghat. Where else will you find such all-renouncing monks? Each of them is equal to a thousand monks." This changed Gopal's mind.

On Tuesday, 12 January 1886 (makar-sankranti), Gopal gave the ochre cloths and rosaries to the Master, who touched them and sanctified them with a mantram. He himself then distributed them among his young disciples. They put on the ochre cloths and saluted the Master. Sri Ramakrishna was pleased to see them in monastic cloth and blessed them. The disciples who received the ochre cloths were: Narendra, Rakhal, Niranjan, Baburam, Shashi, Sharat, Kali, Jogin, Latu, Tarak, and Gopal. The twelfth cloth and rosary, according to the Master's instruction, were set aside for Girish Ghosh. Later Girish touched them to his head and felt the Master's special blessing. In this sense it may be said that the Ramakrishna Order was founded by Sri Ramakrishna himself, although it did not come into official existence until after his death.[24]

M. arrived in the afternoon and went directly to Ramakrishna, who asked M. to rub his stomach with oil.

Wednesday, 13 January 1886: At noon the Master's condition was critical. His breathing almost stopped. M. arrived at 4:30 p.m. and found Dr. Majumdar in the Master's room. Ramakrishna said to the doctor with folded hands: "Too much pain. Please cure this disease."

Ram Datta strongly believed that the Master was an incarnation of God and could cure his disease at any time. The Master said to M.: "I don't like what Ram is saying. You see, when you assume a human body, physical ailments are inevitable."

The disciples were passionately and devotedly serving the Master day and night. M. also stayed that night.

Thursday, 14 January 1886: Dr. Kalachand came to check the Master's condition. M. entered the Master's room and found his own wife seated there. She had dreamt about the Master's critical condition, so she came to see him. M. asked her to go downstairs. Despite his illness, the Master was having fun by imitating women who pretend to be in love. After a while he remarked: "Ram Datta is a doctor and goes to work wearing a turban. He has declared that I am God."

The Master tried to eat some farina pudding, but it was hard for him to swallow anything. Much later, Holy Mother recalled: "Some days farina pudding would come out from his nose and throat. Oh, what suffering he had!"

It was winter, but the Master felt as if he were burning. Shashi was sitting inside the mosquito curtain and fanning the Master. M. was seated outside of the curtain. The Master asked him to sit inside the curtain also as there were too many mosquitoes.

Friday, 15 January 1886: M. hurriedly left work and reached Cossipore at noon. He saw that a piece of thick cloth had been wrapped around Ramakrishna's throat to prevent its swelling. Bhavanath was holding him up in a sitting position and Jogin and Latu were trying to feed him.

Girish, Ram, M., and others were seated in the Master's room. Girish wholeheartedly prayed that the Master's pain be relieved. Shortly thereafter the Master spit up some phlegm and then felt better. He said, "Now I can swallow a little, but the swelling has not gone down." M. stayed at Cossipore that night. At 4:15 a.m. he helped the Master to rinse his mouth with warm water. He left for home at 5:30 a.m.

Saturday, 16 January 1886: M. went to Dr. Sarkar to report the Master's condition to him, and then he went to Vidyasagar's school to carry out his regular duties. At noon he went to Cossipore and informed Ramakrishna that the doctor would come. After lunch the Master had difficulty breathing. M. felt helpless, but he rubbed the Master's feet. Dr. Sarkar arrived soon afterwards, having picked up Dr. Pratap Majumdar in his carriage. Dr. Sarkar gave the Master a dose of Conium, which provided some relief.

Dr. Sarkar told the devotees: "I did not expect the disease to spread so far. There is no earthly remedy that can arrest the progress of the disease. I have been saying this from the beginning and I say this even now. The cancer has spread to the shoulders, neck, and other places."

M. stayed with the Master that night. At midnight Ramakrishna asked for some food. Latu prepared some pudding, and the Master ate a little.

Sunday, 17 January 1886: At 2:00 p.m. Girish, Devendra, and M. gathered under the mango tree on the lawn and discussed the Master's divinity. At 7:00 p.m. M. and Dr. Trailokya Nath Bandyopadhyay were with the Master in his room. The Master was gasping for breath and suffering terribly.

Monday, 18 January 1886: At 7:00 p.m. M., Devendra, and Dwija arrived at Cossipore. The Master went into samadhi while listening to the disciples' singing. M. bowed down to the Master and then returned home with Ram Chandra and Surendra.

Tuesday, 19 January 1886: M. arrived at the Cossipore house in the morning and found the Master asleep. Although he had been coughing, he was feeling a little better. The swelling in his throat had subsided a bit. Ramakrishna was wearing an amulet of Lord Tarakeswar Shiva as requested by Ram Chandra and other devotees. The Master advised M. to visit Tarakeswar Shiva the next Sunday, and M. agreed. He then asked M. to buy a carpet for him. M. stayed the night.

Wednesday, 20 January 1886: At 4:00 p.m. M. went to Barabazar to buy a carpet and a pair of slippers for the Master. He then took a share carriage to Cossipore. He heard that the Master had hemorrhaged twice. M. then went upstairs to show Ramakrishna what he had bought.

Thursday, 21 January 1886: M. went to Cossipore at 4:30 p.m., after attending the Brahmo festival. The Master told him that he had visited Tarakeswar Shiva on three occasions. Baburam's house was near Tarakeswar, so M. got directions from him. Sitting on the southern veranda, Ramakrishna drew some pictures with a piece of charcoal: such as a face of an elephant, a bird, Lord Shiva Taraknath, and so on.

Friday, 22 January 1886: M. arrived at 4:30 p.m. and found Girish waiting in the ground-floor hall. They both went upstairs to the Master's room. Ramakrishna was chewing an amalaki fruit, which helped ease the pain in his throat. Girish asked the Master to eat some food. Shashi and Kali took the Master to the adjacent bathroom. When he returned to the room, he went to bed.

Sunday, 24 January 1886: M. went to Tarakeswar with his wife, his son Nati, and a maidservant. Following the Master's instructions, he touched the deity while performing worship.

Monday, 25 January 1886: At 4:30 a.m. M. left for Cossipore and found the Master in bed. M. gave the Master a detailed account of his pilgrimage to Tarakeswar, which made him happy. The Master asked M. to visit Lord Jagannath in Puri next.

Bhuvaneswari Devi, Narendra's mother, came to see Ramakrishna with her youngest son. She was upset, seeing Narendra in an ochre cloth. The Master consoled her, saying: "The doctor has forbidden me to speak, but I must talk to you. I am glad that you have come. Please take Narendra back home. I told him: 'You will have to look after your mother and younger brothers. It is not the right time for you to put on the ochre cloth.'" Narendra went with his mother by carriage, but got down at Baghbazar to run an errand.

Thursday, 28 January 1886: M. went to visit Sisir Kumar Ghosh, editor of *Amrita Bazar Patrika*, and received detailed information on and directions to Puri. At 5:00 p.m. M. went to Cossipore and found Girish and two actors in the Master's room. Everyone then went downstairs, and M. sang two songs in praise of the Divine Mother. M. then went back upstairs to Ramakrishna's room and told him about his plan to visit Puri. The Master asked M. to consult Balaram also, as he had been to Puri. After that M. returned to Calcutta with Surendra.

Friday, 29 January 1886: The Master had been very ill the night before, but he felt a little better in the morning when M. arrived. That morning Shashi told M. that the Master was upset because Girish was proclaiming him, among his theatre group, to be an avatar. At noon the Master felt much worse, and his throat began to bleed. Shashi cried. When Narendra entered his room, the Master said to him: "This is the condition of your avatar! He is bleeding."

Narendra was angry at God the Creator. "I could create a better world than this one," he declared.

Saturday, 30 January 1886: The Master told Jogin an esoteric truth: "An incarnation of God disappears if people call him an avatar too many times. The king visits the city incognito; but he leaves as soon as people recognize him. If holy people get too many visitors, they leave the place."

Sunday, 31 January 1886: When M. arrived in Cossipore at 4:30 p.m. he was told that the attendants had started restricting visitors. Ram Chandra came to see the Master, but even he was turned away.

M. stayed that night to help serve the Master. At night the Master asked Narendra to rub his chest with a mixture of ghee and camphor. He had terrible pain in his throat and chest and could not sleep. His attendants felt helpless. He chewed a chunk of myrobalan, which helps moisten the throat.

Monday, 1 February 1886: Ramakrishna's disease had become aggravated. M. arrived in the afternoon. When M. entered the room, the Master asked, "How do you see my condition?" M. remained silent. He then went downstairs. At Narendra's request M. sang five songs.

Tuesday, 2 February 1886: When M. arrived at 5:00 p.m. after work, Narendra told him before he could go upstairs that at 4:00 a.m. the Master had hemorrhaged nearly one seer (two pounds) of blood. When M. tried to see the Master, Niranjan forbade him. M. was extremely upset. He left the house and sat on a lower branch of the mango tree in the garden. Niranjan came to M. and apologized for his rude behaviour. As M. was the one coordinating the doctors, he told M. that he had gone to consult with Vaidya Mahafej of Bhawnipur, South Calcutta, who practised naturopathy. When Niranjan left, Narendra went to M. and said: "Do you want to go upstairs? I have not been there for a long while." M. and Narendra went upstairs and found the Master breathing heavily and with some difficulty. M. could not bear the Master's suffering; he and Narendra went back downstairs. Narendra informed M. that the Master asked Kali, "Well, is it true what they say [*that I am an avatar*]?" He indicated that the life of an avatar is beyond human understanding. M. spent the night at Cossipore and returned home in the morning.

Wednesday, 3 February 1886: After work M. arrived at Cossipore. Vaidya Mahafej was in the Master's room. The doctor had brought a medication that the Master was supposed to chew, but he swallowed it instead.

Thursday, 4 February 1886: At 4:30 p.m. M. came to Cossipore, bringing two palm-leaf fans for the Master. The Master told him, "The sides of my ears are swollen." M. remained silent and went downstairs soon after. He heard that Pandit Shashadhar Tarkachudamani had come to see the Master. Swami Saradananda wrote:

> In the course of conversation, the pandit told him: "Sir, we have read in the scriptures that a great soul like yourself can cure his own physical illness by mere willpower. If you but concentrate your mind on the affected part of the body for a while with the resolve that it be healed, you will be cured. Why don't you try it, sir?" The Master replied: "As a pandit, how can you make such a suggestion? This mind has been given up to God

once and for all. How can I withdraw it from Him and make it dwell on this cage of flesh and bone?" Pandit Shashadhar was silenced.[25]

Friday, 5 February 1886: At 4:00 a.m. Navagopal came to M.'s house and informed him that the Master's condition was critical. He had had a terrible hemorrhage at 3:00 a.m. Ram Chandra and Navagopal stayed there that night. Niranjan was supporting the Master when this happened. "Mother, I can't bear anymore," Ramakrishna had said, and fainted in Niranjan's arms. After a while, all saw the Master's fresh blood in Narendra's mouth.* M. recorded in the diary: "Lord's supper — fresh blood."

M. decided that he and his wife would go to Cossipore to help care for the Master. At 8:30 a.m. he hired a carriage and left for Cossipore with his wife. On the way he wept inconsolably. When he arrived, the Master was sleeping. At 10:30 a.m. the Master got up. He said to M.: "So much blood! I am so weak that I can't walk. I have no appetite."

"You will be hungry after a while," said M.

Saturday, 6 February 1886: M. went to Cossipore in the early afternoon after work. He relieved the other attendants and stayed alone with the Master, who indicated that he wanted oil to be rubbed on his abdomen. M. brought Gopal to do this. The Master coughed again and his throat began to bleed. M. poured water on the Master's head to cool his system, then went downstairs to the garden. As he sat in the garden, he prayed to God that he could continue to serve the Master. M. was leaving for Kamarpukur (Ramakrishna's birthplace) at 5:00 a.m. the next day, so he asked Gopidas for directions.

Thursday, 11 February 1886: This was a significant day. The Master commissioned Narendra, drawing a picture and writing the following words: "Victory to Radha, love personified. Naren will teach loudly inside and outside [India]. Victory to Radha." It is assumed that the head in the sketch represents Narendra and the peacock his large following.

M. returned to Cossipore at 11:00 p.m. He went directly to the Master's room and told him in detail the places he had seen and the people he had met in Kamarpukur. Forgetting his pain, the Master was excited and asked many questions. The Master's face was beaming as he listened to M.'s account of his visit to his birthplace. M. gave the Master the prasad of Raghuvir and a flower he had offered, which he joyfully accepted.

---

*It is said that some thought that cancer was a contagious disease, but Narendra wanted to remove that doubt from others' minds by swallowing some of the Master's blood himself.

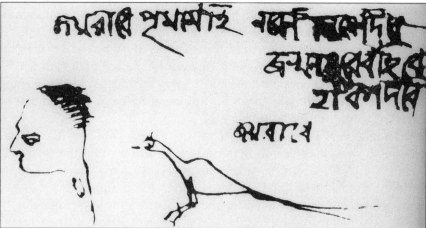

TOP: Kamarpukur: Raghuvir's shrine is on the left. Ramakrishna's room is on the right.
BOTTOM: At Cossipore, Ramakrishna wrote in Bengali: "Victory to Radha, love personified. Naren will teach loudly inside and outside [India]. Victory to Radha." It is assumed that the head represents Narendra and the peacock his large following.

M. heard from the attendants about the Master's own writing and sketch about Narendra. M. copied it in his diary with a comment: "I take without leave something too valuable to be lost."

Friday, 12 February 1886: M.'s wife visited the Master with her brother Dwija. She lamented that she had not been able to accompany M. to Kamarpukur, but Holy Mother consoled her, saying, "You will go with me." Afterwards M. came and met Ramlal downstairs. Both went to the Master's room and found him sleeping. At Baburam's suggestion, M. gave a rupee to Ramlal, who wanted to offer *tulsi* to Krishna in Dakshineswar for the Master's recovery.

Saturday, 13 February 1886: Keshab Chandra Sen's mother, wife, and two sons visited the Master, who greeted them affectionately. M. came in the evening and began to fan the Master. He complained of a throbbing pain in his throat and on his neck. At 7:00 p.m., Girish, Devendra, and other devotees assembled in the hall downstairs, and M. joined their discussion. Pointing to M., Devendra remarked: "I recognized him. He acted in the role of Krishnadas Kaviraj [the recorder] of Chaitanya's divine play." M. left for home at 10:30 p.m.

Sunday, 14 February 1886: At 11:00 a.m. M. went to Dr. Sarkar with the Master's health report. He had a long discussion with the doctor about the mystery of the avatar, death, the Master's influence on the theatre, and other topics. In the early afternoon M. went to Cossipore. He told the Master that Dr. Sarkar would visit him on Wednesday. That night M. stayed in Cossipore to serve the Master.

Monday, 15 February 1886: At 4:30 p.m. M. arrived in Cossipore and met Girish and Surendra. The Master was seated in front of the devotees. He gargled gently and a small amount of ghee was applied to the sore. The Master looked at M. intently. Niranjan told M. and the others, "Let us all go downstairs." M.'s feelings were hurt. He and Surendra returned to Calcutta, where M. visited Ram Chandra, who had not been to see the Master for some days. M. said to him: "Please visit the Master. It will be nice if you can see him. His unbearable pain reminds me of the suffering of Christ on the cross." M. then returned home and passed a sleepless night.

Wednesday, 17 February 1886: At 4:30 p.m. M. arrived in Cossipore. He met Narendra in the downstairs hall and asked, "How is the Master?" Dr. Sarkar came to visit Ramakrishna, whose health was deteriorating rapidly.

Saturday, 20 February 1886: M. visited the Master at 4:00 p.m The Master talked a little with Hazra and M. He told Hazra that M. had brought some of the dust of Kamarpukur. Senior Gopal asked him not to talk anymore. M. and Hazra left the room. Sitting at the ghat of the eastern pond, M. told Hazra about his visit to Kamarpukur.

Monday, 22 February 1886: M. arrived and found Mahima Charan seated in the Master's room. Previously Mahima did not believe that God could be an avatar, but now he had changed his mind. The Master was pleased to see this change.

Tuesday, 23 February 1886: M. arrived and tried to talk with Narendra, but he was a little indifferent. This coldness may have been due to a misunderstanding that had developed among the householder and monastic disciples about the expenses involved in running the Cossipore household. Ram Chandra had asked that the money be spent discreetly, and suggested that careful accounts be kept. Narendra resented Ram Chandra's suggestions.

Friday, 26 February 1886: M. arrived at Cossipore in the early afternoon after work. The Master asked M. to massage his feet, which made M. happy. The Master fell asleep as Shashi and M. fanned him. After a while, he woke up and the attendant applied ghee to the Master's throat. There were some flowers in a tray nearby. The Master worshipped himself by putting some flowers on his own head. He chewed a piece of amalaki and gave a chunk to M. The Master arranged a feast for his attendants and asked M. to buy some meat. M. was delighted to serve them.

Sunday, 28 February 1886: In the morning M. and his younger brother Kishori came to Cossipore. M. then left for Dakshineswar, where he prayed to the Divine Mother: "Mother, what shall I say about your son? You know everything. Mother, I implore you not to give any more suffering to the Master."

When M. returned to Cossipore, the attendants warned him that something bad had happened while he was gone. It had been arranged that Surendra would pay the rent; Balaram would buy the necessities for the Master's diet; and Ram Chandra, Girish, Kalipada, M., and other householders would handle any other expenses. While M. was at Dakshineswar that day, Ram Chandra had proposed cutting the budget. He suggested that two or three full-time attendants were enough for the Master; the others should return home and visit the Master from time to time. Narendra vehemently opposed this idea and a heated argument ensued. Ramakrishna and the attendant disciples supported Narendra, who wanted to continue the Master's service as usual. Narendra decided not to accept money from the householders any longer; he would beg for funds going from door to door to continue service of the Master. The attendants decided that they would not allow any householder devotees to visit the Master. Before the situation worsened, the Master reconciled the two groups of disciples. M. always supported the young disciples.

Wednesday, 3 March 1886: When M. arrived he gave four rupees to Latu to buy a pillow and some refreshments, and then gave six rupees to Gopal to settle a debt.

When M. went to the Master's room that evening, Shashi was reading to Ramakrishna "The Banishment of Ramachandra" from the Adhyatma Ramayana. Surendra arrived and begged forgiveness for the misunderstanding that had happened a few days before. He had not been involved and was upset about the situation. The Master's throat began to bleed, so he indicated that M. should take Surendra downstairs and console him. M. stayed at Cossipore that night.

Thursday, 4 March 1886: It was Shivaratri. M. went home early in the morning. At 5:30 p.m. after work he returned to Cossipore. He went directly to the Master's room and sat near him. Niranjan went to Dr. Sarkar, who suggested bandaging the Master's throat with marigold leaf, which stops bleeding. The disciples observed Shivaratri the entire night by worshipping and singing songs in praise of Shiva.

That night Narendra experimented with his spiritual power on Kali (later Abhedananda). Narendra asked Kali to touch his right knee and began to meditate. After a while, Narendra asked Kali about his experience. Kali replied: "As one feels a shock wave while touching an electric battery, and one's hand trembles, so I felt when touching you."

Swami Saradananda wrote:

> At 4:00 a.m. when the worship of the fourth quarter was over, Swami Ramakrishnananda came to the worship room and told Swamiji [Narendra], "The Master is calling for you." Swamiji immediately went to the second floor of the main building, where the Master was staying. Ramakrishnananda also followed him because he was serving the Master.
>
> Seeing Swamiji, the Master said: "Hello! You are frittering away your power before you have accumulated enough of it. First gather it deep within yourself, and then you will understand where and how you should use it. Mother will let you know. Don't you see what great harm you have done to that boy by infusing your ideas into him? He had been following a specific practice for a long time, and now all is spoilt like a miscarriage in the sixth month of pregnancy. Well, what was supposed to happen has happened. From now on don't do such a thing rashly. The boy is lucky that greater harm did not befall him."
>
> Swamiji said later: "I was completely dumbfounded. The Master had come to know whatever we did during worship! What could I do? I remained silent as he scolded me."[26]

M. kept watch over the Master throughout the entire night. In the morning he went to the Ganges to bathe and then returned to Ramakrishna to bow down to him. The Master felt as if he were burning, so M. fanned him and rubbed oil on his abdomen. Narendra came and informed M. that his breakfast was ready.

Friday, 5 March 1886: M. and Narendra were seated on a mat on the lawn. Seeing Ram Chandra entering the garden, M. suggested, "Let us receive him." But Narendra remained aloof. Since the misunderstanding several days earlier, Ram Chandra had not visited the Master. The following incident may have taken place on this day:

> Ram Chandra Datta wanted to visit the Master, but Niranjan stopped him at the gate. Ram was hurt by this because he was one of the Master's prominent lay devotees. He then said to Latu, "Please offer these sweets and flowers to the Master and bring a little prasad for me." Latu was very touched and said to Niranjan, "Brother, Ram Babu is our very own; why are you putting such restrictions on him?" Still Niranjan was inexorable. Then Latu said rather bluntly, "At Shyampukur you allowed the actress Binodini to visit the Master and now you are stopping Ram Babu, who is such a great devotee." This pricked Niranjan's conscience, so he let Ram go to see Ramakrishna. Later when Latu went upstairs, the omniscient Master said to him: "Look, never see faults in others; rather see their good qualities." Latu was embarrassed. He came down and apologized to Niranjan, saying: "Brother, please don't mind my caustic remark. I am an illiterate person." This shows how the Master taught his disciples to develop close interpersonal relationships.[27]

Sunday, 7 March 1886: M. went to Dr. Sarkar to ask him to visit the Master. They had a long conversation on religion, and then went to Cossipore together in the afternoon. The doctor examined Ramakrishna and announced that the disease was stable. The Master drank some broth made of *masur dal* (pink lentils).

It was Ramakrishna's birthday. M. recorded: "The devotees observed the Master's birthday on a small scale, even though last year it was celebrated lavishly in Dakshineswar. He is not well, and the devotees are submerged in grief."

"The Master's birthday celebration was very brief," Latu recalled. "Brother Naren sang some songs; Surendra Babu brought a beautiful garland and put it around the Master's neck. Balaram Babu and M. gave him a cloth and a shirt. Someone else presented the Master with a pair of slippers."

In the evening there was singing in the ground floor hall. Afterwards

Narendra talked about Christ's self-sacrifice for the good of humanity and Buddha's *parinirvana* (passing away). After supper, at 11:00 p.m., M. left for home.

Thursday, 11 March 1886: It was eight o'clock in the evening. Sri Ramakrishna was in the big hall on the second floor. Narendra, Shashi, M., Sharat, and the Senior Gopal were in the room. Sri Ramakrishna was lying down. Sharat stood by his bed and fanned him. The Master was speaking about his illness.

Master: "If some of you go to Dakshineswar and see Bholanath, he will give you a medicinal oil and also tell you how to apply it."

After a while Sharat set out for Dakshineswar to get the oil from Bholanath.[28]

Sunday, 14 March 1886: M. stayed at home during the day and read *The Life of Jesus* by Renan. He visited Cossipore that evening.

Sri Ramakrishna sat facing the north in the large room upstairs. It was evening. He was very ill. Narendra and Rakhal were gently massaging his feet. M. sat nearby. The Master by a sign, asked him, too, to stroke his feet. M. obeyed.

At midnight M. was seated by his side. Sri Ramakrishna asked him by a sign to come nearer. The sight of his suffering was unbearable. In a very soft voice and with great difficulty he said to M.: "I have gone on suffering so much for fear of making you all weep. But if you all say: 'Oh, there is so much suffering! Let the body die,' then I may give up the body." These words pierced the devotees' hearts. Some thought, "Is this another crucifixion — the sacrifice of the body for the sake of the devotees?"

The devotees wondered what was to be done. One of them left for Calcutta. That very night Girish came to the garden house with two physicians, Upendra and Navagopal.

The Master felt a little better and said to them: "The illness is of the body. That is as it should be; I see that the body is made of the five elements."

Turning to Girish, he said: "I am seeing many forms of God. Among them I find this one also [*meaning his own form*].[29]

Monday, 15 March 1886: In the morning the Master felt somewhat better. He said to the devotees:

"Do you know what I see right now? I see that it is God Himself who has become all this.... Now, I have no pain at all. I am my old self again. If the body were to be preserved a few days more, many people would have their spirituality awakened. Such is not the will of God.... God becomes man, an avatar, and comes to earth with His devotees. And the devotees leave the world with Him."

Rakhal: "Therefore we pray that you may not go away and leave us behind."

Sri Ramakrishna smiles and says: "A band of minstrels suddenly appears, dances, and sings and it departs in the same sudden manner. They come and they return, but none recognizes them."[30]

In the afternoon Ram Chandra brought Dr. J.M. Coates, the head of Calcutta Medical College. He went to the Master's room, but kept his shoes on. He sat on the mat and reclined on a bolster. Before Dr. Coates started to examine his throat, the Master asked him to wait for a minute, and then went into samadhi. After the examination Dr. Coates said that the Master was suffering from cancer and his condition was incurable. Nonetheless, he suggested that the current treatment be continued. A devotee paid the doctor's 32-rupee fee. M. stayed in the Master's room that night.

Tuesday, 16 March 1886: Early in the morning the Master began struggling for breath, so Dr. Trailokya was brought from Baranagore. M. went to bathe in the Ganges. Upon his return, his cousin reported that his wife's mental condition had become worse. When the Master felt a little better that afternoon, M. left for home with Girish and Devendra.

Thursday, 18 March 1886: M. went to Cossipore after work. When he arrived, Atul Ghosh, Girish's brother, told him that Girish was drunk and praying, "The Master must get well." The Master heard about Girish's prayer. Somehow the Master felt better that day.

Friday, 19 March 1886: It was the day before *Doljatra*, or Holi, an auspicious day commemorating Krishna's play with the gopis with coloured powder. That evening Girish, Devendra, M., and the attendants assembled in the Master's room. They all touched the Master's feet with *avir* (red powder), and the Master sprinkled the powder on their chests and heads. They were happy seeing the Master's joyful face. They then began kirtan and danced by the side of the pond.

Saturday, 20 March 1886: It was *Doljatra*, the festival of colours and also Chaitanya's birthday. Girish, M., Narendra, and others assembled in the hall downstairs. Narendra began to sing a song about Chaitanya, which overwhelmed M. The devotees went to Ramakrishna's room and offered *avir* at his feet, and he blessed them. Some women and also some Marwaris came to pay their homage to the Master. After a while the Marwari devotees left, saying, "Victory to Satchidananda, Victory to Satchidananda!" Girish and others covered M.'s head with coloured powder.

In the evening the Master said to M.: "I have no desire to keep this body. I can't eat." M. consoled him, saying, "We wish you weren't in pain."

Master (*to M.*): "If I wish, I could withdraw my mind from this pain, but I have no desire to keep this body anymore. Nevertheless, I get joy when I see you all. That is the reason I endure this suffering."

Then M. had a long conversation with the Master about his divinity.

Ramakrishna said about his intimate devotees, "All of you are part of this place [*meaning himself*]."

M.: "That I have understood. But I am not fully satisfied."

Master: "You will never be fully satisfied."

M.: "Sir, the amount of longing I had at the beginning still remains. I am not fully content."

Master: "None can have full contentment in God [*because He is infinite*]. I am telling you this secret. Please don't divulge it to others."

Meanwhile the Master was served farina pudding for supper. When he saw it, he remarked: "What is the use of eating anymore? I can't digest it."

Seeing M. depressed, the Master said: "Don't worry so much. Make your mind strong."

Sunday, 21 March 1886: Dr. Sarkar arrived at 4:00 p.m. M. and Narendra were in the Master's room. The doctor examined Ramakrishna and advised M. to give him six drops of tulsi juice. Someone asked if the Master could have a boat trip on the Ganges for fresh air, but the doctor didn't approve. He jokingly said, "Jesus Christ would walk on the water."

Seeing the Master smiling, Rakhal remarked: "Despite all this pain, the Master has not lost his smile."

Master: "The Mother is teaching all [*through me*] that this body is transient and so many things are going on; still that pure I-consciousness is unaffected."

Amritalal: "Sir, your suffering is also a lesson for others."

Master: "Is there anything in the scriptures about one person suffering from pain for others?"

M. mentioned that it is recorded in the Christian scriptures, and Sharat corroborated it, saying: "Lord Jesus was crucified in order to expiate sins of the sinners."

Monday, 22 March 1886: While M. was in Cossipore, the Master asked Shashi to bring some sanctified water of the Divine Mother from his father, who was a tantric worshipper. M. gave the carriage fare to Shashi. During M.'s absence, Vijay Krishna Goswami came and the Master blessed him by touching his chest.

Thursday, 25 March 1886: M. went to Cossipore after work and found Dr. Rajendralal Datta, Surendra, and Senior Gopal in the Master's room.

He was feeling better. Dr. Datta examined him, prescribed medicine (Lycopodium 200), and suggested a new diet. That evening the Master had vermicelli and milk for supper.

Tuesday, 30 March 1886: The Master was lying in his bed. A 10-year-old boy named Patu was massaging his feet. "This boy had ecstasy," the Master said to M. "How wonderful! He is so young!" The Master was cold, so the attendant covered him with a chadar.

Wednesday, 31 March 1886: Dr. Rajendralal Datta came to examine the Master, even though the doctor himself was feeling ill. Suresh Chandra Datta also came with his daughter. M. was about to leave the room, but the Master asked him to massage his feet.

Thursday, 1 April 1886: Narendra, Tarak, and Kali left for Bodh Gaya to practise austerities. The Master was concerned. He said: "Narendra is my crown jewel. He will give up his body if he knows who he is. Narendra is one of the seven sages; he is anxious to know his true self."

M. left for Vidyasagar's school and returned to Cossipore in the afternoon. It was an auspicious day for bathing in the Ganges, so he took his bath there and brought some holy water for the Master. At night M. returned home.

Monday, 5 April 1886: When M. arrived at 9:00 p.m. Baburam told him that the Master had cried for Narendra. The Master then consoled the attendants, saying: "Why are you anxious? Where will Naren go? How long will he stay away? Just wait. He will be back soon." Then he said with a smile: "One may travel in all four directions, but one will not find anything [true spirituality] anywhere. Whatever exists is here (*pointing to his body*)."[31] M. stayed the night.

Tuesday, 6 April 1886: Early in the morning M. entered the Master's room and found him sleeping. He silently bowed down to him and left for Calcutta. On his way, however, he saw Dr. Rajendralal Datta coming to Cossipore by carriage, so M. returned with him. Dr. Datta examined the Master and was pleased to learn that his pain had subsided. When the doctor left, Ramakrishna told M. some stories of his boyhood days. They had a long conversation. M. informed the Master that his wife's mental illness had worsened, but she behaved normally when she came to Cossipore. The compassionate Master asked M. to bring her to stay with Holy Mother for a month.

Thursday, 8 April 1886: Narendra, Tarak, and Kali returned from Bodh Gaya and the Master joyfully inquired about their experiences.

Friday, 9 April 1886: At 5:30 p.m. M. arrived and the Master asked him to buy a chadar and a pair of slippers. Narendra explained Buddha's life and experiences to the Master. The Master took the fan from M.'s hand and said: "As I see this fan, *directly* before me, in exactly the same manner have I seen God....I have seen that He and the one who dwells in my heart are one and the same Person."

When the disciples went downstairs, Shashi brought a piece of paper where the Master had written: "Mother, please give knowledge to Narendra." Below that he drew a tiger and a horse. On the reverse page, the Master sketched a woman with a braid.[32]

Monday, 12 April 1886: Narendra criticized Hindu superstitions about food and said that after attaining the knowledge of Brahman one can accept food from anyone. With this in mind he took some of his brother disciples to Piru's Restaurant in Calcutta and fed them chicken curry. When the Master heard of their adventure, he laughed and said, "Very well, you are now free from superstition."

In the evening, when M. was fanning the Master, he said by signs: "Get a stone bowl for me that will hold a quarter of a seer of milk — white stone. When eating from other bowls I get the smell of fish."[33]

Tuesday, 13 April 1886: It was the Bengali New Year's Day and also *Ramnavami*, the birthday of Ramachandra. Dr. Rajendralal Datta, Dr. Srinath, Ram Chandra, and many devotees assembled to pay their homage to the Master. M. had stayed with the Master the previous night. His wife and two daughters, Balaram's wife, Golap-ma, and other women devotees arrived in the morning. The two girls and Golap-ma sang songs and entertained the Master, who was in a great mood.

At 8:00 p.m. Surendra arrived from his office and offered the Master four oranges and two garlands. "Today is the first day of the year," Surendra said. "It is also Tuesday, an auspicious day to worship the Divine Mother. But I didn't go to Kalighat. I said to myself: 'It will be enough if I see him who is Kali Herself, and who has rightly understood Kali.'" The Master smiled and praised Surendra's devotion.[34]

Friday, 16 April 1886: It was evening. Girish, M., Latu, and a few devotees were seated on the steps leading to the pond. They went to the Master's room. He was feeling better. He asked Latu to give some refreshments to Girish and, despite his illness, he poured a glass of water and gave it to Girish himself. He and Girish had a wonderful conversation.

Girish: "Sir, remember what I was before, and see what I have become now by meditating on you! Formerly I was indolent; now that indolence has turned into resignation to God. Formerly I was a sinner; now I have become humble. What else can I say?"[35]

Saturday, 17 April 1886: It was the night of the full moon. M. arrived at

8:00 p.m. He met Narendra, who was going to Dakshineswar to meditate, as he did every night. M. went to the Master's room. The Master asked him to wash his towel and the spittoon. M. washed them in the pond.[36]

Sunday, 18 April 1886: M. had stayed the previous night. In the morning he bathed in the Ganges, and then returned to the Master's room. The Master was feeling well. He asked M. to bring his grief-stricken wife to stay at Cossipore for a couple of days, along with his youngest child. It was about 9:00 a.m. M. and Narendra had a long conversation about the existence of God as Ramakrishna watched. Dr. Rajendralal Datta arrived and examined the Master. Some devotees began to sing kirtan on the ghat of the reservoir, and the Master asked M. and Baburam to join them.[37]

Tuesday, 20 April 1886: Dr. Datta's treatment had temporarily arrested the Master's disease, although he continued to consult Dr. Sarkar as well. The Master had several visitors, including Mani Mallick, Sharat's brother Charu, and Tulsi Babu. M. and Tulsi Babu left for Calcutta together.

Wednesday, 21 April 1886: When M. arrived at Cossipore he saw Hirananda, a devotee from Sindh, in a horse carriage; Narendra and Rakhal were seeing him off. He had come from Sindh to see the Master. M. had a fascinating talk with Narendra about the existence of God. At 4:00 p.m. the Master asked M. to close the window and massage his feet. Purna came to visit the Master; M. gave some money to Gopal for Purna's carriage fare. At 9:00 p.m. M. left with Ram Chandra and Surendra.[38]

Thursday, 22 April 1886: In the evening Dr. Rajendralal Datta and Dr. Sarkar came to evaluate the Master's condition.

> Master (*to Dr. Sarkar and the others*): "The expenses are mounting."
> Dr. Sarkar (*pointing to the devotees*): "But they are ready to bear them. They do not hesitate to spend money. (*To Sri Ramakrishna*) Now, you see, gold is necessary."
> Master (*to Narendra*): "Why don't you answer?"
> Narendra remained silent. Dr. Sarkar resumed the conversation.
> Dr. Sarkar: "Gold is necessary, and also woman."
> Rajendra: "Yes, his [meaning Sri Ramakrishna's] wife has been cooking his meals."
> Dr. Sarkar (*to the Master*): "Do you see?"
> Master (*smiling*): "Yes — but very troublesome."
> Dr. Sarkar: "If there were no troubles, then all would become paramahamsas."
> A few minutes later the physicians took their leave.
> Master (*to M.*): "They say I cannot get along without 'woman and gold'. They don't understand the state of my mind."

Hirananda and two of his friends came to see Ramakrishna. He had a long conversation with Narendra in front of the Master, which M. recorded in the *Gospel*. Finally the Master said to Hirananda: "My mood is changing. I think that I should not say to everyone, 'May your spiritual consciousness be awakened.' People are so sinful in the Kaliyuga; if I awaken their spiritual consciousness I shall have to accept the burden of their sins."[39]

Friday, 23 April 1886: Hirananda and two of his Brahmo friends had lunch at Cossipore. Hirananda massaged the Master's feet and told him that he would send him a pair of pajamas that would be more comfortable during summer. The Master was deeply moved that Hirananda had come to see him from Sindh, which is 2,200 miles from Calcutta.

It was Good Friday, so many devotees came to see the Master.[40]

Saturday, 24 April 1886: The following is the last entry in *The Gospel of Sri Ramakrishna* while the Master was alive.

M. came to the garden house accompanied by his wife and a son. The boy was seven years old. It was at the Master's request that he brought his wife, who was almost mad with grief owing to the death of one of her sons.

That day the Master several times allowed M.'s wife the privilege of waiting on him. Her welfare seemed to occupy his attention a great deal. In the evening the Holy Mother came to the Master's room to feed him. M.'s wife accompanied her with a lamp. The Master tenderly asked her many questions about her household. He requested her to come again to the garden house and spend a few days with the Holy Mother, not forgetting to ask her to bring her baby daughter. When the Master had finished his meal M.'s wife removed the plates. He chatted with her a few minutes.

About nine o'clock in the evening Sri Ramakrishna was seated in his room with the devotees. He had a garland of flowers around his neck. He told M. that he had requested his wife to spend a few days at the garden house with the Holy Mother. His kindness touched M.'s heart.

M. was fanning him. The Master took the garland from his neck and said something to himself. Then in a very benign mood he gave the garland to M.[41]

Monday, 26 April 1886: The Master was feeling better, which gave his attendants and devotees some hope. M. was going to Baranagore with his wife and daughter Manamayi to attend a marriage ceremony. On the way he stopped at Cossipore and visited the Master. After this M. and his wife stayed with the Master for a week.

Thursday, 6 May 1886: M. and his wife came to visit Ramakrishna for the day.

Monday, 17 May 1886: M. went to Darjeeling for a few days. After returning to Calcutta, he went straight to see the Master in Cossipore, where he was told that the Master's condition had worsened. He bowed down to him. It was 5:00 p.m.

The Master asked, "Did the sight of the Himalayas remind you of God?" The Master further inquired about his meditation, vision, and spiritual awakening in Darjeeling. Ramakrishna had once said that one should see the Himalayas and the ocean to get a glimpse of the infinite. Balaram had arranged a festival and a feast, and invited all the devotees. The Master asked M. to go to Balaram's house. After attending the festival, M. returned to Cossipore and stayed with the Master.

Tuesday, 18 May 1886: M. and some attendants were in the Master's room. Narendra pronounced worldly life to be bad and full of selfishness. He advised M. to renounce the world.

Wednesday, 19 May 1886: Early in the morning M. bathed in the Ganges and then bowed down to the Master.

Master: "Will you take lunch here?"

M.: "No, sir. I shall have to return home."

Master: "All right, please go home then."

Thursday, 20 May 1886: This was a difficult day, crucial to M.'s future. The examination results for M.'s school that year were not very good, and Ishwar Chandra Vidyasagar was unhappy. He called on M. to complain. He said that M. was not doing his duty properly as the headmaster and that it was due to his negligence that the students had had such poor results. Vidyasagar also accused M. of visiting Ramakrishna too frequently and neglecting his duties.

M. was deeply hurt because Vidyasagar had included the Master in his complaints. Controlling himself, he went home to make a decision.

Friday, 21 May 1886: M. wrote a letter of resignation to Vidyasagar. He knew very well that without the job, his family would suffer and he would no longer be able to serve the Master financially. However, he could not bear any criticism levelled at his guru. He went to Cossipore and told the Master the whole story. "You have done the right thing," the Master responded.

M. later recalled how the Master's grace saved the situation:

I lost my job. I was pacing on the upper veranda of Thakur Bari like a half-mad person. I was worried about how I could feed my children. But I had not to wait long. Within 15 days I got another job. A teacher at the Hindu School was on leave, so the headmaster called and gave me that job. He also assured me that my post might be permanent.

Still I had some anxiety. Another day as I was pacing absentmindedly on the same veranda, someone called me from downstairs. I went down and found that a man had arrived by phaeton with a letter. Reading the letter I learned that Surendra Nath Banerjee was requesting me to accompany that man to visit him. When I met with him, he said: "I hear you have resigned from Vidyasagar's school. Why don't you join our Ripon College as a professor?" I then joined there as a professor and stayed for five years.[42]

Sunday, 23 May 1886: M. went to Cossipore at 8:00 a.m. The Master was suffering from a burning sensation all over his body, so someone had to fan him day and night. M. bowed down and then began to fan the Master. After 10 minutes, Latu relieved M., who went downstairs.

Dr. Sarkar had not come to see the Master for a long time, and Dr. Datta also was not coming on a regular basis. The attendants and devotees were very concerned.

After supper when everyone went to bed, M. walked alone in the garden house.

M. spent two nights with the Master; at the same time, his wife stayed with Holy Mother. On the morning of 25 May M. and his wife left for home.

*   *   *

M.'s diary was silent from 25 May to 14 August 1886. During this period he must have visited Puri, as in January Ramakrishna had asked him to go there. But M. did not leave Calcutta until May because the Master's condition was serious. M. later recalled his visit to Puri:

Many times the Master told us, "I am Lord Jagannath of Puri." He sent me to Puri and advised me to embrace Jagannath. According to the tradition, one is allowed to embrace Jagannath twice a year — during snan-yatra and before the chariot festival. I arrived there at the wrong time. I was in a dilemma, because pilgrims were not supposed to embrace the Lord on the altar at that time. But when I was inside the temple, the Master inspired me with an idea. I had some coins and other money in my pocket, which I intentionally dropped on the floor of the dark inner sanctuary of the temple. The priests rushed to pick up that money, and in the meantime I jumped onto the altar and embraced Lord Jagannath. Someone saw me and shouted, but I immediately got down and began to circumambulate the Lord. In the dark nobody recognized me.

The Master asked me to embrace Lord Jagannath and gave me the idea of how to do it, and then he made it easy for me by arousing greed in the minds of the priests. Now I wonder how I did that heroic deed! The Master never went to Puri. He said, "My body will not last if I visit Puri."

When I returned from Puri the Master embraced me and said, "Now I have satisfied my desire to embrace Jagannath."[43]

Ramakrishna sang his swan song. He was nearing the ocean of Satchidananda. The end was rapidly approaching. His feeble body was almost daily consumed in the fire of ecstasy and worn out by the constant gift of himself to his disciples. Till the last moment, Ramakrishna gave the final shape to his future Order in Cossipore. He made Narendra the leader of his young disciples and asked him to look after them. During this period, some significant events took place which are not in M.'s diary.

7 or 8 August 1886: Eight or nine days before his passing away, Ramakrishna asked Jogin to read to him from the Bengali almanac the dates from twenty-fifth Shravan (9 August) onwards. Jogin read the events of each day and the positions of the stars until he came to the last day of the Bengali month (16 August), which was Shravan Sankranti, the full moon day. The Master then told him to stop and to put the almanac back in its proper place.[44] Thus Ramakrishna selected the date of his departure from this world.

12 or 13 August 1886: Narendra recalled: "Three or four days before leaving the body, the Master called me alone to his bedside. He asked me to sit before him. Then he looked steadfastly at me and went into samadhi. At that time I really felt that a subtle force, resembling an electric current, was entering my body. I gradually lost outer consciousness. I don't remember how long I was in that condition. When I regained knowledge of the physical world, I found the Master weeping. On questioning him, he answered me affectionately: 'Today I have given you everything I possess — now I am no more than a fakir, a beggar. By the power I have transmitted to you, you will do immense good in the world, and not until it is accomplished will you return.' I feel that power is constantly directing me to this or that work."[45]

*　　　　　*　　　　　*

Saturday, 14 August 1886: Narendra recalled: "It was two days before the Master passed away. His body was about to fall off forever. Sitting at his bedside [probably very early in the morning] I was thinking: 'The Master has said many times that he is an Incarnation of God. If he now says in the midst of the throes of death, in this terrible anguish and physical pain, "I am God Incarnate," then I will believe.' Immediately he looked up towards me and said: 'He who in the past was born as Rama and Krishna is now living in this very body as Ramakrishna.' At this I was dumbfounded."[46]

In the morning Balaram, Ramlal, and an ayurvedic doctor were present in the Master's room. He went into deep samadhi in front of them. After returning to a normal state he said to Balaram: "Do you know what I see? It is Brahman. It looks like a calm ocean of light, like a roof of molten sterling silver."

At noon Rakhal Mukherjee of Baghbazar arrived. The Master went into samadhi again, and then he said, "I see a lake of mercury and I am there as a lead doll."

Latu told this story: In the early afternoon, there was a big noise of thunderbolt. Alarmed, Holy Mother and Lakshmi rushed to the Master's room. When the Master saw Lakshmi's frightened face, he said, "I don't like to see a gloomy face."

Sunday, 15 August 1886: Shashi left an account of the Master's last day, as follows: "The Master had been telling us for some time that the vessel floating in the ocean was already two-thirds full of water, and soon the rest would fill up and it would plunge into the ocean. [He said:] 'Within me are two persons: One is the Divine Mother, and the other is Her devotee. It is the devotee that has been taken ill.' I remember every incident of that last day. Our Master seemed very well and cheerful. For supper he drank a half glass of *payasam* [pudding]."[47]

Lakshmi recalled: "He was reclining against a pillow on his bed. There was silence all around, and all were worried about him. Earlier he could not speak, but when Mother and I went to him, he feebly whispered: 'You have come. You see, I feel I am going somewhere, to a distant land through water.' Mother started to cry. Then the Master said to her: 'Don't worry. You will live as you are living now. As Naren and the others are serving me, so they will also take care of you. Look after Lakshmi and keep her with you. She will manage herself and will not be a burden.'"[48]

At 9:00 p.m. the Master heaved a sigh and went into samadhi. Shashi sent Akshay and Hutko Gopal to give the alarming news to Ram Chandra and Girish. Narendra asked everybody to loudly chant "Hari Om Tat Sat."

At 11:00 p.m. the Master regained normal consciousness. M. entered the room and found the attendants trying to make him sit up so he could eat. The Master said, "If I sit, I may get dizzy." M. suggested putting some water on his head and fanning him." "What?" the Master asked. Senior Gopal said, "M. has come." The Master did not respond. Shashi supported the Master's back with some pillows and made him sit. Some disciples fanned him with palm leaf fans. M. began to gently stroke the Master's feet. Someone soaked a piece of cotton and dripped water in the Master's mouth. He said that he was hungry. He then drank two glasses of rice gruel and said: "I am satisfied. I have no more disease." Narendra was massaging the Master's feet. The Master repeatedly said to him: "Take care of these boys." Narendra asked him to lie down and sleep.

Monday, 16 August 1886: "Suddenly at one o'clock [*in the morning*] his head fell towards one side of the pillow," Shashi recalled. "There was a low sound in his throat, and I saw all the hairs of his body stand on end. Narendra quickly laid the Master's feet on a quilt and then ran downstairs as if he could not bear it. A doctor, who was a great devotee, was taking the Master's pulse. When he found that it had stopped, he began to weep aloud."[49] Alarmed, Shashi sent Jogin downstairs with news of the Master's critical condition. Immediately M. and others rushed to the Master's room. M. recorded: "Paramahamsadev was lying on his left — lower jaw moving — inarticulate sound — his body was still and covered with goose bumps."

When Holy Mother heard the cry upstairs, she could not restrain herself. She rushed to the Master's room and cried out, "O Mother Kali, what have I done that you have left me?"[50] Baburam, Jogin, and Golap-ma tried to console her and then took her to her room. Afterwards she remained silent.

The disciples believed that Ramakrishna was merely in samadhi. Narendra came back into the Master's room and they sat down, some twenty of them, and began chanting: "Hari Om! Hari Om!" Their belief that the Master was in samadhi was dispelled by Dr. Sarkar who arrived at 1:00 p.m. that afternoon. Before the Master's body was taken to the Cossipore cremation ground, two group photographs were taken at the suggestion of Dr. Sarkar, who contributed 10 rupees. M. appears in both pictures.

TOP AND BOTTOM: Two photographs taken on 16 August 1886 at Cossipore garden house before Ramakrishna's body was cremated. M. is marked by an X. The photos have been digitally altered to obscure Ramakrishna's emaciated body with flowers because some devotees consider the sight painful.

—12—
(M.)

After Ramakrishna's Passing Away

R amakrishna passed away on 16 August 1886 at 1:02 a.m. M. was present at the time. The news spread all over Calcutta and the Master's devotees and many Brahmos came to Cossipore. Dr. Mahendralal Sarkar wrote in his diary: "He [Ramakrishna] was lying on the left side with legs drawn up, eyes open, mouth partly open. His disciples, some at least, were under the impression that he was in samadhi, not dead. I dispelled this impression. I asked them to have his photograph taken and gave them Rs. 10/- as my contribution."[1]

At five o'clock in the afternoon the Master's sacred body was carried downstairs and laid on a cot. It was dressed in an ochre cloth and decorated with sandal paste and flowers. Two group pictures were taken of the Master's body with the devotees standing behind. An hour later, the Master's body was carried to the Cossipore cremation ground to the accompaniment of devotional music. A few hundred people joined the procession, shouting, "Victory to Bhagavan Ramakrishna." When the body was placed on the funeral pyre, Shashi began to fan it with a palm-leaf fan. Tears trickled from the eyes of the devotees. The Master was very fond of the singing of Trailokya Nath Sanyal, a Brahmo devotee. Sitting near the funeral pyre, he sang four songs, which were favourites of the Master. Here is one of them:

Thou art my All in All, O Lord! — the Life of my life, the Essence of
    essence;
In the three worlds I have none else but Thee to call my own.
Thou art my peace, my joy, my hope; Thou my support, my wealth, my
    glory;
Thou my wisdom and my strength.
Thou art my home, my place of rest; my dearest friend, my next of kin;
My present and my future, Thou; my heaven and my salvation.
Thou art my scriptures, my commandments; Thou art my ever-gracious
    Guru;
Thou the Spring of my boundless bliss.
Thou art the Way, and Thou the Goal; Thou the Adorable One, O Lord!
Thou art the Mother tender-hearted; Thou the chastising Father;
Thou the Creator and Protector; Thou the Helmsman who dost steer
My craft across the sea of life.[2]

After the body was cremated, the disciples put the sacred relics of
his body into an urn and returned to the Cossipore garden house. M.
returned home from the cremation ground exhausted, grief-stricken, and
broken-hearted. It is hard to imagine the tremendous vacuum that the
loss of his beloved Master caused in M.'s mind.

Swami Prabhananda recorded in his Bengali book *Ananadarup Sri
Ramakrishna* some events that occurred during the first three days after
the Master's passing away. He also described the celebration of 23 August
1886 when a portion of the Master's relics was installed in Ram Chandra
Datta's Kankurgachi Yogodyana. Prabhananda's account is based on M.'s
diary and other sources, and his valuable research puts us all in his debt.

Apart from M.'s diary, we find some detailed information on 16
August 1886 in the reminiscences of Ramakrishna's other disciples, which
they later recounted. Swami Adbhutananda recalled: "Shashi collected
the ashes and bones of the Master and put them in an urn. He placed
the urn on his head and carried it to the garden house, where it was kept
on the Master's bed."[3] Swami Abhedananda recalled: "On that night we
placed the Master's relics on his bed, discussed his pure life, and tried to
relieve our pain of separation from the Master by meditation and japa.
From time to time Narendra consoled us referring to the unconditional
grace of the Master. He said: 'All this will appear like a dream in our lives.
Only its memory will remain with us.' Nonetheless, we felt helpless and
knew not what to do next."[4]

Tuesday, 17 August 1886: Grief is acutely painful when it is fresh.
Time heals grief, no doubt, but the emptiness lingers for a long time. In

the morning M. went to see Ram Chandra, who was planning to install the Master's relics in his garden house retreat, the Kankurgachi Yogodyana. Devendra Majumdar and Surendra Mitra also joined them and they discussed whether cooked food could be offered to the Master in the shrine at Kankurgachi.

In his diary that day, M. wrote: "Acts of the Apostles, He is in them." M. knew the Bible very well. In the forty days between Jesus' resurrection and his ascension to Heaven, Jesus made several appearances to his disciples, described in the Acts of the Apostles. During this period Jesus guided his disciples and finally promised them: "Lo, I am with you always, even unto the end of the world." M. deeply believed that the Master was still with his disciples.

M.'s faith was justified: On the 16th evening after the Master's cremation, Holy Mother started to take off her bangles. Just then the Master appeared and took her hand: "Am I dead, that you are acting like a widow?" he asked. "I have just moved from one room to another."[5]

Swami Vivekananda later said to Sister Nivedita: "Several times in my life I have seen returning spirits; and once — in the week after the death of Ramakrishna Paramahamsa — the form was luminous."[6] Shortly after the Master's passing away, he appeared before Surendra and said: "Oh! What are you doing? My children are wandering in the streets. Look at their sad plight! Make some arrangement for them without delay."[7]

M. and Devendra left Ram's house and stopped at the Kali temple of Shiva Chandra Guha on Brindavan Basu Lane, which was connected with the Master. M. prayed at the temple, and then went to Balaram's house. Girish also came to visit, and released his pent-up sorrow as he shared his memories of Ramakrishna. He remarked: "Now I understand how much suffering the Master had to go through. I knew he was my only God and none else."

After leaving Balaram's house, M. went to the Ganges, took his bath, and then went to Cossipore. The garden house was quiet. Sweet and painful memories arose in M.'s mind. He went upstairs to the Master's room and found the copper urn filled with the Master's remains on his bed and also his picture. M. wrote in his diary: "Samadhi-ghar — the room of the Master's Mahasamadhi." At noon food was offered to the Master and the disciples sang kirtan in his room.

M. and the other disciples went downstairs to the hall, where they shared their reminiscences of the Master. Shashi said to M.: "One day the Master told me: 'Save my pillow and mat. In the future, people will come to see them.'" M. recorded this in his diary, along with the memories that Harish, Tarak, Rakhal, and Amritalal Basu shared that afternoon. Narendra was lying down, covered with a chadar. He told M. that he was not sleeping; he was thinking about the Master.

Jogin recalled that on the 15 August* at 8:00 a.m. the Master had asked him to read from the almanac; he was interested in the lunar day and the position of the stars starting on 25 Shravan (mid-July to mid-August). Jogin had begun reading, but as soon as he read the description of 31 Shravan (16 August), the Master signaled him to stop, and he put the almanac back on the shelf. It was clear that the Master had selected that date for his passing away.

That night the disciples sang kirtan in Ramakrishna's room. Swami Adbhutananda recalled: "At night we offered farina pudding to the Master and sang Ramnam in his room. Then all left for home except Brother Gopal, Brother Tarak, and myself."

Wednesday, 18 August 1886: Several of the Master's disciples assembled in his room at Cossipore. The Master's nephew Ramlal sang some songs recounting Krishna's boyhood days. Kali asked M. to give him five rupees so that he could repay a man from whom he had borrowed money for his return journey from Gaya to Cossipore. M. gave Kali the five rupees. Ishwar Chandra Chakrabarty came to Cossipore to ask his son Shashi to return home, but he refused. At 5:00 p.m. Surendra and Nrityagopal arrived and talked about the Master. Nrityagopal remarked, "Sri Krishna, Chaitanya, and Ramakrishna are the same."

Swami Adbhutananda later recalled that he had gone to Dakshineswar with Holy Mother, Golap-ma, and Lakshmi that day. They returned to Cossipore before evening. He then heard that at noon Shashi, Niranjan, Narendra, Rakhal, and Baburam had come to Cossipore. Ram Chandra arrived in the afternoon. He wanted to close the Cossipore house, and he asked the young disciples to return to their homes. Niranjan and Shashi were shocked by this proposal. They wanted the Master's daily service to continue as usual.

Swami Abhedananda recalled what happened next:

> We asked, "Where shall we place the Master's relics?" Ram Babu answered, "The Master's relics will be buried in my Kankurgachi Yogodyana." He informed us of his decision and then left for home. That night we decided that we should put most of the relics into a casket and secretly take it to Balaram's house. Ram Babu should not know of this at all. When Ram Babu came, we would give him the copper pitcher.

*According to *Sri Ramakrishna Bhakta Malika* by Swami Gambhirananda, Jogin read the almanac to the Master 8 or 9 days before 15 August 1886.

We acted upon our decision. Then Narendra said: "Look, our bodies are the living burial places of the Master. Let us all take a little ashes of the Master's pure body and make ourselves pure." At first Narendra took a little bit of ash from the pitcher and put some in his mouth, saying, "Victory to Ramakrishna!" We followed him one after another and made ourselves blessed.[8]

At 7:30 p.m. Narendra began to sing in the Master's room; he sang thirteen of the Master's favourite songs. Then Nrityagopal and Ramlal shared their memories with the group. According to M.'s diary, the disciples offered lunch and supper to the Master as usual.

Thursday, 19 August 1886: Surendra, Girish, Nrityagopal, and M. met and talked about the Master. Girish was sad that he had not had enough money to pay for the Master's treatment while he was alive. He was now planning to raise 100,000 rupees for a memorial to the Master.

After three days Senior Gopal (later Swami Advaitananda) reported the news of the Master's passing away to the Cossipore Police Station. Here is the entry of the Death Register:

No. 950 Date of entry: 19. 8. 1886
Name and residence of deceased: Ram Kisto Promohongsa; 49 Cossipore Road.
Date of death: 15. 8. 1886; Sex: M; Age: 52 years.
Race or Nationality: Hugli; Caste: Brahmin; Religion: Hindu.
Profession: Preacher; Cause of death: Ulcer in the throat.
By whom reported: Gopal Chandra Ghose, Friend.
Remarks: Cossipore Ghat[9]

Saturday, 21 August 1886: Narendra tried to keep Holy Mother at Cossipore for a few more days, so that she could recover somewhat from her grief. Unfortunately, the householder devotees who were paying the rent and other expenses requested that Holy Mother and the disciples leave immediately. Balaram invited Holy Mother to stay in his Calcutta home. Accordingly she left for Balaram's house by horse carriage in the evening. But the gatekeeper stopped the carriage and demanded the unpaid rent. Narendra was terribly upset and somehow managed to get her released.[10] Then on 30 August Holy Mother left for a pilgrimage to Vrindaban along with M.'s wife, Golap-ma, Lakshmi, Jogin, Latu, and Kali.

Monday, 23 August 1886: The day was Janmashtami, the birthday of Krishna, an auspicious day.

Before Ramakrishna passed away, he had told his attendants that his relics should be installed on the bank of the Ganges. Ram, Haramohan, and another devotee had been searching for a plot of land on both banks of the Ganges, but failed to find anything. Finally, Girish proposed that the Master's relics be installed in Kankurgachi, but some of the disciples objected. Despite this, they realized they had no money to buy land, so they reluctantly agreed and joined the dedication ceremony.

On the evening before Janmashtami, Shashi and Baburam brought the copper pitcher to Balaram's house in Baghbazar. In the morning it was taken to Ram Chandra's house at 13 Simulia Street. The container was smeared with sandal paste and perfume, and decorated with garlands; then the devotees bowed down to it, one after another. At 8:30 a.m. the procession started, with Shashi carrying the pitcher on his head. Narendra and other disciples carried a banner saying "Victory to Sri Ramakrishna." Hundreds of people joined the procession including a group of musicians and actors, who played on drum, cymbals, horn, and harmonium. They sang this song from Girish's *Chaitanya Lila*:

> O Hari, where have you hidden yourself, bewitching my mind?
> I am alone in this world, reveal yourself to me;
> O my beloved, please give me shelter at your feet.
> I was a householder and you made me a mendicant;
> Leaving friends and family, I wander endlessly.
> O Hari, indweller of the heart, where are you?
> My thirsty heart longs only for you.

Finally the procession reached the Kankurgachi Yogodyana. The Master's relics were worshipped according to the Vaishnava tradition and then buried in a concrete chamber. When soil was put on the container holding the ashes, Shashi cried out, "Oh, this is hurting the Master." His passionate outburst brought tears to many eyes in the congregation. The devotees felt that the Master was ever-living and he was with them. Before Ramakrishna passed away, he had told his attendants, "I want to eat pots full of *khichuri*."* Accordingly, Ram Chandra arranged to offer *khichuri* to the Master. Then it was distributed among the devotees and poor people.

So far we have not found any record of this day in M.'s diary.

*   *   *

M. recalled: "As long as one lives with an avatar, one experiences uninterrupted bliss. Nothing but misery and emptiness are left when he departs. I completely forgot the world for five years. I was carried

---

*A food prepared by boiling rice and lentils together with spices.

away by bliss while I lived with the Master. After he left I was tossed between joy and sorrow. There was a mart of joy while we were with the Master — so many feasts, so much singing and dancing. When the Master left his body, I fasted for three days."[11]

"We went through many hardships to visit the Master. And when returning home, we would walk to Baranagore and then go to Shobhabazar by share carriage. If there was no carriage available, we would walk the eight miles to Calcutta."[12]

M. was extremely attached to Dakshineswar, the playground of Ramakrishna. After the Master passed away, M. spent three days every week in Dakshineswar to practise sadhana, while the other four days he lived in Calcutta to be closer to work. "Once I lived in Dakshineswar, renting a room outside the gate of the temple garden," M. recalled. "I lived on flattened rice and sometimes I would cook. After a while I got terrible dysentery and malaria and was forced to return home."[13]

M. at the Baranagore Math

After Ramakrishna's passing away, some of his young disciples had to return to their homes against their wishes, while others had no place to go. They were like orphans. One evening, early in September, while Surendra was meditating in his shrine, Ramakrishna appeared to him and said: "What are you doing here? My boys are roaming about without a place to live. Attend to that before anything else." Immediately Surendra rushed to Narendra's house and said to some of the disciples: "Brothers, where will you go? Let us rent a house. You will live there and make it our Master's shrine; and we householders shall come there for consolation. How can we pass all our days and nights with our wives and children in the world? I used to spend a sum of money for the Master at Cossipore. I shall gladly give it now for your expenses."[1]

Accordingly, a house was rented at Baranagore, near the Ganges, at eleven rupees per month. Surendra paid the rent and provided food and other necessities for the Master's monastic disciples. M. regularly visited the Baranagore monastery and supported the monastic disciples in every possible way. He also used to join them in practising spiritual disciplines, and he was never tired of speaking of their spiritual fervour to others. He would idealize the monk's life of renunciation and purity above all. To him the monks were full-time lovers of God, while the householders were only part-time, because of their worldly obligations. M. regarded Sri Ramakrishna as the embodiment of renunciation and purity and the monks of his Order as those who continued to carry that same lofty banner.

Ramakrishna taught people that one should live in the world, but not let worldliness enter into one. Let the boat be in the water, and not water in the boat; otherwise it will sink. Although M.'s body was in the world, his mind lived with the Master and his disciples. He recalled: "Once [in 1891] I lived at the Baranagore Math for six months. I took my supper at the monastery and lunch at home. I returned to the monastery at 4:00 p.m. and in the morning would go to work. I was the headmaster in three schools and would travel from one to the other by palanquin. When Holy Mother wrote to me about it, I finally returned home."[2]

Mahendra Nath Datta wrote:

In the initial stage of the Baranagore Math M. would visit the monastery every afternoon and stayed the night. In the morning he would return home and then go to school. During this time he took teaching jobs in two schools; he spent the income of his first job for his family and the second one for the monastery. He was a gentle and shy person of few words. He would secretly inquire of the cook and Swami Subodhananda about the needs of the household and supply those things....Some mornings I accompanied M. when he returned to Calcutta. He always stopped in front of the Cossipore garden house and saluted it standing by the street. Then he stopped at Balaram's house and reported the news of the monastery to him. He always loved to listen to others' reminiscences about the Master.

M. then felt that Bhakta, Bhagavata, and Bhagavan — the devotee, the scripture, and God — are one and the same. If you see a devotee, you are seeing God, and whatever they say is God's message, or the Bhagavata. M. realized that the guru and the Chosen Deity are one. Although outwardly he was Mahendra Nath Gupta, inside he was full of Ramakrishna through constant talking, thinking, and meditating on the Master. He put aside his individuality to be identified with the Master, and that was the goal of his life. In fact, his mind was permeated by Ramakrishna.[3]

Section 1

The five volumes of the *Sri Sri Ramakrishna Kathamrita*, recorded by M. (Mahendra Nath Gupta) in Bengali, were not written in chronological order. Moreover, at the end of the first four volumes, M. added some information about the disciples of the Master and the Ramakrishna monastery at Baranagore that was established after Sri Ramakrishna's passing away. A few years ago, some researchers discovered that four of M.'s diary entries (25 August 1886, 2 September 1886, 12 October 1886, and 17 February 1887) had been published in 1904 in the *Navya Bharat* (Jaishtha-Ashar 1311 B.E.), a monthly magazine. Perhaps M. intended to add these entries at the end of the fifth volume of the Kathamrita, but unfortunately that volume was only published posthumously. I have translated this newly-found material from Bengali into English. I must acknowledge that I have used some songs from Swami Nikhilananda's translation in *The Gospel of Sri Ramakrishna*, which I have referred to in the endnotes. In this precious historical record we learn that the Ramakrishna Math at Baranagore was inaugurated sometime before 12 October 1886.

Wednesday, 25 August 1886

It has been ten days since Sri Ramakrishna went to his own abode, leaving his devotees behind. Filled with renunciation, Narendra and his brother disciples have been practising sadhana.

Narendra and the Master's devotees have assembled in the parlour of Balaram Basu's house in Calcutta. They are like motherless orphans. By merely looking at them, one can feel their intense grief as a result of the Master's passing away. One thought fills their minds: The Master has gone to his own abode; what should we do now? The devotees have no place where these young disciples can stay together, so they are forced to return home for food and shelter every day. The thread holding the pearls together, as in a necklace, has broken, and the group is about to fall apart. The disciples continually think: Where shall we go? What shall we do? Sitting in seclusion, they think of the Master and cry for him.

Narendra, Rakhal, Kali, Sharat, Shashi, Tarak, Gopal, Bhavanath, and M. arrived first, and later Niranjan came.

Everyone looks to Narendra. He is planning to send some of his brother disciples to Vrindaban, so he has been collecting some money from the devotees.

Sri Ramakrishna's Advice: Renounce Lust and Gold

Narendra leaves for Girish's house nearby, accompanied by some of his brother disciples. He and M. talk on the way.

Narendra (*to M.*): "Sir, please pay for a one-way fare for Baburam."

M.: "Certainly. I will pay for it."

Narendra: "Right now, if you would, please."

M.: "Right now?"

Baburam is one of those who has been chosen to go to Vrindaban. The group of devotees arrives at Girish's parlour. Narendra asks Girish for some money also.

Girish: "I don't have much money with me at present, but if you want I can contribute ten or eleven rupees right now. Why are they going to Vrindaban?"

Narendra (*gravely*): "The Master told us to renounce lust and gold."

A Devotee: "Are you also going away?"

Narendra: "Let us all renounce our homes first. I have some business at home now. The litigation has not yet been settled. (*After some thought:*) Let the litigation take its own course. I haven't understood the truth. Getting involved in this family affair is useless."

Rakhal: "If I stay here, I shall feel pulled back by my family."

Narendra's father had passed away, and he has two younger brothers and sisters. They have no other guardian and no other means of support. Narendra has passed his B.A. examination, and if he so wishes, he can get a job to maintain his family. Rakhal has his father, wife, and child at home.

The topic of the Kankurgachi garden house [where Ramakrishna's relics were installed] comes up, and they discuss how the trustees should be appointed.

Rakhal: "We will be pleased if they make Narendra a trustee."

Narendra: "No, no. What good is there in being a trustee?"

When everyone asks Narendra to be a trustee, he tells Girish: "All right. Let it be so." But Narendra is not appointed.

The Devotees are Grief-stricken because of the Master's Passing Away

In Girish's room Mani* and a devotee begin to talk. The devotee heaves a sigh and says: "I shall not pray to the Master for anything."

Mani: "Not for anything?"

Devotee: "No, I will not pray for anything — neither for devotion nor for my family."

Having thus spoken, the devotee again sighs deeply.

Devotee: "One day the Master said: 'Why have you given me so much milk? The devotees have their families; how can they afford to pay for it?' How painful! I will never forget it."

While the Master was suffering from cancer at the Cossipore garden house, the householder devotees had borne all the expenses for the Master's service. The Master was always watchful, so that they might not spend too much money.

Devotee: "I wanted to engage a full-time doctor to treat the Master, but I couldn't do it."

The devotee remains silent for a while and then says: "Well, do you think that I would try to improve the condition of my family by chanting

*"M." and "Mani" are pseudonyms for Mahendra Nath Gupta, the recorder of *The Gospel of Sri Ramakrishna.*

the Master's name? What do I care whether people call me good or virtuous?"

Thursday, 2 September 1886

Shashi has come to M.'s house on Guruprasad Chaudhury Lane in Calcutta. He and M. are seated on a wooden cot in the study. Shashi and Sharat live in their family home in Pataldanga. Today Shashi is wearing clean clothes and carrying a new umbrella. Shashi and M. begin to talk about the Master.

M.: "The Master told me that Narendra was the main disciple among the group."

Shashi: "I vividly remember, the Master said that Narendra would be our leader."

M.: "Do you remember what the Master said about further study?"

Shashi (*with a smile*): "Yes, I distinctly remember that the Master told Narendra one day, 'Don't allow them [the young disciples] to study in school anymore.'"

M.: "What about Kali?"

Shashi: "Yes, the Master scolded Kali and said to him, 'You have introduced studies here.' I had begun to study the Persian language, and as a result I got a scolding from him."

Then Sharat and Narendra arrived, and they all began discussing when Sri Ramakrishna's message would be preached and who would preach it first.

M.: "Who has understood the Master? Do you remember what the Master said about Vaishnavcharan's writing?"

Sharat: "Yes, I remember. The Master said: 'Vaishnavcharan understood every one of my spiritual experiences. I thought that he would be the first to make them public.'"

Narendra: "The Master told me, 'The knowledge of Brahman is the goal. Vaishnavcharan was supposed to spread the message first, but it didn't work out. Keshab Sen was the first to make the message public.'"

12 October 1886
Sri Ramakrishna's First Monastery at Baranagore

Nearly two months had passed since the Master left this world, after binding his devotees with a cord of love. Where would they go now? They could no longer enjoy staying at their homes. They wanted to be together always and to spend their days and nights thinking of him and talking about him. Two or three of the disciples had no home. At this

TOP: Baranagore Math
BOTTOM: Standing, left to right: Shivananda, Ramakrishnananda, Vivekananda, cook, Deven Majumdar, M., Trigunatitananda, Haripada Mustafi. Sitting, left to right: Niranjanananda, Saradananda, Hutko Gopal, and Abhedananda

juncture Surendra came forward and told them: "Brothers, you have no place to live, and we [householders] have no place to give rest to our hearts. Let us rent a house in Baranagore, where you will live, and we shall visit from time to time."

Surendra used to pay fifty [actually 80] rupees every month for the Master's service at the Cossipore garden house. He now said: "Brothers, I used to contribute a little money for the Master's service. I shall provide that amount to pay the expenses of this house in Baranagore."

Gradually, Narendra and the Master's other unmarried disciples moved to the Baranagore monastery, and they did not return to their homes. The number of monastic brothers increased over time, and eventually Surendra was donating one hundred rupees per month.

Blessed Surendra! It is you who have laid the foundation of this first monastery. This Ashrama owes its existence to your good wishes! Through you the Master has made it possible for his disciples to live in the world as the embodiment of his central teaching — the renunciation of "woman and gold." Through Narendra and the other young renunciants he has demonstrated the Eternal Hindu Dharma among people. Who can forget the debt owed to you? The brothers lived at the monastery like orphan boys. Sometimes they would not have the money to pay their rent; sometimes they would have no food. They would wait for you to come and settle all these difficulties. Who would not shed tears on remembering your selfless love!

Narendra and Jnana Yoga

Baranagore Math. On this moonlit night Narendra and Mani are walking on the eastern veranda of the Master's shrine. It is the night of the full moon, when the goddess Lakshmi is worshipped.* Narendra and Mani converse about the Master and also about jnana yoga and bhakti yoga.

Mani: "The Master described two paths — knowledge and devotion — and said that both lead to the same goal. The followers of jnana and the followers of bhakti reach the same place."

Narendra: "But the Master told me: 'The Knowledge of Brahman is the goal. Devotion is meant to maintain the external aspect of life. The elephant has outer tusks and inner grinders as well. The tusks are mere ornaments; but the elephant chews its food with the grinders.'"

Mani: "The Master also said that one can attain the Knowledge of Brahman through the path of devotion. The Knowledge of Brahman can

*12 October 1886

be attained through the path of knowledge as well as through the path of devotion. Perhaps you remember that the Master also said: 'After attaining the Knowledge of Brahman, some embrace devotion and live in this world. One can then ascend from the *lila* (Relative plane) to the *nitya* (Absolute plane) and descend from the nitya to the lila.'"

Narendra: "Were you present that day when the Master talked about the Knowledge of Brahman at the Cossipore garden house?"

Mani: "I was not present at that time; but I heard that he talked about it for a long time. Do you remember what he said about Shukadeva?"

Narendra: "No, I don't remember."

Mani: "I have heard that the Master said on that day: 'Shukadeva and sages like him may have been big ants; but even they could carry at the utmost a few grains of sugar. Shiva touched the water of the Ocean of Brahman-Consciousness, or at most drank a handful of that water.' Did you hear such things?"

Narendra: "Yes, the Master said many such things on that day."

Narendra's Vision and Abnegation of Ego

Mani and Narendra begin a discussion about the brothers of the monastery.

Mani: "Now everything depends on you. You will have to look after them."

Narendra: "The ego is very troublesome. The other day I scolded H. a little scornfully. Immediately I had a vision of the Master. Do you know what he told me? He said: 'What are you thinking? Know for certain that I can make any one amongst you who is the smallest, the greatest, and again I can make any one amongst you who is the greatest, the smallest.'* I have been extremely careful since I had that vision. 'The least shall be the greatest and the greatest, the least.'"

Mani: "You are right. One attains God by His grace only. He can make a person great, and also small. Can anyone attain Him by one's own efforts? One needs His grace."

Narendra's Longing for God-vision

Narendra enters the room. It seems that his hope for God-realization has weakened a little. He begins to sing:

Can everyone have the vision of Shyama? Is Kali's treasure for everyone?

---

*Compare: "I teach the Knowledge of Brahman to the gods and human beings. I am endowed with the Knowledge of Brahman. I make a person great if I want to. I can make a person Brahma, a rishi, or a knower of Brahman." — Devi-sukta, 5.

Oh, what a pity my foolish mind will not see what is true!
Even with all His penances, rarely does Shiva Himself behold
The mind-bewitching sight of Mother Shyama's crimson feet.
To him who meditates on Her the riches of heaven are poor indeed;
If Shyama casts Her glance on him, he swims in Eternal Bliss.
The Prince of yogis, the King of the gods, meditate on Her feet in vain;
Yet worthless Kamalakanta yearns for the Mother's blessed feet![4]

Narendra goes to another room in the monastery. What is he thinking? Has Sri Ramakrishna's loving form suddenly come alive in his heart?
He again begins to sing:

Dear friend, my religion and piety have come to an end:
No more can I worship Mother Shyama; my mind defies control.
Oh, shame upon me! Bitter shame!
I try to meditate on the Mother with sword in hand,
Wearing Her garland of human heads;
But it is always the Dark One,* wearing His garland of wild wood-
    flowers
And holding the flute to His tempting lips,
That shines before my eyes.
I think of the Mother with Her three eyes, but alas! I see
Him alone with the arching eyes, and I forget all else!
Oh, shame upon me! Bitter shame!
I try to offer fragrant flowers at the Mother's feet,
But the ravishing thought of His graceful form unsettles my helpless
    mind,
And all my meditations meant for the Naked One** are drawn away
By the sight of His yellow scarf.[5]

After singing this song, Narendra remains silent for a while and
then suddenly announces, "Let us go to the cremation ground." He then
remarks: "My goodness! It seems to be a parlour and not a cremation
ground." (*All laugh.*)
    Paramanik Ghat is near the monastery, and the cremation ground is
near that ghat. The cremation ground is surrounded by walls, and there
is one brick building with three rooms at the east end. Sometimes at night
Narendra and others go there alone to practise sadhana.

*   *   *

    The Holy Mother now lives in Vrindaban. Narendra and M. are talk-
ing about her. One day at the Cossipore garden house, the young devotees

*Krishna.
**Shyama.

told Sri Ramakrishna about the Holy Mother's affection for them. At that time she was living at the garden house to serve the Master. The disciples told the Master that they had never met another woman as large-hearted as she was.

M.: "What did the Master say?"

Narendra: "The Master began to laugh and then said: 'She is my Shakti [Power]. So she loves all.'"

Friday, 17 February 1887

It is 12:30 p.m. at the Baranagore monastery. Narendra and the other monastic brothers are living at the monastery. Haramohan and M. have arrived. Shashi is busy with the Master's worship service. Narendra is about to go to the Ganges for his bath.

Narendra: "Krishna mainly discussed japa and austerity in the Gita."

M.: "How is that? Then why did he give so much advice to Arjuna?"

Narendra: "Krishna did not ask Arjuna to perform family duties."

M.: "When Krishna asked Arjuna to fight, Arjuna was a householder. He, therefore, was advising Arjuna to perform his family duties in a detached way."

[Narendra later changed his opinion about this. While in America he lectured on karma yoga, and there he advised his students to perform action without attachment. When Narendra first took the vows of sannyasa, he was extremely disgusted with the duties of the world, so he said that japa and austerity were the main focus of the Gita.]

A householder devotee is talking with a monastic brother; his intention is to stay at the monastery. The devotee is impressed with the spiritual atmosphere of the monastery, and family life has become distasteful to him. They are talking on the southern veranda of the kitchen, where Niranjan is working.

The Devotee: "If I stay in the monastery, will I be blamed for neglecting my family?"

The Monk: "No one will blame you for living here, but you have a responsibility to look after your family."

Niranjan (*from the kitchen*): "Hello brother, what are you doing? What kind of advice are you giving to him?" (*All laugh.*)

Narendra and Kali have returned from their bath in the Ganges. Kali is always engaged in studying Vedanta. He does not care for the attitude: "You are my Lord and I am Your devotee." He reflects continually: "I am that Brahman. I have no name and form." So after returning from his bath, he goes to his room and starts repeating: "I am beyond name and form. I am that Absolute Being. I salute You, I salute You, I salute You and Myself."

The devotees sit down to have lunch. There is only one cook at the monastery. After lunch everyone clears away his own leaf-plate; but Narendra removes M.'s leaf-plate. When M. objects, Narendra replies, "Here all are equal."

After lunch everyone assembles in the parlour. Some are chewing betel-rolls; some are smoking hubble-bubbles.

Rakhal (*to M.*): "I want to visit you someday. I am eager to hear what you are writing about the Master."

M.: "I have decided that until my life is transformed I will not share those teachings with anybody. Each of the Master's words is like a mantra. Is it not good to translate those teachings into one's life?"

Rakhal: "Yes, indeed. Well, how do you like your family life?"

Shashi: "Look, brothers, Rakhal is lecturing."

Rakhal (*smiling, to M.*): "Previously I was not inclined to come here. Now I see that the company of the brothers is beneficial."

Narendra: "Where is the real substance in human beings? I care for no one, except one. [*Perhaps he meant Sri Ramakrishna.*] Who has his own power? Everyone is subject to circumstances — a slave to maya. Everyone is a slave like me — a sport of circumstances."

Rakhal smiles and whispers to Haramohan. Prompted by Rakhal, Haramohan asks: "What about Brother X?"

Narendra: "Brother X is a wretched fellow. If he wants to be a monk, why is he saving money? A sadhu should be penniless."

A Monk: "Everyone is wretched, and you consider yourself great."

Narendra: "I am also wretched because I am a slave of circumstances. Do I have any power?"

M. (*to himself*): "Is it circumstances or God? The Master used to say, 'Everything happens by the will of Rama.'"

Narendra: "How can a man who has money be a monk? Moreover, he gives lectures to people. Is he not ashamed to preach?"

Narendra and Buddha

Haramohan: "Well, if a man experiences ecstasy or samadhi, he must be great."

Narendra: "Go and study Buddha. According to Shankara the ultimate spiritual experience is nirvikalpa samadhi, which is the first stage that Buddha attained."

A Devotee: "If nirvikalpa samadhi is the first stage, then there must be higher stages than that. Why don't you describe a few to us? Buddha must have said something about it."

Narendra: "I don't know."

A Devotee: "If nirvikalpa samadhi is the first stage of Buddha's experience, then why did he later preach this doctrine: 'Nonviolence is the supreme dharma?'"

Narendra: "It is hard to understand this view, but the Vaishnavas learned their nonviolence from Buddha."

A Devotee: "Is it necessary for one to learn nonviolence from Buddha? It often happens that one gives up eating fish without having any instruction from anybody. It may not be true that the Vaishnavas learned nonviolence from Buddha."

Narendra: "If someone renounces the killing of animals without being asked to, then it is to be understood as hereditary transmission."

A Devotee: "Then what about the people in Europe who have given up killing animals? They were beef-eaters. They have not learned this from Buddha."

Narendra: "However, Buddha discovered this path."

M. (*to himself*): "Wonderful! Each disciple of the Master is a hero. Everyone is an independent thinker, not just Narendra. And why not? They are disciples of the Master and he trained them himself."

Narendra is reading the Gita and explaining it to the brother disciples. He has been elucidating the following verses from the Gita (5:7-9): "He who is devoted to yoga and is pure in mind, who has conquered his body and subdued his senses, who has realized his Self as the Self of all beings — he is undefiled though he acts. 'I do nothing at all,' thinks the yogi, the knower of Truth; for in seeing, hearing, touching, smelling, and tasting; in walking, breathing, and sleeping; in speaking, emitting, and seizing; in opening and closing the eyes, he is assured that it is only the senses busied with their objects."

After reading the Gita for a while, Narendra says: "I am leaving. Now you have the joyful company of M." But Narendra cannot go.

Baburam: "I don't understand the Gita and other scriptures. The Master said the right thing, 'Renounce, renounce.'"

Shashi: "Do you know what the real import of the word 'renounce' is? It means to remain in this world as an instrument in the hands of God."

Prasanna begins to study the Gita in Kali's private room; Sharat is also there reading Lewis' *History of Philosophy*. Another monk is meditating in the Master's shrine.

Narendra and the Vision of God

The discussion turns to the vision of God.

Narendra: "The vision of God is a kind of false perception."

Rakhal: "What do you mean? You have experienced it."

Narendra (*with a smile*): "One gets such a vision because of a derangement of the brain, like a hallucination."

Mani: "Brother, whatever you may say, the Master had visions of divine forms; so how can you say that it is a derangement of the brain? Do you remember when Shivanath remarked that the Master's samadhi was a kind of nervous disorder or mental illness, and the Master replied, 'Does anyone become unconscious thinking of Consciousness?'"

Narendra and the other brothers have assembled in the parlour. Some are chewing betel-rolls, some are smoking hubble-bubbles. It is spring, and nature seems to be pulsating with joy. The monastic brothers are also joyful. They practise celibacy and renunciation and think of God day and night. Always before them is their great ideal, their guru, Sri Ramakrishna. Sometimes out of exuberant joy, they shout the great saying of the Sikhs: "*Wah guruji ki fate!*" — Victory to the guru! Narendra taught them this mantra, prefacing it with "Om."

M. asks Sharat to join him in repeating "Victory to the guru," one hundred times, which makes him happy.

Narendra: "It does not work to just give an order. One should first start repeating the mantra, and then others will join in."

Balaram has sent some sweets and other things from his Calcutta residence. The kachuris (fried bread with a spicy filling) are delicious. All of the brothers enjoy the refreshments. One brother tries to eat more than his share.

Narendra (*to the brother*): "You greedy rascal! It is not good to eat too much."

Vesper Service in the Monastery

It is evening. Shashi burns incense in the shrine and bows down to the Master, glorifying his sweet name. Then he goes to the pictures of the gods and goddesses in each of the rooms, addressing them one after another and waving incense in front of each of them. He chants in his melodious voice: "Salutations to the guru"; "Salutations to Mother Kali"; "Salutations to Chaitanya taking the form of Rama and Krishna"; "Salutations to Radha and Krishna"; "Salutations to the beloved of Radha"; "Salutations to Advaita Acharya and other devotees"; "Salutations to

214 Mahendra Nath Gupta (M.)

Gopala and Mother Yashoda"; "Salutations to Rama and Lakshmana"; "Salutations to Vishwamitra."

The Senior Gopal performs the vesper service by waving the light, conch, cloth, flower, and fan, and the devotees watch him. Narendra and M. are in the main hall. M. had asked Narendra to join the vesper service, but due to some work he could not do so.

After the vesper service, the devotees sing a hymn to Shiva in chorus: "Jaya Shiva Omkara, Bhaja Shiva Omkara; Brahma Vishnu Sadashiva, Hara Hara Hara Mahadeva."

As night falls, everyone sits for a light supper, which Baburam serves. Each person is served a few chapatis, some vegetable curry, and a little bit of molasses. M. is eating with them, sitting next to Narendra. When Narendra sees a couple of burnt chapatis on M.'s plate, he immediately replaces them with good ones. Narendra keeps a vigilant eye on everything.

After supper everyone sits together in the parlour. A monastic brother tells M.: "Nowadays we hardly get to hear any songs on the Divine Mother. Why don't you sing that favourite song of the Master?"

M. sings:

O Mother Shyama, full of the waves of drunkenness divine!
Who knows how Thou dost sport in the world?
Thy fun and frolic and Thy glances put to shame the god of love.
O Wielder of the sword! O Thou of terrifying face!
The earth itself is shaken under Thy leaps and strides!
O Thou Abode of the three gunas! O Redeemer! Fearsome One!
Thou who art the Consort of Shiva!
Many the forms Thou dost assume, fulfilling Thy bhaktas' prayers.
Thou dancest in the Lotus of the Heart,
O Mother, Eternal Consort of Brahman![6]

While talking with M., Rakhal says: "I want to visit Varanasi. I feel I should go there alone."

Rakhal has his father, wife, and son at home, but he has renounced everyone and everything for God-realization. He is endowed with intense renunciation. His mind is longing for God all the time, so he wants to wander alone.[7]

Section 2

M. published eight entries from his diary in the *Kathamrita* that were translated by Swami Nikhilananda in *The Gospel of Sri Ramakrishna* as "After the Master's Passing Away." As this section is already in the *Gospel* in detail, we shall only relate some important events and conversations of

M. with the disciples of the Master at the Baranagore Math. This section is a valuable historical record regarding the inception of the Ramakrishna Order. M. graphically described how the young monks suffered from lack of food and clothing; how they forgot the world by thinking of their guru; how the Master created renunciation, purity, and longing in their hearts; and the daily routine and activities of the Baranagore Math.

M.'s record runs:

Sri Ramakrishna passed away on Sunday, August 16, 1886, plunging his devotees and disciples into a sea of grief. They were like men in a ship-wreck. But a strong bond of love held them together, and they found assurance and courage in each other's company. They could not enjoy the friendship of worldly people and would talk only of their Master. "Shall we not behold him again?" — this was the one theme of their thought and the one dream of their sleep. Alone, they wept for him; walking in the streets of Calcutta, they were engrossed in the thought of him. The Master had once said to M., "It becomes difficult for me to give up the body, when I realize that after my death you will wander about weeping for me." Some of them thought: "He is no longer in this world. How sur-prising that we still enjoy living! We could give up our bodies if we liked, but still we do not." Time and again Sri Ramakrishna had told them that God reveals Himself to His devotees if they yearn for Him and call on Him with whole-souled devotion. He had assured them that God listens to the prayer of a sincere heart.

The young unmarried disciples of the Master, who belonged to his inner circle, had attended on him day and night at the Cossipore garden house. After his passing away most of them returned to their families against their own wills. They had not yet formally renounced the world. For a short while they kept their family names. But Sri Ramakrishna had made them renounce the world mentally. He himself had initiated several of them into the monastic life, giving them the ochre cloths of sannyasis.

Two or three of the Master's attendants had no place to go. To them the large-hearted Surendra said: "Brothers, where will you go? Let us rent a house. You will live there and make it our Master's shrine; and we householders shall come there for consolation. How can we pass all our days and nights with our wives and children in the world? I used to spend a sum of money for the Master at Cossipore. I shall gladly give it now for your expenses." Accordingly he rented a house for them at Baranagore, in the suburbs of Calcutta, and this place became gradually transformed into a math, or monastery.

For the first few months Surendra contributed thirty rupees a month. As the other members joined the monastery one by one, he doubled his contribution, which he later increased to a hundred rupees. The monthly rent for the house was eleven rupees. The cook received six rupees a month. The rest was spent for food.

The Younger Gopal brought the Master's bed and other articles of daily use from the garden house at Cossipore. The brahmin who had been cook at Cossipore was engaged for the new monastery. The first permanent member was the Elder Gopal. After a short time Narendra, Rakhal, Niranjan, Sharat, Shashi, Baburam, Jogin, Tarak, Kali, and Latu renounced the world for good. Sarada Prasanna and Subodh joined them sometime later. Gangadhar, who was very much attached to Narendra, visited the math regularly. It was he who taught the brothers the hymn sung at the evening service in the Siva temple at Benares. He had gone to Tibet to practise austerity; now, having returned, he lived at the monastery. Hari and Tulasi, at first only visitors at the monastery, soon embraced the monastic life and thus completed the list of the Master's sannyasi disciples.

Surendra was indeed a blessed soul. It was he who laid the foundation of the great Order later associated with Sri Ramakrishna's name. His devotion and sacrifice made it possible for those earnest souls to renounce the world for the realization of God. Through him Sri Ramakrishna made it possible for them to live in the world as embodiments of his teaching, the renunciation of "woman and gold" and the realization of God.

Shashi had taken charge of the daily worship in the math. The Master's relics had been brought from Balaram's house and Sri Ramakrishna was worshipped daily in the worship hall. Narendra supervised the household. He was the leader of the monastery. He would often tell his brother disciples, "The selfless actions enjoined in the *Gita* are worship, japa, meditation, and so on, and not worldly duties." The brothers at the math depended on him for their spiritual inspiration. He said to them, "We must practise sadhana; otherwise we shall not be able to realize God."

He and his brother disciples, filled with an ascetic spirit, devoted themselves day and night to the practice of spiritual disciplines. Their one goal in life was the realization of God. They would practise austerity, sometimes alone under trees, sometimes in a cremation ground, sometimes on the bank of the Ganges. Again, sometimes they would spend the entire day in the meditation room of the monastery in japa and contemplation; sometimes they would gather to sing and dance in a rapture of delight. All of them, and Narendra particularly, were consumed with the desire to see God. Now and then they would say to each other, "Shall we not starve ourselves to death to see God?"[8]

Monday, 21 February 1887

It was the day of Shivaratri, the spring festival of Lord Shiva. M. fasted and attended the service the whole night with the disciples of the Master.

The next morning refreshments were served to everyone. M. looked on at this wonderful mart of happiness. The devotees shouted joyfully, "Jai Gurumaharaj!"[9]

Friday, 25 March 1887

M. came to the Baranagore Math to visit his brother disciples. He intended to spend the night in the monastery. He was very eager to observe the spirit of intense renunciation of these young men. He attended the vesper service and then he had a long conversation with Narendra. Narendra shared some important episodes of the Master with M.

> Narendra: "One day, during one of my early visits, the Master in an ecstatic mood said to me, 'You have come!' 'How amazing!' I said to myself. 'It is as if he had known me a long time.' Then he said to me, 'Do you ever see light?' I replied: 'Yes, sir. Before I fall asleep I feel something like a light revolving near my forehead.'
>
> "When he heard that a proposal had been made about my marriage, he wept, holding the feet of the image of Kali. With tears in his eyes he prayed to the Divine Mother: 'O Mother, please upset the whole thing! Don't let Narendra be drowned.'
>
> "He tamed us by his love. Don't you think so?"
>
> M.: "There is not the slightest doubt about it. His love was utterly unselfish."
>
> Narendra: "One day when I was alone with him he said something to me. Nobody else was present. Please don't repeat it to anyone here."
>
> M.: "No, I shall not. What did he say?"
>
> Narendra: "He said: 'It is not possible for me to exercise occult powers; but I shall do so through you. What do you say?' 'No,' I replied, 'you can't do that.'"[10]

Friday, 8 April 1887

It was Good Friday. M. came to the monastery in the morning and planned to spend the night. He had a desire to renounce the world, but the monks tried to persuade him not to do so. M.'s love for the Master was so intense that he always collected every tidbit of information about him from various sources, especially from the monastic disciples. M. recorded:

> Rakhal warned one of the brothers to be careful about the food to be offered to the Master in the shrine.
>
> Rakhal (*to Sashi and the others*): "One day I ate part of his [meaning the Master's] refreshments before he took them. At this he said: 'I cannot look at you. How could you do such a thing?' I burst into tears."

The Elder Gopal: "One day at Cossipore I breathed hard on his food. At this he said, 'Take that food away.'"

M. and Narendra were pacing the veranda and recalling old times.

Narendra: "I did not believe in anything."

M.: "You mean the forms of God?"

Narendra: "At first I did not accept most of what the Master said. One day he asked me, 'Then why do you come here?' I replied, 'I come here to see you, not to listen to you.'"

M.: "What did he say to that?"

Narendra: "He was very much pleased."[11]

Saturday, 9 April 1887

M. was really a wonderful chronicler, interviewer, and a good listener. He not only recorded his personal accounts with the Master in the *Gospel*, but also others' memoirs. Without him we would miss many eyewitnesses' accounts about the Master. As a hemp-smoker loves the company of another hemp-smoker, so the young disciples loved the company of M., who was a genuine devotee of the Master and a seeker of God.

After lunch, sitting under a tree, Narendra recounted to M. his various experiences with the Master. Every word, every tiny incident about the Master, were gems and jewels to M. He collected them in the pages of his diary and left them for all humanity.

M.: "You must remember vividly your first visit to him."

Narendra: "Yes. It was at the temple garden at Dakshineswar, in his own room. That day I sang two songs."

Narendra sang them for M.:

> Let us go back once more, O mind, to our own abode!
> Here in this foreign land of earth
> Why should we wander aimlessly in stranger's guise?...
>
> *   *   *
>
> O Lord, must all my days pass by so utterly in vain?
> Down the path of hope I gaze with longing, day and night.
> Thou art the Lord of all the worlds, and I but a beggar here;
> How can I ask of Thee to come and dwell within my heart?

M.: "What did he say after listening to your songs?"

Narendra: "He went into samadhi. He said to Ram Babu: 'Who is this boy? How well he sings!' He asked me to come again."

M.: "Where did you see him next?"

Narendra: "At Rajmohan's house. The third visit was at Dakshineswar again. During that visit he went into samadhi and began to praise me as if I were God. He said to me, 'O Narayana, you have assumed this body for my sake.' But please don't tell this to anybody else."

M.: "What else did he say?"

Narendra: "He said: 'You have assumed this body for my sake. I asked the Divine Mother, "Mother, unless I enjoy the company of some genuine devotees completely free from 'woman and gold,' how shall I live on earth?"'"

Narendra: "But you must not tell this to anyone else. At Cossipore he transmitted his power to me."

M.: "Didn't it happen when you used to meditate before a lighted fire under a tree at the Cossipore garden house?"

Narendra: "Yes. One day, while meditating, I asked Kali to hold my hand. Kali said to me, 'When I touched your body I felt something like an electric shock coming to my body.'

"But you must not tell this to anybody here. Give me your promise."

M.: "There is a special purpose in his transmission of power to you. He will accomplish much work through you. One day the Master wrote on a piece of paper, 'Naren will teach people.'"

Narendra: "But I said to him, 'I won't do any such thing.' Thereupon he said, 'Your very bones will do it.'"[12]

Saturday, 7 May to Tuesday, 10 May 1887

It was the full moon day of the month of Vaishakh. Narendra and M. were seated on a couch in M.'s study in Calcutta. They were talking. Just before Narendra's arrival M. had been studying *The Merchant of Venice, Comus,* and *Blackie's Self Culture,* which he taught at school.

Narendra frankly expressed his mind to M.: "I shall fast to death for the realization of God."

M.: "That is good. One can do anything for God."

Narendra: "But suppose I cannot control my hunger."

M.: "Then eat something and begin over again."

Narendra remained silent for a few minutes and then continued: "It seems there is no God. I pray so much, but there is no reply — none whatsoever.

"How many visions I have seen! How many mantras shining in letters of gold! How many visions of the Goddess Kali! How many other divine forms! But still I have no peace.

"Will you kindly give me six pice?"

Narendra asked for the money to pay his carriage fare to the Baranagore Math. Just then Satkari arrived in his own carriage. He was Narendra's friend and lived near the Baranagore Math. Narendra returned the money to M. and said that he would go with Satkari in his carriage. He asked M. to give them some refreshments.

M. accompanied the two friends to the Baranagore Math. M. wanted to see how the brothers spent their time and practised sadhana in the monastery. He wanted to see how Sri Ramakrishna was reflected in the hearts of the disciples. After arriving at Baranagore, M. listened to the conversation of the brothers and then joined the vesper service.

The monks and the devotees stood with folded hands near the door of the shrine and sang in chorus the following hymn to Shiva, to the accompaniment of bells and gong:

> Jaya Shiva Omkara, Bhaja Shiva Omkara,
> Brahma, Vishnu, Sadashiva,
> Hara Hara Hara Mahadeva!

Narendra had introduced this song for the evening worship. It is sung in the temple of Shiva in Varanasi. [Later Narendra composed the vesper hymns of the Ramakrishna Order and introduced them in the monastery.]

M. stayed at Baranagore Math from 8 to 10 May 1887. During this period, he discussed the Yogavashistha Ramayana with the monks, observed their dancing and singing, practised meditation and karma yoga with them, listened to their talks on renunciation and resignation, and felt their overwhelming love and devotion to their guru. M. graphically narrated how the disciples were translating the teachings of their Master into their lives. M. was very much moved by Narendra's fiery renunciation and passion, singing and chanting, and inspiring dialogue, which he recorded in the *Gospel* in detail.

The Master forbade M. to become a monk, so he imbibed the monastic spirit — discrimination and renunciation, discipline and the desire for liberation — while staying with the monastic disciples of the Master in Baranagore. Devotion is contagious. Observing the disciples' devotion for the Master, M. could not sleep. He drew a self-portrait in the following passage:

> It was eleven o'clock at night when their supper was over. The brothers prepared a bed for M., and all went to sleep.
>
> It was midnight. M. was wide awake. He said to himself: "Everything is as it was before. The same Ayodhya — only Rama is not there." M. silently left his bed. It was the full-moon night of Vaishakh, the thrice-blessed day of the Buddhists, associated with Buddha's birth, realization, and passing away. M. was walking alone on the bank of the Ganges, contemplating the Master.[13]

—14—
(M.)

Some Early Drafts of
Sri Ramakrishna Kathamrita

T he first volume of *Sri Ramakrishna Kathamrita* (*The Gospel of Sri Rama-krishna*) came out in 1902, volume 2 in 1904, volume 3 in 1908, volume 4 in 1910, and the final volume in 1932. M. based his historic manuscripts on the diaries that he had kept over his years of association with Ramakrishna.

Swami Vivekananda inaugurated the Ramakrishna Mission at Balaram Basu's house in Calcutta on 1 May 1897. Every Saturday for three years the monastic and householder disciples would meet at Balaram's house to reminisce about their guru or discuss the scriptures. In this gathering M. read from his diaries on two occasions: the 18th meeting on 22 August 1897 and the 21st meeting on 12 September 1897. Excerpts from these talks were recorded in the Minutes Book of the Ramakrishna Mission.

These early drafts of the *Kathamrita* reveal new information about Ramakrishna, although they are not properly arranged or edited. The present author has translated these entries from the original Bengali and also, with the help of Swami Nikhilananda's translation, rearranged them following M.'s style. In some places he has added material based on M.'s published versions to complete the theme or story.

18th Meeting: 22 August 1897

[Swami Brahmananda presided over the meeting and Mahendra Nath Gupta read material concerning Sri Ramakrishna from his diary.]

26 November 1883

It was the day of the annual festival of the Sinduriapatti Brahmo Samaj. The festival took place in Manilal Mallick's house. Many Brahmos were present.

Sri Ramakrishna said: "One should keep one's word. Once Shivanath said to me that he would come to Dakshineswar, but he neither came nor sent me word. That is not good."

Soon the service began according to the rules of the Brahmo Samaj. The minds of the devotees were stilled, and they closed their eyes in meditation. The Master went into deep samadhi. He sat there transfixed and speechless. After some time he opened his eyes, looked around, and suddenly stood up, with the words "Brahma! Brahma!" on his lips.

Vijay Krishna Goswami had just returned from Gaya. He was shaven-headed and wore the ochre robe of a monk.

Master (*to the Brahmos*): "Once Pratap said to me: 'Sir, we follow the example of King Janaka. He led the life of a householder in a detached spirit. We shall follow him.' I said to him: 'Can one be like King Janaka by merely wishing it? How many austerities he practised in order to acquire divine knowledge! He practised the most intense form of asceticism for many years and only then returned to the life of the world.'

"Is there, then, no hope for householders? Certainly there is. The mind is like milk. If you keep the mind in the world, which is like water, then the milk and water will be mixed. That is why people keep milk in a quiet place and let it set into curd, and then churn butter from it. Then that butter can easily be kept in the water of the world. It will not mix with the world.

"One needs to live in solitude. If you ask me how long you should live in solitude away from your family, I should say that it would be good for you if you could spend even one day in such a manner. Three days at a time are still better. One may live in solitude for twelve days, a month, three months, or a year, according to one's convenience and ability. One hasn't much to fear if one leads the life of a householder after attaining knowledge and devotion.

"If you break open a jackfruit after rubbing your hands with oil, then its sticky milk will not smear your hands. You must therefore collect oil.

"A magnet attracts the needle when it comes close. Be turned into gold by touching the philosopher's stone. After that you may remain buried underground a thousand years; when you are taken out you will still be gold.

"To realize God, one first needs steadfast devotion. The ancient sages renounced everything and called on God, considering worldly enjoyments to be like crow droppings.

"Then comes *bhava,* intense love. Through bhava a man becomes speechless. His nerves are stilled. *Kumbhaka* comes by itself. It is like the case of a man whose breath and speech stop when he fires a gun.

"But *prema,* ecstatic love, is an extremely rare thing. Chaitanya had that love. When he saw a forest, he thought it was Vrindaban; he thought the ocean was the river Yamuna. When one has prema one forgets all outer things. One forgets the world. One even forgets one's own body, which one holds so dear."

Master (*to Vijay*): "Vijay, have you found your room?

"Let me tell you a story: Once two holy men, in the course of their wanderings, entered a city. One of them, with wondering eyes and mouth agape, was looking at the marketplace, the stalls, and the buildings, when he met his companion. The latter said: 'You seem to be filled with wonder at the city. Where is your baggage?' The first man replied: 'I found a room, put my things in it, locked the door, and felt totally relieved. Now I am going about the city and enjoying it.'

"So I am asking you, Vijay, if you have found your room. (*To M. and the others*) You see, the spring in Vijay's heart has been covered all these days. Now it is open.

"It is necessary for a monk to give up worldly activities. Pray to God to reduce your worldly duties. Whatever duties are left, try to perform them selflessly. Don't think this way: 'Let my guru get sick and then I will serve him without motive.' There is no need for such motiveless action.

"The Avadhuta had twenty-four gurus, one of whom was a kite. In a certain place the fishermen were catching fish. A kite swooped down and snatched a fish. At the sight of the fish, about a thousand crows chased the kite and made a great noise with their cawing. Whichever way the kite flew with the fish, the crows followed it. The kite flew to the south and the crows followed it there. The kite flew to the north and still the crows followed after it. The kite went east and west, but with the same result. As the kite began to fly about in confusion, lo, the fish dropped from its mouth. The crows at once left the kite alone and flew after the fish. Thus relieved of its worries, the kite sat on the branch of a tree and thought: 'That wretched fish was at the root of all my troubles. I have now gotten rid of it and therefore I am at peace.'

"The Avadhuta accepted a bee as another teacher. Bees accumulate their honey by days of hard labour. But they cannot enjoy their honey, for a man soon breaks the comb and takes it away. The Avadhuta therefore learnt from the bee that one should not lay things up.

"Let me tell you one thing, Vijay: Don't trust a sadhu if he keeps his bags with him and a bundle of clothes with many knots. I have seen such sadhus under the banyan tree in the Panchavati. Two or three of them were once seated there. One was picking over lentils, some were sewing their clothes, some had money tied around their waists, and all were gossiping about a feast they had enjoyed in a wealthy man's house. They said among themselves, 'That rich man spent a hundred thousand rupees on the feast and fed the sadhus sumptuously with cakes, sweets, and many such delicious things.'"

(To Vijay) "Renounce everything." Saying this, the Master sang:

Cherish my precious Mother Shyama
Tenderly within, O mind;
May you and I alone behold Her,
Letting no one else intrude.
O mind, in solitude enjoy Her,
Keeping the passions all outside;
Take but the tongue, that now and again
It may cry out, "O Mother! Mother!"
Suffer no breath of base desire
To enter and approach us there,
But bid true knowledge stand on guard,
Alert and watchful evermore.

The Master said to Vijay: "Surrender yourself completely to God, and set aside all such things as fear and shame. This saying is very true: 'One cannot have the vision of God as long as one has these three — shame, hatred, and fear.' Shame, hatred, fear, caste, pride, secretiveness, and the like are so many bonds. Man is free when he is liberated from all these. When bound, one is a jiva and, when free, one is Shiva."

With a glance at the Brahmo devotees who had just arrived, the Master said: "Mere pandits, devoid of divine love, talk incoherently. Pandit Samadhyayi once said in the course of his sermon: 'God is dry. Make Him sweet by your love and devotion.' Imagine! To describe Him as dry, whom the Vedas declare to be the Essence of Bliss! It makes one feel that the pandit didn't know what God really is. That was why his words were so incoherent.

"A man once said, 'There are many horses in my uncle's cowshed.'

From that one could know that the man's uncle had no horses at all. No one keeps a horse in a cowshed.

"Some people pride themselves on their riches and power — their wealth, honour, and social position. But these are only transitory. Nothing will remain with you in death.

"There is a song that runs:

Remember this, O mind! Nobody is your own:
Vain is your wandering in this world.
Trapped in the subtle snare of maya as you are,
Do not forget the Mother's name.
Only a day or two men honour you on earth
As lord and master; all too soon
That form, so honoured now, must needs be cast away,
When Death, the Master, seizes you.
Even your beloved wife, for whom, while yet you live,
You fret yourself almost to death,
Will not go with you then; she too will say farewell,
And shun your corpse as an evil thing.

"One must not be proud of one's money. If you say that you are rich, then someone can remind you that there are richer men than you, and others richer still, and so on. At dusk the glowworm comes out and thinks that it lights the world. But its pride is crushed when the stars appear in the sky. The stars feel that they give light to the earth. But when the moon rises the stars fade in shame. The moon feels that the world smiles at its light and that it lights the earth. Then the eastern horizon becomes red, and the sun rises. The moon fades and after a while is no longer seen.

"If wealthy people would think that way, they could rid themselves of pride in their riches."[1]

21st Meeting: 12 September 1897

[Swami Brahmananda presided over the meeting and Mahendra Nath Gupta read material concerning Sri Ramakrishna from his diary.]

7 September 1884

It was morning. The Master was reclining on the small cot in his room at Dakshineswar. He asked M.: "Where is Narendra? Isn't he coming?" M. told him that Narendra could not come.

A brahmin devotee from Srirampur was reading to the Master from a book of devotional songs by Ramprasad. Sri Ramakrishna asked him to continue. The brahmin read a song, the first line of which was: "O Mother, put on Thy clothes."

Master: "Stop, please! These ideas are outlandish and bizarre. Read something that will awaken bhakti."

The brahmin read:

> Who is there that can understand what Mother Kali is?
> Even the six darsanas are powerless to reveal Her....

Master (*to M.*): "I got a pain because I lay too long on one side while in samadhi yesterday at Adhar's house; my head was bent and no one was there to hold me. So now I'll take Baburam with me when I visit the houses of the devotees. He is a sympathetic soul."

With these words the Master sang:

> How shall I open my heart, O friend?
> It is forbidden me to speak.
> I am about to die, for lack of a kindred soul
> To understand my misery.

> Simply by looking in his eyes,
> I find the beloved of my heart;
> But rare is such a soul, who swims in ecstatic bliss
> On the high tide of heavenly love.

Master: "The Sain sect of Bauls sings songs like that. They hold the attitude of nonduality. They call the Ultimate Truth 'Alekh,' 'the Incomprehensible One.' The Vedas call It 'Brahman.' About the jivas the Bauls say, 'They come from Alekh and they go unto Alekh.' That is to say, the individual soul has come from the Unmanifest and goes back to the Unmanifest.

Saying this, the Master sang:

> Within the petals of this flower there lies concealed a subtle space,
> Transcending which, one sees at length the universe in Space dissolve.

"One day I was taking my meal when a Baul devotee arrived. He asked me, 'Are you yourself eating, or are you feeding someone else?' The meaning of his words was that the siddha [a perfect soul] sees God dwelling within a man. The siddhas among the Bauls will not talk to persons of another sect; they call them strangers.

"A perfect Baul keeps all his spiritual feelings within himself and doesn't show any outward sign of spirituality, but his heart is full. He doesn't even utter the name of Hari. He is not attached to woman. He has completely mastered his senses.

"The Bauls do not like the worship of an image. They want a living man. That is why one of their sects is called the Kartabhaja. They worship the *karta*, that is to say, the guru, as God.

"You see how many opinions there are about God. Each opinion is a path. There are innumerable opinions and innumerable paths leading to God."

Bhavanath: "Then what should we do?"

Master: "You must stick to one path with all your strength. A man can reach the roof of a house by stone stairs, a ladder, a rope ladder, a rope, or even with a bamboo pole. But he cannot reach the roof if he sets his foot now on one and now on another. He should firmly follow one path. Likewise, in order to realize God a man must follow one path with all his strength.

"But you must regard other views as so many paths leading to God. You should not feel that your path is the only right one and that other paths are wrong. You mustn't bear malice towards others.

"Well, to what path do I belong? Keshab Sen used to say to me: 'You belong to our path. You are gradually accepting the ideal of the formless God.' Shashadhar says that I belong to his path. Vijay, too, says that I belong to his — Vijay's — path. The Kartabhajas say that I belong to their path."

Sri Ramakrishna walked towards the Panchavati with M. and a few other devotees. It was midday and time for the flood tide in the Ganges.

They waited in the Panchavati to see the bore of the tide.

Master (*to the devotees*): "The ebb tide and flood tide are indeed amazing. But notice one thing: Near the sea you see the ebb tide and the flood tide in a river, but far away from the sea the river flows in one direction only. What does this mean? Try to apply its significance to your spiritual life. Those who live very near God feel within them the currents of bhakti, bhava, and the like. In the case of a few — the Ishwarakotis, for instance — one sees even mahabhava and prema."

Presently the tide came up the Ganges. They heard the sound of the rushing water as it struck the bank of the river and flowed northward. Sri Ramakrishna looked at it intently and exclaimed like a child: "Look at that boat! I wonder what will happen to it."

The Master and M. sat down for a while in the Panchavati, Sri Ramakrishna placing his umbrella on the cement platform. The conversation turned to Narayan. The boy was a student. Sri Ramakrishna looked upon him as Narayana, God Himself, and was very fond of him.

Master: "Have you noticed Naran's nature? He can mix with all, old and young. One cannot do this without a special power. Besides, all love him. Is he really artless?"

M.: "I think so."

Master: "I understand that he goes to your place. Is that so?"

M.: "Yes, sir. He has visited me once or twice."

Master: "Will you give him a rupee? Or shall I ask Kali about it?"

M.: "Very well, sir. I shall give him the money."

Master: "That's fine. It is good to help those who yearn for God. Thus one makes good use of one's money. What will you gain by spending everything on your family?"

It was about one o'clock in the afternoon. The Master ate prasad from the Kali temple. Then he wanted to rest awhile, but the devotees were still sitting in his room. They were asked to leave, and then the Master lay down. He said to Baburam, "Come here; sit near me."

Baburam answered, "I am preparing betel leaf."

The Master said: "Put your betel leaf aside. Tell me a story."

Some people were singing kirtan in the Panchavati. The Master joined them but he did not experience a spiritual mood. After returning to his room, he remarked: "Shyamdas began the kirtan. He is Ram's music teacher, but I didn't enjoy his singing very much. I didn't feel like dancing. Later I heard about his character. I was told that he had as many mistresses as there are hairs on a man's head."

Sri Ramakrishna asked Nabai of Konnagar to sing kirtan. Nabai was Manomohan's uncle. He lived on the bank of the Ganges, devoting his time to prayer and meditation, and was a frequent visitor to Sri Ramakrishna .

Nabai began the kirtan in a loud voice. The Master rose from his couch and began to dance. Immediately Nabai and other devotees began to dance around him. The atmosphere became intense with spiritual fervour.

After the kirtan, Sri Ramakrishna resumed his seat. With great feeling he began to sing of the Divine Mother:

Cherish my precious Mother Shyama
Tenderly within, O mind;
May you and I alone behold Her,
Letting no one else intrude....

As the Master sang this song he stood up. He was almost intoxicated with divine love. Again and again he said to the devotees, "Cherish my precious Mother Shyama tenderly within." Then he danced and sang:

Is Kali, my Mother, really black?
The Naked One, of blackest hue,
Lights the Lotus of the Heart....

While in this intoxicated mood, he said, "Let me have a smoke." Many of the devotees stood around. Mahimacharan was fanning him. The Master asked him to sit down and recite from the scriptures. Mahimacharan recited from the Mahanirvana Tantra:

Om. I bow to Thee, the Everlasting Cause of the world;
I bow to Thee, Pure Consciousness, the Soul that sustains the whole universe.
I bow to Thee, who art One without duality, who dost bestow liberation;
I bow to Thee, Brahman, the all-pervading Attributeless Reality.
Thou alone art the Refuge, the only Object of adoration;
Thou art the only Cause of the universe, the Soul of everything that is;
Thou alone art the world's Creator, Thou its Preserver and Destroyer;
Thou art the immutable Supreme Lord, the Absolute; Thou art unchanging Consciousness.
Dread of the dreadful! Terror of the terrible!
Refuge of all beings! Purity of purifiers!
Thou alone dost rule over those in the high places,
Supreme over the supreme, the Protector of protectors.
Almighty Lord, who art made manifest as the Form of all, yet art Thyself unmanifest and indestructible;
Thou who art imperceptible to the senses, yet art the very Truth;
Incomprehensible, imperishable, all-pervading, hidden, and without form;
O Lord! O Light of the Universe! Protect us from harm.
On that One alone we meditate; that One is the sole object of our worship;
To That alone, the nondual Witness of the Universe, we bow.
In that One who alone exists and who is our sole eternal Support, we seek refuge,
The self-dependent Lord, the Vessel of Safety in the ocean of existence.

Sri Ramakrishna listened to the hymn with folded hands. After it was sung he saluted Brahman. The devotees did likewise.

Adhar arrived from Calcutta and bowed down before the Master.

Master (*to M.*): "We have had such joy today! How much joy Hari's name creates! Is it not so?"

M.: "Yes, sir."

The vesper services in the Kali and Krishna temples have ended. Adhar, Niranjan, and M. are in the Master's room.

Master (*to Adhar*): "Didn't you get the job?"

Adhar held the post of deputy magistrate, a government post that carried with it great prestige. He earned three hundred rupees a month. He had applied for the office of vice-chairman of the Calcutta Municipality. The salary attached to this office was one thousand rupees. In order to secure it, Adhar had interviewed with many influential people in Calcutta.

Master (*to M. and Niranjan*): "Hazra said to me, 'Please pray to the Divine Mother for Adhar, that he may secure the job.' Adhar made the same request to me. I said to the Mother: 'O Mother, Adhar has been visiting You. May he get the job if it pleases You.' But at the same time I said to Her: 'How small-minded he is! He is praying to You for things like that and not for Knowledge and Devotion.'

(*To Adhar*) "Why did you dance attendance on all those small-minded people? You have seen so much; you have heard so much! 'After reading the entire Ramayana, to ask whose wife Sita is!' That Mallick is of low mentality. He arranged for an ordinary service boat for my going to Mahesh. And as soon as we went to his house, he asked, 'Hriday, do you have a carriage?'"

Adhar: "A man cannot but do these things if he wants to lead a householder's life. You haven't forbidden us to, have you?"

Master: "Nivritti alone is good, and not pravritti. Once, when I was in a God-intoxicated state, I was asked to go to the manager of the Kali temple to sign the receipt for my salary. They all do it here. But I said to the manager: 'I cannot do that. I am not asking for any salary. You may give it to someone else if you want.' I am the servant of God alone. Whom else shall I serve? If you receive something from a man, his tendencies will enter inside you.

"Jadu Mallick noticed the late hours of my meals and arranged for a cook [Sudhamukhi]. He paid one rupee for the cook's monthly salary. It is embarrassing to receive any money from anyone. I had to run to him whenever he sent for me, because he was paying for the cook. It would have been quite a different thing if I had gone to him of my own accord. I said to the Divine Mother, 'I shed tears after eating the food cooked by Sudhamukhi; and I say never again, never again.' Jadu only paid for one month.

(*To Adhar*) "Be satisfied with the job you have. People hanker after a post paying fifty or a hundred rupees, and you are earning three hundred rupees! You are a deputy magistrate. I saw a deputy magistrate at Kamarpukur. His name was Ishwar Ghoshal. He had a turban on his head.

Men's very bones trembled before him. I remember having seen him during my boyhood. Is a deputy magistrate a person to be trifled with?

"Serve him whom you are already serving. The mind becomes soiled by serving but one master. And to serve five masters!

"Once a woman became attracted to a Mussalman and invited him to her room. But he was a righteous person; he said to her that he wanted to use the toilet and must go home to get his water jar. The woman offered him her own, but he said: 'No, that will not do. I shall use the jar to which I have already exposed myself. I cannot expose myself before a new one.' With these words he went away. That brought the woman to her senses. She understood that a new water jar, in her case, signified a paramour."

Narendra's father had died unexpectedly, and the family was in straitened circumstances. He had been seeking a job to support his mother, brothers, and sisters.

Adhar: "May I ask if Narendra would accept a job?"

Master: "Yes, he would. He has his mother, brothers, and sisters to support."

Adhar: "Well, Narendra can support his family with fifty or with a hundred rupees. Will he try for a hundred?"

Master: "Worldly people think highly of their wealth. They feel that there is nothing like it. Shambhu said, 'It is my desire to leave all my property at the Lotus Feet of God.' I told him: 'But does God care for money? It may be a big thing to you, but to God it is heaps of clay — an insignificant thing.'

"After some jewellery was stolen from the temple of Radhakanta, Mathur Babu said: 'O God, You could not protect Your own jewellery! What a shame!' I told him: 'Look, Lakshmi, the goddess of fortune, is God's maidservant. Those few pieces of jewellery may be valuable to you, but they are mere trash to God.'

"Once Mathur wanted to give me an estate and consulted Hriday about it. I overheard the whole thing from inside the Kali temple and said to him: 'Please don't harbour any such thought. It will injure me greatly.'"

Adhar: "I can tell you truthfully, sir, that not more than six or seven persons like you have been born since the creation of the world."

Master: "How so? There certainly are people who have given up everything for God. Lala Babu renounced everything and then lived on alms. As soon as a man gives up his wealth, people come to know about him. But it is also true that there are others unknown to people. Are there not such holy men in upper India?"

Adhar: "I know of at least one such person in Calcutta. He is Devendra Nath Tagore."

Master: "What did you say? Who has enjoyed the world as much as he?"

Niranjan: "But he paid off all his father's debts."

Master: "Keep quiet! Don't torment me anymore. Do you call anyone a man who doesn't pay off his father's debts if he is able to? But I admit that Devendra Nath is infinitely greater than other worldly men who are sunk in their worldliness. They can learn much from him ."

Adhar: "But Chaitanya, too, enjoyed the world."

Master (*amazed*): "What? What did he enjoy in the world?"

Adhar: "Scholarship! Honour!"

Master: "It was honour in the sight of others, but nothing to him. Surendra once said, rather condescendingly, that Rakhal's father could sue me for letting Rakhal stay with me. When I heard about this from Manomohan, I said: 'Who is this Surendra? How does he dare make a remark like that? He keeps a carpet and pillow here and gives me some money. Is that his excuse for daring to make such an impudent remark?'"

(*To Adhar*): "Listen, there is no scarcity of moths when the lamp is lit. When God is realized, He Himself provides everything for His devotees. He sees that they do not lack anything. When God is enshrined in the heart, many people come forward to offer their services.

"Once a young sannyasi went to a householder to beg for his food. He had lived as a monk from his very birth; he knew nothing of worldly matters. A young daughter of the household came to give him alms. He turned to her mother and asked, 'Mother, has this girl abscesses on her chest?' The mother said: 'No, my child. God has given her breasts to nurse her child when she becomes a mother.' Thereupon the sannyasi said: 'Then why should I worry about myself? Why should I beg for my food? He who has created me will certainly feed me.'

(*To Adhar*): "You are an executive officer. What shall I say to you? Do whatever you think best. I am an illiterate person."

Adhar (*smiling, to the devotees*): "Now he is examining me."

Master (*smiling*): "Dispassion alone is good. Attachment to the world brings all troubles. Reduce your activities as much as you can. Let your primary work be to call on God."

Hazra entered the room and sat with the devotees on the floor. Hazra repeated now and then, "Soham! Soham! — I am He! I am He!"

Master: "What you say is a very lofty thought. The aim of spiritual discipline, of chanting God's name and glories, is to realize just that. A man attains everything when he discovers his true Self in himself. The object of sadhana is to realize that. That also is the purpose of assuming a human body. One needs the clay mould as long as the gold image has not been cast; but when the image is made, the mould is thrown away. The body may be given up after the realization of God.

"God is not only inside us; He is both inside and outside. The Divine Mother showed me in the Kali temple that everything is Chinmaya, the Embodiment of Spirit. It is She who has become all this — the image, myself, the utensils of worship, the doorsill, the marble floor. Everything is indeed Chinmaya .

"The aim of prayer, of spiritual discipline, of chanting the name and glories of God, is to realize just that. For that alone a devotee loves God. These youngsters are on a lower level; they haven't yet reached a high spiritual state. They are following the path of bhakti. Please don't tell them such things as 'I am He.'"

Adhar (*smiling*): "We talked about so many things. (*Pointing to M.*) But he didn't utter a word."

Master: "In Keshab's organization there was a young man with four university degrees. He laughed when he saw people arguing with me. He said: 'To argue with him! How silly!' I saw him again, later on, at one of Keshab's meetings. But then he did not have the same bright complexion."

Sri Ramakrishna sat on the floor for his supper. It was a light meal of farina pudding and one or two luchis that had been offered in the Kali temple. M. and Latu were in the room. The devotees had brought various sweets for the Master. He touched a sandesh and asked Latu, "Who is the rascal who brought this?" He took it out of the cup and put it on the floor. He said to Latu and M.: "I know all about him. He is immoral."

M. had received an English education. Sri Ramakrishna said to him: "It is not possible for me to eat things that anyone and everyone offers to me. Do you believe this?"

M: "Gradually I shall have to believe all these things."

Master: "Yes, that is so."

After finishing his meal Sri Ramakrishna washed his mouth.

The moon rose in the clear autumn sky and was reflected in the river. It was ebb tide in the Ganges and the river flowed south towards the sea.[2]

The Gospel of Sri Ramakrishna: A History

The word *gospel* comes from the Old English *godspel*, which means "good news." This good news uplifts human minds.

The Five Gospels of Ramakrishna

Some of Ramakrishna's teachings have been recorded differently by different writers. Although his teachings are basically the same, the wording and language he used changed over time and according to his audience. In addition, writers recorded stories of Ramakrishna in greater or lesser detail, depending on their point of view. We find the same phenomenon in the Bible: The same teachings of Jesus or stories about him were recorded differently by Matthew, Mark, Luke, and John. The wording in each gospel is different, and some stories have more detail than others. It is quite natural for two people to see and hear the same thing at the same time and yet record different descriptions of the event.

Five writers recorded their versions of the gospel of Ramakrishna. In 1878 Girish Chandra Sen, a disciple of the Brahmo leader Keshab Chandra Sen, published 184 of the Master's teachings in *Adi Kathamrita*. In 1884 Suresh Chandra Datta, a householder devotee of Ramakrishna, recorded 950 teachings and published them in *Sri Sri Ramakrishnadever Upadesh*. In 1885 Ram Chandra Datta, a householder devotee of

Ramakrishna, recorded 300 teachings, which were published in *Tattwa-prakashika*. M. (Mahendra Nath Gupta) preserved the Master's teachings in his diary from 1882 to 1886. The resulting *Sri Sri Ramakrishna Kathamrita* was published in five volumes between 1902 and 1932; it has 177 entries. Swami Brahmananda, a monastic disciple of Ramakrishna, recorded the fifth and last gospel. It was published serially in the *Udbodhan* magazine from 1898 to 1900. In 1905 these teachings were collected in a book entitled, *Sri Sri Ramakrishna Upadesh,* and it includes 248 teachings of the Master.

All of these gospels were written in Bengali, Ramakrishna's mother tongue. The first three have not yet been translated into English in their entirety. In 1942 M.'s five volumes were brought together and published in English as *The Gospel of Sri Ramakrishna*. Swami Nikhilananda, of the Ramakrishna-Vivekananda Centre in New York, translated this huge work, and Aldous Huxley wrote the foreword. In 1924 the gospel according to Swami Brahmananda was translated into English and edited by Jnanendra Nath Mukhopadhyay and F.J. Alexander. It was published as *Words of the Master* by the Udbodhan Publication Office, Calcutta.

The Master's words were so impressive and instructive that Swami Shivananda, as a young disciple, felt tempted to take notes. He recalled: "One day at Dakshineswar I was listening to the Master and looking intently at his face. He was explaining many beautiful things. Noticing my keen interest, the Master suddenly said: 'Look here! Why are you listening so attentively?' I was taken by surprise. He then added: 'You don't have to do that. Your life is different.' I felt as if the Master had divined my intention to keep notes and did not approve of it, and that was why he said that. From that time on I gave up the idea of taking notes of his conversations, and whatever notes I already had I threw into the Ganges."[1]

Ramakrishna advised his young monastic disciples to renounce both externally and internally, while he advised his householder disciples to renounce internally. Many years later Swami Premananda described how the Master taught the monastic disciples: "Very little of the Master's teachings are recorded in the *Gospel*," he said. "M. used to visit the Master occasionally and would note down his teachings as he heard them....His teachings to the monastic disciples were given in private. As soon as the householder devotees would leave the room, he would get up and lock the door and then speak to us living words of renunciation. He would try to impress upon our young minds the emptiness and vanity of worldly enjoyments."[2]

The Origin of *The Gospel of Sri Ramakrishna*

M. based his *Sri Sri Ramakrishna Kathamrita* (*The Gospel of Sri Rama-krishna*) on his diary entries from 26 February 1882 to 10 May 1887. He began to develop his diaries for publication within a couple of years after the Master's passing away, but he did not make all of the entries public. On 11 July 1888 M. read a chapter of the *Kathamrita* to Holy Mother, who was then living in Nilambar Babu's garden house in Belur. After she heard this reading from the manuscript, she praised M. and encouraged him to write more. On 15 March 1890 M. read another chapter to Holy Mother and received her blessing and approval to publish it.

In 1892 a small pamphlet of 20 pages was released under the title *"Paramahamsadever Ukti —* Part 3" by "Satchidananda Gitaratna," and collected by "Sadhu Mahindranath Gupta."[3] Swami Vivekananda read this pamphlet* and wrote to M. from Antpur on 7 February 1889: "Thanks! 100,000 times, Master! You have hit Ramkristo in the right point. Few alas, few understand him!!

"My heart leaps in joy — and it is a wonder that I do not go mad when I find anybody thoroughly launched into the midst of the doctrine which is to show peace on earth hereafter."[4]

M. was busy with family duties, so he could not always concentrate on developing his diaries for publication. On 26 November 1895, Holy Mother wrote to M. from Kamarpukur: "Please preserve those teachings of the Master which he left with you." M. was inspired by her letter to publish "Leaves from the *Gospel* of the Lord Sri Ramakrishna," which came out serially in the English-language *Brahmavadin* magazine starting on 15 October 1897.

Swami Vivekananda read the series and wrote to M. from Rawalpindi in October 1897: "Dear M., *C'est bon mon ami* — Now you are doing just the thing. Come out man. No sleeping all life. Time is flying. Bravo, that is the way.

"Many many thanks for your publication. Only I am afraid it will not pay its way in a pamphlet form....Never mind — pay or no pay. Let it see the blaze of daylight. You will have many blessings on you and many more curses but that is always the way of the world, sir. This is the time."[5]

---

*Sunil Behari Ghosh, a researcher and librarian, presumed that *Paramahamsadever Ukti* — Part 1 was compiled and published by Keshab Chandra Sen in 1878, and Part 2 was collected and published by Girish Chandra Sen in 1887, and Part 3 by M. in 1892. Behind his guess is that none could ever find Parts 1 and 2 made by M. (Adapted from *Sri Ramakrishna O Tar Kathamrita*, 219.)

Swami Vivekananda wrote to M. again on 24 November 1897, this time from Dehra Dun: "My dear M., Many many thanks for your second leaflet, it is indeed wonderful. The move is quite original and never was the life of a great Teacher brought before the public untarnished by the writer's mind as you are doing. The language also is beyond all praise — so fresh, so pointed and withal so plain and easy. I cannot express in adequate terms how I have enjoyed the leaflets. I am really in a transport when I read them. Strange, isn't it? Our teacher and Lord was so original and each one of us will have to be original or nothing. I now understand why none of us attempted his life before. It has been reserved for you — this great work. He is with you evidently.

"P.S. Socratic dialogues are Plato all over. You are entirely hidden. Moreover, the dramatic part is infinitely beautiful. Everybody likes it, here and in the West."[6]

After M. began publishing the Master's teachings in English in a pamphlet form, a critic wrote in *Tattwamanjari* magazine: "We have a request to Mr. Gupta to publish these teachings in a big book form instead of in small pamphlets that will benefit the masses. Again, we wonder, why did he publish it in English instead of Bengali? It is needless to remind him that sometimes the spirit of such deep spiritual truths diminishes while translating them into English. It would be difficult for our people to understand these teachings."[7] M. later acquiesced to the critic's request.

This criticism, however, was nothing compared to the appreciation that M. received from many distinguished reviewers. The English-language pamphlets created a tremendous stir because readers found Ramakrishna's teachings new and exciting. But M. eventually decided to publish *The Gospel of Sri Ramakrishna* in Bengali, so that readers could taste the original beauty of the Master's mother tongue. Again, he sought Holy Mother's blessing.

On 4 July 1897 Holy Mother wrote to M. from Jayrambati: "My dear child, whatever you heard from the Master was true. You should not feel any fear in publishing them. At one time he left those teachings in your custody, and now he is bringing them to light through you. Know for certain that people's spiritual consciousness will not be awakened without bringing out those teachings. Whatever words of the Master you collected are true. One day while I was listening to your manuscript, I felt as if the Master was saying all those things."[8]

With this encouragement from Holy Mother, M. earnestly began to develop *Sri Ramakrishna Kathamrita*. He published chapters from the book in many Bengali magazines and newspapers such as *Udbodhan*,

Tattwamanjari, Anusandhan, Arati, Alochana, Utsaha, Rishi, Janmabhumi, Navya Bharat, Punya, Pradip, Prabasi, Prayas, Bamabodhini, Sahitya, Sahitya Samhita, and *Hindu Patrika.*[9] M. then arranged those chapters in chronological order and published them as *Sri Sri Ramakrishna Kathamrita* — Volume I, which was published on 11 March 1902 by Udbodhan Press under Swami Trigunatitananda's supervision. Volume II was published in 1904, Volume III in 1908, Volume IV in 1910, and Volume V in 1932. In its entirety, *Sri Sri Ramakrishna Kathamrita* contains nearly 177 diary entries that M. recorded during Ramakrishna's lifetime and 8 entries that he added after the Master passed away. In addition, M. collected information from other sources that he included in appendices to those volumes.

Swami Nityatmananda described how M. wrote notes to himself in his diary. On Sunday, 1 January 1882,* Ramakrishna went to attend the Brahmo Festival at Jnan Chaudhury's house in Simla, Calcutta. M. wrote only two words in his diary entry for that day: *kamarshalar loha*, meaning "iron in a smithy." Based on those two words, M. wrote the words of the Master: "Why shouldn't it be possible for a householder to give his mind to God? But the truth is that he no longer has his mind with him. If he had it, then he could certainly offer it to God. But, alas, the mind has been mortgaged — mortgaged to 'woman and gold.' So it is necessary for him constantly to live in the company of holy men. Either he should think of God in solitude day and night, or he should live with holy men. The mind left to itself gradually dries up. Take a jar of water, for instance. If the jar is set aside, the water dries up little by little. But that will not happen if the jar is kept immersed in the Ganges.

"The iron becomes red in the forge of a smithy. Take it out and it becomes black as before. Therefore the iron must be heated in the forge every now and then."[10]

On 21 February 1924 a devotee asked M.: "Why did you assume three names — Master, Srima, Mani — in the *Kathamrita* instead of one?"

M.: "Where there is a private conversation, I put 'Mani'; because it is not necessary for the reader to know the person. It is enough to know what the Master said to him. What is the necessity for others to know whether the Master scolded or praised him?"

The devotee: "Will readers understand if your diary is printed as it is?"

---

*This event took place before M. met Sri Ramakrishna. M. collected the information from a reliable source and recorded it in his diary. He later developed and added it in the *Kathamrita* as an appendix.

M.: "No, people won't understand it. It is recorded in a very concise way. Some parts are in my mind and some are in the diary, such as a sub-title in the chapter, 'The Brahmachari and the Snake.'"[11]

On 16 July 1925 Swami Vireswarananda asked M. how he could have written the wonderful *Kathamrita* from such meagre sketches. M. humbly replied: "By the Master's grace alone. People take these incidents to have occurred over forty years ago. But I see them happening this very moment before my very eyes. In meditation the distance of time vanishes. In love and devotion everything is ever-present — there is no past or future."[12]

On 3 November 1927 a devotee asked M.: "Is it true that the Master forbade anyone to record his words, except you?"

M.: "The Master did not allow people to record his words in his presence. No one knew that I was recording the Master's sayings. I habitually maintained a diary, so I went on recording his words accordingly. When the Master was ill at the Cossipore garden house, he learned [somehow] that I was recording his conversations, and he did not forbid it."[13]

M. would listen and absorb the words of the Master, and then return home and write in his diary, sometimes the entire night. On 13 September 1924 M. described the stress this caused: "One day on Badurbagan Street, in front of Vidyasagar's house, I fell unconscious on the sidewalk. Then someone took me home in a horse carriage. When the Master heard about this incident, he said: 'Please sleep more and drink milk. And stop writing for some days.'"[14]

Ramakrishna's Contribution to M.'s Work

Ramakrishna's life was based on truth, so every one of his words was true. He said that the Divine Mother had never allowed an untruth to pass through his lips. The omniscient Master knew that M. was preserving his message, so from time to time he corrected M.'s ideas to make sure they were accurate. The following conversation took place between Ramakrishna and M. on 9 November 1884:

> Master: "How did you like today's conversation?"
> M.: "Very much indeed."
> Master (*smiling*): "How I spoke about the Emperor Akbar!"
> M.: "It was very good."
> Master: "Repeat it to me."
> M.: "A fakir came to visit Akbar. The Emperor was saying his prayers. In his prayers he was asking God to give him wealth and riches. Thereupon the fakir was about to leave the room quietly. Later, when the

Emperor asked him about it, the fakir said, 'If I must beg, why should I beg of a beggar?'"

Master: "What else did we talk about?"

M.: "You told us a great deal about saving up for the future."

Master (*smiling*): "What did I say?"

M.: "As long as a man feels that he must try, he should make an effort. How well you told us about it at Sinthi!"

Master: "What did I say?"

M.: "God takes upon Himself complete responsibility for one who totally depends upon Him. It is like a guardian taking charge of a minor. You also told us that at a feast a child cannot by himself find a place to eat his meal; someone finds a place for him."

Master: "No, that is not quite to the point. I said that the child doesn't fall if the father leads him and holds his hand."

M.: "You also described the three classes of sadhus. The best sadhu does not move about to get his food; he lives in one place and gets his food there. You told us about that young sadhu who said, when he saw the breasts of a young girl, 'Why has she those abscesses?' You told us many other things."

Master (*smiling*): "What else?"

M.: "About the crow of Pampa Lake. He repeated the name of Rama day and night. That is why he couldn't drink the water though he went to its edge. And about the holy man in whose book was written only 'Om Rama.' And what Hanuman said to Rama."

Master: "What did he say?"

M.: "Hanuman said to Rama: 'I saw Sita in Ceylon; but it was only her body. Her mind and soul were lying at Your feet.'

"And about the chataka bird. He will not drink anything but rain-water. And about jnana yoga and bhakti yoga."

Master: "What did I say about them?"

M.: "As long as one is conscious of the 'jar,' the ego will certainly remain. As long as one is conscious of 'I', one cannot get rid of the idea, 'I am the devotee and Thou art God.'"

Master: "No, it is not that; the 'jar' doesn't disappear whether one is conscious of it or not. One cannot get rid of the 'I'. You may reason a thousand times; still it will not go."

M. remained silent a few moments.

M.: "You had that talk with Ishan Mukherji in the Kali temple. We were very lucky to be there."

Master (*smiling*): "Yes, yes. Tell me, what did I say?"

M.: "You said that work is only the first step. You told us that you said to Shambhu Mallick, 'If God appears before you, will you ask Him for a number of hospitals and dispensaries?'

"You said another thing: 'God does not reveal Himself to a person as long as he is attached to work.' You said that to Keshab Sen."

Master: "What did I say?"

M.: "As long as the baby plays with the toy and forgets everything else, its mother looks after her cooking and other household duties; but when the baby throws away the toy and cries, then the mother puts down the rice-pot and comes to the baby.

"You said another thing that day: Lakshmana asked Rama where one could find God; after a great deal of explanation, Rama said to him, 'Brother, I dwell in the man in whom you find ecstatic love — a love which makes him laugh and weep and dance and sing.'"

Master: "Ah me! Ah me!"

Sri Ramakrishna sat in silence a few minutes.

M.: "That day you spoke only words of renunciation to Ishan. Since then many of us have come to our senses. Now we are eager to reduce our duties. You said that day, 'Ravana died in Ceylon and Behula wept bitterly for him.'"

Sri Ramakrishna laughed aloud.

M. (*humbly*): "Sir, isn't it desirable to reduce the number of one's duties and entanglements?"

Master: "Yes. But it is a different thing if you happen to come across a sadhu or a poor man. Then you should serve him."

M.: "And that day you spoke very rightly to Ishan about flatterers. They are like vultures on a carcass. You once said that to Padmalochan also."

Master: "No, to Vamandas of Ulo."[15]

Sometimes Ramakrishna tested M.'s understanding of specific terms that he used. On 3 August 1884 the Master talked about false and real renunciation. Because M. was a family man, it was not possible for him to renounce completely, so the Master asked him to renounce mentally.

M.: "Mental renunciation is prescribed for those who cannot give up the world outwardly. For superior devotees total renunciation is enjoined — both outer and inner."

Ramakrishna was silent for a few minutes and then resumed the conversation.

Master: "How did you like what I said about renunciation a little while ago?"

M.: "Very much, sir."

Master: "Tell me, what is the meaning of renunciation?"

M.: "Renunciation does not mean simply dispassion for the world. It means dispassion for the world and also longing for God."

Master: "You are right. You no doubt need money for your worldly life; but don't worry too much about it. Those who surrender their hearts and souls to God, those who are devoted to Him and have taken refuge in Him, do not worry much about money. As they earn so they spend. This is what the Gita describes as 'accepting what comes of its own accord.'"[16]

The Genesis of *The Gospel of Sri Ramakrishna*

On different occasions M. later related the genesis of the *Gospel* to the monks and devotees:

Once the Master said to me: "The Divine Mother has told me that you have to do a little work for her. You will have to teach the Bhagavata, the word of God, to humanity. God binds the Bhagavata pandit to the world with one tie; otherwise, who would remain to explain the sacred book? He keeps the pandit bound for the good of men. That is why the Divine Mother has kept you in the world."

To what extent can we foresee God's plan? The Master made me start keeping a diary in 1867 when I was a student of class seven at Hare School. Since then I recorded in my journal my daily activities, the places I had visited, and so on. I met the Master in the later part of February 1882. That is when my habit of maintaining a diary really became fruitful. When we look back on our past we realize that God is making us do everything. God determines beforehand what he will do through a particular person and then gets it done through him. There were many people around the Master, but he made me write the chronicle. As a result, *The Gospel of Sri Ramakrishna* came into existence. I was an apprentice for fifteen years. The hard discipline greatly helped me. It sharpened my memory and increased my skill in writing. I could recall the sequence of all of the incidents that had occurred during the day after I returned home at night. I would try to remember the first lines of the songs I had heard. This is the way the Master worked through me.

I was involved in worldly activities, bound to my work, and could not visit the Master whenever I wished. Therefore I used to note down his words so that I could think over what he had said between my visits to him. In this way the impressions made on my mind might not be counteracted by the stress of worldly work and responsibilities. It was thus for my own benefit that I first took notes, so that I might realize his teachings more perfectly.

I used to memorize the Master's words, and then after returning home I would write brief notes in my diary. Sometimes I would spend the whole night in completing my record. Later I would fill in all the details from memory. Sometimes I would spend seven days completing the record of one day's happenings. Thus *The Gospel of Sri Ramakrishna* appeared in book form from the notes of my diary. Sometimes I had to wait for a word of the Master's to come to my mind as a chataka bird waits for a drop of rainwater to fall. Sometimes I meditated on one scene over a thousand times. As a result I could vividly visualize the Master's divine play, though it had happened long before. By the grace of the Master I used to feel that his play had just happened. Therefore one can say that it was written in the Master's presence. At times I would not be satisfied with a particular description of an episode, so I would get absorbed in meditation on the Master. Then the correct picture would vividly appear in my mind. Therefore, from a human standpoint there was a great distance of time, but in my thought world I felt that it had happened just before I recorded it. My account is not culled from other sources. I recorded whatever I heard from the Master's lips with my own ears and whatever I saw of his life with my own eyes.

The Gospel of Sri Ramakrishna is the world's only firsthand record of the life and teachings of an avatar. One can collect materials about Sri Ramakrishna in three ways: First, direct observation recorded on the same day; second, direct observation but unrecorded during the lifetime of the Master; and third, hearsay, also unrecorded during the lifetime of the Master. *The Gospel of Sri Ramakrishna* belongs to the first category. I was present during each scene of the *Gospel*.

I have published my diary very carefully. If there is any mistake in it, then its value will diminish. People do not realize that at one time I had to study the rules of evidence. If a witness makes a single mistake, the entire case becomes nullified. Addressing the judge, the lawyer says, "My Lord, this witness is not reliable." I used to visit the court and observe all these details. The evidence of an eyewitness is very valuable. For that reason the judge asks, "Did you see this yourself?" If a person has seen and heard something himself, his words carry weight. I checked all the facts and details before I published *The Gospel of Sri Ramakrishna.*[17]

When somebody asked M. to remove some of the repetitions from the *Gospel*, he replied:

I cannot do that. The Master told the same parable to different people. If I remove a particular section, the train of the conversation will be broken. Moreover, you won't be able to see the effect of the *Gospel* on a particular person's life. The Master gave the same teaching to five different people in five different places. What he said to Bankim, he said to others also; and whatever conversation he had with Vivekananda, he had with others too.

You see, sometimes the brilliance of a diamond is enhanced by changing its setting. Putting it on the dusty ground produces one effect, and putting it on a green lawn produces another. But putting it in a casket lined with blue velvet produces the most brilliant effect of all. The same is true of the words in the *Gospel*. The rays of the sun look different when they fall on water, on the earth, and on glass, but the maximum brilliance is produced when the sun is reflected on glass. So I cannot avoid the repetitions in the *Gospel*, because removing them would disturb the Master's dialogue.

Once Hriday said to the Master: "Uncle, please reserve some of your best teachings. Otherwise, if you say everything all at once, and then repeat the same thing again and again, people will not come to you anymore." The Master replied: "You rascal! I shall repeat my words fifty times. What does it matter to you?"[18]

M. added the *Kathamrita* to the curriculum of his school. When M. was accused by some people of trying to sell his books to the students, he calmly replied:

The students will understand the effect of reading the *Gospel* when they enter family life. The Master used to say, "The world is a burning fire." And I fully realized it. After the boys enter the world and are tormented by sorrows and sufferings, the Master's immortal words will save them, like a loving mother. If they remember at least one of the Master's teachings, that will be like a boat to ferry them across the turbulent ocean of maya and it will bring peace to their lives.[19]

In spite of his illness, M. read the proofs of the last part of the *Kathamrita* at 1 o'clock in the morning by the light of a kerosene lantern. When lovingly chastised by Swami Nityatmananda, he said:

People are finding peace by reading this book, the Master's immortal message. It is inevitable that the body will meet its end, so it is better that it be used for spreading peace to others. We are in the world and have fully experienced how much pain there is in it, yet I have forgotten that pain through *The Gospel of Sri Ramakrishna*. I am hurrying so that the book may come out soon.[20]

Ramakrishna's Language in the *Kathamrita*

The teachings of Buddha and Christ spread quickly among the masses because they spoke in the language of the people. Buddha used Pali, while Christ taught in Aramaic. Language is the carrier of ideas, and those great teachers explained their ideas through tales and parables that were very effective. Even people who had no formal education could understand their message.

The tenth chapter of the *Lalita-vistara* describes Prince Siddhartha's education under Vishwamitra. Siddhartha (later Buddha) learned 64 lipis — that is, dialects or languages, such as Anga lipi, Banga lipi, Magadh lipi, Shakari lipi, Dravir lipi, Chin lipi, Brahmavali lipi, and so on. He also studied the Vedas in Sanskrit.

Halley's Bible Handbook describes Christ's use of language: "Aramaic was the common language of the people. This was the language Jesus used. He was instructed in Hebrew, the language of the Old Testament Scriptures. He must have known Greek, for it was the language of a large part of the population, and the universal language of the time. Jesus was familiar with both the Hebrew and Septuagint Old Testament. His own language is superb."[21] Before his crucifixion Jesus talked to Pilate, who was a Roman ruler, which indicates he might have known Latin.

Like Buddha and Christ, Ramakrishna taught in the language of the people. His mother tongue was Bengali, but he also knew some English words, including *friend, refine, like, honorary, society, under, tax, cheque*, and *thank you*. Although he had no formal education, he could read and write Bengali. Once he humorously said: "Narendra considers me to be illiterate, but I know the alphabet." Ramakrishna also spoke Hindi with his guru Tota Puri and with monks from western India. He studied Sanskrit "a little" at his brother's Sanskrit School in Calcutta. Again, he once said: "If a pandit speaks to me in Sanskrit, I can follow him, but I cannot speak it myself."[22]

Before we discuss the charm of Ramakrishna's language and how M. recorded it almost verbatim in the *Kathamrita*, it is important to understand the difference between the colloquial mother tongue and the literary language. Children learn their mother tongue spontaneously from their parents, friends, and relatives, but they learn literary language from teachers in school.

As a child Ramakrishna learned his native mother tongue, which was Bengali, but he never learned literary language or "language proper," from his schooling. Thus, when we read the *Kathamrita*, we enjoy the freshness and liveliness of Ramakrishna's colloquial village language. His language is simple and sweet; his words are clear and charming; his examples are apt and beautiful; his descriptions are poetic and graphic; his ideas are profound and meaningful; his style of conversation is original and captivating; his gestures and mimicry are humorous and entertaining. Ramakrishna used short and simple sentences to communicate his profound teachings, so his powerful statements would remain in the minds of his listeners. Even the great savants of India sat spellbound, listening to this uneducated temple priest.

On 28 March 1875, *The Indian Mirror* wrote about Ramakrishna: "We met one (a sincere Hindu devotee) not long ago and were charmed by the depth, penetration, and simplicity of his spirit. The never-ceasing metaphors and analogies, in which he indulged, are most of them as apt as they are beautiful."[23] On 19 August 1886 *The Indian Mirror* wrote again: "He [Ramakrishna] was an unlettered man, but his commonsense was strong and his power of observation keen. He had [a] facility for expressing his ideas in such homely language that he could make himself easily understood by all on intricate points of religion and morality. His child-like simplicity and outspokenness, his deep religious fervour and self-denial, his genial and sympathetic nature and his meek and unassuming manners won the hearts of those who came in contact with him, and music from his lips had a peculiar charm on those who heard him sing."[24]

Swami Vivekananda said: "My ideal of language is my Master's language, most colloquial and yet most expressive. It must express the thought which is intended to be conveyed."[25]

When flowers bloom, bees come of their own accord. In New York Vivekananda gave a lecture entitled "My Master" in which he said:

> People came by thousands to see and hear this wonderful man who spoke in a patois, every word of which was forceful and instinct with light. For it is not what is spoken, much less the language in which it is spoken, but the personality of the speaker, which dwells in everything he says that carries weight. Every one of us feels this at times. We hear most splendid orations, most wonderfully reasoned-out discourses, and we go home and forget everything. At other times we hear a few words in the simplest of language, and they remain with us all the rest of our lives, become part and parcel of ourselves and produce lasting results. The words of a man who can put his personality into them take effect, but he must have tremendous personality. All teaching means giving and taking: the teacher gives and the taught receives, but the one must have something to give, and the other must be open to receive.[26]

It is true that Ramakrishna did not have much formal education, but his words had the force of scripture and he spoke only truth. Vivekananda later said: "The Vedas and other scriptures were so long hidden in the darkness of ignorance, and the light of Sri Ramakrishna has revealed them again."[27] While in America, Vivekananda reminisced to his disciples: "When I think of that man [Ramakrishna], I feel like a fool, because I want to read books and he never did. He never wanted to lick the plates after other people had eaten. That is why he was his own book."[28]

Observing the Master's encyclopaedic knowledge of religion and philosophy, a disciple asked him how he came to have such deep and broad knowledge.

Ramakrishna answered: "I have not read; I have listened and learned. I have made a garland of their knowledge and put it round my neck, and I have offered it at the feet of the Mother."[29]

On 2 January 1884 Ramakrishna said to M.: "At Kamarpukur I have seen grain-dealers measuring paddy. As one heap is measured away another heap is pushed forward to be measured. The Mother supplies devotees with the 'heap' of Knowledge....Weeping, I prayed to the Mother: 'O Mother, reveal to me what is contained in the Vedas and Vedanta. Reveal to me what is in the Purana and the Tantra.' One by one She has revealed all these to me."[30] Ramakrishna used to say that the Divine Mother spoke through his mouth.

M. was blessed with the opportunity to record Ramakrishna's divine language in the pages of the *Kathamrita*. He did not vitiate that wonderful language by paraphrasing it or rewriting the Master's words. Like a skilled craftsman, M. set those divine jewels of the Master's words in the pages of the *Kathamrita*. By resorting to his recorded notes and his meditation, he recreated Ramakrishna's dialogue. I had the opportunity to see some pages of M.'s diary — and from those I could understand that without divine grace, no one could have accurately recorded those divine dialogues of Ramakrishna.

M. emphatically said, "Every word of the Master is a mantra." By this he meant that reflecting upon those words connects individual souls with God. Here I present some of the Master's words as M. recorded them in the *Kathamrita*.

- *Manav jivaner uddeshya ishwarlabh*: The goal of human life is to realize God.
- *Kamini kanchan maya*: Lust and gold are maya.
- *Satya-katha kalir tapasya*: Practising truthfulness is the austerity of this kaliyuga.
- *Bhagavata-bhakta-bhagavan — tine ek*: The scripture, the devotee, and God are all one.
- *Ami mole ghuchibe janjal*: All troubles will cease when the "I" dies.
- *Ami jantra tumi jantri*: I am the instrument and You are the operator.
- *Naham naham, tuhun tuhun*: Not I, not I, but Thou, Thou.
- *Yato mat tato path*: As many faiths, so many paths.
- *Advaita-jnan anchale bendhe ja ichha tai karo*: Tie nondual knowledge in the corner of your cloth and then do whatever you like.

- *Bhakta hobi to boka hobi kena*: Be a devotee, but don't be foolish.
- *Ishwar Kalpataru*: God is the wish-fulfilling tree.
- *Brahma ar shakti abhed*: Brahman and His power are identical.
- *Vedanter sar — brahma satya jagat mithya*: The essence of Vedanta is: Brahman is real and the world is impermanent.
- *Gitar sar — tyagi tyagi*: The essence of the Gita is this: Renounce, renounce.
- *Bishay-asakta mon bhije deshlai*: The attached mind is like a box of wet matches.
- *Nirakaro satya avar sakaro satya*: God without form and with form — both are true.
- *Jeman bhav temni labh*: As is a man's feeling of love, so is his gain.
- *Dhyan korbe mone, bone, o kone*: Meditate in your mind, in the forest, or in the corner of your room.
- *Dub dao*: Dive deep.
- *Satchidanandai guru*: Satchidananda alone is the guru.
- *Ishwarke tushta karo, sakalai thusha hobe*: Please God, then everyone will be pleased.
- *Tini sab hoyechen tabe manushai tini beshi prakash*: God has become everything, but He is manifested to the utmost in human beings.
- *Ishwarer iti karata hina buddhi*: It is petty to limit God.
- *Mon mukh ek karai dharma*: True religion is the union of mind and speech.
- *Bhaver ghare churi koro na*: Let there be no theft [hypocrisy] in the chamber of your heart (i.e., shun hypocrisy).

Translating *Sri Ramakrishna Kathamrita*

M. wrote his first drafts of the *Kathamrita* in Bengali so that he could read them to Holy Mother. In 1888 M. expanded four entries from his diary: (1) 15 June 1884, Surendra's Garden, Calcutta; (2) 25 June 1884, visit to a Hindu Pandit and Preacher (Shashadhar), Calcutta; (3) 5 August 1882, Visit to Pandit Ishwar Chandra Vidyasagar, Calcutta, (4) 3 August 1884, at the Dakshineswar temple. M. then translated these entries into English under the heading *Leaves from the Gospel of the Lord Sri Ramakrishna*, and they were published serially in the *Brahmavadin* magazine (started by Swami Vivekananda in 1895) on 15 October 1897, 16 November 1897, 1 February 1898, and 16 May 1898. He wrote these articles under his pen name: *According to M., a son of the Lord and servant*. He also added a footnote below the title: "Translated by M. from original records kept in Bengali by M. These records are based on notes put down from memory by M. on the very day of the meeting, shortly after the meeting was over, and purport to be an attempt to give the *Lord's own words* as far as possible."[31] Later these four entries were published in two pamphlets in English.

Enthusiastic readers were not satisfied with these pamphlets and demanded that the entire *Gospel* be published in book form. M. worked diligently to develop his diary entries, writing first in Bengali and then translating them into English. In 1907 M. took the four chapters from the *Brahmavadin*, added ten more chapters, and produced a book entitled "*The Gospel of Sri Ramakrishna* (According to M., a son of the Lord and disciple)." M. added a subtitle: "or The Ideal Man for India and for the World." This publication, part one of the *Gospel*, was published by Brahmavadin Office, Madras. It consists of 386 pages. In its second edition, M. deleted the subtitle. Of this *Gospel*, M. wrote: "It is no sentence by sentence translation but M.'s own rendering of his thoughts rather than language, directly into English with many elaborations and elucidating repetitions."[32] In 1912 Swami Trigunatitananda of the Vedanta Society of San Francisco published this first edition of the *Gospel*.

The English of the first edition was archaic, a kind of evangelical language: Thou thinketh, thou comest, thou askest, thou art, and so on. When M. made revisions for the second edition, he freed it of its Biblical turns of expression. This edition was published in 1911 by Ramakrishna Math, Madras. The Madras Math published several more editions, and this work was in circulation until 1942, when the complete translation of *The Gospel of Sri Ramakrishna* (which contained all five volumes of the original *Kathamrita*) by Swami Nikhilananda came out. In 1978 the Madras Math reprinted M.'s version under the title *The Condensed Gospel of Sri Ramakrishna*.

In 1907 Swami Abhedananda of the Vedanta Society of New York published another version, the *Gospel of Ramakrishna*. In the preface Swami Abhedananda wrote: "This is the authorized English edition of the *Gospel of Ramakrishna*. For the first time in the history of the world's Great Saviours, the exact words of the Master were recorded verbatim by one of his devoted disciples. These words were originally spoken in the Bengali language of India. They were taken down in the form of diary notes by a householder disciple, M.

"M. wrote to me letters authorizing me to edit and publish the English translation of his notes, and sent me the manuscript in English which he himself translated. At the request of M., I have edited and remodeled the larger portion of his English manuscript, while the remaining p‹ have translated directly from the Bengali edition of his notes."[33]

Although Swami Abhedananda's edited version of the *Gospel* received many favourable reviews from American papers and was translated into Spanish, Portuguese, Danish, Scandinavian, and Czech, it lacks the flavour and style of M.'s original. M. later remarked that Swami Abhedananda added his own reminiscences to the book.[34] In 1939 Ramakrishna Vedanta Math republished this book as *The Memoirs of Ramakrishna*.

In 1922 Ramakrishna Math, Madras, published an English translation of Volume II of *Sri Sri Ramakrishna Kathamrita*, without consulting M., who was still alive. The material of this volume first came out serially in *Vedanta Kesari*. M. disapproved and requested Swami Shivananda, the president of the Ramakrishna Order, to stop the publication. *Vedanta Kesari* discontinued the series, but the Madras Math published this material as volume two of the *Gospel*. This volume was edited by a Westerner, and the second edition was published in 1928. Then it was withdrawn as it did not meet the author's approval. Regarding this volume two, M. commented: "Even a student of eighth grade translates from Bengali into English. Translation is not an easy thing. One should transmit the idea and mood. A literal translation is not enough. Western people do not understand the Bengali language. . . . While talking, the Master would express an idea with a living feeling. In my translation I have tried my best to convey the same spirit by preserving his words as far as possible. The primary importance is the sense or meaning; words or the language are only secondary. And I have tried to express it in a simple language. In translation, the meaning changes if one overlooks the viewpoint of the Master's saying."[35]

M. was very particular about his record of the Master's words. It was extremely painful for him if his work was translated in a distorted form. Swami Avyaktananda began to publish the translation of other volumes of the *Kathamrita* in *Morning Star*, a magazine in Patna.

On 17 May 1930 M. wrote to him: "Dear Avyakta Babaji, My love and salutations to you all. The translation of the *Gospel* in the *Morning Star*, is, I regret to say, not satisfactory to me. Being an eye-witness, I naturally want the spirit to be kept up in the translation. Moreover, the report of a meeting should not appear in a mutilated form. The translation should be done by myself. You may do the work after my passing, which is by no means a distant contingency. I am 76 and my health is not at all good. It is painful to see the *Gospel* presented in this way. I do not approve of the translation which has appeared as Vol. II from Madras. — M."[36]

In 1942, Swami Nikhilananda of the Ramakrishna-Vivekananda Centre, New York, translated all five volumes of M.'s *Kathamrita* into

English and published the work in one chronologically arranged volume. He did not translate the entire *Kathamrita*. As he writes in the preface: "I have made a literal translation, omitting only a few pages of no particular interest to English-speaking readers." He wrote a long biographical introduction on Ramakrishna, replacing the sketch that M. had written. On the whole, Swami Nikhilananda's translation is superb and elegant. The swami's manuscript was edited by Margaret Woodrow Wilson (a daughter of President Woodrow Wilson) and Joseph Campbell (a famous scholar and orientalist). And John Moffitt, Jr. (a poet and scholar) used his poetical talent on the mystical and spiritual songs of *The Gospel of Sri Ramakrishna*, which enhanced their beauty. Aldous Huxley wrote the foreword to this work. This translation drew the attention of the literary world of the East and the West. Dr. S. Radhakrishnan wrote: "Swami Nikhilananda has done an excellent piece of work. His very readable English translation of the *Ramakrishna-Kathamrita* will enable Western readers to understand the deep spiritual life of Sri Ramakrishna and the homely way in which profound truths are conveyed to ordinary mortals, and I hope that the book will have wide publicity."[37]

This classic translation of *The Gospel of Sri Ramakrishna* has now been translated into most of the major languages of the world. The Bengali *Kathamrita* also has been translated into most of the Indian languages.

M.'s Diary: Lost and Found

Now and then M. would visit Gadadhar Ashrama (a branch of the Ramakrishna Order) in South Calcutta, as he loved to stay with the monks in the monastery. Wherever he went, he carried his diary, which reminded him of the Master. Sometimes he would open it to an entry, meditate on a particular scene, and then talk about it to the monks and devotees. On 16 January 1924 M. was returning by tram from Gadadhar Ashrama to his home in Central Calcutta. Absorbed in thoughts of the Master, he accidentally left his diary next to his seat while changing trams at the Esplanade Station. The diary was found two days later.

On 18 January M. described his agony to the devotees:

What terrible distress I have gone through! It was worse than losing a son. I felt I should not live anymore; otherwise why had the Master taken away his words from me? When I got back my diary, I realized that this body would remain a few days more. Last Tuesday while returning from Gadadhar Ashrama, I left my diary in the tram car. It struck me when I returned home. It was then 11:00 a.m. Immediately I rushed to the Kali temple of Thanthania. I had visited the Divine Mother after getting down

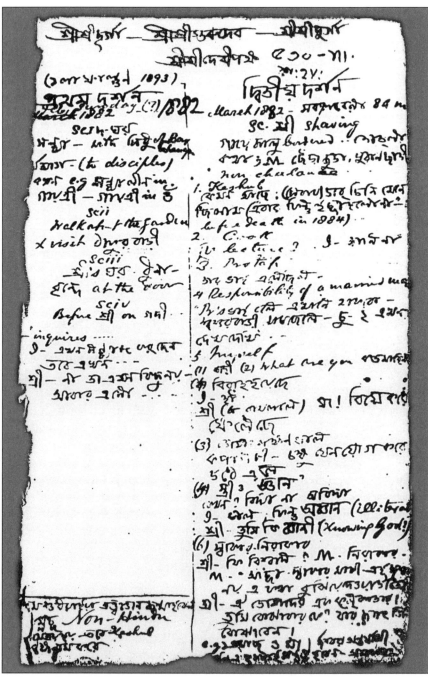

Reproduction of M.'s diary, page 1 (first and second visit, 26 and 28 February 1882)

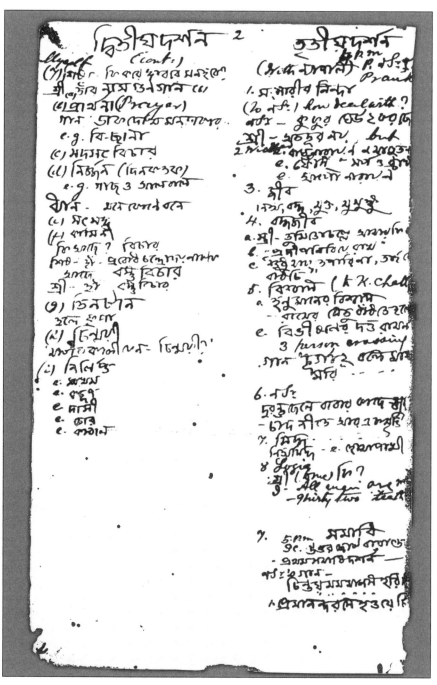

Reproduction of M.'s diary, page 2 (second and third visit, 28 February and 5 March 1882)

Reproduction of M.'s diary, page 3 (fourth visit, 6 March 1882)

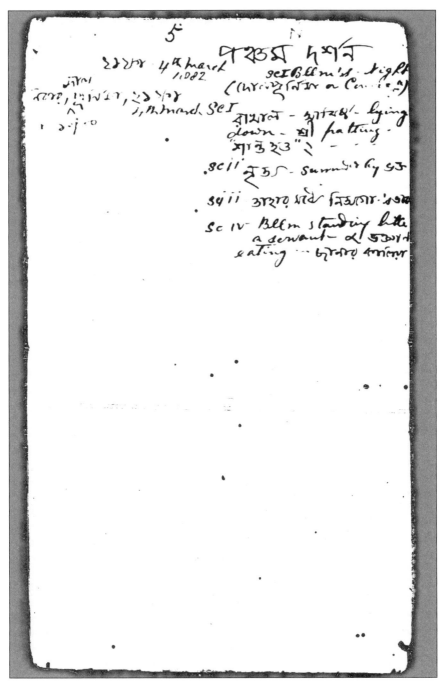

Reproduction of M.'s diary, page 4 (fifth visit, 11 March 1882)

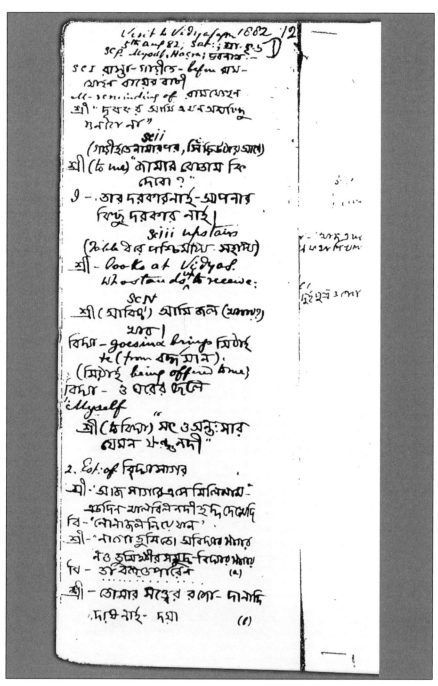

Reproduction of M.'s diary, page 5 (visit to Vidyasagar, 5 August 1882)

Reproduction of M.'s diary, page 6 (visit to Vidyasagar, 5 August 1882)

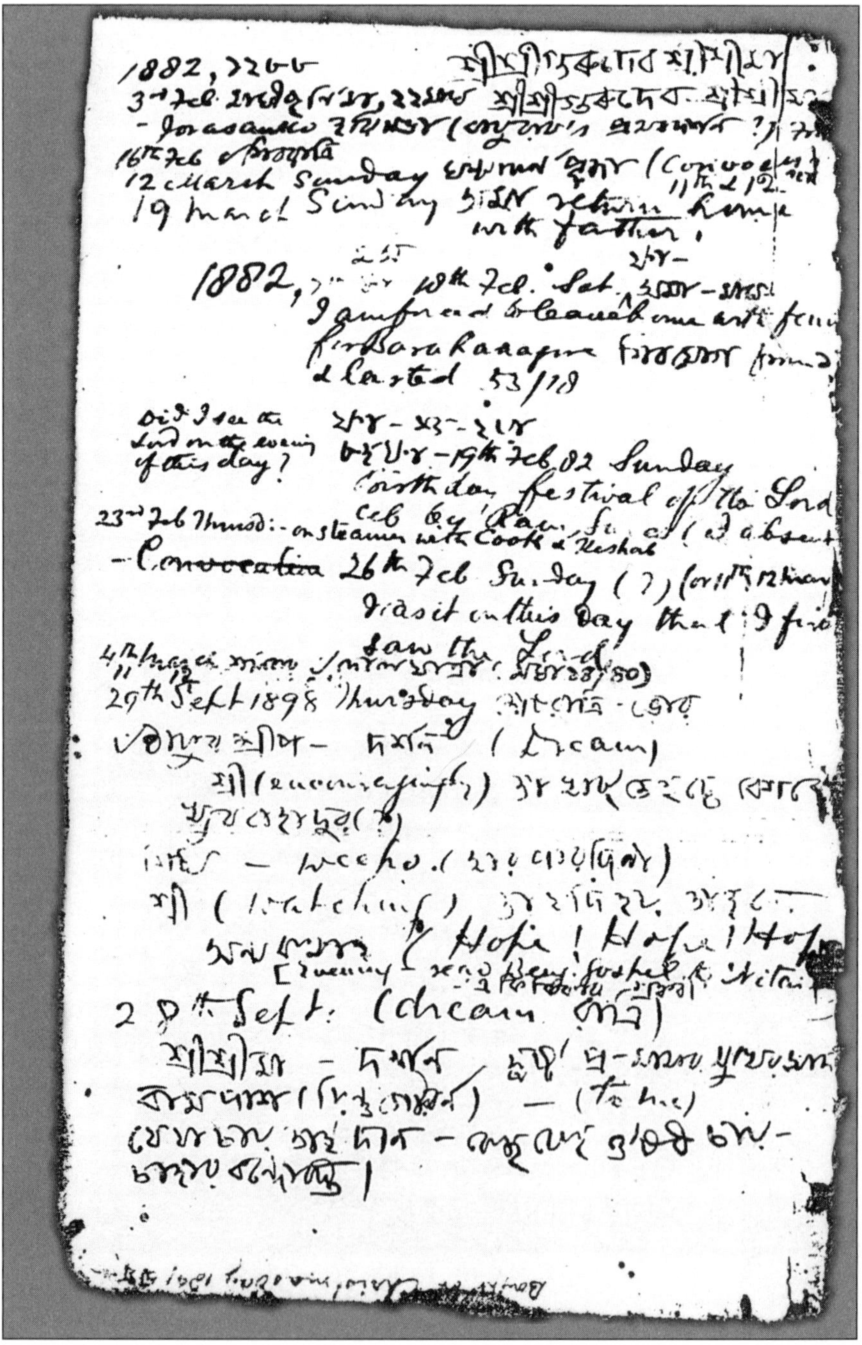

Reproduction of M.'s diary, page 7 (some notes of M.)

from the tram. I thought that I had left the diary there. Some pandits were reading the holy scriptures in front of the temple. I asked them but no one gave me a positive answer. Then I tried to locate my tram ticket, which I had torn and discarded on the sidewalk. It took me 45 minutes to collect those pieces of the ticket and then bring them home. I pasted them on a piece of paper with flour gum and discovered the number of the ticket.

Immediately I went to the Gadadhar Ashrama. In the afternoon the devotees took the ticket and went to the Kalighat tram depot. They discovered the name of the conductor who was on that tram. On Wednesday morning news came that the diary had been found. The conductor had deposited it with the overseer of the tram depot. This overseer was a devotee. He saw the name 'Jayrambati' on the cover of the diary, so he carefully saved it.

In the evening I fervently prayed to the Master. My fear did not go away even after I learned that the diary had been found. I was worried that it might be lost again before picking it up. Oh, how much fear and anxiety I went through for that diary! How sincerely I prayed to the Master for that! What joy I felt when it came to my hand!

Again, another thought arose in my mind: It is not a big deal. I left the diary in the tram car and the conductor deposited it in the office. That is the normal procedure. After receiving the diary, I felt that it had not been necessary to say so many prayers. Such are the vagaries of our minds! It behaved in quite another way once the diary was retrieved. You see, many things could have happened: There could have been a tram accident, or someone could have been run over, or the conductor might not have taken proper care of it.

A Devotee: "It also might have fallen into the hands of the sweeper of the car."

M.: "Yes, it could have, or someone could have taken it and thrown it away on the street. But as soon as I got the diary back, I forgot all those possibilities. What irony! And we live with this mind, which plays tricks on us all the time. So we should always pray: May we not deviate from our goal. May we not forget God when something has been accomplished."

M. presented a copy of the *Kathamrita* to the overseer as a token of his gratefulness.[38]

An Interview with M. at Morton School on 20 March 1924

Swami Madhavananda, the president of Advaita Ashrama in Mayavati, was working on a biography of Ramakrishna. He found some discrepancies between the Kathamrita by M. and the Lilaprasanga by Swami Saradananda, so he went to M. to verify those facts. Furthermore, he wanted to ask M. how he had recorded the Kathamrita *and gathered some other information about the Master.*

Swami Madhavananda (*to M.*): "How many times did Sri Ramakrishna go on pilgrimage? You have mentioned two times."

M.: "Yes, twice. First, the Master went with Mathur; then he went with Mathur's sons. At that time one could go to Varanasi by train. I corresponded with the Railway Company with reference and compared its record of the dates and of who went with him, and they were the same. Moreover, there is some circumstantial evidence. I visited Janbazar and Barrackpore and collected information from the descendants of Rani Rasmani."

Swami Madhavananda: "Did you write in your diary immediately after listening to the Master?"

M.: "No, I didn't write on the spot. After I returned home I wrote from memory. Sometimes I spent the whole night completing an entry. My record [*The Gospel of Sri Ramakrishna*] is not a collection from other sources. I wrote down whatever I heard with my own ears from the lips of the Master and whatever I saw of his life with my own eyes. I didn't collect materials like historians or write like the antiquarians."

Swami Madhavananda: "It is amazing that within such a short period there are so many different versions of the Master's life and teachings!"

M.: "This is nothing to wonder at. It happens that way. Look at the Bible: there is little similarity among the four gospels recorded by Matthew, Mark, Luke, and John. The same thing will happen in the case of the Master. Sometimes I spent seven days recording from memory the events of one day — arranging chronologically the songs, stories, samadhi, and so on."

Swami Madhavananda: "To whom did the Master offer the articles during the night of Kali Puja at Shyampukur house?"

M.: "He offered them to himself."

Swami Madhavananda: "Did he offer them to himself or to Mother Kali?"

M.: "In fact, he offered them to himself. As soon as all of the devotees had offered flowers to the Master, his hands assumed the gestures symbolizing fearlessness and the bestowal of boons [that are seen in images of Kali]. Thus — (*saying so, M. demonstrated those two gestures with his own hands*). Then everyone realized who the Master was."

Swami Madhavananda: "What do you know about the name 'Ramakrishna'?"

M.: "I didn't hear anything from the Master about his name. Probably 'Ramakrishna' was the name given by his family, because the prefix of his brothers' names was 'Rama' (such as Ramkumar and Rameswar). They were all devotees of Ramachandra, and Raghuvir was their household deity. The village people called him 'Gadai.' We did not know that he was called Gadadhar. We learned it later. Tota Puri didn't give him the name 'Ramakrishna,' because long before Tota Puri arrived the name 'Ramakrishna Bhattacharya' was registered in Rani Rasmani's documents."*

Swami Madhavananda: "A knower of Brahman came to Dakshineswar who shared food with the dogs. Who followed that knower of Brahman? Was it Hriday or Haladhari?"

M.: "Haladhari."**

Swami Madhavananda: "Who returned with bel leaves instead of visiting his daughter's house? You have written 'Haladhari's father,' and Swami Saradananda has written 'the Master's father.'"

M.: "I know that way [that is, the version I have written]."

Swami Madhavananda: "Akshay Sen [the author of *Sri Ramakrishna Punthi*] has written about a pandit who sat on the Master's bed with his shoes on. What is your opinion about that?"

M.: "No, that is not correct. I was present. The pandit sat on the floor. As soon as the Master touched his chest with his feet, the pandit exclaimed, 'O guru, please awaken my consciousness.' That man had a very devotional temperament."

Swami Madhavananda: "How many years did the Master go through a spiritual tempest?"

M.: "Seven years. The Master said that his family members then took him back to Kamarpukur for his wedding."

Swami Madhavananda: "Whom did the Master send to Bankim Chattopadhyay?"

M.: "The Master sent Girish Babu and myself to Bankim, saying, 'Please go to Bankim and invite him to come here.' Bankim also invited the Master to visit him, but he could not go."

Swami Madhavananda: "Did Krishnadas Pal [a national leader and the editor of *Hindu Patriot*] visit the Master?"

M.: "Yes, he did. The Master said about him: 'Krishnadas observed the Hindu custom. He entered my room after leaving his shoes outside. I

*Vide Deed of Endowment by Rani Rasmani 1861, 18th February. Tota Puri came to Dakshineswar in 1864.
**It was Hriday, according to the *Lilaprasanga* by Swami Saradananda.

asked him: "What is the goal of human life?" He replied, "It is to do good to the world." I told him: "You see this world? Have you seen innumerable crab eggs floating in the Ganges during the rainy season? As many eggs so many worlds. They are numberless. Who are you to do good to the world? You better try to help yourself. God dwells in every being. Be blessed by serving Him in all beings. The owner of the world will look after his own affairs. You look to your own path.""'

Swami Madhavananda: "When did the Master meet Keshab Sen?"

M.: "In 1875."*

Swami Madhavananda: "Will you include the fifth part of *Sri Ramakrishna Kathamrita*? It would be nice if you would include the Master and Bankim's meeting in it."

M.: "I want to do that. The Basumati publishing house sent a person to me. They are eager to publish it."

Senior Jiten: "Swami Madhavananda and others are writing a biography of the Master."

M.: "Who else will write it? They have practised so much austerity and lived with the disciples of the Master. Moreover they live in the Himalayas [Advaita Ashrama, Mayavati]."

M. continued: "Mayavati Ashrama is doing a marvellous job. It has published many important books. The monks are doing *nishkam karma* (unselfish action) without any personal motive."

Swami Madhavananda left after having some refreshments.[39]

Characteristics of *The Gospel of Sri Ramakrishna*

M. had a photographic memory, artistic talent, and, above all, a poetic imagination. Though one can challenge the historicity of Christ, Buddha, or Krishna, one cannot challenge the existence of Ramakrishna. M. meticulously documented his conversations with the Master, carefully noting the dates and times, the places, and the people who were present, and even any songs that were sung.

Did Ramakrishna say anything new? Not really. He reinterpreted the same ancient Truth. He said, "The money which is used at the time of a Nawab [a Muslim king] becomes outdated with the rule of a Badshah [Muslim emperor]." The coins change according to the rule of different dynasties. Similarly, the ancient avatars brought the message that was needed for their particular age and the conditions in which they lived.

---

*Sri Ramakrishna first met Keshab Sen in 1864 at the Adi Brahmo Samaj, but became closely acquainted with him only in 1875 at Jaygopal Sen's garden house in Belgharia.

Now a new avatar has preached according to the need of our age. One hundred years ago people did not know much about modern medicine. They treated their diseases with herbs and natural medicines. Now we use antibiotics. Herbs and antibiotics are both medicines, but their use changes with the times. Krishna said in the Gita, "Arjuna, I am speaking to you the same Truth again."[40] Tautology is a weakness in logic, but it is not a weak point in scripture. The scriptures never tire of declaring the same truth again and again in different languages in different ages.

In the *Gospel* we find that M. not only preserved the teachings of Ramakrishna, but also described the settings in order to make a deeper impression on the reader's mind. Here is an example of a description from the *Gospel*, dated 22 July 1883: "Sri Ramakrishna had enjoyed a little rest after his midday meal. The room had an atmosphere of purity and holiness. On the walls hung pictures of gods and goddesses, among them being one of Christ rescuing the drowning Peter. Outside the room were plants laden with fragrant flowers, and the Ganges could be seen flowing towards the south. It was the rainy season; the exuberant Ganges was hurrying to meet the ocean and was happy to touch and to see the holy ground where the great saint of Dakshineswar resided."[41]

Here, M. was comparing the spiritual seekers who were coming to meet Ramakrishna to rivers merging in the infinite ocean of Satchidananda. Swami Ritajananda once wrote:

> *The Gospel of Sri Ramakrishna* begins like a novel with a little bit of description of the surroundings in picturesque language, so that the reader can visualize everything around the Master: the large property of the Dakshineswar temple with its gardens, tanks, temples, etc. If anyone desires to make a film, he will find all the directions necessary in the masterly descriptions one reads in the *Gospel*. The place and times, the people present, the positions they took in the room where they met, the songs, and finally every movement of Sri Ramakrishna — these are all presented so vividly that it becomes a special attraction. We have no such presentation of anyone else's life.
>
> In the *Gospel* we find plenty of information about Sri Ramakrishna and how he lived in the world. With him there was plenty of laughter, and it was really fortunate for so many to be near him and feel that the world is really a mansion of mirth in spite of their many painful experiences. Sri Ramakrishna also talked of suffering, the suffering of others and even his own. His health was not perfect and he eventually got cancer of the throat which entailed extreme physical pain. Many who were dear to him left this world, and those who lived with him were not always kind and respectful. Yet he was above all these things. The Divine Mother was

constantly near Her beloved son, answering his questions. M. ignored nothing that took place in the small room of Sri Ramakrishna. He tells us how Ramakrishna ate, how he spoke, how he imitated people and amused the youngsters. Never trying to idolize Sri Ramakrishna, never judging his actions or his words, M. presents a picture of his Master in the most natural way possible. This makes us understand that a highly evolved spiritual person can also be a human being.[42]

The Gospel of Sri Ramakrishna is an authentic record of Ramakrishna's life and teachings, profound and yet very simple and appealing. Moreover, Ramakrishna's language and the expressions he used are fascinating. Many people learn Bengali so that they can read this wonderful piece of literature in its original form and get a taste of how Ramakrishna actually spoke.

When we read the *Gospel*, its vivid descriptions help us visualize Ramakrishna as he moved through his environment. We see the places he saw and the people he came in contact with. This vivid and artistic depiction of an avatar's life is unique. As we read the *Gospel*, we enjoy the holy company of the Master. In the *Gospel*, festivities are always going on, with Ramakrishna at their centre. We enjoy the theatre, music, singing, dancing, humour, worship, meditation, and samadhi. Reading the *Gospel* drives away loneliness and boredom. The *Gospel* presents to us the divine drama of Ramakrishna with various characters representing all types of people: intellectuals, devotees, hypocrites, drunkards, householders, monks, actors, actresses, musicians, and so on.

Swami Bhajanananda once wrote: "Every great religion has its own scripture. There are several scriptures already existing in the world, including the Vedas, Avesta, Tripitaka, the Bible, and the Koran. Do we need one more? Yes, precisely because there are several scriptures: We need just one more to show the validity of every one of them and to establish their overall harmony. *The Gospel of Sri Ramakrishna* compiled by M. serves this purpose admirably well."[43]

M.'s chronicle of Ramakrishna's life is fascinating, in part because he himself played a vital role. Sometimes he was a silent witness to the divine drama of Ramakrishna; other times, an active participant in the play. In addition, M.'s love for the Master was extraordinary. His I-consciousness was saturated with Ramakrishna-consciousness. If this were not so, he never could have produced *The Gospel of Sri Ramakrishna*, which is unique among the world's religious literature. Faithfully and vividly, M. chronicled the Master's samadhi and meditation, his prayer and worship, his dreams and visions, actions and devotion, purity and renunciation, singing and dancing, humour and mimicry, sadhana and pilgrimage, behaviour and psychology, religion and philosophy, and his social and scientific outlook. But most important, M. preserved Ramakrishna's conversations with God, as well as his discussions with the people who came to him, his love and empathy for others, and his fervent concern for his devotees.

M. writes in the *Gospel*: "The Master was weeping and praying to the Mother. In a voice choked with emotion, he prayed to Her with tearful eyes for the welfare of the devotees: 'Mother, may those who come to You have all their desires fulfilled. But please don't make them give up everything at once, Mother. Well, You may do whatever You like in the end. If You keep them in the world, Mother, then please reveal Yourself to them now and then. Otherwise, how will they live? How will they be encouraged if they don't see You once in a while?'"[44]

The Invocation of *The Gospel of Sri Ramakrishna*

According to Indian tradition, the author of a scripture is supposed to introduce the text with an invocation consisting of an auspicious verse or a salutation mantra. Following that custom, M. placed the following verse on the title page of each of the five volumes of his original Bengali *Kathamrita*.

Tava kathāmritam tapta jivanam kavibhir-iditam kalmashāpaham;
Shravana-mangalam shrimad-ātatam bhuvi grnanti ye bhuridā janāh.
          — Bhagavata 10:31:9
"O Lord, your nectar-like words relieve the burning misery of afflicted souls. Your words, which poets have sung in verses, destroy the sins of worldly people forever. Blessed are they who hear of your vast glory. Blessed indeed are those who speak of you. How unparalleled is their bounty!"

The above-quoted invocation is taken from the Gopi-Gita of the Bhagavata. Krishna promised to meet the gopis, the milkmaids of Vrindaban, on a full-moon night in autumn. That night, the gopis came to meet Krishna on the bank of the Yamuna River, and he played affectionately with them. But he sensed that they had become proud and egotistic due to this rare privilege, so he suddenly disappeared from them. Grief-stricken, the gopis wept and prayed to him to return. The above verse is from that prayer.

Tava kathāmritam: "Your words, O Lord, are like nectar." We speak sweet words. We sometimes say, "Oh, your words are so sweet!" But having no nectar ourselves, we do not know how to speak nectar-like words. The Divine Incarnations have this nectar within and so their words are full of sweetness.

Amrita means "nectar" and also "immortality." According to Hindu mythology, the gods and the demons churned the ocean in order to obtain the nectar of immortality. After a hard struggle, they extracted a jar of it. But the gods deceived the demons and drank it all, becoming immortal. This immortality, however, was relative: Absolute immortality comes only from the knowledge of Brahman. That nectar is within all beings. Jesus said, "The Kingdom of Heaven is within you." Dive deep inside. Then you will find that nectar and attain immortality.

God is the ocean of *amrita*, nectar. Once Ramakrishna asked Swami Vivekananda: "Suppose there were a cup of syrup and you were a fly. Where would you sit to drink the syrup?"

Vivekananda replied: "I would sit on the edge of the cup and stretch out my neck to drink it."

"Why?" Ramakrishna asked. "What's the harm in plunging into the middle of the cup and drinking the syrup?"

Vivekananda answered: "Then I should stick in the syrup and die."

"My child," Ramakrishna said to him, "that isn't the nature of the Nectar of Satchidananda. It is the Nectar of Immortality. Man does not die from diving into it. On the contrary, he becomes immortal."[45]

We say that human beings are mortal, but this is not true. The body is mortal. The Atman, our real nature, is immortal. It is this immortality that humankind is always searching for. The Brihadaranyaka Upanishad says that when Yajnavalkya offered wealth to his beloved wife, Maitreyi, she replied: "*Yenāham nāmritasyām, kimaham tena kuryām* — What should I do with that wealth which would not make me immortal?"[46] This is the bold message of Vedanta to modern people. If you want immortality, give up whatever you have. Christ also said the same thing: "Sell what you have and then follow me. Ye cannot serve God and mammon."

The Bengali title of *The Gospel of Sri Ramakrishna* is *Sri Sri Ramakrishna Kathamrita*, which means "Sri Ramakrishna's immortal (or nectar-like) words." We hear the *Gospel*; we read the *Gospel*; we speak about the *Gospel*; but we do not "drink" the *Gospel*. It does not matter if we drink a drop, a glass, a jar, or a barrel of *amrita*. We will be immortal. It is not a matter of quantity, but of the substance itself. If we could actually absorb the *Gospel*, all our worldly desires would quickly dissipate. But it is not easy. We like to hold on to our desires: That is our problem.

Ramakrishna told this beautiful parable:

Once a fishwife was a guest in the house of a gardener who raised flowers. She came there with her empty fish-basket after selling fish in the market, and was given a place to sleep in a room where flowers were kept. But, because of the fragrance of the flowers, she couldn't get to sleep for a long time. Her hostess saw her condition and said: "Hello! Why are you tossing from side to side so restlessly?" The fishwife said: "I don't know, friend. Perhaps the smell of the flowers is disturbing my sleep. Can you give me my fish-basket? Perhaps that will put me to sleep." The basket was brought to her. She sprinkled water on it and set it near her nose. Then she fell sound asleep and snored all night.[47]

Worldly people like the smell of fish. They cannot stand a beautiful divine fragrance. Mere speaking, mere talking, mere hearing won't help us. We may repeat the word "wine" a thousand times but that will not make us intoxicated. We must drink the wine. Christ said, "Whosoever heareth these sayings of mine and doeth them, I will liken him unto a wise man who built his house upon a rock."

Tapta jivanam: "Your words relieve the burning misery of worldly life." The world is burning with misery. When we talk about life we heave a deep sigh. I remember, once when I was a young student of Vedanta I heard a vivid description of this world. Our teacher was expounding the concept of maya. He said: "Do you know what this world is? A traveller was passing through a desert. The sun was scorching hot. He was dead tired, thirsty, hungry, and exhausted. He was trying to find shelter, a shady place where he could take a little rest. At last he found a place where he laid down his head and slept, not knowing that the spot was made shady by the shadow of a poisonous cobra's hood! A single hiss and one drop of poison from that cobra would finish his life. So that is this world." We do not know how the mysterious maya traps, binds, and enslaves us.

Human beings are tormented by desire, doubt, disease, death, passion, jealousy, hatred, and so many other things. This is truly Hell. The word of the Lord alone rescues us from this awful situation. The gospel of the Lord carries solace and succour for suffering humanity. It soothes our nerves and brings us peace and joy. Just as water extinguishes fire, the words of the Lord extinguish the burning misery caused by worldly desires and our enjoyment of them.

Kavibhir-iditam: "Poets eulogize the words of the Lord in many ways." A renaissance begins with the advent of each avatar. Many books and dramas are written, songs and music are composed, and art and sculpture are developed. Ramakrishna spoke but a few words, and Swami Vivekananda expounded that message of the harmony of religions and the divinity of human beings, spreading it throughout the world. M. recorded the Master's immortal gospel, while Girish Chandra Ghosh, the actor-dramatist, wrote several dramas that incorporated the ideas of

Ramakrishna. Again, many poets composed songs based on the teachings of the Master. But Ramakrishna himself had no formal education. His knowledge came straight from God. One day he said: "If you want to understand in one sentence, come to me. If you want to understand the same thing in a thousand words, go to Keshab."[48] Keshab Chandra Sen, the Brahmo Samaj leader, was a famous orator. It was he who first wrote about Ramakrishna in his Brahmo papers and magazines. When the Master came to know about it, he said, "Keshab, by writing about me, you want to make me famous? Don't try. He whom Mother makes famous, becomes famous."

Kalmashāpaham: The words of God "destroy all kinds of sins and their results." God's name purifies our bodies and minds. Try to visualize the world as a room freshly painted with black paint. You are there, dressed in white clothes. You may be extremely cautious, but you cannot be alert all the time. In one moment of forgetfulness, you will spoil your clothes. So it happens in this world: Desire, doubt, pride, anger, jealousy, greed, and lust are continually polluting our minds. Human beings stumble and fall, overcome by temptations. But they should not yield helplessly; they must fight. The Atman manifests in a human being through three powers: wisdom, will, and action. Life is a struggle. Only two groups of people do not have to struggle: the illumined and the dead. *The Gospel of Sri Ramakrishna* helps us develop a strong discriminative faculty and protects us from weakness and temptation.

Shravana-mangalam: Anybody who hears the words of God will undoubtedly be benefited. If one eats a chili, knowingly or unknowingly, one's tongue will burn. It can't be helped. Similarly, these words of the Lord definitely do people good. One may think that just hearing the *Gospel* will not give one the flavour of it, but it will.

Shrimad: Beautiful. The words of the Lord are beautiful; they are truly enchanting and delightful. *The Gospel of Sri Ramakrishna* draws us irresistibly to God.

Ātatam: "Vast and easily available." As we do not need to search for space and air because they surround us, so the words of God are easily accessible. Those who are spiritual aspirants get divine inebriation from the *Gospel*, but it comes gradually and slowly, as the *Gospel* reveals its truths according to the aspirant's spiritual development and understanding. The *Gospel* has an intoxicating effect. We may read it a thousand times, yet it remains an endless source of inspiration. There is no end to spiritual experience, and *The Gospel of Sri Ramakrishna* is a unique chronicle of the highest immeasurable realizations. Once a disciple of Holy Mother said that he had read *The Gospel of Sri Ramakrishna* fifty times and still he was finding new light in it. The message of God is endless. An American student read the *Gospel* and remarked: "There is one defect in this book: it has an end."

Bhuvi grnanti ye bhuridā janāh: You may perform charity in various forms, but the best charity is to distribute the word of God to humanity. This final Sanskrit phrase has another meaning: Those who are spiritual seekers, those who have done spiritual practices in previous lives and also in this very life, get bliss, which is the flavour of spirituality.

Christopher Wood wrote about *The Gospel of Sri Ramakrishna*: "It is a fascinating piece of biography, quite extraordinarily honest. And as for its being long, the truth about anyone is never dull. Try it. I don't think you will be disappointed."[49]

Hundreds of people came to Ramakrishna with their questions and problems. Some came out of curiosity. Scholars came, and so did scientists, doctors, lawyers, teachers, professors, and students. Spiritual leaders and social reformers visited him, as did actors, actresses, dramatists, singers, and dancers. Hypocrites, drunkards, ruffians, and villains also came. *The Gospel of Sri Ramakrishna* is a firsthand account of the conversations that these various characters had with Ramakrishna. Each person can find his or her own personality reflected in a character in the *Gospel*.

Sitting on his wooden cot in the temple garden of Dakshineswar, Ramakrishna offered solutions to the problems of those who came to him because his own life was free from problems. Only a person whose life is troublefree can solve another's problems. Ramakrishna also boosted the spirits of his visitors. As he himself said: "One man makes a fire and others enjoy the heat. I have cooked food for you; you need only come and eat it."

On another occasion he said: "I am the destroyer of karma. I am the French colony."[50] At that time India was divided among three colonial powers: British, French, and Portuguese. If a man did something wrong in British India, he could take shelter in the French colony where the British had no jurisdiction. "I am the French colony" means that whatever sins one may be guilty of, one need only take shelter in Ramakrishna to be free from fear of punishment for them. No worldly rules can bind such a person. Only a saviour has the power to protect people from the consequences of their actions.

The subject of *The Gospel of Sri Ramakrishna* is God and *God alone*. It is concerned with how to realize Him and nothing else. Ramakrishna frequently made this simple statement: "I know only God and nothing else."

In the beginning, in the middle, and in the end of the *Gospel*, you will find only one thing: God.

Ordinary people *preach* religion, but Divine Incarnations like Buddha, Christ, Krishna, and Ramakrishna can *give* religion. Religion means realization. A touch, a glance, or a word from one of the Incarnations can spark a life-altering transformation in a human being. Ramakrishna was a tremendous spiritual force that could awaken God-consciousness in an instant. He was a spiritual phenomenon! In the *Gospel* we find him in samadhi one moment, while the next he is making fun and cutting jokes. He was that prince who could travel through all seven stories of the royal palace (the seven levels of consciousness) without any restriction. Ordinary people live on the first floor and do not know what is on the other six floors. Even Ramakrishna's jokes and frivolities were connected with God. Christopher Wood wrote: "Another side of Ramakrishna which seems to me important is that he had a sense of fun and that he was joyous. It is a tragic mistake that the popular idea of a good person is so often that of someone rather dull and somber, someone who rarely laughs. Whereas in actual fact it seems that the joy, the sheer pleasure even, of approaching God surpasses anything we know."[51] In the *Gospel*, M. notes in many places: "All laugh," or "Laughter."

Ramakrishna never turned anyone away. He said: "Let me be condemned to be born over and over again, even in the form of a dog, if by doing so I can be of help to a single soul. I will give up twenty thousand such bodies to help one man."[52]

Ramakrishna's Teachings in the *Gospel*

The qualifications for studying Vedanta are extremely difficult to meet. A Vedanta student should practise discrimination, renunciation, and control of the senses; and he or she should have a burning desire for liberation. But if you want to read *The Gospel of Sri Ramakrishna*, no qualifications are necessary; no commentator is necessary; no teacher is necessary. It is simple. Simplicity was Ramakrishna's style, so his sentences are seldom complicated. Simplicity is holiness.

Aldous Huxley wrote in the foreword to Swami Nikhilananda's translation: "What a scholastic philosopher would call the 'accidents' of Ramakrishna's life were intensely Hindu and therefore, so far as we in the West are concerned, unfamiliar and hard to understand: its 'essence,' however, was intensely mystical and therefore universal."[53]

Though the background and plots of Ramakrishna's stories and parables are Indian in origin, they are so vivid and simple, so enchanting, that even a child can understand them. A man once came to him and asked, "Sir, how can I realize God?" Ramakrishna answered: "You may see God if your love for Him is as strong as these three attachments put together, namely: the attachment of a worldly man to the things of the world, the attachment of a mother to her child, and the attachment of a chaste and devoted wife to her husband."[54]

Ramakrishna's stories and parables are very positive, instructive, and uplifting. He was always inspiring. His parable of the woodcutter is typical: A holy man told a poor woodcutter, "Go forward." The woodcutter took his advice, advanced further into the forest, and found a sandalwood forest. He sold the sandalwood and became very rich. Then one day he thought to himself: "That holy man told me to go forward. He did not ask me to be satisfied." So he went even further into the forest and found a copper mine. Going further still, he found a silver mine, and then a gold mine. Finally, he found a diamond mine with which he became exceedingly wealthy. Ramakrishna said that there was no end to spiritual bliss, spiritual illumination.

Ramakrishna's teachings are also practical: "To meditate, you should withdraw within yourself or retire to a secluded corner or to the forest."

"Sir, I cannot go to the forest."

"All right. Meditate in the corner of a room."

"Sir, my house is full of people. I cannot get a corner of a room."

"Meditate in the inner chamber of your heart."

There are many alternatives. If you cannot do anything at all, surrender to the Lord and He will do everything for you. "Give me the power of attorney," said Ramakrishna. Only an avatar like Ramakrishna could say that. Ramakrishna gave the example of a mother cat carrying her kitten wherever she wants. The kitten completely surrenders itself.

Another beautiful metaphor that Ramakrishna used concerns three men who were curious to know what was on the other side of a high wall. The first man climbed up a ladder and found Infinite Bliss on the other side. He immediately laughed and jumped into it. The second man did the same thing. The third man also climbed up and saw what was there, but he came back down to tell others of that Infinite Bliss behind the wall, behind maya. That third man is Ramakrishna. In the evening when the sound of the vesper bells reverberated through the Dakshineswar temple compound, Ramakrishna would climb up onto the roof of the kuthi [mansion] and call out for his future devotees: "Come to me, my children! Where are you? I can't bear to live without you!"

The Gospel of Sri Ramakrishna is a large volume, and it is expensive. But whatever the price may be, no price can be put on the value of those words. Ramakrishna had a householder disciple, an Ishwarakoti (godlike soul), whose name was Purna Chandra Ghosh. Long after Ramakrishna passed away, there was trouble in Purna's family and he wanted to commit suicide. He decided to bathe first, and then pay his respects to his guru before killing himself. He took a bath, then went to the shrine and bowed down to the Master. But then he thought: "Let me read a little bit of the *Kathamrita*. Taking the beautiful message of the Master, I shall depart from this world." He opened the book at random and his eyes fell on this sentence: *"Purna balak bhakta. Thakur Purner mangal chinta karitechen."* (Purna is a young devotee. The Master was thinking of his welfare.) "What?" cried Purna. "The Master is thinking of me and I shall commit suicide? Impossible! He is thinking of my welfare and I am contemplating killing myself. It cannot be."[55] He gave up the idea and thus his life was saved. Such is the power of the words of *The Gospel of Sri Ramakrishna*!

A Blessing from Holy Mother

Holy Mother had great appreciation for *The Gospel of Sri Ramakrishna*. On 2 April 1905 Holy Mother, Golap-ma, and Nikunja Devi (M.'s wife) were listening to the *Gospel* being read. When the reading was over, Holy Mother commented: "It is not a small thing to remember the Master's words and ideas, and then write them. I wholeheartedly bless M.: Let his books spread everywhere and let all people know him."

Another day when someone was reading the *Gospel*, Holy Mother was listening with deep absorption. Golap-ma, Nikunja Devi, and some other women were seated there. After some time Holy Mother exclaimed: "How wonderful! How Master Mahashay kept these teachings in his mind! Did he go to the Master with paper and pencil?"

Nikunja Devi: "No, Mother. He would write these things from his memory."

Holy Mother: "What a powerful brain he has! He wrote all these things from memory."

Golap-ma: "Naren also had a powerful mind."

Holy Mother: "He had a different kind of power — for lecturing, writing books, and so on. M. has another kind of power. [*Addressing Nikunja Devi*] My daughter, give your husband more milk [which is supposed to increase mental power]. May he attain more power. Ah, what a great service he is giving to the world!"

The reading continued.

"The Master said to Mani: 'You are all my relatives.'"

Holy Mother commented: "Of course, everyone is in his inner circle."

Another section was read: "Keshab was coughing."

To this, the crazy aunt [Radhu's mother] said, "Why did M. write such a thing?" Holy Mother replied with a smile: "What do you know? It has a purpose."

The reader was reading a passage about the Master's ecstasy: "M. was thinking: Is the Master describing his own state?"

Holy Mother commented: "Yes, M.'s thinking was correct." After a while Holy Mother said to Nikunja Devi: "My daughter, tell your husband that I am blessing him wholeheartedly."[56]

Appreciations

M. tried to hide himself in the pages of *The Gospel of Sri Ramakrishna* by using several pseudonyms, such as Mani, Master, Mohinimohan, a Devotee, a Servant, an Englishman, and so on; but readers quickly discovered him. While intending to make his guru well known, he became famous himself. Truly, *The Gospel of Sri Ramakrishna* made M. immortal. Here we present a few appreciations of his great work.

Swami Premananda wrote to M. on 28 September 1897: "Two copies of your *Gospel* are just at hand, also a p.c. (post card). I am just going to send one copy to Swami Vivekananda. How are you doing now? We are very anxious to see you and hear from you 'the *Gospel* of our Lord,' so carefully kept by yourself. Not only I, but all of us, especially our boys — sannyasins and brahmacharins — are anxious to have your holy company and hear from your *Gospel*."[57]

Girish Chandra Ghosh wrote on 22 March 1909: "If my humble opinion goes for anything I not only fully endorse the opinion of the great Swami Vivekananda but add in a loud voice that the *Kathamrita* has been my very existence during my protracted illness for the last three years.... You deserve the gratitude of the whole human race to the end of days."[58]

Swami Ramakrishnananda wrote on 27 October 1904: "You have left the whole of humanity in debt by publishing these invaluable pages fraught with the best wisdom of the greatest avatar of God."[59]

In December 1897 Satish Chandra Mukhopadhyay wrote in the journal *Dawn*: "We are extremely thankful to our friend M., whom we may introduce to the reader as an unassuming gentleman of high spiritual attainments, and a devoted servant of his Lord and Master, Sri Ramakrishna, for having given us an opportunity of presenting to our readers what we may most appropriately call 'A Modern Gospel' — which breathes throughout a deep catholicity in reference to all forms of religious discipline and is therefore at war with not *one* of them."[60]

Mr. N. Ghosh wrote in the *Indian Nation* on 19 May 1902: "*Ramakrishna Kathamrita* by M. (Part I) is a work of singular value and interest. He has done a kind of work which no Bengalee had ever done before, which so far as we are aware no native of India had ever done. It has been done only once in history namely by Boswell.... What a treasure would it have been to the world if all the sayings of Sri Krishna, Buddha, Jesus, Muhammad, Nanak, and Chaitanya could have been thus preserved."[61]

Nagendra Nath Gupta, who personally knew Ramakrishna, wrote in *Ramakrishna-Vivekananda* in 1933: "*The Gospel of Ramakrishna Paramahamsa* is a record taken at first hand. The words were taken down as they came fresh from the lips of the Master. They were frequently read over to him and he suggested alterations and corrections. There is no room for imagination or exaggeration in anything that concerns Ramakrishna Paramahamsa. Much about the earlier prophets is wrapped in uncertainty and speculation. There are no real likenesses of Buddha, Christ, and Chaitanya. Ramakrishna's photographs are available everywhere. His spoken words are available to all almost just as he uttered them."[62]

The *Brahmavadin* published a review in April 1902: "The life of no prophet has ever been written in the way in which M. has done it in the book under review. Even Boswell's life of Johnson falls into shade before this magnificent record of the Paramahamsa's sayings and doings during the last two years of his life. To the student of psychology and psychic research these conversations are of immense value. They give us a peep into the workings of an extraordinary mind which has risen above the din and incessant devouring activity of this work-a-day world to the eternal presence of the music of the higher spheres. They point out how a Godman who has attained spiritual oneness and realized universal harmony becomes the interpreter of God to man. The dialogues of Socrates resemble to some extent these conversations but without the sublime and tranquil ecstasies of the oriental saint."[63]

Romain Rolland wrote to M.: "*The Gospel of Sri Ramakrishna* is valuable for it is the faithful account by M. of the discourses with the Master, either his own or those which he actually heard for the next four years. Their exactitude is almost stenographic. The book containing the conversations (*The Gospel of Sri Ramakrishna*) recalls at every turn the setting and the atmosphere. Thanks for having disseminated the radiance of the beautiful Smile of your Master."[64]

Aldous Huxley wrote in his foreword to *The Gospel of Sri Ramakrishna*: "M., as the author modestly styles himself, was peculiarly qualified for his task. To a reverent love for his Master, to a deep and experiential knowledge of that master's teaching, he added a prodigious memory for the small happenings of each day and a happy gift for recording them in an interesting and realistic way. Making good use of his natural gifts and of the circumstances in which he found himself, M. produced a book unique, so far as my knowledge goes, in the literature of hagiography. No other saint has had so able and indefatigable a Boswell. Never have the small events of a contemplative's daily life been described with such a wealth of intimate detail. Never have the casual and unstudied utterances of a great religious teacher been set down with so minute a fidelity."[65]

Muhammad Daud Rahbar, a writer and professor of Boston University, wrote: "I have read some delightful portions of the one-thousand-page *Gospel of Sri Ramakrishna*. This marvellous volume has extraordinary revelations. Immediately one recognizes a cherishable friend in Sri Ramakrishna. His open, passionate, and transparent devotion humbles and chastens us. He is no common mortal. He is a man of phenomenal gifts. His presence is a haven. His conversations, recorded abundantly in the *Gospel of Sri Ramakrishna* by his disciple M., are charming, inspired. Their literary merit is due to the inspired goodness of Sri Ramakrishna."[66]

Christopher Isherwood: "M. shows us Ramakrishna by day and by night, chiefly at Dakshineswar but also at the houses of Balaram and other devotees, on river-boats with Keshab Sen, or driving in a carriage through the streets. Usually, there are quite a lot of people present: disciples, householder devotees and casual visitors. Naturally, they tend to ask Ramakrishna the same questions and so Ramakrishna's answers often repeat or paraphrase themselves. M. records these repetitions, as well as the words of all the songs Ramakrishna sings. A newcomer to the *Gospel* may find this tiresome at first. But, if he reads the book straight through from beginning to end, instead of merely dipping into it, he will probably agree that it is these very repetitions which give the narrative its continuity and its sense of life actually being lived from day to day. In any case, a teacher who never repeats himself is a creation of art and editorship rather than a live being!

"The most important function of Ramakrishna as a teacher was available to householder devotee and monastic disciple alike. Both had the opportunity of watching him in the silence of samadhi, in the incoherent mutterings of ecstasy, in the radiant joy of devotional dancing and song. And it was in these manifestations that even some casual visitors to

Dakshineswar caught a glimpse of Ramakrishna's true nature. To those who were not utterly insensitive, this was a demonstration, more convincing than the Master's most eloquent words, of the reality of God's presence.

"The service M. has rendered us and future generations can hardly be exaggerated. Even the vainest of authors might well have been humbled, finding himself entrusted with such a task. M. was the least vain. M. embodies Ramakrishna's ideal of the householder devotee."[67]

N. Bangarayya, a journalist, wrote in his reminiscences of M: "I became fully convinced that it is impossible for anybody to add to the charm of Ramakrishna. M. spoke beautifully; but there was a distinct and ineffaceable barrier between the two styles, the style of the Master as the disciple has recorded and the style of the disciple himself. The originality, suggestiveness, simplicity, and directness of the former are all its own. It soars far above the reach of any human intellect, be it ever so great. It is not possible for anyone to have invented for the world 'The Ramakrishna Art.' It is greatness enough to have preserved it."[68]

Sarala Devi (later Pravrajika Bharatiprana) recalled: "Revered M. presented me a copy of the *Kathamrita* and asked me to read it. He also told me that he would give me other volumes in the future if I liked them. He later gave me the other three volumes. Seeing my set of the *Kathamrita*, the Holy Mother remarked: 'M. is very fond of Sarala and he has presented her his wonderful books. Well, Sarala, please read a little to me from them.' I used to read the *Kathamrita* to the Mother. She would listen very attentively and joyfully tell us the stories of olden days. Recounting the stories of the Master in Dakshineswar, the Mother said: 'M. is so clever that he has recorded the Master's words just as they were. Truly, the Master would speak in that way. Now he is publishing those teachings in book form. Thus so many people are able to know about the Master. I also heard so many things from the Master. I would have recorded them if I had known that these teachings would be published. Well, my child, who could guess that such things would happen?'"[69]

The Centenary of The Gospel of Sri Ramakrishna

The *Gospel of Sri Ramakrishna* was born on 26 February 1882 in the diary of Mahendra Nath Gupta, or "M.," as he preferred to be known. During the centenary celebration of this immortal work of literature, innumerable people worldwide expressed their love and gratitude to M.

M. never realized that the book he had based on his diary would occupy such an exalted position in religious literature. When he was a college professor, he would often hide away on the roof of his college and read his diary in secret. And when the Master's devotees wanted to hear what he had written, he gave them an evasive answer: "It is nothing. I just wrote something for myself." There is a Bengali proverb: "The more it is hidden, the more it becomes firm; and the more it is expressed, the more despicable it becomes."

This universe is beautiful because its Creator has hidden Himself within it. God never comes forward to tell people, "Look, I am the Creator of this universe." M. tried to hide himself in the pages of the *Gospel* by assuming different names, such as Master (schoolteacher), Mani, Mohinimohan, a devotee, a servant, an Englishman (an English-educated man), and other pseudonyms.

Over time, many readers became curious about some of the people who appeared in the *Gospel*, such as Hazra, Mani, and so on. When someone asked M. about Hazra, M. replied: "One day Hazra was on the southeast veranda repeating japa on his rosary. The Master returned from the Kali temple, snatched the rosary from Hazra's hand, and threw it away. He said to Hazra: 'Why do you tell your beads here [*meaning while living with him*]? Many people in Calcutta are repeating the mantra with a rosary — some for twenty years and some twenty-five — but what are they achieving? Without longing one cannot achieve anything. By merely seeing this place [*meaning himself*] one can have awakening of consciousness.'"

A devotee: "What happened to Hazra in the end?"

M.: "Hazra died while repeating the name of the Master."

A devotee: "In the *Gospel* there was a gentleman named 'Mani.' What happened to him?"

M.: "I don't know what will happen to him."[1]

Everyone laughed, because the inquirer did not know that M. and Mani were the same person.

M. used to sit on the foot-mat near the Master's cot in his room. What humility, faith, and love M. had for the Master! One day the Master said to M.: "You don't want anything from me, but you love to see me and hear my words. My mind also dwells on you. I wonder how you are and why you don't come."[2] On another occasion the Master asked for M.'s address. It makes us feel happy to learn how much an avatar thinks of his devotees. We find in the Bhagavata that Krishna sent Uddhava to get news of his devotees in Vrindaban and to console them. In the *Gospel* we find many examples of how Ramakrishna expressed concern for his devotees. This proves that God also thinks of us.

M. was humble and serious, a hidden yogi. He played many roles in the divine drama of Ramakrishna: recorder of the *Gospel*, messenger, close companion, attendant, "kidnapping master,"* and so on.

There are two things that make Ramakrishna unique among incarnations of God: his photographs and the *Gospel*. We have to imagine how other incarnations of God looked, but for Ramakrishna we have three photographs that were taken during his lifetime. Moreover, each one was taken while he was in samadhi. These photos help his devotees in their meditation. We not only have these photos, but we can also learn more about Ramakrishna by reading the *Gospel*, as it vividly describes the Master's daily life, the people he encountered, and what he said. This type of daily record is not available for any other avatar. M. wrote in his

---

*Devotees humorously gave that name to M. because he brought several of his students to Ramakrishna.

introduction to the sixth edition of Volume I of his Bengali version, *Sri Sri Ramakrishna Kathamrita*: "Srima or Master or M. (a son of the Lord and a servant) are the same person. While living with Sri Ramakrishna he recorded whatever he heard and saw. He did not write anything that he heard from other devotees. The subject matter of this book is the daily events of the Master that he recorded in his diary. Whatever he heard and saw on a particular day, he recalled on the same day and recorded in his diary. — Author."

An artist creates pictures on a canvas with a brush and paint. In the *Gospel*, M. used his pen to draw unique portraits of Ramakrishna's daily life.

The main theme of *The Gospel of Sri Ramakrishna* is: "First God and then the world: the goal of life is to realize God." One needs the company of holy people to understand this message. Holy company is rare, but *The Gospel of Sri Ramakrishna* is easily available. This *Gospel* provides holy company, because when we read this book, we feel the presence of the Master and his devotees. Chaitanya said that one can attain devotion by five means: holy company, serving God, study of the Bhagavata, chanting God's name, and living in Vrindaban or some other holy place. M. reminded his visitors repeatedly: "We have no alternative than to have the company of the holy. 'Have the company of the holy' — that was the beginning, middle, and end of the Master's advice to us." Holy company cures householders of worldliness and frees monks from the net of maya. Everyone needs holy company: Even monks need the company of other monks.

There is a Bengali proverb: "Criticism is the ornament of a pioneer." Buddha said in the *Dhammapada* (Verse 228): "There never was, there never will be, nor is there now, a man who is always blamed, or a man who is always praised." M. was not only praised for writing the *Gospel*; some people also criticized him. M. once said:

> Swami Vivekananda wrote to me that after reading the *Gospel*, some would curse me and some would praise me. If these teachings go against someone's self-interest, that person will curse me. Renunciation is the predominant message of this book. Those who desire worldly enjoyment will be angry at me. Perhaps a young man read the *Gospel* and became a monk. His mother will say that the man who wrote that book has brainwashed her son and ruined his life. If a husband becomes spiritual upon reading the *Gospel*, the wife will blame me; if the wife becomes spiritual, the husband will curse me. Only those who no longer desire mere enjoyment will appreciate me. They will say: The words of the *Gospel* are

Ten of M.'s diaries which formed the basis of *The Gospel of Sri Ramakrishna* and the inkpot which M. used to write the *Gospel*.

like nectar. We were burning with misery, but the words of the Master brought peace and joy to our lives.[3]

Many books have been written about *The Gospel of Sri Ramakrishna*, and many more commentaries will be written on it in the future. For many years, I have been watching with amazement how the message of *The Gospel of Sri Ramakrishna* is spreading in the West. This reminds me of something that Swami Premananda once said: "Look, who will preach? No one is needed to preach the Master. He preaches himself. I visit various places and see the glory of the Master. With a view to showing me how he is spreading his ideas among others, he takes me to those places out of his grace."[4]

Many years ago a young American woman who had read *The Gospel of Sri Ramakrishna* wrote a letter to me in St. Louis. I asked her to visit me at the Vedanta Society of Kansas City, Missouri. She was a farmer's daughter and worked on the family farm in the state of Kansas. She drove a few hundred miles to see me. When she was telling me her story, tears came from her eyes. She said: "I bought a copy of *The Gospel of Sri Ramakrishna* from the Vedanta Press in Hollywood and read it. One night I was sleeping in the cottage near our farm. Ramakrishna appeared before me and gave me a mantra." She told me the mantra that she had been given. I was dumbfounded and also happy, knowing the Master had bestowed his grace on her. I marvelled at how the Master was roaming around the vast farmlands in the American Midwest and spotting devotees with sincere longing for God. Yearning for God is the only thing needful in spiritual life.

"Woman and Gold"

A young woman in Kansas City bought a copy of the *Gospel* and read it. I asked her: "Does it bother you when you read in the *Gospel*, 'Woman and gold are maya'?"

She replied: "No, it does not. I mentally change it to 'man and gold are maya.'"

I was pleased to hear that. When I was in Hollywood, I presented a copy of the *Gospel* to a Catholic woman. When she read "Woman and gold are maya," she stopped reading it. She wrote in her will that the book should be returned to me when she died. She died a few years later and her sister sent the book to me.

Swami Nikhilananda wrote an exhaustive note in his translation of the *Gospel*:

The term "woman and gold," which has been used throughout in a collective sense, occurs again and again in the teachings of Sri Ramakrishna to designate the chief impediments to spiritual progress. This favourite expression of the Master "kamini-kanchan," has often been misconstrued. By it he meant only "lust and greed," the baneful influence of which retards the aspirant's spiritual growth. He used the word "kamini," or "woman," as a concrete term for the sex instinct when addressing his men devotees. He advised women, on the other hand, to shun "man." "Kanchan," or "gold," symbolizes greed, which is the other obstacle to spiritual life.

Sri Ramakrishna never taught his disciples to hate any woman, [or] womankind in general. This can be seen clearly by going through all his teachings under this head and judging them collectively. The Master looked on all women as so many images of the Divine Mother of the Universe.[5]

To avoid any misunderstanding, I generally translate the term *kamini-kanchan* as "lust and gold." The root of *kamini* is *kama*, which means desire; one needs gold or money to fulfill that desire. Desires for lust and gold, or sex and money, take the mind away from God — that is why Ramakrishna said that lust and gold are maya.

In 1942, when the English translation of the *Gospel* was published, American society was different from what it is now. When I find a Western woman buying the *Gospel*, I caution her not to get upset when she reads the phrase "woman and gold are maya." I explain that Ramakrishna's Chosen Deity was Mother Kali; one of his gurus was the Bhairavi Brahmani; and his first disciple was his wife, whom he worshipped as the Divine Mother. He was extremely devoted to his own mother: Even though he was a monk, he did not wear ochre robes because he thought this would upset her. Moreover, he preached the motherhood of God, and he taught his disciples to love and respect all women, as they are manifestations of the Divine Mother. He also would feel pained if he found that a woman was fasting. Such a man cannot possibly hate women.

One of our swamis in the United States lent a copy of the *Gospel* to a professor, but he returned the book when he came across the sentence "Woman and gold are maya." The professor told the swami why he had not read the whole book. The swami suggested: "Please read that portion of the book which appeals to you. You will not have to accept everything that Ramakrishna said." Later the professor read the whole book and told the swami: "I think Ramakrishna is the answer to our society. I love this book very much. Our society is guided by two things: Dollar-king and Sex-queen. The teachings of Ramakrishna are a nice solution to those crucial problems."

I have an English friend who is a professor of mathematics. He read the *Gospel* and commented: "I love Ramakrishna for two reasons: First, he never says anything that is irrational. Second, he is an expert at solving problems. He tells his visitors, 'Listen to a story,' and solves their problems. As a professor of mathematics, I cannot accept anything that is irrational and my job is to solve mathematical problems."

I met a woman who was a theology student at Eden Seminary in St. Louis. She was a devout Christian but would sometimes come to our lectures at the Vedanta Society. After reading the *Gospel*, she told me: "Swami, one defect of this book is that it has an end."

Truth and Longing in Vedanta

Ramakrishna was compelled to speak the truth: It was not possible for him to flatter people. He told them what was good for them. Swami Vivekananda said: "The duty of the common man is to obey the commands of his 'God' — society. The children of light never do it. This is an eternal law. The one accommodates himself to his surroundings and to social opinion and gets all good things from his *giver of all good things* — society. The other stands alone and drags society up towards him. The accommodating man finds a path of roses — the non-accommodating, one of thorns. But the worshipper of 'vox populi' goes to annihilation in a moment — the children of Truth live forever."[6]

In 1976 the Catholic Church convened the Eucharistic Congress in Philadelphia. Mother Teresa of Calcutta coined a slogan, "Hunger for God," and this created a tremendous commotion in America. In one of my lectures at the Vedanta Society in Hollywood, I told the audience: "This slogan of Mother Teresa may be new to you, but to us it is an old saying. The avatar comes to create hunger for God in the minds of people. Please open *The Gospel of Sri Ramakrishna*, which consists of 1063 pages. You will see that on almost every page the Master talks about longing for God. He said repeatedly: 'Yearning is like the red sky in the east at dawn. After such a sky the sun must rise. Immediately after that yearning one sees God.'"[7]

In *Sri Ramakrishna and His Divine Play*, Swami Saradananda wrote that when the Master accepted the position of priest in the Kali temple, his longing was so intense that he soon had a vision of the Mother. This first vision resulted from his longing, not through sadhana. Without longing, spiritual life lacks intensity and becomes monotonous.

In the Puranas, we find descriptions of devotees' love and longing for God; but God's love for the devotees is not mentioned. This is because human beings are incapable of describing God's infinite love, and those scriptures were written by human beings. M. once said: "If the Master heard that someone had developed longing for God, he would rush to that person on his own initiative. One dark night the Master hired a carriage and went to a devotee's house in Calcutta. I was with him. As soon as the devotee learned that the Master had come, he said: 'Sir, why did you take so much trouble to come to see me so late at night? If you had called for me, I would have come to you.' The Master told him: 'Look, in the beginning God becomes the magnet, and the devotee, the needle. But in the end the devotee becomes the magnet, and God the needle. One attains God who has longing.'"

Ramakrishna's Influence on the West

For most of the Church's history, Catholics kept themselves separate from adherents of other religious paths and maintained their exclusive identity. They did not even have much communication with other Christian denominations. On 7 December 1965, Pope Paul VI began to change this when he declared: "Let them reflect attentively on how Christian religious life may be able to assimilate the ascetic and contemplative traditions whose seeds were sometimes already planted by God in ancient cultures prior to the preaching of the Gospel."[8]

In August 1981 I had a talk with Swami Bhavyananda of the London Centre. He told me that in 1977 he had been invited to Rome by some Benedictine monks who were hosting a seminar on worship, prayer, and meditation as practised by Buddhists, Hindus, and Christians. On the dais of the monastery's altar, Bhavyananda set a picture of Ramakrishna and then worshipped him with flowers, incense, and candles. He then sang "Hari Om Ramakrishna" with cymbals and other instruments; the Christian monks joined with him. An Italian television station broadcast this event.

Pope Paul VI was in Rome at the time. This great soul met privately with Swami Bhavyananda. When a group photo of the seminar participants was to be taken, he took the swami's hand and made him sit next to him. At that time Swami Bhavyananda presented him with a copy of *The Gospel of Sri Ramakrishna*. He accepted the gift, and he told the swami that he had read about Ramakrishna.*

---

*When I visited Rome in 1990, I met the pope's ecumenical secretary and a monk who was the ecumenical representative for Asia. This monk was from Kerala, South India. He took me to his office and showed me *The Complete Works of Swami Vivekananda* on his desk. He was writing a thesis on Vivekananda's Bhakti Yoga, and

In 1981 I went to Mexico City to visit an unaffiliated Vedanta centre there. Every Monday the devotees met to meditate in front of a picture of Ramakrishna and discuss his life and message. I gave a talk on Vedanta and the president of the Vedanta Society translated it into Spanish.

There are many yogis, gurus, babas, and other religious leaders in America who are tremendously active in teaching Eastern religions and hatha yoga. Many of them use Ramakrishna's teachings in their sermons, directly or indirectly. In addition, I often find Ramakrishna's name in the index of many American books on religion, philosophy, and psychology. A student attending Los Angeles City College gave me a copy of *The Portable World Bible* (edited by Robert O. Ballou, Penguin Books), which is in their curriculum. When I examined that book, I found twelve pages of material taken from *The Gospel of Sri Ramakrishna*. In 1975 Christopher Isherwood presented me with a copy of *A Treasury of Traditional Wisdom* (published by Simon and Schuster, New York). I counted 167 quotations from *The Gospel of Sri Ramakrishna* in this huge volume.

In the *Gospel*, apart from spiritual wisdom, one finds sweetness and humour — and that is the reason it is spreading. One of our friends from the Hollywood Centre was a major in the United States Air Force. He was a disciple of Swami Prabhavananda and a very jovial person. He often said, "Perhaps in my previous life I was that troublemaker Hazra in Dakshineswar," so we called him "Hazra." He later retired and became the editor of *Judo* magazine. He said that he mentally connected himself with the devotees of Ramakrishna in Dakshineswar, and thus enjoyed the company of the Master.

When I was at the Hollywood Centre in 1971, I would shake hands with the members of the audience after the lecture. Once a man came forward and introduced himself, saying, "Swami, I am Girish." When I shook hands with him, I smelled alcohol on his breath. I was delighted to see how the Master's devotees with all their different propensities live on. Let people connect themselves with the Master in whatever way they like. Krishna promised in the Gita: "*Na me bhakta pranashati* — My devotee never perishes."

A friend from Santa Barbara was a staunch devotee of the Master. He was extremely intelligent and very outspoken. A friend of his gave him a book written by a yogi and asked him to read it. Our friend opened the book and counted eighteen "I"s in two pages. He then handed

(*cont.*) asked me for some books on bhakti by other writers. I sent him a copy of *Bhakti Yoga* by Aswini Kumar Datta.

Ramakrishna's *Gospel* to his friend and said: "I see your yogi's book is full
of 'I's; now see this huge volume and count how many times Ramakrishna
used the word 'I.'"

Ramakrishna could not utter the word "I." He would use the term
"here" or "in this place" instead.

In *The Gospel of Sri Ramakrishna*, there are many places in which one
finds, "All laugh," or "Laughter." Sometimes American devotees say,
"Swami, you laugh but we don't find anything there to laugh about." I
reply: "Humour lurks in the language, in gestures, in social customs, and
in the prevailing practices of the people and place. If you want to understand Ramakrishna's humour, you will have to know his language, mood,
behaviour, social customs, interpersonal relationships, and so on. I have
a book, *10,000 Jokes, Toasts and Stories*, which I read sometimes to understand American humour. I don't understand most of the jokes because
I don't get the point or the punch line. You see, if you are not born and
brought up in a particular language, you can't get its subtle meaning, and
you cannot understand the slang and colloquial expressions."

There is a saying: A foolish man laughs three times. At first he laughs
without understanding; second, he laughs when he does understand; and
third, he laughs when he wonders why it took him so long to understand.

Once I was listening to a comedian on the radio. He told a story about
a pastor who was giving a sermon in a village church. The pastor said:
"Only Christ is perfect. You are all imperfect and sinners. Have you ever
seen or heard of anyone who is perfect? If so, please raise your hand."
There was deep silence in the church. At last a middle-aged man from
the back raised his hand. The pastor challenged him: "Are you perfect?"

"No, sir."

"Have you seen anyone who is perfect?"

"No, sir."

"Have you heard of anyone who is perfect?"

"Yes, sir."

"Who is that person?"

"My wife's first husband," replied the man. Everyone laughed
except myself. I then asked a friend, "Where is the humour?" He replied:
"Whatever this man does, his wife says that her late husband was perfect
in that respect." I don't understand many Western customs, especially
courtship, so I can't find any humour in jokes about courtship. Similarly,
Western people do not understand some of Ramakrishna's humour.

Two things are in the blood of the American people: Love of freedom
and a sense of humour. Ramakrishna appeals to both.

We know very little about how Ramakrishna's gospel is spreading throughout the world. Many years ago I went to Washington University to attend a lecture by the famous American writer and Orientalist Joseph Campbell. He finished his lecture by telling the Master's parable of a tiger that was brought up by sheep. Once there was a religious conference at a Baptist Church in Illinois. One minister referred in a speech to the Master's story about the blind men trying to describe an elephant. Neither Joseph Campbell nor the Baptist minister mentioned Ramakrishna's name. That does not matter: the Master never sought name and fame.

It is hard to say how the *Gospel* works on the human mind. In the 1970s I gave a lecture in the Hollywood temple, entitled "Yearning for Illumination." I quoted a saying of Ramakrishna: "It is said, in the Kaliyuga, if a man can weep for God one day and one night, he sees Him." After hearing this, one of the women in the audience, an actress, went to her apartment and began to cry. She cried till midnight and then fell asleep. She said to me later, "I cried for the Master but he did not come." I replied: "You have wept for only seven or eight hours. The Master said that one would have to cry for twenty-four hours. So you will have to cry more."

Truly, tears wash away all impurities of the mind that have accumulated birth after birth.

In 1973 I went to Portland to give a lecture. I quoted the Master: "Cry to the Lord with an intensely yearning heart and you will certainly see Him. People shed a whole jugful of tears for wife and children. They swim in tears for money. But who weeps for God? Cry to Him with a real cry." A middle-aged man said: "In America it is disgraceful for a man to cry. It is a sign of cowardice."

I replied: "The Master asked his devotees to cry to God secretly and in solitude. You do not have to show everyone that you are crying for God."

A young man once asked for some advice from Swami Sankarananda, a disciple of Swami Brahmananda. He replied: "Read *The Gospel of Sri Ramakrishna* every day. It contains the answers to whatever spiritual questions arise in the human mind. If Ramakrishna's words cannot remove doubt from your mind, then do you think my words will?"

Once Swami Vishuddhananda, a disciple of the Holy Mother, joyfully said to a young monk: "Today is a memorable day in my life. I have read the five volumes of *The Gospel of Sri Ramakrishna* in Bengali fifty times."

A young man went to Swami Madhavananda, a disciple of the Holy Mother, and said that he was studying the *Gospel* so that he could be a

monk. The swami remarked: "Look, one cannot become a monk by reading the *Gospel*. Read the books of Swami Vivekananda. They will inspire
you, and then only will you feel the need to join the monastery. One sees
God when reading the *Gospel*. Why should such a person need to become
a monk?"

I know quite a few Westerners who read *The Gospel of Sri Ramakrishna*
every day and try to follow the Master's teachings. The *Gospel* is an anti-
dote for depression and spiritual dryness. This reminds me of a wonderful
incident that took place in 1932. A young monk moaned and complained
to Swami Shivananda, saying: "I have not seen God, nor have I any peace
of mind. Sometimes doubt prevails in my mind, and I even doubt the
instructions that you gave me."

At this, the swami's face turned red. He said excitedly: "Look, my
son, if the Master is true, we too are true. Whatever I say is nothing but
the truth. We have not come to cheat people. If we sink, you too will sink
with us. But by his grace we have realized that we shall never sink, nor
will you."[9]

Like an opium-addicted peacock, M. was always intoxicated with
the nectar of Ramakrishna's words. He distributed the Master's message
to everyone who went to him, and he left his magnum opus for future
generations.

In closing, I shall quote a few lines from Aswini Kumar Datta's memorable letter to M.:

> You are blessed indeed. What heavenly nectar you have sprinkled all
> over the country! I was not born under the lucky star of an M., that I
> might jot down the days, the dates, and the hours of my visits with the
> Master and note down correctly all the words uttered by his holy lips.
>
> I saw the Master not more than four or five times. What I saw and
> received in those few days has sweetened my whole life. That Elysian
> smile of his, laden with nectar, I have locked up in the secret closet of
> my memory. That is the unending treasure of a hapless person like
> myself. A thrill of joy passes through my heart when I think how a
> grain of the bliss shed from that laughter has been sweetening the
> lives of millions, even in distant America. If that be my case, you may
> very well understand how lucky you are.[10]

Pilgrimage and Austerities

R amakrishna repeatedly asked seekers of God to live in solitude from time to time and call on God. On 26 November 1883 the Master gave the householders some wonderful advice:

It is difficult to lead the life of a householder in a spirit of detachment. Once Pratap said to me: "Sir, we follow the example of King Janaka. He led the life of a householder in a detached spirit. We shall follow him." I said to him: "Can one be like King Janaka by merely wishing it? How many austerities he practised in order to acquire divine knowledge! He practised the most intense form of asceticism for many years and only then returned to the life of the world."

Is there, then, no hope for householders? Certainly there is. They must practise spiritual discipline in solitude for some days. Thus they will acquire knowledge and devotion. Then it will not hurt them to lead the life of the world. But when you practise discipline in solitude, keep yourself entirely away from your family. You must not allow your wife, son, daughter, mother, father, sister, brother, friends, or relatives near you. While thus practising discipline in solitude, you should think: "I have no one else in the world. God is my all." You must also pray to Him, with tears in your eyes, for knowledge and devotion.

If you ask me how long you should live in solitude away from your family, I should say that it would be good for you if you could spend even one day in such a manner. Three days at a time are still better. One may live in solitude for twelve days, a month, three months, or a year, according to one's convenience and ability. One hasn't much to fear if one leads the life of a householder after attaining knowledge and devotion.

The mind is like milk. If you keep the mind in the world, which is like water, then the milk and water will get mixed. That is why people keep milk in a quiet place and let it set into curd, and then churn butter from it. Likewise, through spiritual discipline practised in solitude, churn the butter of knowledge and devotion from the milk of the mind. Then that butter can easily be kept in the water of the world. It will not get mixed with the world. The mind will float detached on the water of the world.[1]

M. followed the advice of his guru. During the Master's lifetime he at one time spent more than three weeks at Dakshineswar, practising sadhana. In addition, he visited Darjeeling and Puri. When he was teaching at Ripon College [now Surendranath College], he rented an apartment and lived by himself. The Master had once instructed him to cook rice and eat it first with ghee, and then with milk, because it is sattvic food. As a result of his long absences and pilgrimages, M. lost three jobs. He had a good reputation, however, so it did not take long for him to find a new position each time.

Kamarpukur and Jayrambati

M. visited Kamarpukur and Jayrambati once during the Master's lifetime and nine or ten times after his passing away. M. said: "After the Master's passing away I planned to live in Kamarpukur. But I decided to ask Holy Mother about it first. When I told her about my plan, she replied with a smile: 'My goodness, my son, that place is a repository of malaria. You can't stay there. It is a remote, primitive village. How can you live there?' I then gave up my plan to live in Kamarpukur."[2]

Kalna

In 1884, during the Master's lifetime, M. went to Kalna (in West Bengal) to see Bhagavan Das Babaji, a Vaishnava holy man. Ramakrishna had met him years earlier. After M. returned, the Master said to him: "You went to Bhagavan Das. What sort of man is he?"

M.: "He is very old now. I saw him at Kalna. It was night. He lay on a carpet and a devotee fed him with food that had been offered to God. He can hear only if one speaks loudly into his ear. Hearing me mention your name he said, 'You have nothing to worry about.'"[3]

Vrindaban, Varanasi, Ayodhya, and Hardwar

During Durga Puja in 1887, about a year after Ramakrishna passed away, M. went to Vrindaban and then to Ayodhya, the birthplace of Ramachandra. At that time M. was supposed to grade 1,200 papers from his university students. He graded only 300 papers, and then returned the remaining papers to the registrar with a note that he was leaving on a pilgrimage. The registrar knew M.'s state of mind, so he did not force him to stay and complete the work.[4]

M. recalled: "Ayodhya was then a village. I went to Raghunath Das Babaji's Ashrama. He was like a paramahamsa, and I had a long conversation with him. Swami Vivekananda and some other disciples also met him. He had a great reputation. He said to me: 'My son, why are you roaming here and there? Go to the place of your guru, meditate on him, and glorify his name.' My mind was then empty because of the Master's passing away.

"Raghunath Das Babaji had been a soldier and his duty was to guard the fort. One night he was listening attentively to a recital of the Ramayana and forgot to report for duty. In the morning he was ashamed and went to his European boss to beg for forgiveness. The officer said: 'I don't understand what you are saying. When I did my rounds last night, I saw you there three times. You talked to me and saluted me.' At this, Raghunath's eyes filled with tears, and he said: 'Sir, here is my uniform. I shall no longer work for the government. He [Lord Rama] did duty on my behalf, and I shall serve only him from now on.' He then moved to Ayodhya and served the mendicants."[5]

During this trip M. visited Varanasi and met three holy men. He recalled: "I met Trailanga Swami, Swami Bhaskarananda, and Swami Vishuddhananda. Trailanga Swami was serene and cheerful, but he was suffering from dropsy. He had a childlike nature. Someone offered him some food, and he hid it behind himself so that others might not ask him to share it." M. sang some of the Master's favourite songs for Bhaskarananda and had a long conversation with Vishuddhananda, who was a great scholar.

M. recalled: "There was a famous musician in Varanasi named Mahesh Binkar. He was an excellent vina player. He had played *Ashoyari ragini* for the Master. I also wanted to listen to that particular composition. I asked him every day for three days, and then on the fourth day I insisted that he play for me. He played *Kanada raga*. That music is still ringing in my ears. Later Mahesh became a monk. When he realized that his body would not last, he starved himself in his cottage and gave up his body."[6]

On 5 November 1912 M. and his wife went with Holy Mother to Varanasi. They stayed more than two and a half months, during which time Swamis Brahmananda, Turiyananda, Shivananda and many other monks and devotees were present at both Ashramas in Varanasi. According to Mahendra Nath Datta, Betty Leggett, her daughter Alberta, and her son-in-law George Montague (later the Earl of Sandwich) were then at Varanasi. During the Christmas festival M. read the Bible and discussed Christ's life. It was a festive occasion. M. was exuberant with joy to see and talk with the Master's devotees.

Holy Mother was very pleased to see the Sevashrama (now Ramakrishna Mission Home of Service) and remarked: "Sri Ramakrishna is ever-present in this place, and Mother Lakshmi always casts her benign glance upon it."

When M. arrived, the members of the Sevashrama were talking about how much Holy Mother had appreciated the institution. M. had often said that the Master did not approve of anyone's performing social service before realizing God. One of the monks said to M.: "Mother has just told us that the activities of the Home of Service were service to the Master himself and that he is tangibly present here. Now what do you say?" M. replied with a laugh: "How can I deny it anymore?"[7]

Lavanya Chakrabarty, a disciple of Holy Mother, first met M. at the Ramakrishna Advaita Ashrama in Varanasi. M. asked him to read the Gopi Gita and visit Holy Mother. After a while Lavanya met a monk, who was known to him, outside the Ashrama.

Monk: "Is M. in the Ashrama?"

Lavanya: "Yes, he is. He has been reading the Gopi Gita, and he read it to me also."

Monk: "How is he? Did he seem sad?"

Lavanya: "No, I didn't notice any sadness. Rather he seemed cheerful."

Monk: "This is grace. His favourite daughter has died of cholera, and I carried that news to him a short while ago."[8]

Lavanya recognized M.'s greatness and how the Master's grace had transformed his life.

From February to March 1913 M. stayed in Vrindaban. The Ramakrishna Sevashrama was located near Kala Babu's Kunja on the bank of the Yamuna. Some Vaishnava monks lived in small huts near the Ashrama, surrounded by banyan trees. This place was called *Bangshi*

Bat (because under this banyan tree Krishna played his flute). Mahendra Datta recalled:

"Early in the morning M. would go to the bank of the river Yamuna and sit under a banyan tree. He would meditate on Krishna and his play. He seemed to be intoxicated — as if he was witnessing Krishna's play in Vrindaban with the cowherd boys. At that time his countenance and ges- tures were not of this world, and we were very careful when we talked to him. Slowly he would come back to his normal state. We used to eat together in the Ashrama, but sometimes he would come late so we had to wait for him. One day he said, 'I get ecstatic when I see Bangshi Bat, the river Yamuna and its banks, the trees and the meadow.'

"During Dol Yatra [the festival of colours] there was a fair in front of the Seth's temple, and people would carry the deity around on their shoulders. Many pilgrims would assemble in Vrindaban at that time. In the afternoon M. and I would visit the fairground. M. would buy *daibara* (a fried lentil chop soaked in yogurt) and share it with me. He moved around joyfully, like a boy. I observed that the serious, bearded M. of Calcutta had disappeared, and in his place a young friend of Krishna was moving around and eating pieces of fruit from a carton. I watched him in this condition for a few days. I wondered whether it was bhava samadhi. I was dumbfounded.

"One afternoon M., Nikunja Mallick, and I went to visit Faujdari Kunja [a temple complex], where Sri Ramakrishna had stayed during his visit to Vrindaban [in 1868]. Chaitan Faujdar, the owner of the Kunja, was then alive but quite old. M. asked him many questions and learned that Mathur's family had stayed at his place and a strange man had come with them. Chaitan said that this man would sit at the right side of the image and cry profusely. He was not a normal person. A brahmin [Hriday] would look after him. Chaitan showed us a room downstairs near the veranda, where that man had slept. This much information Chaitan supplied us.

"M. bowed down again and again at the spot where Sri Ramakrishna had sat. Nikunja Mallick and I also bowed down. It seemed that M. was visualizing the Master crying there. He then went into an ecstatic mood and remained still and speechless. After a while we again bowed down to that spot and to the room, and then returned to the Ashrama. In Vrindaban M. also inquired about Gangamayi."[9]

M. stayed in Vrindaban a few weeks and then went to Kankhal and Hardwar. Swamis Turiyananda and Shivananda were then living at the Kankhal Sevashrama, and M. rented a cottage nearby on the bank of the Ganges. M. spent his time talking with the swamis about the Master and other spiritual topics. He then went to Rishikesh and stayed in a hut at Swargashrama, which was on the opposite side of the Ganges. After prac-tising austerities there, he returned to the Kankhal Ashrama and stayed for some more months. During this period he was absorbed in sadhana. At night someone would carry food to his room.[10]

M. recalled: "I went to Hardwar alone and stayed in a hut near the Kankhal Ashrama. Swamis Turiyananda and Shivananda were then in Kankhal. One day we set up a Brahma-chakra and practised sadhana. Once I visited the Gurukul School in Kangri at the invitation of Swami Shraddhananda. Then I went to Rishikesh, first staying at Mayakunda and then at Swargashrama. My hut was adjacent to the boundary wall of Swargashrama. It was a very small hut at the foothills of the Himalayas. Wild elephants would come down from the jungle to drink water from the Ganges. I had heard that animals are afraid of light, so I kept my kero-sene lantern lit outside the room."[11]

For a long time M. had wanted to be a monk and to lead a life com-pletely dependent on God. Now he could partly fulfill that desire by stay-ing in Kankhal and Rishikesh for about five months. He lived on alms like the traditional monks of the Himalayas, studied the Upanishads and the Gita, and meditated on Brahman. The panoramic view of the Himalayas and Ganges overwhelmed him. M. recalled: "One day while I was at Swargashrama, I went for a walk to Lachman Jhola [a bridge over the Ganges] and I saw a monk forcefully inhaling the fresh air of the Ganges. I asked him, 'Maharaj, what are you doing?' He replied, 'I am inhaling the pure air of the Mother Ganges.' One can become pure by inhaling this pure air."[12] M. later told the devotees: "I asked myself how people could leave such a place and go into the world." But after staying in Rishikesh for five months, his mind was drawn back to the playground of Ramakrishna.

M. was nostalgic for the environment of the Vedic sages, so in Calcutta he kept flowering plants and shrubs in tubs on the roof of his school. He regularly meditated there, chanting the Upanishads in the Vedic cadence.

Mihijam

After Holy Mother left her body in 1920, and Swamis Brahmananda and Turiyananda passed away in 1922, M. felt empty and wished to prac-tise sadhana in solitude. In October 1922 M. spent six months in a thatched hut at the Ramakrishna Ashrama in Mihijam (now in Jharkhand State). He was then 68 years old. Mihijam was a quiet place surrounded by hills and trees. Like the ancient forest dwellers, the rishis, M. lived there with some monks and brahmacharins, eating a simple diet — rice and milk at

noon and chapatis and milk at night. He said: "I have come here to practise austerities, so the lifestyle should be simple. One can experience more
divine bliss if one reduces one's wants. Plain living and high thinking
is the ideal of the Indian sages. Because of this ideal, Indian civilization
remains supreme regardless of circumstances."

He did not allow anyone in the Ashrama to wear a watch because
the ancient rishis used the sun to determine time during the day and
they used the pole star at night. The trains that ran near the Ashrama
also helped the monks keep track of time. M. taught the young monks
the Upanishads, Gita, Chandi, Bhagavata, and *Kathamrita*. In the morning
and evening he sent them to meditate under the trees in the Ashrama, so
that they could imbibe the spirit of the Vedic period. M.'s holy company
inspired them with love and longing for God.

One day someone asked M.: "Sir, why does God give us so much
trouble?"

M. replied: "Without tidal waves a person cannot be a good sea captain. Everyone is a pilot in a calm sea. Dangers and troubles are needed,
because the path of Truth goes through them. All great people had to go
through difficulties in life. One develops strength by facing dangers. God
puts a person in hardship whom He wants to make great."[13]

A Brahmachari: "What was unique about the advent of Sri Ramakrishna?"

M.: "The Master came to prove that God exists. He realized God in
many ways — with form and without form. He also made it possible for
his intimate disciples to experience God. If those who have never met the
Master focus their thoughts on him, he will graciously appear to them.
He told us two things: First, 'Those who sincerely call on God, they will
have to come here.' 'Here' means to him, as well as those who will receive
his spiritual ideas. Second, he prayed: 'Mother, please fulfill the wishes
of those who come here with sincerity.' He told his disciples: 'Those who
think of me inherit my treasures, as children inherit their parents' wealth.'
The Master's riches include knowledge, devotion, discrimination, renunciation, love, peace, mahabhava, samadhi, and so on."[14]

As Ramakrishna created hunger for God in people's minds, so did M.
He did not enjoy the mangoes [*Ramakrishna's spiritual treasures*] by himself, like a selfish person. Rather he shared them with others.

Puri

M. preferred the Himalayas for practising austerities, but he liked
Puri next. The Master had told M.: "I am Jagannath and I am Gauranga."

M. therefore had a deep attraction to Puri, the abode of Jagannath. He visited Puri five or six times, once during the Master's lifetime.

In Puri, M. stayed either at the Jagannath priest's house or at Shashi Niketan, the retreat house of Balaram Basu. During one of his visits (probably in 1887) M. was staying at the priest's house when he met Balaram Basu and Baburam in the temple. They took M. to their residence and he stayed with them. M. recalled: "I had the diary of the *Kathamrita* with me and I read from it to them. The women of the house would listen from behind the screen. When the Master passed away I became almost mad. His words brought peace to my heart."[15]

One day M. told the story of Madhav Das, a great devotee of Krishna who lived in Puri. Once Madhav was suffering from dysentery and had to go to the outside toilet again and again. He was so weak that he could not bring water with him to clean himself, but Krishna served him in the guise of a 12-year-old boy. Madhav recognized him, however, and complained, "You could have escaped this service if you had not given me this disease." The divine boy replied with a smile: "What can I do? I can't do anything about the result of your karma."[16]

On 6 October 1925 M. left for Puri with his wife for pilgrimage and to rest from his activities in Calcutta. He was then 71 years old. Sukhendu (later Swami Sukhadananda) and Gopen (M.'s grandson) went with them. M. carried his diaries in a trunk. Many devotees went to Howrah Station to see him off. M. spent nearly four months at Shashi Niketan.

Swami Nityatmananda recorded some incidents and conversations with M. from 25 December 1925 to 1 January 1926.

On 25 December 1925 M. went to a local church to attend the Christmas service. He later said to the monks and devotees: "Today is Christ's birthday. The Master said that he was Christ. So I went to the Church to see the Christian devotees. They are joyful with the spirit of Christmas. One can have awakening seeing those devotees. The pastor said many nice things: 'Christ is the verification of those teachings that the ancient sages spoke five thousand years ago.' Moreover, he chanted: 'Lead us from the unreal to the Real. Lead us from darkness to Light. Lead us from death to Immortality. O Rudra, light us through and through and guide us evermore with Thy loving presence.' And then he concluded, 'Christ was the embodiment of this truth.' Nowadays even Christians are becoming liberal.[17]

"Christ prayed: 'Lead us not into temptation, but deliver us from evil.' The Master also prayed: 'Mother, I don't want any physical enjoyment; Mother, I don't want name and fame; Mother, I don't want the eight occult powers; Mother, I don't want the other hundred powers; Mother, give me pure, unchanging, selfless devotion to you. Mother, may I never be deluded by your bewitching maya.'"[18]

M. pointed out the similarities between Christ's and Ramakrishna's teachings by quoting from the Bible and the *Kathamrita*.

Christ said: "Seek ye first the Kingdom of God and his righteousness, and all these things shall be added unto you. For your heavenly Father knoweth that ye have need of all these things."

The Master said: "Don't worry about the bare necessities of life. Mother knows that you need them."

Christ said: "First take the log out of your own eye; and then you will be able to see clearly to take the speck out of your brother's eye."

The Master said: "Never criticize even a worm. One becomes full of blemishes seeing the blemishes of others. And seeing the goodness of others, one becomes good."

Christ said: "For wide is the gate, and broad is the way, that leadeth to destruction."

The Master said: "Men do not realize how far they are dragged down by women. Once I went to the Fort in a carriage, feeling all the while that I was going along a level road. At last I found that I had gone four storeys down. It was a sloping road."

M. remarked: "See how their teachings concur, because their source is the same. Both are avatars, God in human form. But some of their teachings vary according to the place, time, and person. Christ came 2,000 years ago. During his time people's thinking and social system were different. The Master came in the age of science. Their teachings look a little different, but the essence is the same. The main theme of their messages is that the supreme duty is to realize God."[19]

M. taught the devotees how to pass their time in a holy place. One should visit the deities in the temples and pay respect to holy men during the day, and meditate and study at night. M. told the devotees how the Master held the prasad of Jagannath in high regard: "Every morning the Master would take one particle of Jagannath's prasad before eating anything else. He kept this prasad in a red cloth bag by the side of his bed near the western wall, and gave it to us too. One day he gave it to Narendra, but he refused to eat it. Narendra said: 'It is unclean dry rice.' The Master then said to him: 'Do you believe that some things have effects, such as opium is constipating and *triphala* is a laxative?' Narendra replied, 'Yes, I believe that.' The Master said: 'It is also proven that if one takes this holy mahaprasad, one attains knowledge, devotion, and faith.' Narendra then ate it without further argument. He had complete trust in the Master's words. The Master was truthful and an expert in spiritual affairs. The Master said: 'In this Kaliyuga the mahaprasad of Jagannath, the dust of Vrindaban, and the water of the Ganges are veritably Brahman.'"[20]

On 29 December 1925 M. went to Bhubaneswar with some devotees, where he visited the Ramakrishna Math and the famous Lingaraja Shiva temple. He had lunch at the Math and then returned to Puri that evening. It is amazing how M., who was then 71, led such an austere life in Puri.

Swami Deshikananda spent a few days with M. at Puri and described M.'s daily routine in his memoirs: M. would get up very early in the morning and meditate till 7:00 a.m. He did not eat breakfast. After visiting Lord Jagannath in the temple, he then bowed down to the other deities in the temple complex. He then returned to Shashi Niketan and meditated. At 11:00 a.m. he had his lunch. After that he talked to the devotees and then rested. He would get up at 2:30 p.m. and then to go to the beach with the devotees and talk to them about the Master for a couple of hours. Again at 5:30 p.m., he went to the Jagannath temple, returning to Shashi Niketan at 6:30 p.m. He meditated from 6:30 to 8:00 p.m. and had dinner. Then he talked to the devotees and went to bed at 10:00 p.m.

On the morning of the third day, Swami Deshikananda asked M. how one should meditate. M. canceled his visit to the temple and replied: "During meditation, one should think of the Ishta [Chosen Deity] as living. When the Master would meditate, his Ishta [the Divine Mother] appeared in front of him like a living person. He then would talk to Her, as I am talking to you. I am blessed to have witnessed the Master's meditation and his conversation with the Divine Mother many times."[21] In fact, M. was perfect in meditation on Ramakrishna. Because he had been fortunate to live with the Master, he would see the Master during his meditation.

Gadadhar Ashrama

The Hindu scriptures say: "Those who carry the all-auspicious God in their hearts enjoy festivity all the time, achieve all wealth and prosperity, and attain eternal peace and bliss." M.'s life is a glowing example of this truth. M.'s body became a shrine to Ramakrishna, and the Master's words spontaneously flowed from M.'s mouth. Wherever M. went he created such an atmosphere that all were charmed by his wonderful love and devotion, faith and humility, wisdom and power of speech. Monks and devotees alike were eager to be in M.'s company.

When M. became old, he could no longer go on pilgrimage to distant places, so he often visited Dakshineswar, Belur Math, and other

Ramakrishna Ashramas nearby. From 23 November to 12 December 1923 M. stayed at Gadadhar Ashrama in South Calcutta. Swami Nityatmananda wrote about this visit:

Whenever a devotee came to see M. in Gadadhar Ashrama, he would ask that devotee to go to the Master's shrine first. He said: "The Divine Mother becomes living where many devotees pray wholeheartedly. That place becomes holy where the deity is awakened, such as Dakshineswar. Kalighat [near Gadadhar Ashrama] is also a holy place because the Divine Mother dwells there. Dwarika Babu, Mathur's son, installed the image of the Divine Mother at Chanak in Barrackpore. He then requested the Master: 'You have awakened the Kali of Dakshineswar. Now please awaken the deity here.' The Master replied: 'You first drop the bait. Then a big carp will automatically come there.'[22] He meant that if you have genuine devotion, the Mother will come to you."

Sometimes M. would explain the Upanishads, Bhagavata, and Gita to the monks and devotees who visited him. One day he talked about Nachiketa's renunciation, as described in the Katha Upanishad. Yama, the god of death, offered Nachiketa celestial women, children, a vast empire, long life, and plenty of wealth, but he refused everything. He wanted only the knowledge of Brahman, the eternal source of bliss. He did not care for momentary pleasure.

On 8 December 1923 Swami Kamaleswarananda was performing Kali Puja on the roof of the Ashrama throughout the night. M. asked the devotees to attend the worship: "Please go there. Try to sit at least 15 minutes, and then that time will turn into half an hour. Some people complain that they have no time to practise sadhana. Well, the whole night is at your disposal. You can practise sadhana on your roof."[23]

Holy Mother and M.

Mwas extremely devoted to his mother, who passed away when he was a young man. He felt a terrible emptiness inside. His departed mother then consoled him in a dream: "I shall always be with you, but you will not see me." Shortly after his mother's death, M. began to have difficulties with his extended family. He and his wife, Nikunja Devi, left the family home one night. And this is how, in February 1882, he met his guru, Ramakrishna, in Dakshineswar and found his lost mother in Holy Mother, Sarada Devi.

During that period in India, men and women did not mix freely. Holy Mother led a very private life behind a bamboo curtain at the nahabat in Dakshineswar. Whenever she served the Master and his devotees, she kept her face covered with a veil. Ramakrishna never introduced her to his male devotees, except for his two personal attendants, Latu and Senior Gopal. M. said: "We visited the Master over a period of five years but never saw her. From time to time the Master would refer to 'Ramlal's aunt.' One day I asked, 'Who is Ramlal's aunt?' The Master replied, 'Oh, she lives in the nahabat.' She became the guide and polestar of my life, but at that time I never saw her face. When she became elderly, she lifted the veil a little from her face."[1]

M.'s wife sometimes accompanied him to visit the Master. Two occasions are described in *The Gospel of Sri Ramakrishna*. On 7 March 1885 M. wrote:

The Holy Mother, Sri Ramakrishna's wife, was living in the nahabat. Occasionally she would come to Sri Ramakrishna's room to attend to his needs. Mohinimohan [M.] had brought his wife and Nabin's mother with him to the temple garden from Calcutta. The ladies were with the Holy Mother; they were waiting for an opportunity to visit the Master when the men devotees would leave the room.

Sri Ramakrishna was sitting on the small couch talking to Mohini. Mohini's wife was almost mad with grief on account of her son's death. Sometimes she laughed and sometimes she wept. But she felt peaceful in Sri Ramakrishna's presence.

Master: "How is your wife now?"

Mohini: "She becomes quiet whenever she is here; but sometimes at home she becomes very wild. The other day she was going to kill herself."

When Sri Ramakrishna heard this he appeared worried. Mohini said to him humbly, "Please give her a few words of advice."

Master: "Don't allow her to cook. That will heat her brain all the more. And keep her in the company of others so that they may watch her."

Mohini's wife entered the room and sat at one side.

The Master suddenly addressed Mohini's wife and said: "By unnatural death one becomes an evil spirit. Beware. Make it clear to your mind. Is this what you have come to after hearing and seeing so much?"

Mohini was about to take his leave. He saluted Sri Ramakrishna. His wife also saluted the Master, who stood near the north door of the room. Mohini's wife spoke to him in a whisper.

Master: "Do you want to stay here?"

Mohini's wife: "Yes, I want to spend a few days with the Holy Mother at the nahabat. May I?"

Master: "That will be all right. But you talk of dying. That frightens me. And the Ganges is so near!"[2]

On 24 April 1886 M. recorded in the *Gospel*:

M. came to Cossipore garden house accompanied by his wife and a son. The boy was seven years old. It was at the Master's request that he brought his wife, who was almost mad with grief owing to the death of one of her sons.

That day the Master several times allowed M.'s wife the privilege of waiting on him. Her welfare seemed to occupy his attention a great deal. In the evening the Holy Mother came to the Master's room to feed him. M.'s wife accompanied her with a lamp. The Master tenderly asked her many questions about her household. He requested her to come again to the garden house and spend a few days with the Holy Mother, not forgetting to ask her to bring her baby daughter. When the Master had

TOP: Holy Mother at Calcutta in 1905, BOTTOM: Money Order coupon for ten rupees remitted by M. Holy Mother's thumb print endorsement is on the right.

finished his meal M.'s wife removed the plates. He chatted with her a few minutes.

About nine o'clock in the evening Sri Ramakrishna was seated in his room with the devotees. He had a garland of flowers around his neck. He told M. that he had requested his wife to spend a few days at the garden house with the Holy Mother. His kindness touched M.'s heart.[3]

In the beginning, M.'s wife had disapproved of her husband's close involvement with the Master. When M. reported that to the Master, he said one should give up a wife who was an obstacle to one's spiritual path. But the Master also assured M. that if he had sincere faith in the Divine Mother, She would change his wife's mind. Soon Nikunja Devi became an ardent devotee of the Master and Holy Mother, and it was through her that M. learned more about Holy Mother.

On 6 April 1886, when the Master was ill in Cossipore, M. reported to the Master about his wife's condition: "My wife has temper tantrums from time to time, and has no feeling for the children. She feels fine when she comes to you. She says that sometimes she sees you. But she was lamenting the other day that you had bestowed grace on Balaram's wife and not on her. She has no peace. She becomes upset if I don't come here, and again if I do come here. The other night she had a dream that your disease had become worse and she began to cry, saying, 'O Master, I became rid of all my pain by visiting you.' I share your teachings with her, but she does not listen to me. She works according to her whims."[4]

Nikunja stayed with Holy Mother both at Dakshineswar and at Cossipore. It was through Nikunja that M. learned of Holy Mother's patience, perseverance, forgiveness, renunciation, service, and motherly affection for all. He became convinced that the Master and the Mother were manifestations of the same divine power.

At Belur Math on 18 December 1924, Miss Josephine MacLeod asked M.: "Mr. M., today is Holy Mother's birthday. Well, what was she to you?"

M. replied: "The same as Sri Ramakrishna, God-incarnate on earth. He and the Holy Mother are one as 'I and my Father are one.' The Master said, Brahman and Shakti are one. He illustrated this fact by the example of a serpent. When the serpent is coiled up, it is like Brahman in Its undifferentiated Absolute state. And when the serpent moves in a zigzag manner, that is when She creates, preserves, and destroys the world, and that is the illustration of Shakti, or the Primordial Energy.

"It is this Ultimate Energy, or Brahma-shakti, which now and then incarnates in a human body for the good of the world. It is this Ultimate

Energy which incarnated in a dual form as Sri Ramakrishna and Holy Mother. So these two forms — Thakur and Ma — are one and the same in essence."[5]

On 30 August 1886, after the Master's passing away, M. sent Nikunja on pilgrimage with Holy Mother. They visited Vaidyanath, Varanasi, Ayodhya, and Vrindaban. However, within a month Nikunja contracted malaria and had to return to Calcutta with Kali (later Swami Abhedananda). In August 1887 Holy Mother returned to Calcutta and then in September left for Kamarpukur. She again returned to Calcutta towards the end of 1888. In Calcutta Holy Mother stayed either in Balaram's house or M.'s house, and sometimes she later stayed in rented homes. Regarding the rented houses, M. wrote: "First Holy Mother stayed at Raju Gomastha's house; second, near the cremation ground; and third, at Nilambar Mukherjee's house. These three places are in Belur. Fourth, she stayed on the second floor of a warehouse in Baghbazar. It was a jute warehouse and she had to enter her quarters through it. Fifth, she stayed in a house in front of Girish's house; sixth, near Nivedita's house [on Bosepara Lane]; but finally she stayed at her own house in Udbodhan."[6]

When Holy Mother was staying at M.'s house, his sister-in-law Krishnamayi one day said to Holy Mother: "M. says, 'I have forgotten my previous father and mother. Now Paramahamsadeva is my father and Holy Mother is my mother.'"

Holy Mother replied: "He is right. He is feeding us. I can talk to him but I feel shy."

Holy Mother seldom spoke directly to any male devotee or disciple of the Master. Sometimes she communicated to them through Golap-ma or her other female attendants. Nikunja was the medium of communication between Holy Mother and M. Gradually, M. realized that Holy Mother was an extended spiritual entity of Ramakrishna and there was no separation between them.

On 23 April 1890, M., Narendra, Jogin, and others were at Balaram's house. Narendra pointed out, "The Master said so many things, but he rarely talked about Holy Mother."

Jogin said: "What do you say? If the Master is God, the Mother is the Goddess."[7]

Later Narendra wrote of Holy Mother that she was the "Living Durga." Her divinity and greatness touched the hearts of the devotees and disciples.

M. and Nikunja were fortunate to have received the grace of both the Master and Holy Mother. On 30 October 1888 Nikunja received initiation from Holy Mother, who was then staying at Nilambar Mukherjee's house in Belur. When the Master was alive, he wrote a seed mantra on M.'s tongue; and then on 15 May 1887 M. received a mantra from the Master through a dream. From May to June of 1891 M. and Nikunja lived at Jayrambati with Holy Mother. Holy Mother and the women devotees lived in her brother Prasanna's house, and the male devotees stayed in his parlour. One night after dinner, Holy Mother had a vision. She saw M. as a 5-year-old boy running naked on the streets of Jayrambati. The Master then appeared, pointed to him, and said, "Initiate him." Holy Mother wondered: 'Didn't the Master already initiate him?' Nonetheless, she immediately summoned M. and gave him initiation.[8]

M. served Holy Mother as his own mother. For her part, Holy Mother felt free while living with M.'s family. When the Master was in Cossipore, M. wanted to perform Durga Puja at his home. The Master said that this desire would be fulfilled later. In October 1888 Holy Mother was staying at M.'s house. Just before Durga Puja, the Master said to her in a dream: "M. told me that he had a desire to perform Durga Puja. Now you arrange Durga Puja and install the ghat [the consecrated pitcher]."[9] Accordingly, on Saturday, 8 October 1888, Holy Mother installed and worshipped Sri Chandi Mangal Ghat (the Durga Ghat) and Sri Ramakrishna's photograph in M.'s shrine and arranged for their daily worship, which continues even today. At that time M. named his house, "Thakur Bari" (The Master's House). This historic event inspired M. to write *The Gospel of Sri Ramakrishna*.

Holy Mother initiated many devotees in M.'s holy shrine, and Swami Vivekananda and many other direct disciples meditated there. Once Shyamasundari, Holy Mother's mother, visited M.'s shrine. When she saw the Master's shoes in a glass case, she remarked: "When Saru was married, did I know that my son-in-law was God and his shoes would be worshipped in this way?"[10] M.'s house is now a museum, where devotees can see an original print of the Master's picture, his shirt, his shoes, Holy Mother's footprints, and many other precious relics.

After Ramakrishna passed away, the monastic disciples practised austerities and travelled all over India. They had no means for supporting Holy Mother. Both Balaram and Surendra, who had financially supported the Master, died in 1890, and Holy Mother suffered as a result. Other householder devotees were not aware of Holy Mother's financial condition. At that time, M. took three jobs and distributed his salaries to Holy Mother, Baranagore Math, and his own family respectively. In 1894 he purchased a rice field of more than one acre in Jayrambati for Holy

Mother. He also contributed 1,000 rupees to build Holy Mother's new house in Jayrambati and to dig a well. In addition to this support, M. gave Holy Mother 10 rupees every month without fail. M. and his wife also accompanied Holy Mother when she went for pilgrimage to Puri (1904), to Varanasi (1912), and several times to Jayrambati.

Holy Mother was very fond of M. and his family, as Ramakrishna had been. She praised M.'s loving service and steadfast devotion. Once Holy Mother said to Nikunja: "I know that Master Mahashay has many noble qualities." On another occasion she said, "The way Master Mahashay walks reminds me of how the Master would pace in the same way." One day, as she heard M. read the *Kathamrita*, she remarked, "It seems as if the Master is saying those words."

During Kali Puja in 1904, Holy Mother was staying at a rented house on Bosepara Lane. M. had informed her earlier that he would visit her that day. It was late at night. When someone said that perhaps M. would not come, Holy Mother replied: "Is he a cheap ordinary man? He has a deep passion for truth. You will see, he will definitely come." M. arrived shortly thereafter. On another occasion Holy Mother said to Nikunja: "Master Mahashay's love and devotion are phenomenal. His letter forced me to come to Calcutta from Kamarpukur. He is a rare devotee. He is endowed with knowledge and devotion. His mind is pure, and the blood, bones, and flesh of his body are pure." Once a devotee bowed down to Holy Mother in Udbodhan. She said to that devotee: "Master Mahashay is downstairs. Please go and bow down to him. Know for certain, he is a great soul."[11]

Again, Holy Mother once remarked about M.: "Is he an ordinary man? He has recorded so many teachings of the Master. Is there any other avatar whose picture and conversations have been taken or recorded in such detail? It is as if the Master himself is speaking in M.'s book."

A Conversation between Nikunja Devi and Holy Mother

Generally women talk among themselves more freely than they talk with men. Nikunja was a close companion of Holy Mother, so on many occasions she told Nikunja many incidents of her life with the Master. Nikunja related those stories to M., and he recorded them in his diary.

Nikunja: "Mother, in family life there is only suffering and no peace. When I come to you, I get a little peace in my arid heart. It calms my soul when I address you as 'mother.'"

Holy Mother: "My daughter, you have seen the Master, so you have nothing to worry about. He was very fond of you. He said to me: 'M.'s wife is simple and open-hearted. She looks at me with wonder.' Let me tell you, child — happiness and misery, good and bad — both exist in this world. They come in due course of time and people reap the results of their karma. One should make the mind strong and keep it on God. It is no good to always harp on 'suffering, suffering.'"

Nikunja: "Mother, when I talk to you I feel strong and my mind becomes peaceful. That is why when I feel restlessness, I long to come to you."

Holy Mother: "Child, when I was 18 or 19 years old [at Dakshineswar in 1872], I used to sleep with the Master. One day he asked me, 'Who are you?' I replied, 'I have come to serve you.'

"One day there was no salt during lunch, so I said, 'There is no salt.' He scolded me, saying: 'What is this? Never say negative words. Try to collect everything.'

"When I was at Kamarpukur [probably in 1866], Ramlal's father asked me to go to the Master's room to sleep at night. The Master would laugh. At that time we slept together but spent the night talking about God. He taught me how to perform household work and how to behave with people, and to try to know that God is our own and is the only reality.

"When my mother visited Kamarpukur, the Master treated her with love and care, and asked her, 'Please make some pickles for us.'

"When I was at Jayrambati, the Master came there one day. He asked me to wash his feet with fuller's earth (*saji-mati*). At this other women commented about my loving service to my husband.

"When my mother-in-law was grief-stricken over the demise of her son [Rameswar], the Master would mostly stay with her and console her. One day he prayed to the Divine Mother: 'Mother, I want to chant Your name, but if my mother always grieves and cries, how is it possible to call on You? Please change my mother's mind.' Actually this prayer was answered, and my mother-in-law remained most of the time in an ecstatic mood.

"Shambhu Mallick made a cottage for me [on 11 April 1876], but I was reluctant to live there alone. When I told this to the Master, he said to Hriday, 'Hride, bring your wife here [from Sihar].' Hriday replied, 'Did Shambhu Mallick build that cottage for my wife?'

"At that time there was a brahmachari [Tantric Sadhak] in Dakshineswar. I was scared of him, thinking that he might do some harm to the Master; so I offered 10 rupees to him. Learning about it, he [the Master] came to the nahabat and said: 'Don't worry. I have the Divine Mother. Who can harm me?'

"One day the Master said to Ram Datta and others: 'You see, she talks about children. You all go to the nahabat and tell her, "Mother, we are your children."'"

"Once we went together to Kamarpukur by boat via Bali-Deoanganj [in 1877]. We ate wonderful prasad and he sang so many songs on the way. Ah, what a great mood he was in! And he said to me: 'I know who you are, but I will not tell you now.' (*Pointing to himself*) He said, 'Everything is inside this place.'

"When my mother-in-law was dying [on 13 February 1877], he said: 'O Mother, who are you that you carried me in your womb? Mother, you looked after me in this form; henceforth please do the same.'

"One day, after his mother's passing away, he told me before lunch: 'Please wait. Let me go to the Panchavati and cry for my mother.'

"About his monthly salary of 7 rupees, he said to the manager: 'If you wish, give that money to her [*meaning Holy Mother*]; otherwise throw it into the Ganges, or spend it for the guests. Do whatever you like.'

"When I was living in the nahabat, I once spent the whole day making a beautiful garland. I requested him to put the garland on. He then put it around his neck and sang a song: 'Is there anything left to decorate me with? I have put on the necklace of universal jewels.'

"Before returning to Jayrambati, I went to see him [in his room] several times, which he did not like. He said to Hriday: 'Why is she coming so many times? Ask her to go.'

"One day he said to Golap-ma about me: 'What power of forbearance she has! I salute her.'

"One day he said: 'I know who you are and who Lakshmi is, but I won't tell you. To pay my debt to you, I shall be born as a baul and take you as my companion.'

"Hearing that Lakshmi was fasting on Ekadashi Day, he said, 'I am beyond the injunctions of the scriptures. Please eat well.' He did not care to see women wearing a cloth without a border. He commented, 'It is a dress that an ogress would wear.'

"During his sadhana, he saw Sita in the Panchavati with bangles having a diamond-cut pattern. Observing that pattern of the bangles, he got some made for me. On the other hand, he could not touch money.

"One day I said to him, 'I have not had any spiritual ecstasy.' To this, he remarked: 'What do you expect? Does ecstasy mean that one will dance, letting one's cloth drop? Who will then manage to keep one's cloth in the proper place?'

"A few days before his passing away, the Master said, 'It is better to be miserly than to be an extravagant wretch.'"[12]

On different occasions M. recounted stories about Holy Mother to the devotees, and they were recorded by Swami Nityatmananda:

When the Master passed away, Holy Mother said, "His gross body is gone, but his spiritual body exists eternally." Once Hriday teased Holy

Mother, saying, "Aunt, if you call uncle 'father,' I shall give you five seers of sandesh [sweets]." Holy Mother replied: "You will not have to give me sandesh. I tell you on my own that he is my father, mother, guru, friend, and husband — he is everything to me." She found the Master in every type of relationship. What faith she had!

Sometimes the Master talked to Holy Mother in front of the nahabat. Golap-ma, Yogin-ma, and Gauri-ma occasionally stayed with her. Brinde would help her do the household work.

The Master said to Holy Mother: "This mud hut of Kamarpukur is yours. Live on spinach and rice, and chant God's name the entire day." He gave Holy Mother his cottage in Kamarpukur and 400 rupees. Mathur gave some jewellery to the Master when he was practising sadhana as a confidante of Radha. That jewellery was sold for 400 rupees and the money was invested in Balaram's estate. It earned an annual interest of 30 rupees. The Master would sometimes ask us: "Well, are 2 rupees a month enough for a brahmin widow? What do you think?" [Actually 600 rupees were invested and Holy Mother would get 6 rupees per month from the interest.] On the other hand, he was oblivious of day and night, even of his wearing cloth. He was so concerned about Holy Mother. He set the example, so that others would follow his example.

One day Holy Mother was meditating and someone loudly called for her. Her meditation broke and she cried out. Hearing this the Master rushed to the nahabat, and gradually Holy Mother became calm. The Master said to others: "During meditation, one should neither call nor make any noise near that person."

The Master slept with Holy Mother in the same bed for eight months in Dakshineswar. Why? To teach the devotees. They slept together but had no physical relationship. His action was meant to bring strength and encouragement to the devotees so that they would try to live with spouses like brothers and sisters. His marriage was an example for others. He demonstrated how to lead a married life.

The Master suffered in Dakshineswar after Mathur's passing away. There was no one to look after him. He would eat the cold spicy food at 1:00 p.m. His mat was torn, and his pillowcase and bedsheet were dirty; but his mind was in God. Gradually his health broke down. He wrote to Holy Mother: "There is no one to look after me here. I shall appreciate it if you come here." Holy Mother returned to Dakshineswar and began to cook for him.

Once Holy Mother said to a woman devotee: "I have seen so many holy people, but none can be compared with the Master." The woman devotee replied: "What do you say, Mother? Other holy men come to be liberated and the Master came to liberate others." Holy Mother said with a smile, "You are right." Holy Mother made that statement to test that devotee.

Those who search for genuine monks get confused. They do not see their own imperfections. The Master would say, "Both good and bad qualities exist in human beings; only God — an avatar — is free from blemishes." Holy Mother said, "There is even a stain on the moon, but there is no stain on the Ramakrishna-moon."

Sometimes we would send some food and other things to Holy Mother [in Udbodhan] through our servant. She would feed him the Master's prasad with great care. She would not discriminate like other people, who make one kind of food for themselves and another kind for the servants. All were equal to her.

Once it was proposed to bring a cow from Belur Math to Udbodhan so that Holy Mother could have fresh milk. But she immediately protested: "No, no. Those cows are grazing freely in the holy atmosphere of the monastery compound and seeing the Ganges. Here the cow will be tied with a rope and kept in a room! I can't bear it. I can't drink that milk." It proves that Holy Mother was the mother of all.

Holy Mother once said to a young man: "My son, never get married. If you are not married, you will be able to sleep peacefully at night. My child, never enter this burning fireplace." As she initiated a young man into brahmacharya, she said, "My child, now you will be able to sleep happily."

Once Holy Mother arrived at Dakshineswar on an inauspicious day. After two days the Master sent her back to Jayrambati to change her journey. This hurt Holy Mother's feelings, so she did not return to Dakshineswar for two years. Afterwards the Master wrote to her: "Hriday has left. I am passing through great difficulties. There is no one to look after me. Please come as soon as possible." When she got this message, Holy Mother immediately returned to Dakshineswar. Ah, how Holy Mother tied the devotees with her love and affection!

Once at Jayrambati five male devotees went to have initiation from Holy Mother. One of them belonged to a low caste. He was asked to sit outside because his presence might pollute the shrine. He began to cry. When Holy Mother entered the shrine, she found four men and inquired about the other person. They replied, "He belongs to the washerman's caste; he is outside." She rushed to that devotee and escorted him into the shrine. He was reluctant to enter, but Holy Mother took him inside and initiated him with the others.

Holy Mother said four things:

1. "Those who are desireless have unconditional devotion. They are *Ishwarakotis* (god-like souls)."

2. "For those who have money, give in charity; and for those who have nothing, repeat the mantra." Charity means worshipping and serving others as God with money. Otherwise, spend your time repeating the mantra.

3. "Things are overflowing all around but human nature is hard to change." People listen to the words of God, but nothing happens. Why? Because human nature is pulling those people back.

4. Someone asked Holy Mother, "What happens if a person dies after losing outer consciousness?" Holy Mother replied: "There is nothing wrong in losing consciousness while dying. It is enough if a person remembers God just before becoming unconscious. That brings good results."

One should serve others when one visits an Ashrama. The monks are busy taking care of the devotees, and the devotees are practising japa and meditation — this is not right. Once several women devotees went to visit Holy Mother in Jayrambati. They were meditating with closed eyes while Holy Mother was mopping the mud floor. A woman devotee [*probably M.'s wife*] got up from meditation and went to help Holy Mother. She responded: "The others are meditating. Why have you come?" The woman devotee replied: "Shame! I don't care for that meditation. You are mopping the floor and I shall close my eyes and meditate? I can't do that." That devotee understood what the right thing to do was.

Some fortunate devotees saw Holy Mother in samadhi. Her body remained motionless and her eyes did not blink. She was extremely bashful. Ah, what a rare scene!

The Master was sometimes criticized. Once someone offered a small amount of money to Holy Mother as a gift. Trailokya commented, "The young priest has brought his wife here to earn money." The Master went to the Kali temple and cried to the Divine Mother, saying, "Mother, the authorities of the temple are saying such things."

Holy Mother said to a monk: "During your last moments the Master will come and take you with him. You belong to him, so you will go to him. But if you want peace while living, practise austerities and meditate on him." "Grace dawns on one who practises austerities. Of course, his grace is not subject to any condition."

Holy Mother said:

1. To those who have taken refuge in the Master he will appear at the time of death.

2. Misery is inevitable for an embodied being; even the creator has no power to stop it. If you want peace, practise spiritual disciplines.

3. There is no certainty when death will come, so it is better to visit holy places soon without discriminating between auspicious or inauspicious times.

4. Someone asked, "Why is my karma not ending?" Mother replied: "There is plenty of string in the spool of the kite; the spool will be empty when all of the string comes out.

5. The Master never caused me pain, even for a day.

The Master promised: "I swear that those who think of me will attain my spiritual wealth, just as children inherit their parents' wealth." He said this with such emphasis, yet people still do not believe it. Holy Mother had so much love for the devotees! Once when a devotee was leaving Jayrambati after receiving initiation, she came out from her room to see him off, in tears. She watched that devotee walk away, as far as she could see him. Although she had known him for only a couple of days, her love surpassed even that of a biological mother.

She had strong common sense. On one hand, she said, "You will not have to practise japa and meditation"; and on the other, she said, "If you want peace in this life, you will have to practise sadhana." How nicely she reconciled two opposite things!

These two aspects we learn from Holy Mother's life: (1) Brahmacharya and absorption in God, (2) Self-control and service. She did not know anything other than God. Seeing God in every being, she served Him day and night. All her teachings are mantras. Many highly educated women, including Nivedita, would sit at her feet with folded hands. Modern ideas and education were subordinate to her towering personality.

Holy Mother was then in Vrindaban. One day we were talking about Holy Mother in Baranagore monastery. Swamiji related this incident: One day at the Cossipore garden house the devotees mentioned to the Master about Holy Mother's affection for them. She was there to serve the Master. The devotees said, "We have never seen such a noble heart." I asked Swamiji, "What did the Master say about it?" Swamiji replied: "The Master laughed and then remarked: 'She is my shakti. That is why she is noble.'"[13]

It is quite natural for parents to think about the future of their children. Sometimes Shyamasundari felt anguish for her daughter Sarada. She often lamented: "I have married my daughter to such a madman that she will never know the happiness of a householder's life. She will not have any children and feel the joy of being addressed as 'Mother.'" The Master heard these words and said: "Mother, please do not worry about that. Your daughter will have so many children that her ears will burn from her constantly being called, 'Mother.'"[14] The Master also reassured Holy Mother: "Why should you worry? I shall leave you many children, all pure as gold, the like of whom women do not get even through the prayers and austerities of millions of lives. So many people will call you mother that you will find it hard to look after them all."[15] The Master's promise was fulfilled.

Although Ramakrishna was the polestar of M.'s life, M.'s love and devotion for Holy Mother were truly phenomenal. He not only provided whatever she needed, but was also ready to lay down his life for her. In 1907 there were Hindu-Muslim riots in Calcutta, and there was a blackout in the city. Holy Mother was then at Jayrambati and had been intermittently suffering from malarial fever when she was invited to attend the Durga Puja at Girish's house. To keep Holy Mother safe on her journey, M. and Lalit Chattopadhyay left Calcutta and went to the Vishnupur railway station, where they met Mother, who had travelled there by bullock cart from Jayrambati. Their train arrived at Howrah Station late in the evening.

Holy Mother, accompanied by Radhu and her mother, got into Lalit's waiting carriage. M., Lalit, and some devotees then escorted them, sitting on the top of the carriage or standing on the footboard. M. was relieved when Mother reached Balaram's house, which was close to Girish's house.

M. recalled: "Once Holy Mother lived with us for a month. Before leaving our home, she presented a pair of cloths and money to the brahmin cook and bowed down to him. She also asked blessings from him with folded hands. Observing her humility, we were all amazed. Thus she taught us how to show respect to others."[16]

M. and Swami Vivekananda

M. and Swami Vivekananda

Mhad a close relationship with each of Ramakrishna's disciples, and he served them in every possible way. After the Master passed away, the disciples established the Baranagore Math and formed the Ramakrishna Order under the leadership of Narendra (later Swami Vivekananda).

M. first met Narendra on 5 March 1882 at Dakshineswar and observed the Master's affection for the young man. M. and Narendra soon became close friends, and remained close all through their lives. When Narendra's father died and his family faced a terrible financial crisis, M. came forward to help Narendra so that his spiritual journey might not be impeded.

During those early days Narendra talked candidly to M. about his spiritual struggles and experiences. On 9 April 1887 at the Baranagore Math, Narendra described the awakening of his kundalini and how the Master had transmitted power to him. He said to M.: "You must not tell this to anybody else. Give me your promise." Fortunately for us, M. did not give that promise. However, he did not divulge this secret during Narendra's lifetime. M. published those beautiful dialogues between Swami Vivekananda and himself in the pages of *The Gospel of Sri Rama-krishna,* long after the swami had passed away.

Vivekananda had great love and respect for M. because of his devotion and faithful service to the Master and his disciples. While he was in America, he acknowledged his indebtedness to M. in one of his letters to

Swami Vivekananda at Cossipore garden house in 1886

Swami Brahmananda: "Only people like Balaram, Suresh, Master (M.), and Chuni Babu were our friends at that hour of need. And we shall never be able to repay our debts to them."[1] Swamiji asked M. to speak during Ramakrishna's birth anniversary in 1898 at Belur Math, saying: "Master Mahashay, you will have to relate to us something about the Master."[2] At Balaram's house on 23 January 1898, M. asked Swamiji to sing a song. Swamiji sang: "Cherish my precious Mother Shyama, tenderly within, O mind...." A devotee recalled: "It seemed as if a vina were playing. After singing the entire song, Swamiji said to M.: "Well, are you satisfied now? No more singing; otherwise I will be carried away by its intoxication. My voice has become hoarse because of frequent lecturing in the West. Moreover, my voice trembles."[3]

After Swamiji returned from the West in early 1897 he founded the Ramakrishna Mission, which emphasized serving human beings as God. At first, M. did not approve of it, because the Master had told him again and again: "The goal of human life is to realize God." So one day M. said to Swamiji: "You talk about service, charity, and doing good to the world: those are after all in the domain of maya. When according to Vedanta the goal of man is to attain mukti [liberation] by breaking the bondage of maya, what is the use of preaching things which keep the mind on mundane matters?" Without a moment's hesitation Swamiji replied: "Is not the idea of mukti also in the domain of maya? Does not the Vedanta teach that the Atman is ever free? What is striving for mukti to the Atman, then?"[4] The conversation ended there. M. recognized Swamiji's greatness and the importance of his mission. Ramakrishna had said that he was nityamukta, an ever-free soul. Swamiji was not born for his own liberation; rather he came to liberate others.

Although the Master had asked M. to remain a householder, he admired and promoted the Ramakrishna Math. Swami Vijnanananda once remarked, "Ninety percent of the monks joined the Ramakrishna monastery after reading *The Gospel of Sri Ramakrishna*." M. encouraged devotees to keep in touch with the disciples of the Master in the monastery because it would benefit them immensely. He said: "The ideal of the Math is the Master, the Avatara — indivisible Satchidananda — who came as a human being. The monks perform various works — worship of the Master, and relief, hospital, publication, educational work — as service to the Master. The whole atmosphere of the monastery is permeated with spirituality."[5]

On different occasions M. made various statements about the Ramakrishna Math:

The Ramakrishna Math is an oasis in the desert. People who are tormented in this world can go there for peace.

The Ramakrishna Math is a hospital that treats the disease of ignorance. Just as people go to a hospital to be cured of a disease, so people should go to the monastery to get rid of ignorance. No one could find a better way to cure mental illness.

The Ramakrishna Math is a factory for manufacturing knowers of Brahman. I have seen that those who live in the monastery after renouncing everything become gods within two or three years.

The Ramakrishna Math is a university postgraduate program. One's training will be completed if one gets admitted there. The service attitude of the monastery supplements university education. One can see there how the Master's words become manifest in the lives of those monks. They renounce everything to live at Belur Math.[6]

Whenever M. had the opportunity, he would visit Belur Math and other monasteries with devotees, and sometimes he would receive information about the monks from the devotees. M. secretly sent money to monks who were sick or practising austerities in the Himalayas. He also taught the devotees how to visit the monastery. He said to them:

1. Don't seek any favour from, or take advantage of, the Ashrama.

2. Monks collect food by begging and subscription, so be satisfied with a little prasad and don't be demanding.

3. Don't take away a monk's meditation time by conversing with him.

4. If any monk scolds you in the monastery compound, please forbear it with humility.[7]

Later in M.'s life he recalled some interesting incidents concerning Swami Vivekananda:

Nowadays many gurus do not teach their disciples the path of renunciation; rather they encourage them to make more money. The Master did not care for those worthless gurus. Once Swamiji came to the Master with his hair well kempt. The Master mussed his hair, saying, "My child, we have not come to this world for enjoyment."[8]

Swamiji was truly a great soul. When he was a student, he never went to the theatre. After meeting the Master, however, he saw Girish's *Chaitanya Lila, Vilwamangal,* and a few other plays.[9]

Swamiji's longing for God was phenomenal. One day he arrived at Cossipore, having wept all the way from Calcutta. He was so oblivious of his body that he lost his sandals on the way. The Master asked him, "Will you not appear for the law examination?" Swamiji replied, "Sir, I would be relieved if I could forget whatever I have studied."[10]

The Master scolded Swamiji twice: first at Dakshineswar and second at Cossipore. When Swamiji first began visiting Dakshineswar, he frequently criticized Kali. Finally the Master said gravely, "Don't come here anymore." Despite this scolding, Swamiji did not become upset. He immediately began preparing a smoke for the Master. Later in Cossipore the Master scolded Swamiji when he said something about the views of Tantra. The Master said, "I have seen that those who practise those esoteric sadhanas in the name of religion go astray."[11]

After being propitiated, whatever God gives us is prasad (sanctified food). One should accept prasad with love and respect; this unites one with God. It works on the subconscious mind and also purifies the mind. To rid oneself of a craving for a particular food, one should offer it to God, then eat it. The craving will go away. The Master held prasad in high regard. He said, "The prasad of Lord Jagannath, Ganges water, and the dust of Vrindaban are veritably Brahman." He used to take one particle of Jagannath prasad (dry rice) every day and advised his devotees to do the same. He once gave it to Swamiji, but he refused to take it. Swamiji said: "It is merely a particle of dry rice. What good will it do?" The Master answered: "Do you believe in the medicinal property of a thing — such as opium is constipating and *triphala* is a laxative? Prasad is like that. It enhances devotion and faith." Without further argument Swamiji took the prasad.[12]

Once the Master taught Vedanta to Narendra [Swami Vivekananda]. Master: "There are ten cups of water and the sun is reflected on them. How many suns do you see?"

Narendra: "Ten reflected suns and one real sun."

Master: "Well, if one cup is broken, then how many remain?"

Narendra: "Nine reflected suns and one real sun."

Master: "If among ten cups nine are broken, how many remain?"

Narendra: "One reflected sun and one real sun."

Master: "If this cup is broken, what will you see?"

Narendra: "One real sun."

Master: "No, that is not correct. Who can then say what remains? The person who is supposed to say this is not there."

For that reason, the Master said to Vidyasagar: "Everything has been defiled except Brahman. None can express Brahman by speech."[13]

It takes time for a big flower to bloom. Narendra was a thousand-petalled lotus. Such a flower takes a long time to bloom but lasts many days. Other flowers bloom, and then wither the next day. Oh, Swamiji absorbed so many shocks in his life. His father died and he needed to support his whole family. His father had spent more than he earned, so the family was in debt. I asked Vidyasagar to give Narendra a job. He appointed Narendra as the headmaster of Bowbazar School, but within a month he lost the job. Vidyasagar's son-in-law was the secretary of that school and he did not get along with Narendra. He tried to control Narendra, but failed. Then he devised a plan: He secretly incited the upper-class students to say that the headmaster was a poor teacher. Vidyasagar then told me that Narendra had been fired. At this, I felt as if a thunderbolt had fallen on my head. I did not know how I would give Narendra this news. However, when I finally informed him, he did not protest. He was surprised, and said: "The students said such a thing! I worked hard, prepared the class, and then taught them." He did not defend himself, nor did he blame anyone. As I observed his serene attitude, I realized that Narendra was a noble soul. It is hard to believe that a person who would be a great teacher of the world was not able to teach schoolboys! The Master wanted to make him a great captain, so he put him through all kinds of difficult tests.[14]

Swamiji suffered terribly when he saw his mother and brothers starving. Every day he searched for a job, going from place to place without eating. In the evening he would return home and go to bed, saying: "I have eaten. You please eat whatever food is there." One of his friends secretly gave some money to his mother and told her, "Please don't tell Narendra my name; otherwise he will return the money." He had tremendous self-esteem, and no suffering could perturb his strong-willed nature.[15]

Swamiji also suffered greatly during his itinerant days. Once he and Gangadhar were seated under a tree. Swamiji had not eaten for two days. When they saw a man coming towards them, Swamiji told Gangadhar that he would feed them. The man approached and asked, "Maharaj, have you eaten anything?"

"No," replied Swamiji.

The man took them to his home and fed them joyfully. In exchange for his food, Swamiji chanted some verses of the Gita.

On another occasion he fainted because he hadn't eaten in three days. A Muslim fakir saved his life by giving him a cucumber. Swamiji used to say: "We have established this monastery so that the monks can get some food and shelter here after practising spiritual disciplines."

Why did Swamiji introduce philanthropic activities in the Ramakrishna Mission? Unselfish action purifies the mind. Not everyone can remain absorbed in meditation all the time. Each person's samskaras (tendencies) are different. If a person sits idle, he will become unstable and suffer from worry and anxiety. For that reason Swamiji established all these Ashramas and launched selfless activities.[16]

Aswini Datta said to Swamiji: "Why did you criticize the Theosophists so much? The Master never criticized anyone." [The Theosophists had tried to disrupt Swamiji's work in the West, so he made some critical remarks against them in Madras after returning from the West.]

Swamiji replied: "Please accept only those words of mine which are compatible with the Master. Sometimes I lose my temper and say things."

Swamiji was a *nityasiddha*, an ever-perfect soul, who practised spiritual disciplines after realizing God. He was like the gourd or pumpkin vine — first fruit, then the flower. An elephant has two sets of teeth — external and internal. He protects himself with the external tusks and masticates his food with his inner teeth. Similarly, Swamiji's activities are like the tusks of an elephant, and his meditation and austerities, and his love and devotion for God and guru, are like the elephant's inner teeth. No one can refute Swamiji's words. One purifies one's mind through unselfish action; then comes love for God."[17]

On 2 April 1924 two American women devotees visited M. They had met Swamiji in San Francisco in 1900. One of them said to M.: "When we heard Swamiji we felt his spirit was lifting our soul perforce, much against all our intellectual barriers, to a serene and beatific stage. This living religion we hankered after, and Swamiji quenched that long thirst. So pure, so high and yet so humble, he was."[18] M. then told them his reminiscences about the Master and Swamiji.

Afterwards, referring to the American devotees, M. said: "Those who have seen Swamiji are blessed. Those are our intimate relatives who have loved and respected Swamiji and served him. We are indebted to them, because Swamiji and the Master are one and the same. I heard that the Master always followed Swamiji like a shadow in the West. When Swamiji was tired, he would sometimes try to enter samadhi, but the Master would appear before him and inspire him to continue to spread his message so that people could attain peace. All of Swamiji's activities were part of a master plan. The Master was an avatar, so he was concerned with the whole world, but he was especially interested in the West. Science has helped Western people to become advanced on the material plane, but this wealth and prosperity have made them forget God. The Master engaged Swamiji to turn their minds to God."[19]

M. witnessed Ramakrishna's and Vivekananda's ways of life and was fully aware of their teachings. He also observed that Vivekananda's message was nothing but a commentary on his Master's teachings. Actually Vivekananda was "His Master's Voice." Swamiji himself acknowledged it in his lecture on *My Life and Mission*: "All the ideas that I preach are only an attempt to echo his [Ramakrishna's] ideas."[20]

Many monks and Miss Josephine MacLeod asked M. to write something about Swami Vivekananda. On 22 August 1924 M. began to dictate to Brahmachari Jagabandhu (later Swami Nityatmananda) a series of articles that tried to show how Swamiji's lectures echo the Master's teachings. These articles were published in the journal *Basumati* and later incorporated into an appendix in the fifth volume of the *Kathamrita*, which was published after M.'s passing away. Swami Nikhilananda did not translate this appendix in *The Gospel of Sri Ramakrishna*. Below we have translated that appendix with M.'s comments, abridging the parallel teachings that he quoted from the *Gospel* and Vivekananda's *Works*.

1. Ramakrishna and Narendra

M. first recorded what the Master told him about Narendra:

Narendra belongs to a very high plane — the realm of the Absolute. He has a manly nature. So many devotees come here, but there is not one like him.

Every now and then I take stock of the devotees. I find that some are like lotuses with ten petals, some like lotuses with sixteen petals, some like lotuses with a hundred petals. But among lotuses Narendra is a thousand-petalled one.

Other devotees may be like pots or pitchers; but Narendra is a huge water barrel.

Others may be like pools or tanks; but Narendra is a huge reservoir like the Haldarpukur.

Among fish, Narendra is a huge red-eyed carp; others are like minnows or smelts or sardines. Tarak of Belgharia may be called a bass.

Narendra is a very big receptacle, one that can hold many things. He is like a bamboo with a big hollow space inside.

Narendra is not under the control of anything. He is not under the control of attachment or sense pleasures. I feel great strength when Narendra is with me in a gathering.[21]

M. wrote how Narendra implicitly followed his guru's advice. The Master knew that Narendra would carry his message, so he trained him accordingly. The Master said to him:

What can you achieve by mere lecturing and scholarship without discrimination and dispassion? God alone is real and all else is unreal. First of all set up God in the shrine of your heart, and then deliver lectures as much as you like. It is difficult to teach others. Only if a man gets a command from God, after realizing Him, is he entitled to teach.[22]

Following the advice of his guru, Narendra renounced the world and practised austerities in solitude. In Cossipore the Master transmitted power

to him, and then wrote on a piece of paper, "Narendra will teach people."
After the Master passed away, Narendra, then Swami Vivekananda, went
to the West to preach the spiritual message of India. Appreciating his success in the West, people of Madras held meetings and sent him addresses
of thanks and congratulations. Swamiji replied from America:

> It was your generous appreciation of him [Ramakrishna] whose message
> to India and to the whole world, I, the most unworthy of his servants,
> had the privilege to bear; it was your innate spiritual instinct which saw
> in him and his message the first murmurs of that tidal wave of spiritual-
> ity which is destined at no distant future to break upon India in all its
> irresistible power.[23]

In 1897 after returning from the West, Swamiji gave several lectures in
Madras, and in his third lecture, *The Sages of India*, he said:

> Let me conclude by saying that if in my life I have told one word of truth
> it was his and his alone; and if I have told you many things which were
> not true, correct, and beneficial to the human race, it was all mine and on
> me is the responsibility.[24]

In his Calcutta address at Radhakanta Dev's house, Swamiji said:

> If this nation wants to rise it will have to come enthusiastically round
> his [Ramakrishna's] name....Within ten years of his passing away this
> power has encircled the globe. Judge him not through me. I am only a
> weak instrument. His character was so great that I or any of his disciples,
> if we spent hundreds of lives, could do no justice to a millionth part of
> what he really was.[25]

Swami Vivekananda was always overwhelmed when he would talk
about his guru. Blessed was his devotion for the guru!

2. Realization of God

Vivekananda preached the universal, eternal Hindu religion that he
had learned from Ramakrishna.

On 26 October 1884 the Master said to Mahimacharan:

> How much of the scriptures can you read? What will you gain by mere
> reasoning? Try to realize God before anything else. What will you learn
> of God from books? As long as you are at a distance from the market-
> place you hear only an indistinct roar. But it is quite different when you
> are actually there. Then you hear and see everything distinctly. You hear
> people saying: "Here are your potatoes. Take them and give me the
> money."

One cannot get a true feeling about God from the study of books. This feeling is something very different from book learning. Books, scriptures, and science appear as mere dirt and straw after the realization of God.[26]

Swamiji addressed the Parliament of Religions in Chicago:

The Hindu does not want to live upon words and theories. He must see God, and that alone can destroy all doubts. So the best proof a Hindu sage gives about the soul, about God, is "I have seen the soul; I have seen God."[27]

In a lecture in Hartford, Connecticut, Swamiji said:

Religion does not consist in doctrines or dogmas. The end of all religions is the realization of God in the soul. Ideas and methods may differ, but that is the central point. A man may believe in all the churches in the world, he may carry on his head all the sacred books ever written, he may baptize himself in all the rivers of the earth, still if he has no perception of God I would class him with the rankest atheist.[28]

In New York on 9 January 1896, Swamiji gave a lecture entitled *The Ideal of a Universal Religion*, in which he said:

Religion is realization, not talk nor doctrine nor theories however beautiful they may be. It is being and becoming, not hearing or acknowledging; it is not an intellectual assent.[29]

3. Harmony of Religions

Ramakrishna had taught Swamiji the unique message of the harmony of religions. On 13 August 1882 the Master said:

God can be realized through all paths. All religions are true. The important thing is to reach the roof. You can reach it by stone stairs or by wooden stairs or by bamboo steps or by a rope. You can also climb up by a bamboo pole.[30]

It is not good to feel that one's own religion alone is true and all others are false. God is one only and not two. Different people call on Him by different names: some as Allah, some as God, and others as Krishna, Shiva, and Brahman. It is like the water in a lake. Some drink it at one place [and] call [it] 'jal,' others at another place and call it 'pani,' and still others at a third place and call it 'water.' The Hindus call it 'jal,' the Christians 'water,' and the Mussalmans 'pani.' But it is one and the same thing. Opinions are but paths. Each religion is only a path leading to God, as rivers come from different directions and ultimately become one in the one ocean.[31]

In an address to the Parliament of Religions in Chicago, Vivekananda said:

Sectarianism, bigotry, and its horrible descendant fanaticism have possessed long this beautiful earth. They have filled the earth with violence, drenched it often and often with human blood, destroyed civilizations and sent whole nations to despair.

If anyone here hopes that this unity will come by the triumph of any one of the religions and the destruction of the others, to him I say, "Brother, yours is an impossible hope." Do I wish that the Christian would become Hindu? God forbid. Do I wish that the Hindu or Buddhist would become Christian? God forbid. The Christian is not to become a Hindu or a Buddhist, nor a Hindu or a Buddhist to become a Christian. But each must assimilate the spirit of the others and yet preserve his individuality and grow according to his own law of growth.[32]

4. Vivekananda's Patriotism

Vivekananda's heart cried for suffering humanity. Being a monk, he tried to collect money for the poor people of India, and at the same time he showed his love and sympathy for the African-American poor. Ramakrishna said:

To love these objects, regarding them as one's own, is maya. But to love all things is daya, compassion. To love only the members of the Brahmo Samaj or of one's own family is maya; to love one's own countrymen is maya. But to love the people of all countries, to love the members of all religions, is daya. Such love comes from love of God, from daya. Maya entangles a man and turns him away from God. But through daya one realizes God.[33]

During an interview with the *Chicago Tribune*, Swamiji said:

The crying evil in the East is not religion. They have religion enough; but it is bread that these suffering millions of burning India cry out for with parched throats. I came here to ask aid for my impoverished people and fully realized how difficult it was to get help for heathens from Christians in a Christian land.[34]

5. Is God with Form or Formless?

Once Keshab Sen, a Brahmo leader, came to Dakshineswar with his followers. The Master talked to them about God without form. He said: "I don't consider the image of Kali to be made of clay or stone. She is conscious. Brahman and Kali are the same. When that consciousness is actionless, it is Brahman; and when it creates, preserves, and destroys, it is Kali."

A Brahmo Devotee: "Sir, has God forms or has He none?"

Master: "No one can say with finality that God is only 'this' and nothing else. He is formless, and again He has forms. For the bhakta [devotee] He assumes forms. But He is formless for the jnani, that is, for him who looks on the world as a mere dream. The bhakta feels that he is one entity and the world another. Therefore God reveals Himself to him as a Person. But the jnani — the Vedantist, for instance — always reasons, applying the process of 'Not this, not this.' Through this discrimination he realizes, by his inner perception, that the ego and the universe are both illusory, like a dream. Then the jnani realizes Brahman in his own consciousness. He cannot describe what Brahman is.

"Do you know what I mean? Think of Brahman, Existence-Knowledge-Bliss Absolute, as a shoreless ocean. Through the cooling influence, as it were, of the bhakta's love, the water has frozen at places into blocks of ice. In other words, God now and then assumes various forms for His lovers and reveals Himself to them as a Person. But with the rising of the sun of Knowledge, the blocks of ice melt. Then one doesn't feel anymore that God is a Person, nor does one see God's forms. What He is cannot be described. Who will describe Him? He who would do so disappears. He cannot find his 'I' anymore."[35]

Some Christian missionaries of the West considered the people of India to be uncivilized because they worshipped idols. Swami Vivekananda said to them:

At the very outset I may tell you there is no polytheism in India. In every temple, if one stands by and listens, he will find the worshippers applying all the attributes of God to these images.

Then he continued:

Why does a Christian go to Church? Why is the Cross holy? Why is the face turned towards the sky in prayers? Why are there so many images in the Catholic Church? Why are there so many images in the minds of Protestants when they pray? My brethren, we can no more think about anything without a mental image than we can live without breathing....If a man can realize his divine nature with the help of an image, would it be right to call that a sin? Nor even when he has passed that stage, should he call it an error? To the Hindu, man is not travelling from error to truth, but from truth to truth, from lower to higher truth.[36]

6. The Doctrine of Sin

The doctrine of sin is a big issue to many people in all religions. Ramakrishna said: "As one spark of fire can burn a mountain-size bale of cotton, and the clapping of the hands can drive away the birds in a tree, so if a person sincerely chants God's name and thinks of Him, all sins will disappear."

Once the Master told Keshab Chandra Sen and the Brahmo devotees:

> Bondage is of the mind, and freedom is also of the mind. A man is free if he constantly thinks: "I am a free soul. How can I be bound, whether I live in the world or in the forest? I am a child of God, the King of Kings. Who can bind me?" If bitten by a snake, a man may get rid of its venom by saying emphatically, "There is no poison in me." In the same way, by repeating with grit and determination, "I am not bound, I am free," one really becomes so — one really becomes free.
>
> Once someone gave me a book of the Christians. I asked him to read it to me. It talked about nothing but sin. (To Keshab) Sin is the only thing one hears of at your Brahmo Samaj, too. The wretch who constantly says, "I am bound, I am bound" only succeeds in being bound. He who says day and night, "I am a sinner, I am a sinner" verily becomes a sinner.
>
> One should have such burning faith in God that one can say: "What? I have repeated the name of God, and can sin still cling to me? How can I be a sinner anymore? How can I be in bondage anymore?"
>
> If a man repeats the name of God, his body, mind, and everything become pure. Why should one talk only about sin and hell, and such things? Say but once, "O Lord, I have undoubtedly done wicked things, but I won't repeat them." And have faith in His name.[37]

At the Parliament of Religions in Chicago, Swamiji said:

> Ye are the children of God, the sharers of immortal bliss, holy and perfect beings. Ye divinities on earth — sinners! It is a sin to call a man so. Come up, O lions, and shake off the delusion that you are sheep; you are souls immortal, spirits free, blest and eternal; ye are not matter, ye are not bodies; matter is your servant, not you the servant of matter.

In Hartford, Swamiji said in a lecture:

> Shall we advise man to kneel down and cry, "O miserable sinner that I am!" No, rather let us remind them of their divine nature. If the room is dark, do you go about striking your breast and crying, "It is dark!" No, the only way to get into light is to strike a light and then the darkness goes. The only way to realize Light above you is to strike the spiritual light within you and the darkness of impurity and sin will fly away. Think of your higher Self, not of your lower.[38]

7. Renunciation

Vivekananda was a man of true renunciation and he followed in his guru's footsteps. "Everything in this world is fraught with fear. It is renunciation alone that makes one fearless."

Ramakrishna told Vijay Krishna Goswami:

One cannot teach people without renouncing woman and gold. Being entangled with woman and gold, if one preaches, "The world is unreal and God is real," no one will listen to that person.[39]

Again, he said to Vidyasagar:

Vultures soar very high in the sky, but their eyes are fixed on rotten carrion on the ground. The book-learned are reputed to be wise, but they are attached to "woman and gold." Like the vultures, they are in search of carrion.[40]

Pointing to Narendra, the Master said:

You all see this boy. He behaves that way here. A naughty boy seems very gentle when with his father. But he is quite another person when he plays in the Chandni. Narendra and people of his type belong to the class of the ever-free. They are never entangled in the world. When they grow a little older they feel the awakening of inner consciousness and go directly towards God. They come to the world only to teach others. They never care for anything of the world. They are never attached to "woman and gold."[41]

Swami Vivekananda was not only a scholar but a great soul. He was a true disciple of his guru. The stain of "woman and gold" never touched his body. In the *Song of the Sannyasin,* he wrote:

Truth never comes where lust and fame and greed
Of gain reside. No man who thinks of woman
As his wife can ever perfect be;
Nor he who owns the least of things, nor he
Whom anger chains, can ever pass through maya's gates.
So give these up, sannyasin bold! Say,
　"Om Tat Sat Om!"[42]

8. Karma Yoga

Ramakrishna used to say that everyone has to perform karma. One can reach God through the paths of jnana, bhakti, and karma. According to the Gita, the monk and the householder should work in a detached way for the purification of the mind. It is ignorance to think: "I am the doer, and this money and family are mine." One should perform action after surrendering its fruit to the Lord. The Gita also says that one can do karma after attaining illumination and receiving God's command, as did King Janaka. Karma Yoga is difficult. One cannot perform unselfish action without practising sadhana for a long period in solitude.

Swami Vivekananda renounced lust and gold and practised sadhana, in solitude, according to the instructions of his guru. He was an ideal karma yogi.[43]

Swamiji wrote in the *Song of the Sannyasin*:

"Who sows must reap," they say, "and cause must bring
The sure effect: good, good; bad, bad; and none
Escape the law — but whoso wears a form
Must wear the chain." Too true; but far beyond
Both name and form is Atman, ever free.
Know thou art That, sannyasin bold! Say,
    "Om Tat Sat Om!"

In London on 10 November 1896 Swamiji explained Karma Yoga according to Vedanta:

Curiously enough the scene is laid on a battlefield where Krishna teaches this philosophy to Arjuna; and the doctrine which stands out luminously on every page of the Gita is intense activity, but in the midst of it, eternal calmness. And this idea is called the secret of work, to attain which is the goal of Vedanta.[44]

9. Left-Handed Tantra

At Dakshineswar on 29 September 1884 Narendra asked about some left-handed or esoteric religious sects of Bengal. Ramakrishna described their beliefs and condemned their immoral practices. He said that they could not follow the true course of spiritual discipline, but enjoyed sensual pleasures in the name of religion.

The Master said to Narendra:

You need not listen to these things. The bhairavas and the bhairavis of the Tantric sect also follow this kind of discipline. While in Varanasi I was taken to one of their mystic circles. Each bhairava had a bhairavi with him. I was asked to drink the consecrated wine, but I said I couldn't touch wine. They drank it. I thought perhaps they would then practise meditation and japa. But nothing of the sort. They began to dance.

(*To Narendra and the others*) Let me tell you this. I regard woman as my mother; I regard myself as her son. This is a very pure attitude. There is no danger in it. To look on woman as a sister is also not bad. But to assume the attitude of a 'hero,' to look on woman as one's mistress, is the most difficult discipline. In this form of sadhana one cannot always maintain the right attitude.[45]

At the Cossipore garden house, the Master told Narendra:

My child, let no one drink any alcohol here. It is not good to drink in the name of religion. I have seen that those who are involved with this kind of practice have fallen.[46]

After returning from the West in 1897, Swami Vivekananda echoed his guru's message in his lecture on *The Vedanta in All Its Phases*:

Give up this filthy Vamachara that is killing your country. You have not seen the other parts of India. When I see how much the Vamachara has entered our society, I find it a most disgraceful place with all its boast of culture. These Vamachara sects are honeycombing our society in Bengal. Those who come out in the daytime and preach most loudly about *Achara* [code of conduct], it is they who carry on the horrible debauchery at night and are backed by the most dreadful books. They are ordered by the books to do these things. You who are of Bengal know it. The Bengali Shastras [scriptures] are the Vamachara Tantras. They are published by the cartload, and you poison the minds of your children with them instead of teaching them your Shrutis [Upanishads]. Fathers of Calcutta, do you not feel ashamed that such horrible stuff as these Vamachara Tantras, with translations too, should be put into the hands of your boys and girls, and their minds poisoned, and that they should be brought up with the idea that these are the Shastras of the Hindus? If you are ashamed, take them away from your children, and let them read the true Shastras, the Vedas, the Gita, the Upanishads.[47]

10. Ramakrishna as an Avatar

M. witnessed the spiritual and intellectual evolution of Narendra. In his early days Narendra did not care for the doctrine of the avatar, but after coming in contact with the Master, he gradually started to have faith in it.

On 7 March 1885 Ramakrishna said:

The other day, when Harish was with me, I saw Satchidananda come out of this sheath. It said, "I incarnate Myself in every age." I saw that it is the fullest manifestation of Satchidananda; but this time the Divine Power is manifested through the glory of sattva.[48]

In early March 1885, Girish Chandra Ghosh began declaring publicly that Ramakrishna was an avatar. On 1 March 1885, the Master asked Narendra: "Do you agree with Girish about me?"

Narendra: "He said he believed you to be an Incarnation of God. I didn't say anything in answer to his remarks."

Master: "But how great his faith is! Don't you think so?"[49]

After a few days the Master asked Narendra: "Well, some call me an avatar. What do you think of this?"

Narendra: "I shall not accept anything based on another's opinion. Only when I understand and believe it myself shall I give my opinion."[50]

A couple of days before Ramakrishna's passing away, when the Master was in excruciating pain, a thought flashed across Narendra's mind: "Well, if you can now declare that you are God, then only will I believe you are really God Himself." Immediately the Master looked up at Narendra and said distinctly: "O my Naren, are you still not convinced? He who in the past was born as Rama and Krishna is now living in this very body as Ramakrishna."[51] Narendra was dumbfounded. Later he practised sadhana and realized the Master's divinity.

In his book *Bhakti Yoga*, Swamiji expressed his conviction:

Higher and nobler than all ordinary ones are another set of teachers, the avatars of Ishvara, in the world. They can transmit spirituality with a touch, even with a mere wish. The lowest and most degraded characters become in one second saints at their command. They are the Teachers of all teachers, the highest manifestations of God through man. We cannot see God except through them. We cannot help worshipping them; and indeed they are the only ones whom we are bound to worship.

As long as we are men, we cannot conceive of Him as anything higher than man. The time will come when we shall transcend our human nature and know Him as He is; but as long as we are men, we must worship Him in man and as man. Talk as you may, try as you may, you cannot think of God except as a man. You may deliver great intellectual discourses on God and on all things under the sun, become great rationalists and prove to your satisfaction that all these accounts of the avatars of God as man are nonsense. But let us come for a moment to practical common sense. What is there behind this kind of remarkable intellect? Zero, nothing, simply so much froth. When next you hear a man delivering a great intellectual lecture against this worship of the avatars of God, get hold of him and ask what *his* idea of God is, what *he* understands by "omnipresence," or "omnipotence," and all similar terms, beyond the spelling of the words. He really means nothing by them; he cannot formulate as their meaning any idea unaffected by his own human nature; he is no better off in this matter than the man in the street who has not read a single book."[52]

In his lecture on *Christ, the Messenger*, Swamiji expressed how a true avatar speaks:

"'Thou hast seen me and not seen the Father? I and my Father are one. The kingdom of Heaven is within you.' That was what Jesus of Nazareth said.

"Let us, therefore, find God not only in Jesus of Nazareth, but in all the Great Ones who preceded Him, in all who have come after Him, and in all who are yet to come. Our worship is unbounded and free. They are all manifestations of the same infinite God."[53]

After returning from the West, Swamiji said in his lecture in Madras on *The Sages of India*:

The time was ripe for one to be born who in one body would have the brilliant intellect of Shankara and the wonderfully expansive, infinite heart of Chaitanya; one who would see in every sect the same spirit working, the same God; one who would see God in every being, one whose heart would weep for the poor, for the weak, for the outcast, for the downtrodden, for everyone in this world, inside India or outside India; and at the same time whose grand brilliant intellect would conceive of such noble thoughts as would harmonize all conflicting sects, not only in India but outside of India, and bring a marvellous harmony, the universal religion of head and heart into existence.

Such a man was born, and I had the good fortune to sit at his feet for years. He was Sri Ramakrishna Paramahamsa. Let me now only mention the great Sri Ramakrishna, the fulfillment of the Indian sages, the sage for the time, one whose teaching is just now, in the present time, most beneficial.[54]

During Narendra's early meetings with Ramakrishna, he considered him to be mad. Later, however, he declared the Master to be an avatar. He composed the vesper hymns on Ramakrishna, and in the salutation mantra he declared: "O Ramakrishna, establisher of righteousness, embodiment of all religions, best of avatars, salutations to Thee."

An Ideal Householder Devotee

The ancient sages of the Vedas based the Hindu view of life on spirituality. Thus, its main goal is *moksha,* or liberation. According to the Hindus, there are four stages of life, or ashramas: *brahmacharya āshrama* (student), *gārhasthya āshrama* (householder), *vānaprastha āshrama* (forest dweller), and *sannyāsa āshrama* (monk). In the West, an ashrama is generally considered to be a religious retreat or a place where people practise spiritual disciplines, study, and perform their duties under the guidance of a guru, but an ashrama is also a stage of life. The Hindu begins life as a student; then he or she marries and becomes a householder; in old age he or she retires; and lastly he or she gives up the world and becomes a sannyasin or sannyasini.

Although each stage of life is equally important, only householders earn money and support the other three ashramas. In fact, the entire structure of society depends on householders. If their lives are unstable, society itself becomes unstable. Nowadays family life in both the West and the East is unsteady because of economic distress and social ills such as divorce. Children of broken homes live in turmoil. Distracted by selfishness and greed, many householders forget their duties, and so society descends into chaos. Regarding the householder's duties, the Mahanirvana Tantra says: "The householder should be devoted to God; knowledge of God should be the goal of his life. Yet he must work constantly and perform all his duties; and he must give the fruits of his actions to God."

Front row, left to right: Tarak Datta, Akshay Sen, Girish Ghosh, Swami Adbhutananda, M., Middle row: Kalipada Ghosh, Devendra Majumdar, Swami Advaitananda, Back row: Devendra Chakrabarty, unknown, unknown, Abinash Mukhopadhyay, Mahendra Kaviraj, Vijay Majumdar

Ramakrishna trained one group of his disciples to be ideal monks and another to be ideal householders. When M. visited the Master for the second time, Ramakrishna learned that he was married and had children, so he began to train M. accordingly. At that time M. asked him: "How ought we to live in the world?"

The Master replied: "Do all your duties, but keep your mind on God. Live with all — with wife and children, father and mother — and serve them. Treat them as if they were very dear to you, but know in your heart of hearts that they do not belong to you.

"A maidservant in the house of a rich man performs all the household duties, but her thoughts are fixed on her own home in her native village. She brings up her Master's children as if they were her own. She even speaks of them as 'my Rama' or 'my Hari.' But in her own mind she knows very well that they do not belong to her at all."[1]

During his third visit M. asked: "Sir, is there no hope for a bound soul in the world?"

The Master replied: "Certainly there is. From time to time he should live in the company of holy men, and from time to time go into solitude to meditate on God. Furthermore, he should practise discrimination and pray to God, 'Give me faith and devotion.' Once a person has faith he has achieved everything."[2]

Buddha emphasized renunciation and encouraged men and women to become monastics. Christ said, "You cannot serve both God and Mammon." He also said, "Sell all you have and give the money to the poor and then follow me." Chaitanya said: "Listen, Brother Nityananda, the bound souls of this world have no chance for liberation."

Ramakrishna knew that it was not possible for householders to renounce completely, so he advised them to adopt *gārhasthya-sannyās*, which means to perform the duties of a householder but inwardly practise renunciation and keep the mind focussed on God — like the gopis, who performed their household duties and kept their minds focussed on Krishna. M. used to say: "The Master dyed my mind with ochre [the color of sannyas]."

M. once said: "The Master would say: 'It is not possible to ask the people of Calcutta to renounce everything; they would stop coming here. So I tell them to do their family duties and at the same time practise spiritual disciplines. Hold on to God with one hand and your family with the other. I tell them to mentally practise detachment. After visiting this place again and again, they will realize that the relationships of friends and family last only for a few days, and then the spirit of renunciation will develop automatically.'"[3]

M. recorded in *The Gospel of Sri Ramakrishna*:

Neighbour: "Sir, is it ever possible to realize God while leading the life of a householder?"

Master: "Certainly. But as I said, one must live in holy company and pray unceasingly. One should weep for God. When the impurities of the mind are thus washed away, one realizes God. The mind is like a needle covered with mud, and God is like a magnet. The needle cannot be united with the magnet unless it is free from mud. Tears wash away the mud, which is nothing but lust, anger, greed, and other evil tendencies, and the inclination to worldly enjoyments as well."[4]

Money is a big issue for householders. Some people earn money by ruining their health, and later they spend that money to restore their health. Some think that money will bring happiness in life, so they work hard, save money, and become extremely attached to it. During his sadhana Ramakrishna mentally analyzed the purpose of money: It provides food, clothing, comforts, and so on, but God cannot be attained by it. So he threw some money into the Ganges, saying, "Money is clay and clay is money." But he did not give that advice to householders.

M. asked the Master many important questions that householders quite often face. Once he asked: "Sir, may I make an effort to earn more money?"

Master: "It is permissible to do so to maintain a religious family. You may try to increase your income, but in an honest way. The goal of life is not the earning of money, but the service of God. Money is not harmful if it is devoted to the service of God."

He further said to M.: "You no doubt need money for your worldly life; but don't worry too much about it. The wise course is to accept what comes of its own accord. Don't take too much trouble to save money. Those who surrender their heart and souls to God, those who are devoted to Him and have taken refuge in Him, do not worry much about money. As they earn so they spend. The money comes in one way and goes out the other. This is what the Gita describes as 'accepting what comes of its own accord.'"[5]

The Master also reminded householders: "Many people regard money as their very life-blood. But however you may show love for money, one day, perhaps, every bit of it will slip from your hand."[6]

"Those who have money should give it to the poor and needy. Jaygopal Sen is well-to-do. He should be charitable. There are some who are miserly even though they have money. There is no knowing who will enjoy their money afterwards.

(*To Surendra*) "I cannot eat anything offered by miserly people. Their wealth is squandered in these ways: first, litigation; second, thieves and robbers; third, physicians; fourth, their wicked children's extravagance. It is like that.

"Your giving money away in charity is very good. Those who have money should give in charity. The miser's wealth is spirited away, but the money of a charitable person is saved. He spends it for a righteous purpose."[7]

M.: "How long should a man feel obliged to do his duty towards his wife and children?"

Master: "As long as they feel pinched for food and clothing. But one need not take the responsibility of a son when he is able to support himself. When the young fledgling learns to pick its own food, its mother pecks it if it comes to her for food."[8]

M.: "What should one do if one's wife says: 'You are neglecting me. I shall commit suicide.'?"

Master: "Give up such a wife if she proves an obstacle in the way of spiritual life. Let her commit suicide or anything else she likes. The wife that hampers her husband's spiritual life is an ungodly wife."

M. was shocked and bewildered by Ramakrishna's harsh response. He was an honest and dutiful family man and needed an answer to the problem that he was facing. But the Master understood M.'s situation and shortly afterwards told him privately: "If a man has sincere love for God, then all come under his control — the king, wicked persons, and his wife. Sincere love of God on the husband's part may eventually help the wife to lead a spiritual life. If the husband is good, then through the grace of God the wife may also follow his example."[9] This assurance soothed M.'s worried mind.

Sometimes people misunderstand nonviolence, and get confused about right and wrong. In this connection M. asked: "At meal-time, sometimes a cat stretches out its paw to take the fish from my plate. But I cannot show any resentment."

The Master replied: "Why? You may even beat it once in a while. What's the harm? A worldly man should hiss, but he shouldn't pour out his venom. He mustn't actually injure others. But he should make a show of anger to protect himself from enemies. Otherwise they will injure him. But a sannyasi need not even hiss."[10]

Ramakrishna was a very practical teacher and he knew that it was almost impossible for a married man to practise absolute continence. So he said: "You should not renounce woman completely. It is not harmful for a householder to make love with his wife. But after the birth of one or two children, husband and wife should live as brother and sister."[11] On another occasion the Master said to M.: "As long as one has a body, a little lust remains. There is nothing wrong in it."

M. responded: "Sir, I want to be free from lust completely."

The Master answered: "Is it possible? It is only possible when one realizes God."[12]

M. later said that he overcame lust by making tremendous self-effort, following the Master's instructions, and surrendering to him. Thus by the Master's grace, he achieved self-control.

A householder has duties to his elderly parents, because he is the bread-earner of the family. M. and his wife could not get along with the members of their joint family, so they moved out of the house and lived in a separate rented place. The Master said: "Are father and mother mere trifles? No spiritual practice will bear fruit unless they are pleased."

(*To M., reproachfully*) "And let me say this to you. Your father and mother brought you up. You yourself are the father of several children. Yet you have left home with your wife. You have cheated your parents. You have come away with your wife and children, and you feel you have become a holy man. Your father doesn't need any money from you; otherwise I should have cried, 'Shame on you!'"[13]

After that scolding, M. returned to his ancestral home. Ramakrishna was pleased and said to him: "You have done well. It will be convenient for you to live at home. Since your parents live there, you won't have to worry so much about the family."[14] The Master's intention was that M. be released from some of the responsibility for his wife and children, so that he could devote more time to practising spiritual disciplines and spending time with holy people.

Every human being has responsibilities according to place, time, and circumstances. These duties are dictated sometimes by one's conscience, but the scriptures frequently determine what is right or wrong. These duties differ from person to person, society to society, country to country, and religion to religion. Swami Vivekananda said: "To give an objective definition of duty is thus impossible. Yet one can define duty from the subjective side. Any action that makes us go Godward is a good action and is our duty; any action that makes us go downward is evil and not our duty."[15]

In the *Gospel*, M. carefully recorded the Master's universal teachings concerning a householder's duties, so that people from all over the world could practise them.

Subjudge: "Sir, we are householders. How long should we perform our worldly duties?"

Master: "Surely you have duties to perform. You must bring up your children, support your wife, and provide for her in case of your death. If you don't, then I shall call you unkind."

Subjudge: "How long should one support one's children?"

Master: "As long as they have not reached their majority [full legal age]. When the chick becomes a full-grown bird and can look after itself, then the mother bird pecks it and doesn't allow it to come near her."

Subjudge: "What is a householder's duty to his wife?"

Master: "You should give her spiritual advice and support her during your lifetime and provide for her livelihood after your death, if she is a chaste wife. But if you are intoxicated with the Knowledge of God, then you have no more duties. Then God Himself will think about your family if you are intoxicated with Him."[16]

Although the Master dwelt most of the time on a lofty spiritual plane, he gave practical advice to the householders who came to him. M. carefully recorded those teachings for himself as well as for others.

Regarding living with bad or difficult people, the Master told the story of the brahmachari and the snake. The brahmachari advised the snake to practise nonviolence and not to bite people; as a result some cowherd boys badly injured the snake. Later when the brahmachari came to know about the whole situation, he said to the snake, "I asked you not to bite but you could hiss and frighten the boys." If anyone wants to harm you, you should "hiss and not bite." God dwells in all beings, but one should not embrace the tiger god. Salute him from a distance.

Moreover, while living in this world one should develop the power of forbearance, and one should learn to forgive others. The Master said: "Forbear, forbear, forbear; he who forbears, prospers and he who does not, perishes." This is a very practical lesson for community life.

Then again, it is important to be flexible and to adjust to changing circumstances in everyday life — otherwise one will meet with resistance at every step. So the Master said: "One should learn to adjust according to time, place, and person."

The Master also gave M. private instructions on which to build his spiritual life. He asked M. to fast on the eleventh day of the lunar fortnight [ekadashi] to purify his mind and to develop love of God. Because a complete fast might have been difficult for M., the Master told him that he could have milk and puffed rice on fast days. Regarding food, the Master advised him to eat sattvic food and to follow Krishna's instructions in the

Gita: "Yoga is not for him who eats too much nor for him who eats too little." During his sadhana, M. ate rice with a little ghee and milk as per the Master's instruction.

Ramakrishna also taught the English-educated M. to have the company of holy people, because their association enhances longing for God. But a householder should not visit a sadhu empty-handed, as sadhus also need the bare necessities of life.

The Master told M. to keep pictures of monks and saints in his room in order to create a spiritual atmosphere. It is better to see the faces of holy people when one rises in the morning, rather than to see worldly people. He also told M. that one must keep one's home clean and orderly. Uncleanliness and disorderliness are signs of tamas, or inertia. The Master could not bear careless people. Once a devotee bought, with one pice, 6 betel leaves instead of 10. The Master scolded him, saying: "Be a devotee, but don't be foolish. Don't get cheated. If you have extra, distribute them to others but never be cheated."[17]

Although the Master's mind was mostly absorbed in an ecstatic state, he was very careful about small things. On 5 April 1884 M. recorded in the *Gospel* how the Master had humbled him for his forgetfulness. After having his bath in the Ganges, M. returned to the Master's room and sat near him. Seeing that he had bathed, the Master offered him fruits and sweets (prasad) to eat, so M. went to the semi-circular veranda to eat them. After eating the prasad and drinking some water, he rushed back to the room to sit near the Master, leaving the water pot behind. Sri Ramakrishna said, "Are you not bringing the water pot back?"

M.: "Yes sir. I am going to get it."

Master: "Bah!"

M. was embarrassed. He went to the veranda and brought the water pot back to the room.

M. often said that he had wanted to renounce family life, because the Master repeatedly said in the *Gospel*, "One cannot attain God if one has even a trace of attachment to 'woman and gold.'"[18] After he had been visiting the Master for some time, M. felt the urge to become a monk. But Ramakrishna discouraged him, as he had set out a different path for him. He told M.: "You are well established in God already. Is it good to give up all?"[19]

One evening when M. and Ramakrishna were alone at Dakshineswar, the Master said in an ecstatic mood: "Let nobody think that if he does not do Mother's work, it would remain undone. The Mother can turn even a straw into a teacher."[20] This erased any doubt left in M.'s mind.

He understood that he should surrender completely to the Master's will, so he resolved within himself to live as a hidden yogi in the family setting. He practised inner *sannyasa* (renunciation), yet he did not neglect his responsibilities. M. was a successful schoolteacher, but he maintained the calmness of a yogi. He was very humble and served monks and devotees with deep sincerity. Thus he combined the virtues of a householder with the spiritual intensity of a monk.

One day, however, the Master finally fulfilled M.'s longing for sannyasa. M. wrote: "The Master initiated a devotee [M.] and Baburam into Tantric sannyasa together. That devotee had pestered the Master again and again for sannyasa. But he kept that devotee at home at the behest of the Divine Mother and wiped out attachment and worldly desires from his mind. The Master made everything favourable for that devotee. He prayed to the Mother to give that devotee a vision, so that he could teach people.…He further said: 'Mother, since you are keeping him at home, then from time to time reveal Yourself to him; otherwise it will be hard for him to stay at home.'"[21]

M. later told the devotees how the Master had guided and protected his life as a householder. One day the Master took M. inside the Kali temple and taught him to pray: "O Mother, you are the destroyer of danger and obstacles. Please remove my obstacles."

M. said: "The greatest obstacle in spiritual life is body-consciousness and attachment to the sensual world. As long as the Mother keeps one conscious of the body, one should pray to her, 'Mother, remove my obstacles.'"[22]

As a Hindu mother teaches her children how to bow down to deities in a holy place, similarly the Master helped M. develop devotion in his discriminating mind. One day in the Panchavati the Master bowed down to the spot where a branch of the old banyan tree had fallen. He said to M.: "I had so many divine visions here. Please bow down at this place." Another day he prayed for M.: "Mother, this person is very simple. He sits near me quietly. I am praying to you for him so much; Mother, please attract him." Then the Master gave M. a private instruction: "Sing this song in solitude, with a longing heart. It will rouse your Kundalini power.

'Waken, O Mother! O Kundalini, whose nature is Bliss Eternal!
Thou art the serpent coiled in sleep, in the lotus of the Muladhara.'"[23]

As his guru had instructed, M. remained in the world like a servant who only serves others. Once at Dakshineswar M. cleaned the dishes after the Master's lunch. The Master commented: "This is very good. It is nice to learn all kinds of work — cooking, dishwashing, washing clothes, sweeping, and cleaning the room." Later M. used to cook his own food, so one day his wife complained to Holy Mother that her husband was not eating her cooking. When Holy Mother asked M. to eat the meals that his wife prepared, he obeyed her in his own fashion: When his wife served a meal, M. joyfully tasted each dish and praised her cooking.[24] In truth, however, he ate practically nothing of it. He ate only the simple food that the Master had prescribed for him. He also washed his own clothes. He seldom accepted personal service from others. M. followed this teaching from the scriptures: "Dependence is misery and independence is happiness."

Swami Nityatmananda once described how M. lived like a servant in his own home. During his school's summer vacation, M. went for a retreat at the Gadadhar Ashrama in South Calcutta. One night at 10 o'clock he returned to his residence at the Morton Institution. His wife and children lived on the third floor, and he lived in an attic room on the fourth floor. M. had not eaten supper that night. Nityatmananda was about to awaken M.'s wife so that she could prepare a meal, but M. forbade him to do so. When Nityatmananda insisted, M. begged him: "Please allow me to obey the behest of the Master. If a maidservant arrives at a house at night, does the mistress cook for her?"

Nityatmananda: "Sir, then what will you eat?"

M.: "The sweet shop on the corner is still open. Please buy some hot milk and a piece of Punjabi bread for me."[25] Thus he had his supper.

M. provided the necessities of life for his wife and children, and also served the devotees by sharing with them his knowledge and devotion. He explained the true meaning of service: "Service to others means that one must know that God dwells in all beings. When serving others, one is truly serving God. One should do it oneself and not through others. The greatest devotee sees God within himself, so he serves the indwelling God himself."[26]

One day M. introduced his eldest son, Nirmal, to the Master, saying, "My son." Immediately the Master affectionately cautioned him: "Never say, 'My son.' You should think that he is God's child and that He has kept him with you to receive your service. Why? Because if something happens to the boy or if God takes him away, you will be beside yourself with grief." This actually happened. Nirmal died and both M. and Nikunja Devi suffered terribly from grief. Through his guru's grace, M. recovered, but his wife suffered for the rest of her life.[27]

M. was a dutiful, compassionate, and humble householder devotee, yet he was uncompromising about moral and ethical values. His youngest son, Charu Chandra, was a bachelor, well-educated, and a disciple of Holy Mother, but he had a terrible habit of gambling. When this came to M.'s attention, he told Charu to give it up or leave home. Piqued, Charu left. M. was unperturbed and never showed any anxiety about his son.

Charu took shelter with his maternal uncle, who was wealthy and had no children. He lived with his maternal uncle and aunt for a long period and continued to gamble. After some time his uncle died, and then his aunt passed away during a pilgrimage to Badarika Ashrama in the Himalayas. Charu's other cousins then forced him to leave the house, and he became homeless, without food and clothing.

One day Swami Nityatmananda was walking on Amherst Street, carrying the proofs of the *Kathamrita* to the printer, when he met Charu. Seeing his pitiable condition, Nityatmananda asked, "Are you sick?"

"No, I am not sick. I have not eaten for two days. Will you give me 30 rupees?"

Charu knew that Nityatmananda was his father's cashier and secretary. The swami could not give him money without M.'s consent, however. He asked Charu to wait there while he went to M. and explained the situation. M. calmly said, "All right, give him 30 rupees on condition that he pay it back within 31 days." Charu took the money and repaid M. within the stipulated time. On another occasion Charu sent a letter through his nephew: "Father, I am on the verge of starvation. Please give me some money."

M. replied, "Yes, I will give you whatever you want but you are to stop going to the horse races." As Charu would not give any such promise, he did not take any money.[28] However, Charu later followed his father's advice and reformed himself.[29]

Although M. was sensitive and loving, he never deviated from his ideals. He was convinced that everything he could call his own actually belonged to the Master. And he felt he had no right to give money to a son who would only use it to support a terrible addiction. M. freely spent money for the Master, Holy Mother, and the monastic disciples, but he was extremely reluctant to spend anything on himself. While in Calcutta he travelled by tram in second class (there was no third class), and on trains he travelled in third class. He led a simple, unostentatious life. He had three dhotis (wearing cloths), three shirts, one chadar (shawl), and one pair of sandals. The same simple clothing he wore when he first met Ramakrishna, he wore the rest of his life.

M. idealized the monastic life of renunciation and purity. He regarded monks as full-time lovers of God, and householders as part-time, because of their worldly obligations. M. considered Ramakrishna to be the embodiment of renunciation and purity and the monks of his Order as those who continued to carry his lofty banner. When a monk came to visit M., he would set aside his work and sit near him like a servant, saying: "A holy man has come. The Lord himself has come in one form, as it were. Shall I not postpone my eating and bath for him? Absurdity can go no further if I cannot do that."[30]

Though outwardly M. was a householder, inwardly he was like a monk, full of intense devotion to God and renunciation of things of the world. Sometimes he would get up at night and leave his home, taking his bed roll with him, to sleep on the open veranda of the Calcutta University Senate Hall among the homeless people of the city. When asked why, he explained, "The idea of home and family clings to one and does not leave easily."[31]

Sometimes he would go to the railway station to watch the stream of pilgrims returning from the Jagannath temple at Puri. He liked to see their bright, serene faces, and occasionally he would ask for a little prasad from them. The Master had told him that one who eats prasad attains devotion. If anyone brought him prasad, he would even save the container in which it was carried, thinking that it would remind him of God. He would bow down to the place on Bechu Chatterjee Street where the Master's elder brother had once conducted a school, and also to the house of the Mitra family at Jhamapukur, where the Master had once worked as a priest. In response to his companions' surprise, M. would say, "Do you know that anyone who walks through this street will become a yogi?"[32] Sometimes when he went to Dakshineswar after the Master's passing away, he took a towel with him to soak in the Ganges. When he returned, he would squeeze the water from it and sprinkle that water on the devotees, saying, "I brought this water from the ghat on the Ganges where the Master used to bathe."[33]

Everything is in the mind. A man may live alone in a forest retreat, but if his mind is engrossed in family ties and attachments, he remains a worldly householder. However, if a person lives in a family situation, yet his mind is controlled and free from family attachments, he is considered to be a yogi. Such a home turns into a hermitage. M. made his home an abode of God and he lived there as a *sthitaprajna*, a man of steady wisdom. Krishna described the signs of a *sthitaprajna* in the Gita (2:56): "He who is not perturbed by adversity, who does not long for happiness, who is free from attachment, fear, and wrath, is called a *muni* of steady wisdom."

One afternoon Swami Atmananda, a disciple of Vivekananda, visited M. at home. M. received him in his parlour and sent his attendant to buy some sweets. He then served the swami refreshments and they began to talk. The swami observed several people entering the house barefoot, with towels on their shoulders. He could also hear some people crying upstairs. Curious, Atmananda asked, "Master Mahashay, what is the matter?"

M. calmly replied: "It is nothing. Please have your refreshments."

M. never allowed any monk to leave his house without having some refreshments. When the swami finished eating, M. said, "A girl [his own daughter] of this house has passed away, so those people have come to take the body to the cremation ground."

Amazed, Atmananda said to M.: "Sir, blessed you are! Unperturbed by grief and danger, you have served a monk. Blessed you are! Victory to the Master!"[34]

When M.'s other daughter was married, he gave her away during the ceremony, as was the custom, and also received the visitors and relatives and made arrangements for the wedding feast. Thus the wedding celebrations continued till 2:00 a.m. Afterwards M. went to his attic shrine and began to read his diary by the light of a kerosene lantern. He remained absorbed in meditation on the Master until 6:00 a.m.[35] As a maidservant does her own work after finishing her duties in her master's house, so M. remained absorbed in his own work after discharging his family responsibilities.

Ramakrishna listed the five signs of a jnani householder: First, a householder devotee must maintain calmness under all circumstances; second, he must be humble; third, he must act like a lion (meaning, as an efficient and energetic leader) in the working field; fourth, he should be lighthearted and make people happy; fifth, he should regard himself as a servant of monks and devotees. All these signs were present in M.'s life.

M. remained in the world as a hidden yogi. On 14 December 1884 Ramakrishna described the hidden yogi: "Some attain knowledge of God in the world. Mention is made of two classes of yogis: the hidden and the known. Those who have renounced the world are 'known' yogis: all recognize them. But the 'hidden' yogis live in the world. They are not known. They are like the loose woman who performs her household duties zealously but whose mind constantly dwells on her lover."[36]

Vedanta says: God alone is real, and the world is illusory. Everyone, except for illumined souls, is entangled in the meshes of illusion, or maya. After realizing God and becoming illumined, how does a hidden yogi remain in the world? The Master told the secret: "Suppose an office clerk has been sent to jail. He undoubtedly leads a prisoner's life there. But when he is released from jail, does he cut capers in the street? Not at all. He gets a job as a clerk again and goes on working as before. Even after attaining Knowledge through the guru's grace, one can very well live in the world as a jivanmukta."[37] Thus did Ramakrishna reassure M. and others who were living as householders.

The Morton Institution and Naimisharanya

M any people have a problem reconciling their day-to-day activities with their spiritual disciplines. Even monks face this dilemma; in their case it is between action and contemplation. Some monastics think that the contemplative life is better than the active life. In the Gita, however, Krishna reconciled all four yogas: karma (action), jnana (knowledge), bhakti (devotion), and raja (meditation). He pointed out that liberation is possible through each one of them, as seen in the Gita quotes below.

Karma Yoga: "Therefore always do without attachment the work you have to do; for a man who does his work without attachment attains the Supreme." (3:19)

Jnana Yoga: "And those who have completely controlled their senses and are even-minded under all conditions and thus worship the Imperishable, the Ineffable, the Unmanifest, the Omnipresent, the Incomprehensible, the Immutable, the Unchanging, the Eternal — they, devoted to the welfare of all beings, attain Me alone, and none else." (12:3-4)

Bhakti Yoga: "But by devotion to Me alone may I be known in this [Cosmic] form, O Arjuna, realized truly, and entered into, O dreaded prince." (11:54)

Raja Yoga: "Shutting out all external objects; fixing the gaze of his eyes between his brows; equalizing the outward and inward breaths moving in his nostrils; controlling his senses, mind, and understanding; being ever bent on liberation; ridding himself of desire, fear, and anger — such a man of contemplation is indeed always free." (5:27-28)

Is it possible for a householder with a full-time job and a family to realize God? Ramakrishna was asked this question repeatedly, and he always answered it the same way: "Everybody will surely be liberated. But one should follow the instructions of the guru....Sages like Janaka performed worldly duties. They performed them, bearing God in their minds, as a dancing girl dances, keeping jars or trays on her head. Haven't you seen how the women in northwest India walk, talking and laughing while carrying water pitchers on their heads?"[1]

Ramakrishna often expanded on this, as in the following excerpt from the *Gospel*:

> To live in the world in a detached spirit is very difficult. By merely saying so you cannot be a King Janaka. How much austerity Janaka practised! You don't have to practise these extreme disciplines. But you need sadhana; you should live in solitude. You may lead the life of a householder after having attained divine knowledge and love in solitude....Janaka was a great hero. He fenced with two swords, the one of knowledge and the other of work.
>
> You may ask, "Is there any difference between the realizations of two jnanis, one a householder and the other a monk?" The reply is that the two belong to one class. Both of them are jnanis; they have the same experience. But a householder jnani has reason to fear. He cannot altogether get rid of his fear as long as he is to live in the midst of "woman and gold." If you constantly live in a room full of soot, you are sure to soil your body, be it ever so little, no matter how clever you may be....Although a jnani living in the world may have a little blemish, yet this does not injure him. The moon undoubtedly has dark spots, but these do not obstruct its light.
>
> After realizing God, some souls perform work in order to teach men. Janaka, Narada, and others like them, belong to this group.[2]

M. also belonged to this group. Ramakrishna trained him to be a householder jnani. As King Janaka ruled his kingdom yet remained absorbed in Brahman and talked about Him, so also M. did his work, teaching and supervising a school, while the remaining time he was absorbed in God-consciousness, writing the Master's gospel, and talking about him to seekers of God.

The Morton Institution

As described in Chapter 2, M.'s first job was in 1879 as a headmaster in Narail High School, in Jessore (now in Bangladesh), where he worked for nearly a year. In 1880 M. became the headmaster and superintendent of Metropolitan High School, Shyampukur branch, which was owned by the great educator and social reformer Ishwar Chandra Vidyasagar. M. stayed at the Metropolitan until 1886. From then until 1905 he worked as a professor and headmaster in different colleges and schools in Calcutta, and finally in 1905 he bought the Morton Institution at Jhamapukur (in Calcutta) from the son of Nakri Ghosh. The school soon became so popular that one house could not accommodate all its students, so M. rented a four-storey building at 50 Amherst Street. This building looked like a chariot and was painted red. At that time the streets in Calcutta were not overcrowded, and they were lined with flowering trees such as *bakul, kadamba,* and *krishna-chura.* M. became the rector, and the teachers and students called him "Rector Mahashay." M.'s eldest son, Prabhas, was the headmaster, and Fakir Babu was the superintendent. Classes for grades one through five were held at a house on Panchanan Ghosh Lane, close to the main building; and classes for grades six to ten were held at the Amherst Street building. Later on, all classes were held in the latter building. The school was only for boys.

M. divided his time between the Morton Institution, where he stayed in a room on the fourth floor of the Amherst Street building, and Thakur Bari, his family home. After M. bought the Morton Institution in 1905, he slowly withdrew himself from regular teaching. He made decisions about the school's management and also watched the students when they entered the school, during lunch, and when they left. Sometimes, however, he taught classes on religion, morality, and patriotism, and also substituted for absent teachers.

Mahimaranjan Bhattacharya, a student of the Morton Institution in 1921, recalled:

> Our Geography teacher was absent one day, so the Rector Mahashay taught the class in his place. The topic of the lesson was Arabia. He taught us in a manner I can never forget. The main fruit of Arabia is the date. The story of how a merchant threw away the pit after eating the fruit, the Red Sea, the Suez Canal, Mecca and Madina, and the story of the Prophet — how beautifully he narrated all these!
>
> Besides these casual classes, the Rector would sometimes come for lessons on morals and ethics. He would also tell us the teachings of Sri Ramakrishna and stories of great men, and explain in simple language

ABOVE: M.'s room in the attic; Left: Morton Institution at 50 Amherst Street (now Rammohan Sarani)

verses from the Gita. In M.'s school, the study of Sri Ramakrishna's life and the *Kathamrita* were compulsory. I can still hear the deep voice: *Manushatvam mumukshatvam mahapurusha samshrayah* — human life, longing for liberation, and the company of the holy — these are the three essentials of spiritual life. I knew this by heart. Nobody ever saw the Rector reprimanding anybody. He would never lose his temper, let alone inflict bodily punishment. But his personality was such that hearing his deep voice even from a distance, saying, 'Please place your hands on your knees and sit up erect,' we would immediately place our hands on our knees and sit up straight. The whole class would become so quiet that one could hear one's own breathing. We never saw him raise his voice at anybody.

Along with his solemn and loving personality, his dress was also notable. A kurta with a folded cloth round his back, its two ends hanging over his shoulders opening out on his chest, long hair, ample beard reaching his chest, and big eyes — peaceful and patient as if turned inwards. On his feet he wore polished shoes or sometimes sandals; his gait was firm and patient. Sometimes he would hold his hands clasped behind his back. At the tiffin hour in school or at the close of the day or at the time of coming to school he would stand and keep on watching the boys. Either he would be in the schoolroom going over the papers during the day or he would walk up and down with his hands behind his back. I felt awed on approaching him but later on when I came in closer contact with him I realized what a gentle, loving soul lay hidden behind the outer veil, a touch of which has blessed me forever.

The place M. occupied in the midst of the devotees of Sri Ramakrishna was beyond my ken at that age. But I was old enough to see that M. was far above the common man. Many a high-class sadhu and saint used to visit M. from Belur Math and elsewhere and so did many seekers who came to him for instruction and to dispel their sorrows. I can still recall the faces of some of those persons. Much later I came to know their identity. But then I had the simplicity of a child with his unshakable faith and unique curiosity. I have now lost that longing, and regret that I did not go nearer the Rector Mahashay. Had I at least spent some more time in closer contact with him, my life would have become meaningful.

One day I entered the room of the Rector Mahashay during the recess period, full of trepidation. He was then seated on a blanket with both of his hands clasped on his lap; perhaps he was meditating. On entering I immediately saw that it was not a residential room, nor even the usual puja room. It was a temple. There were pictures all around — that of the Paramahamsa Deva, the Holy Mother, Swami Vivekananda, Mother Bhavatarini, and so many pictures of other gods and goddesses, and even a picture of Jesus Christ. On each of the pictures there were devotional marks of sandal paste and flowers, and the perfume of burning incense. I felt something — this something cannot be expressed in words.

He had seen me, so he asked me to take my seat. He offered me some fruit as prasad which I accepted with a mind full of devotion. The Rector gave me some advice before I left. According to the present reckoning it was perhaps banal but to us of the older generation so invaluable: adoration of parents, complete dependence on God, compassion for created beings — these were his main instructions.

Seen superficially, M. looked like a worldly person. He would keep a perfect account of profit and loss of his money. He also ran his school so efficiently. In the matter of spending also he was so thrifty. Not only did he believe in thrift for himself, he would also teach his pupils not to spend needlessly. How could such a man be a realized soul, and the winner of the grace of the Supreme Person? To understand this, one had to know M. more intimately.... Many outsiders could not see how indifferent M. was to physical comforts. And they did not know, possibly do not know now, how unbounded was his charity. And yet his left hand did not know what his right hand gave away. When Swamiji's family was passing through terrible times because of want of money and was actually starving, it pulled through for three months with M.'s financial help. At the end of every month he was seen filling out a number of money-order forms. It can only be surmised that they were meant for the needy fellow-disciples of his guru who had fallen into straitened circumstances. There were those among them who could not afford a medically prescribed diet, others who needed medical care, yet some other saintly persons depended on charity for their living. M. knew them all — I believe he must have been noting down in his diary or some other notebook what and how much these persons needed. No doubt, he had a phenomenal memory."[3]

M's notebook later revealed that he used the income he earned from the *Kathamrita* to support several monks* of the Ramakrishna Order who were either sick or practising austerities.

The Morton Institution was a reputable school, and the students had good results in their final examinations and university entrance examinations. Sometime in the late 1920s, when Sir Jadunath Sarkar was the vice chancellor of Calcutta University (1926-1927), this university withdrew its affiliation with the Morton Institution. We do not know the exact reason. It may be that M. had introduced religious education into the curriculum

---

* At Kashi (Varanasi): Sri Jagadananda, Sri Shantananda, Sri Shakti, Sri Chandra, Sri Divyananda Puri, Sri Shashi, Sri Gadadhar, Sri Chitprakash (Tarini), Sri Prabuddha, Sri Siddhananda, Sri Swaprakash. At Rishikesh: Sri Gopesh, Sri Tanmayananda, Sri Divya Chaitanya (Hari). At Almora: Sri Mokshananda, Sri Parananda. At Bangalore: Sri Hemendra and others.

and instilled patriotism among the students during that British period. It is also said that there was a difference of opinion between M. and the university authorities regarding how the school committee was formed. M. then had to cancel the 9th and 10th grades. The Institution remained a private school, but limited to grades one through eight. This reduced his income significantly, but the alternative was to lose his freedom, which he did not want to do.[4] M.'s friends and well-wishers advised him to take legal action; he could have easily won the lawsuit, but he refused. M. renamed the school Ramakrishna-Vivekananda Institution and continued leading it until he passed away in 1932.[5] When Prabhas died in 1934, the school changed ownership.[6] It is now called the Hindu Academy.

M. as an Educator

M. was an excellent teacher, held in high esteem by the great educators of the day as well as by national leaders. Here are three recommendations from well-known academics of the time:

I have known Babu Mahendra Nath Gupta, since his appointment as Headmaster and Superintendent of the Shyampukur Branch of the Metropolitan Institution in January 1880. He has given me satisfaction by diligent and attentive discharge of the duties entrusted to him. He is proficient in the art of teaching and is a remarkably intelligent and well informed gentleman of amiable disposition and an exceptional character.
Ishwar Chandra Sarma [Vidyasagar]
Calcutta, 26 June 1882

Certified that Babu Mahendra Nath Gupta was Professor of English and Political Economy and Moral Philosophy in the Ripon College and satisfactorily discharged his duties. He has a high sense of his responsibilities. Professor M.N. Gupta was employed in the Ripon College for about six years.
Surendra Nath Banerjee
The Ripon College, 60 Mirzapur Street
Calcutta, 6 April 1898

Babu Mahendra Nath Gupta, B.A., was a professor of English, History and Political Economy in the Metropolitan Institution for one academic Session. He had to teach the B.A. classes (Pass and Honours) and also F.A. classes. He did his work thoroughly well, commanded the respect and affection of his pupils, and inspired the confidence of the College authorities.
N.N. Ghosh
Principal, Metropolitan Institution
Calcutta, 31 May 1900[7]

M. was not just an ordinary teacher who taught the university curriculum as outlined by the British government. He had his own thoughts regarding education and was greatly inspired by Ramakrishna's mode of teaching, which he incorporated into his own teaching. Because the Morton Institution was a private school, M. had the freedom to incorporate his method of teaching in addition to the curriculum of the university.

Mahimaranjan recalled: "Why did M.'s teachings go straight to the heart? So many people teach, but their teachings have little effect. The reason is that M. would teach only what he himself believed in and had practised in his life. Without being determined true to one's vows, nobody can do it."[8]

M. emphasized national education, man-making education, and the goal of education. He said: "One should know first the contents of human beings, and then have a philosophy or the plan of education. Each human being has three bodies: gross or physical, subtle or intellectual, and causal or spiritual. It is extremely important to feed all three bodies so that they become strong. Our schools and colleges are feeding only the subtle body. The educational system must be connected with the spiritual body, which will form character and will bring peace and joy. If education is not connected with the Highest Ideal, the moral character will not be strong. India's culture is grand and great because of her educational system. In olden days students would live with their gurus and received broad training that developed all three levels of their bodies. Before planning for education, we should first set the ideals of a human being, the ideals of national life. Otherwise it will be like water poured from a pitcher, which is falling on the floor because the glass is far away. It turns into fruitless toil."[9]

Regarding the goals of education, M. emphasized building character first, and second, passing the university entrance examination. A student should be idealistic and at the same time practical. Without a university education, a student cannot get a good job with a decent salary. Until one attains the highest spiritual realization, one should not neglect materialistic prosperity following scientific advancements.

In addition to building character and enabling students to enter the university, M. also sought to provide a "man-making education" for the boys whom he taught. The following were his guidelines:

1. It is essential to present the goal of human life to students from an early age. We need genuine human beings to build the nation. Under the influence of the British, students learn that the goal of education is to achieve fame, prestige, and money.

2. The students should be brave and physically strong. A butter-doll is good for nothing. They should be taught manliness from their childhood onward.

3. Students should learn the dignity of labour; there is no shame in doing one's own work. The British educational system did not emphasize the dignity of labour; rather it trained a few Indians to imitate the British, who used the natives to do menial jobs. Even in his old age, M. demonstrated to his students how to remain active. He did his own chores, contributed to the household work, and even repaired the roof of the school building himself.

4. M. worked to develop perseverance and tenacity in his students. He said: "Try, try again. If at first you don't succeed, try, try again. Never give up until you reach the goal."

5. M. emphasized moral and spiritual education, and he introduced his students to the lives of the great teachers of the world and to the *Sri Ramakrishna Kathamrita*. He believed that Ramakrishna's catholic views about religion could eradicate religious fanaticism.

6. In M.'s time there were no teacher-training colleges, so he recommended that teachers get good training. He also advocated training for parents or guardians because students lived at home, not with a guru as in ancient times.

7. "Teaching is an art," said M. The teacher should be a person of good character and must be tactful enough to handle students without scolding and caning them, as was common in his time. M. also said: "The Master said, 'It is better to hear than to read, and better to see than to hear.' So a teacher should read, and then teach students verbally instead of forcing them to read books themselves. Teachers should use pictures, diagrams, and maps, so that students can visualize what they are learning. And from time to time teachers should take students to various places so that they can see what is actually being discussed.

M. said: "Some professors who lecture in English in colleges have no clear idea of what they are teaching, because they do not know that language well enough. So how will the students learn? They memorize the lessons without understanding them, then pass the examinations and receive a B.A. or M.A. degree. When the British authorities encouraged Vidyasagar to spread their method of education, he replied with a smile, 'Yes, the students will pass the examinations but learn very little.'"[10]

According to M. the medium of education should be the students' native language. Students must learn English and Sanskrit, of course, but before teaching in these languages the teacher should first explain the theme in the mother tongue. During the classes the teacher should check from time to time to ensure that students are absorbing the subject.[11]

Swami Nityatmananda, a teacher in the Morton Institution, wrote: "I worked with M. in the school and realized that he was a teacher of a high caliber. Although he was such a great scholar, while teaching he would come down to the level of the students. He would study the minds of the students and find out how much they could absorb and how they could learn properly. He would use maps, pictures, diagrams, and other methods so that the students could learn well. He introduced Bengali as the medium of instruction in the Morton Institution. He was not only a teacher of students; he also taught the teachers the methods of proper teaching."[12]

Regarding the method of teaching, M. said: "An ideal method of learning is when a student learns using all five organs of knowledge."[13] When teachers give lectures, students use only one organ of knowledge — the ears. They use their eyes and ears if diagrams and maps are also provided. Likewise they learn more by using other organs of knowledge — nose, tongue, and skin.

On the first and second floors of the Morton Institution, M. taught *apara vidya,* or regular education, to his ordinary students, and on the fourth floor (in Naimisharanya) he taught *para vidya,* or supreme knowledge, to seekers of God.

One needs an education to improve one's standard of living, so M. always encouraged his students to apply themselves: "Study well. It helps us get acquainted with various thoughts of the world, and the interactions of thoughts develop our mental culture. Finally, the mind resorts to sublime thoughts. Furthermore, when one is always engaged in learning higher thoughts, that develops brahmacharya and eventually that enhances love and attraction for God."[14]

About education, Socrates said: "They who provide much wealth for their children, but neglect to improve them in virtue, do like those who feed their horses high, but never train them to the manage."[15] M. advocated a curriculum that emphasizes human values. He said: "Is the aim of education only to earn money? See, how good education helps to develop noble qualities. It enhances (1) Patience, (2) Perseverance, (3) Accuracy or carefulness, (4) Attention or focus, (5) Concentration, (6) Sense of responsibility, (7) Breadth of vision, (8) Perception or clear understanding, and (9) Application or skill in action."[16]

M. managed the Morton Institution for 27 years, trying out his ideas of education on his students with wonderful results. This school earned an excellent reputation in Calcutta, and M. himself commanded love and respect from his teachers and students through his magnanimous personality, his integrity, and his deep spirituality. By nature he was very softhearted. Once a neighbour's son shot a bird, which fell on the roof of the Morton Institution. He immediately put the bird in a cage, applied medicine to its wound, and fed it. After a few days of this treatment, the bird improved. However, when the cage door was opened it tried to fly but fell into a drain. M. again began to nurse the bird but unfortunately could not save its life.

M. was also extremely patriotic. He was fully convinced that India would someday win her freedom. Although he never played an active role in politics or in India's freedom movement, he inspired his students to love and serve the motherland, which he considered to be a spiritual country. He had deep respect for two national leaders, Mahatma Gandhi and Chittaranjan Das. M. said that although Mahatma Gandhi was involved in politics, his life was imbued with spirituality and fully dedicated to the service of the nation. Gandhi was a man of renunciation. Chittaranjan Das was a famous barrister who earned a huge amount of money (1.2 million rupees every year), but he gave up his profession to join the Indian freedom movement. M. greatly appreciated his renunciation and dedication to the motherland. When Das died in 1924, M. wrote in the circular book of the Morton Institution: "The school will remain closed for three days on account of the sad and untimely demise of the great patriot saint of Bengal."[17]

Naimisharanya in Calcutta

The Legend of Naimisharanya: Naimisharanya is the holy forest where Vedavyasa taught the Vedas and all the Puranas to his disciples. Later it was in this very holy place that Romaharshana (alternatively Lomaharshana), Vedavyasa's disciple, narrated the Puranas to several rishis (sages). It is also the blessed place where Ugrasrava (Suta Goswami), the son of Romaharshana, narrated the story of Shrimad Bhagavatam to several rishis.

According to legend, in the Satya Yuga (golden age), the first of the four yugas (cycles), the rishis wanted to perform uninterrupted yajnas (fire sacrifices) for the benefit of mankind, and asked Lord Brahma for a suitable place. Lord Brahma created a huge wheel (called Manomaya chakra), released it, and instructed the sages to follow it. He also told them that the place where it broke down would be very auspicious for doing penance. The sages followed the Manomaya chakra, which after travelling for a long time fell down on a large segment of land, and its circumference (Nemi) broke down as predicted by Lord Brahma. This segment of land became famous as Naimisharanya.

As soon as it was destroyed, from the spot a huge gush of water spurted up in the form of a Shiva-linga. As the water was flooding the place, the rishis prayed and Mother Shakti appeared and absorbed and stopped the flow of water. Hence Naimisharanya is also a Shakti-Pitha and has a famous ancient Lalita Devi temple. It is situated in the Sitapur district of Uttar Pradesh, 100 kilometer from Lucknow.[18]

M. recreated Naimisharanya on the roof of Thakur Bari, his family home, as well as on the roof of the Morton Institution. He lived both in Thakur Bari and in the attic room of his school. To create an atmosphere like that of a Vedic Ashrama, he planted tulsi, plumeria, and other flowering plants in tubs on the roofs of both buildings. He also had his shrine on the roof of Thakur Bari that still exists. Here he wrote and published *Sri Ramakrishna Kathamrita*, volumes one, two, three, and four. He wrote volume five in 1932 at the Morton Institution.

The Vedic sages lived in the forest, where they taught the knowledge of Brahman to their disciples. These teachings are now known as the Upanishads. M. was nostalgic for those ancient Vedic times in the forest, so he went to Rishikesh, Hardwar, and Mihijam to perform austerities, and then he created miniature forests on the roofs of his residences. Swami Nityatmananda wrote: "It appeared that the soul of a great rishi lived in M. He had a tremendous longing to live in a hermitage throughout his life. For that reason, he planted various flowers and fruit trees in tubs on the roofs of both his Calcutta residences — Thakur Bari and the Morton Institution. When he recited the Upanishads in his deep voice, it seemed as if an ancient sage of the Satya Yuga had been born in a new body. The Upanishads were his soul and the Gita was next to them. He was also an authority on the Bible. While talking with the devotees, he would quote from these three — the Upanishads, Gita, and Bible — without interruption. The attic room and the adjacent roof of the Morton Institution were veritably Naimisharanya, and resounded continually with the words of God. M. was like the great sage Narada, proclaiming the glory of Ramakrishna with a thousand mouths."[19]

In later years, people would say: "If you want to forget the world, go to see M. He knows how to remove worldly desires from the mind and instill the thought of God there." People flocked to him, and he would talk to them only about God. When they would say, "Please tell us something about Sri Ramakrishna," he would quote the conversation between the disciple and the teacher in the Kena Upanishad: The disciple said, "Teach me the Upanishad," and the preceptor replied, "I have already told you the Upanishad." By this, M. meant that as he knew only Ramakrishna and nothing else, whatever came through his lips was about him.[20]

Some rishis in ancient times were married; nonetheless, they practised severe austerities in the forest, and lived on fruit or begged for their food like mendicants. Generally M. lived in the school building while his family lived in Thakur Bari, a half mile away, and he used to walk there for his meals as if he were a mendicant begging for food from someone else's house. He was a light eater and his food was very simple: rice with ghee, milk, and fruit during the day, and bread with milk at night. He followed his guru's ideal of plain living and high thinking.

Swami Raghavananda wrote: "The abstemiousness and the extreme simplicity of his life struck his visitors forcibly. Although able to live more lavishly, he limited himself to the strictest frugality. In food and dress and external surroundings he was very simple. He would say that one of the great teachings of the Master was the simplification of life; otherwise the external incidents of life would increase, engross the mind, and completely smother the spirit, leaving no time for thinking about God. Thus living in simple, almost tattered garments, on food simple to bareness, in surroundings the most commonplace, he lived the life of absorption in God, and was an example of high thinking and plain living. His food was the simplest — only rice and milk. This he continued for many years and did not ask for any variation. He was truly 'devoid of rasa,' which meant he completely controlled the craving of the palate. Living this simple life and being merged in God, he was a blessing to innumerable souls and a hope and a stay to many a lost wanderer on this planet."[21]

Fortunately we have some photographs of M. that help us to visualize him. Swami Nityatmananda also described his appearance: "M. had a well-built, tall body and fair complexion. His forehead was prominent; chest, expanded; eyes, large and protruding and tinged with love; and arms, long enough to reach the knees. His long white beard overflowed on his chest, and his countenance was calm and deep in thought. He was a handsome, humorous, and sweet-speaking person. Being absorbed in the thought of Ramakrishna, it was as if this great yogi had been born to glorify the Master day and night. Although he was a great soul and a man of wisdom, he was an embodiment of humility. He was god-intoxicated and free from desires and doubts. He was truly a great rishi."[22]

In 1923, when M. was 69 years old, Swami Chidbhavananda met with M. on the roof of the Morton Institution. He left this account:

Advanced as he was now in age, it was but natural that he should retire from the teaching work and take to spiritual pursuits exclusively. His dutiful son had now taken up the responsibility of running the school. Master Mahashay, whom I was seeing for the first time, looked like a patriarch of yore. He was neither tall nor short — a middle-sized, venerable person he was. Calmness and serenity were the distinguishing features of his face. The bald head bespoke of his advanced age. The beard added to his venerable appearance. The prominent and lotus-like eyes sparkled with spiritual luminosity. The lips indicated the ethical chiseling they had undergone.

Master Mahashay utilized all his learning for the service of his Lord, Sri Ramakrishna Deva. His body, property, and life were all completely at the disposal of Sri Ramakrishna. His delight, sustenance, and purpose in life were the presentation of the godly career of his Lord to the daily thronging devotees. Soon after a preliminary talk, he would switch to his favourite theme — the Master's earthly lila in the Kali temple at Dakshineswar. Man delights in recounting his favourite memories in life. The invaluable treasure in the life of Master Mahashay was his own Master, the Paramahamsa Deva. He was at his best when he was giving a verbal presentation of his Master. Blessed are they who got the opportunity of listening to such talks. The narrator, the listeners, and the topic chosen coalesced for the time being. This divine gift in Master Mahashay was a boon to mankind as long as he was in his mortal coil. In the presence of assembled devotees he would recapitulate his holy contact with the Godman of Dakshineswar. Then it would transform itself into verbal expression. By this act he mentally took the devotees to the realm of joy. What was not physically possible due to the barrier of time was more than compensated for by the mental union. Day after day this good shepherd escorted the religiously inclined ones to the presence of his Chosen Ideal. The presence of the Paramahamsa would be tangibly experienced by the listeners. They would feel themselves personally presented to the God-absorbed superman. Time and space are no barriers for one enlightened soul introducing the other ardent one to his intimately known Godman. This rare cosmic function Master Mahashay was very efficiently discharging all through his earthly career.

Evenings, between five and seven, was the time when devotees would resort to the residence of Master Mahashay for spiritual repast. One evening the parlour was full with devotees to its maximum capacity. They were all inclined more to silence than to gossip. At five sharp the apostle emerged from his room. With eagerness looming large on their faces, the assembled people stood up to greet the holy man. The formal exchange of greetings was over. The day's topic was not always decided

ce. As chance and circumstances would impel, the theme
velop of its own accord. "The grace of God" was the topic that
........geu from the mouth of the holy man on that day. He spoke of it very
eloquently because of his own experience: "The sun and the rain are the
sources of life on earth. Even so the grace of God is no less a life-giving
factor to the devotee. But for it, life would be dreary on earth. The breeze
of the grace of God is eternally blowing. The devotee is only to avail
himself of it. After tasting the mercy of the Lord the devotee becomes
completely changed. Earthly tribulation is no bar to his career on earth.
The more he meets obstacles, the more his devotion increases. Grace is to
the devotee what air is to the worldly man. Life becomes unbearable for
him if he forgets the grace of his Maker."

Womenfolk had free access to Master Mahashay in the manner in
which daughters approach their fathers for the solution of their domestic
problems. Master Mahashay was always kind to them and spared no
pains in attending to the problems. The gravity of a problem was more
subjective than objective. Master Mahashay knew it, but his complete
identification with the person helped mitigate the poignancy of the problem. Invariably he would take up the attitude of the father. A young
woman in tears once presented her family complication. She put it to
the holy man that her mother-in-law was always harsh to her and her
husband paid no heed to this. This was her serious handicap. Master
Mahashay sympathized with her and asked her to accept the order from
her mother-in-law as a mandate from the Maker Himself. Once that
attitude was assumed all her difficulties would vanish as trifles. Young
age was the time to practise fortitude. This world is a training ground.
The Cosmic Mother Kali is assuming millions of forms and shaping the
careers of beings in tune with their dispositions. She is both kind and
stern alternately. As the mother of this young woman, She was kind. But
as her mother-in-law She was stern, which is absolutely necessary. All
commands that came from her were to be taken as orders from Mother
Kali. By implicitly obeying the mother-in-law, the woman was building
her character. Such an attitude would change her distress into discipline.
Earnestness would take the place of weariness and disgust. This revela-
tion from Master Mahashay opened her eyes. She turned a new chapter
in life. Henceforth she had no problems.

A young widow came to him dazed with her problems. Death had
suddenly snatched away her loving husband. The woman had no children. The relatives of her husband were all callous about her future. On
her parental side also there was hardly any who could help her. The
means at her disposal were meager. She thought of suicide, but did
not have the courage to resort to it. Life was gloomy. In that sad plight
she approached Master Mahashay staggering and afflicted. The sage,

however, received her calmly and with all love and affection. And that was the first ray of hope and consolation for the forlorn young widow.

Master Mahashay said: "The apparent blow is an act of mercy that has come to you from God. A few years back you did not know anything about your departed husband. You were an utter stranger to him. A social usage brought you in contact with him. Providence has now kindly broken your bonds with him. There are other ways of making life more useful. The husband-and-wife life is good in its own way. But God has in his mercy provided a woman with innumerable other avenues, more useful and greater in purpose. Daughter, sorrow not. Please listen to the message of hope and benediction that has come to all of us from the Paramahamsa Deva of Dakshineswar. A chartered libertine who became a staunch disciple of the Master put it to him this wise:

Question: If you happen to be enmeshed in an earthly career but have the freedom to choose a life to your liking within bounds, what sort of life would you like to have?

Master: I would choose to be a young widow.

Question: Why so?

Master: All earthly obligations are over for a widow with no family. She can therefore chalk out a career of her choice. A cottage in a village, a bit of land adjoining it, and a cow are sufficient to provide her with earthly needs. She can then remain heart and soul immersed in Godly pursuits. She can forget all her worldly concerns. She can create a divine world of her own. That would be a blessing to herself and to the world. There is nothing happier than this in this world of impermanence and uncertainty.

"Daughter, ponder over this message of the Great Master. It seems he has given this benediction to you in particular. Dependence upon human beings is always uncertain. Whereas dependence on God and his grace is everlasting."

This analysis by the aged sage opened a new vista on human life in the mind of the erstwhile depressed and forlorn young widow. She acted on the advice of Master Mahashay and carved a new chapter in her life. There have been many such stranded souls who were put on the right path by this noble and enlightened Master.[23]

Swami Raghavananda left a vivid description of M.'s Naimisharanya:

In the sweet and warm months of April and May, sitting under the canopy of heaven on the roof garden at 50 Amherst Street, surrounded by shrubs and plants, himself sitting in their midst like a rishi of old, the stars and planets in their courses beckoning us to things infinite and sublime, he would speak to us of the mystery of God and his love, and of the yearning that would rise in the human heart to solve the eternal riddle, as exemplified in the life of his Master. The mind melting under the influence of his soft sweet words of light would almost transcend the limits of the finite existence and dare to peep into the Infinite. He himself would take in the influence of the setting and say, "What a blessed privilege it is to sit in such a setting (*pointing to the starry heavens*), in the company of devotees discoursing on God and his love." Those unforgettable scenes will long remain imprinted on the minds of his hearers.[24]

Bees fly from flower to flower to gather nectar and create honey from it. People then extract the honey from the honeycomb and enjoy it. M. used to visit the temple garden of Dakshineswar as well as places in Calcutta to gather Ramakrishna-honey, the Master's immortal words. He gathered Ramakrishna-honey over a period of five years, recorded it in the *Gospel*, and dispensed it himself for nearly fifty years. He strongly believed that anyone who imbibes these immortal words of the Master will become immortal.

Holy company is like a ferry boat that helps people cross the turbulent ocean of maya. M. lauded holy company in many ways. For instance, he said:

Holy company is the panacea, the remedy for all worldly diseases. It is like an oasis in the desert. As thirsty travellers in the desert rush to the oasis and save their lives by drinking water, so being tormented with worldly sufferings, human beings take refuge in holy company....One can achieve a new life by keeping company with the holy; otherwise one cannot fathom the spiritual world. If one can hold on strictly to the association with the holy, all favourable things of spiritual life come automatically. It is like the mother cow who comes spontaneously to a person who holds her calf....Lust or animal passion diminishes spontaneously through the company of the holy. And again, it enhances longing for God....We have no alternative than to have the company of the holy. "Have the company of the holy" — that was the beginning, middle, and end of the Master's advice to us....Not only did the Master ask us to have the company of the holy, he also created some wonderful sadhus. The monks of Belur Math are the greatest sadhus in this age, because their ideal is Sri Ramakrishna.[25]

M. always encouraged devotees to visit Belur Math and enjoy the company of the holy monks there.

M. himself realized the value of holy company by associating with Ramakrishna from 1882 to 1886; and from then until his death in 1932 he was always surrounded by monks and devotees. As the ancient sages talked only about God and His glory in Naimisharanya, M. did the same thing in his rooftop gardens in Calcutta.

Swami Raghavananda recalled:

M.'s great love for sadhus [monks] and devotees was phenomenal. He would idealize sadhus and their lives above all and could not bear to class them in the same category with householders. Sadhus — those who are trying to devote their whole time and energies to God, without giving their energies to anything else — he would consider the *beau ideal* of life. If the realization of God is the end of life, then that realization is possible only to those who give their all to God — who, leaving all other preoccupations, with single-minded devotion wait upon God for a spark of the Divine Fire which will set their hearts aflame with divine love. Householders, even if they are devotees, have a thousand distractions, a hundred necessary setbacks, which put a limit to their allegiance to God. They cannot be compared with those who have set their whole mind and face towards Him — that is what he would say.

He would say again that all the teachings of Sri Ramakrishna tended towards sannyasa [renunciation], even in his teachings to the householders; he sowed the seeds which will ultimately sprout up in the form of sannyasa either in this life or another. According to him without outer-sannyasa, inner-sannyasa was not possible; and without inner-sannyasa, realization of God was impossible. Thus he would idealize sadhus — wholetime men, as he would call them — and set them apart in a category by itself and would resent the least slight shown to them or their life and would always preach the glory of sadhu-sanga [holy company] — the only practical means of spiritual realization.

When a sadhu would come, he would sit near him for hours, forgetting everything and say: "A sadhu has come. The Lord Himself has come in one form as it were, and shall I not postpone my eating and bath for him? Absurdity can go no further if I cannot do that." He would love to feed the sadhus and sit by them and watch and say, "I am offering food to Thakur [the Master]; I am partaking in and seeing a Puja [worship]." He would paint in brilliant colours the life of the sadhu, his great ideal and mission of life, his great sacrifice for the highest end, and would show infinite regret if any sannyasin neglected his rare opportunity of realizing the *summum bonum* of life. Sadhus learned from him the glory of their mission."[26]

In the divine drama of Ramakrishna, M. played two important roles: He acted in the role of the sage Vyasa by recording the modern Bhagavata (*The Gospel of Sri Ramakrishna*), and he performed the part of the sage Narada, who always sang the glory of God. Swami Shivananda said:

"M. is a great soul. He is Vedavyasa in the Ramakrishna Incarnation."[27] He was born to spread his Master's mission. Ramakrishna told M.: "The Divine Mother has told me that you have to do a little work for Her. You will have to teach the Bhagavata, the word of God, to humanity. God binds the Bhagavata pandit to the world with one tie; otherwise, who would remain to explain the sacred book? He keeps the pandit bound for the good of men. That is why the Divine Mother has kept you in the world."[28]

M. accepted his guru's assignment and fulfilled it with his heart and soul. Sitting in his Calcutta Naimisharanya, he recorded *The Gospel of Sri Ramakrishna* and taught its message to monks and devotees for nearly half a century.* The whole of humanity is indebted to this humble householder and wise rishi, whose whole being was saturated with Ramakrishna-consciousness.

---

*Some of his conversations are recorded in Bengali by Swami Jagannathananda in two volumes (*Srima Katha*) and Swami Nityatmananda in sixteen volumes (*Srima Darshan*). Swami Chetanananda compiled and edited all available reminiscences in one volume (*Srima Samipe*).

M. as a Guide at Dakshineswar and Cossipore

Blessed are the places where incarnations of God are born and raised, where they live, travel, and pass away. Those spots become holy, and they attract pilgrims, historians, writers, poets, artists, and tourists throughout the ages. One of the most wonderful gifts of God is that of inquisitiveness, the desire to know. When children begin to talk, they ask questions: Who? Why? When? How? Where? What? Similarly when we visit those holy places, we ask a guide to tell us every detail of the stories connected with those divine beings. Thus we try to visualize the divine play of the avatars through the guide's descriptions.

Of course there is a gulf of difference between the tourists and the pilgrims visiting a holy place. On one hand, tourists bring a camera, take pictures of themselves with a temple in the background, buy souvenirs and mementos, shop for loved ones, eat in good restaurants, and tell their stories to friends upon returning home. On the other hand, pilgrims fast and bathe in holy rivers or springs, buy flowers and fruits to offer the deity, engage a priest-guide to perform worship of the deity, and learn from him the significance of that vibrant place. Pilgrims practise austerities, pray and meditate for some days, and finally return home with a deep impression of God.

In the Ramayana we come across a few places connected with Rama-chandra: He was born in Ayodhya; he married in Mithila; and during his 14-year banishment he lived in Chitrakut, Dandakaranya, Panchavati, Rameswaram, and Sri Lanka. And in the Bhagavata we find that Krishna was born in Mathura, raised in Gokula and Vrindaban, and spent his adult life in Mathura and Dwaraka. But we also find him in other places such as Hastinapur, Kurukshetra, and Prabhas. In the Bible we learn that Jesus was born in Bethlehem and raised in Nazareth, and that he travelled through Judea, Samaria, Galilee, and Jerusalem. The scriptures, however, give us no detailed description of those holy places. Again, when we visit holy places, the priests or tour guides tell us things about those places that may be only partly true; they often embellish or distort history, concoct stories about the avatars, and describe some miracles that they performed.

In *Sri Ramakrishna and His Divine Play* Swami Saradananda described how Chaitanya discovered the sacred places in Vrindaban:

It is said that Chaitanya was the first to experience a manifestation of the divine presence in Vrindaban. Long before his advent, the holy spots of Vraja were almost forgotten. When Chaitanya travelled in those places, he ascended to the higher plane of consciousness and experienced whatever divine sport had occurred there. In fact, Bhagavan Krishna had enacted the same sport long before in the same place. His disciples — Rupa, Sanatan, and others — were the first to accept these revelations, and later all Indians believed what the disciples told them.[1]

Chapter 8 presented a description of the Dakshineswar temple garden and some stories of Sri Ramakrishna based on M.'s writings. In the *Gospel,* M. immortalized many persons and places connected with Ramakrishna; if he had not done this, they would have passed into oblivion. M. lived for 46 years after the Master passed away. During this period, he visited Dakshineswar and Cossipore many times and acted as a guide to devotees and distinguished guests. His eyewitness accounts of the Master penetrated deeply into the hearts of those visitors and still have a profound effect on all of us. M. had a tremendous passion for truth, a love for history, and an objective mind. He did not dilute the freshness of the original story. M. told visitors, "The avatar has just come, so here everything is fresh."[2]

Swami Nityatmananda paid seven visits to Dakshineswar and Cossipore with M., and in *Srima Darshan* he recorded his experiences in detail. M. pointed out the areas in those two holy places that were connected with the Master. This record is extremely precious to devotees and admirers of Ramakrishna. While reading it, they can visualize what happened in these locations so important in the Master's life. They will not have to depend on a priest or on tour guides. I have compiled and translated these entries from *Srima Darshan** below, so we can see those holy places through the eyes of M.

Visiting the Dakshineswar Temple Garden

Ramakrishna often encouraged his disciples and devotees to have picnics in the Panchavati, and these were festive occasions for the young disciples. Swami Vivekananda recalled:

> The solitude of the Panchavati, associated with the various realizations of the Master, was also the most suitable place for our meditation. Besides meditation and spiritual practices, we used to spend a good deal of time there in sheer fun and merrymaking. Sri Ramakrishna also joined in with us, and by taking part enhanced our innocent pleasure. There we used to run and skip about, climb on the trees, swing from the rope-like madhavi vines, and sometimes have a picnic. During our first picnic, the Master noticed that I had cooked the food, and he partook of it. I knew that he could not eat food unless it was cooked by brahmins, so I had arranged prasad from the Kali temple for him. But he said, "There is no harm in my taking cooked food from a pure and sattvic person like you." He ignored my repeated objections and ate the food I had cooked that day.[3]

After Ramakrishna's passing away, the devotees sometimes held picnics in the Dakshineswar temple garden as they had done during his lifetime. One such occasion was on 18 October 1923, which was during the Durga Puja celebrations. M. joined the devotees at the temple, arriving at 11:30 a.m. with Dr. Durgapada Ghosh. M. removed his shoes and went to the Master's room, where he sat on a foot-mat near the north side of the small cot. This is where he used to sit during the Master's lifetime. One can see the Ganges through the western door from that spot. M. sat there and meditated along with the devotees. From the west side he put his hands under the mattress of the big cot where the Master used to sleep. The Master used to sit at the centre of the small cot facing the east, so M. touched his head on that spot, just as he used to bow down to him in those days.[4]

Someone asked M.: "Which pictures were here during the Master's time?"

M. pointed out the pictures of Rama and Sita, Prahlada, Dhruva, Jesus, and Chaitanya singing Sankirtan.

*1. 1 December 1923, vol.4:61-70; 2. 18 October 1923, vol. 3:235-244; 3. 14 January 1924, vol. 8:18-29; 4. 21 March 1924, vol.4:78-85; 5. 30 March 1924, vol. 5:109-124; 6. 30 November 1924, vol. 10: 166-193; 7. 28 January 1926, vol. 13:220-227.

TOP: Mother Kali of Dakshineswar, BOTTOM: Left to right: Krishna Temple, Kali Temple, Natmandir of Dakshineswar

M. then left the Master's room and went to the northern veranda. Jagabandhu asked him, "Where did the Master go into samadhi while listening to Swamiji sing?"* M. pointed out the southeastern corner of the veranda and bowed down to that spot.

He said: "The Master stood here, leaning his back against the wall. His eyes became still and a divine bliss spread over his face. His form was an embodiment of peace and love.... This was the first time I saw samadhi — a state of uninterrupted bliss beyond happiness and misery."[5] He then pointed to the upper step of the veranda's northeast corner and said: "The Master would stand there and say good-bye to the devotees."

M. then came to the southeast veranda of the Master's room and pointed out where Hazra would sit on his asana. Now there is a mat where the Master's nephews sit and talk to devotees.

M. went to the Radhakanta temple and received sanctified water from the priest.

Readers of Ramakrishna's life know the story of Krishna's broken foot and how the Master repaired it. Nirmal Kumar Roy supplied an important piece of information about that image in his book *Dakshineswar Kali Mandirer Itivritta*:

> The present image of Krishna is made of black stone and its height is 21½ inches, and Radha's image is made of eight metals and its height is 16 inches. These two images are now on the main altar and worshipped daily. This image of Krishna was made during Rani Rasmani's time but was kept in a separate room, because the Master advised her to continue worshipping the broken Krishna. Now that original broken Krishna is in the north room of the Krishna temple. It was worshipped till 1929. Then while the image was being refurbished, the foot again broke and it was temporarily repaired. Finally in 1930, the trustees of the Kali temple decided to install the spare one on the main altar and replace the broken one.[6]

M. bowed down to Lord Shiva from the courtyard and then went to the Kali temple. He then bowed down to the Divine Mother and meditated in front of Her. Nakul, Ramlal's son, gave sanctified water to M. and put a vermillion mark on his forehead.

*Meditate, O my mind, on the Lord Hari,
The Stainless One, Pure Spirit through and through.
Ever more beauteous in fresh-blossoming love
That shames the splendour of a million moons,
Like lightning gleams the glory of His form,
Raising erect the hair for very joy.

When M. was in the Natmandir, Amrita asked, "Where was the Master when you asked him if there would be any more singing on that evening during your fourth visit?" M. showed him the spot in the middle of the Natmandir. Pointing to the second pillar to the left, from the north, M. said: "As he listened to Nilkantha's Yatra performance, the Master embraced this pillar and wept." M. then embraced the pillar.

M. was a wonderful guide. He showed visitors to the temple garden important spots as well as those that are less significant, so that they could have a complete picture of that holy place. He took devotees to the kitchen where Mother Kali's food is cooked and to the room where it is stored. He also showed them the western ghat of the Gazi-tala pond, east of the Kali temple, where the Mother's puja utensils are washed. From the ghat he pointed out Jadu Mallick's garden house, where the Master would go for a walk. The Master was fond of Jadu Mallick, and the caretaker of his garden house was very devoted to the Master.

Mr. Jinwala said to M.: "It is said that Ramakrishna tried to kill himself with Kali's sword when he did not have the vision of the Divine Mother. Have you heard this from the Master?"

M.: "No, I didn't hear that."

Dr. De Mello: "Is it in the *Gospel* that you recorded?"

M.: "No, it is not in the *Gospel*. Someone might have written about it, but I didn't."

Dr. De Mello: "The Master himself was God. Then why did he try to kill himself in order to see God?"

M.: "The Master said that the Divine Mother had taken the cosmic form. She Herself was manifest in the Master's body. The Goddess said to him that his form was a special manifestation among all forms. Out of longing for Mother, as a devotee, the Master tried to kill himself. He himself was a devotee and also God."[7]

M. crossed the courtyard to the Chandni Ghat, and then walked down the steps to the Ganges. He sprinkled the holy Ganges water on his head, bowed down to Mother Ganges, and repeated a mantra. On his way to the nahabat, he touched his head to the semicircular veranda of the Master's room. Pointing to the northwest corner of the northern veranda, M. said: "One day I saw the Master himself sweeping this place with a broom. Seeing me, he said, 'The Divine Mother walks here.' He used to see the Mother's divine play with his open eyes."[8]

Next M. bowed down to the front steps of the nahabat, saying: "Holy Mother, the Master, and the devotees walked over these steps while entering the room. This nahabat is the new Shakti-pith [a holy place consecrated to the Divine Mother]. It was Holy Mother's place of tapasya. She lived here for a long time. She was extremely shy. There were bamboo curtains all around the veranda, and she lived here like a bird in a cage. Setting aside her personal comfort, she served the Master. In this small room she lived with Golap-ma, Yogin-ma, Sister Lakshmi, and sometimes with Gauri-ma. Here also she stored the Master's groceries and other necessities. Once a day at 3 o'clock in the morning she would go to the jungle to answer the call of nature and then bathe in the Ganges. She would practise japa and meditation, and then cook for the Master. What superhuman patience, forbearance, self-control, renunciation, and self-sacrifice she had!"[9]

M. bowed down to the first step of the stairs to the upper floor of the nahabat and remarked: "Holy Mother used to sit here and repeat her mantra. Sitting here for long hours caused her to develop rheumatism, which continued throughout her life."

M. then went to the Bakul-tala ghat and pointed to a cement platform to the west of the path leading to the Panchavati. He said: "I saw the Master seated here 41 years ago. I vividly remember it now, and it feels like it happened yesterday."

M. touched his head on the middle of the Bakul-tala ghat and said: "Just before Chandramani passed away, her body was brought here. She was lying on a rope cot. Two legs of the cot were in the Ganges and the other two legs were on the cement ghat. Holding his mother's feet, the Master said tearfully, 'Mother, who are you who carried me in your womb?' He meant that she was not an ordinary mother. She must be like Kaushalya, Devaki, Mayadevi, Mary, and Shachi — who were mothers of Rama, Krishna, Buddha, Jesus, and Chaitanya respectively."[10]

"Narendra sat on the south embankment of this ghat and sang for the Master an Agamani song [a special song that is sung inviting the Mother Durga to come for Her worship] that he had learned shortly before." M. bowed down to that spot.[11]

Seeing a Shiva image inside the Sadhan-kutir, he remarked: "During the Master's time, this brick building and the Shiva image were not here. There was only a thatched hut with a mud floor."

M. circumambulated the altar that surrounded the banyan tree in the Panchavati; then he touched the second, third, and fourth steps of its southern stairs and bowed down. He said: "The Master used to sit here and put his feet on the lower step. He would talk about God with Keshab Sen, Vijaykrishna Goswami, and other devotees." Standing at the northwest corner of the Panchavati, M. related one of his sweetest memories: "One day from here I saw the Master coming from the pine grove. There was a thick dark cloud behind him and it was reflected on the Ganges."[12]

M. touched and bowed down to the ashwattha tree in the Panchavati, which the Master had planted himself. He then went under the madhavi vine, which is nearly 50 feet long and connects the banyan and the ashwattha trees. The Master brought that plant from Vrindaban and planted it there himself. M. bowed down to it and said: "This madhavi is very dear to us. The Master took care of it like a mother and helped it to grow. The divine touch of his hand lives within this vine. Blessed is this plant! Perhaps this vine is a great soul, living incognito like the Yamala and Arjuna trees who were Jaya and Vijaya, the gatekeepers of Vishnu, but were cursed and became trees."[13] Pointing to the southwest step of the Panchavati, M. said: "On his birthday, the Master sat on this step and gave advice to Vijaykrishna Goswami and Kedar Chattopadhyay, who were seated to his left. Tota Puri lived in the open space of the Panchavati and the Master visited him there quite often."[14]

On the way to the bel-tala from the Panchavati, M. pointed out a spot on the east side of the path and mentioned: "There was a fence here in which one of the Master's feet became stuck. He fell down and broke his left arm. He was in ecstasy and had no body-consciousness."

M. then went to the bel-tala, where the Master had practised Tantric sadhana. Around the bel tree is a circular altar that is 2 feet high. M. circumambulated it, keeping the altar to his right.

Pointing to a spot to the east of the altar, M. said: "One day according to the instruction of the Master, a devotee [M. himself] was meditating facing the east. A few hours passed. The Master came to see the devotee and stood in front of him. Seeing the Master, the devotee was overwhelmed with joy and bowed down to him. He saw his Chosen Deity on whom he had been meditating in his heart."[15] He bowed down to that spot where he had once seen the Master standing. He then sat on the altar to meditate and asked the devotees to do the same.

Later, M. pointed to the embankment next to the Ganges and said, "At midnight the Master would pace back and forth here and listen to the anahata sound [music of the sphere]."

M. went to the kuthi (mansion) and entered the southwest room. He bowed down and said: "The Master lived in this room for 16 years. His mother also lived here. He had many visions and spiritual experiences in this room. Trailokya, Mathur's son, used to live upstairs when he visited Dakshineswar. The Master's nephew Akshay died here in

TOP: Bel-tala where Ramakrishna practised Tantra Sadhana.
BOTTOM: Panchavati at Dakshineswar

1869, and in 1871 the Master moved to the room in the northwest corner of the temple complex and his mother moved to the upper floor of the nahabat."

Nirmal Kumar Roy wrote in *Dakshineswar Kali Mandirer Itivritta*: "In the early days, Rani Rasmani and Mathur arranged for the Master's stay in the kuthi; but when Akshay died, the Master did not want to stay there anymore. However, an opportunity soon came for the Master to move from the kuthi, as Mathur wanted to repair and paint the building. So it was arranged that the Master move temporarily to the northwest corner room of the temple complex, which had been used as the storeroom for the Vishnu temple, while his mother would move to the upper room of the nahabat. When the repairs and painting were done, the Master said that he did not want to return to the kuthi. Mathur granted the Master's request and moved the Vishnu temple supplies to one of the rooms in the eastern complex."[16]

M. stood on the southern ghat of the goose pond, which is located just to the east of the Panchavati. He said: "The Master always filled his water pot at this goose pond and used it after answering the call of nature. He never used Ganges water, because it is holy. Once as the Master stood on this ghat he said to Narendra: "Come a little more often. You are a new-comer. Haven't you noticed how a man and a woman meet frequently after their first acquaintance? It intensifies love."

A picnic was arranged at the Gazi-tala, because the temple manager would not allow the devotees to have it in the Panchavati. M. was a little hurt. A devotee then talked about this to Kiran Chandra Datta, the receiver* of the Dakshineswar temple. He immediately wrote a strong memo to the temple manager: "Please allow Revered M. and the devotees to have a picnic wherever they want. And clean that place."

M. was very pleased and remarked: "You see, every spot of Dakshineswar is holy. But God himself had picnics there with the devotees, so that place is saturated with joy. If we have our picnic there, then that joy will be awakened in our minds. One can experience bliss by imitating a particular lila enacted by God. The Master experienced the bliss of Brahman while sitting under that banyan tree, and it still bears witness to those events. The memory of the Master's joyful picnics in that place will intensify the joy of our own picnic. Thus one can connect oneself with God. Otherwise, mere eating is nothing but worldly enjoyment."[17] According to Swami

*A person appointed by a court administrator to take into custody the property or funds of others, pending litigation.

Nityatmananda, M. had picnics with the devotees in the Panchavati on 14 January 1924, 30 November 1924, and 28 January 1926.

On 30 November 1924 M. made a comment about the picnic: "It is a joyful function. We shall be able to stay at Dakshineswar for a long time because of this picnic. The minds of the devotees will get deep impressions of the trees, gardens, ponds, ghats, temples, and so on. Later these will remind them of Mother Kali and the Master. Sometimes the Master would encourage devotees to arrange picnics in the temple garden. An impression becomes deeper if it is connected with good food. The Master would adopt many methods to direct the devotees' minds towards God. Whenever any devotee would come, the Master served him some prasad or gave him something to eat. This would serve two purposes: First, that devotee would remember the food he had eaten; people generally forget verbal advice. Second, the devotee would develop love for the Master unconsciously. His mind would think of the Master's affection because he had given him some food to eat. Eventually this memory would protect him, and give him strength when he struggled for breath in the ocean of maya, almost drowning. Every one of the Master's actions was meant to set an example for others."[18]

While M. and the devotees were returning to Calcutta, M. remarked: "Every particle of dust of the Panchavati is holy and vibrant because it was touched by the feet of God. The trees, plants, and vines of Dakshineswar are gods, ancient rishis, and devotees who are still seeing and enjoying the divine play of God. Truly, they are witnesses of the avatar's lila." Whenever M. visited Dakshineswar, he always embraced and bowed down to the trees.[19]

M.'s Farsightedness

M. was a farsighted rishi. By the Master's grace he sensed what would happen in the future. M. wrote in the *Gospel*:

> The Master started for the Panchavati accompanied by M. No one else was with them. Sri Ramakrishna with a smile narrated to him various incidents of the past years of his life.
>
> Master: "You see, one day I saw a supernatural figure covering the whole space from the Kali temple to the Panchavati. Do you believe this?"
>
> M. remained silent with wonder. He plucked one or two leaves from a branch in the Panchavati and put them in his pocket.
>
> Master: "See there — that branch has been broken. I used to sit under it."

M.: "I took a young twig from that tree — I have it at home."
Master (*with a smile*): "Why?"
M.: "I feel happy when I look at it. After all this is over, this place will be considered very holy."[20]

M.'s *Gospel* has made Dakshineswar a place of pilgrimage like Ayodhya, Vrindaban, Varanasi, and Rameswaram. His vivid description has drawn people from all over the world to visit Dakshineswar and to know more about Ramakrishna. Moreover, inspired by the *Gospel*, many young people have also left home and joined the Ramakrishna Order. Thirty-five years after that conversation he recorded in the *Gospel*, M. witnessed a remarkable result of his detailed chronicle.

In October 1918 M. told devotees about the following incident: "Lord Ronaldsey, the present governor of Bengal, read *The Gospel of Sri Ramakrishna*, and then went to Dakshineswar with his wife and secretaries. He saw those places which had been mentioned in the *Gospel*. He also greeted Ramlal, knowing that he was the Master's nephew."[21]

The world is always changing, but truth never changes. Dakshineswar is very different now from what it was during Ramakrishna's time, yet M.'s chronicle of the Master's message is for all time and will remain vital as long as the sun and moon exist.

Visiting the Cossipore Garden House

On 30 March 1924 M. visited Dakshineswar and the Cossipore garden house with Dr. De Mello, Mr. Jinwalla and his wife (a Parsi couple), and some other devotees. In the car on the way to Cossipore, Swami Nityatmananda pointed out the Cossipore cremation ground where the Master's body had been cremated and whispered something to Dr. De Mello. The doctor then asked M., who was in the backseat, "Shall we stop at the Cossipore cremation ground?" Hearing the words "Cossipore cremation ground," M. felt deep pain, as if he had been stung by a scorpion. His face turned grave. Nityatmananda asked De Mello not to raise that topic again, because this would cause M. great pain.[22]

The car stopped at the western side of the Cossipore house. M. bowed down at the entrance. An Armenian Christian family was renting the house at the time. They were very hospitable and allowed people to visit the house where the Master had lived.

While waiting for permission to enter the house, M. took the group and showed them the kitchen, the servants' quarters, and the room where Holy Mother had lived in the northeastern corner of the house.

He pointed out three rooms that had previously been the stable where young attendants of the Master had stayed. M. removed his shoes, entered one of the rooms, and said: "One morning here the young disciples of the Master who later became monks sang this song about Shiva: 'Lord Shiva is adorned with the crescent moon on his forehead, the Ganges in his matted hair, and a trident in his hand. His body is besmeared with ashes, a garland hangs around his neck.' The all-renouncing Shiva was their ideal. This was the training place of future teachers."

M. then walked to the pond that was to the east of the house. He went to its southern ghat and said, "Sometimes we used to sit here." He then pointed to a mango tree to the south of the ghat and said: "Narendra would sit under that tree and light a dhuni fire, then practise meditation. During the summer the devotees would meditate on this ghat. It has been 37 years since I last visited this place."

M. walked to that holy mango tree and embraced it, and then bowed down. When he arose, he continued: "One night Narendra was meditating near the dhuni fire and his body was covered with mosquitoes, but he had no body-consciousness. His mind was absorbed in Brahman."

When the group reached the garden path to the east of the house, M. pointed out a pine tree and said, "This is our old friend." M. and his companions thus circumambulated the Cossipore house where the Master had lived during his last days.

When M. and his companions received permission to enter the house, they climbed the steps to the Master's second-floor room and entered it. M. prostrated on the floor at the southwest corner, where the Master had rested while he was alive. There is a door on the south wall of the room and a shuttered window on the west. M. pointed to an area 2 yards from the western window and said, "The Master's bedding was here." The Master would lie on a mattress with his head near the southern wall and feet towards the north. M. sat near where the Master's feet would have been and meditated for some time.

He then went out the door on the south side of the room and walked out onto the roof overlooking the garden compound; he stood near the western railing and held onto it. Then he and the devotees went downstairs to thank the host. After that, the party and M. left for his Calcutta residence at the Morton Institution.

In the evening gathering, Dr. Bakshi asked: "Why didn't the Master sleep on a bed?"

M.: "It was convenient for the Master to sleep on the floor. His body was weak. There was a mat on the cement floor, then on top of that a cotton carpet, and over that a mattress."

Jagabandhu: "Did the Master ever walk on the roof?"

M.: "Seldom."

Jagabandhu: "Did he go for a walk in the garden?"

M.: "A few times. He walked on 1 January 1886, of course. The Master fulfilled his wish." [On that day Sri Ramakrishna became the wish-fulfilling tree and blessed the devotees, saying, "Be illumined."][23]

On 30 November 1924 M. revisited Cossipore with Dr. Bakshi, Binay, and Jagabandhu, but this time they were not allowed to enter the house. The Christian gentleman was a patient of Dr. Bakshi, who had presented him with a picture of Ramakrishna and asked him to hang it on the wall of the Master's room. The man later did so, but his pastor had objected and asked him to remove the picture. Moreover, the man did not want to do anything that would make his Christian community upset. However, M. gave the Christian gentleman a copy of *The Gospel of Ramakrishna — Part 1*, and asked, "May we have a look around the garden?"

"Of course," he replied.

The devotees were upset because they were not allowed to see the Master's room. With a heavy heart, M. said to Dr. Bakshi, "Here one should come as a learner and not as a preacher."

As they walked around the garden surrounding the house, M. said: "Every particle of dust in Dakshineswar and Cossipore is pure. These trees are gods and rishis incognito. They are hiding their true forms to watch and enjoy the divine play of the avatar." M. pointed to an old tree at the southeast corner of the garden, near a bend in the path, and remarked: "This tree felt the same air that touched Sri Ramakrishna's body." M. then embraced that tree.

M. stopped near the bend in the path. All of a sudden he became indrawn and his eyes became moist. He said: "What a great event took place on this spot! It was 1 January 1886, a holiday. Girish and other devotees were visiting from Calcutta. The Master felt a little better, so he came down from his room and walked in the garden. It was 3 o'clock in the afternoon. The devotees followed the Master. When the Master stopped at this spot, the devotees bowed down to him one after another. He blessed them, saying, 'May you be illumined.' This blessing awakened their inner consciousness and they each had a vision of their Ishta [Chosen Deity]. Everyone was overwhelmed with bliss."

M. then became quiet and still. When he regained his normal mood, he prostrated himself on the garden path where the Master had become the Kalpataru, the wish-fulfilling tree, and put some dust from the path onto his head. He slowly got up and walked to the car, giving the garden one last lingering look.[24]

In the Footsteps of Ramakrishna

Throughout the world there are many holy places frequented by people on pilgrimage who desire to draw closer to God. The life of Ramakrishna is made more real and immediate when it is visualized against the landscape that was its setting. Goethe said: "If you want to understand the poet, you must visit his country."

Following the footsteps of Ramakrishna, in 1997 Nirmal Kumar Roy wrote a book in Bengali called *Charan Chinha Dhare* (Holding the Footprints of Ramakrishna). In this book he wrote the history of the places that Ramakrishna had visited, their present condition, and how to reach them. He described Calcutta, North 24-Parganas, Howrah, Hooghly, Bankura, Burdwan, Nadia, Khulna in East Bengal, Vaidyanath, Varanasi, Prayag, Mathura, and Vrindaban. In 1979 he wrote another important book in Bengali called *Sri Sri Ramakrishna Samsparshe* (People Who Came in Contact with Ramakrishna). The main source for these two books was M.'s *Sri Sri Ramakrishna Kathamrita*.

After closely associating with M. for a number of years, Swami Nityat-mananda wanted to visit the places in Calcutta and its suburbs where Ramakrishna had gone. He considered them to be modern places of pilgrimage. When he first approached M. with his plan, M. discouraged him. But later, observing Nityatmananda's enthusiasm for seeing the holy places connected with the Master, M. joyfully gave him permission and guidance. When Nityatmananda asked where he should start, M. replied, "Be quick! Please start from this area [Central Calcutta]."

On 27 May 1932 (8 days before he passed away) M. dictated a list of places that Nityatmananda recorded:
1. Rajendra Mitra's house on Bechu Chatterjee Street, which Ramakrishna visited. Keshab Sen came there to meet the Master.
2. Thanthania Kali Temple: When the Master was 16 years old, he used to sing there for the Divine Mother.
3. The Master's brother Ramkumar's Tol [Sanskrit school] on Bechu Chatterjee Street. It is now a Radha-Krishna temple.
4. A hut with a tiled roof on Bechu Chatterjee Street, where the Master and Ramkumar lived. It is opposite the Laha's house.
5. Digambar Mitra's house on Jhamapukur Lane, where the Master performed rituals for the family shrine.

6. Vijaykrishna Goswami's residence at 27 Mechua Bazar Street, which the Master visited when he became ill.
7. The Navavidhan Brahmo Samaj in Mechua Bazar, which the Master visited. He also went to Ishan Mukhopadhyay's house on the same street and had lunch there.
8. Keshab Sen's Lily Cottage, at the junction of Mechua Bazar Street and Circular Road [now Acharya Prafulla Chandra Roy Road], which Ramakrishna visited many times. Keshab worshipped the feet of the Master in the shrine upstairs.
9. Badurbagan, where the Master went to visit Ishwar Chandra Vidyasagar.
10. The Sadharan Brahmo Samaj on Cornwallis Street [now Bidhan Sarani], where the Master went to meet Narendra.
11. Narendra's house in Simulia.
12. Ram's house behind the Oxford Mission. [It has since been demolished to make way for a road.]
13. Manomohan's house on Simla Street.
14. Kashi Mallick's temple on Harrison Road [now Mahatma Gandhi Road], where the Master went to visit Mother Simhavahini.
15. Mani Mallick's house in Sinduriapatti, where Ramakrishna attended a Brahmo festival. It has since been replaced by a Jain temple.
16. Sutapatti, in Barabazar, where he visited Lakshminarayan Marwari.
17. The Chaitanya Sabha and Navin Sen's house in Colootola.
18. Rani Rasmani's house in Jan Bazar.
19. The Methodist Church in Taltala, where the Master attended a service.
20. The Kalighat temple in South Calcutta.
21. The Museum
22. Alipore Zoo
23. Jagannath Ghat
24. Koila Ghat
25. The Maidan, where the Master saw a circus perform.
26. The Viceroy's palace. The Master saw it and made a remark: "The Mother revealed to me that it was made merely of clay bricks laid one on top of another."
27. Jaygopal Sen's house in Ratan Sarkar Square in Barabazar.
28. Jadu Mallick's house in Pathuriaghata.
29. The Adi Brahmo Samaj in Chitpur.
30. Devendra Nath Tagore's house in Jorasanko.
31. The Harisabha in Jorasanko.

32. A devotee's house in Haritaki-bagan.
33. Ram's garden and Suresh's garden in Kankurgachi.
34. Dr. Kali's house in Shyambazar.
35. The house in Shyampukur where Ramakrishna received treatment.
36. The following devotees' houses in Baghbazar: Nanda Basu, Golap-ma, Yogin-ma, Balaram Basu, and Girish Chandra Ghosh.
37. The following temples in Baghbazar: Siddheswari Kali, Madanmohan.
38. The Master came to M.'s rented house at Kambuliatola in Shyampukur.
39. Vishwanath Upadhyay's house in Shyampukur.
40. Deven Majumdar's house on Nimu Goswami Lane in North Calcutta.
41. The Star Theatre on Beadon Street, where the Master saw *Chaitanya Lila* performed.
42. Adhar Sen's house in Shobhabazar.
43. Dinanath Mukhopadhyay's house near the Baghbazar bridge, which Ramakrishna visited with Mathur.
44. The Master attended the festival of the Brahmo Samaj at Kashi Mitra's house in Nandan-bagan.
45. Mahendra Goswami's house in Simulia.

    That very day Swami Nityatmananda visited several places in the morning, afternoon, and evening. He reported his experiences to M. in detail the next day so that M. could visualize those places that had been touched by the feet of Sri Ramakrishna.

    On 28 May 1932 M. told Nityatmananda about some other places connected with the Master. These are located in various Calcutta suburbs.
1. The Cossipore garden house.
2. Beni Pal's garden house in Sinthi.
3. The Sarvamangala temple in Cossipore.
4. The Cossipore cremation ground.
5. The Dasha Mahavidya temple in Baranagore.
6. The house of Thakur Dada (Narayan Das Bandyopadhyay), who was a narrator of the scriptures in Baranagore.
7. Joy Mukhopadhyay's shrine and the Ganges ghat at Baranagore.
8. Two houses in Baranagore belonging to Haramohan and Mani Mallick.
9. Patbari of Bhagavata Acharya (a Vaishnava Ashrama) in Baranagore.
10. Natabar Panja's oil mill in Alambazar.
11. Two garden houses in Dakshineswar belonging to Shambhu Mallick and Jadu Mallick.

12. The Dakshineswar temple garden, the playground of Sri Rama-krishna.
13. Swami Yogananda's house in Dakshineswar.
14. Rasik's house. Rasik was a sweeper of the Dakshineswar temple. The Master secretly cleaned the privy in Rasik's house with his own hair and prayed to the Divine Mother, "Mother, destroy the ego of my brahminical caste."
15. Krishnakishore's house in Ariadaha
16. Gadadhar's Patbari in Ariadaha.
17. Mati Sil's Thakur-bari and lake in Belgharia. To demonstrate how to meditate on the formless God, the Master took a devotee [M.] and showed him big fish swimming freely in the lake. One can imagine the fish as human souls playing in the ocean of Satchidananda.
18. Panihati: Mani Sen's house, the festival grounds, and Raghav Pandit's Thakur-bari.
19. Kamarhati: The Krishna temple and Gopal-ma's place.
20. Kalna, where the Master visited Bhagavandas Babaji.
21. A garden house in Sinthi where the Master met Dayananda Sara-swati.
22. Navachaitanya Mitra's house in Konnagar.
23. The timber yard of Vishwanath Upadhyay in Belur, which is now the present Belur Math.[25]

Although Swami Nityatmananda had already visited with M. many of the places listed, he began to revisit those places and report back to M. At that time M. would relate many anecdotes about the Master in which those places had played a part. The swami observed that M.'s health was failing day by day, so he tried to collect from M. information about those holy places and anecdotes about the Master concerning them. He also wanted to list their old and new addresses. Nityatmananda could not complete the project, however. The unique guide, the chronicler and cus-todian of Ramakrishna's life and message, left this world on 4 June 1932, a week after Nityatmananda began his project.

What Ramakrishna Taught

Introduction

In the Vishnu Purana it is said: "Those who do not perform their duties and practise religion, but say 'O Lord, O Lord,' are ignorant and are to be considered enemies of God, because God has to take human birth to show them how to practise religion."

Avatars, or divine incarnations, have a special mission in each age. Sometimes their teachings are specific to a particular time, and sometimes they are eternal and universal. For example, Ramachandra killed the demon Ravana, and he also established the religion of Truth. Krishna killed Kamsa and other demons, and he also established Dharma (righteousness) and harmonized the four yogas. Buddha censured the violence and hatred endemic to his time, and he also taught morality, ethics, and service. Christ attacked the hypocrisy of the established religious authorities and taught the religion of love and compassion. Ramakrishna destroyed the greatest demon that plagues the human mind: doubt in God's existence. He also taught the importance of purity and renunciation, and he preached the harmony of religions.

Avatars do not write autobiographies or record their teachings. They bring devotees with them who are ordained to write their biographies and record their messages. As the same moon rises again and again, so in every age the same God comes to earth to eradicate evil and establish the eternal religion. Perhaps the chroniclers of the avatars are actually the same soul, who is reborn over and over to record the avatars' lives and teachings.

Sage Valmiki wrote the Ramayana, the life and teachings of Ramachandra. It is said that once Valmiki went to the Sage Narada and asked:
"O great Sage, is there any human being living on this earth who is
endowed with all divine qualities and with great power, who is filled
with gratitude, truthful, firmly resolved, of noble character, and is the
benefactor of all beings? And who is learned, skillful, handsome, brilliant,
steady, and who has conquered anger and jealousy; and to whom even
the gods are respectful? I am eager to know about such a person." Narada
then described Ramachandra, who had just returned to Ayodhya after
conquering Ravana. Later, at Brahma's command, Valmiki wrote a great
epic, the Ramayana, consisting of 24,000 verses.

Sage Vyasa compiled the four Vedas, composed the greatest epic, the
Mahabharata, which consists of 100,000 verses, and also wrote 18 Puranas.
Vyasa chronicled the life of Krishna and his different incarnations in the
Bhagavata, which contains 18,000 verses. He also recorded Krishna's
main teachings in the Bhagavad Gita, which is part of the Mahabharata.
Krishna's last message was recorded by Vyasa in the Uddhava Gita, which
is part of the eleventh canto of the Bhagavata.

Buddha did not have a single chronicler, but immediately after his
death 500 chief *arhats* (illumined disciples) held a convention under the
leadership of Mahakassapa in Rajagriha to record the doctrines originally
taught by their Master. Ananda, Buddha's cousin and attendant, knew
82,000 teachings of Buddha by heart, and he collected 2,000 sayings from
other disciples.[1] Ananda recited the *Dhamma,* and Upali recited the *Vinaya.*
Later the arhats recorded the profound philosophy of the Buddha's teachings in the *Abhidhamma.* The Buddhist scriptures are called *Tripitaka,*
which means "three baskets." They are the Basket of Disciplines (*Vinaya
Pitaka*), the Basket of Discourses (*Sutta Pitaka*), and the Basket of Ultimate
Doctrine (*Abhidhamma Pitaka*).

In the beginning Buddha's teachings were recited by monks and
spread in an oral tradition. Towards the end of Buddha's life, Ananda
said to him: "After Buddha enters nirvana we want to compile the Sutras.
What words should we introduce them with to show that they are the
Buddha's?" Buddha replied: "Use the four words 'Thus I have heard.'"[2]

The *Tripitaka* was compiled and arranged in its present form by those
arhats of old. During the reign of the pious Sinhala King Vattagamani
Abhaya in Ceylon (now Sri Lanka), about 83 B.C., the *Tripitaka* was, for the
first time in the history of Buddhism, committed to writing. The volumi-
nous *Tripitaka,* written on palm leaves, contains the essence of the Buddha's
teachings and is estimated to be about eleven times the length of the Bible.

The life and teachings of Christ are recorded in the New Testament of the Bible. The authors of the Four Gospels were Matthew, a publican (tax collector); Luke, a physician; John, a fisherman; and Mark, whose profession is unknown. Matthew and John were companions of Jesus. Mark was a companion of the disciple Peter, and his Gospel seems to contain what Peter told him about their master. Luke was a companion of Paul, and his Gospel seems to contain what he had heard Paul preach throughout the Roman Empire, and verified by his own investigation.[3]

The scriptures of different religions, therefore, are based on the lives and teachings of various avatars throughout the ages. How *The Gospel of Sri Ramakrishna* emerged from the diary of M. was discussed in Chapter 15. As Valmiki and Vyasa were the chroniclers of Ramachandra and Krishna, so M. was the recorder of Ramakrishna's divine play. Some of Ramakrishna's teachings were also published by the Brahmos and by other disciples during his lifetime. In addition, the Master's monastic disciples, householder devotees, and Brahmo admirers left eyewitness accounts, which were translated and published in the book *Ramakrishna as We Saw Him*.

If someone were to ask for the quintessence of Ramakrishna's teachings in one sentence, the answer would be: "The goal of human life is to realize God (*Manav-jivaner uddeshya ishwar-labh*)."

How? Ramakrishna has the answer: "Repeat God's name and sing His glories. Have the company of the holy. Go into solitude now and then and think of God. To meditate, you should withdraw within yourself or retire to a secluded corner or to the forest. Discriminate between the Real and the unreal — God alone is real and all else is unreal, that is, impermanent. Cry to the Lord with an intensely yearning heart and you will certainly see Him."

People in general are content with worldly life and are not interested in knowing God. This reminds me of a story:

Brahma was the creator of the universe and every creature within it. After creating human beings, He generously gave them every worldly enjoyment, except peace and bliss. He wished to play a game with His children. Brahma put peace and bliss in a jar and asked the other gods and goddesses where he should hide it.

Indra, the god of heaven, suggested keeping the jar in outer space. Brahma said: "My American and Russian children will come here with the space shuttle and get it."

Varuna, the god of water, suggested putting the jar at the bottom of the ocean. Brahma said: "It won't work. Many countries will have submarines and they will dive into the ocean and find it."

Dharitri, the goddess of the earth, suggested that the jar be kept underground. Brahma said: "No, that will not work. Most of the countries have dynamite and they will blast the beautiful earth to get at it."

Finally, Brahma made a decision: "I shall hide this jar in the heart of each human being. If they want peace and bliss in life they must search within themselves."

Peace and bliss are indispensable. Without them, life is dull and dreary, empty and sorrowful. One can buy everything except peace and bliss. Throughout human history, people have experimented by seeking peace and bliss in money, sensual pleasures, family, friends, home, car, and name and fame. In every case they have failed. When their external efforts bring no success, people finally begin to search within and realize the hidden Self, or God, the embodiment of peace and bliss.

The great teachers have taught human beings the way to attain peace and bliss after they themselves had gone within and discovered the Creator's game. Buddha taught his disciples mindfulness. He said: "The disciples of Gotama are always wide awake and thoughtful, and their minds day and night ever delight in meditation. . . . Be ye lamps unto yourselves. Rely on yourselves, and do not rely on external help."[4] Christ proclaimed: "The Kingdom of heaven is within you. . . . Blessed are the pure in heart for they shall see God."[5] Krishna said in the Gita (18:61): "The Lord dwells in the hearts of all beings, O Arjuna, and by His maya causes them to revolve as though mounted on a machine." The Taittiriya Upanishad says (3:1:1): "Brahman is bliss and It is established in the heart."

Most of the avatars were well versed in the scriptures, and some were great scholars, but Ramakrishna was different. The sage Vashishtha and the sage Sandipani instructed Ramachandra and Krishna respectively. Buddha, Shankara, and Chaitanya studied the scriptures and were great scholars. But Ramakrishna could hardly read or write, yet great scholars were struck dumb while discussing philosophical matters with him. Once he told them the source of his knowledge: "I wept before the Mother and prayed, 'O Mother, please tell me, please reveal to me what the yogis have realized through yoga and the jnanis through discrimination.' And the Mother has revealed everything to me. She has shown me everything that is in the Vedas, the Vedanta, the Puranas, and the Tantra."[6]

Ramakrishna taught what he himself had experienced and not what he learned from scriptures. But his life was the living demonstration of the truths of the Upanishads, the Bhagavad Gita, and other scriptures. In Ramakrishna's life can be found a synthesis of the four yogas (karma, jnana, bhakti, and raja); and the philosophies of the three main schools of

Vedanta — dualism, qualified nondualism, and nondualism — were harmonized in his teachings.

Ramakrishna came to make religion simple enough for everyone to practise. He not only taught religion, but he also demonstrated religion to all. For example, while explaining samadhi, he went into samadhi. After he had renounced money, he could not even touch it. Once he told one of his physicians, Dr. Bhagavan Rudra, "Put some money in my hand to test me." As soon as the doctor placed a coin in the palm of Ramakrishna's hand, his breathing stopped and his hand became numb. The doctor was dumbfounded; such an experience had never been recorded in the annals of science.[7]

Ramakrishna incorporated into his teachings parables, symbols, songs, stories, folklore, myths, scientific reasoning, anecdotes from ordinary life, and examples from nature as well as the behaviour of humans and animals. He seldom quoted the scriptures. He taught from his personal experience and explained the deep truths of spiritual life in an utterly simple way. This captivated M.; never before had he met such a man.

Ramakrishna described two types of illumined souls: "Some eat mangoes secretly and remove all trace of them by wiping their mouths with a towel. But some share the fruit with others. There are sages who, even after attaining Knowledge, work to help others and also to enjoy the Bliss of God in the company of devotees."[8] M. belonged to this second group. He unselfishly distributed the immortal teachings of Ramakrishna to humanity through *The Gospel of Sri Ramakrishna* and also by talking to devotees. M. was often surrounded by monks and devotees, and his conversations with them centred on Ramakrishna and spiritual life. Swami Nityatmananda recorded these conversations from 1923 to 1932, and had them published in sixteen volumes under the title *Srima Darshan*. The following teachings and reminiscences from those volumes have been translated from the original Bengali.

My First Meeting with Sri Ramakrishna

What a great event it was when I first met Sri Ramakrishna. At that time I could not get along with my father and brothers at home. Though I tried my best to serve them, they mistreated me very much. Unable to bear the mental agony any longer, I decided to leave home and commit suicide. One night at ten o'clock I left with my wife in a hired carriage. I asked the driver to take us to Baranagore, where my sister lived, but on the way, near Shyambazar, a carriage wheel came off. We then went to a friend's house, where we got a cold reception. He thought we wanted to stay at his house overnight. Finally I was able to get another carriage, and we reached Baranagore at midnight.

The next afternoon I went for a walk with my nephew Sidhu, and we visited several gardens on the bank of the Ganges. Feeling tired and depressed, I sat down in a garden. Sidhu then said: "Uncle, let us go to Rasmani's garden. A holy man lives there." We entered through the main gate of the temple garden at Dakshineswar. It was half an hour before sunset.

Having a poetic mind, I was deeply impressed with the beautiful flower garden. I picked some flowers and was overwhelmed by their fragrance. After some time we entered Sri Ramakrishna's room.

The Master was seated on his small cot and the devotees were on the floor. I didn't know any of them. The first thing I heard from the Master's lips was: "When, hearing the name of God once, you shed tears and your hair stands on end, then you may know for certain that you do not have to perform any more karma."[9]

My Ego Was Crushed

During my second visit, the Master asked me, "Well, do you believe in God with form or without form?" I had a tendency to argue about religious matters. I answered, "Sir, I like to think of God as formless." And I further said: "It is meaningless to worship a clay image. One should explain to those who worship a clay image that it is not God, and that while worshipping it, they should have God in view and not the clay image." At that time there were many lectures on this topic in Calcutta.

The Master immediately silenced me by saying: "That's the one hobby of you Calcutta people — giving lectures and bringing others to the light. Nobody ever stops to consider how to get the light himself. Who are you to teach others?"

He continued: "You do not have to rack your brain on this matter. Look at the world, how it moves in an orderly way. It is God who sends the sun to shed light, the rain to give water, and the seasons to rotate. The earth produces crops that help human beings survive. God arranged everything for us. Look at religion. You can see temples and holy places all over the country. He created the scriptures and the holy people. These He arranged for people who want to lead a spiritual life. He thinks about everyone. We do not have to think of anything." Listening to this, I was speechless. My inclination for argument ended forever. I realized that the Lord is the doer and we are His instruments.[10]

Live at Home like a Maidservant

The Master used to say: "There are two types of devotees — the inner circle and the outer circle. Those of the inner circle easily get spiritual awakening, but those of the outer circle are a little egotistical. Those of the latter group think that they will not attain knowledge without practising austerity." The Master used to compare the two types of devotees with the inner and outer pillars of the natmandir [the hall in front of the Kali temple]. Those of the inner circle were like the inner pillars, and those of the outer circle, like the outer pillars. He had special love for devotees of the inner circle because they would carry on his mission.[11]

The Master asked some of the devotees to live at home, like a maidservant in a rich man's house. And some of them he trained to set an example for others. He said to me, "The Divine Mother has told me that She will make you do some teaching work for Her." The Master even prayed to the Mother to give me a little power, because one cannot teach people without the power of the Divine. At that time I wanted to renounce the world, and I told the Master about this.[12]

One night at nine o'clock the Master was alone in his room and I was standing on the western veranda. He left his room and stood next to me. In front of us the Ganges flowed with a sweet murmuring sound. All was quiet. Suddenly he said to me: "Look. Let no one think that without him the Divine Mother's work will stop. She can make great teachers out of straws." He further said: "If a faucet in the bathroom leaks, the plumber replaces it with a new one. He has many spare parts. Similarly the Divine Engineer [God] can bring a new person to do His work. His work never stops." I wholeheartedly accepted what the Master said to be the will of the Mother.[13]

The Master prayed for me: "Mother, as you are keeping him in the world, please give him a vision of You from time to time. Otherwise, how will he live in the world?"[14]

A Boyhood Memory

Once I went to Rishra with my mother, and from there we visited the Chariot Festival of Jagannath at Mahesh. On our way back we stopped at the Dakshineswar Kali temple. I was then four years old. Standing in front of the Kali temple, I began to cry because I could not see my mother in the crowd. She was visiting the other temples. I heard people saying, "This is the Kali temple of Rani Rasmani." In the meantime a man came and consoled me. Most probably it was Sri Ramakrishna. It was 1858 and he was then a priest of the Kali temple and practising austerity there. My next meeting with the Master was twenty-four years later.[15]

The Master's Training

Once the Master accompanied me to the Panchavati grove, and he bowed down at the spot where a branch of the old banyan tree had fallen. He then said: "I have had so many visions here. Please bow down." He was like my loving mother. Another time the Master asked me to buy a shirt for him, and I got three. He took one and returned the others to me. Lest I should feel hurt, he affectionately asked, "How many shirts did I ask for?"

"One," I replied.

Then he said: "Please keep these extra shirts with you. When I need another one, I shall tell you. You are my own."

What renunciation he had! He could not hoard anything. His mind dwelt only on divinity. He further told me, "Never do anything that would disturb my mind." The Master warned me that if he were disturbed it would be harmful for the devotees.

Another time he asked me to buy a carpet. He knew that I might ask someone else to get it, so he said, "You yourself should go and buy it." Why did he say this? Because the impression of serving the Master would stay in my mind, and I would be able to meditate on him throughout my life, thinking, "I presented a carpet to the Master."[16]

Kali, the Mother

Once somebody asked the Master, "Is God with form or without form?" The Master answered: "I have seen the Mother both ways. She is the indivisible Satchidananda, and again she assumes various forms for the devotees. At Kalighat [in South Calcutta] I saw the Divine Mother playing with some children and chasing a butterfly. Another time I saw her walking on the Adi Ganges."

On one occasion the Master told us: "Mother has come. She is wearing a red-bordered sari and has tied a bunch of keys in the corner of her cloth." He said this in the presence of Keshab Sen and others in his room at Dakshineswar. People heard the Master's words, but the Master alone heard the Mother's words.

Another day he said: "The Mother is going up and down the stairs in the temple. Her hair is dishevelled, and her anklets are making a *jhun-jhun* sound."

Once in Cossipore he said, "Today I saw the Mother playing a vina [a stringed instrument]."

The Master was absorbed in the formless aspect of the Mother for six months at the time of his sadhana.[17]

One day I went to Dakshineswar and found the Master sweeping the garden path to the north of his room. Seeing me, he said, "The Mother walks here, so I am cleaning the path."[18]

The Master used to say, "Sculpture, painting, poetry, music — all these fine arts make one thoughtful." He also told us that Navin, a sculptor, used to eat only once a day, at three o'clock in the afternoon, a vegetarian meal of rice, boiled vegetables, and clarified butter.

When Navin made the image of Mother Kali at Dakshineswar he practised self-control and harsh austerities for six months. That is why the image looks alive. Only when the sculptor is absorbed in the Divine can he project divinity in a stone image.[19]

The Master Talked with God

Before I met the Master I had been connected with the Brahmo Samaj for seven or eight years. During their formal service they would talk about God, and as I listened to their sermons, I would think that God was far away. But when I went to the Master, I saw that he would talk with God directly.

What a great ideal the Master presented before us! He said, "The goal of human life is to realize God." Without that, life is meaningless. Not only did he see God, but he also used to talk to the Divine Mother, as we talk among ourselves.[20]

One day he said, "The Mother has come." Then he began to talk to Her, saying: "Well, Mother, to whom should I listen? This person is saying this and the other person something else." Then the Divine Mother said something to him. Again the Master said: "I understand, Mother. I shall listen to you and no one else."

At the beginning of his years of sadhana he would cry to the Divine Mother: "Mother, I cannot bear these worldly people. My body is burning."

The Mother said to him: "Wait for some time. The pure-souled devotees will come." The Master had to wait nearly twenty-two years for his devotees.[21]

From the Infinite to the Finite

Once when the Master was going to Vidyasagar's house he asked me: "My shirt is unbuttoned. Will that offend Vidyasagar?"

I assured him: "Oh, no! Don't be anxious about it. Nothing about you is offensive."

What a wonderful person the Master was! When he was in the carriage only a few minutes earlier, he had been in samadhi; when he alighted he was still absorbed in that mood, so his steps were faltering. But yet he was quite aware of social formalities, such as the condition of his clothes. What a fantastic mind he had!

At that time two opposite ideas were harmonized in his behaviour. On one hand his mind had transcended the world and was merged in God, and on the other he was inquiring about human affairs. This should be the ideal: "True to the kindred points of heaven and earth." This we find in the lives of the avatars [divine incarnations]. The avatar brings the message of the Infinite to the finite world.[22]

"What Do You Think of Me?"

Once there was a big gathering at Jadu Mallick's house and Keshab Sen gave a lecture. The Master repeatedly asked Keshab: "Please evaluate my knowledge and devotion. How much am I worth?"

Keshab was reluctant to answer, but at last he hesitantly said, "Sir, your knowledge is one hundred percent."

Then and there the Master said: "I don't trust your words. You are attached to wealth, name and fame, and other worldly things. If the great sages like Narada and Shukadeva were to evaluate me, I would value their judgement."

The Master sometimes uttered unpleasant truths for the sake of truth and justice. He spoke frankly about Keshab before others. At that time Keshab was highly admired. The Master loved him, so he told him the truth without compromising. When Keshab died, the Master wept.[23]

Another time the Master said, "It is the Divine Mother within who is making me do everything."

Once he asked me: "Some say that I am the full manifestation of the Godhead. What do you say?"

I replied: "Sir, I don't understand whether the manifestation is full, partial, or the like. But I have understood one thing that you said: 'There is a round hole in a wall and through it one can see a vast field on the other side.' You are that hole. Through you everything can be seen — that Infinite Meadow without end." The Master was extremely pleased and said, "Yes, one can see quite a bit."[24]

Living with the Master

The Master could see a person's inherent tendencies. When he first met each of his disciples, he immediately recognized him and tried to improve his mental tendencies. He used to say: "There are some who have gold [i.e., knowledge of the Self] hidden beneath half a pound of earth, but for others it is beneath forty pounds. So, let it be! Who is going to dig out forty pounds of earth?"

The Master knew the past history and samskaras [impressions from previous lives] of his intimate disciples and would mould them accordingly. For example, suppose he felt that a particular disciple should live with him for his spiritual growth. At that time he would not let the disciple visit his home in Calcutta. If the Master were told that a relative of the disciple was sick at home, he would say: "Let it be. If there is any emergency, the neighbours will take care of it. You do not need to go." What he meant was that trials and tribulations, sorrow and suffering, have always existed and will continue to exist, but the Master would not live forever. For this reason he forced his disciples to stay with him while they had the chance. As Christ said, "Me ye have not always."

Once the Master sent me to practise meditation under the bel tree at Dakshineswar. I closed my eyes and sat facing east. When I opened my eyes after meditation I found the Master, the object of my meditation, standing in front of me. Immediately I bowed down to him. He did not merely give instructions; he also kept an eye on each person to see whether he was practising the instructions or not. If somebody was unable to do it, he would help him like a loving mother.

I once lived at Dakshineswar for a few days at the Master's request. One day a messenger came from my Calcutta home with a letter for me. As soon as the Master saw the letter he cried out as if he were afraid of a snakebite: "What is this? What is this? Throw it away."

I immediately threw it away as if it were poison. He did not allow me to read it, thinking that the spiritual mood I was acquiring by living with him would be destroyed by worldly news. He led his disciples against the current of maya, so he was extremely cautious. The path of the world goes downward, but the Master went in the opposite direction and guided his disciples the same way.

Once the Master asked a devotee: "How is everybody in your family? Are they all right?"

The devotee answered: "They are so-so. You have told us that here there will be no talk other than about God."

The Master was pleased to hear this reply. Later he would get information about the welfare of this devotee's family through someone else.

Girish Chandra Ghosh once said to the Master: "Sir, my servant was down with a fever for six days. Your prasad cured him."

At once the Master scolded him: "Fie on you! What a small-minded person you are! You are asking for pumpkins and gourds from God! You should ask for immortality from Him."[25]

One day a visitor came to see the Master and was introduced as an atheist. The Master patted him on the back and said, "Oh no, how can he be an atheist?" The Master knew what was inside the man. He used to say, "I can see what is inside each person, just as I see what is inside this glass case." The Master understood that since that person had come to see him, he could not be an atheist.[26]

There was another person whose monthly salary was twenty-five rupees. He used to bring *rabri* [pieces of thickened milk, soaked in syrup] and other fancy sweets for the Master. The Master later told us: "Look, the things that man brought for me seem like filth."

Afterwards we found out that though the man's regular salary was twenty-five rupees, he was making an extra thirty rupees by presenting false bills. The Master saw his food to be filth and could not eat it.[27]

Once Ishan Mukherjee visited the Master wearing a gold ring on his finger. He was then fifty years old. Nothing escaped the Master's eyes. Seeing the ring, he remarked with a smile, "There was an old prostitute who lost all her physical beauty, but she always adorned herself with earrings." Hearing the Master's comment, everybody laughed loudly.[28]

An Evening with the Master at Dakshineswar

It was almost dusk. The Master said to me: "The mind of the yogi is always fixed on God, always absorbed in the Self. You can recognize such a person by merely looking at him. His eyes are wide open, with an aimless look, like the eyes of a mother bird hatching her eggs. Her entire mind is fixed on those eggs, so there is a vacant look in her eyes. Can you show me such a picture?"

"I shall try to get one," I said.[29] [M. was not able to find such a picture during the Master's lifetime, but he fulfilled the Master's wish later.]

We Watched the Master Twenty-Four Hours a Day

The Master was in such a state that he could accept things only after offering them to the Divine Mother. If someone presented a new cloth to the Master, he would first offer it to the Mother in the temple and then use it himself. In this way the Master demonstrated how one could be immersed in yoga while living in this world.[30]

Once the Master was staying at Mathur's Calcutta residence. One morning at two o'clock he suddenly said to Mathur, "I want to go back to Dakshineswar."

Mathur said: "Father, where shall I get a carriage now? You can go at daybreak."

"If you don't get a carriage now I shall go on foot," said the Master.

Mathur was compelled to go to his coachman and ask him to get the carriage ready and take the Master to Dakshineswar. After arriving at the Kali temple the Master said, "Mother, here I am." The Divine Mother was his all in all.[31]

The Master said, "Gauranga and I are one." One day he was humming and chanting the name "Gaur, Gaur." A person asked, "Sir, why are you saying 'Gaur, Gaur' instead of chanting the Mother's name?"

The Master replied: "What can I do? You people have many resources — wife, son, daughter, money, home, and so on — but I have only one resource, God. For that reason I sometimes say 'Gaur,' sometimes 'Mother,' sometimes 'Rama, Krishna, Kali, Shiva.' This is the way I spend my time."[32]

The Master experienced the truth of Brahman as described in the scriptures not just once or twice but all the time. We lived with the Master and watched him closely twenty-four hours a day. He never deviated from God-consciousness. Even while lying in bed at night he would chant "Mother, Mother." He had very little sleep. He never slept more than fifteen to thirty minutes at a stretch. Such a thing is not possible for an ordinary God-realized person. Only when God incarnates in a human body is such a thing possible.

The Master declared that in his body Satchidananda had manifested on earth. One day he told me, "Christ, Chaitanya, and I are one and the same entity." Is this the temple priest or God? We were bewildered when his real nature was revealed to us. "The Mother of the Universe," he said, "speaks through my mouth." He spoke out of inspiration. "I am an illiterate man," he said on several occasions, "but the Mother supplies knowledge from behind."[33]

Days in Cossipore

Once when Sri Ramakrishna was ill in the Cossipore garden house, somebody said to him, "Sir, why don't you go to Dakshineswar?"

"Why?" asked the Master.

"Because Mother Kali is there," was the reply.

"Is not the Mother here?" said the Master.[34]

On the eve of the Holi festival, the Master touched his heart with the palm of his hand and then made a circle around himself with a finger. He then said to Narendra, "Tell me what I meant by that."

Narendra replied, "Sir, the whole universe has emanated from you."
The Master was pleased and said to Rakhal: "Just see. Now he understands me." Previously Narendra had not accepted the concept of avatar,
or Incarnation of God. But now he did, so the Master was happy.[35]
Narendra sang this song at Cossipore:

O Lord, I am thy servant, I am thy servant!
    Thy servant am I!
O Lord, thou art my Master, thou art my Master!
    My Master art thou!
From thee I have received two pieces of bread and a loincloth;
When I sing thy name, devotion wells up in my heart and
    shields me from harm.
Thou art the Master, the All-compassionate; this I repeat, O Lord!
Thy servant Kabir has taken refuge at thy feet.

When the Master heard this song, tears fell from his eyes.

Oh, what a sweet voice Narendra had! The Master also had a beautiful, sweet voice. After hearing them, I don't enjoy anybody else's singing.
Their singing was not only sweet but sublime and charming. It would
raise the mind to a higher level of consciousness and unite it with God.
I will never hear such singing again. During the last year of his life, the
Master could not sing. Usually Narendra and some devotees would sing
and the Master would listen. The frequent bleeding in the Master's throat
reduced his body to a skeleton. By enduring this physical pain, he showed
humanity that physical suffering is inevitable when one takes a body, and
that there is no escape from it.

The Master was in terrible pain, but he never forgot God even for a
minute. This is possible only when one attains supreme love. Whenever
he listened to a song or talked about God, his mind would transcend the
body and merge into God-consciousness. Saying "Mother, Mother," the
Master would lose outer consciousness. This state is possible only for an
incarnation of God and none else.[36]

Even during his last illness at Cossipore, he played as he used to do
when he was a child. There was a fair in the neighbourhood in celebration
of the last day of the Bengali year. The Master had sent a devotee to the
fair to buy a few articles, and when he returned the Master asked, "What
have you bought?" The devotee replied, "Candy, a spoon, and a vegetable
knife."[37]

At Cossipore the Master's body was so emaciated that it appeared
bent like a bow. Once I was seated near his bed, dejected in mind. Seeing

me the Master said: "Why are you seated like that? It is not right. Be strong and gird your loins. Give up this melancholy."[38]

Once at Cossipore the Master asked me to buy a stone bowl. Someone said, "Master, we have a bowl." But he said, "Let him buy another one." It was noon. Without eating lunch, I went to Jorasanko [in West Calcutta] and returned to Cossipore after purchasing the bowl. The Master took the bowl in his hands and looked at it. Why did he do this? The Master knew I would remember this incident all through my life and that it would be helpful to me. The remembrance that I had bought a bowl for an avatar would inspire my mind and become a living meditation.[39]

My Crisis

While the Master was lying sick in the Cossipore garden house, I was working as headmaster of Vidyasagar's Shyampukur High School. I visited the Master quite often, and as a result I could not pay sufficient attention to the activities of the school. The students' test scores suffered a little. Vidyasagar was displeased with this and said to me, "You are visiting Sri Ramakrishna too much, so the results of the examinations are not good." I immediately resigned my job and informed the Master. He said three times, "You did the right thing." He knew that I did not have any savings and that I might have to starve, but still he said that I had done the right thing. Whatever one does for God is the right thing to do. First serve God and then the world.

When I quit that job I was worried about how I would feed my children. Within fifteen days I got another job. A teacher of the Hindu School was on leave, and the headmaster of that school called me and appointed me in his place, saying that the post was likely to be permanent. Even then I was worried. Another day I was abstractedly pacing back and forth on the veranda when I heard someone calling me from downstairs. I went down and found a messenger who gave me a letter from Surendra Nath Banerjee requesting me to visit him. When I met him, he said to me: "I hear you have given up your job. Why don't you work in our college?" So I joined the Ripon College [now Surendra Nath College] as a professor and worked there for five years.[40]

My Visit to Kamarpukur

I went to Kamarpukur during Saraswati Puja in 1886, when the Master was living at Cossipore. At that time the Master had raised my mind to such a high state that I perceived light everywhere in Kamarpukur. I saw trees, plants, birds, beasts, and human beings as luminous forms and I bowed down to them.

While travelling on the road to Burdwan I reflected that the Master had walked on this road, so every bit of its dust was pure. Part of the way I went by bullock cart and the rest on foot. On the way I saw a man carrying weapons. I immediately rushed to the cart and asked the driver, "Is this man a robber?"

The driver replied: "No, he is not a robber. He is a mailman. He has money with him so he carries a weapon. We are the robbers."

I was scared when I heard that.

When I returned the Master asked me, "How did things go in that place of robbers?" I told him everything in detail, including how I had seen everything there as luminous. When I told him that I had bowed down to a cat on the street in Kamarpukur, he laughed. I then expressed my desire to visit Kamarpukur again and he whispered, "Let me get well." But the Master was very sick by then, so my desire was not fulfilled.[41]

Pray in Solitude

The Master used to talk quite often about living in solitude. In a solitary place one develops a sense of infinity. There, nature imparts education. This cannot be understood unless one lives in solitude. The Master said: "The trees of the temple garden would remind me of the forest hermitages where the ancient sages practised their austerities. They would observe the infinite sky, the morning sun, and the beauty of nature." The Upanishads originated in the forest, so they are also called *Aranyakas* [forest treatises].

When I see clouds in the sky, I am reminded of those ancient rishis. They passed through all the six seasons — summer, rain, autumn, fall, winter, spring — and realized God. The descriptions of these seasons are found in their hymns and conversations. The six seasons have also been mentioned in *The Gospel of Sri Ramakrishna*. Reading between the lines, one can find out what was spoken when. The Master said: "During my early days, a monk came to Dakshineswar. As soon as he would see the clouds in the sky, he would begin to dance."

The river, the ocean, the vast fields — all these awaken God-consciousness. After I returned from Darjeeling, the Master asked me, "Did you experience the presence of God when you looked at the Himalayas?" He said nothing else.

I told the Master that when I saw the Himalayas from a distance I had burst into tears. At that time I did not realize the significance of it. Later on I read in the Gita where Krishna said, "Among the immovable things,

I am the Himalayas." Without knowing it, I had had that awakening. The Master used to say, "If you bite a chili, knowingly or unknowingly, your tongue will burn."[42]

The Way of Meditation

The Master described three ways to meditate: First, imagine a windless sky overcast with clouds. Second, think of a big lake with motionless water. Third, mentally visualize the unflickering flame of a lamp in a windless place.

Once the Master told me, "If you meditate on me that will do." Another time he taught me meditation on the formless Brahman. He took me to Mati Seal's lake at Belgharia. There were tame fish in the lake. Nobody harmed them. Visitors threw puffed rice and other bits of food into the water, and the big fish came in swarms to eat it. The fish swam fearlessly and sported joyfully in the water.

The Master said to me: "Look at the fish. Meditating on the formless God is like swimming joyfully like these fish in the ocean of Bliss and Consciousness." He also gave an illustration of a bird flying freely in the infinite sky. Thus he pointed out how to impose the mood of meditation on the formless aspect of God. Meditation on the Master is the same as meditation on the nondual Satchidananda [Existence-Consciousness-Bliss Absolute], which is beyond mind and speech.

The Master would sometimes pace back and forth like a lion on the embankment of the Ganges at two or three in the morning. He could hear the *anahata* sound [music of the spheres, or Om] at that time. He said that yogis could hear it too.

One day in Dakshineswar there was a fierce thunderstorm. The Master was pacing in his room and repeating his mantra. Perhaps he was watching the terrible form of the Divine Mother. He began to hum these two lines of a song: "O Mother, when assuming your terrible form you dance with your sword, and the earth trembles. Mother, you are the embodiment of the three gunas, the destroyer of demons, the saviour, the consort of Shiva."[43]

Plain Living and High Thinking

About food the Master used to say, "Eat a little rice and spinach and chant God's name the whole day." What is the need for many dishes, such as meat, fish, vegetables, and sweets? Those who are earthbound focus on external things and worldly enjoyments. However, those who have some knowledge about spiritual life or have a guru don't need many material things. They should be content with bare necessities and should practise sadhana as long as they live.

Once the Master's ancestral home was being repaired by the Laha family. Seeing that ornamental designs were being put on the door, the Master said: "What is the need for all those decorations? Just put up a door so that the jackals cannot enter." But who has such insight?

The Master solved various human problems through the example of his own life. Eat simple food and the rest of the time chant the name of Rama. He used to say: "My ideal is a brahmin widow who lives in a cottage, grows her own vegetables, eats simple food, and chants God's name all the time." When Swami Vivekananda's family was suffering from starvation, the Master blessed him, saying, "You will get rice and lentils — that is, plain food — and nothing more."

A beginner should practise japa and meditation daily at fixed times. Even when busy, he must sit for meditation in the morning and evening. Practice makes everything easy. The Master used to say: "One should get up at four in the morning, if not at three. Four or five hours of sleep is enough. One should think of God early in the morning. Holy people meditate at that time. This is called *Brahma-muhurta*, or the time of Brahman, when a spiritual current flows all around."

One should be careful about one's evening meal. If you eat too much then, you won't be able to get up early. So the Master used to say, "One may fill one's stomach at lunch, like a cannon which has been loaded with gunpowder, but supper must be light." He told me at Shyampukur: "Read the Bhagavad Gita. There you will find instructions concerning moderate eating for a yogi." Yogis eat neither too much nor too little. They eat food that is simple, substantial, and easily digestible. The Master advised some devotees to eat rice with ghee [clarified butter] and milk, saying that it was the food of the ancient sages.[44]

Be a Devotee, But Don't Be Foolish!

The Master taught devotees how to be practical in daily life. It is extremely difficult for a person to make any progress in spiritual life if he is careless and unmindful in small matters. A person has to reach God with the help of the mind, so there should be no insincerity or carelessness. The Master scolded Swami Yogananda when he once bought a cracked cooking pot.

The Master said: "Why did you buy the pot without examining it? The shopkeeper was there to conduct his business, not to practise religion. Why did you believe him and get deceived? Be a devotee, but don't be foolish!"

The Master then sent him back to exchange the pot.

What a watchful eye the Master had! He did not miss any detail. Once a disciple paid a pice for six betel leaves instead of ten. Immediately the Master scolded him: "Why do you allow yourself to be cheated? You must get the right quantity. If there is any extra amount offered, take it to distribute among others. But by no means be cheated." This saying of the Master's has a deep significance. If a person is not careful, maya will use lust and gold to cheat him. Some people are heedless and develop a personality that permits them to be cheated by others.

Once I forgot to bring the Master's umbrella from the Panchavati. As soon as I reached his room he said to me indignantly, "While in ecstasy it is hard for me to keep the cloth on my body, yet I do not make such a mistake."

Since the Master's whole life was based on dharma [religion], every action of his was perfect. It will not do to behave in a religious manner part of the time and in the opposite manner later. Whether eating, walking, sleeping, dreaming, telling beads, concentrating, worshipping, or reading the scriptures — in every condition, the mind should remain centred on one thought, one ideal — realization of God.

Nowadays some people consider dharma to mean an indifference to external matters. But the Master could not tolerate this. He said, "Such indifference is the result of *tamoguna* [laziness]."

He was very particular about several things: First, cleanliness and tidiness. Generally people are unclean because of habitual laziness. How many people forget their bodies because they are thinking of God? God does not manifest Himself to an unclean person. Both external and internal purity are necessary. Second, one should not be wasteful. The Master could not bear to see anyone waste anything. Once at Cossipore he scolded a devotee who had cut six pieces of lemon instead of one. He said: "You are wasting the devotees' hard-earned money, which they are giving for my service. It is better to be miserly than extravagant." The Master also did not like it if anybody wasted food. Third, he could not bear people wearing torn or dirty clothes. He said, "The goddess of fortune leaves a person who wears patched clothes." Fourth, he could not bear disorderliness. He wanted everything to be put in its proper place and handled artistically. Fifth, he liked to see self-reliance, such as cooking one's own food. He said: "A spiritual aspirant should cook his own food and then eat the prasad after offering it to God. Thus he will not have to depend on others, nor will he lose his spiritual excellence."

He used to say: "A great worship is going on all the time. Nothing should be neglected. One should think of God during all activities of life, such as eating, walking, moving, talking, and sleeping. This is called true religion."[45]

Be Perfect

[*M., noticing the orderliness of the kitchen storeroom at the Mihijam retreat, made these following comments.*] It looks beautiful, as if it were a shrine. When the Master came to Shyampukur from Dakshineswar for treatment, he first visited the kitchen storeroom to check on the household supplies. He noticed that the earthen pots didn't have coil stands and lids, so he immediately sent somebody to the market to buy those things. The Master couldn't tolerate disorderliness. He insisted on arranging things properly and putting them in their respective places. On one hand, he was in samadhi day and night, forgetting even his wearing cloth; and on the other, he was keenly alert to the details of everyday life. The Master used to say, "He who can keep an account of salt can also keep an account of sugar candy."[46]

Three Practical Lessons

The Master taught us three practical lessons: First, have a charitable attitude towards all. One should remember that human beings are a mixture of good and evil. Second, show your manliness. Sometimes it is necessary to scold somebody if he does something wrong; otherwise he may exploit your goodness. Hiss but don't bite. Once I said to the Master, "My nature is so tender that I cannot hit a cat even if it steals the fish from my plate." He immediately protested and said firmly: "Don't be like that. If you push the cat away, it will not die." I had thought the Master would appreciate my pacifist attitude, but instead he was advising me to resist. Failure to act is not considered nonviolence; rather it is *tamas,* or inertia. Third, if you find a person with predominantly evil tendencies, salute him from a distance as people do the tiger god. All are gods, but maintain a safe distance from the tiger god; otherwise, it may kill you.[47]

Sri Ramakrishna, an Exemplar

The Master told me this story, which took place during his early years at Dakshineswar when he was twenty-five years old. Before the arrival of Tota Puri, various monks visited the Master. One of these monks lived for a time in the Panchavati and served Gopala [the child Krishna]. The Master used to visit him and listen to his teachings. According to tradition, one should serve the guru for three days. The Master served the monk by bringing him water, food, and so on for three days and then stopped going to him.

The monk asked, "Why are you not visiting me anymore?"

The Master replied, "I decided to serve you for three days and now that time is up."[48]

Once a hatha yogi [one who practises postures] was staying at the Panchavati. He was addicted to opium and also required one and a half seers of milk daily. He asked Rakhal to collect some money for his needs, so Rakhal said he would mention it to the Calcutta devotees. When the devotees arrived at the Master's room, the hatha yogi also arrived there, clattering in his wooden sandals. As soon as the yogi reminded Rakhal about the money, the Master said to the devotees, "Will you give him something?" Perhaps the devotees felt he was not a worthy recipient, so they kept quiet. Then the Master continued: "Oh, you do not wish to give him anything. I see nobody is responding." The Master spoke tactfully, so that the devotees might not feel pressured.[49]

A young disciple [Latu] used to live at Dakshineswar with the Master and serve him. Once a householder devotee presented him with a new pair of sandals. As he was busy most of the time serving the Master, he had no time to wear them. One night a jackal took one of them away. When the Master learned about it, he searched around the garden and finally found the sandal after an hour. The Master returned it to his young disciple. At once the latter exclaimed: "Sir, what have you done? I am supposed to serve you — not the other way around." Saying this, he took the sandal from the Master's hand. What affection the Master had for the devotees!

Adhar Sen was an English-educated person. Once he went to Jadu Mallick's house with the Master. He bowed down to the goddess Simhavahini but did not make an offering. At once the Master said to Adhar, "You have not offered anything to the Mother!"

Adhar said, "Sir, I didn't know that one should make an offering after saluting the deity." He then offered a rupee.

Occasionally the Master would say: "I don't usually say this lest you think I am egotistical, but when you come here bring a pice worth of cardamom or myrobalan or something." He did not ask for anything expensive, lest the devotees should stop coming.[50] The Master said this for the welfare of the devotees. [According to the Hindu custom, a person is supposed to offer a piece of fruit, a flower, or some money when visiting a deity or a holy person.]

Shashi, a young disciple of the Master, used to live in Central Calcutta.

As the Master was very fond of ice, he asked Shashi to bring one pice of ice from Calcutta. During summer Shashi would walk nearly six miles with the ice wrapped in a cloth to bring it to the Master. He ignored the scorching sun. He felt tremendous joy in serving the Master. The Master would mix the ice with water and greatly enjoy it. What service Shashi gave to the Master till the end! He offered his body, his mind, and everything else at the Master's feet, and thus he became great.[51] [He later became Swami Ramakrishnananda.]

There Are Two Paths

Once a man came to the Master and said that he was feeling great sorrow. The Master told him: "Look. Misery is better than joy. *Nivritti* [renunciation] is better than *pravritti* [attachment to sense objects]. Misery directs the mind towards God."

Another time a woman came from Kamarpukur and said to the Master, "I have no one in this world." At this the Master began to dance with joy. He said to her, "One who has nobody has God." The woman returned home, at peace.[52]

The Master told us that there are two paths: *vidya-maya* [the path of knowledge] and *avidya-maya* [the path of ignorance]. Through avidya-maya one can have money, home, name, fame, sensual enjoyments, and so on. These things divert the mind from God. Compassion, holy company, austerity, study of the scriptures, and pilgrimage belong to the category of vidya-maya. They help one to realize God.[53]

The Value of Prasad (Sanctified Food)

The Master used to say, "In this Kali Yuga, the prasad of Jagannath, Ganges water, and the dust of Vrindaban are veritable manifestations of Brahman."

It is not possible for us to understand his divine outlook. Every morning the Master would eat a particle of Jagannath prasad [cooked and dried rice] before eating anything else. He kept this prasad in a small cloth bag near the western wall of his room, and he used to share it with us. One day he gave a particle to Narendra, who refused to eat it, saying, "It is unclean rice."

The Master then asked him: "Do you believe in the effect of food on the human body? For example, opium causes constipation, whereas *triphala* [myrobalan, amalaki, and baira — three kinds of tropical fruits] has a laxative effect."

Narendra replied, "Yes, I believe that."

Then the Master said, "In the same way, anybody who eats this prasad of Jagannath will attain knowledge, devotion, and faith."

Narendra ate it and did not argue any further. He trusted every word of the Master's. He knew that the Master was truthful and an expert in metaphysical science.

Many times the Master told us, "I am Lord Jagannath of Puri." He sent me to Puri a few times and advised me about what to do in a holy place. Once he said, "Embrace Lord Jagannath." I was in a dilemma, because pilgrims are not supposed to embrace the Lord on the altar. But when I was inside the temple, the Master inspired me with an idea. I had some coins and other money in my pocket, which I intentionally dropped on the floor of the dark temple sanctuary. When the priests rushed to pick up the money, I jumped onto the altar and embraced Lord Jagannath. Someone saw me and shouted, but I immediately got down and began to circumambulate the Lord. Nobody could recognize me in the dark.

It was the Master who asked me to embrace Lord Jagannath and gave me the idea of how to do it, and then he made it easy for me by arousing greed in the minds of the priests. Now I wonder how I did that heroic deed! The Master never went to Puri. He said, "My body will not last if I visit Puri." When I returned from Puri the Master embraced me and said, "Now I have satisfied my desire to embrace Jagannath."[54]

Once a Vaishnava monk came to Dakshineswar. The Master sent him some luchis [fried bread] and sweets that had been offered to Mother Kali. But the monk was such a fanatic Vaishnava that he threw away the prasad because it had been offered to Kali. The Master became angry. He said, "It would be good if somebody beats this rascal from head to foot and throws him out of this place." Three days later that monk quarreled with the gardeners, and they beat him and threw him out. Later the Master lamented: "That rascal threw away the Mother's prasad! If a person doesn't want to eat it, he should either give it to someone else or return it."[55]

Advice to Worldly People

Samadhi is the natural state of all human beings, but it seems to be unnatural. Why? Because of our craving for worldly enjoyment. When desires cease, samadhi begins.

People are drowned in maya. When the Master took a carriage to Calcutta, he would watch people on the street through the windows. Once he said: "I saw only one person with a high spiritual outlook, near the corner of the Criminal Court Building. All others had a worldly outlook." People with a worldly outlook are busy eating, sleeping, and begetting children.[56]

Another time the Master went to Barabazar and found that a man had
opened a shop in a small basement. Neither sunlight nor moonlight could
penetrate there. One could not possibly enter it without bending one's
head. The man was selling earthen cups and pipes for smoking tobacco.
I did not pay any attention to the man, but later the Master told me: "See
how people undergo so much hardship with intense concentration to
earn money? They could divert this austerity and concentration towards
God." But who has this perspective and who thinks this way? The Master
came to do good to humanity. His mind was always on God, whereas
people's minds are on the world.[57]

The Master used to say that those who have an oily physical appearance want both God and enjoyment, yoga and bhoga. Those who have a
dry physical appearance are devoted only to yoga.[58]

The Path of Degradation

In the Gita, Krishna describes the seven steps of a man's downfall
from spiritual life.* The Master used to say, "The path of degradation
is like a slope. A man has no inkling that he is going downward." The
Master went to visit Fort William [a military barracks built several storeys
below ground] in Calcutta. He said: "In the beginning I did not realize
that I had descended so far. My goodness! When I looked up, I found
myself below the level of a three- or four-storeyed building. Likewise, the
mind, thinking of sense objects, unconsciously sinks to the depths."

Once the Master visited the Kali temple of Thanthania [in central
Calcutta] and saw that the priests were playing cards on the veranda. He
plaintively said, "Look, in such a holy place they are playing cards!" A
bound soul goes to his neighbour's house and wastes the whole afternoon
playing cards, but he will never call on God.[59]

Worldly Talk

When Aswini Datta's father retired from his position as subjudge, he
came to visit the Master. Observing his good nature and physical traits,
the Master asked him to stay at Dakshineswar for three days. One day the

*Thinking about sense objects
Will attach you to sense objects;
Grow attached, and you become addicted;
Thwart your addiction, it turns to anger;
Be angry, and you confuse your mind;
Confuse your mind, you forget the lesson of experience;
Forget experience, you lose discrimination;
Lose discrimination, and you miss life's only purpose. (2:62-63)

Master's room was full of visitors and Mr. Datta began to talk about some secular subject. At that time the Master was in samadhi. As soon as he regained outer consciousness, he heard that secular conversation. With folded hands he said humbly to Mr. Datta, "Sir, I don't like to hear talk about anything other than God."[60]

Another time a man came to the Master and asked, "Sir, tell me how to realize God." The Master had previously heard that this person didn't have a job, so he immediately said to him, "First try to get a job and then I shall tell you how to realize God."[61]

Sri Ramakrishna and Girish Chandra Ghosh

The Master went to see the drama *Chaitanya Lila* [The Life of Chaitanya] in September 1884. We went with him. Girish Ghosh arranged a box seat for the Master and engaged a man to fan him with a big palm leaf fan. The Master asked, "How much will they charge?"

"Nothing," I replied. "They are happy that you have come to see the performance."

Then the Master said joyfully, "I chant Mother's name, so they are doing all these things for me."

It is amazing that he was reluctant to take any credit for himself. The Mother was doing everything.[62]

On another occasion Sri Ramakrishna went to see Girish perform at the Star Theatre. He gave him a rupee since he did not want to see it for free. Girish put the coin on his head and began to dance. He regarded it as prasad from the Master and preserved it in his shrine.[63]

One day while going to Balaram's house, the Master passed near the home of Girish Ghosh, who was then seated on his veranda. Pointing to him, Narayan, a young devotee, said to the Master, "There is Girish Ghosh, who wrote *Chaitanya Lila*." As the Master was by nature humble, he saluted Girish with folded hands. Girish followed the Master to Balaram's home. There the Master said to him: "The play is well written. Many people will derive joy from it."

Girish replied: "Sir, I am an unworthy person. I do not deserve such a compliment. Wherever I sit, the earth becomes impure seven cubits deep."

Immediately the Master entered into an ecstatic state and sang this song:

If only I can pass away repeating Durga's name,
How canst thou then, O Blessed One,

Withhold from me deliverance,
Wretched though I may be?
I may have stolen a drink of wine, or killed a child unborn,
Or slain a woman or a cow,
Or even caused a brahmin's death;
But, though it all be true,
Nothing of this can make me feel the least uneasiness;
For through the power of thy sweet name
My wretched soul may still aspire
Even to Brahmanhood.

This song consoled Girish, and the Master blessed him. After that Girish would inquire about the Master's Calcutta visits and would wait for him at those places. Gradually his life was changed. Once he and a friend went to Dakshineswar by carriage. Both were dead drunk. Girish took hold of the Master and began to sing, "O Lord, where is your sweetheart Radha?" Later the Master said: "What faith Girish has! It is so deep that it cannot be measured."[64]

One day the Master asked Girish to take a dip in the Ganges and pray, "O all-purifying Mother Ganges, please bless me." Girish unwillingly did what the Master said. But after he immersed himself in the Ganges, his mind was filled with bliss. Such was the greatness of Mother Ganges! The Master said, "In this Kali Yuga, Ganges water is the veritable manifestation of Brahman."[65]

Another time Girish asked the Master, "Why do I feel depressed from time to time?"

The Master replied: "As long as you are in the world, the cloud of maya will arise. Don't be afraid of it. It is the nature of the mind to sometimes go up and sometimes go down."[66]

Girish said: "Sir, you have the power to make everybody pure and unattached, whether he is a householder or a monk. You are beyond all laws." What faith he had!

The Master agreed and said to him: "Yes, it is possible. Exuberant devotion transcends all scriptural injunctions." Here the Master gave himself away. Who can admit such a thing except an avatar?

Girish got whatever he asked for from the Master. He said to the Master, "Sir, what I was and what I have become — just by thinking of you!"[67]

What faith Girish had! The Master used to say, "Girish has one hundred and twenty-five percent faith." The Master didn't give importance to external behaviour: He saw a person's inside. Once he said, "I can see the inside of each person as one sees an object in a glass case." He could see not only the present life of a person but his past and future lives too. Though Girish's external life was to some extent unconventional, basically he was a spiritual person.

Once the Master visited Girish's house. Girish bought some refreshments at the market and served them on plates that were placed directly on the carpet where the devotees were seated. Balaram Basu, a staunch devotee of the Master, was also present. Girish's style of service upset Balaram, because in his opinion it was not the proper way to serve the Master. Sri Ramakrishna looked at Balaram and told him with a smile: "This is the custom here. When I go to your house, you may serve me in your way." Balaram was a strict orthodox Vaishnava devotee.[68]

The Story of Rasik

Rasik was a sweeper in the temple garden of Dakshineswar. The Master told us about him.

One day Rasik asked him, "Master, what will happen to me?" [The Master blessed him and said, "You will see me at the time of death."] Rasik built a tulsi grove in his courtyard where he would practise spiritual disciplines. Later he became ill, and at last one day at noon he asked his wife to call his sons and have them carry him to the tulsi grove. There, fully conscious, he gave up his body while chanting the Master's name.

Rasik was a great soul. He not only saw the Master over a long period of time, but he also recognized him as an Incarnation of God. Through the Master's grace he was prompted to ask that vital question, "What will happen to me?" Though Rasik was a sweeper, the Master gave him immortality. The Master himself told us that once he cleaned the open drain of Rasik's house with his own hair while praying with tears in his eyes, "Mother, destroy my pride of being a brahmin."[69]

Sri Ramakrishna's Humour

Sometimes the Master would tell funny stories that made the devotees laugh. One day he said: "Do you know how young boys talk among themselves? One says: 'Brother, once I was walking along a street flooded with water. Do you know what I saw? There were many shad fish jumping over the open drain near the street.'" [Usually shad are confined to rivers.]

The Master could accurately imitate the voice, gestures, and movements of a person. At such times it seemed to us that he had become identified with that person. He knew the devotees might not like to hear only talk about God, so he used to tell many humorous stories. When their tension had subsided, he would lift their minds to a higher plane again. Wit and humour are necessary in the initial stages of spiritual life. They have the same effect as pickles. A person relishes his food more if he takes a little pickle with it now and then. The Master adopted various means for inspiring the devotees.[70]

Once I went to Dakshineswar and found the Master lying on his small bed. It was a hot summer day and I was perspiring quite a bit. Mani Mallick was seated on the floor, and the Master said to him, "Since all these Englishmen [meaning, people who have an English education] are coming here, it proves there must be something within me." Thus, even through humour he disclosed his true nature.[71]

The Master often went to Calcutta from Dakshineswar by horse carriage. If the horse was old and weak, it would pull the carriage only a short distance and then stop. Once when this happened he asked the coachman, "Hello, what happened?"

The coachman replied: "There is nothing wrong, sir. My horse is just catching his breath." Everybody laughed.

What a humorous person the Master was! He used to say that if a man were old and weak like that horse, he would not be able to see God. In an amusing way he would teach others.[72]

The Master often told this story: When farmers go to the market to buy bullocks, they test each one by touching its tail. A gentle one closes its eyes and lies down on the ground, but a strong one jumps up as soon as its tail is touched. This indicates its mettle. A spirited bullock costs seventy-five rupees, whereas a gentle bullock is only five rupees. A seeker of God should be like the strong bullock, which does not care for comfort.[73]

When the Master travelled by horse carriage, it would usually cost three rupees and two annas for a round trip. One day Balaram arranged for the Master's return trip to Dakshineswar at a cost of only one rupee and four annas.

The Master asked Balaram, "Why is the fare so low?"

"Sir, I got it at a cheaper rate," answered Balaram.

On the way to Dakshineswar near Baranagore, the carriage lost one of its wheels, and the Master was stranded on the street. Just then Trailokya, Mathur's son, passed by in his luxurious phaeton. He was on his way to Dakshineswar. The Master was embarrassed and covered his face with his cloth. Later he would tell us about Balaram's miserliness and the accident, and we would all laugh.[74]

The Slide Show

Once a magician came with a magic lantern box, which contained many slides. There were two projectors to magnify the pictures. As soon as he pulled a string, the picture would change. He charged each child a pice to see them. The magician announced in a musical tone: "Look. This is Calcutta city, and this is Bombay. Here is the court of the king and queen." He thus showed various pictures. When he announced, "Now see Badri Narayan [a famous holy place in the Himalayas]," the Master immediately became curious like a child and peeped through the viewer. When he saw Badri Narayan, the Master went into ecstasy. What was the need of a picture then? Afterwards, when he came back to the normal plane, he asked a devotee to pay the magician. The devotee gave four pice. Then the Master said indignantly: "What! He showed Badri Narayan and you paid only four pice! Please give him a rupee."

What a mind the Master had! Day and night he was in a god-intoxicated state. The slightest stimulation would plunge him into samadhi. I have never seen another person like him in my life.[75]

Sri Ramakrishna at the Circus

One winter a circus company came to Calcutta. We bought tickets for the cheapest seats [half a rupee] and went to see it with the Master. Sitting on a bench in the upper gallery, the Master said: "Ha! This is a good place. I can see the show well from here." Like a child, he could not contain his joy. There were exhibitions of various feats. A horse raced around a circular track over which large iron rings were hung at intervals. The circus rider, an Englishwoman, stood on one foot on the horse's back, and as the horse passed under the rings, she jumped through them, always alighting on one foot on the horse's back. The horse raced around the entire circle, and the woman never missed the horse or lost her balance.

When the circus was over the Master and the devotees stood outside in the field near the carriage. Since it was a cold night he covered his body with his green shawl.[76]

The Master then said to me: "Did you see how that Englishwoman stood on one foot on her horse, while it ran like lightning? How difficult a feat that must be! She must have practised a long time. The slightest carelessness and she would break her arms or legs; she might even be killed. One faces the same difficulty leading the life of a householder. A few succeed in it through the grace of God and as a result of their spiritual practice. But most people fail. Entering the world, they become more and more involved in it; they drown in worldliness and suffer the agonies of death. A few only, like Janaka, have succeeded, through the power of their austerity, in leading a spiritual life as householders. Therefore spiritual practice is extremely necessary; otherwise one cannot rightly live in the world."[77]

Sri Ramakrishna: An Ideal Teacher

The Master used to advise us to practise japa and meditation at fixed hours. He taught that one should follow one's routine rigidly. When he was ill in Cossipore, he said to one of his disciples, "In the evening practise japa and meditation." One should give up all activities in the evening and call on God. He further said: "The ancient rishis realized God after hard struggle. Early in the morning they would leave their Ashramas and go into the deep forest so that nobody could disturb their spiritual disciplines. Then they would return in the evening. Thus they had visions of God." Their words have become Vedic mantras. Whatever the Master said is also a mantra.

Once someone asked the Master, "What is the way?"

Without hesitating for a moment, he replied, "Faith in the words of the guru." He further said: "What are the words of the guru like? Suppose a man is being tossed up and down in a rough, choppy ocean and he is gasping for breath. Just at the critical moment a lifeboat arrives. The words of the guru are that lifeboat." One should have faith in the words of one's guru.

The Master also said, "One should thoroughly scrutinize a person before choosing him as the guru." Once you have accepted a guru, you should not leave him. You cannot change gurus as you change the cleaners that wash your clothes.

Regarding initiation, the Master told someone: "Just visit this place [*meaning himself*]. That will do." Sometimes he would write a mantra on a person's tongue, or he would give someone specific instructions.

Once the Master said, "He who has seen the avatar has seen God." Christ said: "He that hath seen me hath seen the Father." (John 14:9); "I and my Father are one." (John 10:30) The Master knew who he was, so he said: "Just visit this place. That will do." One could get spiritual awakening just by seeing the Master. Why do people practise japa and meditation? For this awakening.

One day Hazra was repeating the mantra with his rosary. The Master took the rosary from his hand and threw it away. He said to Hazra, "Even sitting here you are counting beads!" In other words, the aim of counting beads is to see God, and here the avatar is in front of you. What other purpose does japa have?

A devotee would come and look at the Master intently without blinking. Once after he had left, the Master told the others, "He has fixed his whole mind on me, so what else has he to do?" In other words, that man had achieved the goal of his spiritual disciplines.

Another time the Master told me: "Please tell that person in Calcutta to meditate on me. Then he will not have to do anything else." At night the Master asked the Mother: "Well, Mother, did I do anything wrong in sending that message to the devotee? I see, Mother, that you have become everything — the five elements, mind, intellect, mind-stuff, ego — all the twenty-four principles." He was aware of his Divine nature. Who else could speak like this except God?

When his mother was dying at the bakul-tala ghat on the Ganges, he held her feet and cried, saying, "Mother, who are you that carried me in your womb?" He knew that he was the Supreme Brahman. He was telling his mother that she was not an ordinary mother because she had given birth to an avatar.[78]

A devotee used to secretly practise spiritual disciplines in seclusion at Haritaki-bagan, in Calcutta. One day, without giving any intimation, the Master went to his house. The devotee was dumbfounded. He humbly said to the Master, "Sir, I am supposed to visit you, but instead you have found me after a long search and have come to my home."

The Master said to him: "Call on God. Then someone will come forward to help you." That is why he was very anxious for the devotees.[79]

Only Longing Is Needful

No external objects are needed to attain God. The Master used to say, "Cry to the Divine Mother secretly in solitude and pray, 'Mother, please reveal Yourself to me.'"

A wealthy devotee built a large cottage for practising *purashcharana* [the repetition of the name of a deity a fixed number of times, according to a vow]. When the Master heard about it he scolded him, saying: "Fie on you! What low intelligence you have! You want to call on God by putting a signboard outside your house? God, the priceless treasure, dwells within the heart. Once should call on him secretly."

Once I was carrying some dried chickpeas [grams] to keep count of my japa. I had decided to set aside one chickpea after each repetition of 108 japa. When the Master found out about it, he said: "This will lead to vanity. You will only dwell on how you have repeated the name fifty thousand times, or have performed so much purashcharana. God is a hidden treasure. Give me those grams. I would rather soak them and eat them."

The Master's mind remained in samadhi most of the time. Once a person closed an umbrella before him, and he at once went into samadhi. It reminded him of yoga, which teaches how to gather in the scattered mind. He had tremendous concentration. Another time, in an ecstatic mood, he fell into a fire and burned his hand. When he regained external consciousness, he prayed like a boy, "Mother, heal my wound."

A person gave up eating fish and betel leaf. At this the Master said: "Do you consider this a big thing? Real renunciation is renunciation of lust and gold. What will one achieve by renouncing fish and betel leaf? Blessed is he who can fix his mind on God even while eating pork. On the other hand, wretched is he who, though eating sanctified vegetarian food, feels lustful and greedy."[80]

Call on God Secretly

Once the Master visited Navin Sen's [a relative of Keshab Sen] house in Coolootola. Keshab Sen had passed away. I was living nearby at Shyampukur. When the people of my household fell asleep that night, I left for Navin Sen's house. I sat on the outside veranda and listened to the Master singing upstairs. Ah, what singing! I could not hear the conversation, but I heard the songs. Nobody knew I was sitting on the veranda. It was a full-moon night, and I returned home alone. It seems to me as if it happened just the other day. The next day when I visited the Master, his room was full of people. I sat at a distance. Suddenly the Master came near me and said, "Secretly — very good." He knew that I had gone to Navin Sen's house. He then said, "It is good to call on God secretly." He thus encouraged me.[81]

Sri Ramakrishna's Prayers

Every word of the Master's is a great mantra. Repetition of any one of them leads to perfection. His prayers too are mantras. Is it necessary that all mantras be in Sanskrit? A mantra can be in Bengali too. The Master used to pray:

> Mother, here is thy virtue, here is thy vice;
>   take them both and grant me only pure love for thee.
> Here is thy knowledge, here is thy ignorance;
>   take them both and grant me only pure love for thee.
> Here is thy purity, here is thy impurity;
>   take them both and grant me only pure love for thee.

Here is thy dharma, here is thy adharma;
   take them both and grant me only pure love for thee.[82]

The Master used to repeat the following prayer in a voice filled with
pathos:

Mother, I don't want any physical enjoyment;
Mother, I don't want name and fame;
Mother, I don't want the eight occult powers;
Mother, I don't want the other hundred powers;
Mother, give me pure, unchanging, selfless devotion to you.
Mother, may I never be deluded by your bewitching maya.

This is our Lord's Prayer or universal prayer. Jesus Christ also taught
his disciples a prayer:

Our Father, who art in heaven, hallowed be thy name.
Thy kingdom come, thy will be done on earth as it is in heaven.
Give us this day our daily bread, and forgive us our debts as we forgive
   our debtors.
And lead us not into temptation, but deliver us from evil.
For thine is the kingdom, the power, and the glory forever.[83]

The Master used to say another prayer:

O Mother, thou art the operator and I am the machine.
Thou art the indweller and I am the house.
Thou art the driver and I am the chariot.
I move as thou movest me.
I do as thou makest me do.
I speak as thou makest me speak.
Mother, not I, not I, but thou, thou.
Mother, thou art my refuge!
Thou art my refuge! Thou art my refuge![84]

The Master's Samadhi

After renouncing karma one attains samadhi. Who knows what happens in samadhi? Only one who has experienced it knows. It cannot be
described in words. Avatars and some great souls have reached this state.
We are really fortunate that we lived with a person who was immersed in
samadhi most of the time. Now by his grace I understand a little. It is not
a matter of talk, but is felt in the depth of one's being. The Master could
transmit this experience of samadhi by a touch or a mere wish.
   It is extremely difficult to have samadhi even once, whereas the

Master would experience samadhi many times a day — as if he were possessed by a spirit. While coming down from samadhi he would say, "The pandits are like straw to me." [He meant that they were dry intellectuals and could not taste the bliss of Brahman.] We are indeed fortunate. By his grace we got a little glimpse of his message. A salt doll went to measure the depth of the ocean and got dissolved there. Who could bring back the information? This [samadhi] is the *summum bonum* of life.[85]

While the Master was in samadhi, Dr. Mahendra Sarkar touched one of his eyeballs with his finger. There was no response. The Master was devoid of body-consciousness.[86]

Hold on to the Truth

The person who holds on to the truth has nothing to fear. He has already achieved seventy-five percent of his goal. I vividly recall one memorable night when I was riding in a carriage with the Master. As we came near the junction of Shobhabazar [in West Calcutta], the Master said to me, "If you hold on to truth, you will see God." What a great message!

Jadu Mallick had promised that he would arrange for the recital of the Chandi, but he forgot. The Master reminded him, saying: "Jadu, what is the matter with you? You have not yet arranged the Chandi recital."

Vidyasagar once gave his word to the Master that he would visit him at Dakshineswar, but he never came. One day the Master asked me: "What kind of man is this Vidyasagar? He has not kept his promise."

The Master used to say, "The words of a person should be like the tusks of an elephant." He meant that just as the elephant never retracts his tusks, in the same way, whatever comes from one's lips should be followed.[87]

The Master's Forbearance

The Master had to endure much criticism from the temple officials. Once a devotee offered a little money to Holy Mother as a gift. Trailokya, Mathur's son, remarked: "The young priest [Sri Ramakrishna] has brought his wife to the temple garden to earn money." The Master was shocked to hear Trailokya's comment. He said to the Divine Mother with tears, "Mother, the temple people say so many things that are not true." What can be done? Worldly people talk like that, and one has to adjust accordingly.

Another time Trailokya ordered his guards to remove Hriday, the Master's nephew, from the temple compound for misconduct. But by mistake the guard also went to the Master and asked him to leave. Without a word of protest, the Master left the room, putting his towel over his shoulder. Seeing the Master walking towards the gate, Trailokya asked, "Sir, where are you going?"

The Master said with a smile, "You have ordered your guard to ask me to leave the temple garden."

Trailokya was embarrassed and said: "No, sir, I didn't say that you must go. Please come back. The guard made a mistake."

The Master again returned to his room, with a smile on his face. The Master was unconcerned about his dwelling place. The Divine Mother was always with him, so he was fearless.[88]

The Master's Renunciation

What a state the Master had to pass through! He could neither touch nor accept money, and hoarding it was out of the question. Mahendra Kaviraj of Baranagore once gave five rupees to Ramlal for the Master's service. At first the Master thought the money could be used to pay the milk bill. But after a couple of hours he got up and called Ramlal, who was sleeping.

The Master asked: "To whom did Mahendra give that money? Is it for your aunt [*meaning Holy Mother*]?"

"No, it is for you," answered Ramlal.

Immediately the Master said: "No, don't accept it. Go right now to Baranagore and return the money."

It was midnight. Ramlal pacified the Master for the time being by promising to return the money the next morning, which he did.

Later the Master told the devotees: "Because of that money, I could not sleep at night. I felt as if a cat were scratching my chest."[89]

The Master's Compassion

The Master used to pray to the Divine Mother for the devotees, with tears falling from his eyes, "Mother, fulfill their desires."

He had so much compassion for the devotees! They could not serve him to their heart's content while he was ill because of their family obligations, so he prayed to the Mother on their behalf: "Mother, they are very busy and have so many problems at home. Don't consider their shortcomings. Bless them, Mother."[90]

Sometimes soldiers of the Dum Dum cantonment would take a few hours of leave to visit the Master. The Master used to pray for them: "Mother, be kind to them. They come to you, undergoing so many difficulties."[91]

Once some ornaments were stolen from the Radhakanta temple of Dakshineswar. Haladhari, a cousin of the Master, was then the priest of that temple, and the police arrested him as a suspect. The Master prayed: "Mother, your name is Durga [one who saves devotees from danger]. Your name will be tarnished if misfortune befalls your child. Mother, remove all obstacles."[92] [As far as we know, Haladhari was released.]

A man came to the Master and said: "Sir, I am incapable of practising spiritual disciplines. If you wish, give me some experience."

Immediately the Master went into samadhi. After some time he began to talk to the Divine Mother, saying: "Mother, this person does not want to do anything. Do I have to make curd from milk, butter from curd, and then put the butter into his mouth?" This attitude towards spiritual practice is prevalent in the modern age.[93]

The Master's Forgiveness

Christ prayed, "Father, forgive them, for they know not what they do." He said this prayer for those who were responsible for his death. The Master, too, prayed for evildoers. Mathur Babu's family priest lived at Kalighat, but he would conduct the worship service at Janbazar, Mathur's Calcutta home. This priest was very jealous of the Master because of Mathur's devotion to him.

One day the Master was lying on the floor in ecstasy at the Janbazar house when the priest came to him and said, "Tell me, how did you cast a spell on Mathur Babu?" But the priest could not get any response, so he kicked him and left. The Master, knowing the priest would have been severely punished, never reported this incident to Mathur.

One day the Master attended the annual festival of the Brahmo Samaj at Nandan Bagan [in Calcutta]. The head of the family responsible for the festival had passed away, so his sons were conducting it. They did not treat the Master respectfully, but the Master was unconcerned. Other people began eating, but the young hosts ignored the Master. Some of the devotees were very upset and wanted to leave, but the Master said to them: "It is late. Where shall we get food at this late hour? Moreover, who will pay our carriage fare?" Later, he made a little room to eat in a dirty corner where people put their shoes. He ate a couple of luchis [fried bread] with some salt. Why did he do that? The Master understood that the boys were young and did not know him, so he compassionately accepted their food.[94]

Once Trailokya arranged a garden party at the kuthi [mansion] in Dakshineswar, and he invited some young women. He sent a messenger to the Master asking him to come to the kuthi. The Master immediately went there and asked, "Why did you call me?"

"Sir, we want to hear your singing," replied Trailokya.

"Why?" said the Master. "Let these girls sing and we shall listen."

Later the Master sang, and so did the women. They offered some refreshments to him, but he did not eat anything. Someone later brought refreshments to his room.[95]

One night an officer of a rich man arrived at Dakshineswar in a phaeton. He approached the Master and said: "Sir, you will have to come with me right now. Our master at home is extremely ill."

The Master told him: "You have made a mistake. There is a monk in the Panchavati who distributes medicines. I don't know those things. I simply eat and live in this temple garden."

One day a girl was waiting at the corner of the temple courtyard. When the Master passed by, she beckoned him. The Master went to her and she said: "My paramour has not visited me for some days. You are a holy man. Why don't you teach me some mantras or tricks so that I can attract him?" The Master replied, "Mother, I don't know such things."[96]

The Master's Simplicity

Once the Master ate at Keshab Sen's house, though Keshab was not a brahmin. He forbade us to tell anyone about it, lest the temple officials refuse to let him enter the Kali temple. The next day, however, when the temple manager was passing by, the Master told him: "Yesterday I went to Keshab's house and he gave me a sumptuous feast. I don't know whether the food was served by a washerman or a barber. Will it harm me?"

Smiling, the manager replied: "No, sir, it is all right. Nothing can pollute you." The Master was as simple as a child.[97]

Most people call on God to fulfill their desires. As long as they get wealth and prosperity, they continue their worship. As devotees they are all right. But real devotees, those who love God for love's sake, are few in number. The Master's whole life was one of pure devotion. Wealth and power could not touch him. It was often difficult for him to keep his cloth around his body. Most of the time he would call "Mother, Mother," as if he were a child of the Mother.[98]

Most of the Master's devotees were not well-to-do, and some were even penniless. He would often say things to amuse them. One day he asked, "How many carriages have come today?" "Nineteen," replied Latu. The Master laughed and said: "Only nineteen! That is nothing. Had there been many cabs, horses, and devotees, people would think this place must really be something."[99]

"I Am an Avatar"

Standing in the pine grove of Dakshineswar, the Master said to me: "I am an avatar. I am God in human form." He also told me, "I will have to be born again."

The Master proclaimed again and again, "The greatest duty of man is to realize God." And he himself fully demonstrated this ideal in his own life.[100]

When an avatar descends, a current of bliss flows everywhere. So Christ said, "Can the children of the bride chamber mourn as long as the bridegroom is with them?" Christ was an avatar. One day the Master told me, "Christ, Gauranga, and I are one." A person experiences uninterrupted bliss while he lives with an avatar. But when the avatar departs, sorrow and gloominess come. I forgot the world for five years. When the Master was with us we floated in bliss. Now I experience happiness one day and misery another. What a wonderful time we had with the Master — festivals, feasts, singing, dancing! When the Master passed away I fasted for three days.[101]

If anybody asks me what the greatest event of my life was, I would say that I met Sri Ramakrishna Paramahamsa — my Master.[102]

—24—
(M.)

From Death to Immortality

Death is the only certain thing in this uncertain world. Union must always end in separation. The wheel of life and death is continually rotating and Time (Mahakala) is the controller of that wheel. There is none dear or hateful to Time. It is indifferent to all.

After 78 years, M. realized that he needed to prepare to depart from the world stage; his performance in the divine drama of Ramakrishna was nearing its end. He was extremely happy that he had acted in his role very well, and was satisfied that he would be remembered throughout the ages. In truth, although Time devours everything, It will never be able to touch *The Gospel of Sri Ramakrishna*, M.'s immortal work.

A true lover always loves to talk about or listen to his or her beloved. M.'s life is a glowing example of a true lover and devotee of his beloved Master. One day in an inspired mood, he was trying to describe Sri Ramakrishna. He said:

The Master was like a five-year-old boy always running to meet his Mother.

The Master was like a beautiful flower whose nature is to bloom and spread its fragrance.

The Master was like a bonfire from which other lamps are lighted.

The Master was like a celestial vina always absorbed in singing the glory of the Divine Mother.

The Master was like a big fish joyfully swimming in calm, clear blue waters, the Ocean of Satchidananda.

421

The Master was like a bird which had lost its nest in a storm and then, perched on the threshold of the Infinite, was joyfully moving between the two realms, singing the glory of the Infinite.

After trying to describe the Master in many ways, he said that all these similes were inadequate. The Infinite cannot be expressed in words.[1]

Tulasidas said: "Without holy company, there is no talk about God; without talk about God, there is no chance of getting rid of delusion; and without getting rid of delusion, there is no possibility of seeing God."

During a discussion, on the evening of 20 June 1931, M. quoted from the Gita (6:3): "For a sage who wants to attain yoga, action is said to be the means; but when he has attained yoga, serenity is said to be the means." He then explained the mystery of karma to the assembled devotees: "Krishna also described the secret of work thus: '*mām anusmarah yuddhya cha* — remember me and fight.' This is called karma yoga — unite yourself with the Lord through karma. First think of Him, then work, and again think of Him and offer the fruit to Him. This is karma yoga."[2]

M. continued: "Swamiji was a hero. Look at his life: He attained samadhi, then performed action, and again he remained in samadhi. He had no attachment for action. He was commanded to perform his divine mission — working for the welfare of humanity. Work is not the goal — it is the means to realizing God."

Excitedly, M. said: "What a great hero! How boldly he proclaimed, 'I will tear up the net of maya!'"

Upon saying this, M. got up and went to his room, as if he were about to tear up his own maya. When the monks and devotees entered the room, they found M. in excruciating pain: His right hand, with which he had written five volumes of the *Kathamrita,* was hurting terribly. Swami Nityatmananda warmed a salt bag on the top of a hurricane lantern and pressed it on the damaged nerves. His son and grandsons rushed to him. At 11:00 p.m. Dr. Durgapada Ghosh arrived and gave him medicine to alleviate the pain. M. then fell asleep at midnight. Hearing about M.'s condition, Swami Shivananda remarked: "This time M.'s life has been saved by God's grace."[3]

Swami Raghavananda recalled:

Three months before the finale, M. came to humbler rooms in 13/2 Guruprasad Chaudhury Lane, to pass his days in the midst of devotees and monks, personally attending to the worship of Sri Ramakrishna, conducted in this place for the last 40 years. Here he lived as before, but still more abstemiously — cooking his own simple *havishya* food, doing all his

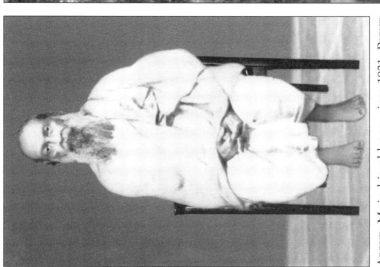

ABOVE: M. in his old age, circa 1931, RIGHT: M. with Brahmachari Balai (without chadar) and another unknown person (with chadar and near M.)

things with his own hands, and writing the fifth part of the *Kathamrita*, which he had taken in hand in January (1932) last. He looked more tired than before, but his nerve-spasms, though frequent, were not so acute now. His enthusiasm for devotees and love for talking about God were unabated; they rather increased. His face wore a greater brightness. When he would dictate the *Kathamrita*, Part V (now published), from his diary, many would cluster around him to listen to his words. Sometimes he would get up at dead of night, say to any devotee found nearby, "Let us listen to the words of the Master in the depth of night as he explains the truth of the *Pranava*," and the dictation and writing of the book would proceed for more than an hour. This happened also three or four days before the end.

There were discourses every morning and evening. In the morning he would get up and sit in the shrine in deep meditation — the eyes half-closed and the beautiful face beaming with heavenly light. Then he would sing some songs, the sweet refrain and tune of which still linger and haunt our mind. Every evening he would come up, take his accustomed seat on the roof, listen to the even-song, and bow down to the Lord; sometimes he would talk to the assembled devotees and sometimes listen to the hymns sung by the devotees after *aratrika* (vesper). Sometimes he would request some particular hymns to be sung.

A few days before his passing away a devotee was singing some song, the tune of which M. heard from his room below. This was a song of the devotees of Nadia bewailing the departure of Sri Chaitanya previous to his Sannyas (monastic vows). M. called the singer to his room and had the song sung in his presence. But he fell into deep meditation and asked the singer to retire. Alas, the song cruelly proved prophetic of the finale!

Sometime earlier, when one of the devotees [*probably Raghavananda, who was then living with M.*] was meditating in front of the shrine, all at once he saw a vision: He saw M. in leisurely gait mounting to a very elevated position and from there trying to jump into the Infinite Vastness; at this the devotee got up and catching him said, "Where are you going?" He narrated this to other devotees; but it was all in fun and he made light of it, thinking that the end would not be so near.[4]

Although M. had been suffering from that neuralgic pain in his hand over a period of eight months, he continued to give final shape to the last volume of the *Kathamrita*. On 8 May 1932 Swami Nityatmananda visited M. at Thakur Bari and noticed his broken health. M. was having milk and bread for his supper. A devotee was heating the salt bag on the top of a hurricane lantern; M. then pressed it to his right elbow with his left hand. Sometimes the pain would start just when M. began a writing session on the *Kathamrita*. When his attendant would ask him to rest, M. would say: "I forget pain when I meditate on the words of the Master. It transports my mind into bliss."[5]

Despite his ill health, every afternoon many visitors would come to M. to listen to his inspiring talk and reminiscences of the Master. On 14 May 1932 M. was working on the fifth volume of the *Kathamrita*, so the devotees were waiting for him on the roof adjacent to the shrine. When he had finished writing, Nityatmananda entered the room. He was alarmed by M.'s emaciated condition. When he expressed his concern, M. replied: "The human body decays and dies at the end — this is an eternal law. The One who is within this body — Satchidananda — is alone free from disease and death. As long as one has a body, one will have to undergo misery. Having this knowledge a devotee should stay in this world. The Master said, "Tie the nondual knowledge in the corner of your cloth and then do as you please in this world."

Nityatmananda: "It is almost dark and you are still writing!"

M.: "Yes, I was really enjoying myself. A fish was taken out of the water and it was about to die; all of a sudden it jumped into the water and swam away. While writing the *Kathamrita*, I forgot my excruciating pain."

M. then attended the vesper service in the shrine.

15 May 1932: M. supervised some plastering and painting work done on Thakur Bari — the Master's house. He never claimed ownership of his own house. He sensed his days were numbered, so he worked quickly to finish his duties. People around him wondered at his tremendous energy and willpower. It is said that a dying swan sings a song. During this time, Nityatmananda heard M. singing the following song of Ramprasad:

I have surrendered my soul at the fearless feet of the Mother;
Am I afraid of Death anymore?
Unto the tuft of hair on my head
Is tied the almighty mantra, Mother Kali's name.
My body I have sold in the market-place of the world
And with it have bought Sri Durga's name.
Deep within my heart I have planted the name of Kali,
The Wish-fulfilling Tree of heaven;
When Yama, King of Death, appears,
To him I shall open my heart and show it growing there.
I have cast out from me my six unflagging foes;
Ready am I to sail life's sea,
Crying, "To Durga, victory!"[6]

M. said: "The Master told me that I would have to do a little work for the Divine Mother. I have been doing that work for the last 50 years, yet She is still not giving me any leave." M. passed away 21 days later.

On the afternoon of 25 May 1932 M. was in his room on the second floor of Thakur Bari. He decided to finish the last appendix of the fifth volume of the *Kathamrita*, so he opened his diary to the entry describing the Brahmo festival at Simulia in Jnan Chaudhury's house, dated 1 January 1882 (18 Paush 1288 B.E). M. had not been present on that occasion, but he had collected a description of the day's events from Manomohan Mitra. Nityatmananda was with M., and he was amazed by M.'s god-given memory and writing ability, and by how he could develop the scene and complete the dialogue with only brief and cryptic notes. He felt that M. had become one with the Master, and he was writing what was appearing in his pure mind. Nityatmananda noticed that M. wrote four pages of the finished description from one and a quarter pages of the diary.

All of a sudden the pain in M.'s arm became acute, and he lay down on the bed. Nityatmananda fanned him, then gave him a piece of rock candy and a glass of water. Slowly the pain subsided and he went to the shrine to attend the vesper service. Afterwards he sat on the roof and met with the devotees. At 9:30 p.m. M. took his supper.

M. lived in two places. Sometimes he stayed in the attic room on the fourth floor of the Morton Institution at 50 Amherst Street. His wife and children lived on the third floor of that building. At other times he lived in Thakur Bari, his ancestral home at 13/2 Guruprasad Chaudhury Lane. When he stayed in Thakur Bari, M. prepared his own food. His menu consisted of rice, a boiled potato, one boiled *patal* [a kind of vegetable], boiled *mung dal* with a little turmeric and salt, and milk and rice for dessert. He ate his lunch at 10:00 a.m. and then rested. Even in his old age, M. was very independent and did not allow others to serve him. He made his own bed and attended to all of his personal tasks.

On the afternoon of 26 May 1932 M. continued his work on the *Kathamrita*, ignoring his pain. That evening he attended the vesper service in the shrine of Thakur Bari. He suffered from excruciating pain that night.

The next morning, M. insisted on removing the rubbish that had been left behind by the masons working on his bathroom in Thakur Bari. Nityatmananda tried to stop him, but M. paid no heed.

After lunch M. dictated to Satinath the chronology of the *Kathamrita*, which was added in the fifth volume. While dictating, M. remarked: "These incidents took place 49 years ago. It seems to me that they happened yesterday. What a deep impression the Master left in our minds!"[7]

Afterwards Nityatmananda told M.: "It is not possible to practise japa and meditation all the time. So I am thinking of visiting the places sanctified by the holy feet of Sri Ramakrishna."

M. joyfully gave his permission and said: "That is a wonderful project. Finish it soon."

Nityatmananda asked: "I need your blessing and guidance. Where shall I start?"

M. suggested that he begin in central Calcutta, where the Master first lived when he moved from Kamarpukur in 1852. M. mentioned 85 places in Calcutta and Dakshineswar, and also on the west bank of the Ganges. Nityatmananda visited those places connected with Sri Ramakrishna and reported to M. every day. Thus M. could mentally revisit those places associated with the Master and get immense joy.

One day Nityatmananda went to visit the Chaitanya Sabha at Colootola, where he met Kunja Mallick, who recounted his encounter with Ramakrishna:

> I was then 16 years old. One day Mani Mallick asked me to go with him to Dakshineswar to see a holy man. Mani Mallick was a friend of my grandfather. When I went to Dakshineswar, the Master gave me some sweets to eat, and another day he fed me a sandesh. Despite receiving his affection, I have achieved nothing. (*Tears came from his eyes.*)
>
> A few things I recall about the Master: His childlike behaviour, blissful mood, and unearthly love. I have never experienced such love in my life.
>
> I vividly remember these two incidents: One afternoon I went to him in Dakshineswar and he was about to go to Calcutta to see Girish Chandra's *Chaitanya Lila*. Seeing me he said: "You have come. Very well. I shall leave now." Saying so, he took a sweet from the cabinet and gave it to me, and blessed me while putting his hand on my head. I was overwhelmed with joy.
>
> Another day Narendra was singing on the floor of the Master's room and he was seated on his small cot — immersed in samadhi. When he regained outer consciousness, he came down and sat on the floor near the southeastern door. Moved with tears, Narendra touched his head to the feet of the Master.[8]

In the early morning of 28 May 1932 M. went for a walk; he returned at 6:00 a.m. Nityatmananda asked him, "Why did you go alone?"

M. replied: "I feel nervous if I do not walk. Perhaps I won't be able to move anymore."

M. then went to the third floor and read the page proofs of Chapters 13 and 14 of Volume 5. He made some additions, altered some sections, and then gave the pages to Nityatmananda who carried them to the Sudha Press.

Ramakrishna had asked M. to work for the Divine Mother, and he did so for fifty years. Even though his health was delicate, he never gave up. Nityatmananda described a touching incident in his memoirs:

I was responsible for the printing of the *Kathamrita* [the Bengali *Gospel*] while it was at the printer's, but I had many things to do and was unable to finish the proofreading in time. At 1:00 a.m. I saw a light in M.'s room. I entered and found he was reading the proofs of the *Gospel* by a kerosene lantern. He was not well at all, and moreover, as he was working at an odd hour, his eyes were watering. I was pained at this. I lovingly chastised him and he replied with affection: "People are finding peace by reading this book, the Master's immortal message. It is inevitable that the body will meet its end, so it is better that it is used for spreading peace to others. We are in the world and have utterly experienced how much pain is there, yet I have forgotten that pain through *The Gospel of Sri Ramakrishna*. I am hurrying so that the book may come out soon." Indeed, M. died while the last portion of the last volume was at the press. He was born to write and teach *The Gospel of Sri Ramakrishna*.[9]

On the morning of 3 June 1932, M. left Thakur Bari and walked to his residence in the Morton Institution (probably a 15-minute walk). He spent some time with his family and then returned to Thakur Bari. After that he prepared and ate his meal as usual, and then rested for a while. In the afternoon he swept his room and the ground floor. When questioned by a devotee, he said, "I am cleaning this place a little." Then he sat down and said, "I am having a little spasm now."

That evening he visited his family in the Morton Institution for a second time, and at 7:30 p.m. he returned to Thakur Bari with his grandson. He became exhausted on the way back to Thakur Bari and had to sit down on the footpath near City College. With great effort he continued his journey on foot. The vesper service was beginning at Thakur Bari. He went to the shrine on the third floor, bowed down to the Master, and then went to his room.

It was Amābashyā, the new moon night, and the auspicious night of Phalaharini Kali Puja. M. sent Raghavananda and Satinath to Gadadhar Ashrama in South Calcutta, saying: "There will be Kali Puja at the Ashrama all night tonight. Please go and attend the worship. One can achieve the result of a thousand years' austerity by doing sadhana on this auspicious night." When they had left, M. returned to the shrine. Brahmachari Balai was then putting the Lord to bed. M. bowed down to the Master for the last time. He went to the open roof and looked at the bright stars in the dark night, which transported his mind to the realm of the Infinite. He then looked in all directions from the roof of his dear Thakur Bari as if to say "good-bye" to everything. He noticed that a wedding ceremony was being held on the roof of his neighbour's house to the south, and the pandal was beautifully decorated with multi-coloured lights.

At 9:30 p.m. M. came downstairs and ate his last supper: Two pieces of Punjabi bread with milk, some vegetables, and two pieces of *Langra* mango that were prasad. After supper he washed his hands and rinsed his mouth. He then said to Balai: "Please put the hurricane lamp on the table. I shall read the proof."

M. loved holy company and enjoyed talking about the Master, so he was always surrounded by monks and devotees. Some of them even lived with him. On that night, however, M. had sent everyone except Brahmachari Balai to Belur Math, Dakshineswar, and Gadadhar Ashrama. At 9:45 p.m. Balai went to his home nearby for supper and returned at 10:30. He found M. asleep under his mosquito curtain. He then went upstairs to the shrine and began repeating his mantra. Within five minutes M. loudly called to Balai, who came immediately. He helped M. to use the toilet.

M. was suffering from excruciating pain, so Balai heated the salt bag on the top of the kerosene lantern and pressed it to his arm. M. tossed around on the floor, leaning on the wall till 12:00 p.m. He was perspiring profusely. Finally, he asked Balai to call Sidu and Nishu, M.'s closest neighbours. Sidu did not respond but Nishu came. Balai asked Nishu to summon Ami, M.'s nephew, who also lived nearby. Ami was told that M. was stricken with nausea, so he brought some carbonated soda water. M. drank the entire bottle.

Ami then went to the Morton Institution to inform Prabhas, M.'s eldest son, who rushed to see his father along with M.'s two grandsons. M. asked them to spread a white blanket on the floor of his room; and he lay there on his right side, facing the east. He was having terrible pain in both of his elbows. One person pressed the heated salt bag to the spots that were paining, while someone else fanned him, another massaged him, and another attendant wiped away perspiration from him with a towel. From time to time he prayed, "Mother, my work is done." He was trying to sit in a yoga posture, but the pain prevented him. He prayed, "Gurudeva, Mother, please take me in your arms." Thus he struggled till 2:30 a.m. His upper body was bare and he was rolling on the floor, pressing his chest.

Dr. Dhiren arrived at 4:00 a.m. He offered a pill to M., but he refused to take it. He was fully conscious. Throughout his life he had been reluctant to accept service from others, and now seeing so many people caring for him, he told his grandchildren, "You go and sleep." At 5:00 a.m. his wife, Nikunja Devi, arrived. M. felt a little chilled, so a chadar was spread over him. Then M. asked to be put in bed. At 5:15 he threw up, and then slowly his restlessness began to subside. His body became calm, and his face became serene and luminous. He began having difficulty breathing, and he said, "This body will not last." He then turned on his left side and said in a clear voice: "Guru Deva — Mother — take me up in your arms." Five minutes later, M. passed away of a heart attack. It was 5:30 a.m. on Saturday, 4 June 1932 (21 Jaishtha 1339 B.E.).

M.'s mind had always dwelt in the Master, so his soul flew to the eternal abode of Ramakrishna. The enchanting voice of the Bhagavata Pandit, which had spread the divine message of Ramakrishna for nearly half a century, became silent.

Within an hour the sad news of M.'s passing away was phoned to Belur Math, and then it spread all over Calcutta and to the other centres of the Ramakrishna Order. Swami Shivananda, the president of the Ramakrishna Order, sent from Belur Math a silk cloth and chadar for M.'s funeral. Many monks from Belur Math and other Ramakrishna centres and also devotees rushed to the Thakur Bari to pay their homage and to have a last glimpse of a great soul. M.'s wife, sons, grandchildren, and other family members and neighbours wept bitterly. They all talked about M.'s love and care for them.

M.'s body was in his room. The monks were continually singing devotional songs, and then at 11:00 a.m. they began to prepare M.'s body for the final journey. Swami Pranavananda wiped M.'s face with a wet towel soaked in Ganges water; others carefully replaced his cloth with the silk cloth and chadar sent by Swami Shivananda. One monk put sandal paste on M.'s forehead and a garland around his neck. His body was covered with lotuses and roses. Swami Raghavananda waved a lamp with five wicks and also a camphor lamp before M.'s body. Swami Pranavananda also offered incense. Monks, a German devotee named Miss Feper, as well as teachers and brahmacharinis from the Nivedita School, offered flowers. A new cot and a bed with a canopy were made ready outside on Guruprasad Chaudhury Lane (because the entrance of Thakur Bari was very narrow). M.'s body was transferred to a new thin carpet and the monks carried it from his room to the cot outside. People showered his body with flowers and perfume.

The journey began. Despite the summer heat and the hot pavement, the monks and devotees carried M.'s cot on their shoulders, barefooted, chanting, "Victory to Bhagavan Sri Ramakrishna." A kirtan party followed behind the cot, singing continuously. Thousands of people followed the procession, with even more people joining on the way as they heard that M., the author of the *Kathamrita*, had passed away. Prabhas asked the coffin bearers to stop at the Morton Institution, where M. had lived for 25 years. The cot was placed in the courtyard of the school, and M.'s eldest sister tearfully hugged her brother one last time. Other neighbours also visited him.

The funeral procession resumed, passing through Maniktala and Beadon Street. When it arrived at Cornwallis Street (now Bidhan Sarani), traffic stopped for some time. The procession then crossed Tala Bridge, passed near the Cossipore garden house, and finally arrived at the Cossipore cremation ground where Ramakrishna's body had been cremated on 16 August 1886. M.'s body was placed to the east of Ramakrishna's monument, with his head towards the south. Some footprints were taken with red paint. Many men, women, and young people then offered flowers at M.'s feet.

Monks and devotees rubbed M.'s body with pure ghee, placed it on a carpet, and carried it into the Ganges for a bath. Meanwhile the funeral pyre was set up with heaps of sandalwood just to the south of Ramakrishna's monument, and M.'s body was placed on it with his head towards the north. At 6:00 p.m. Prabhas offered sacrificial cakes and then set the pyre alight. Monks and devotees waved incense and lighted camphor, and chanted "Hari Om Ram Ram." Swami Kamaleswarananda stood near the funeral pyre and chanted Rudra mantras from the Vedas.

By 8:00 p.m. M.'s body had been consumed by the fire god, and the monks came forward to extinguish the fire with coconut water, yogurt, and Ganges water. They then recited the peace mantra of the Yajur Veda: "Filled with Brahman are the things we see. Filled with Brahman are the things we see not. From out of Brahman floweth all that is: yet is He still the same. Om Peace, Peace, Peace."

Swami Shivananda had sent a message that M.'s remains were to be preserved in Belur Math, so the monks had brought two copper containers. Balai, along with two monks, collected the bones, washed them with Ganges water, and put them in the containers. An altar was made with Ganges mud on the spot where M.'s body had been cremated and a fence was set up all around it. Before this, the devotees had received permission from the Calcutta Corporation to preserve that spot for M.'s monument.

M.'s monument at Cossipore cremation ground, next to Ramakrishna's on the right. Belur Math is visible on the west side of the Ganges.

Charu, M.'s youngest son, was out of town. When he received the sad news, he came straight to the cremation ground. But as it was too late to see the body, he returned with his brother and other relatives to their home.

Swamis Jitatmananda and Nityatmananda crossed the Ganges with the copper containers containing M.'s relics; a portion of the remaining relics was immersed in the middle of the Ganges. The next day M.'s relics were worshiped along with the worship of the Master. Swami Shivananda then asked Swamis Jitatmananda and Nityatmananda to carry the containers to Swamiji's temple. Later, when Ramakrishna's new temple was built, M.'s relics were taken to the upper floor of the temple, where the relics of the Master's other disciples are kept.

Once Girish Ghosh had asked M.: "What is the foremost ambition in your life?"

M. replied with a smile, quoting a Bengali proverb: "If I go to my father's house, I shall take my husband with me."*

M.'s greatest desire was to always remain in the Master's company. So the Master fulfilled his wish: Even after M.'s death, the Master kept his remains near him.

On 5 June 1932 Swami Shivananda consoled the bereaved Nityatmananda, who had been very close to M. for many years. Shivananda said: "M. belonged to the Master, and he came to fulfill Sri Ramakrishna's mission. When M.'s task was over, the Master took him in his arms. Indeed, M.'s physical body is gone, but look at those volumes [*pointing to the set of the* Kathamrita *in his shelf*]. They will proclaim his immortal glory forever. As long as there will be a sun and a moon, Sri Ramakrishna's name will be acclaimed on this earth, and along with it M.'s name — the recorder of *The Gospel of Sri Ramakrishna*."[10]

---

*This refers to a bride speaking to her friends, indicating that she does not want to be separated from her husband.

ABOVE: Steps leading from the second floor up to M.'s shrine. LEFT: Entrance to M.'s house with the sign "Kathamrita Bhavan." M. called it Thakur Bari (the house of the Master).

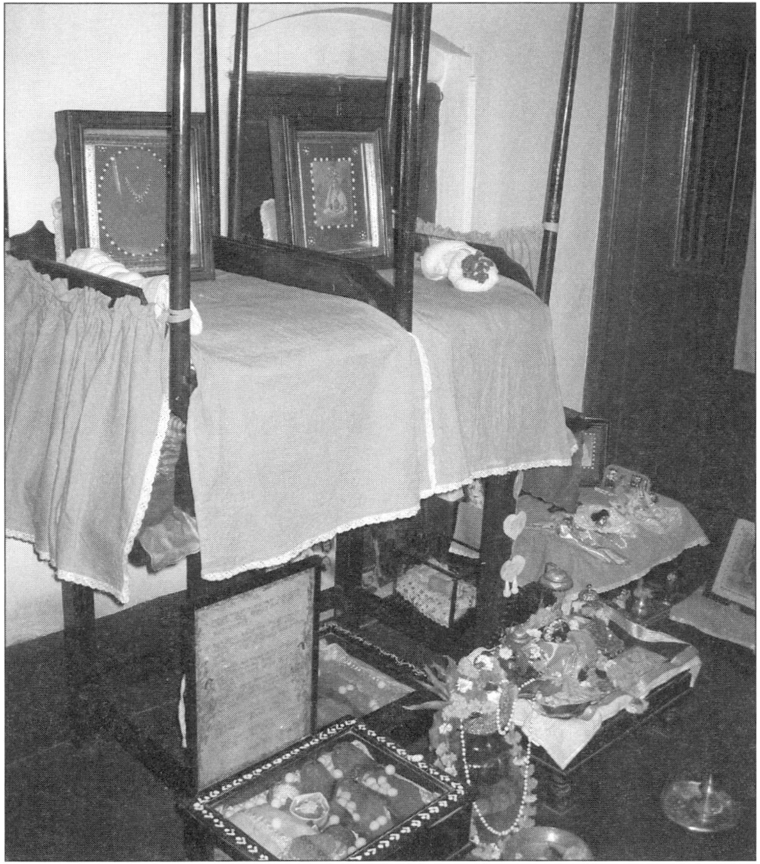

ABOVE: Sri Chandi Mangal Ghat installed by Holy Mother on 6 October 1888. LEFT: M.'s shrine with one of the original pictures of Ramakrishna and some of the Master's relics (ashes, nail, and hair) in the glass case

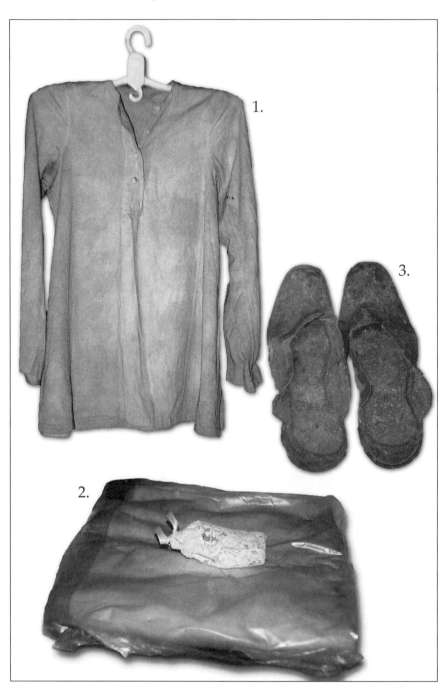

Articles used by Ramakrishna: 1. Shirt, 2. Moleskin Shawl, 3. Shoes

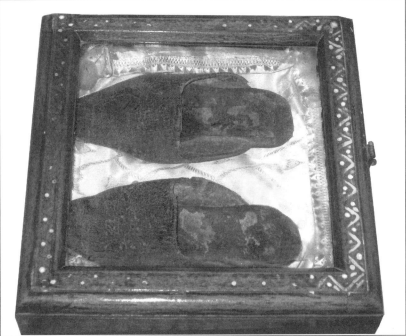

Top: M.'s bedroom on the second floor where Holy Mother stayed and where M. later passed away. Bottom: M.'s shoes

ABOVE: A painting of a nesting bird visualized by Ramakrishna which M. commissioned after his passing away. Regarding the background of this patinting, see page 43.

RIGHT: Roof garden at M.'s house where M., Vivekananda, and other disciples meditated.

Photos in the order that they appeared in the 1920 Bengali edition of *The Gospel of Sri Ramakrishna* published by M:

TOP LEFT: Ishwar Chandra Vidyasagar, TOP RIGHT: Keshab Chandra Sen
BOTTOM LEFT: Vijaykrishna Goswami, BOTTOM RIGHT: Dr. Mahendralal Sarkar

Reminiscences of
Mahendranath Gupta

Swami Satprakashananda

It was at the end of January 1908 that I first had the opportunity to leave my home city, Dhaka — at that time the capital of the province of East Bengal and Assam — for a trip to Calcutta, which was then the capital of British India and of West Bengal. I was in my first year at an intermediate college located in Dhaka that was affiliated with the University of Calcutta. I came to Calcutta, accompanied by a relative, with a concession travelling ticket of about ten days, mainly for the purpose of pilgrimage.

While Dhaka is situated on the river Budiganga, Calcutta is situated on the Ganges, which derives from the Bhagirathi, the main stream of the Ganges. According to Hindu astrology there was to be a rare auspicious day for a sacred bath in the Ganges on account of a solar eclipse at dawn. The auspicious day happened to be, as far as I can recall, on Monday, 3 February 1908. The day was further sanctified by the special position of a notable constellation. Most probably I arrived in Calcutta on Saturday, 1 February.

Being closely connected with the Ramakrishna movement at Dhaka from an early age, I was familiar with the names of most of the people and places associated with the life of Ramakrishna, and within the reach of Calcutta. I had had the good fortune to see Swami Vivekananda for three days when he visited Dhaka in March 1901. I also had the privilege of carrying on the work of the Ramakrishna Association of Dhaka since the autumn of 1905. In our meetings held every Saturday evening we used to read *The Gospel of Sri Ramakrishna* (the *Kathamrita*), and then sing some devotional songs.

Upon my arrival in Calcutta, I naturally felt compelled to meet M., Master Mahashay, the author of *The Gospel of Sri Ramakrishna*, who lived in the city not far from where I was staying. It was early evening (probably Saturday, 1 February) when I went by streetcar to his residence in Calcutta. As I entered the house I inquired about Master Mahashay. I was told to walk up to the fourth floor by way of the brick stairway in front of the building.

When I reached the fourth floor I found Master Mahashay seated with a group of devotees inside a porch before the attic, which was used as the shrine. I was surprised to see a close friend of mine, known as Sagar Babu, reading *The Gospel of Sri Ramakrishna*. I thought to myself, "How strange, he who has written the *Gospel* has been listening to it being read, like a pupil!

I was very happy to see my friend there. Sagar Babu had come from Dhaka to Calcutta to study medical science. After the reading was over there was a short discussion and then the devotees left, except for Sagar Babu, who greeted me and introduced me to Master Mahashay as a close friend of his who was intimately connected with the Ramakrishna Association at Dhaka.

After he had also left, Master Mahashay talked with me and inquired about the Ramakrishna Association at Dhaka. Then he told me to go inside the shrine and get the small metal glass of offered water and a piece of offered sandesh on a small metal plate. As directed by him, I went outside on the porch and drank the offered water and ate the offered sandesh.

As I was going to sit down before Master Mahashay again within the porch, he inquired: "Where did you put the plate? Where is the glass?" I told him that I had left them outside on the porch. "No, no," he said. "This will not do. You should wash them." Then I walked down the stairs to the ground floor, where there was a faucet. With quick steps I returned. Master Mahashay told me to dry the glass and the plate and put both of them in their proper places, in the proper order. At the same time he told me that Thakur [Ramakrishna] was very orderly, neat, and clean. He used to put things in such a way that one could find them even in the dark of night. (In those days there were no electric lights.)

Then Master Mahashay made further inquiries about me and our activities at Dhaka. I said: "We are trying to establish an Ashrama at Dhaka on the outskirts of the city. Our friend, Sagar Babu, who has married into a very wealthy family, has granted us several acres of land for this purpose. We have already started a centre there with a cottage, and one of our young associates who wants to be a monk has been living there."

I further told Master Mahashay that our plan was to establish temples there of different religions in accordance with Thakur's teaching of the harmony of religions. With great enthusiasm I said that there would be on the same site a Hindu temple, a Muslim mosque, a Christian church, and a Buddhist temple. I added that gradually there would be temples of other religions, and that there would be an appropriate sign on each of the temples. Further, at the monastery gate a big signboard "The Temple of Harmony of Religions" would be fixed. I spoke with youthful enthusiasm and Master Mahashay listened quietly.

When I stopped speaking, Master Mahashay responded: "This is what you want, signboards and advertisements — self-advertisement. This is not Thakur's idea. According to Thakur one should gather something here within the heart [*pointing his finger to his heart*] before one launches into public work. First of all you should have devotion to God. Until you have that you are nowhere. You are simply *frittering away* your energies, *frittering away* your energies. Thakur said, again and again, that one should pray to God in solitude and secrecy (*nirjane gopane*)."

"*Nirjane gopane,*" he repeated several times. He then quoted a parallel passage from the Bible: "But thou, when thou prayest, enter into thy closet, and when thou hast shut thy door, pray to thy Father which is in secret; and thy Father which seeth in secret shall reward thee openly." (Matthew 6:6) I kept quiet. I could not say a single word.

Then Master Mahashay said to me: "Since you have come to Calcutta for the first time you should see the Holy Mother, Rakhal Maharaj, and Baburam Maharaj. You must visit Belur Math and Dakshineswar." I already had planned to visit these holy places and bow down to the holy personages.

I had to return to Dhaka in about a week. But each time I had an occasion to go to Calcutta I made it a point to see Master Mahashay and bow down to him. However, that was the first and last time that Master Mahashay scolded me. After that he always received me cordially and often treated me with two rasagollas (cheese balls soaked in syrup) offered to Sri Ramakrishna. From the second time on, I usually met him on the fourth floor of the Morton Institution on Amherst Street [now Rammohan Sarani], of which he was the proprietor and rector. Once I met him at Belur Math. I do not remember the details of each visit but he invariably talked about Sri Ramakrishna.

In December 1911 I visited Calcutta for the second time. I was a fifth-year graduate student. I came to Calcutta on a concession ticket with a group of my classmates, on the occasion of the visit of Emperor George V of England.

I took the earliest opportunity to see Master Mahashay, and walked up to the fourth floor of the Morton Institution to meet him. He was alone at that time. In the course of conversation I said that Thakur used to see the Divine Mother. Master Mahashay gravely told me: "No, not *seeing* only! The Divine Mother *talked* with him and he used to talk with the Divine Mother, just as we are talking!"

On several occasions I found him reading one or another Vedanta book. On my arrival he would pass the book to me, asking me to read some of the pages. After the reading was over he would talk a little while on the topic and then on Sri Ramakrishna. His purpose was to avoid vain talk. One day I found him reading *Yogavasistha Ramayana* (the Bengali translation). When I came in he asked me to read a few pages of the book.

One other occasion I remember as well as the first one. It was in 1924, in early winter. I was returning from a pilgrimage to the Himalayas and to several holy places in northwestern India. From Hardwar I had gone to Badarika Ashrama on the Alakananda, and then visited the temple of Kedarnath on the Mandakini. On my return I lived for about a month at Hardwar on the Ganges, and I spent the next month in our Sevashrama (Home of Service) at Kankhal. Then after a short stay at our Kishenpur Ashrama, a monastic retreat near Dehradun, I went on a pilgrimage to Amarnath in Kashmir with a party of four monastic brothers.

On my way back to Calcutta I visited a number of holy places in Kashmir, the Punjab, and the northwestern provinces. I particularly wanted to visit Naimisharanya, where Suta Goswami had related the Srimad Bhagavata before an audience of sixty thousand people, including many saints and sages. The main story of the Srimad Bhagavata was narrated originally by Shukadeva (a born-free soul) to King Parikshit on the eve of his leaving the body. Suta Goswami was present among the audience.

From Lucknow I came to the small railroad station in Balamo. From Balamo I walked up to Naimisharanya. There I saw the extensive meadow where the audience of sixty thousand had gathered. In one part of this meadow there were a few water tanks and temples.

On my way back I visited a few other places, including Varanasi, and then came to Calcutta. When I went to see Master Mahashay, he inquired about my pilgrimage. He showed particular interest in Naimisharanya, and asked me how I went there and what kind of place it was. Then he remarked, "Ah, so many holy places you have seen! Had Thakur seen you, he would have gone into samadhi, but I do not go into samadhi!"

From this time on I lived for several years at the Dhaka Ashrama, Mayavati Ashrama, and the Delhi centre. Whenever I happened to be in Calcutta I invariably saw Master Mahashay. During most of my visits I met one or more of the three devoted pupils of Master Mahashay: Gadadhar, Vinay, and Jagabandhu.

Master Mahashay had deep regard for the monastic ideal. After he came to know of my decision to enter into monastic life he would never allow me to touch his feet when I bowed down to him. He spoke very highly of sincere monks. In his opinion a householder and a monk can both be highly advanced in spiritual life, yet there will still be a difference between the two as between two ripe mangoes (or apples) of two different grades.

The last time I saw Master Mahashay was in the summer of 1931, when Mahapurush Maharaj (Swami Shivananda) sent me back to Delhi to take charge of the work there. On the eve of my departure for Delhi, one evening I came to the Morton Institution on Amherst Street and asked to see Master Mahashay. Someone escorted me to his bedroom with his permission. He was ill and in bed. When he came to know about my going to Delhi, he greeted me as I bowed down to him. He passed away on 4 June 1932.

[Taken from *Sri Ramakrishna's Life and Message in the Present Age* by Swami Satprakashananda (Vedanta Society: St. Louis, 1976), 106-12]

Gokuldas Dey

I first met M. (Master Mahashay) one afternoon in March 1910 on the fourth floor of the Morton Institution. A devotee opened the door and escorted me to him. He was seated wearing an ordinary dhoti (cloth), half around his waist and half covering his upper body. He was tall and had a fair complexion, a broad chest, large eyes, and a long beard falling down his chest like that of a rishi. His ecstatic mood created a deep spiritual atmosphere there. He would not allow anyone to bow down to him, so when I saluted him with folded hands, he saluted me in the same way and said, "Please sit down."

After exchanging a few words, he said: "Do you know what the Master [Sri Ramakrishna] has given us — what we have received from him? Burning faith." This he indicated with a gesture of his hand, which I still can clearly see. Shortly afterwards he began to hum a song, gazing upward and with one hand on his head. He then sang:

> O King of Kings, reveal Thyself to me!
> I crave Thy mercy. Cast on me Thy glance!
> At Thy dear feet I dedicate my life,
> Seared in the fiery furnace of this world.

After finishing the song, M. said: "When Swamiji sang this song the Master went into samadhi. Do you know how to sing? Please learn. In the beginning I was very shy and could not sing in front of the Master. Later he made me sing with him. The Master said: 'Shame, hatred, and fear are bondages. As long as one has these, one cannot have God-realization.'"

M. knew one of my brothers. He inquired about me and expressed his joy that I had finished my intermediate examination. He then offered some sweets to the Master and gave me that prasad. I shall never forget his loving care.

A few days later I returned and found him preparing the manuscript of *Sri Ramakrishna Kathamrita*, Volume 4. Holding some old papers with small type, he was dictating and a young devotee was writing. When he came to a song, he sang it as he dictated. He continued: "The sight of Kedar awakened in the Master's mind the episode of Vrindaban in Sri Krishna's life. Intoxicated with divine love, the Master stood up and sang, addressing Kedar:

> Tell me, friend, how far is the grove
> Where Krishna, my Beloved, dwells?
> His fragrance reaches me even here;
> But I am tired and can walk no farther."

M. sang this song to a kirtan tune and it sounded very sweet to me.

When the dictation was over, M. said: "You see, I have never heard as sweet a voice as Swamiji's, but the Master's voice was even sweeter than his." I asked how many volumes of the *Kathamrita* he expected there to be. He replied, "If the Master wishes, it could be eight to ten volumes."

He asked me: "Do you meditate? Do you go to Udbodhan? Please visit Belur Math — it is the fort of the Master's battalion. Wherever there is famine, epidemic, flood — these monks go there to fight. Their goal is to save human beings from natural calamities. Don't think they enjoy an idle life there. First one should realize God by practising japa and meditation in solitude, and then sacrifice one's life for others. God-realization is not possible without renouncing lust and gold. For that reason Swamiji set the ideal of renunciation and sent the boys to the Himalayas for practising japa and meditation. The monks of Belur Math have practised many spiritual disciplines. You should have their company." I listened quietly to him.

I secretly wished to take dictation of the *Kathamrita* from him, and I expressed my desire to him. He gave me permission and asked me to come another day. After a couple of days, I returned and wrote a page of the *Kathamrita*. M. dictated it slowly and seriously, and it took half an hour to write one page.

One year passed. I went to Rangoon to study for my B.A. degree. In April 1911 I returned to Calcutta and again visited M. He lived in the school building on the fourth floor, with his family on the third floor. M. presented me a copy of the *Kathamrita*, Volume 4. From the high roof of the school building one could see a great distance, and this would, according to him, give one an idea of the infinite. Sitting on the roof every evening till 9 or 10 o'clock, M. would meet devotees and practise sad-hana with them. Here are two of the songs that M. would sing with those devotees:

Chant, O mind, the name of Hari,
Sing aloud the name of Hari,
Praise Lord Hari's name!
And praising Hari's name, O mind,
Cross the ocean of this world.
Hari dwells in earth, in water,
Hari dwells in fire and air;
In sun and moon He dwells,
Hari's ever-living presence
Fills the boundless universe.

*   *   *

Can everyone have the vision of Shyama? Is Kali's treasure for everyone?
Oh, what a pity my foolish mind will not see what is true!
Even with all His penances, rarely does Shiva Himself behold
The mind-bewitching sight of Mother Shyama's crimson feet.
To him who meditates on Her the riches of heaven are poor indeed;
If Shyama casts Her glance on him, he swims in Eternal Bliss.
The Prince of yogis, the King of gods, meditate on Her feet in vain;
Yet worthless Kamalakanta yearns for the Mother's blessed feet!

M. used to sing slowly and his beautiful voice had sweetness and power. He would sing with closed eyes and keep one hand on the top of his head as if he was seeing someone inside. Afterwards he would make a brief comment: "The Master said: 'Is it possible to understand God? We cannot understand either His good aspect or His bad aspect. Is it possible to hold ten seers of water in a one-seer jar? What can you do? Meditate on Him and sing His glories. Practise this kind of devotion.'"

I heard that Ramakrishna would provide travelling expenses to the schoolboys who visited him. M. followed that tradition. After kirtan (devotional singing) he would ask his school superintendent, "Fakir Babu, please follow our custom." Fakir Babu gave six pice to M., who then handed that to me and said: "You return home by tram car. Don't think it is a luxury. The energy that you will spend for walking use instead for your study and meditation." When I objected one day, he said: "Look, when you become a deputy magistrate, then you can return this money." Then he interjected, "I hope you will never become a deputy magistrate."

M. loved to live alone. Although he had a substantial income at that time, his room was simple. There was a bed on a small cot, heaps of books and papers on a table, and a mat on the floor. If one or two people came to see him, he would sit with them on the mat and talk about God. His style of living and dress were simple, as were his eating habits. At night he would eat a small loaf of Great Eastern Hotel [bread] with milk.

In the evening, when a devotee lit the lamp and burned incense in his room, he would stop talking and silently repeat the mantra. He did not go to a separate place for meditation. Afterwards he would start to talk about God and sing kirtan. Quoting from the Mundaka Upanishad (2:2:5), he said, "'Know that nondual Atman alone and give up all other talk.' Don't talk about anything other than God. The Master said, 'The goal of human life is to realize God.' All other activities should be performed in order to achieve that goal. Christ said: 'Seek ye first the kingdom of God and his righteousness and all these things shall be added unto you.'" (Matthew: 6:33)

M. considered Belur Math and Dakshineswar to be the two most important holy places. If any visitors came from there to him, he would stop talking and remark: "Ah, blessed you are! You are coming from those holy places. I am old and cannot go there, so I am blessed with your company." We were amazed by his unfathomable faith and devotion. During festival times he would visit Belur Math. As he watched the devotees eat the Master's prasad, he would remark, "The Master is eating through so many mouths." Upon seeing the huge crowd he said, "One can have an awakening of God-consciousness when one sees such a vast crowd."

M. visited the Udbodhan house frequently whenever Holy Mother returned from Jayrambati. One day he saw me at the Udbodhan and remarked, "At the advent of spring, the cuckoos come." M. realized that Holy Mother was the veritable Divine Mother, and this was apparent in his actions and behaviour. The devotees would wait downstairs to make obeisance to Holy Mother; but when M. came he would bow down and touch his head to the floor of the Udbodhan house for a while, with tearful eyes. Then, when visiting time began, M. would go upstairs to bow down to Holy Mother. She looked upon M. as her son and treated him affectionately, touching his chin. It was worth seeing how the elderly M. behaved with Holy Mother as though he were a child.

Generally *prasad* means offered food that God has accepted; and if anyone partakes of it, God is pleased and does good to him. One day at Udbodhan M. explained: "Do you know what prasad is? Prasad means that God is pleased, not that He will be pleased later."

How M. would use various means to make God his own! When he went near the Ganges, he bowed down for a long time with his head touching the ground. He considered the river Ganges to be the Divine Mother Herself. One day he said: "It is as if Mother Ganges is saying, in the words of Jesus Christ, 'Come unto me all ye that labour and are heavy laden, and I will give you rest.'" At that time some labourers were bathing in the Ganges after a long day of hard labour. They returned home after thus easing their weariness. We see this kind of scene every day, but how many of us are reminded of the Divine Mother's blessing by seeing people bathe?

M. was very particular about discipline in the school. One day he brought a student into his office and said to me, "This boy is not amenable to discipline." He also required the office workers to obey their leader's orders wholeheartedly. He humorously called modern democracy a "mobocracy." Because he had a difference of opinion with the authorities of Calcutta University regarding the formation of the school committee, the university revoked his school's affiliation. As a result, he gladly closed the ninth and tenth grades at his school, which reduced his income substantially. When I asked why he had not agreed to the university's proposal, he replied: "Who wants to live without freedom?" He ultimately maintained his own policy and held to the ideals of his institution.

I never heard him say anything about his family. One day his eldest son (Prabhas Gupta) was pacing in the courtyard with a big stack of ten rupee notes (bills) and waiting for the gatekeeper to bring his bag from upstairs. He was going to the bank to deposit the money. Pointing to him, M. said to me: "See the power of money! Its heat is making him pace back and forth in the courtyard and not allowing him to stand still. Is money an ordinary thing? Sometimes a son shoots his father for money." Dumbfounded, I thought that an ordinary father could not say such things, citing the example of his own successful son. I could not figure out how he considered his own dutiful son to be a stranger.

Every evening M. would meet devotees on the roof of the fourth floor of the Morton Institution and spend time in meditation and singing the glory of God. Sometimes he would talk about the Master, Swamiji, and himself. The following statements of his were deeply imprinted on my mind:

"Listen, those who sincerely call on God have to come to the Master.

"If the devotees tell their own stories, you will understand what we did. When I was tormented with worldly problems, I called on God wholeheartedly and then tried to commit suicide when I thought that there was no God. At that juncture the Master came into my life.

"Human beings crawl over this earth like short-lived worms. Watching them, what will you decide to do [with your life]? Call on God and shed tears. He will reveal Himself to you. Then only will you understand what your duty is.

"Some people are eager to give lectures. But who will listen to them? Swamiji gave lectures after receiving the command from God. He once said to me: 'People fight for different ideologies, but knowing God one knows everything, for all contradictions meet in Him.'

"Have you seen the mango tree in the courtyard of the old shrine at Belur Math? There was a wooden bench under that tree and Swamiji quite often used to sit there. One day as Swamiji sat on that bench he said to me: 'Master Mahashay, Western people have taken away all my energy. This present body has broken down.' He was not well at that time, and he was hinting to me that he would not live long." As M. said that, tears came from his eyes. He thought awhile and then said: "Do you think they [*meaning the direct disciples*] have gone away? They still exist. We shall see them again."

[Translated from *Srima Samipe*, edited by Swami Chetanananda (Udbodhan Office: Calcutta, 1996), 49-58]

Lalit Bandyopadhyay

One of my lawyer friends came to see me one day and accidentally left a copy of the first volume of *Sri Ramakrishna Kathamrita* at my house. Providence smiled. It is amazing what transpired because of this insignificant event. Like other Westernized Bengalis, I was very fond of English literature and did not care for Bengali writers. After supper, I began reading the *Kathamrita* out of curiosity. I was so moved that I continued reading till 3:00 a.m. My eyes forgot sleep; my body forgot rest; and my mind was full of joy and sweetness. I finished the first volume quickly, and when my friend returned, I asked him, "Could you lend me the other volumes of the *Kathamrita*?"

My friend sarcastically replied: "My goodness! You enjoyed reading a Bengali book as much as the books of Western writers! I am glad that you have changed your mind. It is the Master's grace. I shall give you the other three volumes." After reading the other volumes of the *Kathamrita*, I wanted to meet the author.

One afternoon I went to the Morton Institution to meet M. The gatekeeper directed me to his room. There an old man was seated on the floor, grading students' papers, and a young man was seated near him. I saluted him; he also saluted me and asked me to sit on a grass mat. He asked me several questions: "Where do you live? What do you do? Are you married? How many children do you have?"

When I answered all those questions, he asked: "Why have you come here? Do you have any questions?"

I replied: "Yes, sir. I have no peace of mind."

M. laughed and addressed the young man: "Did you hear what this gentleman says? He is living in the world and complaining that he has no peace. He is drinking a big bottle of wine and asking, 'Why am I drunk?'"

Then M. asked me: "Do you know any songs? Why don't you sing a song to the Master?"

"Sir, I don't know any songs," I replied.

M. smiled and said: "Generally everyone knows some songs, but some are too shy to open their mouths. Do you know the song that Narendra sang when he first met Sri Ramakrishna?"

"I don't know it, sir."

"Then please listen:

Let us go back once more, O mind, to our own abode!
Here in this foreign land of earth
Why should we wander aimlessly in stranger's guise?...
Companionship with holy men will be for you
A welcome rest-house by the road;
There rest your weary limbs awhile....
If anything along the path should frighten you,
Then loudly shout the name of the Lord;
For He is Ruler of that road,
And even Death must bow to Him."

It was a long song and M. sang it in its entirety. This song revealed what was in his heart. I was very impressed and my heart grew full as I watched M.'s joyful face.

M. smiled, and said: "The idea behind this song is wonderful! Can anyone be happy leaving his own home and living in a foreign land? In this world sufferings never end. For that reason, God created monasteries, where worldly people can get peace by listening to His words. It is like the government installing drinking water faucets by the side of the road, so that travellers can drink water when they are thirsty."

After a while, M. said: "The Master was very fond of Narendra's singing. Narendra also sang this song:

Immerse yourself for evermore, O mind,
In Him who is Pure Knowledge and Pure Bliss."

M. then sang the song, creating a wonderful divine atmosphere.

Although I have not seen Sri Ramakrishna, I saw M., who recorded the Master's words and so many beautiful scenes in the *Kathamrita*.

It was evening. We heard the sound of conches from the neighbouring homes.

"This is the time for prayer," M. said, smiling. He set aside the students' examination papers, and continued: "The Muslims are very particular with their prayers: They pray to Allah punctually five times a day. A Muslim mason may be working on a roof or a Muslim driver may be driving a car, but at the time for prayer, they stop work and pray. The

Master was very fond of them for that reason. It is important to think of God in the evening."

M. sat on an asana and began to repeat his mantra silently. There was a picture of Chaitanya hanging on the wall. The young devotee lit the kerosene lantern and waved incense in front of the gods and goddesses. Other devotees came and sat on grass mats to join the group meditation. A peaceful silence pervaded the room. I had found an oasis in the desert of the world. When the meditation was over, I got up.

"Do you want to go now?" M. asked. "All right. Whenever you have time, please visit us."

"Sir, please bless me so that I shall come back soon."

"Please pray to the Master."

After four or five days I returned to M., who was talking to devotees at the time. I bowed down to him. When he saw me, he smiled and remarked, "He has come again." He then recounted that old story of the opium-addicted peacock that the Master had told on his second visit. That day I stayed till the end of his evening gathering. From then on I attended M.'s holy gatherings regularly and learned many things about spiritual life.

March 1917, Shivaratri (Spring Festival of Shiva)

In the morning I went to the fourth floor of the Morton Institution and found M. seated on a bench with two monks and some devotees. He was listening to the song of Shiva that Swami Vivekananda had composed:

> There Shiva dances. Striking both His cheeks; and they resound *ba-ba-bom*!
> *Dimi-dimi-dimi* sounds His drum; a garland of skulls from His neck is hanging!
> In His matted locks the Ganges hisses; fire shoots from His mighty trident!
> Round His waist a serpent glitters, and on His brow the moon is shining!

Everyone sang that song in chorus three times as M. clapped to maintain the rhythm.

"What a wonderful song!" M. said. He continued: "And what a great idea! Today is Shivaratri, an auspicious day. Lord Shiva will be worshipped in Nepal, Vaidyanath, Varanasi, Tarakeswar, Dakshineswar, and Belur Math. The devotees will fast all day and then perform worship four times throughout the night. The story of the hunter in the Purana is wonderful. The cruel hunter committed many sins killing innocent animals, but without being aware of it, he worshipped Lord Shiva on Shivaratri night.* When he died, Shiva's attendants pushed aside the minions of Yama [the god of death] and took the hunter's soul to the abode of Shiva. So the Master would say, 'Whether you know it or not, your mouth will burn if you bite a chili.'

"Once on Shivaratri I went to Tarakeswar, gave the priest a rupee, and worshipped the Lord by touching the image. When the Master heard my story, he joyfully said, 'Very well, you paid one rupee to touch Lord Mahadeva.'

"Lord Shiva will be worshipped all night in Dakshineswar and at Belur Math. It is wonderful to see the monks and devotees fasting and worshipping the Lord. The Master would tell his devotees, 'Those who work in an office should eat some fruit instead of a regular meal of rice.' He could not bear to hear of women fasting. If any woman devotee, especially a widow, visited the Master on Ekadashi [a day of fasting], he would first feed her prasad and then talk to her. He considered all women to be part of the Divine Mother. The Master also said, 'If someone's mind remains on the stomach, that person cannot concentrate on God.' Let us go and visit Mother Siddheswari in Thanthania."

M. and the devotees crossed Amherst Street and then walked through Bechu Chatterjee Street. M. pointed to the Shyamsundar Temple and said: "Ramkumar's [the Master's brother] school used to be there. The Master lived there when he first came to Calcutta. At that time he performed worship in the house of Raja Digambar Mitra. He would carry the offered rice, fruits, and sweets that he had received from that house and sit in front of the Kali temple, where we are going. People knew that the handsome young man had a good voice, so they would ask him to sing. He would sing to the Mother, then return to his apartment distributing the prasad to the people."

As we walked through the street, some people saluted M. and he inquired about their welfare. M. stopped in front of a big red building [14A, Bechu Chatterjee Street] and said: "This house belonged to Ishan

*On the day of Shivaratri, a hunter, who had killed many animals in a forest, was chased by a hungry lion. The hunter climbed a bilva tree to save himself from the lion's attack. The lion waited throughout the entire night at the bottom of the tree for its prey. The hunter had had no food the whole day and in order to stay awake to avoid falling from the tree, the hunter kept plucking the leaves of the bilva tree and dropping them below. The leaves fell on a Shiva Linga that happened to be located at the bottom of the tree. Shiva was pleased by the offering of the bilva leaves by the hunter, although inadvertently, and saved the hunter in spite of all the sins the hunter had committed by killing animals. This story emphasizes the auspiciousness of worshipping Shiva with bilva leaves on Shivaratri.

Chandra Mukhopadhyay. He visited the Master, and the Master also came to this house. Ishan's son also once met the Master." From the street M. saluted Thakur Bari, his own home, which he called the Master's house. We then crossed Cornwallis Street [now Bidhan Sarani] to gather in front of the Siddheswari Kali temple. M. removed his shoes and bowed down. Then he put on his glasses and looked intently at the Mother for some time. After that he went to the entrance and took a little sanctified water, and then put two pice on the collection plate. The priest put a vermillion mark on the foreheads of M. and the devotees. Afterwards we all visited the adjacent Shiva image, pushing through the crowd to bow down to Lord Shiva. M. and the devotees then sat at the temple portico.

M. surveyed the crowd and remarked: "It seems there will be a heavy crowd in the evening. It is always good to sit in front of the Mother. One feels as if She is talking to Her children. She is not a godmother, but instead a real Mother. Some come to the temple and leave after merely bowing down to Her. That is like waving to Her to say 'good morning.'"

M. watched the people who came to the temple. A young man smoking a cigarette with one hand touched his forehead with the other to salute the Mother. A middle-aged woman took a big bundle down from her head and fervently prayed to the Mother. A Hindu widow got out of a motor car and brought a basket filled with fruits and flowers to offer to the Mother. A non-Bengali man bowed down to Shiva, saying, "O Shiva, please remember me." Some people were chanting the Gita and the Chandi in front of the temple, and some were silently repeating their mantra.

The rest of the devotees took leave of M., but I remained with him. He took me to Thakur Bari, opened the shrine on the third floor, and showed me his precious collection: the Master's picture on the altar; the Master's sandals; a lock of the Master's hair in a container; and the Mangal Ghat of Mother Durga that Holy Mother had installed. M. offered me prasad — a piece of sandesh and an orange. He then closed the shrine and said: "We have enjoyed ourselves immensely today. If possible, please visit Belur Math tonight and bring me a little prasad."

That evening Dr. Bakshi and I crossed the Ganges at Baranagore to visit Belur Math. We attended vespers in the upper shrine. Shiva Puja was arranged in the hall downstairs. The monks sang many songs, and some danced around the image of Shiva, chanting, "Hara Hara, Bom Bom." Worship continued throughout the night and then prasad was distributed. We were fortunate to meet Swamis Brahmananda, Premananda, and Shivananda, all disciples of the Master. Swami Brahmananda told us: "Very happy to see you. I believe that Master Mahashay has sent you. Please keep his company and sometimes come here."

The next morning, while we were crossing the Ganges to return home, I said to Dr. Bakshi: "How wonderfully we passed the night! It must be M.'s grace."

Dr. Bakshi replied: "You are right. I recently came in contact with M. He has so much love and feeling for the devotees! Let us go to Udbodhan and salute Holy Mother, and then visit M." I agreed.

We met Swami Saradananda and Vaikuntha Nath Sanyal on the first floor of Udbodhan and bowed down to them. Meanwhile, a brahmachari called the devotees to visit Holy Mother. We bowed down to her, took prasad, and went to see M. at the Morton Institution.

M. was about to have his lunch, but when he saw us he sat down on a bench. He knew that we had spent the night at Belur Math. "Blessed you are!" he said. "It is your great fortune to spend the night with the holy monks on an auspicious day at a holy place. You have gotten the result of ten years' austerities in one night. Please tell me how you passed the night."

M. was delighted as we described the night's events. His grandson kept reminding him: "Grandpa, the food is getting cold. Please come and eat." We realized that we should not detain him any longer. M. then asked, "Have you brought some prasad?" I handed the prasad to him. He removed his sandals and took the prasad. We then left for home.

At the Morton Institution

M. asked me: "Are you initiated? Is your family guru alive? You can receive a mantra from him."

I replied: "I have no desire to take initiation from my family guru. My father died within a year after receiving initiation from him."

M. said calmly: "Birth and death are in the hands of God. Well, one thing you can do: Take your wife to Udbodhan someday. Holy Mother is there. It would be nice if your wife approached Holy Mother for initiation."

I joyfully replied: "Will she bestow grace on us? I also feel that way."

M.: "She does as she wishes. Sometimes she takes a child on her lap who is covered in dirt and mud. Please let me know."

M. went to bed and I returned home with a peaceful mind.

5 November 1917, Morton Institution

Following M.'s instructions I went to the Udbodhan house in Bagh-bazar with my wife and widowed sister to bow down to Holy Mother.

That afternoon I visited M., who was then listening to a boy from Orissa sing a song about Jagannath.

"Please tell me your news." M. said. "What transpired between your wife and Holy Mother?"

I replied: "My wife and sister are talking about Mother and counting the days until they receive initiation, which will be on Kartik Sankranti, an auspicious day. They also want to see you. They are waiting in the car on the street."

M. immediately went to the car, met them there, and said to them, "If God is pleased, the whole world is pleased."

When the car left, we went upstairs.

M. said: "If one bows down to the feet of Holy Mother, one receives the result of visiting every holy place. Please tell me about your meeting with the Mother. It is good to think about initiation. But it is not enough to have initiation. One should develop a spiritual life by practising the guru's instructions. There is a saying: 'A man may receive the grace of God, the grace of the guru, and the grace of the devotees, but nothing will avail if he does not receive the grace of his own mind.' Please tell me what transpired between your wife and Holy Mother."

I replied: "When my wife and sister went upstairs, Holy Mother inquired: 'Where is your home? What does your husband do? Who else do you have?' Meanwhile, Holy Mother became busy with the women devotees and the worship service. After the worship, she distributed prasad.

"Finally, Holy Mother reminded my wife and sister, "You have not said why you have come here."

"'Will you kindly initiate us?' they said.

"Holy Mother said with a smile: 'Very well. The day of Kartik Sankranti is coming soon. Lord Kartik will be worshipped on that day and it is an auspicious day for initiation.' Later, she called me upstairs and informed me also of our initiation date. I bowed down to her and she blessed me, touching my head."

M. said joyfully: "Wonderful! There is no more worry if the Divine Mother looks after you. This is in *Chaitanya Charitamrita*: 'So many iron rods became gold by touching the philosopher's stone.' If Holy Mother is gracious and accepts responsibility for a person, he or she will achieve everything. Now please pray, and wait for that auspicious day. Practise self-control. Jesus said: 'Unless ye be born again, ye cannot enter the kingdom of God.' Initiation brings new life and shows the path of God-realization."

It was evening. A devotee waved incense in front of the pictures of the gods and goddesses in M.'s room. Several devotees arrived and all sat on grass mats. Everyone silently repeated their respective mantras.

M.: "It is a rare chance to be born during the time of an avatar. One can attain his grace with just a little effort. The Master said, 'The breeze of God's grace is always blowing; only unfurl the sail.' Although the Master's physical form is no longer amongst us, he is now performing his *lila* through Holy Mother. He now bestows mercy through her. She is distributing many precious spiritual gems."

A devotee: "The guru is also a mine of gems, like the ocean."

M.: "The ocean looks awesome and dreadful from a distance, but if you sit on the beach, its gentle waves will refresh and invigorate your body. We shall not gain anything by merely counting the waves; we must collect gems from the ocean floor. What great spiritual treasures we received by living with the Master!"

A devotee brought prasad from Mother Kali of Dakshineswar and gave it to M. He touched it to his head, took a little, and then distributed it amongst the devotees. When he saw a devotee drop a bit of sandesh on the floor, M. asked him to wash that spot with water.

"Do you know the meaning of prasad?" M. asked. "It destroys old samskaras, or tendencies, and makes the mind calm. While taking prasad, one should think: 'Let all my accumulated samskaras from birth after birth be wiped out.'"

It was 10:00 p.m. The devotees took leave of M.

15 November 1917, Morton Institution

It was Kartik Puja. My sister, wife, and I received initiation from Holy Mother. We had lunch and Mother's prasad in Udbodhan and then returned home after meeting Swami Saradananda and other monks. In the afternoon I went to see M., who was then filling out money orders. Every month M. sent remittances to Kankhal, Varanasi, and other centres, and also to some monks. I bowed down to M. and sat on a grass mat.

M.: "Today I was thinking of you off and on. Please tell me how you received the grace of Holy Mother. What was she doing when you arrived? And what happened next?"

"It is your grace, sir, that the impossible became possible," I replied. "We got up at 4:00 a.m., bathed, and went to Udbodhan at 6:30 a.m."

"Very good! It is not good to delay in this respect. One needs longing. Then what happened?"

"When we bowed down to the Mother, she said: 'I have not been feeling well since yesterday. However, since you have come, please wait. Let me finish my bath in the Ganges.' When she heard this, Golap-ma [Holy Mother's attendant] objected: 'My goodness! Mother, you had a fever yesterday. Let them come another day.' Holy Mother replied: 'You see, they have come with great expectation. Today I shall initiate them. It will be all right if I have a quick bath in the Ganges.' She then left for her bath and we waited downstairs. She returned shortly and called me to enter the shrine."

"Ah, how compassionate is the Mother! What next?"

"We carried flowers, fruits, and sweets for the offering. Those were arranged on trays in front of the Master. Holy Mother sat on an asana [small rug] and asked me to sit on another asana nearby. I asked my wid-owed sister to receive initiation first, and I sat in the corner. When her initiation was over, Mother called me. But when I asked her to initiate my wife beforehand, she said: 'No, it is not the custom. The wife gets initia-tion after the husband. She will be initiated after you.'"

"That is true. Then?"

"I sat on the asana next to Holy Mother. She asked me to sip a little Ganges water for purification and repeat the Gayatri mantra ten times. Then she whispered the seed mantra and showed me how to practise it on my fingers. Before initiation she asked about our family tradition. When I hesitated, she said: 'I understand, your family worships Shakti.' She then pointed to an oil painting of Kali on the wall, and said, 'She is your Chosen Deity.' Pointing to the Master's picture on the altar, she said: 'He is your guru. Now bow down.' Then after initiating my wife, Holy Mother gravely said: 'From today onward your human birth is over. I am taking on the burden of all of your sins.'"

"You are blessed! Today you have received the grace of the Mother of the Universe. Have you noticed the blessing that she bestowed on you all? She took upon herself the burden of your sins rather than your virtues. Be careful from now on: Don't do anything that would cause her pain. Did you give any guru *dakshina*?*

"Yes, we did. Each of us gave Mother five rupees and a red-bordered silk cloth. She sent everything to Swami Saradananda and did not keep anything for herself. When my wife had asked her before whether she should wear a Varanasi sari [which is expensive] for initiation, Holy Mother replied: 'Are those who do not have such a cloth denied initiation?'"

---

*After initiation the disciple is supposed to give something, such as money or a cloth or a fruit, to the guru, according to his or her means.

"Yes, Holy Mother is right. She does not consider money to be the primary thing. Do you know who the guru is? The guru is God Himself. He lives in heaven but He takes human birth out of His mercy, to remove human delusion. A spiritual aspirant feels blessed finding Him in front as the Chosen Ideal because of his or her good karma in previous lives. After the guru passes away, He waits in the other world, becoming a saviour for His disciples. He is the ocean of mercy. The more you have faith in the words of your guru, the easier your liberation will be."

"Today I made a mistake. Out of egotism, I used a disrespectful word to a monk in Udbodhan. Please bless me so that I may get rid of this bad habit."

"Please pray to the Master. If you pray sincerely, he will listen."

It was evening. A kerosene lantern was lit and a devotee waved incense in front of the deities on the wall. M. sat for meditation and said to me: "Today is the first day of your initiation. Please obey your guru's instruction." Gradually other devotees came and filled the room.

After meditation a devotee asked: "What is the way for householders?"

M. replied: "The Master said: 'There is a constant disease [i.e., ignorance] in family life. One needs the company of the holy.' Whenever you have an opportunity, please visit a holy place. One should have faith in the words of the guru. It is sinful to consider the guru to be a human being. The guru is the compassionate form of God. Human beings do not always see God, so He sometimes descends as a human being like us and plays His divine play. Human beings understand a little about God by associating with the avatar [divine incarnation] and by loving him and tasting his divine love. While explaining Bhakti Yoga in the Gita, Krishna said: 'Fix your mind on Me alone. If you are unable to do that, then devote yourself to My service.' And finally: 'Abandon all duties and come to Me alone for refuge. I will deliver you from all sins; do not grieve.' People die for lack of water, and they get it in plenty in their courtyard when the avatar comes. The Master is now bestowing blessings through Holy Mother."

M. then sang these two lines from one of the Master's favourite songs:

O Mother, Thou my Inner Guide, ever awake within my heart!
Day and night Thou holdest me in Thy lap.

M. picked up a towel and wiped away his tears of joy, and then continued: "This is not an artificial relationship. And this idea that the

Mother is there and I am here is false. She always dwells in the heart. She is the mother of all, but she thinks more about her weak and destitute children. As the Master said, 'If water falls on the hilltop, it flows downward and accumulates on low ground.' When King Guhaka was busy serving Rama, Rama told him: 'Please take care of my two horses first. They carried me here. I shall be happy if they are fed first.'"

M. then spoke directly to me: "One should not be angry at the attendants of Holy Mother. They look after Holy Mother's convenience and inconvenience. So before visiting the Mother one should listen to her attendants and try to please them.

As the night advanced, the devotees bowed down to M. and left for home.

October 1918, Thakur Bari

It was Maha-Ashtami (Durga Puja). That morning my wife and I went to see Holy Mother in Udbodhan. In the afternoon I visited M., who was then seeing the images of Mother Durga in the neighbourhood with the devotees. Afterwards he went to Thakur Bari, entered the shrine on the third floor, and bowed down to the Master. He then went to the big room downstairs to meet with devotees.

M. said to me: "It would be good if you could visit Holy Mother during Durga Puja."

I replied: "Yes, this morning I went to Udbodhan with my wife to pay our respects."

"Very good. Today is a very auspicious day and you have visited your guru. Please tell me something about your visit to her."

"My wife and sister finished cooking early and then we went to Udbodhan at 10:00 a.m. The Mother was seated on the roof in the sun. She was rubbing medicated oil on her feet, because she has arthritis. My sister rubbed oil on one foot, and then Mother asked my wife to rub it on the other. Then she said to my wife: 'It is not proper to touch only one foot. Please rub the other also.'"

"Oh, how compassionate she is! What happened then?"

"She went to her room and called for me. I bowed down to her and she blessed me and talked to me for a while. I was a little hurt that only the women could stay with her for a long period. Shall I tell you something personal?"

"Of course."

"I said to Holy Mother: 'While repeating the mantra, I don't like to visualize the Master's form. Your form appears in my mind instead, and I feel good. Is there anything wrong with this?' She said with a smile: 'No, there is nothing wrong. You meditate on that form which appeals to you most.'"

"Yes, the Master would also say that. Then what happened?"

"I asked her whether one should pray to the Master to solve one's family problems. She replied: 'Of course, one can let the guru know about one's problems. If a person chants the Master's name, all of his or her sufferings go away.'"

"Ah! How compassionate is the Mother!"

"Then she gave us the Master's prasad and we returned home."

A devotee said: "There is a saying: 'O Lord, teach me how to love Thee more.'"

M. commented: "Without simplicity, one cannot reach God who is the embodiment of simplicity. The parents of the avatar are always simple, like Nandaraja and Yashoda."

A devotee: "But nowadays if a person is too simple, he or she will be cheated."

M. smiled and said: "A scholar from Oxford University wrote in a book directed at the English: 'You have brought so much gold and gems from India and now all the men are gone for the war [the First World War, 1914-1919]. You could not bring the great spiritual treasures from India. You built fancy homes with their wealth, but could not bring their religion.' Lord Ronaldsey, the present governor of Bengal, read *The Gospel of Sri Ramakrishna*, and then went to Dakshineswar with his wife and secretaries. He saw the places that were mentioned in the *Gospel*. He also greeted Ramlal, knowing that he was the Master's nephew."

A devotee: "The same blood of the Master's family flows in Ramlal."

M.: "Yes, it is true. The scriptures say that one should respect not only the guru but his family members also. The Master would say: 'Those who have a little attraction for God will have to come here.'"

It was late evening. The devotees bowed down to M. and left for home.

[Translated from *Srima Samipe*, edited by Swami Chetanananda (Udbodhan Office: Calcutta, 1996), 235-88]

Ramesh Chandra Sarkar

Morton Institution: Sunday, 2 February 1919, 5:30 p.m.

My friend Banabihari and I visited M. in his bedroom. He was reclining on his bed. He asked us to sit down, and then he sang some songs in a low voice. "What do you do?" he asked me.

I responded: "I want to give up my studies."

"Why?"

"I have many problems and no peace."

"Well, that is natural. As long as you have a body, you will face unrest and anxiety."

"I need your blessing."

"Pray to God wholeheartedly. He will definitely listen."

M. gave us some rock candy prasad, then continued: "Why do we experience suffering? It is so we can realize that this world is like a dream. God put lust and anger and other things into our minds so that He could make us great souls. Only an expert boatman can save his boat from a storm. One or two boatmen are happy when they face tidal waves. They boast, 'Watch how we can break through these waves and save our boats.' Weaklings weep and wail as they sit in their boats. There is a kind of bird named the stormy petrel. When a cyclone starts in the ocean, the animals onshore become afraid and hide in the forest. At that time the stormy petrel emerges from the cleft in the cliffs and flies joyfully against the strong wind. [*M. demonstrated by spreading his arms.*] Likewise, we all must go through difficulties in life, and we need courage and self-effort to do so.

"'Lakshmi, the goddess of fortune, bestows favour on bold and enthusiastic people; cowards say that luck brings favour.' Self-effort is a small part of that infinite power. If you lack strength, please apply to the head office — i.e., God. God does everything. As a snake, He bites; and again as a doctor, He cures. He traps human beings with maya, yet as the guru He awakens their consciousness. It is impossible to understand His lila [play]."

Morton Institution, 3 February 1919, 4:00 p.m.

M. asked me to sit on the carpet and gave me a copy of *Sri Ramakrishna Punthi* to read. Then he asked Banabihari to sing a song. Banabihari sang: "O black bee of my mind, be absorbed in the nectar of the lotus feet of Ramakrishna."

"Very good!" M. exclaimed. "Devotional songs lead the mind to God. Yogis keep their minds focussed on God. One will float in bliss if one can develop a little love for Him. So yogis do not let their minds wander to other objects. Direct your mind towards God and try to love Him. What will you gain if you only love your family members and concentrate upon them all the time? One day they will all die; and when you lose them you will suffer from grief.

"One of my friends built a hut on the bank of the Narmada River. There he has been chanting the name of Rama for the last thirteen years, striving to realize God."

He then sang:

Raghupati raghava raja ram, patita pavana sita-ram.
Ram ram jaya raja ram, ram ram jaya sita-ram.
[O Rama, King of the Raghu dynasty, you are the saviour of the soul.
    Victory to Rama and Victory to Sita.]

When the elderly attendant wanted to light the kerosene lantern, M. said to him: "Not now. It is not yet evening." Then I got up to close the window, and M. saw *Sri Ramakrishna Punthi* lying on the carpet. He said: "Never put holy books on the floor near the feet. Paying respect to the scriptures is a sign of devotion." He then sprinkled Ganges water on his head and on the others present. Now and then he checked to see if he could see the hair on his arm; when he could not, he asked that the lantern be lit.

A brahmachari arrived who had received prasad at the temple of Siddheswari Kali of Thanthania, which Sri Ramakrishna had visited many times. M. said to the brahmachari: "You are blessed to have received prasad in that temple. Every day during meditation, you should think of that place and mentally bow down to the Divine Mother. Thus you will achieve meditation on the Master. A place where the Master has visited even once becomes holy. He is the avatar, the Lord of the Universe."

M. then put his hand under his chadar and began to repeat his mantra, becoming deeply absorbed.

Morton Institution, 4 February 1919, 4:00 p.m.

I bowed down to M. and sat on the carpet. After handing me an issue of the *Udbodhan* magazine to read, he began to cough.

"I see you are not well today," I said.

M. replied: "You see, I am now an old man. This body will get a disease and then die. This is nothing to wonder about. I am an old man. Why should I worry about something that is inevitable? A raw fruit does not fall even during a storm, whereas a ripe fruit falls even when the wind is still. When lust and anger appear in the mind during one's youth, one should not be discouraged or think that one's spiritual life is doomed. At that time, one should resolve: 'I must overcome these obstacles.' When some people experience lust and anger, they think they are great sinners and become depressed. Don't pay any attention to those things. They are natural impulses, normal to the human system. In one's youth one should fight against such animal instincts, as the stormy petrel fights against the wind. For this reason, our sages introduced brahmacharya [celibacy] to prepare us to face these obstacles. There are so many obstacles in this world! God has created these obstacles, yet as a guru He rescues us and tells how to overcome them. He created great souls so that we can have the company of the holy.

"In the Gita, how did Arjuna ask Krishna for the signs of a great soul? 'How does the man of steady wisdom speak; how does he sit; how does he move?' Their actions, their words, even their facial expressions — all are exquisite. Have you not read in the *Gospel* how one moment the Master would be laughing and the next he would continue talking on exalted spiritual topics? Everything about him was connected with God. There have been so many great souls born in this country, and so many seers of God! There are so many holy places on the banks of the Ganges and in the Himalayas. We are blessed to have been born in this country. Look at the West, how they are killing each other in the war. [This was during the First World War.] Life is empty to them. Now they may try to accept the Master's message that God alone is real.

"Do you think the world will accept this idea?" I asked.

"Why not? The idea of God is common to all. Is the Master limited to a small body? He is God and sees everyone equally. He loves everyone in every nation. But we are fortunate that He was born amongst us."

Thakur Bari, 6 February 1919, 11:00 a.m.

I asked M.: "When did you write the *Kathamrita*? Did you write at night after working all day? It must have been exhausting."

M. replied: "Is it possible to achieve anything without hard labour? Yes, I used to write at night. Sometimes I listened to the Master's conversation, and then wrote it down in my diary the next day after meditation." Then he opened a page from the Chandi (4:11) and recited, "'O Devi, you are the intelligence by which the essence of all scriptures is comprehended.' Have I done this work? It was the Master's work. He did it. He appeared in me as *medha* [the power of remembrance]. He is the doer and makes others act. We may or may not realize this."

8 February 1919, Evening

I visited M. in the evening; a few devotees were present.

M. said: "What divine intoxication the Master experienced! What attraction for God! Ah, those days are gone. One day the Master came to Calcutta, but he was eager to return to Dakshineswar. He was like a fish floundering on the ground, desperate to return to the water. Calcutta was infested with lust and gold, but Dakshineswar was the abode of Mother Kali — free from worldly things. When the Master saw the attendants of the Divine Mother, he would experience Her presence.

"One day Rasik, the temple sweeper, bowed down to the Master with folded hands and asked, 'Master, shall I achieve anything in this life?' The Master replied: 'Of course you will get something. You will have a divine vision. You are a servant of the Mother and you keep this temple clean.'

"Once I saw the Master sweeping the garden path in Dakshineswar. He remarked, 'Mother walks on this path.' As he said this he went into ecstasy, repeating, 'Mother, Mother.' He would talk to the devotees for their welfare. The Master said: 'It is normal for this mind [i.e., his mind] to remain absorbed in God; the reverse is abnormal.' The normal state of bamboo is to be straight, but due to gravity it bends — that is abnormal. You see, one should accept the Master's words. He said that Chaitanya was an avatar; therefore we should believe this firmly.

"One day after samadhi he touched his chest and said, 'I am the avatar in every age.' God has form and is also formless. He comes as an avatar. The Master said this, so it must be true. What do you think?"

A devotee asked: "Does anybody achieve anything by visiting a holy place?"

M. replied: "One should not cultivate a negative attitude, such as, 'It is useless to visit a holy place' or 'I have no devotion.' One should have self-confidence. Please develop faith in the scriptures and holy places. The Master said, 'If you bite a chili, whether you know it or not, your tongue will burn.' It is the quality of the chili and not of the eater. Similarly, if one associates with the holy people in a sacred place, one comes under their influence automatically and new samskaras [impressions] grow. A holy place is not an ordinary place: it is where the deities, avatars, and holy people live. Their influence is palpable there."

11 February 1919, Afternoon

After visiting Swami Saradananda at Udbodhan and Swami Brahma-nanda at Balaram's house, I went to see M. I raised the topic of reliance on God.

M.: "God takes responsibility for human beings. There are so many birds and beasts. Who takes responsibility for them? Men? Men cannot even take responsibility for themselves.

"One should learn to endure pain and suffering. At one time the Master's arm broke. Some devotees tried to cover it up so that people would not know that such a holy man had broken his arm. But the Master would show people his injury and say, 'Look, my arm was fractured.' Ah, he embraced suffering, so that others could learn to endure suffering. This was a song he sang then:

> Mother, this is the grief that sorely grieves my heart,
> That even with Thee for Mother, and though I am wide awake,
> There should be robbery in my house.

"He could have cured himself with a mere wish. But he could not force his mind away from the Divine Mother and come down to the cage of flesh and bone."

A monk had sent a devotee to M. with some string beans from the Belur Math garden. When the beans were cooked, M. offered them to the Master. He took a little and distributed the rest among the devotees. What great regard he had for Belur Math!

Wednesday, 12 February 1919, 1:30 p.m.

A devotee from Ballygunj said to M.: "You are very fortunate to have touched, seen, heard, and served Sri Ramakrishna."

"I am not the only fortunate one," M. responded. "The Master said that all his children would inherit his treasures: discrimination, renunciation, knowledge, devotion, and love. Those who think of the Master develop good qualities."

Friday, 15 February 1919

A brahmachari said to M.: "You were the first person to preach the Master's teachings."

M. replied: "The Master preached his own teachings. Arjuna said in the Gita [10:12-13]: 'All the sages have declared You to be the eternal, self-luminous Person, the first of the gods, unborn and all-pervading; likewise have the divine sages Narada, Asita, Devala, and Vyasa proclaimed. So, too, have You said unto me.'"

A gentleman asked M.: "Did you visit Paramahamsadeva? Are you his disciple?"

"It is hard for me to say that I am his disciple," M. said. "I am the servant of his servants. My Lord is the Lord of the Universe. Did he come for one person only? He came for the whole of humanity. We are all his children. He is an avatar."

Tuesday, 18 February 1919, 4:30 p.m.

I arrived at M.'s at 4:30 p.m.

M. was speaking on the *Kathamrita*: "What a wonderful thing the Master produced! Such a thing does not exist for other avatars. The *Kathamrita* is like a photograph, an exact reproduction. It depicts the place, time, *tithi* or lunar day, even the high and low tides of the Ganges. If someone reads this book after visiting Dakshineswar, he or she will experience deep meditation.

"We need the company of the holy. I wanted to visit those places where the Master went and to have the company of the holy. But I am old and it is hard for me to walk. What to do? So I meditate on the monks, which is akin to holy company. After visiting sadhus, one should meditate on them. It is marvellous to meditate on the avatar, the King of the Sadhus. Paramahamsadeva was an avatar. One cannot reach God without meditating on the avatar."

M. then read from Swami Vivekananda's *Bhakti Yoga*: "We cannot conceive of God except through these human manifestations."

He continued: "Some say that God is formless. How can one think of a formless God? While thinking of a formless God, some imagine a Being seated on a big throne with his feet hanging down. We are limited, so how can we conceive of That which is unlimited? Can you put six ounces of water in a one-ounce pot? Although God is infinite, He becomes finite when he takes a form as an avatar. He does this so that devotees can meditate on Him. The Master told some of his devotees: 'It is not necessary to think of other deities. Just think of me.'

"When the Master was ill in Cossipore, one night at 1:00 a.m. Swamiji came to him besmeared with ashes. He said to the Master, 'Would you like to hear a song?' With his beautiful voice he sang a hymn asserting that the Master was God Himself in human form. When a person like Swamiji accepts the Master as an incarnation of God, we have no other option than to admit this. To the man whom the Master loved and considered to be a good vessel for his teachings, he revealed his true nature. He told Swamiji: 'I am an avatar. It will be enough if you meditate on me.'"

[Translated from *Srima Samipe*, edited by Swami Chetanananda (Udbodhan Office: Calcutta, 1996), 69-87]

Swami Dharmeshananda

First Meeting

In 1920 or 1921 I went to see M. with my friend Surendra Nath Kundu and Brother Bhupati, who was a householder devotee of Sri Ramakrishna. At the time I was living in North Calcutta and was in my second year at City College. Surendra had given me a copy of the fourth volume of the *Kathamrita*, which I read with great attention. He also told me that the author of this book was still alive, and that it would be wonderful if we could hear the Master's words directly from him.

One afternoon Surendra and I went to the fourth floor of the Morton Institution and met M., who was surrounded by devotees. He received us cordially. It was the rainy season, a few days after the Chariot Festival of Jagannath. M. put Jagannath's prasad (dry rice) into our hands and said, "When one has this prasad one attains devotion for God." I used to go to the Brahmo Samaj and was moreover under the influence of Western education, so I considered such faith to be superstitious.

I remarked: "Yes, if one eats this prasad with faith, one may attain devotion."

M. replied: "No, there is a sure effect of an object. In whatever way you eat this prasad, your mind will become pure and you will attain faith and devotion."

"How is that possible? The mind is everything," I replied. "If there isn't any faith in one's mind, how can one attain devotion?"

"The Master said that whatever way you take prasad, you will attain devotion."

"I can't accept that."

M. became grave and turned his chair towards the devotees. Pointing at me with his left index finger, he said indignantly: "The Master said, 'One attains devotion,' and this person does not accept the Master's words." Everyone remained silent. Surendra was looking at me, and I hung my head and kept quiet. I was ashamed of my audacity.

M. then told me affectionately: "Listen, one day in Dakshineswar the Master said to me, 'The Chariot Festival is over. The pilgrims are now returning from Puri. You go to Howrah Station and beg for some prasad for me. One attains devotion if one takes this prasad.' I went to Howrah Station. When I saw pilgrims getting off the train, I pleaded like a beggar, 'Will you give me a little prasad?' Some were amazed by the sight of a well-dressed gentleman begging for prasad. Some walked away quickly without paying any attention, and some devotees realized my sincerity and gave me some grains of dry rice from their bundle. When I carried that prasad to the Master, he was very happy. 'When God is pleased, the whole world becomes pleased.' I was truly blessed. The Master used to eat one or two grains of that dry rice every day and asked me also to do so. Have faith in his words. There is no other way."

I took one or two grains of that prasad. Starting in 1924, my faith gradually developed after I began visiting M. regularly.

Encouragement

In 1924 I went to see M. with Brahmachari Tarak of the Vivekananda Society. I was then a student in my fifth year of college. I used to stay at the Society and perform worship there. We went to visit M. at the Morton Institution.

M. asked Tarak: "What do you do?"

Tarak replied: "I collect subscriptions for the Vivekananda Society, help the secretary, and arrange religious classes and kirtans in devotees' houses once a month. And every week there are two classes in the Society on Ramakrishna-Vivekananda literature."

"Very good," M. said. "This is real karma yoga as described by Swamiji. If you can perform this service without any motive, you will attain knowledge and devotion."

This encouragement made Tarak happy, and he rededicated his life to the Vivekananda Society.

M. then asked me: "What do you do?"

I replied: "I perform daily worship in the shrine of the Society and conduct the vesper service."

"You have gotten a very good job," M. said. "This work will give you devotion. Look, flowers have a beautiful fragrance — and you are offering them to the feet of the Lord. When you make sandal paste, it generates a sweet fragrance and you offer that to the Lord. You are also meditating upon Him in your heart. Don't give up this work. One can attain God's grace quickly by means of worship. Perform worship with a pure and concentrated mind, and then pray and offer yourself at the feet of the Lord. When one listens to vesper songs, one's mind becomes one-pointed and meditation comes automatically. You are doing marvellous work."

Many devotees were present. M. praised our jobs though they were different.

Devotion for Holy Mother

M.'s devotion for Holy Mother was indescribable. He considered her to be Mother Lakshmi. In 1931, long after Holy Mother had passed away, I had an opportunity to go with M. to Udbodhan, Mother's house. He brought a big basket of sandesh to offer to the Master. We arrived at 9:00 a.m. and entered the room where Mother passed away, which is now the shrine. Mother's bed is still there, as it was during her lifetime. M. sat near the bed and meditated for a long time. Then a monk gave M. prasad and we returned to his residence.

Alone with M.

Early one afternoon (at 1:30 or 2:00) in 1931, I went to the Morton Institution. I was then staying at Udbodhan, and almost every evening I would go to M. to listen to him speak about the Master. In the evening he would meditate with devotees in the tulsi grove on the roof. I would bring my own asana [meditation carpet], but one night I forgot to bring it back with me, so I returned at that odd time to retrieve it. M. saw me.

M. loved solitude so he would stay alone in the attic room of the school building. But he also loved to talk about the Master with devotees. When he saw me, he called out, "Please come here." I went to his room. He asked me to sit on his bed and inquired about my welfare. I said: "I have to leave now. There is a class on the Chandogya Upanishad at Udbodhan. I need to attend it. I forgot to take my asana with me, so I came to get it."

"Please sit down," M. said, but I got up and bowed down to him. When I was about to leave, he said: "Dhiren, all Vedas and Vedanta are at the Master's feet. One can attain knowledge by meditating on those feet."

Like a fool, I did not understand the deep meaning of his words, so I returned to Udbodhan. Later I lamented that I had lost a chance to enjoy his rare holy company all by myself. Perhaps he intended to raise my mind to a higher realm of consciousness, which he did for one of my friends.

About Ramakrishna's Centenary

Sri Ramakrishna's centenary celebration was to be held from 1936 to 1937. For five years the Centenary Committee was planning to publish a centenary memorial volume on Ramakrishna. The committee was collecting articles from great thinkers of India about their experiences with and concepts about the Sanatana Dharma [Eternal Religion]. Swami Avinashananda, the organizer of the Centenary Committee, came to M. one day with another monk to consult with him about articles for that volume. I was present at that time.

M. said: "The soul of dharma [religion] is tapas [austerities]. Sri Ramakrishna was the embodiment of tapas. If you can travel all over India and collect descriptions of spiritual experiences from all-renouncing monks, that collection would be the best memorial volume on Sri Ramakrishna. The Ramakrishna Order is based on the austerities of Swamiji, Swami Brahmananda, and other monastic disciples of the Master."

Morton Institution, Christmas Eve 1930, 7:00 p.m.

M. was seated on his chair and surrounded by nearly twenty devotees. A devotee from Sind had sent a basket of fruit wrapped in red paper. M. was very pleased, and he showed the basket to the devotees.

M.: "Today is an auspicious day to think of Christ and the Master. The Master said, 'I am Christ.' Let us first think of the Master and then we shall be able to understand Christ.

"Christ had 12 disciples from Galilee and most of them were fishermen. He was the son of a carpenter and did not have a formal education. The Master also said, 'I am an unlettered fool.' They did not teach by virtue of their education. 'A learned ignorance is the end of philosophy and the beginning of religion.' Renunciation is necessary.

"The Master said openly that it would be enough if people came to him; they didn't need any spiritual disciplines. Then the Divine Mother took him away from this world. The Master produced butter and gave it to everyone to eat, without any need for making an effort. Now he will make us work, and this is the beginning of spiritual life. The goal is love for Satchidananda. Love is God. The vision of God means unconditional love and devotion for God. There may be one or two exceptions, but everyone will have to work and practise sadhana. Krishna said in the Gita (18:11): 'It is indeed impossible for an embodied being to renounce action entirely.' The goal of action is to attain love and devotion. Western people are very busy collecting enjoyments; they will not be able to preach

Christ. The people of the East will preach Christ. Moreover, he belonged to Asia. He considered himself to be a lamb; he surrendered himself like a sacrificial animal. And he incarnated to take away the sins of all. By the grace of the Master, I understand a little of Christ's message. Is it easy to understand the words of an avatar? One cannot understand Christ if one's mind is attached to lust and gold."

M. then opened his Bible and showed us pictures of the Madonna and Christ, Jerusalem, and so on. He touched the Bible to his head and then read from Matthew, John, and Luke. He read the following sections: Christ's birth in the manger; his escape from Herod; the wise men of the East who found Christ and then fled; Christ's preaching; the pure life of his parents; his baptism by John; and so on. We left at 9:30 p.m.

Morton Institution, 4 January 1931, 7:30 p.m.

M. was seated with some swamis, devotees, and an English journalist from London who was curious to learn about God.

M. told the journalist: "God incarnates as an avatar."

Journalist: "Is it true that when a person becomes one with God, he becomes an avatar?"

"No, there is a belief in this country that God comes down as an avatar. Our scriptures tell us of ten, twenty-four, and again numerous avatars. Christians do not believe Christ was an avatar, but we do."

"Then godmen are chosen as avatars?"

"Who would choose?"

"I have used the wrong words. Pardon me."

"Christ is the same as Krishna, Chaitanya, and now Ramakrishna. He himself says so. This is the proof."

"How do people know whether this or that avatar is authentic?"

"If they pray, they will know. Some false prophets profess themselves to be avatars, but the sincere devotee recognizes the genuine avatar. You went to Dakshineswar. It is as sacred as Jerusalem. Prayer is the essential thing. Pray. Knock and it will be opened. Be eager."

"How should we pray?"

"O Father, let us know You. Give us Your love. Make us perfect devotees. Give us eternal life — true life."

"In which way? Praying aloud?"

"There is no need for that. One may or may not do it aloud. If one is hungry and cannot give it proper expression, is one not hungry? The Father knows one's inner yearning."

"How can we have love for God so that we may pray?"

"The company of holy people who have renounced the world will make you feel love for God. This is the first step towards religion and the alpha and omega of spiritual life. The intellect cannot understand all this. Your scientists are engaged in seeking sense knowledge. A human being's intellect is feeble, very weak. Only faith and prayer are needed — these are all. Depend on His mercy. He will let us know in time. We are under Him; He is not under us. We need His grace. If you ask, when should one renounce, the answer is given in Christ's words. Once he asked someone to come and follow him. The man answered: 'A relative of mine died. I have to bury him first; then I will join you.' Christ replied: 'Follow me, and let the dead bury the dead.' Worldly-minded people are truly dead. The sadhus live real lives. All others are dead. Those people will take care of the dead. Pray without ceasing and keep company with holy people."

The journalist wanted to take a picture of M., but M. declined. Instead, he presented the journalist with a copy of *The Gospel of Sri Ramakrishna* as a memento.

[Translated from *Srima Samipe*, edited by Swami Chetanananda (Udbodhan Office: Calcutta, 1996), 88-132]

Swami Kamaleshwarananda

18 October 1921

M. (Master Mahashay) said: "Sri Ramakrishna would wait at the ghat for devotees. Sometimes he would watch the boats.

"Once he scolded Latu Maharaj because he slept too long and got up late in the morning. He told him: 'Get up early. After practising japa and meditation, you may take a little rest.'

"The Master once praised a woman devotee, and as a result, some devotees went to visit her. But when Rakhal Maharaj went to see her, the Master scolded him and forbade him to go there again.

"Swamiji used to visit his friend Annada Guha at his garden house. The Master did not approve, however, because Annada was a worldly man. During the Chariot Festival at Balaram's house, when Swamiji wanted to leave, the Master remarked: 'The words of those who have gold in their ears are valuable. No one listens to him who hasn't even a rag around his waist.'

"Once the Master stayed at Mathur's Jan Bazar house. One night he got up and said to Mathur, 'I must go to Dakshineswar.' Mathur arranged for a carriage and the Master returned to Dakshineswar. He then said, 'Mother, I have come.'

"The Master did not sleep well at night. He would pace back and forth. Once at midnight he said to me, 'One can hear the *anahata* sound at this time.'

"The Master once told me, 'Please tell that person that it will be enough if he thinks of me.' Actually he was indirectly saying that to me. The Master said to Adhar: 'Preparatory devotion is not real devotion. Be up and doing; achieve something. No one knows when death will come.'

"Sometimes the Master would cover himself with a thick chadar, so that the air that surrounds worldly people would not touch his body.

"God speaks through the avatar. During Kali Puja at the Shyam-pukur house, Girish and other devotees worshipped the Master with flowers and other articles. The Master then went into samadhi and his hands assumed gestures symbolizing fearlessness and the bestowal of boons.

"Once the Master touched Baburam Maharaj and went into samadhi. He said, 'I can determine who has made progress in spiritual life, and how much.'

"Every evening the Master would say: 'I am the house, You are the indweller. I am the instrument, You are the operator.'

"During his early days at Jhamapukur in Calcutta, the Master would go to the Thanthania Kali temple every evening and practise japa and meditation for a long time.

"Lust and anger are inherent in every human being. Ordinary people succumb to them. Some try various methods without knowing how to counteract them. They do not know that the correct way to overcome lust and anger is to think of God.

"It is possible to miss the goal if one is attached to worldly or wealthy people. Everyone — both monks and householders — needs the company of the holy.

"A devotee [M.] brought some gram [dried chickpeas] to Dakshineswar to use for counting the japa that he performed. But the Master asked him to give the gram to him so that he could soak it in water and eat it.

"Ishan Mukhopadhyay built a cottage in which to practise *purashcha-rana* [a vow to do japa a certain number of times]. Hearing this, the Master remarked: 'What is this? He wants to tell everyone that he is calling on God!'

"On Kali Puja night the Master had goose bumps while in ecstasy. He remarked, 'You see, many people are calling on God tonight, so I am having these horripilations.'

"The Master observed the lunar days, both auspicious and inauspi-cious, such as *maghā, ashleshā, sankrānti*. The first day of the Bengali month is very inauspicious for travel. Once, on that day, a devotee came to see the Master on his way to another place, but the Master did not fully approve of this.

"To save our lives, God provided milk in our mother's breasts. And for the welfare of our souls, He created sadhus, scriptures, and temples in different places. The Master told me, 'Give up all work in the evening and think of God.'

"The Master said to Vijay Goswami: 'Pray to God and He will reveal

His true nature to you. What is the need for discussing whether God is formless or with form?'"

10 October 1925

M. said: "Sometimes seed mantras would burst forth from the Master's mouth. Unconsciously he would utter those mantras. Once Tarak Maharaj [Swami Shivananda] heard a mantra from the Master."

M. did not like monks bowing down to him and touching his feet. Once he said to me, "If you bow down, people will wonder why monks are touching the feet of a householder."

I replied, "I consider you to be a venerable man."

M. said, "It is good to maintain that attitude mentally."

In 1924 when M. stayed with us at Gadadhar Ashrama in South Calcutta, I made his bed. He rolled up the bedding and said: "What is this? I am a householder. How can I sleep on a bed that was made by a monk?"

While eating lunch one day, M. said: "We live in eternity. 'Man does not live by bread alone. He who loves his father or mother more than Me is not worthy of Me.'"

[Translated from *Srima Samipe*, edited by Swami Chetanananda (Udbodhan Office: Calcutta, 1996), 133-35]

Mahendra Kumar Chaudhury

In 1921 I was staying at 47 Amherst Street, which was very close to M.'s school, the Morton Institution. I heard that the recorder of *The Gospel of Sri Ramakrishna* lived there and that many devotees met with him in the evenings. I was anxious to see him and enjoy his holy company. One day I arrived at twilight, and no devotees were there. M. cordially received me and asked me to meditate. I was impressed by his dignified appearance and his overflowing beard. Gradually other devotees arrived and M. began to narrate to us the history and teachings of the *Gospel*.

Here are some of M.'s sayings, as I remember them:

Either keep company with the holy or live alone like a lion. Pray to God in solitude, secretly with a longing heart.

What will you gain by chatting with others? One should spend that time practising meditation and spiritual disciplines.

A human being has three bodies: gross, subtle, and causal; or body, mind, and spirit. The spiritual body does not care for worldly enjoyment; it enjoys only divine ecstasy. When a spiritual person hears about God, he or she gets goose bumps and tears flow from the eyes. The spiritual body merges into Brahman through meditation and samadhi.

When someone asked the Master about reincarnation, he replied that it is true and one should not doubt it.

The goal of human life is to realize God. One should adopt any means to attain Him. Too much talking and planning are useless. The Master said: "You have come to eat mangoes. What is the need for counting the trees and fruits?" If you know God, He will teach you everything. If you meet Jadu Mallick, he will tell you how much money and how many stocks and bonds he has. Some think that one should first learn by reading books, and then try to know God. First try to know God and then He will make you know everything.

Holy company is the best means to attain God.

God incarnates in every age and makes the difficult and inscrutable spiritual path simple and easy. As a guru the avatar makes the way to God-realization smooth. The Master said that one could reach God by meditating on him [*meaning Ramakrishna*].

It is better to follow the avatar's teachings than to talk about God. Jesus said: "Thou sayest O God, God, God, but why dost thou not do what I say unto you?"

A disciple should not have any worries once he receives the guru's grace. A magician threw a string with many knots into a large audience and asked someone to untie the knots, but no one could loosen them. Finally, he shook the string once or twice, and immediately all the knots came undone. Similarly all fetters fall off in a moment by the grace of the guru.

Practise meditation and spiritual disciplines in solitude and study holy books. Hearing is better than reading.

Do not disturb another's faith; rather one should help others on their own path. All paths lead to God.

It is true that God can be reached through many paths, but one cannot walk on many paths at the same time. One should begin one's spiritual journey with faith and devotion. One can climb to the roof by means of a staircase, a ladder, a bamboo pole, or a rope. While descending also one should adopt only one means. Similarly, one should follow one path for God-realization.

[Translated from *Srima Samipe*, edited by Swami Chetanananda (Udbodhan Office: Calcutta, 1996), 136-39]

Sailendra Kumar Gangopadhyay

I saw M. three times. The first time I saw him was in 1922 at Belur Math during the birth anniversary of Sri Ramakrishna. M. was calm and dignified, like a rishi. He was seated on a wooden chair. I did not dare go near him.

The second time was in 1924 at Belur Math, during Sri Ramakrishna's birth anniversary. M. was seated on a wooden bench. I was with my father, who asked me to bow down to him. I saw his large eyes filled with grace. He talked to my father a little. His voice was very sweet.

The third time I saw M. was in 1932, when I visited him at the Morton Institution. I was then 24. It was evening. I saw a stone plaque on the wall that read: "Ramakrishna-Vivekananda Institute." I hesitated to enter, but a young man asked me to go upstairs. I went to the roof and found some gentlemen seated on a bench near the door. There was an easy chair; I guessed that it was M.'s chair. I also sat on the bench.

Meanwhile, someone brought a kerosene lantern. I learned later that he was M.'s son. After a while M. slowly came upstairs and sat in his chair. His son put a book wrapped with red cloth into his hands. M. touched the book to his head and meditated for a while. Then he gave that volume of the *Kathamrita* to me and gravely said: "Today you are the reader. Please read to us." I was overwhelmed.

"From where shall I read?" I asked.

A gentleman replied, "From any place."

I looked at M. and found him calm and motionless, with his eyes closed. It was a copy of the second volume of the *Kathamrita*. It was a great test for me to read the *Kathamrita* in front of M. I read for nearly 45 minutes. I read with great attentiveness, and as a result every scene became vivid to me. From time to time I looked at M. and saw tears of joy coming from his eyes. I have never since met such a wonderful man, nor have I seen such a wonderful scene.

When the reading was over, I handed the book back to him. I tried to bow down to him but he forbade me, saying, "You are the Bhagavata — the reader of the holy book." He wrapped the book with the red cloth again and said: "This book is the fifth Veda. Every word in it is a mantra. It awakens consciousness in human beings, brings peace to their minds, and soothes the burning pain of family life."

M. gave me two rasagollas and one mango to eat and then asked me to wash my hands in the water tank at the corner of the roof. He then asked my name and learned that I had come from Kanpur. He knew my father, who was the founder of the Ramakrishna Mission there. In parting I bowed down to him. He blessed me by touching my head. I am blessed that I met M., who was faith and devotion personified.

[Translated from *Srima Samipe*, edited by Swami Chetanananda (Udbodhan Office: Calcutta, 1996), 146-48]

Satish Chandra Nath

Gadadhar Ashrama, Calcutta, 30 January 1924

M. was staying at Gadadhar Ashrama for a few days. Early every morning he went to the shrine and meditated for hours. He took care of his own needs and would accept service from no one. The Master had taught him that holy company is vital to spiritual life, so he had come to stay in the Ashrama to associate with the monks.

M. said: "Vidyasagar took English lessons from a teacher for one week. Later, when he heard that the teacher had passed away, he took responsibility for his family. Just see his gratitude! Holy Mother used to say, 'Is he a man who is ungrateful?' Lalit Maharaj [Swami Kamaleshwarananda] served people and taught the scriptures for the welfare of all. Now we should look after him. [He was suffering from mental illness.]

"Once some women devotees went to Jayrambati to visit Holy Mother. In the morning while everyone was absorbed in meditation, Holy Mother mopped the mud floor by hand. When one of the women saw that, she came forward and began to mop the floor. Holy Mother asked, 'Will you not meditate?' She replied, 'Mother, how can I meditate when you are mopping the floor?'"

1 February 1924

It was winter. M., the monks, and the devotees sat on the roof for lunch.

M. said: "Once when Nivedita visited Holy Mother, she took her dog along. But Holy Mother would push the dog away with a fan so that it would not enter her room, which was also her shrine. Nivedita said: 'Mother, do you love me? Then why will you not love my dog? It is said in the Bible: Love me, love my dog.'"

M. pointed to me and said: "What a precious statement! Memorize it."

M. told me privately: "Let me give you a secret task. From today onward, keep a diary and record the sayings of great personalities. Be sure to note the time, subject, place, and who is talking to whom. Don't record discussions about politics. In this manner you will develop the power of judgement and insight into human nature. You will be able to discern right from wrong. In the future, this will help your meditation. I started to write my diary when I was in the seventh grade. Fifteen years later I met the Master. My habit was to make brief notes in the diary; later the *Kathamrita* emerged from it. The Master's message to the world remained hidden, like seeds, in the pages of that ordinary diary."

That night M. asked a devotee: "Do you meditate?"

"No, I cannot meditate," the devotee replied.

"Please try," M. said. "The mind will run around in the beginning, but gradually it will come under control. Try to practise meditation for at least 15 minutes a day. There is another kind of meditation — thinking of the Master's divine play. Meditation is nothing but uninterrupted thought of God."

3 February 1924

After lunch M. rested for a bit and then he talked to us.

"It is a difficult discipline to say, 'I am Brahman,'" M. began. "Listen to a story. A drunkard pretended that he was dead, and some of his drunken friends carried him on their shoulders. The man said, 'I am dead.' The people on the street said, 'No, you are not yet dead, as you are still talking.' When a man experiences 'I am Brahman,' he becomes silent and no words come from his mouth."

The night before, we had studied *Bhakti Yoga.* The topic was "A knower of Brahman becomes Brahman."

M. said: "What will you achieve by repeating 'I am Brahman?' Brahman has the power of creation, preservation, and destruction. Do you have that power? So the Master said, 'It is good to have the attitude of a devotee, such as "I am His child, or I am His servant."'"

In the afternoon we went with M. to walk in Harish Park, in South Calcutta. A public meeting associated with Swamiji's birth anniversary had been scheduled, but it was cancelled for some reason.

"What happened to that meeting?" M. asked. "It is good that it was cancelled. The Master taught us: 'Call on God in solitude and in secret.' This is the truth. There is no need to put up a signboard: 'This place is meant for calling on God. All are welcome to call on God.'"

"The Master used to say: 'A flower blooms in the deep forest. It has a sweet fragrance and is full of honey. Is it necessary to inform the bees that such a flower is blooming in that spot in the forest? The bees go there of their own accord. Learn how to gather honey [spirituality].'"

Gadadhar Ashrama, Calcutta, 27 February 1924

In the evening many devotees came to listen to M. talk about spiritual matters.

A brahmachari asked: "Shall we achieve something in this life?"

M. replied: "Suppose you are asleep on a cot and others carry you a great distance. Can you know how far you have gone? There is a great power [Ramakrishna] behind you who is thinking of you."

A devotee asked him: "Could you tell us why people go to a holy place with great difficulty and then endure humiliation? In the Puri temple priests humiliate the pilgrims and even beat them with broomsticks."

M. replied: "People go through various ordeals to realize God. Is it not a great blessing to be touched by a broom that is used to clean the temple and the Lord's chariot? For that reason, people who visit Puri are willing to be beaten with that broomstick.

"Some ask, 'What miracle did Sri Ramakrishna perform?' I answer: 'The Master turned the worldly current in the opposite direction — towards God. He made the pleasant (*preyas*) into the good (*shreyas*). Is there any greater miracle than this? He changed the current of life for those who went to him."

A swami asked: "How can we get rid of our old samskaras [tendencies]?"

After a brief silence, M. replied: "Listen to a story: A Hindu was forcibly converted to Islam and was made to repeat the name of Allah. Out of fear, he repeated 'Allah,' but from time to time he said 'Jai Jagadamba.' When the Muslims beat him, he said: 'Look, your Allah's name is on my lips — but inside I am full of Jagadamba [the Divine Mother]. So Jagadamba's name comes out, pushing Allah's name aside. What can I do? You had better kill me.' Such is the influence of samskaras."

M. then began to read from the Bible. He said to the audience: "Do you know the meaning of spirit, water, and blood? It means Christ, baptism, and crucifixion. Everything happens by God's will. If a man cannot love his own brother, how can he love God?

"After Swamiji returned from the West, one day we were talking on the roof of Balaram's house. It is extremely difficult to understand the principle of the avatar [the doctrine of divine incarnation]. Swamiji said: 'I read so much in the Vedas and Vedanta; and I heard so many things from the Master; yet I still cannot fathom this mystery of the avatar.'"

Morton Institution, 29 September 1924

In the afternoon a gentleman came from the Basumati Publication Office to meet M., the rector of the school. He had read excerpts from the *Kathamrita* in the *Basumati* and *Manasi* magazines, and he was curious to meet the author who had written under the pseudonym of Srima. I met the gentleman downstairs and told him: "Mahendra Babu did not want people to know who he was, so in the *Kathamrita* he used several pen names, such as Srima, Master, Mani, and M. In fact, he wanted to spread the message of Sri Ramakrishna to the world. On the title page of the *Kathamrita* is written 'Srima Kathita,' or 'As Told by Srima.' This has a deep meaning: He would open his old diaries; meditate on those episodes concerning Sri Ramakrishna, and then give dictation. Some designated people would write down his words. Thus the *Kathamrita* came into existence. So it is written on the title page, *as told* by Srima and not *written* by him."

The gentleman replied: "My goodness! Sir, this is something unprecedented."

When we came to M., two devotees were with him.

A devotee asked: "When I sit for meditation, my mind wanders to worthless things."

M. responded: "One needs to practise meditation regularly, and then gradually the mind will come under control."

Another devotee asked: "What was the Master's complexion like?"

M. said: "Holy Mother told me that the Master's complexion was like milk and red paint combined. When we met him, his complexion was not like that, and his beard was turning a little grey."

The gentleman now said: "I wish you would touch my head. Your blessed hands have served the Master, and the touch of his feet remains on your hands."

"What will you achieve from the touch of these ordinary hands?" M. responded. "Please visit Dakshineswar from time to time. The blessed feet of the Master touched every particle of dust in that place. The Panchavati, the bel tree, and the pine trees have seen the Master. Blessed are the births of those trees. You will be inspired by the Divine Mother's temple. Please visit that place."

The gentleman from the Basumati office was speechless and overwhelmed.

Morton Institution, 2 December 1924

I reached the Morton Institution at 8:00 a.m. M. was reading the proof of the *Kathamrita* and asked me to sit on a bench.

M. said: "A free soul loves to see long roads, expansive skies, and vast meadows, and also to have the company of the holy. He does not like to be caught in bondage. The Master could not tie a knot, tuck the mosquito curtain under his mattress, or stitch a cloth. He could not even write. His mind always dwelt in God. It was necessary for him to bring the mind down to write something, so he could not write. When he tried to, it turned into scribbles.

"Again the Master could not eat his meal mixing various dishes together, because this required him to bring the mind down. But to please the devotees, he would bring his mind down and eat. Sometimes to bring his mind down, he would say, 'I shall drink some water.' One day he asked me, 'Could you tell me why I am in such a state?' I replied: 'Your mind remains in a higher state. You bring it down to play with the devotees.' Immediately he corrected me, saying: 'No, I don't bring the mind down. It is the Mother who does that.'"

I asked: "In the *Kathamrita* it is written that Govinda Roy initiated the Master into an Allah mantra. Who is this Govinda Roy?"

M. replied: "Govinda Roy's house was near Dum Dum. He was not a Muslim, but he used to practise Islam."

Morton Institution, June 1925

It was evening. Devotees silently meditated with M. Afterwards M. asked someone to read from the *Kathamrita*. The topic was: "One should realize one's true nature."

M. said: "God's true form manifests in the hearts of the devotees. Whatever you see in this world is nothing but pretense, like actors performing on a stage. It is a dramatic performance. The actress who is dressed like Sita must act like the all-suffering Sita — always crying. Sometimes she cries so much that it is hard for her to perform.

"There are three ways one can destroy the false show of this world. First think: 'This is not my true nature. I have assumed this form. I am that free soul.' This is *jnana yoga*. Second: 'I have dressed as You wished me to. Please don't make me wear this false garb anymore. I cannot perform anymore. Reveal Yourself to me.' This is *bhakti yoga*. Third: Sitting in the green room, one thinks, 'Now I am putting makeup on myself. When the play is over it will be removed.' Thus one gets rid of delusion. This is called *abhyasa yoga*, or the yoga of practice."

The devotees left at 10:00 p.m.

Morton Institution, 19 December 1926

It was winter. M. was seated on a bench, covered with a woolen shawl. During that evening's gathering he talked about the Master and Holy Mother.

M. said: "In Jhamapukur, the Master studied in his brother's *Tol* [Sanskrit school]. That Tol was closed long ago and the Shyamsundar temple was erected in its place. You will feel awakening if you sit there for a while. Genuine devotees will go there and think of the Master."

Meanwhile, a devotee came from Belur Math. M. inquired: "Who is the worshipper in the Master's temple? Who is worshipping Holy Mother? What kind of sari was used to decorate the Mother's picture? Does she have a shawl? How is the flower garden at Belur Math? Did you feel joy there?"

The devotee answered: "Yes, I did."

"There are various signs of bliss," M. said. "One of them is to visit a holy place again and again. The minds of those who are not married will be drawn to God, and will be inspired to renounce everything and join the Ramakrishna monastery. There is a gulf of difference between the garhasthya ashrama and the sannyasa ashrama. Light comes into a householder's life through a chink, and a flood of light comes from all directions into a monastic's life. They are full of light, inside and out."

Meanwhile, a devotee brought offered sweets and fruits from the Shyamsundar temple. M. touched the prasad to his head and then distributed it amongst the devotees.

M. said: "The Master used to say, 'Whoever thinks of me, I think of him.' We think of him very little, and now just see how much prasad he has sent us. I can't imagine what the Master would do for us if we offered our body, mind, and everything at his feet."

Morton Institution, 27 December 1927

In the evening M. was seated, surrounded by devotees. As different water channels lose their identity when they meet with the Ganges, so people of different temperaments and views lost their individualities when associating with M.

M. said: "On Christmas day I went to the Roman Catholic Church in Dharmatala [central Calcutta] to pray as well as to see their manner of praying. I knelt down with the Indian and foreign Christians. The next day also I joined in their prayers, and I had an opportunity to talk about

Christ with the pastors. Their idea about the Holy Bible is different from ours. You see, we have seen Christ. If you ask: 'How? He lived nearly 1900 years ago.' Well, the Master said: 'I am Rama, Krishna, Christ, and Chaitanya.' Thus have I seen Christ.

"On the same day I went to Dakshineswar and had prasad of the Divine Mother. The priest kindly opened the western door and I entered the Mother's temple. I saw the Mother standing from three positions — south, southwest, and west — and each angle of vision was different.

"You see, we have seen the Master. Those who have seen him speak about him in one way; those who have heard about him speak of him in a different way; and those who have read about him speak in yet another way. A man who has seen the ocean describes it in a detailed way, whereas the man who has merely heard about the ocean cannot speak as impressively as the eyewitness. Some have seen milk, heard about milk, and drunk milk. We belong to the last group. In other words, while drinking the milk, we have seen, heard, and tasted it.

"The Master accepted all religious views. In fact, he not only accepted them but also practised those religious paths. He practised Islam and realized that God has made all paths. While practising Islam, he dressed like a Muslim. He also did not go to the Kali temple, and he wanted to eat Muslim food. So Mathur arranged to have Muslim meals prepared by Hindu cooks.

"Some ask: 'What miracle did Sri Ramakrishna perform?' Is there any dearth of the Master's miracles? One of his miracles is Girish Ghosh — what he was and what he became. The current of his life was moving in one direction and the Master reversed it. Another miracle is Gauri-ma. The Master made her practise sadhana and did much work through that woman. Latu Maharaj [later Swami Adbhutananda] was another of the Master's miracles. He was truly phenomenal: a piece of rusty iron turned into gold by the Master's touch. He was a servant of Ram Datta and would carry various things for the Master. Later he began to serve the Master at Dakshineswar. Seeing him asleep one evening, the Master said to him, 'If you sleep in the evening, then when will you do spiritual disciplines?' From then on, Latu Maharaj gave up sleeping at night and practised sadhana.

"It is a great miracle to change a person's life current."

Saying this, M. became serious and silent. It was late evening and the devotees took their leave of him.

[Translated from *Srima Sarada* magazine, recorded by Satish Chandra Nath (Sri Sri Yogeswari Ramakrishna Math: Howrah), 5:1,7,10 issues and 6:1,2,6 issues]

Shanti Kumar Mitra

Morton Institution, fourth floor, March-April 1925, 7:00 p.m.

M. said: "Today is an auspicious day, the Holy Mother's temple in Jayrambati was dedicated on this day [two years earlier]. Thus, many memories of the Mother are coming to my mind. I had the Master's company for only 5 years, but Holy Mother protected me from all dangers over a period of 35 years. She was the Mother of the Universe. Once just before I returned home from Jayrambati, she served me my meal. She pressed a large quantity of rice onto my plate so that it looked like a small amount. I said, 'Mother, shall I be able to eat so much rice?' She replied: 'My son, it is not much. Please eat. You don't know when you will get your next meal.' He who has received the Mother's affection even once will never forget her. I observed that the Master could not control his bhava samadhi, although he tried. But Holy Mother was the embodiment of great power. She served food to the devotees, cooked in the kitchen, and looked after her niece Radhu; and yet she went into samadhi seated on the veranda. She was like the Phalgu River: there is sand above, and no one knows that water flows beneath it. Who can understand Holy Mother?"

A young devotee was staying with some relatives while he was going to school, but he was ill-treated because of his association with the monastery. He said to M.: "Please tell me how I can get peace. Perhaps it is because I committed great sins in my past life that I am undergoing this humiliation."

M. said: "Whomever you stay with, give some service to them and try to satisfy them. But if they obstruct your spiritual practices or keep you from visiting the monastery, do not listen to them. Just keep quiet and forbear. The Master said: 'He who forbears, survives; and he who does not forbear, perishes.' The nature of worldly people is strange: if their sons are immoral, they joyfully accept that; but if their sons want to be monks, that is unpardonable. You see, human character is formed through sufferings and obstacles. The more you face those obstacles, the more your mind will long for God. The great devotee Prahlada went through so much suffering for God. Look at how the gopis suffered. They knew no one but Krishna. There is an English proverb: 'Good comes from evil.'

"It is true that your suffering is due to either bad karma from a past life or some other reason, but yet you have the holy company of the Master's disciples. The Lord is showing you the true nature of worldly life and then leading you to his disciples. Just see how suffering is pushing you towards God, the source of infinite bliss. Let pain and suffering come. Focus your mind on the Master and depend on him. Be content with whatever condition he keeps you in. The mother spanks the child and it cries, but it still holds on to its mother. You talk about peace: the more you go towards God, the more you will get peace. Complete peace comes when you attain God. Monks in the western part of India ask other monks, 'Have you attained peace?' In other words, have you attained God? Pain and suffering are all in the mind. There is a blissful state where worldly suffering cannot reach."

M. told Jiten Babu: "You see, the body needs food to function. One needs air to breathe. God keeps us dependant in such a way that a man still feels that he is the doer."

Dr. Kartik Bakshi said: "Breathing and the heartbeat do not stop until death."

M. responded: "Yes, they can stop when one is alive. When the Master was in deep samadhi, doctors examined his lungs and heart and found that their functions had halted. That is why, the day the Master passed away in samadhi, we did not recognize it at first. He quite often went into deep samadhi, so we did not realize that he had left his body."

As M. said this, tears trickled from his eyes and his voice became hoarse. He could no longer speak. His attendant Ramlal brought his supper. It was 9:30 p.m. when the devotees left.

Morton Institution, 1925, 5:00 p.m.

A devotee said: "There is no escape from the results of bad karma. Shall we have to experience the results of all karma?"

M. replied: "You are studying to pass an examination, and when you pass, you get the result. A thief steals, and then he goes to jail. There are also some actions that were done in a previous life but did not produce any result then, so they remain in the storehouse. Some of those actions bear results in this life and give you misery. But if you follow your guru's instructions, and practise japa and meditation, your suffering will be reduced. For example, you are walking through the scorching sun. You have no umbrella and your head is burning; you are perspiring profusely; your chest feels as if it is splitting with thirst; and your feet are covered with blisters. At that time a man comes forward and gives you an umbrella, a pair of shoes, a glass of cold water, and a hand fan. You cool yourself with the fan, drink the water, put on the shoes, and hold the umbrella over your head. When you begin to walk, the heat of the sun remains the same, but you do not feel so much pain. Holy Mother used to say: 'Japa and meditation destroy the results of bad karma. Providence changes His writing with His own pen.' She further said, 'Suppose you are destined to lose a leg; you will get a scratch instead.' Don't worry about all these things. Just take refuge in Him. Krishna said in the Gita (18:66): 'I will deliver you from all sins; do not grieve.'"

Another devotee asked: "What can I do if my mind does not like to repeat the mantra?"

"In the beginning japa seems to be dry," M. said. "But one should continue to repeat the mantra even if the mind does not like it. *Japāt siddhi* — perfection comes through japa. The mind does not become concentrated in one day. One should pray to the Master wholeheartedly. Then by his grace the mind becomes calm automatically. Once this happens it is hard to stop japa and leave your seat.

"A dog bites a bone and its mouth bleeds, yet it does not give up biting it. If it can break the bone and get to the marrow, it forgets all pain. Anyone who gets the taste of japa does not like anything else. He or she becomes irritated if someone disturbs the chanting. God and His name are not separate — they are one. The wheel of the mantra destroys all worldly bondages, all bad impressions of past lives, and all kinds of sins. The mantra purifies the body and the mind. The Lord's name removes the fear of death and one experiences only bliss."

A devotee said: "We get peace when we come to you. At least for the time being we are free of our pain and suffering. But you are now old and your health is not good. I sometimes wonder how this vast Ramakrishna Order will continue. What will happen to us, who are burning in this world, when you people depart?"

"Why? The Master is the goal." M. said. "As long as a genuine monk exists in this Order, the Master will remain in the Order and guide it. Some of his disciples are still living. Have their company as much as you can. This will change the samskaras of your past lives. The Master lived in

Dakshineswar for 30 years, and Swamiji gave up his body in Belur Math. So many monks have practised sadhana in those places, so they are truly holy. One's mind moves easily towards God in those places. The bodies of the avatar and his associates are not everything: their gross bodies may disappear, yet they help humanity through their subtle bodies."

Three monks arrived from Belur Math, two of whom were from Kerala. One of them asked: "The Master said that Bhakti Yoga was the zeitgeist of this age, whereas Swamiji emphasized Karma Yoga. Which one should we follow?"

M. replied: "You have read Swamiji's *Karma Yoga*. He also wrote *Bhakti Yoga*. If you read *Bhakti Yoga*, you will understand what he meant. When he talked about Karma Yoga, he emphasized that. In other words, he taught according to his audience. The activities of the Ramakrishna Mission are pursued to purify the mind. If one performs action in the spirit of service to God, one will develop devotion. If one works unselfishly in the hospital and dispensary, these altruistic actions help one to attain liberation."

Another devotee said: "Sir, we find all the teachings of the avatars in the Gita and other scriptures. Then why do they come again and again and undergo all these troubles?"

"Sugar and sand are mixed in the scriptures," M. replied. "Commentators put their own ideas into the words of God. When the avatar departs, his messages get jumbled and lead to confusion within a short time. If the avatar does not come, who will explain the scriptures? Krishna said in the Gita (4:7): 'Whenever there is a decline of dharma, and a rise of adharma, I incarnate Myself.' Who is the avatar? He is the highest manifestation of Divinity among human beings. Philip said to Jesus, 'Rabbi, show me the Father.' Jesus immediately replied: 'Philip, hast thou seen me and not seen the Father? I and my Father are one.' The Master also said: 'Now I am not finding myself within me. Sometimes I think "I am He, and He is I."' The Master told us: 'If anyone cries with a longing heart, God cannot stay still. He hurriedly reveals Himself to that person.' Jesus also said: 'Seek, and ye shall find; knock, and it shall be opened unto you.'"

A devotee asked: "Sir, is there any hope for a married man?"

M. said: "Why not? If a householder moves one step towards God, He comes forward walking ten steps. He knows that he has put 20 maunds* of weight on their heads [*meaning heavy responsibility*]. Suppose a dandy

---

* One maund is equal to 82 pounds.

is walking with a stick in hand and on his way he bows down to Mother Kali at Thanthania. And a porter, carrying a two-maund weight on his head, puts it down with great effort with both hands and then bows down to the Mother with devotion. The Mother accepts the porter's salutation before the dandy's. Can everyone renounce? Jesus also had monastic disciples and householder devotees. He did not ask everybody to renounce. He said to some people: 'Some are eunuchs for the sake of God.' And again he said to others: 'Thou art in the world but not of the world.'

"If one does not renounce externally, one should practise nonattachment mentally. This is the worldly disease: We think that something that is impermanent, is permanent. That is the problem. It is extremely important for a householder to associate with holy people and the guru. They help us to understand our real condition. They show us our duties and point the way to the goal. It is like using a correct watch to adjust a watch with the wrong time.

"You see, although the highest ideal is renunciation, the guru knows our path. Does the doctor give the same medicine to everyone? The prescription differs from disease to disease. 'The same coat does not fit Henry, Jim, and John alike.' The guru guides some to the path of renunciation and some to the path of family life according to their tendencies. Finally, he accepts all and removes their impurities. The guru is the helmsman in this ocean of maya."

Morton Institution

A monk and a brahmachari arrived from Gadadhar Ashrama.

"Welcome, welcome, please come in," M. said. "When monks come here it indicates that the Master has not forgotten us."

The monk said: "Today on the bank of the Ganges I saw a holy man who looked like the Master, but he was observing the vow of silence. Then a desire came to see you and listen to the words of the Master."

M. said: "That happened to me once also. It was a long time ago, but after the Master's passing away. I was near the Howrah Bridge when I met a monk who looked like the Master. I unfolded my umbrella to protect his face from the scorching sun. He smiled a little. Then I asked, 'Can I do anything for you?' That monk replied, 'I will be happy if I can get a ticket to Varanasi.' I took him to the railway station, bought him a ticket to Varanasi, and escorted him to the train. Pleased, the monk gave me a special rudraksha bead and said, 'Please keep this; it will do you good.' I humbly accepted his loving gift. But afterwards, while crossing the Howrah Bridge, I thought about how the Master had taken on all of my responsibilities, my good and bad [actions], my fortune and misfortune, my life and death, and this life and the next life. Why then did I accept that rudraksha bead? What kind of faith do I have in the Master? I threw that rudraksha bead into the Ganges. When the Master is looking after me and protecting me day and night, why would I depend on those things?

"When I first met the Master, it seemed to me that he was an ordinary man. As time passed, I realized that he was the indivisible Satchidananda covered with a veil of maya, beyond our comprehension.

"The Master is beyond the injunctions of the Vedas. In his mercy, he gave me shelter at his feet. He left so many years ago, but amazingly it seems those incidents happened yesterday. The Master is our all in all. When the trolley pole of the tram car is connected with the overhead electric wire, the tram runs, gives light, and the fan moves; but everything stops if the trolley pole is down. Now I see the Master is walking with me and holding my hand. I believe he will be with me till the end."

In the evening M. waved the lamp in front of the pictures of gods and goddesses. Coming to the picture of the mother bird hatching her egg, M. said: "Let the work continue, but the mind should be on God. Look at this bird: her whole mind is on hatching her egg; her eyes are open but she sees nothing external. One finds fulfillment in life if, by His grace, one can keep one's mind on God. The goal of japa and meditation, austerity and sadhana, discrimination and renunciation is to attain God. But He does not reveal Himself if one does not have intense longing for, concentration on, and absorption in Him."

Everyone present began to practise japa and meditation. After a while, the brahmachari sang a song: "Sing the name of Ramakrishna. Victory to Ramakrishna." M. listened to the song with folded hands. Then the brahmachari sang another song: "O my mind, see no difference in Ramakrishna, Krishna, Kali, and Shiva." As M. listened to this song, tears trickled from his eyes. He wiped them, and then calmly said: "The Master is the embodiment of all gods and goddesses. By thinking of him one thinks of all of them."

[Translated from *Srima Samipe*, edited by Swami Chetanananda (Udbodhan Office: Calcutta, 1996), 148-64]

Amulya Krishna Sen

I met M. in the fall of 1922. One evening I went to the fourth floor of the Morton Institution in Calcutta, where I found a serene gentleman with a long beard seated on a chair on the veranda. He was facing north and some devotees were sitting in a bench nearby. I recognized him immediately. I tried to bow down and touch his feet, but he stopped me and asked me to sit on the bench in front of him. I began to listen to the conversation.

There had been a solar eclipse that morning. A devotee had gone to Belur Math, where he saw many people bathing on both sides of the Ganges. He was describing the scene to M.

M. said: "How wonderful! You are very fortunate to have seen that — so many people bathing and thinking only of God. It is a sight for the gods to see. You see, Krishna mentioned four kinds of devotees in the Gita (7:16): 'Four types of virtuous men worship Me, O Arjuna: the man in distress, the man seeking knowledge, the man seeking enjoyment, and, O best of the Bharatas, the man endowed with wisdom.' Although Krishna gave the highest position to jnanis, he also stated 'noble indeed are they all.' Afflicted souls also call on God. And the seekers are moving around to know God, and thus finally they also attain knowledge in the course of time."

M. continued: "See the glory of God! He is so compassionate! He created temples in various places, monasteries nearby, and devotees all around, so that people have opportunities to call on Him. He made Belur Math for us as an invitation to visit Him. If we do not respond to His call, He will close the door." M. then told a story adapted from the Bible.

"Once Christ invited some householders to a banquet. He sent messengers to them to join the feast, but no one came. One person declined, saying, 'I must bring in the harvest.' Another man said: 'I am newly married. How can I go without my wife?' Yet another person said: 'I have some urgent business. I can't go.' Everyone refused Christ's invitation.

He then told his disciples, 'Call in people from the street and feed them this food.' When they came in and the food was served, Christ asked that the door be closed. When the grand feast was going on, the people whom he had previously invited came to their senses. They realized that they should not have turned down the Lord. So they came one after another and began to knock at the door, saying: 'Lord, Lord, please open the door. We have come.' Christ replied from inside, 'Who are you?' They answered: 'We are those devotees whom you invited. Don't you recognize us?' Christ replied: 'Why didn't you come when I sent you the invitation? I will not open the door now.' The Lord did not open the door.

"The Master created the monastery nearby. It is as if he is inviting us, and also cautioning us. If we do not respond to his invitation, he will close the door. In other words, if we do not take advantage of the holy company in the monastery, he will close the door."

Again, referring to seekers of God, M. commented: "A devotee went on vacation, travelling to various holy places in search of God-realization. It is hard for a devotee who hungers for God to remain idle. The devotee's father-in-law told him: 'Why do you move here and there? Just relax and enjoy your vacation.' The father-in-law was a wealthy man." Referring to him, M. said: "Look, rich people like this are worthless. Such people seek only comfort. They are not self-reliant. Their servants rub oil on their bodies and bathe them. They seek only comfort."

M.'s remark struck me deeply. I resolved to become self-reliant and not depend on others.

M. then inquired about me. I said that Swami Shuddhananda had sent me to him and that I needed his blessing. He replied that the Master would bless me.

After listening to M.'s wonderful conversation I returned home. His serene look and childlike simplicity left a deep impression on my heart. It seemed to me that he had achieved divine bliss. I lamented that I had not come to him earlier.

Morton Institution, 15 June 1931

I arrived before evening and found M. walking on the roof of the school building. The walls of the roof were so high that one could not see the buildings around. The devotees were seated under the blue sky. I bowed down to M.

M. said: "You see, the Master said to the devotees, 'Bhagavata, bhakta, Bhagavan — the scriptures, devotees, and God are one.' God is the Bhagavata scripture; He is the devotee; and He is God Himself.

Krishna said in the Gita (9:30-31): 'Even the most sinful man, if he worships Me with unswerving devotion, must be regarded as righteous; for he has formed the right resolution. Proclaim it boldly, O son of Kunti, that My devotee never perishes.' Is a devotee an ordinary person? A devotee does not know how great he or she is."

A devotee responded: "It is better not to know; otherwise one may develop pride."

"That is not so." M. disagreed. "A true devotee has no ego. The Master compared the ego of a devotee to a burnt rope. If you blow on it, the ashes will fly away.

"Ah, the clouds were beautiful at noon today! There was a monk in Dakshineswar who would dance when he saw a cloud. God has become everything: 'From Him are born prana, mind, all the sense-organs, space, air, fire, water, and earth, which supports all.' (Mundaka Upanishad, 2:1:3)

"A monk from the Himalayas would remark when he saw a waterfall, 'Ah, what a wonderful thing you have created!' The sight of the waterfall would awaken God-consciousness in that monk.

"Today I received a letter from Darjeeling. A Western woman wrote to me, saying, 'I wish you would enjoy the cold weather here.' She belongs to the West, so she prefers a cold climate. The people of our country are eager to see the vastness of the mountains and become awakened thereby. Once when the Master was at the Cossipore garden house, I went to Darjeeling. When I returned, he asked, 'Well, did you have an awakening when you saw the Himalayas?' When I was on the train ascending from Siliguri, tears automatically fell from my eyes. I did not know why at that time, but when the Master asked me about awakening, I understood the reason for my tears. Krishna said in the Gita (9:25): 'Of sacrifices I am the sacrifice of japa; of immovable things I am the Himalayas.' He has become the Himalayas. You see, if you eat a chili, whether you know it or not, you will feel that burning sensation."

It was evening. M. invited us to his room, saying, "Please come inside and see the deities." He showed us the pictures of Ramakrishna, Holy Mother, and a picture of monks at the Kumbhamela. He then left his room, bowed down to the tulsi plant on the roof, and sat down to meditate. The devotees sat for meditation near him. After half an hour, M. quoted from the Gita (9:19): "'I give heat; I hold back and send forth rain.' Just see, we were suffering from heat; then came rain, and now we feel cool. Please notice how God has set the seasons on this earth: summer, rain, autumn, fall, winter, and spring rotate automatically.

"God created human beings, birds, and beasts. He created our hands, feet, ears, nose, and eyes. That is on the outside. And now see inside: He created the heart, the spleen, the liver, the nervous system, consciousness, and perception. We survive by breathing, so He created air. If He were to withdraw the air, let us see how long our free will would survive.

"And what about food? Who created this food? We eat breakfast, lunch, and dinner so that this body can survive; otherwise we would be nowhere.

"God has also created sleep. People work hard the entire day. When their bodies are exhausted, they sleep at night and are refreshed the next morning. When I go for a walk early in the morning, I see some people sleeping on the footpath. Police do not disturb them because they understand that everyone needs sleep.

"The sun rises every morning in the east. Is this not a great miracle? It happens every day, so we don't consider it to be a wonder. Well, think about that day when the sun rose for the first time upon this earth!"

*   *   *

A devotee remarked: "The Master said, 'If an aspirant practises a little spiritual discipline, then someone comes forward to help him."

M. said: "I didn't understand what he meant at that time. Later, I understood the real meaning: 'He who is beyond mind and speech takes a human form and comes to help us.'

"The Master told us this story: 'A woman considered herself to be a knower of Brahman. She wore stockings and high-heeled shoes when she went walking, and she did not care for gods and goddesses. But then her son became seriously ill. First she took him to an allopathic doctor, then to a homeopathic doctor, and finally to an ayurvedic doctor. Unfortunately her son's condition did not improve, but instead became worse. One of her relatives suggested: "Sister, you have consulted with many doctors, but none could cure him. Why don't you go to Tarakeswar Shiva and pray for a divine favour? I think your son will be cured." Then that proud mother rushed barefoot to Tarakeswar. She did not discriminate any longer. By God's grace her son recovered.'

"One needs deep faith to succeed in spiritual life. One should believe that God dwells in all hearts: 'I am the Goal and the Support; the Lord and the Witness; the Abode, the Refuge, and the Friend.'" (Gita, 9:18)

[Translated from *Srima Samipe*, edited by Swami Chetanananda (Udbodhan Office: Calcutta, 1996), 140-45]

Swami Jagannathananda

Morton Institution, 27 May 1929

M. said: "The Master passed away 43 years ago, but it seems that it happened just the other day. Those images remain vivid in my mind. The entire report of the Master's illness is in my diary. I recorded the amount of blood from each hemorrhage, the intensity of his pain, what he ate, and other things. Every day I carried that report to Dr. Mahendralal Sarkar."

Hari Babu asked: "Did the Master tell Dr. Sarkar, 'It will be enough if you think of me,' and 'I am the avatar'?"

M. replied: "He did not say that to him directly because the doctor might have become irritated, so he asked me to tell him. Thus we both received the lesson."

Morton Institution, 12 June 1929, 6:30 p.m.

Bhutnath, Kartik Maharaj of Baranagore Ashrama, and some devotees were present.

Bhutnath asked M.: "Shall I meditate on Swamiji or the Master?"

"Swamiji asked people to meditate on Sri Ramakrishna," M. answered. "First meditate on the Master and then on Swamiji."

Bhutnath said: "Swamiji's form is bright and heroic, and he wears a turban. The Master looks very ordinary."

M. replied: "Well, Swamiji has many other pictures — one in which he wears only a loincloth, another he wears a cloak, and still another with a staff and a water pot. People meditate on the form that they prefer."

M. addressed a monk from Baranagore Ashrama: "The Ashrama grounds are spacious. Whenever you have no work, please sit under a tree and meditate. Is it necessary to work throughout one's life? One should work to attain devotion. It is important to go into solitude and meditate on God. Only then can one detect one's shortcomings. The Ashrama is for monks, but the monks are not for the Ashrama. Jesus said: 'The Sabbath was made for man, and not man for the Sabbath.'" (Mark 2:27)

M. served some refreshments to Kartik Maharaj and Bhutnath, and then they left. It was evening. M. and the devotees meditated on the roof for a while.

M. said: "The Master told this story: 'A man took some gold to a goldsmith to make some jewellery. The goldsmith was very shrewd. He instructed his beautiful wife to put on a nice dress and some makeup, and then said: 'When I am mixing the customer's gold with brass, you suddenly open the door behind me. Be sure to make some noise. The customer will stare at you with an open mouth and at that time I shall steal a chunk of gold.'"

With a smile, M. continued: "One day the Master said to the devotees: 'A young girl has come to the Panchavati. She is a devotee and spiritual aspirant. Please go and see her.' Most of them rushed to see her, including a young boy devotee. When he returned, the Master asked, 'Why did you go? The others belong to that group of curious people.' The young devotee said, 'Sir, you asked everyone to go.' The Master replied, 'I was testing people to see what kind of devotees they are.' Some did not go although the Master asked them to. Later I asked someone who had gone to see that young woman, 'What is she like?' He replied, 'She is greater than the Master.' I was shocked. God in human form is here in front of us, and this fellow says that girl is greater than the Master.

"The Master was very fond of Suresh Mitra and visited his home many times. Once Suresh took a blanket and came to Dakshineswar to stay the night. When he returned home, his wife said to him: 'You may stay there during the day, but at night you must return home.' After that Suresh did not dare stay overnight in Dakshineswar again. His wife pulled him away from the company of the Master.

"Mahamaya, the great enchantress, traps everyone — the king, the people, and even monks. Alexander the Great, who humbled many kings and conquered many countries, finally lost his life in Persia under the influence of alcohol and women. Napoleon was like that. The whole of Europe was afraid of him. He supervised the war and advised his generals. One day he said to his main general, 'Last night I saw you enter a woman's tent.' The man replied, 'I saw a woman entering *your* tent.' Napoleon laughed and then rode away on his horse. You see, the whole world trembles in fear of these people!

"I once knew a man who had been a monk for 20 years, and then gave up the ochre cloth and got married. If you are attracted to lust and gold, your attachment may live inside your mind — but finally Mahamaya will pull you into the world of maya. The Master repeated this great mantra: 'Lust and gold are maya. Mother, may I never be deluded by them.' Every one of his words is a mantra. Christ said, 'Heaven and earth shall pass away, but my words shall never pass away.'"

Seeing a cloud in the northwest, M. recalled: "I remember, one day the Master was returning from the pine grove. There was a thick cloud in the sky, northwest of the Ganges. The Master was returning from the pine grove, walking southward. That scene is deeply imprinted in my mind."

It was evening. M. and the devotees meditated among the tulsi plants on the roof. After meditation, M. sat in his chair.

"The gods and demons fight for an object of enjoyment," M. said. "After they churned the ocean, they began to fight to possess the pitcher of nectar that would make their bodies immortal. The demons practised austerities so that they could maintain their worldly enjoyments. But the rishis were people of a different calibre. They did not care for any worldly pleasures. They went into the forest and remained absorbed in the thought of God. This was their aim: 'Only by knowing Him does one pass over death. There is no other way to the Supreme Goal.' (Svetasvatara Upanishad, 3:8) The Master created a group of renunciants who remained untouched by lust and gold."

Morton Institution, 28 June 1929

It was a cloudy morning. M. was seated in his chair. A few days earlier, Dr. Kartik Bakshi, a great devotee and an admirer of M., had passed away.

M. said: "Dr. Bakshi visited this place for ten years. He longed for God, so God did not keep such an unselfish and loving soul in this world of misery." M. suggested that his family perform the *shrāddha* ceremony. Then he said: "During the Master's last illness, his relatives suggested: 'The Master has a terminal disease. A ritual for expiation must be performed.' The Master told them, 'All right, do it.' Balaram's priest recited the hymn of *Aparādha-bhanjana* (Forgiveness of transgressions). The Master told his close devotees: 'You will not have to do those things. Avatars are free from all transgressions. Those who have egos, let them do it.' It is difficult to understand through whom the Master will work. If he wishes, he can make a person a *jivanmukta,* a living-free soul, or a great devotee of God."

A brahmachari asked him: "Could the rishis see these subtle truths?"

M. replied: "They visualized some of these truths through sadhana, and God revealed some to them. Who has the power to absorb a transcendental truth? One cannot comprehend that truth without finishing one's karma. Some do not even want to listen to it. The Master did not teach the highest truth to all. He would sometimes say, 'The Mother is pressing my mouth shut and not allowing me to speak.' Each spiritual aspirant is different: One person is a like a small water pot, another like a pitcher, and yet another like a big jar. One can go higher and higher in space — it is limitless."

*   *   *

In Dakshineswar sometimes the Master would walk in the gardens belonging to Shambhu Mallick or Jadu Mallick.

M. recalled: "When the Master visited Jadu Mallick's garden, the caretaker would fan him. The Master once went into samadhi as he witnessed that man's devotion. One day the caretaker invited the Master to lunch, and he accepted. The Master went to his place accompanied by Rakhal Maharaj, me, and a young brahmin boy from Orissa [M.'s cook]. Perhaps he would not have accepted an invitation from a rich man.

"The Master's samadhi was so unpredictable that he needed someone to stay with him at all times; there was a chance that he could have an accident. One day when he was in an ecstatic mood, he had a vision of Jagannath. The Master tried to embrace Him, but fell down and broke his arm."

M. said, "While listening to the temple music [*rasun chauki*] being played at the nahabat, the Master would go into samadhi.... The Master would also merge into samadhi when he saw someone closing an umbrella. It reminded him of withdrawing the mind from the world and giving it to God."

[Translated from *Srima Samipe,* edited by Swami Chetanananda (Udbodhan Office: Calcutta, 1996), 165-76]

Tarani Purakayastha

In 1930 after Durga Puja I went to Puri and Bhubaneswar with a friend. After our pilgrimage we returned to Calcutta and visited M. on the fourth floor of the Morton Institution. He had a large room with ordinary furniture. His bed was a simple cot with a deerskin covering. There was a table, a canvas easy chair, and a couple of benches. A glass of water was on the table. Pictures of Ramakrishna, Chaitanya, and Nityananda were hanging on the wall, and there was also a *mridanga* [a drum]. Some books were on a shelf.

We were blessed to see him in his room. His face was calm, serene, and full of humility and devotion. His hair and beard were like sterling silver. His form was like that of a hermit. His eyes were loving and luminous. Sri Ramakrishna had once seen him in a vision in the company of Gauranga.

M. was alone in his room. When he learned that we had brought him some prasad of Jagannath, he got a clean container and asked us to put the prasad in it. Then he asked us to wash our hands outside the room. We were amazed by his faith and his devotion for the prasad of Jagannath. He taught us how one should respect prasad.

Because we were carrying prasad, we had not yet bowed down to him. We now bowed down. He asked us to sit on the bench, and said: "Now, please tell me about your visit to Puri, the holy place of Lord Jagannath, so that I can visualize the Lord in my mind." We briefly described our visit to the deity while he listened very attentively.

Then M. asked us whether we knew any monks of the Ramakrishna Order. We knew a few monks and we mentioned their names. Then he said: "Please keep in touch with those monks either directly or through correspondence. There are some monks who are absorbed in deep meditation and tapasya. They don't like to spend time answering letters. When you write letters to that type of hermit monk, please say this: 'I am not expecting an answer from you.' As soon as that monk reads your letter and thinks of you, you will be greatly benefitted. Thus always keep in touch with the monks." This is how M. taught us the glory of holy company and how to maintain it.

Then M. removed a letter from an envelope and said: "A monk wrote this letter to me. Please listen." He began to read: "Most revered Master Mahashay, I left my parents, my home, and everything else, and took the vow of sannyasa in order to experience the Truth and to realize God. I have been misusing my time and could not achieve anything. I have no peace of mind and am filled with sorrow. For that reason, I have come to Uttarkashi [a hermitage in the Himalayas] to practise austerities. Please bless me so that by the Master's grace my mind will be focussed on the goal." After reading that letter M. said: "Yes, this time he will make it. He will make it. Because his mind is remorseful, his spiritual journey will be favourable." M. did not mention the name of the writer.

M. then told us: "Let us meditate now." He gave each of us a folded blanket to use as an asana, and he sat on the deerskin on his cot. We meditated till 10:00 a.m. M. got up and said to us: "Perhaps this is your lunch time. You may go now." We then bowed down to him and returned to our home.

M. was a born teacher. Before saying good-bye, he taught us how to meditate. I saw M. again several times after this meeting, but I still cherish the blissful memory of my first visit.

[Translated from *Srima Samipe*, edited by Swami Chetanananda (Udbodhan Office: Calcutta, 1996), 177-80]

Brahmachari Yatindranath

M. loved the songs that Sri Ramakrishna used to sing. M. sang:

I have made Thee, O Lord, the polestar of my life;
No more shall I lose my way on the world's trackless sea.

He then said: "Without His grace, is it possible for us to make Him the polestar of our lives? The songs that put the Master into samadhi are mantras. There is tremendous power in them. India is a wonderful country: Here if a person's actions or songs lead him or her to God, those actions or songs are acceptable; otherwise they are rejected. If certain foods enhance sattva qualities, they are acceptable; otherwise they are rejected.

"The other day I saw a wonderful scene: A gorgeous marriage procession was going along one side of the street. On the other side was a funeral procession, accompanied by the chant, '*Ram nam satya hai* — the Lord's name is the only reality.' The man who died had many hopes and aspirations, and they all disappeared. People still believe that they will not die. In fact, that death alone is the real death, after which there will be no more death. [*He meant liberation here.*] Otherwise human beings are born again and again.

"Lust takes on terrible dimensions when one lives alone. Some desires that do not raise their head in front of others will attack viciously when one lives in solitude. One comes to know one's own nature in solitude, and this makes the aspirant cautious. It is dangerous for a restless aspirant to live in solitude.

"He is blessed who passes his whole life in the Ramakrishna Order and tries to realize God, unselfishly serving others without considering his own comfort. This Order is the body of the Master, and his ideal manifests through it. The message of the avatar does not spread without the Order. Rather it disappears. The main aim is God-realization, and the Order functions well if the spirit of renunciation is present. The fall of the

Order is inevitable if any one of these two is absent."

It was worth seeing M. when he received prasad. He would remove his shoes, wash his hands and mouth, chant that particular deity's name, touch the prasad to his forehead, and then put a little of the prasad into his mouth. He behaved as if he were in the presence of that deity. He would say: "What good fortune! We sit in Calcutta and receive prasad from those distant holy places — Rameswaram, Dwaraka, and Puri. Now we are connected with those holy places. It is enough to get a little prasad."

But M. looked serious when he visited Dakshineswar. Observing his demeanor and actions, one felt that M. was in the Dakshineswar of old and walking with his beloved Master, Sri Ramakrishna. M. would sit in those places where he used to sit to listen to the Master. He would embrace a pillar in the natmandir that the Master had embraced while remarking that the devotees of the inner circle were like this inner pillar. M. would embrace the trees that the Master had touched. He would visit the rooms in the mansion where Rasmani and Mathur had lived. When M. visited the Master's room, the Panchavati, or the bel-tala, he was in a different mood, as if he were in the company of the Master. Some of the devotees could not understand this, so they were cautious around him at those times. One day an arrangement was made to take a group photo in front of the Kali temple. M. sat on the terrace and a devotee tried to sit next to him. He told him: "No, you can't sit here. The Master sat here. We are sitting around him. The photographer is taking his photo and not ours."

Wherever M. had once spoken with the Master, from the temple to the bel-tala, he would stop and describe to the devotees the incidents that had occurred there, referring to the dates and occasions.

Once a picnic was arranged in the Panchavati. Before they began eating, M. heard that Brother Ramlal, the Master's nephew, had not been invited. He became sad and immediately sent curd and sweets to his house. He remarked: "They belong to our guru's family and as such are worthy of our respect. God has taken birth in their family. How fortunate they are!"

If any devotee came to M. after visiting Kamarpukur, M. would excitedly say to the other devotees present, "He is coming from the Holy Land — Jerusalem." When one such devotee visited, M. joyfully served him refreshments. He then reminisced: "When I first went to Kamarpukur, I asked the villagers and farmers all about the Master. I wanted to embrace them because they were my own people. I considered the birds, beasts, and trees of Kamarpukur as blessed because they had seen and touched the Master. When someone told me anything about the Master, I bowed down to him. The Master changed my outlook!"

Because the Master had visited the Brahmo Samaj, M. would also go there. M. would sit in the section of the Navavidhan Brahmo temple where the Master had sat. Every year M. went to the temple on the day that the Master had visited it.

Once, on the night of Kali Puja, M. wanted to visit Kalighat in South Calcutta. Some devotees objected because there would be a heavy crowd. M. said: "Well, that crowd did not gather to buy a ticket in the railway station or at the cinema. The aim of each person there is to see the Divine Mother, which is a noble cause. It would be good if the body were to die in the crush of that crowd. Today is a special day. Every householder should observe these festivals. A nonstop religious festival flows in Hindu life from birth to death. Great souls and avatars are born to those devout families who faithfully observe the injunctions and prohibitions of the scriptures, and not to dissolute families."

One day during Durga Puja M. went to see the deities on Cornwallis Street (now Bidhan Sarani). As he watched some young children joyfully playing, M. commented: "Please see Mother Durga. The blissful Mother is expressing Her joy through them. Is the Mother in the image only? Wherever there is bliss, there the Mother manifests." When he saw the vegetables displayed in the College Street market, M. said: "Just see how the Mother is manifested here as vegetables. We eat these things to survive. In this way, to keep us alive, the Divine Mother pervades everything."

One night M. said: "Let us go and see Vrindaban." He then led the devotees to the roof and remarked: "Look at that moon. This very moon rose in Vrindaban and witnessed the Raslila [Krishna's play with the gopis]. As we gaze upon this moon, we are connected with Vrindaban. So we are now in Vrindaban. The mind transcends the barrier of space and time.

"Long ago the Master prepared me to record the *Kathamrita*. I was unaware of this. I began to keep a diary when I was in the seventh grade [in 1867]. I would listen attentively to the lectures of distinguished people speaking in the Town Hall and Senate Hall, and then record them in my notebook with the date, time, and name of the lecturer. I met the Master after practising this kind of recording for 15 years. What an auspicious moment it was! My whole life changed.

"I was fond of Keshab Sen's lectures, which he would deliver with great passion. After I met the Master I realized why I liked Keshab Babu's lectures. Keshab Babu had been visiting the Master for years, and he would deliver the Master's message in his own powerful language. That is why his speeches inspired me.

"One day I was stung by a scorpion and the pain was unbearable. Then I remembered the Master's long suffering from cancer and my pain immediately subsided, as if water had fallen on fire.

"This is in the Chandi (11:29): 'No calamity befalls those who have taken refuge in You, O Mother, and those who resort to You become a refuge to others.'

"Worship is a direct connection with God. It is better to simplify the elaborate external aspects of worship and increase silent japa."

Someone sang this song:

Oh, when will dawn the blessed day
When Love will waken in my heart?
As I repeat Lord Hari's name,
And all my longing be fulfilled?...
When becoming mad I will make others mad?

M. commented: "Everyone is busy trying to 'make others mad,' to teach others. If you sincerely cry for God, then those who come in contact with you will also do the same. You do not have to worry about that. If you want to make others cry [for God], your own tears will stop."

M. relentlessly distributed Ramakrishna's message. It was late at night and someone kept reminding him about his supper. But he was absorbed in talking about the Master. He said: "Wait, I eat that ordinary food every day, but the company of devotees is a real feast. How can I leave this banquet?

"Food is of three kinds: [gross, subtle, and spiritual]. Can a man live by gross food only? The subtle foods — art, literature, science, and philosophy — are for intelligent people. Those who are real human beings eat spiritual food (para vidya), the highest knowledge that leads one to realize the Imperishable Brahman.

"The purpose of gross food is to realize God through this body. Birds and beasts also eat food. One should first offer pure food to the Lord and then partake of this prasad. That is the proper way to eat. As the Gita (4:24) says: 'Brahman is the offering and Brahman is the oblation.' The Brihadaranyaka Upanishad (3:8:10) says: 'Whosoever departs from this world without knowing the Imperishable is miserable.' One should not misuse a single moment in useless action. A monk is a full-time worker. A monk without renunciation is akin to a penniless householder; he needs to preserve his precious renunciation as one preserves grapes in a cotton box. It is because of his intense renunciation that a monk is worshipped by all."

If someone brought prasad from Belur Math and Dakshineswar, M. would take the Belur Math prasad first and then the prasad from Dakshineswar. He said: "In Belur Math all-renouncing monks perform worship without any motive, whereas in Dakshineswar householders perform worship to achieve some end."

In 1926, during the first convention of the Ramakrishna Mission, M. went to Belur Math to meet with the monks. When the steamer landed, M. was told that some monks were staying in a house nearby. He went into the bedroom and found no one there. Then he bowed down to their beds and said: "The monks' beds are pure. They pray, practise japa and meditation, and cry for God from these beds."

When M. observed someone with steadfast devotion to holy company, he felt that the Master's grace had dawned upon that person.

M. said: "I noticed that the Master would think more often of that devotee who was burdened with family responsibilities."

A man once tried to argue with M., but M. asked that person to go to the roof and look at the vast sky. When the man returned, M. asked: "What have you seen? What have you understood? Is it possible to understand the mystery of God? This earth is like a lump of clay and we are like small worms. Is it possible to understand the Creator of this universe by means of argument?

"We are breathing; but if we stop, all our proud talk will soon end. Again, we see the sun rise every day, and how incredible that is. We live every day in this miraculous universe; still people want to see miracles.

"Do you know why jnanis have compassion and the desire to act? Consider, for example, a poor man who has become wealthy through the help of others. It is natural for him to be compassionate to poor people. In the same way, great souls come forward to help the ignorant, remembering the suffering that they endured when they were in that state.

"Swamiji did so much work for the world, but it was the Master who prompted him to act and spoke through him. He was endowed with tremendous power, and Swamiji used the Master's power to conquer the world. Arjuna won the battle of Kurukshetra through the power of Krishna. When Krishna departed, Arjuna could not even lift his bow, *Gandiva*. The Master's disciples were educated and came from good families. Christ's disciples were farmers and fishermen — yet see what great work he did through them."

A devotee said: "We are not sincere and the mind is engrossed in worldliness. Is there any hope for us?"

M. answered: "Please pray to the Master for longing for God."

"I don't feel the desire to pray," the devotee replied.

M. said: "Well, then repeat the mantra that you received from your guru. Despite your restless mind, why don't you repeat the mantra 10 to 15 thousand times a day? Devotion comes from chanting the mantra. Then gradually renunciation develops, and finally the kundalini awakens."

The devotee said: "I don't even care to repeat the mantra."

"Then your case is serious," M. replied. "There is little chance you will survive. Tasting the divine name is the last treatment for the disease of worldliness. You will be free from fear if you have love for God's name. Gradually you will develop longing, devotion, and meditation. Meditation is not possible if one wants to enjoy the senses. When you close your eyes during meditation, the things that you desire appear in beautiful forms. Chanting God's name is very effective in this Kaliyuga.

"When Sanaka and other sages went to Brahma to be instructed in the knowledge of Brahman, He said: 'I am busy with creation now. My mind is restless. Please wait a little; let me calm my mind first.' Brahma went into samadhi, and then gave them advice. If one is busy with too many activities, it is difficult to calm the mind.

"Krishna said to Uddhava: 'I have told you what I have to say. Now go to Badarika Ashrama and practise austerities there. Then you will realize everything.' After doing that, Uddhava understood Krishna's message. If God comes to you and says, 'You have the knowledge of Brahman,' you won't fully experience it without practising austerities. The Master said to Keshab Sen, 'If I tell you more — that nondual truth — your organization will fall apart.' Keshab Babu was a great soul, yet even he was scared. If one has a secret desire to enjoy the senses, one is afraid to listen to teachings on renunciation and nondualism.

"The nondualistic teachings of Vedanta are meant for all-renouncing monks who practise the inner disciplines of hearing, reflection, and meditation on Brahman. These teachings are not for everyone. Nowadays most people have weak stomachs; they cannot digest even sago, barley, and cheese water [whey]. They would die if they ate *kaliya, pilaf, rabri,* and other rich dishes."

[Translated from *Srima Samipe*, edited by Swami Chetanananda (Udbodhan Office: Calcutta, 1996), 181-87]

Jitendranath Chattopadhyay

In M.'s life we observed the culmination of devotion. His heart was filled with faith in and devotion for Ramakrishna. Although he had had a Western education and was a proud teacher, his life was transformed when he came in contact with the Master. His transformation was truly remarkable. When the Chariot Festival of Puri was over, M. would wait in Howrah Station to ask pilgrims for prasad from Jagannath. If someone sent some prasad in an envelope or a basket, he would save the containers in his room after eating the prasad. He said, "They will remind me of the deities." Whenever M. passed through Bechu Chatterjee Street and Jhamapukur, he would bow down and touch his head to the ground where Ramkumar's school had been, and at Digambar Mitra's house, because those places were connected with the Master. When his companions wondered at M.'s unusual behaviour, he would reply, "You see, if a man walks through these streets, he will become a yogi." Again, when he visited Dakshineswar, he would soak his towel in the river at the Chandni Ghat and take it back to Calcutta. When the devotees arrived in the evening, he would squeeze the towel and sprinkle the Ganges water onto their heads, saying, "This water is from the Ganges at Dakshineswar where the Master bathed." What wonderful devotion M. had! Our lives would be blessed if we could achieve a particle of that devotion.

Ramakrishna was in M.'s mind in all three states: waking, dreaming, and sleeping. If anyone asked him to speak about the Master, he would reply: "You see, in olden days students would go to the rishis with sacrificial wood in hand and say, 'Please tell us the Upanishads.' The rishis replied: 'Our words are the Upanishads.' My situation is the same. The Master's words are my words." This is true indeed. Whatever topic M. discussed, even concerning the war, he would connect it with the Master's words.

I shall tell a story that illustrates the love and faith M. had for his Master. His mind was completely occupied with the thought of his guru and he was unaware of the world. Whenever he had a short break during class hours, he would rush to see his guru at Balaram's house or at Shyampukur. M. was then the headmaster of the Metropolitan School of Shyampukur, which was owned by Vidyasagar. One year the matriculation examination results were not good. From this, Vidyasagar concluded that M. was not paying sufficient attention to his duties at the school, due to his excessive devotion for his guru. But when Vidyasagar discussed this with M., M. resigned. Although M. knew that his family would suffer due to a terrible financial crisis, he could not bear any criticism of his guru.

Chaitanya said: "Be humbler than a blade of grass. Be patient and forbearing like a tree. Take no honour for yourself; give honour to all. Chant unceasingly the name of the Lord." M. was the embodiment of this teaching. He addressed everyone as *āpani* [a respectful form of *you*]. He took care of his own personal chores — from washing his clothes to cleaning his dishes after meals. If someone tried to arrange his mosquito curtain, he said, "Please don't meddle in my routine." He did not care for luxury, nor did he crave for worldly things. Once a devotee presented him with an expensive Italian blanket. He remarked: "What have you done? This blanket is like a beautiful young girl. My mind will be always occupied with looking after it." He completely gave up physical comforts, as well as any desire for good food. He would rinse rich food with water so that his tongue could not taste the flavour. If any devotee brought him a delicacy, he would say: "What have you done? Please take these dishes to the Advaita Ashrama for the monks."

In 1925 M. went to Puri to visit Lord Jagannath. One evening he and the devotees went to the temple to see the deity. Standing near the Garuda pillar, M. began to wave an oil lamp. He was then in a different world. His mind had merged into the transcendental realm. The lamp went out, yet he still continued to wave it. After a long time he came back to the normal plane. This kind of deep absorption helped M. to write the *Kathamrita*. M. took a vow to lead human beings towards God. He answered all questions with the Master's words.

M. was self-controlled and deeply spiritual. And he was extremely frugal. Every penny that he earned, he spent for a holy purpose. He regularly sent money to monks of the Ramakrishna Order who were practising austerities in the Himalayas. Moreover, he would send money to Belur Math from time to time. M. gave 100 rupees to Swamiji's mother so that

Swamiji could concentrate on spiritual disciplines without any financial worry. When Holy Mother lived in Jayrambati after the Master passed away, M. sent 10 rupees to her every month. Holy Mother was very fond of M., and she did not hesitate to ask him for anything that she needed.

M. often used to sing this song:

O Hari, You are the life and friend of all the lowly.
The scriptures say that seeing Your divine face, one is never reborn.

Seeing that face of the Lord, M. left for the divine realm. It is said, "A person lives through his achievements." M. will live forever through his achievement: the *Kathamrita*.

[Translated from *Srima Samipe*, edited by Swami Chetanananda (Udbodhan Office: Calcutta, 1996), 188-91]

Abinash Sharma

Twenty years ago a friend gave me a copy of the *Kathamrita*. After reading that book, I went one spring afternoon to see M. He was in his living room then, grading his students' papers. A teacher, who is now a monk of the Ramakrishna Order, was also seated there. When I bowed down to M., he joyfully received me and asked me to sit down. He then asked, "Do you have a question?"

I said: "Yes, sir. I don't have any peace of mind."

At this, he burst into laughter like a child. Addressing the young teacher, he said: "Did you hear what he said? He lives in the world and complains that he has no peace. A man drinks a whole bottle of wine and wonders why he is drunk!" Everyone laughed. This was his method of teaching.

M. then told me: "When Swamiji first went to Paramahamsadeva, he sang this song. Please listen." He then began to sing slowly, in a low voice:

Let us go back once more, O mind, to our own abode!
Here in this foreign land of earth
Why should we wander aimlessly in stranger's guise?...

When he finished singing, he wiped his tears of joy with a towel. He then sang another song:

Meditate, O my mind, on the Lord Hari,
The Stainless One, Pure Spirit, through and through.
How peerless is the Light that in Him shines!
How soul-bewitching is His wondrous form!
How dear is He to all His devotees!

It was evening. A gentle spring breeze was coming through the window. Moonlight reflected on the floor. It was a heavenly atmosphere. After

the song, M. said with a smile: "It is evening. Let us all meditate t
The Master used to say, 'It is good to chant God's name in the morn   ᵤ ₋.₋ᵤ
evening.'" M. silently began to repeat his mantra. Meanwhile, a young
man lit the kerosene lantern, and then began to wave incense in front of
the deities hanging on the wall. I saw the following pictures: Mother Kali
of Kalighat, Sita and Rama, Chaitanya seated on his knees, Ramakrishna,
Holy Mother, Swami Vivekananda, and Kali of Dakshineswar. When M.
finished repeating his mantra, I took leave of him, and he said with a
smile, "If you pass through this area, please visit me." From then on I
visited M. many times.

When M. talked about Sri Ramakrishna, he lost all body-consciousness. It seemed as though his soul was trying its utmost to break out of
its cage of name and form, trying to encompass the Infinite. His love and
devotion for Sri Ramakrishna was so great, it would spread to those who
heard him speak. One day in an inspired mood, M. was trying to describe
his Master. He said: "Blessed is he who can surrender everything at the
feet of his guru. The guru sees Eternal Life, so he tells his disciples, 'Ye
children of Immortal Bliss, I can give you Eternal Life.'

"The Master was like a five-year-old boy always running to meet his
Mother.

"The Master was like a beautiful flower whose nature was to bloom
and spread its fragrance.

"The Master was like a bonfire from which other lamps were lit.

"The Master was like a celestial vina always absorbed in singing the
glory of the Divine Mother.

"The Master was like a big fish joyfully swimming in calm, clear,
blue waters, the Ocean of Satchidananda.

"The Master was like a bird that had lost its nest in a storm and then,
perched on the threshold of the Infinite, was joyfully moving between the
two realms, singing the glory of the Infinite."

After trying to describe the Master in many ways, he said that all these
similes were inadequate. The Infinite cannot be expressed in words.

[Translated from *Srima Samipe*, edited by Swami Chetanananda
(Udbodhan Office: Calcutta, 1996), 192-94]

N. Bangarayya

It looks as though Incarnations of God often bring their own recording angels. Valmiki accompanied Rama, and Vyasa came with Krishna. Who accompanied Ramakrishna?

I can never forget the day in November 1916 when a copy of the glorious *Gospel* was first placed in my hands. It came as a present from especially holy hands — a monk who had dedicated his life to the service of others and the quest of Truth, one who, even in this Iron Age, had lived all the four traditional *ashramas* (stages of life) in an exemplary way, and had at last reached the Goal of life. His disciple, who actually brought it, was also a great lady — a life-long celibate given to austerity, pilgrimage, and *sadhana*.

But for that *Gospel*, I would have perhaps missed Ramakrishna. No doubt, there are other books — great in themselves — giving an account of Ramakrishna's life and sayings. But the *Gospel* stands unique among the Ramakrishna literature, if not among the scriptures of the world. In it we are face to face with the Lord — no veil of interpretation standing between. Ramakrishna speaks, and we listen. How it was possible to preserve the freshness and inspiration, God alone knows. My artistic temperament would not have been attracted to Sri Ramakrishna, but for the fascinating picture in the *Gospel*. For some time, I entertained a doubt whether the English-educated disciple did not polish up and smarten the crude speech of his illiterate Master. But when I met Master Mahashay or M. (as the modest pen-name goes), I became fully convinced that it was impossible for anybody to add to the charm of Ramakrishna. M. spoke beautifully; but there was a distinct and ineffaceable barrier between the two styles, the style of the Master as the disciple has recorded and the style of the disciple himself. The originality, suggestiveness, simplicity, and directness of the former are all its own. It soars far above the reach of any human intellect, be it ever so great. It is not possible for anybody to have invented for the world "The Ramakrishna Art." It is greatness enough to have preserved it.

The *Gospel* prompted me to visit M. For this literary curiosity apart, I had an intense longing to meet the great benefactor who presented a hero after my heart. I lived in a corner of South India when I actually decided to go and meet him. I had been corresponding with him for about three or four years on questions pertaining to my *sadhana*. At my insistence and in spite of his advanced age and neuralgic pains, he wrote a whole card in his own hand, blessing (praying for the Master's blessings as he put it) and encouraging me. I have kept the letter as a precious memento.

*　　　*　　　*

On 1 August 1930, I with two companions started for Calcutta. We reached there on the 2nd and went to a South Indian hotel on Chittaranjan Avenue. We met M. for the first time on the 3rd of August. Early in the morning we took a guide from the hotel and started to find M.'s residence on Amherst Street, at which he was then living, and which was very near our hotel. The roads were still wet with the rain of the previous night, and by the time we started (early morning) a slight drizzle had begun. When we reached the house of M., we were immediately directed to the fourth floor where M. was residing. It was a big building in which a school was run, of which M. was the proprietor. The stairs led us to a very tiny apartment, where stood two or three rickety old chairs and a bench. The apartment opened on one side onto a pretty spacious open terrace. On the other side there was a very big room which we later discovered to be the meditation room. When we occupied the chairs in the apartment, there was nobody there. We had brought with us a garland of fresh jasmine and sat meditating upon Sri Ramakrishna. It must have been about 9:00 a.m., quite a long time after we had arrived, when the door of the meditation room suddenly opened.

There stood before us a tall and stately figure with an overflowing silvery beard. Is it a *mantra drashta* [rishi] that has stepped out of the Vedas? We fell prostrate on the ground before him. He bade us rise up and take our seats. "I shall be coming presently," he added, and went downstairs. He came back shortly after and sat on a bench opposite to us. He spoke for about an hour. There was first a dialogue between us and then an uninterrupted speech by him. The speech was replete with quotations from the *Gita* and the *Upanishads*. It was at once fluent and sparkling. There was a singsong intonation in it such as is found among the Christian missionaries of our parts. If I had a mind, I could have recorded the whole speech from memory after I returned to my hotel. But at that time I did not take it into my head to record it, and now I regret it very much. When he was still going on with his speech, a lean Bengali boy who was waiting upon him spoke to him something in Bengali. Then M. turned to us apologetically, saying: "I am sorry. Recently I fell ill. My heart is weak and the doctors have advised me not to speak." Upon this we said: "We are very sorry to have troubled you. We would beseech you to follow the instructions of your medical advisers strictly."

This was the first day. I recorded what I thought important in the dialogue. Though the record is a little fragmentary, I would like to share it with the reader. After the introductions were over, I started the conversation.

I (*pointing to one of my companions*): "He is suffering very much from lust. Can you give him any helpful advice?"

M.: "Every man can be a pilot in a calm sea. He is an expert who can steer his ship in stormy weather. In the same way he is a real *sadhaka* who manages to remember God in spite of lust and other passions assailing his mind. There is true greatness in it."

I: "We are far from greatness, and the suffering is too much for us."

M.: "After God-realization, not the slightest trace of it will be left. You will not feel embittered because you have suffered so much. You will only laugh at all this struggle."

I (*within myself*): "God realization! Goodness gracious! How far away it must be!" There was a short silence.

M.: "Have you gone to Belur Math? Have you paid your respects to Swami Shivananda?"

I: "Yes."

M.: "Have you come to take initiation from him?"

I: "For me there is a point of pride. I have made up my mind that I should not take initiation from anybody else except Sri Ramakrishna. Will my desire be fulfilled?"

M.: "What objection can there be if there is God's grace?"

My companion (*Narsu*): "Do you advise us to take initiation from Shivananda?"

M.: "How can I give any advice in the matter? It is for individuals to decide for themselves. It has been a fashion to take initiation and then to remain in the vortex of worldliness. What purpose is served by such an initiation? After all, your *guru* must appeal to you and you must appeal to your guru."

Narsu: "We cannot stay here for more than a week; we have no money with us to do so."

M.: "Is God-realization such a light thing as to be decided in a week? If once you take initiation the consequences follow for lives. You must think very carefully in this matter. Have you not heard the proverb: 'Marry in haste and repent at leisure'? So be careful. You must observe your guru for at least ten or fifteen days before you take initiation from him. Then if he appeals to you, you can have initiation."

I: "Is Shivananda a realized soul?"

M.: "How can I say? Do not depend upon my opinion. 'Lean not on a broken reed: for man is such.' If you depend upon man, you may be totally misled. Suppose I say he is a realized soul. What guarantee is there that you will have faith in it? You must decide for yourselves."

M.: "Have you seen Dakshineswar — the scene where Sri Ramakrishna played his divine drama?"

I: "No. We have not yet been taken there."

M.: "Oh, no, no. You must not delay it. You can see the temple's pinnacle even from Belur Math. Have you seen it?"

I: "Yes. Every inch of the land in that temple —"

M.: "Why, every particle of dust in that temple is instinct with spirituality. If you just step into that temple, you will make spiritual progress."

I: "But we may also feel pain that Sri Ramakrishna is not physically present there."

M.: "Wherever there is pleasure there is pain also. He who transcends both is a yogi. Even though you cannot feel the physical presence of Sri Ramakrishna, you can try to imagine the presence of his sat-chit-ananda (spiritual) form there."

I: "Can imagination give satisfaction? We must see Him face to face. Otherwise how can the thirst be quenched?"

After this the sage, who was facing us, turned a little sideways and exclaimed: "We have become known to each other! We are all of one family. This is all due to the grace of Sri Ramakrishna. Through the grace of an Incarnation, people belonging to different nations and races forget their differences and behave as though they are blood brothers."

When he exclaimed, "We are all of one family," a spring of joy welled forth from within us.

With a glow on his face he asked us, "Have you seen our Thakurs (gods)?", and then rose to take us into his worship room. As we were going, I said: "You are not doing well. Otherwise I would have requested you for some reminiscences of the Master." He turned around and exclaimed: "All that I have spoken to you today are reminiscences of the Master. Take away the Master, the disciple is nothing!" I have already referred to a

continuous speech made by M., of which, unfortunately, I did not keep
a record. That was a bit general and no personal incident was narrated
therein. So I failed to understand how it could have come under the head
of reminiscences, and I added, "I mean personal reminiscences." Still the
sage insisted, "They are intensely personal," and repeated, "Take away
the Master, the disciple is nothing." I did not like to pursue the point
further.

The meditation room was very spacious. But it was not neatly kept.
The floor was full of some unbound printed forms; and books lay scattered here and there. I was reminded of the Master's description of a
sattvic devotee's surroundings. On the walls were hung some pictures.
But they were so very old that it was hardly possible to decipher them.
Pointing to a photo he said, "This is Vivekananda at twenty-three." We
put faith in his words and took it to be a picture of Vivekananda, for,
left to ourselves, we could not see much of a picture there. Similarly he
pointed at other pictures, naming each. But one thing gave us very great
delight. Pointing to each picture, the venerable sage bowed before it, and
we had the good fortune to be with him at that heavenly moment. It gave
us a thrill of joy.

He next took us onto the open terrace. From there he pointed, saying, "That is our flower garden." On the terrace was the sacred *tulsi*, basil
plant. He fell prostrate before it, and we followed suit.

My companion Narsu wanted to place the jasmine garland round his
neck, but as he attempted to do so the apostle gave a start as though he
were shocked. He asked the young Bengali boy standing by his side to
take it and place it on the picture of Sri Ramakrishna in the worship room.
As he was doing so, M. exclaimed in Bengali, '*Sugandhi*' (very fragrant).
At our home for many years we had been decorating the picture of Sri
Ramakrishna with garlands of flowers. But when we saw the writer of
the *Gospel* decorating the picture in his worship room with the garland we
had brought with us, we counted it a unique moment in our lives.

Then we took our leave of him. Before we parted, I pleaded: "It is
unfortunate that you are not doing well. We intend to come here now
and then. You need not exert yourself. But please allow us to sit in your
company for some time. That boon you must grant us."

He replied, "Please do come."

As we were parting I wanted to say how happy we felt to have met
him. But before I could finish my sentence he exclaimed: "Speech is silver,
but silence is golden. So I did not like to give expression to my joy. This
meeting is a blessing to me."

His modesty silenced us.

*   *   *

In the evening of that very day at about seven, we again repaired to that tiny apartment. It was dark and there was no lamp in it. He was meditating along with some devotees. As we entered, a devotee ran downstairs, brought a lamp and accommodated us on one of the benches. Another devotee whispered to me in broken and faulty English, "He is prays." The meditation continued, and we too sat meditating. After about half an hour he opened his eyes.

M. (*turning to us*): "Have you been to Dakshineswar?"

I: "No."

M.: "Have you been to Belur Math again?"

I: "No. Tomorrow we propose going to Dakshineswar."

M.: "Before you go there you should prepare yourselves for the visit."

I: "Today we have been busy preparing ourselves. That is why we did not go either to the Math or to any other place."

After a short pause, he burst into what I would call an inspired utterance. It was meant to be an introduction to our pilgrimage to Dakshineswar.

M.: "Seeing Dakshineswar you can have an idea of what Sri Ramakrishna's surroundings were. The temple was the background of divine scenes and incidents. At Dakshineswar you will find the bel tree under which the Master practised great *tantric sadhanas*. There is also the Panchavati where he went through many spiritual exercises. You will also see the Master's chamber. When you enter the Master's chamber you will see with your mind's eye the Master seated with his disciples and talking to them on divine subjects. We always found the Master absorbed in spiritual moods. Sometimes he would be in samadhi. Sometimes he would be singing and dancing. At other times he would be talking to the Divine Mother. We have seen a man who actually talked to the Divine Mother. We were fortunate enough to see a man whose experiences form, as it were, a living Veda. It is revelations from such people that we have to fall back upon and not on our 'ounce of reason.' Intellect cannot go far into spiritual matters. Intellect has been weighed and found wanting. Christ said to his disciples, 'I speak of things which I have seen with my own eyes, and yet you believe me not.' One has to put faith in the words of a man of realization. When you go to the temple you must purify yourselves and strip yourselves of all sensuality. Only the pure in heart can see God. You must also prepare yourselves to receive wireless messages from the Master. This pilgrimage to Dakshineswar will help you a good deal towards God-realization."

He went on talking like this, when a devotee whispered into my ear: "Master Mahashay has recently fallen ill. So please don't allow him to go on. The doctors have warned us that there is danger if he is allowed to speak too much." Upon this I interrupted M., saying: "Revered sir, you are suffering from heart trouble. If you go on speaking like this, it will do you harm. I would request you to stop." He at once realized the situation and, in a gentle and tender voice, pleaded, "Yes, it is true that I am ill" and stopped. He afterwards spoke something in Bengali to someone sitting by his side. A lamp was brought there from downstairs. A devotee gave us prasad.

I cannot describe in words the impression made on our minds that night. Each sentence of his speech was a diamond. How much he must have been absorbed in the Master may be gleaned from the fact that he forgot altogether about his illness. He risked his health for our sake, and earnestly prepared us for the unique pilgrimage of our life. I thought within myself: "Suppose I now go on a pilgrimage to Vrindaban. Shall I find an Uddhava or a Vyasa to introduce me to the place? How fortunate I am!"

We knelt before him and prayed, "Please bless us that we may be fit to enter the temple of Dakshineswar and receive the Master's wireless messages." But it was impossible for him to slip from his exalted humility even casually. He replied quickly: "Let us all pray for His blessings. Who am I to bless? 'Lean not on a broken reed, for man is such.'" The repetition of the last sentence sounded like one of the epic repetitions of the Ramayana.

*   *   *

Our third and last visit was after we had finished our pilgrimage to Dakshineswar. It was probably on the 5th of August. The climate of Calcutta did not suit me, and I fell ill. So lest we should be troubling the sanyasins of the Math [*monastery*], we wanted to cut short our stay there and return home.

It must have been nearly 5:30 p.m. when we reached M.'s apartment for the third time. It was evening, and the sunset was beautiful to watch. The mellowed light of the evening sun enveloped the open terrace. Some boys and girls were flying kites and shouting merrily. Undisturbed, the sage was meditating within the room. We sat on the bench and after some time he came out and greeted us cordially. Saying that he would return shortly, he went downstairs. After a short interval there came a young man of about twenty-five. He had a smiling appearance and had over-flowing hair. We entered into a conversation with him.

I: "Are you a son of Master Mahashay?"

He: "No. But you can take me for one from the reverence I bear towards his spiritual instructions."

I: "How many sons and daughters has he?"

He: "Two sons and two daughters." (*He then pointed to a boy and a girl playing there who were the grandchildren of M.*)

I: "Does Master Mahashay give initiation to anybody?"

He: "No. He does not."

It must have been about 7:30 p.m. when M. again came upstairs. By that time about a dozen devotees had gathered in that apartment, evidently to bask in the soulful company of M. and spend the evening in prayer and kirtan. M. requested to be excused, saying that he had delayed us long. We gave a suitable reply.

With a glow on his face he said: "Come in. You shall visit our Thakur." We went into the meditation room and that evening we again bowed down before the pictures of Sri Ramakrishna, Vivekananda, and other deities. Pointing to a picture he said, "These are *Saptarshi Maharajas.*" It was a picture of a rather old type, and there was not much art in it to admire. He then showed us some cuttings of pictures from newspapers. They were pictures of the *kumbhamela* at Hardwar, which had taken place that very year. "This is Sitapati Maharaj conversing with the sadhus at Hardwar," he explained. I asked, "Who is Sitapati Maharaj?" He replied, "Swami Raghavananda." Both the names were equally unfamiliar to us. He then led us to the terrace, and we all prostrated before the sacred basil plant. I narrate this in detail to show that, though he was an illumined sage, how punctiliously he observed these practices with a view to setting an example for others, and fulfilled the dictum of the Gita in this respect.

That day was *ekadashi* (the eleventh day of the fortnight), considered particularly auspicious by Hindus. It must have been a day of fasting for him. He had a harmonium brought there by one of his attendant devotees and asked us to sing some Telugu songs. Our only qualification seemed to be that none of us knew anything about music, and we had never touched a harmonium or any other instrument. But there was one thing, namely — that we were deeply devoted to the kirtans of Tyagaraja. I explained to him that we did not know anything about music. However, at his insistence I recited the texts of some three or four kirtans of Tyagaraja. I explained their meaning in English to him. On hearing them he burst out: "Oh! He is a great seer. A *mantra drashta.* He is a God-realized soul."

After that he asked the young man with whom we had had a conversation before to sing some Bengali songs for us. In the *Gospel* we had read the translation of many a Bengali song which the Master used to sing, but that was the first time for us to hear Bengali songs of Ramprasad and Kamalakanta among the ancients, and Girish Chandra Ghosh among the moderns. We considered ourselves particularly fortunate to hear the favourite songs of the Master sung under the direction of a direct disciple. I said smilingly, "We are exchanging bad for good music." At this M. blushed and exclaimed, "Oh! No, no."

We stayed on till 9:00 p.m. The kirtan was still proceeding. We rose up to take our leave. I explained to him how our stay had to be cut short. He felt sorry for my ill-health, and placed two beautiful oranges in my hand with a prayer in his heart for our spiritual well-being and progress.

It will be presumptuous for anybody to attempt to assign the place of M. among the Master's disciples. Maybe he is the least among them. But this much is certain, namely, that he has achieved what no other (not excluding even the great Vivekananda) has done. He has built an indestructible shrine in letters to his Master, which shall stand as a Wonder of the World to the admiring gaze of posterity. As Vivekananda put it, it must be that the Master was with him in this unique achievement. The self-effacement, the love of humanity, and the immense tapasya that stood behind the achievement will be adored by mankind forever.

The relics of two disciples of Buddha, Sri Sariputta and Mahomoggalana, are, at the time of writing this, being received with great éclat. And in this context we cannot but feel how fortunate we are to have seen with our own eyes an intimate disciple of an equally great One!

[Taken from *Prabuddha Bharata*: 1949:228-34]

Paul Brunton

In the onward-rushing train I have picked up another thread of guidance in this quest. Like most mainline trains in India, it is packed to the point of fullness. The compartment in which I have been fortunate enough to find a berth — for all trains carry sleeping berths, except in the lowest class — contains a mixed crew. They discuss their affairs so openly that soon one learns who and what they are. There is a venerable son of Islam who is attired in a long, black silk coat, which is buttoned around his neck. A round black cap, neatly embroidered in gold, rests on his thinly thatched head. White pajama trousers are gathered around his legs, while his shoes provide an artistic finish to his dress for they are daintily made with red and green threadwork. There is a beetle-browed Marathi from Western India; a gold-turbaned Marwari who, like many members of his race, is a moneylender; and a stout Brahmin lawyer from the South. They are all men of some wealth for they are attended by personal servants who dart out of their third-class carriages at most stopping-places, to enquire after their masters' welfare.

The Muslim gives me a single glance, closes his eyes, and drifts off into vacuous sleep. The Marathi busies himself in conversation with the Marwari. The Brahmin has recently entered the train; he has yet to settle down.

I am in one of my talkative moods, but there is no one to whom I can talk. The invisible barrier between West and East seems to divide me from all the others. I feel cheered, therefore, when the rubicund Brahmin pulls out a book whose English title, *Life of Ramakrishna*, I cannot help seeing, so boldly is it printed upon the cover. I seize the bait and bring him into conversation. Has not someone once told me that Ramakrishna was the last of the rishis, those spiritual supermen? Upon this point I engage my fellow-traveller, and he is eager to respond. We ascend the heights of philosophical discussion and descend into talk on the homelier aspects of Indian life.

Whenever he mentions the name of the rishi, his voice fills with love and awe and his eyes light up. The reality of his devotion to this long-passed man is indubitable. Within two hours I learn that the Brahmin has a master who is one of the two or three surviving disciples of the great Ramakrishna himself.

This master of his is nearly eighty years old and lives, not in some lonely retreat, but in the heart of Calcutta's Indian quarter.

Of course, I beg for the address and it is freely given.

"You will need no introduction other than your own desire to see him," says the lawyer.

And so I am now in Calcutta itself, searching for the house of the Master Mahashay, the aged disciple of Ramakrishna. Passing through an open courtyard which adjoins the street, I reach a steep flight of steps leading into a large, rambling old house. I climb up a dark stairway and pass through a low door on the top storey. I find myself in a small room, which opens out onto the flat, terraced roof of the house. Two of its walls are lined with low divans. Save for the lamp and a small pile of books and papers, the room is otherwise bare. A young man enters and bids me wait for the coming of his master, who is on a lower floor.

Ten minutes pass. I hear the sound of someone stirring from a room on the floor below out into the stairway. Immediately there is a tingling sensation in my head and the idea suddenly grips me that that man downstairs has fixed his thoughts upon me. I hear the man's footsteps going up the stairs. When at last — for he moves with extreme slowness — he enters the room, I need no one to announce his name. A venerable patriarch has stepped from the pages of the Bible, and a figure from Mosaic times has turned to flesh. This man with bald head, long white beard, and white moustache, grave countenance, and large, reflective eyes; this man whose shoulders are slightly bent with the burden of nearly eighty years of mundane existence, can be none other than the Master Mahashay.

He takes his seat on a divan and then turns his face towards mine. In that grave, sober presence I realize instantly that there can be no light persiflage, no bandying of wit or humour, no utterance even of the harsh cynicism and dark scepticism which overshadow my soul from time to time. His character, with its commingling of perfect faith in God and nobility of conduct, is written in his appearance for all to see.

He addresses me in perfectly accented English.

"You are welcome here."

He bids me come closer and take my seat on the same divan. He holds my hand for a few moments. I deem it expedient to introduce myself and explain the object of my visit. When I have concluded speaking, he presses my hand again in a kindly manner and says: "It is a higher power which has stirred you to come to India, and which is bringing you in contact with the holy men of our land. There is a real purpose behind that, and the future will surely reveal it. Await it patiently."

"Will you tell me something about your master Ramakrishna?"

"Ah, now you raise a subject about which I love best to talk. It is nearly half a century since he left us, but his blessed memory can never leave me; always it remains fresh and fragrant in my heart. I was twenty-seven when I met him and was constantly in his society for the last five years of his life. The result was that I became a changed man; my whole attitude towards life was reversed. Such was the strange influence of this Godman Ramakrishna. He threw a spiritual spell upon all who visited him. He literally charmed them, fascinated them. Even materialistic persons who came to scoff became dumb in his presence."

"But how can such persons feel reverence for spirituality — a quality in which they do not believe?" I interpose, slightly puzzled.

The corners of Master Mahashay's mouth pull up in a half smile.

He answers: "Two persons taste red pepper. One does not know its name; perhaps he has never even seen it before. The other is well acquainted with it and recognizes it immediately. Will it not taste the same to both? Will not both of them have a burning sensation on the tongue? In the same way, ignorance of Ramakrishna's spiritual greatness did not debar materialistic persons from 'tasting' the radiant influence of spirituality which emanated from him."

"Then he really was a spiritual superman?"

"Yes, and in my belief even more than that. Ramakrishna was a simple man, illiterate and uneducated — he was so illiterate that he could not even sign his name, let alone write a letter. He was humble in appearance and humbler still in mode of living, yet he commanded the allegiance of some of the best-educated and most cultured men of the time in India. They had to bow before his tremendous spirituality which was so real that it could be felt. He taught us that pride, riches, wealth, worldly honours, worldly position are trivialities in comparison with that spirituality. They are fleeting illusions which deceive men. Ah, those were wonderful days! Often he would pass into samadhi of so palpably divine a nature that we who were gathered around him then would feel that he was a god, rather than a man. Stangely, too, he possessed the power of inducing a similar state in his disciples by means of a single touch; in this state they could understand the deep mysteries of God by means of direct perception. But let me tell you how he affected me.

"I had been educated along Western lines. My head was filled with intellectual pride. I had served in Calcutta colleges as Professor of English Literature, History, and Political Economy, at different times. Ramakrishna was living in the temple of Dakshineswar, which is only a few miles up the river from Calcutta. There I found him one unforgettable spring day and listened to his simple expression of spiritual ideas born of his own experience. I made a feeble attempt to argue with him but soon became tongue-tied in that sacred presence, whose effect on me was too deep for words. Again and again I visited him, unable to stay away from this poor, humble but divine person, until Ramakrishna one day humorously remarked: 'A peacock was given a dose of opium at four o'clock. The next day it appeared again exactly at that hour. It was under the spell of opium and came for another dose.'

"That was true, symbolically speaking. I had never enjoyed such blissful experiences as when I was in the presence of Ramakrishna, so can you wonder why I came again and again? And so I became one of his group of intimate disciples, as distinguished from merely occasional visitors. One day the Master said to me: 'I can see from the signs of your eyes, brow and face that you are a Yogi. Do all your work then, but keep your mind on God. Wife, children, father and mother, live with all and serve them as if they are your own. The tortoise swims about in the waters of the lake, but her mind is fixed on where her eggs are laid on the banks. So, do all the work of the world but keep the mind in God.'

"And so, after the passing away of our Master, when most of the other disciples voluntarily renounced the world, adopted the yellow robe, and trained themselves to spread Ramakrishna's message through India, I did not give up my profession but carried on with my work in education. Nevertheless, such was my determination not to be of the world although I was in it, that on some nights I would retire at the dead of night to the open veranda before the Senate House and sleep among the homeless beggars of the city, who usually collected there to spend the night. This used to make me feel, temporarily at least, that I was a man with no possessions.

"Ramakrishna has gone, but as you travel through India you will see something of the social, philanthropic, medical, and educational work being done throughout the country under the inspiration of those early disciples of his, most of whom, alas, have now passed away too. What you will not see so easily is the number of changed hearts and changed lives primarily due to this wonderful man. For his message has been handed down from disciple to disciple, who have spread it as widely as they could. And I have been privileged to take down many of his sayings in Bengali; the published record has entered almost every household in Bengal, while translations have also gone into other parts of India. So you see how Ramakrishna's influence has spread far beyond the immediate circle of his little group of disciples."

Master Mahashay finishes his long recital and relapses into silence. As I look at his face anew, I am struck by the non-Hindu colour and cast of his face. Again I am wafted back to a little kingdom in Asia Minor, where the children of Israel find a temporary respite from their hard fortunes. I picture Master Mahashay among them as a venerable prophet speaking to his people. How noble and dignified the man looks! His goodness, honesty, virtue, piety, and sincerity are transparent. He possesses that self-respect of a man who has lived a long life in utter obedience to the voice of conscience.

"I wonder what Ramakrishna would say to a man who cannot live by faith alone, who must satisfy reason and intellect?" I murmur questioningly.

"He would tell the man to pray. Prayer is a tremendous force. Ramakrishna himself prayed to God to send him spiritually inclined people, and soon after that those who later became his disciples or devotees began to appear."

"But if one has never prayed — what then?"

"Prayer is the last resort. It is the ultimate resource left to man. Prayer will help a man where the intellect may fail."

"But if someone came to you and said that prayer did not appeal to his temperament, what counsel would you give him?" I persist gently.

"Then let him associate frequently with truly holy men who have had real spiritual experience. Constant contact with them will assist him to bring out his latent spirituality. Higher men turn our minds and wills towards divine objects. Above all, they stimulate an intense longing for the spiritual life. Therefore, the society of such men is very important as the first step; and often it is also the last, as Ramakrishna himself used to say."

Thus we discourse of things high and holy, and how man can find no peace save in the Eternal Good. Throughout the evening different visitors make their arrival until the modest room is packed with Indians — disciples of the Master Mahashay. They come nightly and climb the stairs of this four-storeyed house to listen intently to every word uttered by their teacher.

And for a while I, too, join them. Night after night I come, less to hear the pious utterances of Master Mahashay than to bask in the spiritual sunshine of his presence. The atmosphere around him is tender and beautiful, gentle and loving; he has found some inner bliss and the radiation of it seems palpable. Often I forget his words, but I cannot forget his benignant personality. That which drew him again and again to Ramakrishna seems to draw me to Master Mahashay also, and I begin to understand how potent must have been the influence of the teacher when the pupil exercises such a fascination upon me.

When our last evening comes, I forget the passage of time, as I sit happily at his side upon the divan. Hour after hour has flown by; our talk has had no interlude of silence, but at length it comes. And then the good master takes my hand and leads me out to the terraced roof of his house where, in the vivid moonlight, I see a circling array of tall plants growing in pots and tubs. Down below a thousand lights gleam from the houses of Calcutta.

The moon is at its full. Master Mahashay points up towards its round face and then passes into silent prayer for a brief while. I wait patiently at his side until he finishes. He turns, raises his hand in benediction and lightly touches my head.

I bow humbly before this angelic man, unreligious though I am. After a few more moments of continued silence, he says softly: "My task has almost come to an end. This body has nearly finished what God sent it here to do. Accept my blessing before I go."*

He has strangely stirred me. I banish the thought of sleep and wander through many streets. When, at length, I reach a great mosque and hear the solemn chant, "God is most great!" break forth upon the midnight stillness, I reflect that if anyone could free me from the intellectual scepticism to which I cling and attach me to a life of simple faith, it is undoubtedly the Master Mahashay.

[Taken from *A Search in Secret India* by Paul Brunton (E.P. Dutton: New York, 1935), 181-85]

_____

long I was apprised of his death.

Paramahamsa Yogananda

"Little sir, please be seated. I am talking to my Divine Mother."

Silently I had entered the room in great awe. The angelic appearance of Master Mahashay [M.] fairly dazzled me. With silky white beard and large lustrous eyes, he seemed an incarnation of purity. His upraised chin and folded hands apprised me that my first visit had disturbed him in the midst of his devotions.

His simple words of greeting produced the most violent effect my nature had so far experienced. The bitter separation of my mother's death I had thought the measure of all anguish. Now an agony at separation from my Divine Mother was an indescribable torture of the spirit. Abandoned in some oceanic desolation, I clutched his feet as the sole raft of my rescue....

"Holy sir, thy intercession! Ask the Divine Mother if I find any favour in Her sight!" ... "I will make your plea to the Beloved." The master's [M.'s] capitulation came with a slow, compassionate smile.

What power in those few words, that my being should know release from its stormy exile?

"Sir, remember your pledge! I shall return soon for Her message!" Joyful anticipation rang in my voice that only a moment ago had been sobbing in sorrow.

Descending the long stairway, I was overwhelmed by memories. This house at 50 Amherst Street, now the residence of Master Mahashay, had once been my family home, scene of my mother's death. Here my human heart had broken for the vanished mother: and here today my spirit had been as though crucified by absence of the Divine Mother. Hallowed walls, silent witness of my grievous hurts and final healing!...

The sun on the following morning had hardly risen to an angle of decorum when I paid my second visit to Master Mahashay. Climbing the staircase in the house of poignant memories, I reached his fourth-floor

533

room. The knob of the closed door was wrapped around with a cloth: a hint, I felt, that the saint desired privacy. As I stood irresolutely on the landing, the door was opened by Master Mahashay's welcoming hand. I knelt at his holy feet. In a playful mood, I wore a solemn mask over my face, hiding the divine elation.

"Sir, I have come — very early, I confess — for your message."...

"Think you that your devotion did not touch the Infinite Mercy? The Motherhood of God, that you have worshiped in forms both human and divine, could never fail to answer your forsaken cry."

Who was this simple saint, whose least request to the Universal Spirit met with sweet acquiescence? His role in the world was humble, as befitted the greatest man of humility I ever knew. In this Amherst Street house, Master Mahashay conducted a small high school for boys. No words of chastisement passed his lips: no rule and ferule maintained his discipline. Higher mathematics indeed were taught in these modest classrooms, and a chemistry of love absent from the textbooks. He spread his wisdom by spiritual contagion rather than impermeable precept. Consumed by an unsophisticated passion for the Divine Mother, the saint no more demanded the outward forms of respect than a child.

"I am not your guru; he shall come a little later," he told me. "Through his guidance, your experiences of the Divine in terms of love and devotion shall be translated into his terms of fathomless wisdom."

Every late afternoon, I betook myself to Amherst Street. I sought Master Mahashay's divine cup, so full that its drops daily overflowed on my being. Never before had I bowed in utter reverence; now I felt it an immeasurable privilege even to tread the same ground which Master Mahashay sanctified.

"Let us go tomorrow to the Dakshineswar Temple, forever hallowed by my guru." Master Mahashay was a disciple of a Christlike master, Sri Ramakrishna Paramahamsa.

The four-mile journey on the following morning was taken by boat on the Ganges. We entered the nine-domed Temple of Kali, where the figures of the Divine Mother and Shiva rest on a burnished silver lotus, its thousand petals meticulously chiseled. Master Mahashay beamed in enchantment. He was engaged in his inexhaustible romance with the Beloved.

This was the first of many pilgrimages to Dakshineswar with the holy teacher. From him I learned the sweetness of God in the aspect of Mother, or Divine Mercy. The childlike saint found little appeal in the Father aspect, or Divine Justice. Stern, exacting, mathematical judgment was alien to his gentle nature.

"He can serve as an earthly prototype for the very angels of heaven!" I thought fondly, watching him one day at his prayers. Without a breath of censure or criticism, he surveyed the world with eyes long familiar with the Primal Purity. His body, mind, speech, and actions were effortlessly harmonized with his soul's simplicity.

"My Master told me so." Shrinking from personal assertion, the saint ended any sage counsel with this invariable tribute. So deep was his identity with Sri Ramakrishna that Master Mahashay no longer considered his thoughts as his own....

Another day found me walking alone near the Howrah railway station. I stood for a moment by a temple, silently criticizing a small group of men with drum and cymbals who were violently reciting a chant.

"How undevotionally they use the Lord's divine name in mechanical repetition," I reflected. My gaze was astonished by the rapid approach of Master Mahashay. "Sir, how come you are here?"

The saint, ignoring my question, answered my thought. "Isn't it true, little sir, that the Beloved's name sounds sweet from all lips, ignorant or wise?" He passed his arm around me affectionately; I found myself carried on his magic carpet to the Merciful Presence....

One afternoon a brisk walk brought us to the garden fronting Calcutta University. My companion indicated a bench near the Goldighi or pond.

"Let us sit here for a few minutes. My Master always asked me to meditate whenever I saw an expanse of water. Here its placidity reminds us of the vast calmness of God. As all things can be reflected in water, so the whole universe is mirrored in the lake of the Cosmic Mind. So my gurudeva often said." ...

If anyone observed the unpretentious M. and myself as we walked away from the crowded pavement, the onlooker surely suspected us of intoxication. I felt that the falling shades of evening were sympathetically drunk with God. When darkness recovered from its nightly swoon, I faced the new morning bereft of my ecstatic mood. But ever enshrined in memory is the seraphic son of the Divine Mother — Master Mahashay!...

[Taken from *An Autobiography of a Yogi* by Paramahamsa Yogananda (Self-Realization Fellowship: Los Angeles), 87-95]

Dilip Kumar Roy

Whenever I visited a monk or a great personality, I would report to my father [Dwijendralal Roy, a famous poet and dramatist] what I had observed and heard, and what I had learned from them. He would listen enthusiastically. As a result of listening to my conversations with Sri Ramakrishna's disciples, his mind was drawn to him whom I loved whole-heartedly. At my request my father read two volumes of the *Kathamrita* recorded by M.

The greatest spiritual personality whom I met during my father's lifetime was M.

I told my father: "Father, I went to visit M."

Father smiled and said: "Oh, your Master's Boswell? Very well. Tell me everything."

"Oh, father, he is really wonderful and beautiful. Anyhow, I had an argument with Brother Nirmal [Nirmalendu Lahiri, a famous actor and cousin of Dilip Roy] yesterday. I told him that, based on your statement, I believe in Ramakrishna."

"What do you mean?"

"Well, you told me the other day, 'As that door is a real door, so it is the living truth that Ramakrishna is a true sadhu.'"

"Yes, what I said is true," Father replied. "Not only that, I shall add this: His ecstatic image [in his picture] convinces me that he was a great soul."

I joyously replied: "I shall inform M. of your conviction tomorrow."

Father agreed: "Please tell him. But is there any value in the statement of an atheist like me to a great believer like M.?"

I said to Father: "Brother Nirmal possesses phenomenal faith and sometimes he acts like a fanatic. He said to me, 'Every word of the *Kathamrita* is the gospel truth (*veda-vakya*).' Is that possible, Father?"

"What do you think?" he asked.

"It is impossible," I replied. "No human being can be free from error, except Krishna — but he is God himself and not a human being."

"As I understand, Nirmal thinks that Ramakrishna is God, so you had a fight with him."

"That is correct. I said that I considered Ramakrishna to have been a great soul, an avatar, and free from sin — but he was not God. Tell me, is it not bigotry to call him God?"

"What can I say? Fourteen generations of my family have not seen God. You are free to express your opinion. But it is not proper to insist that God is this and God is not that. This is not what I mean. I read Ramakrishna's remark in the *Kathamrita* that those who held this kind of view are dogmatic. All right. Tell me what happened next."

"When Brother Nirmal said that every word of the *Kathamrita* is the gospel truth, I protested vehemently, saying, 'I don't agree.' Then he said: 'The Master does not care whether you believe in his words or not. Even Swamiji said that the Master was incomparable.' I angrily replied: 'The Master may be incomparable but it cannot be proven that whatever M. recorded in the *Kathamrita* are the Master's own words and not some of his own input.' Enraged, Brother Nirmal said: 'Keep quiet! You are too saucy. Don't try to understand this world with your puny intellect. How do you know that those words in the *Kathamrita* are concocted? Do you know who M. is? It is rare to find a man as truthful as M. His power of memory is incomparable — he remembers everything he hears." I said: 'Well, he might have a fantastic memory, but that does not mean he could remember everything the Master said. Moreover, he did not record the Master's words in his diary immediately.' Brother Nirmal then joyfully said: 'Yes, whatever M. heard from the Master, he recorded that in his diary on the same day. I saw his diary with my own eyes. Come with me and I shall show you also.'"

"My goodness!" Father exclaimed. "M. recorded the events in his diary on the same day! This is interesting. I didn't know that. Tell me what happened next."

I continued: "M.'s house is not very far from ours. Brother Nirmal took me directly to M.'s living room. I saw him seated on his cot surrounded by books. Incense was burning in front of the Master's picture. There was a row of Morocco leather–bound books on a shelf. I was told that those were his famous diaries. Father, M.'s face was bright and calm. His eyes were large and moist. Furthermore, his sweet smile was so wonderful that it cooled my heart."

"Tell me more."

"When we entered the room, Brother Nirmal bowed down to M. He joyfully said: 'Welcome, Nirmal. Who is this boy?' When Brother Nirmal introduced me, M. excitedly said: 'Ah, he is a son of D.L. Roy, who wrote *Sita*, *Pashani*. Sit down, my child. Blessed you are!' Now, are you happy?"

"I am delighted to hear that."

"Please listen. M. asked me to sit near him and he affectionately rubbed my back. He then asked why I had come. I was ashamed to raise the topic of my arguments with Brother Nirmal. I simply said, 'I have come to hear about the Master.' Father, I didn't lie; truly, I wanted to ask him about the Master. Moreover, what would I gain by seeing his diary?"

"I trust you. Tell me what happened next."

"Anyhow, when he heard my request, he shivered and loudly called out: 'Prabhas [M.'s son] — O Prabhas, please come here. Just see, this little boy has come to me to hear the words of the Master!' He then said to Brother Nirmal: 'My child, this happens as a result of good karma from a previous life. Otherwise, why would he have such a spiritual question at a young age?' Turning to me, M. said, 'Look, my child, I am covered with goose bumps.' As he said that he extended his hands towards me and I saw it was true. Moreover, tears trickled down his face, which he wiped off with a corner of his dhoti. He then said in a choked voice, 'My child, live long — a hundred years.'

"Meanwhile, three or four people came from the inner apartment to see me. I was dumbfounded. Just imagine, I went to see M., whereas some people came to see me."

Father smiled and said: "This seems to be a drama. Then what happened?"

"M. went on talking about Sri Ramakrishna," I continued. "Father, it is amazing how passionately he spoke! From time to time he wiped tears from his eyes. He described how the Master would sing and dance, make jokes with the young ones and feed them, and how while singing in ecstasy his cloth would drop from his body. Finally, he talked about the Master's love and affection. He said: 'My child, it was not human love; no human being can love that way. His love was so intense, it seemed that he had been known for a long time — that he was our very own. God exists afar and hidden, whereas he gave himself up to us as a human being.' Father, M. said many wonderful things like this. However, I was more impressed by his devotion for his guru than by his description *of* his guru. As you know I am afraid to make anyone my guru, but while I was returning home my eyes filled with tears when remembering M.'s devotion for his guru. I don't know how much the Master loved M., but today I witnessed M.'s love for the Master. Just imagine, so many years after the Master's passing away, he had goose bumps when he uttered his guru's name. I have never seen such devotion to the guru in anyone else. What do you say?"

"What can I say? I am ignorant about the doctrine of the guru. But after listening to your description, I am moved that M. loved the Master so intensely."

The next morning I visited M. again with Brother Nirmal. M. cordially received me and made me sit next to him. Soon someone brought two cups of tea for us. Observing me to be a little hesitant, M. said: "My child, please drink the tea. Yesterday I didn't serve you refreshments. You see, I forget everything when I talk about the Master."

Brother Nirmal asked M.: "Will you kindly show him your diary?"

M. got up, carefully took one volume from the shelf, and said: "My child, please see this diary. Ah, how I passed those days with the Master! I never forgot to write in my diary for a single day, when my memory was very fresh."

I began to turn the pages of that diary and became absorbed. I felt a sensation in my heart. I reflected: "This *Kathamrita* removes the afflictions of millions of people, showing the path to those whose lives lack focus, bestowing faith on those who are bereft of devotion, and shedding light on those who roam in the darkness of despair. This great message emerged from the lips of Sri Ramakrishna, the avatar of this age. He came to distribute divine nectar in this materialistic world. He lived his life in an ordinary room like a humble and modest person and carried this message to the lowly. God is always the friend of the downtrodden."

I remember that M. told me on that day: "One day a destitute man came to Sri Ramakrishna and lamented, 'Master, I have no one.' When he heard this, the Master was overjoyed. He called out to his nephew Hriday: 'O Hridu, look, look! Today a great and fortunate man has come to me. Listen, God belongs to him who has no one to call his own.' What sweet and hopeful words! These are truly words soaked in nectar."

Brother Nirmal was reading another diary and suddenly said to M.: "Yesterday Dilip told his father everything you said about the Master."

M. asked me: "Tell me, child, what your father said?"

I replied: "My father said that the Master was a great soul. This is obvious when one sees the photo taken when he was in samadhi."

"Ah, it is a great fortune to have such a father! Listen, my child, let me tell you something. Every day, write down what your father says in a notebook, as I did. Not only that, whenever you hear something inspirational from any great man, please record it in your diary."

I nodded my head and said, "I will."

M. continued: "Let me tell you another thing: your father is not an ordinary man. If he were, he could not say that the Master was a great soul. What a wonderful statement your father made! Only a great soul can recognize another."

[Translated from *Smriticharan* by Dilip Kumar Roy (Surakavya Samsad: Calcutta, 1987), 229-38]

Swami Shivananda

Swami Shivananda had not been at all well. He had high blood pressure and did not sleep very well the previous night. The morning brought very bad news: Revered M. (Mahendra Nath Gupta, author of The Gospel of Sri Ramakrishna) *left his mortal body on 4 June 1932 at 5:30 a.m. and was united with the Master. He was seventy-eight years of age when he passed away. Upon hearing this news Swami Shivananda was grief-stricken and sat silent. Unable to control his feelings any longer, he gently remarked to the sadhus and devotees who were close by:*

The Master has placed me in such a position that I could not even go and see M. [before his death]. One by one the Master is taking away his devotees, leaving me here to bear the brunt of the grief. He alone knows what he wills. Ah! M. lived in Calcutta, illumining the entire city, as it were. How many devotees would visit him and hear from him the Master's words, and be filled with peace! This loss will never be made good. He had nothing else to discuss but the words of the Master. His life was filled with the Master. How dearly the Master loved him! He spent many days at Dakshineswar.

M. was very simple as regards his food, living mostly on milk and rice. The Master himself arranged, through the maidservant, for a pint of good milk for him every day. M. had a very strong body. That is why he could do so much of the Master's work. Whatever he would hear from the Master he would note down in his diary after going home. Later from those notes he wrote that wonderful *Gospel of Sri Ramakrishna*. He had a prodigious memory. He jotted down just meager notes and later from those notes, by exercising his memory through meditation, he developed the *Gospel*. He belonged to the group of Sri Ramakrishna's intimate disciples. The Master brought M. with him for that particular work, so to say. M. would visit him every Saturday and Sunday or on any holiday. He would also see him when the Master would come to Calcutta or wherever the Master would be visiting. When interesting subjects were being discussed and there was a big crowd, all of a sudden Sri Ramakrishna would say to M.: "M., did you understand? Note that point well." Sometimes the Master would repeat certain points. We did not realize then why the Master spoke to M. that way.

The Master's words were so impressive that I too started taking notes. One day at Dakshineswar I was listening to the Master, looking intently at his face. Many beautiful things were being discussed. Noticing my attitude and divining my intention, suddenly the Master said: "Look here! Why are you listening so attentively?" I was taken by surprise. The Master then said: "You don't have to do that. Your life is different." I felt as if the Master had divined my intention to take notes and that was why he spoke that way. From that time on, I gave up the idea of making notes of his conversations and whatever notes I had I threw into the Ganges.

The next morning some devotees came to the monastery from Calcutta. All of them had associated with M. and had served him devotedly for a long time. They were all grief-stricken over his passing away. Upon hearing from them the details of M.'s death, Swami Shivananda affectionately remarked:

Ah! It is a great blow to you. This bereavement is fresh. No words from anyone will assuage this grief. Where is Benoy [Swami Jitatmananda]? It must be a great blow to him also. He stayed with him for a long time and served him very devotedly. What is to be done? No one has any control over this. Sri Ramakrishna himself is taking away his devotees, but we know that the relationship of M. with us and with the Master is eternal. Do you understand? This relationship is imperishable. Never think for a moment that M. passed away and that there has been an end of everything. Never!

What fear is there, my children? The Master is living [in a spiritual sense]! And we are still in the flesh. Whenever you find time, do come to the monastery.

Ah! M. was like a refuge to the devotees — a haven of peace to many. Especially after Sharat Maharaj's [Swami Saradananda] passing away many devotees used to go to M., and he would give peace to the hearts of many by speaking untiringly to them about the Master. This loss cannot be filled! He was a holy soul. What great work of the Master he accomplished! Even if he had written only one volume of the *Gospel* it would have immortalized him. His work is imperishable.

[Translated from *Srima Samipe*, edited by Swami Chetanananda (Udbodhan Office: Calcutta, 1996), 210-12]

Appendices

Illustration of the Dakshineswar temple complex is from the Bengali *Gospel* published by M. in 1920.

Correspondence of Romain Rolland with M.

Villeneuve (Vand), Switzerland
Villa Olga
10 October 1928

Dear Mr. Mahendra Nath Gupta,

Perhaps you may have heard from the Ramakrishna Mission about the study which I wish to dedicate in French to Sri Ramakrishna. It is doubtless, rather a rash undertaking for a Western writer, but I have brought to it great respect (love) and a sincere piety.

I owe much naturally to your admirable *Gospel* "Evengale," and I have affectionate regard for it. Thank you for having transmitted to us the benefit of the benign smile of your Master. Will you allow me to ask you some points which I want to know. The lack of literary culture of Ramakrishna is commonly spoken of. It is said that he was very nearly illiterate and that his culture was oral. To an Indian there is no need of emphasizing — for his own experience enables him to grasp what this oral culture is, but a European cannot exactly picture it to himself. In what did this culture consist in the case of Ramakrishna? Was it in the classical foundations of great religious teachings and the popular lyrical songs of Bengal? I wish specially to question in regard to this last point. When Ramakrishna was a child what were the principal sources of poetry and music upon which he was brought up? Those pastoral songs about Krishna, the love songs about Radha, were they by well-known poets, did they belong to the Vaishnavite literature? What were the religious dramas in which he acted or which he saw enacted?

In your *Gospel*, you mention a certain number of poets, whose hymns Ramakrishna used to sing. I find amongst them frequently the name of

Ramprasad and two or three times that of Kabir. I know those two, but who were Premdas, Kamalakanta, Nareshchandra, Bodha-charita? To what epoch do they belong?

1. By whom is the hymn of the "Sacred name of God and His power" quoted several times with different variations? (pages 65, 125, 129 or 193 in your Fourth Edition 1925, vol. I).

2. By whom is the "well known" hymn of Radha quoted by you in volume I, page 382.

3. By whom are the hymns of the Gopis in the Kirtan in vol. II, page 309.

4. The beautiful hymn of the "Machine" vol. I, page 296, vol. II, page 113 impressed me. Is it well known in Bengal?

5. I never see mentioned the names of Chandidas, Vidyapati, and other great old poets of Bengal. Did not Sri Ramakrishna know them? It seems to me that he ought to have loved intensely these wonders of mystic love which seemed to me, the greatest achievements of Bhakti art (specially the songs of Chandidas).

Have the dramas of Girish been translated and published in English?

I also would like to question on a historical point. Have you any knowledge of the date on which Ramakrishna met Devendra Nath Tagore? Swami Ashokananda first told me that it was in 1869 or 1870. Afterwards he said, in 1863. This last date seems to me logically to be less probable, for it belongs to a period of his life in which Ramakrishna seemed too much occupied with his own inward researches to go visiting other people. But logic is not an infallible rule of life, and I should hope to be enlightened by you on this subject. Excuse me, for having recourse to your personal memories for which you have my affectionate envy, and would you accept, dear Mr. Mahendra Nath Gupta, my respects and my fraternal feeling in the memory of Sri Ramakrishna.

Romain Rolland

Supplementary questions:

1. Is it a fact that some of the songs (specially certain sung by Naren) belong to the collection of the Brahmo Samaj?

2. One sometimes hears of the influence of Chaitanya on Sri Rama-krishna. How has that influence been brought to bear on him? By what intermediaries? Were not certain works of Girish dedicated to Chaitanya?

Again, pardon my taking advantage of your scholarship and your kindness.

*   *   *

Sri Gurudeva
50 Amherst Street
Calcutta, 28 November 1928

Dear Monsieur Romain Rolland,

Many many thanks for your kind and affectionate greetings and your holy message — a message which has kept us meditating upon our loving Master with the benignant smile beaming from his sweet radiant face.

May the Lord bless the noble task you have imposed upon yourself, viz., to tell the spiritual as well as the literary world how this Godman lived and how he taught to solve the problem of this mysterious enigmatic life; and what his relation is to humanity as well as to India and his immediate disciples.

My affectionate greetings herewith to your good self and the members of your family — all enjoying the blessing of retirement — and to all your friends.

In the following type-written pages I have attempted to answer some of your interesting questions.

I remain with love and namaskar,

Ever yours in the Lord,
M.

I

You ask, "In what did this (oral) culture consist in the case of Sri Ramakrishna?"

The Master used to say, "Jesus or Chaitanya or myself is not the fruit of culture or *sadhana* (book-learnt or oral)."

As you say (*Prabuddha Bharata*, April 1928): "The Eternal has sown Himself with full hands over the whole field of humanity.…He is sometimes awake and often goes to sleep."

The Godman (the Avatar) is the highest manifestation of the Eternal. The words that fall from the lips of the Godman are inspired … are spoken, as the Master used to say, by the Divine Mother. "My doctrine is not my own, but His that sent me."*

His words are Vedas or Revelations.

Did not the Doctors assembled in the Temple wonder and say, "Is this Joseph's son — the Carpenter? He knoweth not letters but never man spake like that man." And Jesus was then only a boy of twelve.

---

*John 7:16

Europeans are quite familiar with the picture of this boy Jesus, illiterate as he was.

The Master too assured the *bhaktas*, his disciples, that he had seen God when eleven years old, in a state of samadhi (God-consciousness) while going to Anur on his way to a certain shrine in company with his mother, and other women-folk, all pilgrims.

"*Tasmin vijñāte sarvamidam vijñātam bhavati* — Once He is realized all else is known." (Upanishad)

Did not Jesus also say to his disciples, "Blessed are the pure in spirit, for they shall see God."*

The Godmen realized the kingdom of heaven both within and without — realized God. Once the rod on the electric tram is connected with the electric wires overhead the car starts going, has life, is illuminated both within and without by a flood of light!

Of course it is difficult for us all to realize the divine equipment of these Godmen, manifested even in their infancy as a result of God-vision. But "there are more things in heaven and earth, Horatio, than are dreamt of in your philosophy!"

Did not Jesus say, "I thank Thee, O Father, because Thou hast hid these things from the wise and prudent ... and hast revealed them unto babes." (Matthew 2:25). It was indeed a rare unique privilege given unto his disciples to come in touch with such a Godman for five long years — long, but alas all too short!

Europe, as the Lord wills it, is now busy with many things. She finds it difficult to realize Jesus even as a historical personage. "Martha, Martha, thou art troubled with many things! But one thing is needful, and Mary has chosen the good part that shall not be taken away."

Europe relies on canons of historical evidence and criticism to establish the personality of Jesus! How futile, how infructuous, all these are in the case of Godmen! It is a Maha-yogi, a Godman alone, who can understand and interpret a Maha-yogi or Godman — not our historians steeped in the common pursuits of life. The yogi has not been understood. He does not play to the gallery. "Let me a fit audience find, though few," says

---

*To see God! Is it by the senses or by Yoga (perfect detachment from the sense-world and communion with the Lord)? The Godmen who had realized knew it all! One must be "pure — stripped of one's sensuous nature" (Kant) — to be able to see God. The Godmen are Nitya-siddha or Ever-perfect, always pure. They always see God. Did not Jesus say "Father, You have given to me to conquer the flesh that I may give Eternal Life to those that seek it." Did not Sri Ramakrishna also teach renunciation of sense-enjoyments, riches, honours, titles, sense-pleasures (derived from "women and gold") to the seekers of God?

he. What is more, the Yogi was crucified in Jesus. He was found guilty of laying hands on "vested interest."

It is not the fact, therefore, as the Master assured his disciples that he was, "brought up" upon his cultural environments. In his case as well as in the case of Jesus, as the Master pointed out, it was the fruit (God-realization) that first came out on the tree of life. The flowers came after. The sadhana, the culture, the struggles for realization, the teachers, the lyric songs, the Shastras, the Scriptures, were all meant to "fulfill all righteousness." Did not John the Baptist say to Jesus, "I have need to be baptized of thee and comest thou to me!" Did not Jesus say in reply, "Suffer it to be so now, for thus it becomes us to fulfill all righteousness"? (Matthew 3:15)

Thus too Sri Ramakrishna was asked by the Divine Mother to go through those sadhanas, those spiritual researches, those austerities, all those wonderful prayers and meditations in order to point out to future aspirants the path to realization. These were meant by the Divine Mother to be milestones for future travellers longing to reach the goal.

The programme of service — altruistic work based on renunciation — chalked out by the Ramakrishna Mission under the guidance of Swami Vivekananda has this great object in view, viz., *chitta shuddhi* or purification of the soul by work based on renunciation of sense-enjoyments — the ultimate objective being the realization of God. Such *nishkāma karma* (disinterested work) is, as the Master repeatedly pointed out, the *means* of attaining true life but not the *end* of life, which is "to see God." As Jesus said, "Blessed are the pure in heart, for they shall see God." Selfless work leadeth to purity: Purity leads to God-realization. Such work is the means: The end is to see, to realize God.

Mahatma Gandhi's patriotic work is equally *nishkāma,* disinterested. The difference from the altruistic philanthropic work of the Ramakrishna Mission consists in this: The Mission emphasizes alike by word and deed (1) that its social-service work is based on the renunciation of sense-enjoyments, and (2) that its work is thus only a means of attaining, realizing, seeing God. Mahatma does not appear to emphasize this in so many words, but the goal is the same, emphasized, expressed or understood.

Again, the glow of the morning sun lends a golden hue to the face of nature. The Godman too, as the Master taught, throws a charm on his environments — scriptures, personalities, places, motherland and all.

He revives and expounds the deep spiritual meaning of life — life lived by former Godmen with their spiritual experiences preserved by the scriptures or the poets. He alone comes down as an interpreter of former Godmen — he, the divine interpreter. "*Swayameva ātmanātmānam vettha twam purushottama* — It is Thou, O best of men, that knowest Thyself by Thyself." (Gita)

The Godman does not learn either from the scriptures or from the divine teachers. He interprets them — for he has realized God. Jesus interpreted the Law and the Prophets: Sri Ramakrishna was the divine interpreter of the Vedas, the Puranas, the Tantras, the Bible, and the Koran etc., as well as of Christ, Buddha, Chaitanya and other Godmen. Thus, in the tree of his life in this world, flourished first the fruit and then the flowers, as he said.

The Divine Mother brought to him after realization, men, scriptures, songs for him to put in his transcendental crucible, and to separate the gold from the dross — to deal a blow to discord, intolerance, sectarianism on the one hand and deliver a twofold message to humanity, viz., (1) That God can be realized, seen, talked to, communed with and (2) that all religions lead to the same goal — God-realization. Only let us pray unto Him without ceasing with a longing, yearning heart for life, for realization.

Did not the Divine Mother place the Master in the midst of other environments too — money, honours, titles, sense-pleasures, etc.? Is the Godman influenced by them? No, he would have none of them. Jesus, tempted, rejected the offers of Satan in the wilderness. As to the *siddhis*, the power of working miracles, the Master was convinced of their worthlessness by the Divine Mother and he set his face against them. Did not Jesus also say, "It is a vile adulterous generation that looks for signs, for miracles"? And the message of the New Testament is love, the one thing needful, pure unadulterated love for God which seeks no return in the shape of little things in this world, material goods — enjoyments of the flesh, power, pelf, fame, and the rest of them.

Thus, as the Master taught, the Godman shakes himself free from the influence of environments which almost overpower ordinary mortals. The Godman, the son of God, is a born "eunuch for the Kingdom of Heaven."

II

I must apologize for not having until now attempted to answer the rest of your interesting questions:

(a) Re. meeting with Devendra Nath Tagore.

I suggested to Swami Ashokananda the year 1863 on the ground that the Master had said to us that he had seen Keshab Sen seated on the pulpit of the Adi Brahmo Samaj at the time of the visit. Now Keshab was appointed Minister of the Adi Samaj in 1862.

Keshab seceded from the Adi Samaj in 1865: so it must be between 1862 and 1865. The Master practised in 1864-65 *Sakhi-bhava*, the role of the handmaiden of the Divine Mother, wearing woman's clothes, dancing and singing before Her and before Radha and Krishna — God-incarnate as love. He was filled with the madness of divine, ecstatic love during these eventful years. At that time he was put in a state of samadhi many times in the course of the day.

Between 1858 and 1862 he was in the midst of his sadhana, or as you put it, "He was occupied with his own inward researches." Notwithstanding, he would oftentimes go about earnestly to listen to the Ramayana, the Mahabharata, the Bhagavata, sung or recited by pandits near about the temple. He would avoid the company of worldly men and was eager to hear of God and God alone.

(b) Re. dramas of Girish.

So far as it is known to us they have not been translated into English. Girish joined the Master towards the end of 1884, i.e., about two years before the Master's passing. The Master witnessed the performance of *Chaitanya-Lila*, *Daksha-yajna*, *Prahlada-Charitra*, *Dhruva-Charitra*, and *Brishaketu*, towards the end of 1884 and in 1885. These dramas were all written by Girish.

(c) *Buddha-Charita* or the life of Buddha dramatized by Girish is the name of a play, not of a poet.

(d) Premdas, Kamalakanta, Nareshchandra, and Kabir.

Premdas: Premdas was the name assumed by the late Trailokya Sannyal, a follower of Keshab. He had the advantage of often meeting Sri Ramakrishna and witnessing his wonderful God-consciousness (samadhi), his communion with the Mother of the Universe, his dancing and singing songs relating to the mystic love for the Mother, and for Radha and Krishna, and for Chaitanya. Some of his songs were thus inspired by Sri Ramakrishna.

Kamalakanta: He was a devout pandit employed about 1810 as sabhapandit or president of an assembly of literary men attached to the court of the Maharaja of Burdwan. His songs were specially addressed to the Divine Mother.

Nareshchandra: It is said that he came from the Navadwip Raja family; a devout composer of hymns mostly addressed to the Divine Mother. It is said he flourished in the beginning of the 19th century.

Kabir and Kubir:

Kabir — the well-known disciple of Ramananda of Southern India.

Kubir — the Vaishnavite Bengali saint, probably flourished in the beginning of the 19th century. He is known by some popular songs bearing his name.

(e) Re. songs of Jayadeva, Vidyapati, Chandidas, Govindadas, Jnanadas and other Vaishnavite poets.

Yes, the Master was familiar with them too. There will be reference to some of these songs in the future volume of the *Gospel* to be published in English. The Master was often put in a state of samadhi whenever he heard the songs describing the ecstatic love of the Gopis. Some of the songs were adapted in yatras (indigenous theatrical performances), conducted by Govinda Adhikari, Nilkantha, and other yatrawallas. Sri Ramakrishna was very familiar with them also.

(f) Re. the well-known song of Radha.

"O my friend, how far is that blessed woodland!" (*Gospel*, 1924, vol. I:381)

The song appears to be an adaptation in the yatras from the Vaishnavite poets Jayadeva, Vidyapati, and Chandidas.

(g) Re. "The sacred name of God and His power" and "The song of the Machine."

These two songs referring to the Mother of the Universe are sung in connection with "Chandi" (i.e., the Divine Mother sporting in this play-world of Hers with her devotees, Kalketu, Srimanta, etc.). (Vide *Chandi* by Kabikankan translated by Cowel)

We are making enquiries as to the composers of the songs.

By the "Machine" constructed by the Divine Mother is as you see, meant the human being. The "Machine" is a beautiful hymn as you observe, striking at the root of the doctrine of free will. The golden touch of the Master who used to sing this hymn has made the song of the "Machine" well known in Bengal. Till then it was known to a limited few.

(h) Re. the song of the Gopis, "O Madhavi" (*Gospel*, vol. II:309).

This is also a song adapted from the Vaishnavite poet for the yatras. The yatras here are popular and are largely resorted to specially by the masses.

(i) Re. Sri Ramakrishna and the yatras.

As the Master told us, he would often witness these yatras (dramatic performances, presented principally in songs).

He acted the part of Shiva, (called *yogiraj*, the king of yogis) when he was a boy, upon the special invitation of the Manager, the actor to whom the part had been allotted being away or taken ill. This was the only occasion on which he presented himself as an actor. But in the course of the acting he was found lost in samadhi! People thought he had passed away and the yatra was about to come to an end.

(j) Re. the songs of the Brahmo Samaj.

Yes, some of the songs sung before the Master were songs composed by the members of the Brahmo Samaj, e.g., "The full moon of divine love..." (*Gospel*, vol. I, section 3)

This song and some other songs bearing the name of the composer Premdas were composed under the inspiration of Sri Ramakrishna's personality — for Keshab and his followers used to meet him off and on and were struck by the Master's strange and unique God-consciousness.

Naren (Vivekananda) used to attend the meetings of the Samaj when a boy before he first met the Master towards the beginning of 1882.

The following song from the Brahmo Samaj sung by Swami Vivekananda (*Gospel*, vol. I, section 6) also put the Master in samadhi.

Song: "When shall we realize in the temple of the heart the all-good, all-gracious form of God, the only Reality..." (*Gospel*, vol. I)

(k) Re. the influence of Girish's dramas.

The Master heard *Chaitanya-lila* towards the end of 1884 in which year the drama was first brought out, i.e., only one year and a half before the Master's ascension in August 1886.

Now the Master was found intoxicated with Chaitanya's madness of ecstatic love (prema) ever since 1858 or even earlier. *Chaitanya-lila* was published 26 years after.

(l) Re. influence of Chaitanya.

Ever since 1858, this ecstatic love for the Divine Mother, for Radha and Krishna, for Ramachandra, and for Chaitanya as God incarnate made the Master "mad" and he was found all these long years singing, dancing, and what is more, losing sense-consciousness in samadhi.

The Master's life, his deep intense religiousness, his ecstatic love, explained the true meaning of Chaitanya's mystic love of Radha for Krishna. Hitherto people could hardly understand the true significance of that love.

When Swami Vivekananda, then a lad of 19, first saw him, the Master said to him, "Have you heard of Gauranga (Chaitanya of Navadwip)? Well, the same was myself in a previous incarnation." Vivekananda, then a mere boy, was puzzled. He wondered and was speechless. He regarded him at the time as a madman, as he told us shortly after.

To us also the Master said, "He who was Rama, Krishna, Chaitanya, Jesus, the same is Sri Ramakrishna in the present age."

Did not Jesus also say, "Before Abraham was I am!" (John 8:58). And again, "My doctrine is not mine but His that sent me." (John 7:16)

Bahuni me vyatitāni janmāni tava cha Arjuna
Tānyaham veda sarvāni na tvam vettha parantapa.

"Many have been my incarnations and yours too. I know (remember) them all; you do not." (Gita)

Yes, the bard of Stratford was after all right, "There are more things in heaven and earth than are dreamt of in one's philosophy." Greek culture, Roman culture, the six systems of Indian philosophy — all have been weighed in the balance and found wanting! Until new life, new blood, is infused into them by the Godman, the Avatar, the divine interpreter, they are mere dry bones — dumb, lifeless apparatus for mere intellectual gymnastics!

The strangest thing of all is that the Divine Mother, the Logos, made the Master realize not only Her manifestations, Her emanations, but also Her transcendental Reality! Not only the Divine Incarnations, Ramachandra, Krishna, Jesus, Chaitanya, Sri Ramakrishna but also Herself as the absolute, the unconditioned, the super-sensual, the noumenon, the substantia, the Nirguna Brahman of the Vedanta — realized by the Godman in the depths of nirvikalpa samadhi, mystic God-consciousness, in which vanishes even the last trace of the finite phenomenal, conditioned ego! (Vide also *Gospel* 1924, vol. I, sec. 2:86-127)

With love and namaskar,

Ever yours in the Lord,
M.

[Taken from *Vedanta Kesari*: 1953:3-10]

—Appendix 2—

A Brief History of M's House

M.'s (Mahendra Nath Gupta's) ancestral home is situated at 13/2 Guru-prasad Chaudhury Lane in Central Calcutta. M. called this house *Thakur Bari,* or The Master's House. It is also called *Kathamrita Bhavan,* or The House of the *Kathamrita.*

Thakur Bari is very near the famous Siddheswari Kali temple at Bidhan Sarani in Central Calcutta, an important place of pilgrimage for the devotees of Ramakrishna, as he practised japa and meditation here when he first came to Calcutta in 1852. It is said that Ramakrishna visited M. in this house, as did Swami Vivekananda, Swami Ramakrishnananda, and other monastic disciples.

M.'s Room

After Ramakrishna's passing away, Holy Mother lived with M.'s family on many occasions, sometimes for a week, a fortnight, or even a few months at a time. Nikunja Devi (M.'s wife) and her two sons received initiation from Holy Mother. (In 1909 Holy Mother's permanent home, the Udbodhan House, was built.)

During one such visit in October 1888, Ramakrishna appeared to Holy Mother in a dream and commanded her to worship Goddess Durga in M.'s shrine. Later M. chose to use this small room on the second floor, where Holy Mother had stayed, as his own bedroom. In this very room, he wrote a substantial portion of *The Gospel of Sri Ramakrishna,* and finally on 4 June 1932, M. completed the fifth volume of the *Sri Sri Ramakrishna Kathamrita* (the last volume of the Bengali *Gospel*) and passed away.

M. collected precious relics of Ramakrishna and Holy Mother, including the Master's shirt, his moleskin shawl, his water pot, and a small jug owned by Holy Mother. These articles — as well as the ink pot that M. used when writing the *Gospel* — are all preserved in this room on the second floor. A very old picture of Chaitanya and his kirtan party dancing in

555

ecstasy is hanging on one of its walls. The Master presented this picture to
M. on 24 September 1885. The cot that M. slept on, and on which he passed
away, is on the east side of this room. On it rests a large picture of M. that
was taken on 23 February 1927 at the foot of the bel tree in Dakshineswar.
It was placed there shortly after M.'s death, and it remains there today.

M.'s Shrine

M.'s shrine is on the third floor of the house, which can be reached by
the same wooden staircase that was used by Holy Mother, Swami Vivekananda, M., and other disciples of Ramakrishna.

On 6 October 1888 Holy Mother installed an original photograph of
Ramakrishna on the altar, and also installed the Sri Chandi Mangal Ghat,
a sacred urn filled with water in which the Goddess Durga is invoked. She
then dedicated M.'s shrine by worshipping the Master's photograph and the
Ghat. This historic event inspired M. to write *The Gospel of Sri Ramakrishna*.

In this very shrine, Holy Mother blessed and initiated many devotees.
Some of Ramakrishna's disciples spent many hours here in deep meditation. Some sacred relics of the Master and Holy Mother are also preserved
here in glass cases: the Master's sandals, a bundle containing hair and nail
clippings of Ramakrishna and Holy Mother, a silk bag containing Holy
Mother's rudraksha beads (japa-mala), and a box holding her vermilion,
as well as Holy Mother's footprints. These sacred articles are adored and
worshipped every day.

Adjacent to the shrine is an annex, and next to that is the roof where
M. planted flowering trees in tubs. At one corner of the roof stands a cen-
tury-old plumeria (gulancha) tree; even today it bears beautiful and fragrant flowers. Swamiji, M., and others meditated on this roof for hours.

Daily Activities

To preserve this historical landmark and holy place, M.'s descendants
handed the house over to the Ramakrishna Order, although M's descendants still watch over it with great love and care.

The worship service that Holy Mother introduced still continues three
times a day. The birthday celebrations of Ramakrishna, Holy Mother,
Swami Vivekananda, M., and others are observed every year. On the
Maha-Ashtami day of Durga Puja, a special worship is performed to the
Sri Chandi Mangal Ghat.

Every day between sixty and eighty monks, devotees, and other visitors come to M.'s house. The visiting hours are 8:00 to 11:30 a.m. and 4:00
to 7:30 p.m.

M's Family Tree

Madhusudan m. Swarnamayi
1. Kailashchandra
2. Kshirodvasini
3. Saudamani
4. Kshetramohan
5. Ramanmohini
6. Manmohini
7. Akshaykumar
8. Binodini
9. Mahendranath m. Nikunja Devi (died in 1941)
10. Durgamani
11. Kishorimohan
      1. Nirmal (died at 8 in 1884)
      2. Prabhas (died in 1934) m. Kamalini
      3. Charu (unmarried, died in 1933)
      4. Sarojini (Habi, Handu; died at 22 in 1890)
      5. Mrinalini (Mrinmayi, Gondi)
      6. Manmayi (Mani)
      7. Radharani
                     1. Arun m. Shanti
                     2. Ajay
                     3. Ajit
                     4. Shobha
                     5. Anil
                     6. Ramchandra
                           1. Tapas
                           2. Manas
                           3. Dipak
                           4. Gautam
                           5. Anjan

Chronology of M.'s Life

1854 Birth of Mahendra Nath Gupta: Friday, 14 July at Simulia, Calcutta.

1858 During the Chariot Festival in July, M. and his mother visited Mahesh and on their way back stopped at Dakshineswar, where he most likely met Sri Ramakrishna.

1862 M. studied for two or three years at Vidyasagar's school on Shankar Ghosh Lane.

1864 On 5 October M. prayed to God during the cyclone. Saw Vidyasagar.

1865 Admitted to Hare School, where he studied till 1870. Saw Keshab Chandra Sen speak for the first time.

1866 Met Michael Madhusudan Datta.

1867 Started to keep a diary while in the seventh grade at Hare School.

1870 Passed the matriculation examination.

1871 Admitted to Presidency College and visited Varanasi with friends.

1872 Passed the F.A. examination.

1873 Married Nikunja Devi, a cousin of Keshab Sen.

1874 Graduated from Calcutta University.

1875 Admitted to Law College but did not complete a degree.

1877 Took a job in a merchant's office.

1879 Became headmaster of Narail School, Jessore District.

1880 Became headmaster and superintendent of Vidyasagar's Metropolitan High School, Shyampukur Branch, Calcutta. His mother passed away.

1882 On 18 February left home, and met Sri Ramakrishna on Sunday, 26 February. There are 22 entries in *The Gospel of Sri Ramakrishna* for this year.

1883 There are 60 entries in *The Gospel of Sri Ramakrishna*.

1884 There are 39 entries in *The Gospel of Sri Ramakrishna*. In November, M.'s eldest son, Nirmal, died.

1885 There are 41 entries in *The Gospel of Sri Ramakrishna*.

1886 There are 15 entries in *The Gospel of Sri Ramakrishna*. Developed 3 more entries after the Master's passing away that are not in the *Gospel* (see Chapter 13). Visited Kamarpukur from 7 to 11 February, Darjeeling 17 May, and Puri in June. Resigned from Vidyasagar's school on 21 May and on 10 June accepted a position at the Hindu School, and in July began working at Ripon College. Sri Ramakrishna passed away on 16 August at 1:02 a.m. Visited Baranagore Math on 12 October.

1887 After the Master's passing away, there are 8 entries in *The Gospel of Sri Ramakrishna*. Besides these, another entry was published in the *Navya Bharat* magazine (see Chapter 13). Holy Mother stayed at M.'s house from 1 to 15 September and installed the Durga Mangal Ghat. In September Nikunja Devi and Holy Mother went to Kamarpukur. In October M. visited Vrindaban, Varanasi, and Ayodhya.

1888 On 11 July M. read the manuscript of the *Gospel* to Holy Mother at Nilambar Mukherjee's garden house. On 30 October Nikunja Devi received initiation from Holy Mother.

1889 In May M.'s father died.

1891 Left Ripon College and became headmaster of Oriental Seminary.

1897 Published a pamphlet entitled *The Gospel of Sri Ramakrishna* in English.

1902 Published *Sri Sri Ramakrishna Kathamrita*, volume 1.

1904 Published *Sri Sri Ramakrishna Kathamrita*, volume 2.

1905 Retired from headmastership, bought the Morton Institution, and became the rector of the school.

1907 Madras Math published the English translation of the *Gospel*.

1908 Published *Sri Sri Ramakrishna Kathamrita*, volume 3.

1910 Published *Sri Sri Ramakrishna Kathamrita*, volume 4.

1912 Went to Varanasi, Hardwar, and Rishikesh to practise austerities.

1913 Returned to Calcutta via Delhi.

1922–23 Lived in Mihijam Ashrama from 21 October to 10 May.

1925 Visited Puri with Nikunja Devi.

1932 Passed away on Saturday, 4 June at 5:30 a.m. On 24 August *Sri Sri Ramakrishna Kathamrita*, volume 5 was published.

Photographs from the 1920 Bengali edition of the *Gospel* published by M.
TOP: Cossipore garden house, BOTTOM: Balaram Basu's house in Calcutta

References

Prologue

1. Christopher Isherwood, *Ramakrishna and His Disciples* (Methuen & Co.: London, 1965), 277-82
2. Swami Prabhananda, *Amritarup Sri Ramakrishna* (Udbodhan Office: Calcutta, 1991), 240
3. Swami Nityatmananda, *Srima Darshan* (General Printers and Publishers: Calcutta, 1970), 7:24-27

1. Early Life (1854-1874)

1. Swami Nityatmananda, *Srima Darshan* (General Printers and Publishers: Calcutta, 1968), 5:326-27
2. Ibid., 7:198 and Swami Chetanananda, *They Lived with God* (Vedanta Society: St. Louis, 2006), 210
3. M., *The Gospel of Sri Ramakrishna*, trans. Swami Nikhilananda (Ramakrishna-Vivekananda Centre: New York, 1969), 801
4. Abhay Chandra Bhattacharya, *Srimar Jivan Darshan* (Grantha Bharati: Calcutta, 1990), 37
5. Ibid., 39
6. *Srima Darshan*, 1:22
7. Ibid., 1:13
8. *They Lived with God*, 211
9. Jagannathananda, *Srima-Katha* (Udbodhan Office: Calcutta, 1941), 1: (6)
10. *Jivan Darshan*, 45
11. *Srima Katha*, 1: (7)

2. As a Householder and School Teacher

1. Abhay Chandra Bhattacharya, *Srimar Jivan Darshan* (Grantha Bharati: Calcutta, 1990), 50

2. Ibid., 52
3. Ibid., 53
4. Swami Chetanananda, *They Lived with God* (Vedanta Society: St. Louis, 2006), 221
5. *Jivan Darshan*, 366
6. Swami Nityatmananda, *Srima Darshan* (General Printers and Publishers: Calcutta, 1967), 1:339-40

3. First Meetings with Ramakrishna

1. M., *The Gospel of Sri Ramakrishna*, trans. Swami Nikhilananda (Ramakrishna-Vivekananda Centre: New York, 1969), 77
2. Ibid., 78
3. Ibid., 79
4. M., *The Condensed Gospel of Sri Ramakrishna* (Sri Ramakrishna Math: Chennai, 1978), 30
5. Ibid., 31
6. *Gospel*, 84
7. Ibid., 84
8. Ibid., 85
9. Ibid., 86
10. Ibid., 86-87
11. Ibid., 87
12. Ibid., 89
13. Ibid., 90
14. Ibid., 91

4. The Guru and the Disciples

1. Swami Nityatmananda, *Srima Darshan* (General Printers and Publishers: Calcutta, 1968), 1:340-41
2. Katha Upanishad, 1:2:7
3. M., *The Gospel of Sri Ramakrishna*, trans. Swami Nikhilananda (Ramakrishna-Vivekananda Centre: New York, 1969), 98

4. Ibid., 95
5. Ibid., 95
6. *The Complete Works of Swami Vivekananda* (Advaita Ashrama: Calcutta, 1968), 6:64
7. *Gospel*, 112-14
8. Ibid., 122-23
9. Abhay Chandra Bhattacharya, *Srimar Jivan Darshan* (Grantha Bharati: Calcutta, 1990), 97
10. Ibid., 98
11. *Gospel*, 126
12. Ibid., 127
13. Ibid., 459
14. *Jivan Darshan*, 71
15. Shatapatha Brahmana, 10:5:2:20 (Brihadaranyaka Upanishad, 2.1.2)
16. Bible, John 3:3
17. *Gospel*, 237-38
18. Ibid., 256
19. Ibid., 247
20. Ibid., 300-01
21. Ibid., 331-34
22. Ibid., 506
23. *Complete Works of Swami Vivekananda* (1966), 4:177
24. Swami Saradananda, *Sri Ramakrishna and His Divine Play*, trans. Swami Chetanananda (Vedanta Society: St. Louis, 2003), 805-06
25. *Gospel*, 376-77

5. With Ramakrishna in Various Places

1. M., *The Gospel of Sri Ramakrishna*, trans. by Swami Nikhilananda (Ramakrishna–Vivekananda Centre: New York, 1969), 591
2. Swami Chetanananda, *They Lived with God* (Vedanta Society: St. Louis, 2006), 221
3. Swami Saradananda, *Sri Ramakrishna and His Divine Play*, trans. Swami Chetanananda (Vedanta Society: St. Louis, 2003), 649
4. *Gospel*, 99-100

5. Ibid., 110
6. Ibid., 833
7. Ibid., 133
8. Ibid., 144
9. Ibid., 154
10. Ibid., 253
11. Ibid., 259-60
12. Ibid., 261
13. Ibid., 281
14. Ibid., 286-87
15. Ibid., 365-66
16. Ibid., 366-67
17. Ibid., 462
18. Ibid., 463-64
19. Ibid., 466
20. Ibid., 471-72
21. Ibid., 546-47
22. Ibid., 550
23. Ibid., 550-51, 556-57
24. Ibid., 637-38
25. Ibid., 641-42
26. Ibid., 724, 730-32
27. Ibid., 762
28. Swami Akhandananda, *Smritikatha* (Udbodhan Office: Calcutta, 1937), 24
29. *Gospel*, 738-39
30. Ibid., 742
31. Ibid., 815-20
32. Ibid., 822-23
33. Ibid., 825-26
34. Swami Chetanananda, ed. & trans., *Ramakrishna as We Saw Him* (Vedanta Society: St. Louis, 1990), 208-09
35. *Gospel*, 391
36. Ibid., 400-401
37. Ibid., 1018-19

6. Christmas Vacation with Ramakrishna

1. M., *The Gospel of Sri Ramakrishna*, trans. by Swami Nikhilananda (Ramakrishna-Vivekananda Centre: New York, 1969), 331
2. Ibid., 331-32
3. Ibid., 338-39
4. Ibid., 337-38

5. Ibid., 334-40
6. Ibid., 341
7. Ibid., 341
8. Ibid., 342
9. Ibid., 343-44
10. Ibid., 345-46
11. Ibid., 346
12. Ibid., 347
13. Ibid., 348
14. Ibid., 349
15. Bible: Matthew 21:13
16. *Gospel*, 348-49
17. Ibid., 349
18. Ibid., 350
19. Ibid., 351
20. Ibid.,,352
21. Ibid., 353
22. Ibid., 353
23. Ibid., 353
24. Ibid., 353
25. Ibid., 357
26. Ibid., 358-60
27. Ibid., 360
28. Ibid., 362-63
29. Ibid., 364
30. Ibid., 365
31. Ibid., 366
32. Ibid., 370
33. Ibid., 371
34. Ibid., 371
35. Ibid., 81-82
36. Ibid., 372
37. Ibid., 372
38. Ibid., 373
39. Ibid., 375
40. Ibid., 375-77
41. Ibid., 377
42. Ibid., 378-79
43. Ibid., 381-82

7. Two New Entries from M's Diary

1. Amiya Kumar Majumdar, *Punya Darshan Srima* (Gangotri Parishad: Calcutta, 1985), 1:60-66
2. *Ramakrishna Mission's Minute Book* (Calcutta: 22 August 1897), 31-34

8. The Stage for Ramakrishna's Divine Play

1. Swami Saradananda, *Ramakrishna and His Divine Play*, trans. by Swami Chetanananda (Vedanta Society: St. Louis, 2003), 182-83
2. *The Complete Works of Sister Nivedita* (Nivedita Girls' School: Calcutta, 1967), 1:191
3. Swami Chetanananda, ed. & trans., *Ramakrishna as We Saw Him* (Vedanta Society: St. Louis, 1990), 475-77
4. Swami Nityatmananda, *Srima Darshan* (General Printers and Publishers: Calcutta, 1970), 4:116-17
5. Ibid., 6:90
6. *Rk as We*, 478
7. *Srima Darshan*, 4:200-201
8. Ibid., 12:175
9. Ibid., 6:91
10. *Rk as We*, 479
11. *Srima Darshan*, 12:174
12. *Gospel*, 92
13. *Rk as We*, 477
14. *Srima Darshan*, 4:67
15. *Rk as We*, 477
16. *Divine Play*, 487
17. Swami Chetanananda, *They Lived with God* (Vedanta Society: St. Louis, 2006), 223
18. *Rk as We*, 480
19. *Srima Darshan*, 1:252
20. *They Lived*, 202
21. *Rk as We*, 484
22. *Gospel*, 89
23. *Srima Darshan*, 3:240, 9:119
24. *They Lived*, 35
25. *Rk as We*, 483
26. *Srima Darshan*, 3:236
27. *Rk as We*, 483-84
28. Ibid., 481
29. *Srima Darshan*, 4:64
30. *Rk as We*, 481
31. *Srima Darshan*, 3:237, 5:113
32. Ibid., 6:292

33. *Gospel*, 504
34. *Srima Darshan*, 8:22
35. *Rk as We*, 482
36. Ibid., 482
37. Ibid., 482
38. *Divine Play*, 274-75
39. *They lived*, 223-24

9. Service to the Master

1. Bhagavad Gita, 4:34
2. M., *The Gospel of Sri Ramakrishna*,
   trans. Swami Nikhilananda
   (Ramakrishna-Vivekananda Centre:
   New York, 1969), 458
3. Swami Chetanananda, *God Lived with
   Them* (Vedanta Society: St. Louis,
   1997), 185
4. Abhay Chandra Bhattacharya, *Srimar
   Jivan Darshan* (Grantha Bharati:
   Calcutta, 1990), 122
5. Ibid., 144
6. *Gospel*, 238
7. Ibid., 719-22
8. Ibid., 724-25
9. Ibid., 800-01
10. Ibid., 809
11. Ibid., 940-41
12. Gita, 9:22
13. Ibid., 9:26
14. *Gospel*, 642
15. Ibid., 655
16. Ibid., 655-56
17. Ibid., 932
18. Ibid., 950-51
19. Ibid., 543
20. Ibid., 847
21. Swami Jagannathananda, *Srima-
    Katha* (Ramakrishna Math:
    Bhubaneswar, 1953), 2:160, 163, 221
22. *Gospel*, 973
23. Ibid., 973-74
24. *God Lived*, 338

10. Ramakrishna's Love for M.

1. M., *The Gospel of Sri Ramakrishna*,
   trans. Swami Nikhilananda

(Ramakrishna-Vivekananda Centre:
   New York, 1969), 331
2. Ibid., 591
3. Ibid., 355
4. Bhagavad Gita, 10:9-11
5. Swami Chetanananda, *How a Shepherd
   Boy Became a Saint* (Vedanta Society:
   St. Louis, 2000), 174-75
6. Bhagavata, 10:32:17-22
7. *Gospel*, 839
8. Ibid., 761
9. Ibid., 341
10. Ibid., 463
11. Ibid., 720
12. Ibid., 260
13. Ibid., 282
14. Ibid., 345-46
15. Ibid., 932
16. Ibid., 270
17. Ibid., 381

11. Last Days with Ramakrishna

1. Romain Rolland, *The Life of
   Ramakrishna* (Advaita Ashrama:
   Calcutta, 1931), 294
2. Anonymous, *Life of Sri Ramakrishna*
   (Advaita Ashrama: Calcutta, 1943), 541
3. Swami Saradananda, *Sri Ramakrishna
   and His Divine Play*, trans. Swami
   Chetanananda (Vedanta Society: St.
   Louis, 2003), 869
4. M., *The Gospel of Sri Ramakrishna*,
   trans. Swami Nikhilananda
   (Ramakrishna-Vivekananda Centre:
   New York, 1969), 719-20
5. *Divine Play*, 900
6. Ibid., 875
7. Swami Jagannathananda, *Srima-Katha*
   (Ramakrishna Math: Bhubaneswar,
   1953), 2:160, 163, 221
8. *Gospel*, 848-56
9. Ibid., 856-67
10. Ibid., 868-76
11. Ibid., 876-79
12. Ibid., 879-85
13. Ibid., 886-95

14. Ibid., 895-906
15. Ibid., 907-12
16. Ibid., 912-20
17. Ibid., 920-24
18. Ibid., 924-30
19. Ibid., 931-35
20. *Divine Play*, 826
21. *Gospel*, 935-37
22. Ibid., 937-39
23. Swami Chetanananda, *God Lived with Them* (Vedanta Society: St. Louis, 1997), 539
24. Ibid., 519-20
25. *Divine Play*, 431
26. Ibid., 149
27. *God Lived*, 252
28. *Gospel*, 939-40
29. Ibid., 940-41
30. Ibid., 941-46
31. *Divine Play*, 607
32. *Gospel*, 947-50
33. Ibid., 950
34. Ibid., 950-54
35. Ibid., 954-58
36. Ibid., 959
37. Ibid., 959-61
38. Ibid., 962-63
39. Ibid., 963-70
40. Ibid., 970-73
41. Ibid, 973-74
42. Swami Nityatmananda, *Srima Darshan* (General Printers and Publishers: Calcutta, 1968), 4:309, 7:37
43. Ibid., 7:20, 13:205, 14:72
44. Advaita Ashrama, *Life of Ramakrishna*, 594 and Swami Gambhirananda, *Bhakta Malika* (Udbodhan Office: Calcutta, 1963), 1:167
45. Sharat Chandra Chakrabarty, *Swami Shishya Samvad* (Udbodhan Office: Calcutta, 1961), 2:90 and Swami Nikhilananda, *Vivekananda, The Yogas and Other Works* (Ramakrishna-Vivekananda Centre: New York, 1953), 34
46. *Swami Shishya Samvad*, 1:54 and *Yogas and Other Works*, 35
47. *God Lived*, 273
48. Swami Chetanananda, *They Lived with God* (Vedanta Society: St. Louis, 2006), 83-84
49. Swami Chetanananda, ed. & trans., *Ramakrishna as We Saw Him* (Vedanta Society: St. Louis, 1990), 158
50. Swami Chetanananda, *How a Shepherd Boy Became a Saint* (Vedanta Society: St. Louis, 2000), 52

12. After Ramakrishna's Passing Away

1. Swami Chetanananda, ed. & trans., *Ramakrishna as We Saw Him* (Vedanta Society: St. Louis, 1990), 474
2. M., *The Gospel of Sri Ramakrishna*, trans. Swami Nikhilananda (Ramakrishna-Vivekananda Centre: New York, 1969), 207
3. Swami Chetanananda, *How a Shepherd Boy Became a Saint* (Vedanta Society: St. Louis, 2000), 53
4. Swami Abhedananda, *Amar Jivankatha* (Ramakrishna Vedanta Math: Calcutta, 1964), 122
5. Swami Nikhilananda, *Holy Mother* (Ramakrishna-Vivekananda Centre: New York, 1962), 93-94
6. *The Complete Works of Sister Nivedita* (Nivedita Girls' School: Calcutta, 1967), 1:268
7. His Eastern and Western Disciples, *The Life of Swami Vivekananda* (Advaita Ashrama: Calcutta, 1979), 1:193
8. *Amar Jivan Katha*, 122-24
9. Mahendra Nath Datta, *Gurupran Ramachandrer Anudhyan* (Mahendra Publishing: Calcutta, 1958) Appendix, 61
10. Swami Saradeshananda, *Sri Sri Mayer Smritikatha* (Udbodhan Office: Calcutta, 1982), 21

11. Swami Nityatmananda, *Srima Darshan* (General Printers and Publishers: Calcutta, 1968), 16:29
12. Ibid, 5:50-51
13. Ibid., 1:370

13. M. at the Baranagore Math

1. Swami Chetanananda, *They Lived with God* (Vedanta Society: St. Louis, 2006), 136
2. Ibid., 1:153
3. Mahendra Nath Datta, *Master Mahashayer Anudhyan* (Mahendra Publishing: Calcutta, 1954), 13-19
4. M., *The Gospel of Sri Ramakrishna*, trans. Swami Nikhilananda (Ramakrishna-Vivekananda Centre: New York, 1969), 679
5. *Gospel*, 873
6. Ibid., 808
7. *Udbodhan*, vol. 102, issue 10 and vol. 103, issues 2 and 3.
8. *Gospel*, 975-77
9. Ibid., 977-80
10. Ibid., 980-83
11. Ibid., 983-84
12. Ibid., 984-87
13. Ibid., 987-90

14. Some Early Drafts of Sri Ramakrishna Kathamrita

1. Minute Book of the Ramakrishna Mission, 22 August 1897, 30-31
2. Ibid., 12 September 1897, 44-46

15. The Gospel of Sri Ramakrishna: A History

1. Swami Chetanananda, *Ramakrishna as We Saw Him* (Vedanta Society: St. Louis, 1990), 125
2. Swami Chetanananda, *God Lived with Them* (Vedanta Society: St. Louis, 1997), 189
3. Brajendra Nath Bandyopadhyay & Sajani Kanta Das, *Samasamayik Drishtite Sri Ramakrishna Paramahamsa* (General Printers and Publishers: Calcutta, 1968), 122
4. Srima, *Sri Sri Ramakrishna Kathamrita* (Kathamrita Bhavan: Calcutta, 1951), 3:vi
5. Ibid., 3:vii
6. Ibid., 3:vii
7. Sankari Prasad Basu, *Vivekananda O Samakalin Bharatvarsha* (Mandal Book House: Calcutta, 1976), 2:275
8. *Kathamrita*, 3:v
9. Anonymous, *Sri Ramakrishna O Tar Kathamrita* (Ramakrishna-Vivekananda Ashrama: Howrah, 1983), 220
10. M., *The Gospel of Sri Ramakrishna*, trans. Swami Nikhilananda (Ramakrishna-Vivekananda Centre: New York, 1969), 1019 and D.P. Gupta & D.K. Sengupta, ed., *Sri Sri Ramakrishna Kathamrita Centenary Memorial* (Srima Trust: Chandigarh, 1982), 142
11. *Srima Sarada* magazine (Sri Sri Yogeswari Ramakrishna Math: Howrah), 4:135
12. Swami Nityatmananda, *Srima Darshan* (General Printers and Publishers: Calcutta, 1972), 13:97
13. *Srima Sarada*, 6:8
14. *Srima Darshan*, 13:184
15. *Gospel*, 662-64
16. Ibid., 506
17. *Ramakrishna as We Saw Him*, 321-23
18. Ibid., 323
19. Ibid., 323
20. Ibid., 323
21. H.H. Halley, *Halley's Bible Handbook* (Zondervan Publishing House: Grand Rapids, 1965), 493
22. *Gospel*, 407
23. *Samasamayik Drishtite*, 3
24. Ibid., 46-47
25. *The Complete Works of Swami Vivekananda* (Advaita Ashrama: Calcutta, 1968), 5:259
26. Swami Nikhilananda, ed.,

Vivekananda: Yogas and Other Works
(Ramakrishna-Vivekananda Centre:
New York,1953), 708

27. *Belur Math Rule Book*, 10
28. *Complete Works of Swami Vivekananda*,
    6:64
29. Romain Rolland, *The Life of
    Ramakrishna* (Advaita Ashrama:
    Calcutta, 1931), 89-90
30. *Gospel*, 376
31. *Brahmavadin*, 3:104
32. D.P. Gupta & D.K. Sengupta, ed., *Sri
    Sri Ramakrishna Kathamrita Centenary
    Memorial* (Srima Trust: Chandigarh,
    1982), 147
33. *Gospel*, preface, vii-ix
34. *Srima Darshan*, 5:126
35. Ibid., 3:295-97
36. Abhay Chandra Bhattacharya,
    Srimar Jivan Darshan (Grantha
    Bharati: Calcutta, 1990), 351
37. From the back cover of the Gospel
38. *Srima Darshan*, 5:55-57 and *Srima
    Sarada* 1959:251
39. *Srima Darshan*, 6:103-110
40. Bhagavad Gita, 10:13
41. Srima, *Sri Sri Ramakrishna Kathamrita*
    (Kathamrita Bhavan: Calcutta, 1957),
    1:129 and *Gospel*, 266.
42. *Ramakrishna Kathamrita Centenary
    Memorial*, 77, 79
43. Ibid., 85
44. *Gospel*, 381
45. Ibid., 675
46. Brihadaranyaka Upanishad, 4:5:4
47. *Gospel*, 433-34
48. Suresh Chandra Datta, *Sri Sri Rama-
    krishnadever Upadesh* (Haramohan
    Publishing: Calcutta, 1968), 162
49. Christopher Isherwood, ed., *Vedanta
    for the Western World* (George Allen &
    Unwin Ltd.: London, 1961), 266
50. *Udbodhan*, 37:359
51. *Vedanta for the Western World*, 267
52. Romain Rolland, *The Life of
    Ramakrishna*, 294-95
53. *Gospel*, vi
54. Ibid, 83
55. Swami Abjajananda, *Swamijir
    Padaprante* (Ramakrishna Mission
    Sarada Pitha: Belur Math, 1972), 37
56. Swami Prabhananda, *Amritarup
    Sri Ramakrishna* (Udbodhan Office:
    Calcutta, 1991), 201-02
57. *Jivan Darshan*, 344
58. *Kathamrita*, 3:viii
59. Ibid., 3:viii
60. *Samakalin*, 2:302
61. Ibid., 3:viii
62. *Samakalin Bharatvarsha*, 2:306
63. *Amritarup Sri Ramakrishna*, 184
64. *Kathamrita*, (1st edition), 5:iv
65. *Gospel*, v
66. Swami Lokeswarananda, ed., *World
    Thinkers on Ramakrishna-Vivekananda*
    (Ramakrishna Mission Institute of
    Culture: Calcutta, 1992), 13
67. Christopher Isherwood, *Ramakrishna
    and His Disciples* (Methuen & Co.:
    London, 1965), 279-82
68. *Prabuddha Bharata*, 1949:228-29
69. *Udbodhan*, 60:95

16. The Centenary of The Gospel of Sri Ramakrishna

1. Swami Jagannathananda, *Srima Katha*
   (Udbodhan Office: Calcutta, 1953),
   1:146
2. M., *The Gospel of Sri Ramakrishna*,
   trans. by Swami Nikhilananda
   (Ramakrishna–Vivekananda Centre:
   New York, 1969), 591
3. Swami Nityatmananda, *Srima Darshan*
   (General Printers and Publishers:
   Calcutta, 1972), 9:18
4. *Udbodhan*, 35:11
5. *Gospel*, 82
6. Swami Nikhilananda, *Vivekananda: The
   Yogas and Other Works* (Ramakrishna-
   Vivekananda Centre: New York,
   1953), 903
7. *Gospel*, 338
8. Vatican Council II (Ad Gentes, 7
   December 1965)

9. Swamis Vividishananda and Gambhirananda, trans., *For Seekers of God*
(Advaita Ashrama: Calcutta, 1975), 296
10. *Gospel*, 1021-27

17. Pilgrimage and Austerities

1. M., *The Gospel of Sri Ramakrishna*,
trans. Swami Nikhilananda
(Ramakrishna-Vivekananda Centre:
New York, 1969), 313
2. Swami Jagannathananda, *Srima Katha*
(Udbodhan Office: Calcutta, 1941), 1:
intro, 19
3. *Gospel*, 449-450
4. Swami Nityatmananda, *Srima Darshan*
(General Printers and Publishers:
Calcutta, 1972), 11:104-05
5. *Srima Darshan*, 7:191-92
6. Ibid., 14:195
7. Swami Nikhilananda, *Holy Mother*
(Ramakrishna-Vivekananda Centre:
New York, 1962), 307
8. Swami Chetanananda, ed.& compiled, *Srima Samipe* (Udbodhan Office:
Calcutta, 1996), 61-62
9. Mahendra Nath Datta, *Master
Mahashayer Anudhyan* (Mahendra
Publishing: Calcutta, 1954), 25-35
10. Ibid., 36-37
11. *Srima Darshan*, 7:192-93
12. *Srima Katha*, 1: intro 22-23
13. *Srima Darshan*, 1:7
14. Ibid., 1:185, 189
15. Ibid., 3:120, 14:82
16. Ibid., 14:87
17. Ibid., 14:115
18. Ibid., 14:131
19. Ibid., 14:134-37
20. Ibid., 14:243
21. Ibid., 14:289
22. Ibid., 3:264
23. Ibid., 3:272

18. Holy Mother and M.

1. Abhay Chandra Bhattacharya, *Srimar
Jivan Darshan* (Grantha Bharati: Calcutta, 1990), 314-15

2. M., *The Gospel of Sri Ramakrishna*,
trans. Swami Nikhilananda
(Ramakrishna-Vivekananda Centre:
New York, 1969), 715-23
3. *Gospel*, 973-74
4. *Jivan Darshan*, 315-16
5. Swami Nityatmananda, *Srima Darshan*
(General Printers and Publishers:
Calcutta, 1972), 11:132
6. *Srima Darshan*, 4:262-63
7. Swami Prabhananda, *Amritarup
Sri Ramakrishna* (Udbodhan Office:
Calcutta, 1991), 190
8. Ibid., 192 and Brahmachari Akshay
Chaitanya, *Sri Sri Sarada Devi* (Calcutta
Book House: Calcutta, 1972), 119
9. *Udbodhan*, 108:795
10. Ibid., 108:795
11. Ibid., 108:797
12. Swami Purnatmananda, ed & comp.,
Sri Sri Mayer Padaprante (Udbodhan
Office: Calcutta, 1995), 2:431-35
13. Ibid., 4:889-900
14. Swami Nikhilananda, *Holy Mother*
(Ramakrishna-Vivekananda Centre:
New York, 1962), 54
15. Ibid., 80
16. *Srima Darshan*, 1:167

19. M. and Swami Vivekananda

1. *The Complete Works of Swami
Vivekananda* (Advaita Ashrama:
Calcutta, 1968), 6:342
2. Ibid., 7:110
3. Ibid., 3:335
4. His Eastern and Western Disciples,
Life of Swami Vivekananda (Advaita
Ashrama: Calcutta, 1961), 2:230
5. Swami Nityatmananda, *Srima Darshan*
(General Printers and Publishers:
Calcutta, 1968), 1:15
6. Abhay Chandra Bhattacharya, *Srimar
Jivan Darshan* (Grantha Bharati:
Calcutta, 1990), 299
7. Ibid., 300
8. Swami Jagannathananda, *Srima Katha*
(Udbodhan Office: Calcutta, 1941), 1:24-25

9. Ibid., 95
10. Ibid., 304
11. *Srima Katha*, 1:196.
12. *Srima Darshan*, 13:93-94, 7:19-20
13. Ibid., 3:62
14. Ibid., 5:231-32, 4:56
15. *Srima Katha*, 1:102-03
16. Swami Jagannathananda, *Srima Katha* (Ramakrishna Math: Bhubaneswar, 1953), 2:42
17. Ibid., 2:269-70
18. *Srima Darshan*, 4:152
19. Ibid., 4:157
20. *Complete Works of SV*, 8:79
21. M., *The Gospel of Sri Ramakrishna*, trans. Swami Nikhilananda (Rama-krishna-Vivekananda Centre: New York, 1969), 810-11
22. *Gospel*, 125-26
23. Srima, *Sri Sri Ramakrishna Kathamrita* (Kathamrita Bhavan: Calcutta, 1957), 5: Appendix 4
24. Ibid., Appendix 5:4
25. Ibid, 4-5
26. *Gospel*, 645-46
27. *Kathamrita*, 5: Appendix 7
28. Ibid., 5:7-8
29. Ibid., 5:9
30. *Gospel*, 111
31. Ibid., 264-65
32. *Kathamrita*, 5: Appendix 13-14
33. *Gospel*, 456
34. *Kathamrita*, 5: Appendix 17
35. *Gospel*, 148
36. *Kathamrita*, 5: Appendix 27-28
37. *Gospel*, 138
38. *Kathamrita*, 5: Appendix 30-31
39. Ibid., 5: Appendix 31
40. *Gospel*, 101
41. Ibid., 88
42. Swami Nikhilananda, ed., *Vivekananda: Yogas and Other Works* (Ramakrishna-Vivekananda Centre: New York,1953), 864
43. *Kathamrita*, 5: Appendix 36
44. Ibid., 5: Appendix 39-40
45. *Gospel*, 571-72
46. *Kathamrita*, 5: Appendix 43
47. *Kathamrita*, 5: Appendix 42-43 and *Complete Works of SV*, 3:340-41
48. *Gospel*, 720
49. Ibid., 711
50. *Kathamrita*, 5: Appendix 46
51. Swami Chetanananda, *God Lived with Them* (Vedanta Society: St. Louis, 1997), 37
52. *Complete Works of SV*, 3:53-54
53. *Kathamrita*, 5: Appendix 51-52
54. *Complete Works of SV*, 3:267-68

20. An Ideal Householder

1. M., *The Gospel of Sri Ramakrishna*, trans. Swami Nikhilananda (Ramakrishna-Vivekananda Centre: New York, 1969), 81
2. Ibid., 87
3. Swami Nityatmananda, *Srima Darshan* (General Printers and Publishers: Calcutta, 1972), 9:24
4. *Gospel*, 98
5. Ibid., 506
6. Ibid., 958
7. Ibid., 398, 696
8. Ibid., 114
9. Ibid., 126
10. Ibid., 247
11. Ibid., 874
12. *Srima Darshan*, 2:297-98
13. *Gospel*, 424
14. Ibid., 761
15. Swami Nikhilananda, ed., *Vivekananda: Yogas and Other Works* (Ramakrishna-Vivekananda Centre: New York,1953), 477
16. *Gospel*, 628
17. Abhay Chandra Bhattacharya, *Srimar Jivan Darshan* (Grantha Bharati: Calcutta, 1990), 93
18. Ibid., 524
19. Anonymous, *The Disciples of Sri Ramakrishna* (Advaita Ashrama: Calcutta, 1955), 421
20. *Srima Darshan*, 9:43
21. Ibid., 9:43-44, 6:222

22. *Jivan Darshan*, 105
23. Ibid., 105
24. Ibid., 129-30
25. Ibid., 122
26. Ibid., 122
27. *Srima Darshan*, 15:5-6
28. *Jivan Darshan*, 124-25
29. Ibid., 132
30. Swami Chetanananda, *They Lived with God* (Vedanta Society: St. Louis, 2006), 221
31. Ibid., 221
32. Ibid., 221
33. Ibid., 221
34. Swami Jagadiswarananda, *Navayuger Mahapurush* (Ramakrishna Ashrama, Raghunathpur: 1951), 2:330-31
35. *Jivan Darshan*, 131
36. *Gospel*, 681
37. Ibid., 233

21. The Morton Institution and Naimisharanya

1. M., *The Gospel of Sri Ramakrishna*, trans. Swami Nikhilananda (Ramakrishna-Vivekananda Centre: New York, 1969), 98
2. Ibid., 856-57
3. D.P. Gupta & D.K. Sengupta, ed., *Sri Sri Ramakrishna Kathamrita Centenary Memorial* (Srima Trust: Chandigarh, 1982), 304-14
4. Swami Chetanananda, ed.& compiled, *Srima Samipe* (Udbodhan Office: Calcutta, 1996), 57
5. Amiya Kumar Majumdar, *Punya Darshan Srima* (Gangotri Parishad: Calcutta, 1985), 2: Intro. 19
6. Abhay Chandra Bhattacharya, *Srimar Jivan Darshan* (Grantha Bharati: Calcutta, 1990), 285
7. Ibid., 284-85
8. *Kathamrita Cent. Memorial*, 320
9. Swami Nityatmananda, *Srima Darshan* (General Printers and Publishers: Calcutta, 1968), 4:38
10. Ibid., 11:12

11. *Jivan Darshan*, 290
12. *Srima Darshan*, 1: Intro. 12
13. Ibid., 4:248-49
14. *Jivan Darshan*, 295
15. *Webster's Encyclopedia of Dictionaries*, 866
16. *Jivan Darshan*, 295
17. Ibid., 272
18. Google website
19. *Srima Darshan*, 1: Intro. 32-33
20. Swami Chetanananda, *They Lived with God* (Vedanta Society: St. Louis, 2006), 220
21. *Prabuddha Bharata*, 1932:500
22. *Srima Darshan*, 1:4-5
23. *Kathamrita Cent. Memorial*, 207-18
24. *Prabuddha Bharata*, 1932:497
25. *Jivan Darshan*, 156-57
26. Ibid., 498-99
27. *Jivan Darshan*, 415
28. *Gospel*, 718-19

22. M. as a Guide at Dakshineswar and Cossipore

1. Swami Saradananda, *Sri Ramakrishna and His Divine Play*, trans. Swami Chetanananda (Vedanta Society: St. Louis, 2003), 636
2. Swami Nityatmananda, *Srima Darshan* (General Printers and Publishers: Calcutta, 1968), 3:223
3. His Eastern and Western Disciples, *Life of Swami Vivekananda* (Advaita Ashrama: Calcutta, 1979), 1:132-33
4. *Srima Darshan*, 4:70
5. Ibid., 3:240, 5:118
6. Nirmal Kumar Roy, *Dakshineswar Kali Mandirer Itivritta* (Lokmata Rani Rasmani Foundation: Dakshineswar, 2005), 59
7. *Srima Darshan*, 5:116-17
8. Ibid., 4:84
9. Ibid., 10:184-85
10. Ibid., 10:183-84
11. Ibid., 10:184
12. Ibid., 5:113
13. Ibid., 10:179-80

14. Ibid., 5:113
15. Ibid., 5:114-15
16. *Dakshineswar Kali Mandirer Itivritta*, 66
17. *Srima Darshan*, 10:178
18. Ibid., 10:174-75
19. Ibid., 3:235-44
20. M., *The Gospel of Sri Ramakrishna*, trans. Swami Nikhilananda (Ramakrishna-Vivekananda Centre: New York, 1969), 332
21. Swami Chetanananda, ed. & compiled, *Srima Samipe* (Udbodhan Office: Calcutta, 1996), 276
22. *Srima Darshan*, 5:118-19
23. Ibid., 5:119-24
24. Ibid., 10:166-72
25. Ibid., 15:412-36

23. What Ramakrishna Taught

1. Hellmuth Hecker, *Ananda, the Guardian of the Dhamma* (Buddhist Publication Society: Kandy, Sri Lanka, 1980), Foreword
2. *The Middle Way*, The Buddhist Society, London: vol. XLVIII: 3, November 1973
3. H.H. Halley, *Halley's Bible Handbook* (Zondervan Publishing House: Grand Rapids, 1965), 414
4. Irving Babbitt, *The Dhammapada* (New Directions Pub. Corporation: New York, 1965), 46 and Paul Carus, *The Gospel of Buddha* (The Publications Division, Govt. of India: New Delhi, 1961), 189
5. Bible: Luke 17:21 & Matthew 5:8
6. M., *The Gospel of Sri Ramakrishna*, trans. Swami Nikhilananda (Ramakrishna-Vivekananda Centre: New York, 1969), 579
7. Swami Nityatmananda, *Srima Darshan* (General Printers and Publishers: Calcutta, 1970), 2:79
8. *Gospel*, 500-01
9. *Srima Darshan*, 1:139-40
10. Ibid., 2:36
11. Ibid., 2:247

12. Ibid., 943
13. Ibid., 2:247
14. Ibid., 9:43
15. Ibid., 7:198
16. Ibid., 2:84
17. Ibid., 8:166
18. Ibid., 9:119
19. Ibid., 3:96, 4:200-01
20. Ibid., 6:193
21. Ibid., 2:154-55
22. Ibid., 6:265
23. Ibid., 1:100-01
24. Ibid., 6:177
25. Ibid., 1:40-42
26. Ibid., 1:55
27. Ibid., 1:64
28. Ibid., 1:241
29. Ibid., 4:100, 7:225-26
30. Ibid., 5:34-35
31. Ibid., 13:212
32. Ibid., 7:178
33. Ibid., 11:84, 130-31
34. Ibid., 3:225
35. Ibid., 15:161
36. Ibid., 4:322-24
37. Ibid., 5:209
38. Ibid., 4:19
39. Ibid., 8:190
40. Ibid., 4:308-09, 7:37
41. Ibid., 12:154, 7:189-90
42. Ibid., 1:38,84,30
43. Ibid., 1:183, 231, 252, 370
44. Ibid., 1:23-24, 28, 36
45. Ibid., 1:29-30 ,145-47
46. Ibid., 1:330-31
47. Ibid., 1:97
48. Ibid., 3:176
49. Ibid., 4:18-19
50. Ibid., 3:247-49
51. Ibid., 12:91
52. Ibid., 5:225
53. Ibid., 10:115
54. Ibid., 14:243, 7:19-20, 14:76
55. Ibid., 7:76
56. Ibid., 2:135-36
57. Ibid., 7:141
58. Ibid., 3:320

59. Ibid., 1:274, 337
60. Ibid., 4:267
61. Ibid., 7:38
62. Ibid., 6:130
63. Ibid., 7:156
64. Ibid., 1:108-09
65. Ibid., 3:86
66. Ibid., 2:107
67. Ibid., 210-11
68. Ibid., 4:39-40
69. Ibid., 7:170-71, 168
70. Ibid., 6:163
71. Ibid., 7:182
72. Ibid,, 1:69
73. Ibid., 1:71
74. Ibid., 6:55-56
75. Ibid., 9:83
76. Ibid., 1:72
77. *Gospel*, 154
78. *Srima Darshan*, 2:53-58
79. Ibid., 2:34
80. Ibid., 3:26-27
81. Ibid., 2:247-48
82. Ibid., 1:199-200
83. Ibid., 3:22
84. Ibid., 2:145-46
85. Ibid., 2:88
86. Ibid., 3:91
87. Ibid., 10:94-95
88. Ibid., 6:74, 79-80
89. Ibid., 2:79
90. Ibid., 3:68

91. Ibid., 3:214
92. Ibid., 3:26
93. Ibid., 5:72-73
94. Ibid., 1:175-76
95. Ibid., 3:151
96. Ibid., 6:15
97. Ibid., 2:59
98. Ibid., 4:286-87
99. Ibid., 4:283-84
100. Ibid., 6:224
101. Ibid., 16:29
102. Ibid., 7:25

24. From Death to Immortality

1. Swami Chetanananda, *They Lived with God* (Vedanta Society: St. Louis, 2006), 226
2. Swami Nityatmananda, *Srima Darshan* (General Printers and Publishers: Calcutta, 1974), 15:355
3. Ibid., 357
4. *Prabuddha Bharata*, 1932: 500-501
5. *Srima Darshan*, 15:363
6. M., *The Gospel of Sri Ramakrishna*, trans. Swami Nikhilananda (Ramakrishna-Vivekananda Centre: New York, 1969), 302
7. *Srima Darshan*, 15:416
8. Ibid., 15:421-22
9. Ibid., 1: Life (11)
10. Ibid., 15:457-58

Index

Nityatmananda, Swami (*continued*)
on M. at Dakshineswar, 375; on M.'s
appearance, 358; on M.'s diary entries,
238, 426; on M.'s final illness, 424–25;
on M.'s humility, 341; on M.'s pain,
Cossipore, 376; and M.'s son, 342; on
printing of *Gospel*, 428; recorder, M.'s
words, 13, 17, 112, 387; visits Rk sites,
379, 381–82, 427; writings on SV, 321
Nivedita, Sister, 196; with dog at HM's,
484; on importance of Dakshineswar,
109; reverence for HM, 312

Panchavati, 77–78, 80–81, 85–86, 88–89,
119–22, 227–28, 366–67, 371–72, *373*,
374–75, 401–3; changes to, 85; hatha
yogi in, 403; M., devotees picnicking at,
374–75, 508; M.'s description, 120–21,
371–72; M.'s reverence for, 487; M.'s
sadhana in, 81, 86; M. with Rk in, 78;
Rk on picnics in, 367; Rk praising, 80;
Rk's reverence for, 89, 340, 390; Rk's
sadhana in, 77, 122, 523; Rk's vision in,
Sita, 308
Pandavas, 63, 100
Panihati, *59*
paramahamsa, 88, 109, 133, 152, 186, 291,
359
Paramahamsa Yogananda, 533–35
Parliament of Religions, 323–24, 326
Paul (Christ's apostle), 385
Peter (Christ's disciple), 385
Philip (Christ's disciple), 494
Pope Paul VI, 284
Prabhananda, Swami, 16, 145, 195
Prabhas Gupta (M.'s son), 348, 352, 429,
431, 450, 538, 557
Prabhavananda, Swami, 285
Prahlada, 105, 116, 156, 367
Pranavananda, Swami, 430
Pratap Majumdar, 55, 103–4, 146–47, 149,
159, 168, 170, 172, 222, 289
prayer, 10, 71, 84, 93, 136, 214–15, 233,
259, 414–15, 475–76
Premananda, Swami (Baburam), 67,
69, 117, 137, 177, 212, 226, 478; to M.

on *Gospel*, 273; moves Rk's relics, 199;
on M.'s donation, 203; prepares betel,
228; on Rk crying for SV, 184; on Rk
initiating, 340; on Rk spreading own
word, 281; on Rk's teachings, 235; on
staying with Rk, 125; student at M.'s
school, 126
Presidency College, 17, 21–23, 558
Puranas, 22, 26, 50, 54, 247, 283, 356, 384,
386, 454
Puri, 173, 472, 508; M.'s visit to, 189–90,
290, 295–96, 298, 405, 505, 514, 559; M.'s
visit to with HM, 306
Purna Chandra Ghosh, 72, 146, 150, 186;
saved from suicide, 272

Radha, 98, 119, 309, 545, 551–53
Radhakanta temple, Dakshineswar, 30,
58, 83, 108, 115, 417
Radhakrishnan, Dr. S., 251
Raghavananda, Swami, 424, 428,
525; arati at M.'s death, 430; on M.'s
Ashrama, 361; on M.'s last days, 422;
on M.'s love, sadhus, 363; on M.'s
simplicity, 358
Raghunath Das, Chaitanya's disciple, 58
Raghunath Das Babaji, soldier, Rama's
devotee, 291
Raghuvir, 88, 175, 261
Rama; Ramachandra: 15, 100, 105,
213–14, 220–21, 241, 261, 291–92,
383–86, 553–54; his chronicler, Valmiki,
384; name of, 30, 240, 400, 465
Ramakrishna (the Master), *41*
[*These index subentries appear after
general entries:*
    illness and death
    M.
    Narenda/SV
    parables and stories
    personal qualities
    teachings
    visions]

Binodini visits, 151; birth centenary,
474; blesses Rasik, 409; Chaitanya's

Works by Swami Chetanananda

Books

Ramakrishna and His Divine Play, by Swami Saradananda
  (*Translated by Swami Chetanananda*)

God Lived with Them: Life Stories of Sixteen Monastic Disciples of Sri Ramakrishna

They Lived With God: Life Stories of Some Devotees of Sri Ramakrishna

How to Live with God: In the Company of Ramakrishna

Ramakrishna as We Saw Him

Ramakrishna: A Biography in Pictures
  (*Biographical Introduction by Swami Smaranananda*)

Sarada Devi: A Biography in Pictures
  (*Biographical Introduction by Swami Smaranananda*)

Vivekananda: East Meets West (*A Pictorial Biography*)

Vedanta: Voice of Freedom

Meditation and Its Methods: by Swami Vivekananda
  (*Edited by Swami Chetanananda*)

A Guide to Spiritual Life — Spiritual Teachings of Swami Brahmananda

Spiritual Treasures: Letters of Swami Turiyananda

How a Shepherd Boy Became a Saint: Life and Teachings of Swami Adbhutananda

Girish Chandra Ghosh: A Bohemian Devotee of Sri Ramakrishna

Avadhuta Gita: The Song of the Ever-Free
  (*Translated by Swami Chetanananda*)

CDs

(*Sanskrit Chants with English translation*)

Echoes of the Eternal: Peace, Bliss, and Harmony

Breath of the Eternal: Awakening, Reflection, and Illumination

DVDs

Ramakrishna (*A Documentary*)

The Parables of Ramakrishna (*40 Parables of Ramakrishna*)

Vivekananda as We Saw Him (*A Documentary*)